White Burgers, Black Cash

WHITE BURGERS, BLACK CASH

Fast Food from Black Exclusion to Exploitation

Naa Oyo A. Kwate

University of Minnesota Press
Minneapolis
London

The University of Minnesota Press gratefully acknowledges financial assistance provided for the publication of this book by research funding from the National Library of Medicine of the National Institutes of Health.

Time line on pages x–xi by Kudos Design Collaboratory

Published by the University of Minnesota Press
111 Third Avenue South, Suite 290
Minneapolis, MN 55401–2520
http://www.upress.umn.edu

ISBN 978-1-5179-1109-6 (hc)
ISBN 978-1-5179-1110-2 (pb)

A Cataloging-in-Publication record for this book is available from the Library of Congress.

Printed in the United States of America on acid-free paper

The University of Minnesota is an equal-opportunity educator and employer.

32 31 30 29 28 27 26 25 24 23   10 9 8 7 6 5 4 3 2 1

For my parents

Contents

Part II. Racial Turnover

Part III. Black Catastrophe

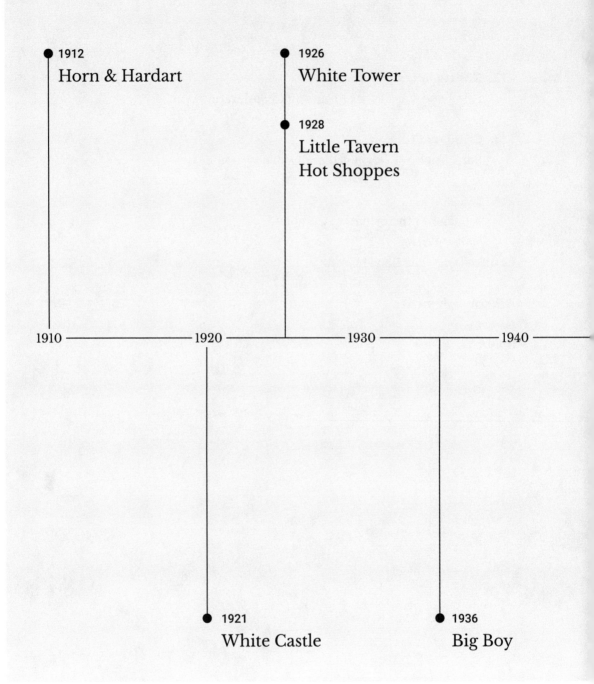

1912
Horn & Hardart

1926
White Tower

1928
Little Tavern
Hot Shoppes

1910 —————— 1920 —————— 1930 —————— 1940 ——

1921
White Castle

1936
Big Boy

Time line of American fast food restaurants

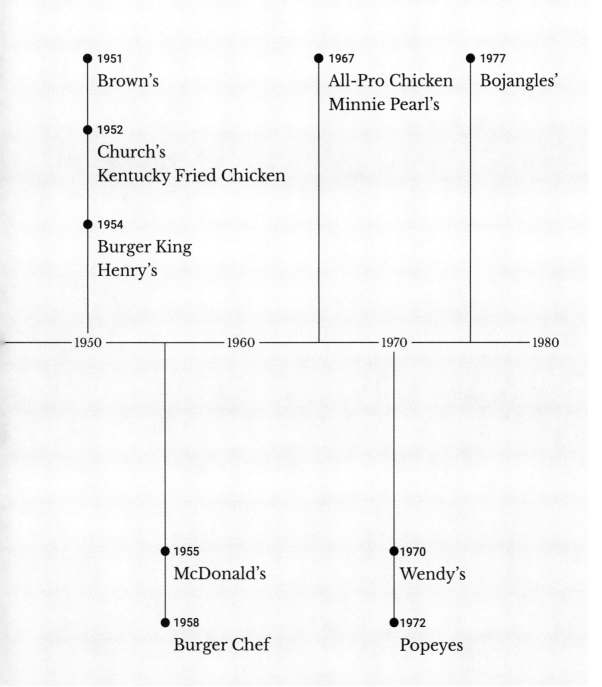

● 1951
Brown's

● 1952
Church's
Kentucky Fried Chicken

● 1954
Burger King
Henry's

● 1967
All-Pro Chicken
Minnie Pearl's

● 1977
Bojangles'

1950 ———— 1960 ———— 1970 ———— 1980

● 1955
McDonald's

● 1958
Burger Chef

● 1970
Wendy's

● 1972
Popeyes

Introduction

How Did Fast Food Become Black?

Fast food has always been a fundamentally anti-Black enterprise.

Today, fast food—by which I mean take-out restaurants serving primarily burgers, fries, and fried chicken, like McDonald's, Burger King, and KFC—is everywhere in America, and even around the world. Carrying brand recognition that few food retailers can match and boasting about the billions its restaurants have served, fast food is a core part of the American social fabric. But fast food is especially everywhere in Black communities. And Black communities contend with worse health profiles than do their White counterparts for myriad health conditions. Over the past couple of decades, as researchers, policymakers, and community residents have turned increasingly to local environments to explain health risks, fast food has come under scrutiny and critique for its role in obesity and chronic illness. So an argument about fast food being anti-Black would at first blush appear to reference health inequities. That is, "fast food is anti-Black because it causes shorter and sicker lives among Black folks." It is true that fast food constitutes a community-based health risk; but it is not anti-Black primarily because of that. Fast food is anti-Black because it has subordinated Blackness throughout its history.

With fast food as ubiquitous in Black neighborhoods as it is today, it is ironic that Black people were once hard-pressed to buy a burger in this country. James Baldwin writes in *Notes of a Native Son* about the time he spent living in New Jersey, working in defense plants. Never having experienced the strictures of Jim Crow directly, he was unprepared when ordinary excursions to restaurants provoked racial animus that barred him from patronizing them. In all instances, he sought a hamburger and coffee. In Princeton, thrice he visited a "self-service restaurant," unaware that the establishment did not serve Black folks. The restaurant format allowed him to simply pick up plates of food without recognizing that the staff had purposefully not served him. He found out on the fourth visit. In Trenton, his last night in the state punctuated a year of indignities at all manner of eating and drinking places. He and a White friend ventured into the American Diner, and when the counterman asked what they wanted, Baldwin replied curtly, "We want a hamburger and cup of coffee, what do you think we want?"[1] Again he was met with the racial refrain of the day, and the pair retreated. Later that night, at a "glittering and fashionable restaurant," he was not so easily cowed; and his refusal to capitulate to yet another instance of discrimination, had events gone otherwise, might have cost him his life.

As striking as Baldwin's repeated rejection while in search of a hamburger is the fact that he wanted one at all. His retort to the counterman—"what do you think we want?"—reveals both the ordinariness and value afforded to hamburgers, and Baldwin's inability to obtain one stands in poignantly for the rest of Black America. In the main, what he experienced in 1942 was a pattern of exclusion that extended to potential Black fast food consumers across the country. Even when fast food outlets were not denying individual Black diners, they were operating in exclusionary White space and remained intensely focused on Whiteness for decades. More symbolically, the burger Baldwin called for wasn't all that was at stake. It isn't self-evident that Baldwin and his friend should want burgers; why not chicken potpies or ham sandwiches? No—only a hamburger would do, that quintessentially American meal. Baldwin was essentially ordering a portion of ordinary American life. Black consumers would not have ready access to such a dish until the 1970s, when fast food switched from a posture of absolute exclusion to a pattern of Black exploitation.

Black communities, residents, activists, and policymakers wrestle today with the toxic consequences of retail corridors littered with fast food outlets. By sheer force of number, by aggressive marketing (often leaning on Black cultural productions), and by corporate attempts to establish themselves as benefactors for communities that the state continually forgets, fast food has colonized the restaurant landscape in Black neighborhoods. Having done so, the ubiquity of these outlets has transmuted into judgments about the communities in which they multiply. A city neighborhood with a high density of fast food is commonly understood to be a Black neighborhood, and likely a troubled one as well. In January 2016, the *New York Times* wrote about a new restaurant in Minneapolis's Near North neighborhood, a community reportedly facing a high incidence of violent crime, describing the eatery as an anomaly in a neighborhood "otherwise dominated by fast food restaurants."[2] These varied elements are supposed to make sense collectively—crime, fast food, Blackness, and a community on the disadvantaged side of an entrenched racial and socioeconomic divide. Similarly, fast food, unhealthiness, and Blackness have become entwined in the public imagination as assumptions about demand, deviance, and disorder become shorthand explanations for the shape of the food environment on one end, and obesity and poor health on the other.

But fast food hasn't always been endemic in Black space. Once upon a time, it occupied the exclusively White terrain that pushed James Baldwin to the periphery. The Blackness so strongly coded in contemporary fast food is a remarkable departure from its origins. Burger restaurants that literally embodied Whiteness with names like White Castle and White Tower emerged in the 1920s, creating an urban restaurant landscape that catered to White, primarily male pedestrians. When fast food was born again in the 1950s, restaurateurs explicitly sought out the exemplary domesticity of White, middle-class suburbs, inviting families in their automobiles to shiny, new drive-thrus. *White Burgers, Black Cash* traces the long racial and spatial path fast food has traveled: from a starting point in the early twentieth century to the contemporary moment, where it landed heavily in Black communities.

I initially came to this book from a public health perspective. In the early 2000s, behavioral approaches to dietary intake were predominant. The CDC showed that more and more of the country was putting on more and more weight, and that obesity prevalence was especially acute among African Americans. The conclusion was often to implement behavioral interventions to induce African Americans to change their consumption, making health status out to be an individual issue. Implicitly and explicitly, funders, health professionals, and the general public understood diet and body weight to be the result of Black people's bad behavior, Black people's failure to take charge of their health, or, seemingly more charitably, Black people's lack of nutrition knowledge. But context matters in determining who benefits from good health and who does not, since access to flexible resources such as money, power, prestige, knowledge, freedom, and social support act as accelerants or brakes on disease.[3] This does not mean that attention to individual health behaviors is irrelevant for public health, but rather that it is unlikely to have much of an effect when the broader context is missing. If we are concerned with diet, obesity, and chronic disease, the food environment must be interrogated; and for Black neighborhoods, that means a landscape where segregation quarantines disproportionate densities of fast food.

In 2009, my colleagues and I took on this question and examined the distribution of fast food across New York City's five boroughs. To look at it from the street, that there was a surfeit of outlets compared to predominantly White neighborhoods seemed obvious. There were multinational chains and small, dubious restaurants often following the naming convention "X Fried Y and Z," where X is a personal pronoun, Y is chicken or fish, and Z is ribs, pizza, or ice cream. We set out to test whether what passersby could observe at street level bore out empirically across the city. Gathering all the fast food restaurant addresses from the city's restaurant health inspection database, we mapped their locations and analyzed the census demographics to determine what was driving fast food density.[4]

It was Blackness. No other variable came close. Not income, not population density, not consumer expenditures on dining out. The percentage of Black residents determined where fast food was located; the more Black people there were, the more fast food was present. And, dispelling the notion that it was about economics, affluent Black neighborhoods were just as likely to be exposed to fast food as their low-income counterparts. Presenting these findings to scholarly and community audiences elicited dismay but not surprise, and researchers elsewhere in the country reported the same findings.[5] But how did these patterns come to pass? How was fast food racially transformed, and what were the consequences for Black communities?

Fast food followed a trajectory in the ghetto much like the racial stratification in housing, which shifted from market exclusion to market exploitation.[6] I use *ghetto* here and throughout the book not as a colloquial term meant to comment on a neighborhood's danger, poverty, or cultural behavior, but as a sociological indicator of the racial segregation that characterizes American cities. The ghetto refers to a set of neighborhoods where most or all residents are Black, and where most Black people in a given city reside.[7] Having ignored the Black ghetto for years, fast food would eventually come to see these spaces as necessary for business. Purveyors of fast food have become national icons whose meaning has been exported around the world; theirs is a purportedly democratic institution where all may partake of simple pleasures. But fast food has also acted as enforcer for a range of complex racial needs: as border security, as analgesic, as disciplinary measure. The impulse to keep fast food White pervaded its early history; and once the color line was breached, the industry retooled to extract as much as it could from Black communities. Fast food has imagined both a world without Blackness and one that tethers Blackness to the corporate bottom line.

Why did the industry ignore Black people? Was it because of racism? Yes. Then why did it start moving into Black neighborhoods? Wasn't that also racism? Yes. But it's too simple to begin and end there. The undercurrent and texture of that racism changed over time. Fast food passed over Black neighborhoods not simply because the industry was ignorant or dismissive of a profitable consumer group (though it was and it did), but because these communities were incompatible with the racial logics and symbolic meanings of these restaurants. At different points in time, fast food pursued different goals, all of which were a reflection and furtherance of the country's racial projects.[8] To manage them, the industry made strategic choices about how to engage or reject Black communities.

Sometimes chains excluded Black people altogether by locating in communities where they did not and could not live, thanks to the swath of institutional policies and practices that kept White space White. Other times the industry included Black folks as consumers but not as franchisees. Once the doors to Black franchising opened, they yielded passage to redlined business ownership. Fast food was not only subject to racial notions but created them, picking up racialized tropes (such as those around hygiene) and deploying them as foundational to the business concept. Time-varying racial narratives and stereotypes necessitated a changing posture, and corporations melded with the racial currents eddying around fast food's product image and the lifestyle it was meant to support. That lifestyle changed over time—food for the working man, wholesome leisure for suburban families—but all the while, fast food acted to protect and serve Whiteness, defending its sanctity and suppressing intrusions by Black persons to the benefits it conferred.

Tracing fast food's racial transformation reveals what is true about food in general: it looms large in how Americans make sense of race, gender, and citizenship. Fast food is the closest thing the United States has to a national cuisine (albeit as a standardized, industrially produced product antithetical to the very definition of cuisine), and it has helped draw lines around who belongs and who does not.[9]

From White Utopia to Black Catastrophe

Fast food took almost one hundred years to remake its color line. The industry took root in the early 1900s, when the earliest restaurant chains began. First-generation fast food emerged in the Automat, a precursor to what the industry would become; it continued with burger outlets such as White Castle and knockoffs like White Tower; and it included the first drive-ins, as in D.C.'s Hot Shoppes. All these urban operations were temples to Whiteness literally and figuratively. Early fast food facilitated a White public that existed across space and had little room for racial error. Second-generation fast food, arriving in the early to mid-1950s, became the biggest chains we know today. KFC, Burger King, and McDonald's arose in White suburbia, pursued families and children, and remade fast food from cheap fuel for laborers to domestic oasis. Fast food pursued, with near total exclusion of Black people, a White utopia in different forms.

From the 1960s to the early 1970s, chinks began to appear in fast food's racial armor. While White America closely guarded fast food as a family treat, most of the interest Black communities expressed in fast food in the late 1960s was deadly serious. Well into the decade, advertising firms had not yet awakened to the fact that Black people were fully human, with a diversity of demographic groupings and interests. White corporate America maintained a stance of studied bewilderment about what Black people bought and did in their day to day lives. Who would have thought there were "Negro women, Negro teens, Negro gourmets, Negro surfers, Negro garden lovers," as Donald A. Wells, executive vice president at the advertising agency BBDO, realized in 1966?[10] The broader misrecognition of the Black market meant that consumers and entrepreneurs were shut out of the booming franchise business. But over the course of the 1960s came Black (men) franchisees, predicated on fast food corporations' fear of urban rebellions and the federal government's infusion of money into "minority" franchising. Black franchisors also entered the fray, as celebrities lent their names or their time to new enterprises meant to empower Black communities. Black folks refused to go quietly into a fast food–less night, seeing in the enterprise a means to economic opportunity, political empowerment, and community development. Fast food elicited diverse responses from Black people as consumers, political activists, and owners; but they are best summarized not as the pursuit of leisure, but as a battering ram to topple structural inequities.

Eventually, the industry moved away from fast food as a solution to social unrest, and toward extraction of what it saw as the gold mine in the ghetto. Over the course of the 1970s, fast food finally began marketing targeted to African American consumers; and as it entered the 1980s, the number of outlets exploded under conditions of privation and instability in Black communities. Fast food was fully racialized as Black by the 1990s, and those who consumed it were constructed as part of a spectacle of deviance. Fast food's trajectory of Black catastrophe entered the 2000s with public health studies documenting the deleterious impact of fast food saturation—but also with continued Black agency to push back against corporate interests.

This book charts the change in fast food's color line nationally, but with particular focus on three cities: Chicago, New York, and Washington, D.C. A number of factors coalesce to make them particularly important to this story. They are among the country's most populous cities and have large proportions of Black residents. Though distinct, all three show how fast food intersects with other industries, institutions, and social problems that affect daily Black life. These cities are also instructive in the urban changes that shaped fast food's trajectory, were home to major franchises and Black advertising firms, and were pivotal in the marketing strategies created to reach Black audiences. Other Rust Belt cities appear across the narrative—Philadelphia, Cleveland, Baltimore. All of these cities come into greater focus at particular points in the narrative in support of different aims: to discuss unique events (e.g., the experience of a Black franchisee); to examine fast food siting and change at the level of neighborhoods; to reveal fast food's particular presence in Black space (e.g., the aesthetics of storefronts); and to illustrate trends playing out elsewhere in the nation. Regions that figure minimally in the book are the West, which did not have the same density of Black urban centers as the Rust Belt; and the South, where the story of restaurant location is complicated by Jim Crow laws and the civil rights movement's targeting of lunch counters and restaurants. Attempting to study fast food siting and marketing across North and South would conflate major differences in the institutionalization of race.

A study of this scope also necessitates a narrow definition of fast food; in this book it encompasses hamburgers and fried chicken almost exclusively. The chains serving those items have dominated the industry for its entire history and have taken on an iconic perch in the notion of what fast food is, both in the United States and around the world. Restaurants featuring pizza, submarine sandwiches, tacos, and other items have neither the stature nor the evidentiary base the others do, and their addition reveals little over and above burger and chicken joints alone. National chains (which became multinational) also dominate the narrative more than local chains or independent outlets, despite the prevalence of the latter in Black neighborhoods. That is because overwhelmingly these are the businesses that are most discussed by journalists and scholars, that have the longest histories, and whose records are most accessible in archives. To be sure, the evidence for the major chains has its own limits; existing archives only reveal so much about the motivations, conflicts, goals, failures, and successes of fast food's projects of racial exclusion and exploitation.

What clearly emerges in this story, however, is that fast food has left disorder in its wake that extends beyond obesity, and its impact cannot be reduced to a causal relationship between consumption and health. If fast food is quintessentially American, it is equally implicated in all the troubles with which the country has reckoned. If fast food stands as a symbol of Americana, that includes the anti-Blackness at the center of the nation's history.

Part I

White Utopias

Little Rock, Ark., March 22. Senator McKnight introduced a bill in the Senate, making it unlawful for negroes to wait upon white persons. "It is to prevent negroes from taking white women about the waist and helping them off trains."

—"Against Negro Servants," *Charlotte News,* March 22, 1907

A Fortress of Whiteness

First-Generation Fast Food in the Early Twentieth Century

The August 24, 1929, issue of the Salt Lake City *Deseret News* ran an advertisement from the A&W Root Beer Company. It testified that its "stations"—drive-in outlets that served snacks and drinks—hewed to the highest sanitation standards possible. The ad pointed out that local courts had decreed the company compliant with health laws, and that all their glasses were "sterilized after each individual service with a chlorine disinfecting solution recognized as positive by the best sanitation authorities." It closed by informing the public that all were welcome to inspect A&W's sterilizing methods whenever they chose. Chlorine disinfection, court rulings, and health department officials are not the most appetizing characteristics a restaurant chain might elect to include in a newspaper ad, but the late 1920s was a time in which allaying concerns about food safety at casual take-out restaurants was critical. J. Willard "Bill" Marriott (of later hotel fame) and his wife, Allie, both originally from Utah, bought an A&W franchise and opened their own stand in Northwest Washington, D.C., in 1927. Later they added hot food to the menu, and with that, one of the first-generation fast food restaurants was born—Hot Shoppes. The drive-in offered a diverse menu of meals to a nondiverse clientele of Washingtonians and D.C. suburbanites at locations within the city limits and beyond.

Marriott sought to re-create a drive-in reminiscent of those he knew as a youth in Utah and opened his first Hot Shoppes at 5103 Georgia Avenue NW. This was a major artery that would attract commuters, and the little building stood in a sea of asphalt where customers ate curbside meals served on a tray clipped to the car door. Hot Shoppes' waiters were called "curbers" and earned wages only from tips.[1] They were all White.

That Hot Shoppes actively sought motor traffic was evident in the multitude of auto-related businesses that surrounded the restaurants, including used car sales

Figure 1.1. Hot Shoppes curbers were mostly women, but this photograph shows a male worker delivering food to customers in Washington, D.C. Photographed by John Collier for the Farm Security Administration in 1941. Library of Congress, Prints & Photographs Division, FSA/OWI Collection, LC-USF34–081717-E.

dealerships, filling stations, and parking lots. An automobile- and family-centric business plan set this chain apart from its first-generation peers, which targeted pedestrian workers. The immediate area around the Hot Shoppes in Southeast D.C.'s Congress Heights sported no less than three gas and service stations and an auto sales shop. Hot Shoppes locations also maximized nearby retail and attractions from which hungry patrons might emerge, including drug and liquor stores, supermarkets, theaters, barbershops, and bowling alleys.[2] In 1930, the flagship location opened at 4340 Connecticut Avenue, still within the District but suburban in feel (today it's known as the Van Ness neighborhood). Quickly a trendy teenage destination, 4340 drew in patrons from a nearby ice rink and recreation center who enjoyed menu items ranging from simple sandwiches and hamburgers to full meals such as roast leg of lamb, potpie, and Sunday roast. By 1933 there were six Hot Shoppes, together grossing $1 million per year ($20.5 million in 2020 dollars). The business was growing rapidly and becoming a fixture of middle-class, White Washington's sphere of leisure.

Hot Shoppes was actually late on the scene, as the first generation of fast food began in the early 1900s. It counted among its ranks a set of restaurants awash in Whiteness, figuratively and literally. Some of the buildings were painted white and brands bore names featuring the word *white* (e.g., White Castle). The outlets were staffed by White male workers who served White patrons in exclusively White neighborhoods. Even the bread was white.[3] First-generation fast food such as Horn & Hardart, White Castle, White Tower, Little Tavern, and Hot Shoppes reflected and created transformations in how White residents in midwestern and East Coast cities ate. Located squarely in urban cores, these restaurants catered to White customers ranging from those of moderate means to the middle class, serving simple fare in an informal atmosphere. By doing so, they helped forge a national White identity. These restaurants did not seek out Black customers and equally spurned Black staff, or else kept them out of sight. Excluding Black people as customers and subordinating them as employees made quick service restaurants an institution that helped define American racial boundaries.

In a Racial Nadir

First-generation fast food restaurants varied in the extent to which they excluded Black patrons, which also varied in explicitness over place and time. But overall, the earliest iterations of fast food did not include Black folks. Hot Shoppes' easygoing veneer belied the racial exclusion that blemished its operations. The chain has garnered racial acclaim from contemporary food commentators who argue that it welcomed African American customers when other restaurants would not.[4] But by the 1950s, long-standing discriminatory treatment began to be challenged in court. Charles E. Williams, a District of Columbia resident, filed a civil suit after he was refused service from Hot Shoppes in Alexandria, Virginia. And when the NAACP conducted audits, it found that Black patrons were served in Silver Spring, Maryland, but refused at two District locations and in suburban Bethesda, Maryland. In the words of a Hot Shoppes spokesperson, "Naturally we do not wish to embarrass our guests. Our policies are dictated by customs in the area." Similarly, vice president and treasurer Robert F. McFadden argued that this was not a company-wide policy, but that the facilities were small and it was difficult to "pioneer": "We watch the neighborhoods and follow the trends."[5] Local custom meant abiding by the exclusion of Black patrons. Management at the suburban tearoom of D.C. metro area department store Woodward & Lothrop was unapologetic after being caught by the NAACP's audit: "We do not serve Negroes at the Chevy Chase store. No explanation is necessary." Court rulings expressed the same in lawsuits involving other establishments, such as Howard Johnson in Alexandria and White Tower in Baltimore, which in 1957 refused to serve Sara Slack, a reporter for the *Amsterdam News*.[6]

The long history of exclusion that preceded Slack's encounter reflected the fact that first-generation fast food arrived during the Nadir of race relations, the period ranging from the end of the Civil War to the 1930s in which Black folk were cast back into noncitizenship.[7] During this time, African Americans were disenfranchised, *Plessy v. Ferguson* ushered in legal segregation, lynchings reached their highest point, African Americans were expelled everywhere from skilled trades to professional sports, the outspoken White supremacist President Woodrow Wilson segregated the federal government, minstrel shows mocking Black humanity flourished, D. W. Griffith's 1915 film *The Birth of a Nation* spurred the rebirth of the Ku Klux Klan, and Tulsa, Oklahoma, witnessed the 1921 destruction of the successful Black enclave in a nearly weeklong, state-sanctioned White race riot leaving dozens dead and hundreds homeless.[8] Fast food came into being at a time when cities were undergoing seismic changes in population as Black migrants arrived from the South in droves. The first Great Migration of Black southerners to cities in the North and West, seeking work and fleeing the severity of American apartheid, began in the mid-1910s; by the close of the 1930s, the country had seen more than 1.6 million Black southerners on the move.[9] Those who arrived in cities such as Chicago, New York, and Detroit found bitter contests in racial terrorism waged against them by Whites. What have been termed race riots, but are more accurately described as collective anti-Black violence,[10] came to a head in 1919, across the country but most notably in Chicago.

White Castle opened two years after that so-called Red Summer of 1919. One of the most well-known campaigns of racial terrorism took place when Eugene Williams, a Black boy, dared to raft across an invisible racial line demarcating Chicago's 29th Street beachfront, and was murdered by George Stauber, a young White man.[11] Even before such incidents of mob violence, Black Chicago residents faced racist attacks in the form of house and real estate office bombings and aggression by White "athletic clubs," which were gangs meant to defend neighborhoods from the incursion of Black neighbors. The Hamburg Athletic Club of Bridgeport produced the city's most powerful mayor, Richard J. Daley. These gangs, comprising young working-class men who had fathers often working in stockyards or as police officers, were able to attack Black communities with impunity.[12]

The Nadir also was the time of the urban ghetto's formation, between 1900 and 1940. Before 1900, Black residents of northern cities lived in communities with high levels of Black–White contact. The values for many of the indices social scientists use today to quantify segregation—such as dissimilarity and isolation—were but a fraction in 1860 of what they would become in 1940. In New York City, the value for isolation, which measures the extent to which minority members are exposed only to one another, was but a scant 3.6 in 1890 (meaning the average Black person lived in an area whose population was only 3.6 percent Black); in 1910 it was 6.7; in 1920, 20.5; and in 1930, 41.8. The same trend was repeated in cities across the North.[13]

Amid such racial storms and hardening segregation first-generation outlets were born. At the hands of the White men who came of age during the Nadir, the first fast food brands created—and for some chains nationalized—a new brand of consumable Whiteness, one that made fast food the exclusionary province of White America. Fast food's enduring selling points—quick service and convenience—found traction among White urbanites in its earliest years because food shopping and cooking was challenging in early twentieth-century cities. European immigrants who had immigrated to northern urban centers from rural homelands found it a hassle to put food on the table, what with immense, hectic outdoor markets that required judging food quality and haggling for a good deal. These residents lacked both space at home and abundant cash; for instance, Polish residents in Chicago's Packingtown community spent more than half of their income on food and made frequent shopping trips.[14] They at least had the opportunity to do business with proprietors of the same ethnicity who spoke the same language. Social ties were critical in fostering interpersonal interaction and maintaining dietary customs, which is why chain stores, despite their lower prices, did not always win out.[15]

Eating out became a handy solution to many of the constraints inherent to shopping and cooking in the late 1800s and early 1900s. Meals at home could be supplemented with ready-made local food from vendors of various kinds, such as saloons and taverns, lunchrooms, delicatessens, bakeries, and small restaurants. Roadside stands were unpretentious eating places, little more than sheds, but made popular as the mass production of automobiles brought car ownership to households with modest incomes. However, these tended to operate seasonally, serving customers year-round only in California and Florida.[16] Among male diners, saloons were immensely popular because they offered free—if rather salty—hot and cold lunches with the purchase of beer. Despite the influx of African Americans in the Great Migration, photographic evidence suggests that such establishments were segregated by race. Saloons numbered in the thousands; Chicago sported over 6,200 of them in 1901, and New York City's Lower East Side alone had 1,000.[17] Many of New York's saloons were interracial spaces, but Black men who visited predominantly White saloons could expect to encounter racist speech and violence. Black men created their own locations (often illegal due to discrimination in regulation) where they could avoid the "censorious and possibly hazardous gaze" of White people, drink, and engage in the underground economy; however, even here, Black women could not freely socialize or drink on equal terms.[18] Lunchrooms were less attractive than saloons because the prices were at least twice as high, and that did not even include beer. By 1918, half of Chicago workers were eating out at least occasionally, and more than two-thirds of those in New York did the same.[19]

New types of eating establishments then began to attract customers on a similarly segregated basis. Beginning in 1912, one of the places New Yorkers frequently dined out was the Automat, the first dining format in America that could be called fast food. Many of its novel features, such as an emphasis on technology, standardized service, and hygiene, became central in the fast food chains we know today. As will be discussed in part III, decades later, once the concept became obsolete, it was subsumed by contemporary (second-generation) fast food; Horn & Hardart was bought out by Burger King and its Automats transformed into the new chain.

The Automat

The Hardy Boys series, originally published in the late 1920s but reissued and popular in the late 1950s and 1960s, recounted the adventures of Frank and Joe Hardy, two "all-American" teenage brothers and amateur detectives who lived in the Long Island town of Bayport. Long Island, that "slender, riotous island which extends itself due east of New York,"[20] comprises numerous New York City suburbs across the counties of Nassau and Suffolk. Suffolk, the geographically larger but less densely populated of the two, was in 1950 a sparsely populated expanse. With 296 persons per square mile compared to Manhattan's 85,078, it was more rural than suburban. The entire county also had too few Black residents for them to be counted in the census. It is home to the real town of Bayport and the fictional one depicted in the Hardy Boys adventures. In *What Happened at Midnight*, Chet Morton, close friend of the Hardy Boys, marvels at the food service of the Automat that had just arrived in town. "For a dime," he declares, "one may have nourishment. For two dimes, one may feast. For a quarter, one may have a banquet."[21] Presiding over a half-dozen high school peers, Chet explained how the system worked: "'There is the sandwich. Here is my nickel. There goes my nickel,' he added, inserting the coin into the slot. 'Here comes my sandwich. Very simple.'"[22] Although unnamed as such, this Bayport location would have been one of the many Horn & Hardart Automats in the New York metropolitan area.

Introduced in 1902 by Joseph Horn and Frank Hardart in Philadelphia, the Automat originally served meals to patrons via dumbwaiter. After placing an order, customers waited for food to arrive from the basement kitchen. Though their orders were plated sumptuously, middle-class diners soon tired of the wait at the dumbwaiter. The company therefore abandoned luxury and opted for speed, creating a new system that arrived in New York City in 1912.[23] Large food machines displayed a variety of foods, such as sandwiches, salads, baked beans (one of the biggest sellers), beef stew, baked macaroni, soups, and pies—all behind glass-fronted, individual slots. Prices were quantified in nickels, and customers without exact change turned their money over to women known as "nickel throwers."[24] In sum, Automats were essentially live-action vending machines stocked by workers offering freshly prepared food. The quick service, uniform food, high-tech infrastructure, and inexpensive meals made them America's first fast food.[25]

Like Chet Morton, the public was awed by the technology and the presentation of menu items.[26] After the Automat had been in operation for many years, Edward O'Brien, a writer for the Federal Writers Project, probed the unique experience of dining on offer: "Here, the man-in-a-hurry is worried by no middle-men; his relationship with his fodder, over which he may gloat, ruminate, or despair, is strictly private. He selects, pays, conveys, eats, and departs, leaving no tip, uttering no sound."[27] Though O'Brien's account suggested a somewhat lonely experience, he seemed more taken with the serene, unbothered, and above all private context in which individuals made their selections. An earlier and more ambiguous review of Horn & Hardart portrayed the Automat's functioning as mysterious. Whether the New York reporter was inspired by the technology or found it a suspicious sleight of hand was unclear: "All you have to do is deposit a coin in a tiny slot in the wall, and before you can say 'National League for the Improvement of Urban Conditions

Figure 1.2. Interior of the Airline Terminal Automat at 80 East 42nd Street. The individual slots on the back wall are for sandwiches, bread, and rolls. Photograph by Drucker-Hilbert Co. Inc., Commercial Photography. Manuscript and Archives Division, New York Public Library.

Among Negroes' the catch is sprung, the golden cord is loosed, and by reaching into the letter box you may withdraw the twin tea biscuit."[28] The reporter's reference to a so-called Black organization is puzzling because nothing about Horn & Hardart bore evidence of a connection to Black, urban life.

Above all, the Automat emphasized a deluxe meal at a low price. The interior décor included stained glass, beveled mirrors, and neon lights; and because food was delivered from a central commissary, there was no possibility of a potentially unclean or sloppy attendant handling it.[29] The centralized cooking and exacting recipes also enabled consistency in the taste of each dish no matter which location the

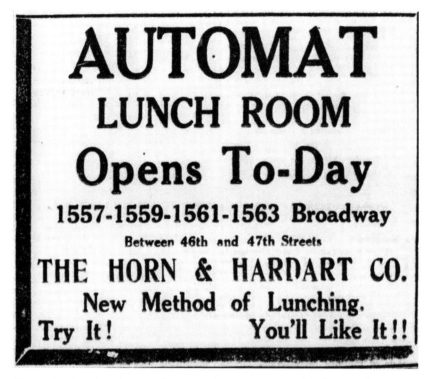

Figure 1.3. An advertisement for a new Automat, *New York Tribune,* July 2, 1912.

customer patronized—a hallmark of today's fast food dining.[30] However, unlike contemporary fast food, menu items at the Automat numbered in the several hundred.

Automats were prevalent across New York City, but only in White space. The first location, at 1557 Broadway (the heart of Times Square), quickly became a focal point for popular culture.[31] Others scattered in Midtown, Lower Manhattan, and into the outer boroughs tended to locate near large apartment buildings, residential hotels, and blocks of row houses. Uptown locations, such as 2710 Broadway (at West 104th Street), 611 West 181st Street (Manhattan), and 121 East 170th Street (the Bronx), bracketed—but avoided—Harlem. Black patrons did eat at Automats in neighborhoods other than where they lived. For example, in one market research study, two African American respondents reported having eaten at the Automat for decades, during their high school years, near their places of work, and while moving about the city.[32] But it is doubtful that Black customers dined at Automats in large numbers. Archival photographs of crowded interiors depict almost exclusively White customers, and popular accounts of the restaurant chain routinely made no mention of Black visitors.

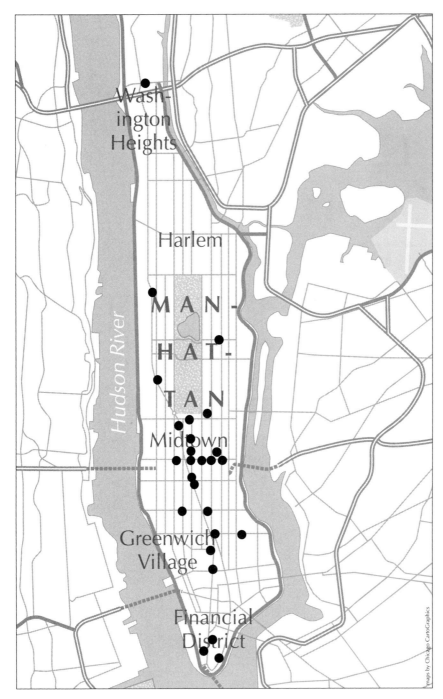

Map 1.1. Selected Horn & Hardart Automat locations in Manhattan. The company also operated retail stores and ran Automats in the outer boroughs, but depicted here are some of the key addresses. All were in operation by the early 1930s. Harlem, where almost all of Manhattan's Black residents lived, had no outlets. Map by Dennis McClendon, CartoGraphics.

Automats presented a competitive challenge to New York's inexpensive restaurants. They operated alongside saloons and their free lunches; but as the temperance movement grew stronger, several cities moved to prohibit saloon lunches to reduce the number of drinking customers. Once Prohibition was enacted, saloons closed altogether. As a result, lunchrooms serving lighter and more quickly prepared food such as sandwiches or soup did so "in environments dominated by clean, sanitary white tile."[33] Such restaurants became popular among white-collar workers in central business districts. Following lunchrooms were cafeterias (basically simplified versions of lunchrooms). Neither of these outlets served alcohol and were therefore spaces amenable to women, unlike saloons.[34] In fact, Horn & Hardart made it a point to advertise its women-friendly environment when it opened a new location at 68 Trinity Place in Lower Manhattan, stating it was "Specially equipped for ladies."[35]

Regardless of a customer's gender identity, the Automat system was enjoyable because it was quick and easy, customers could see the food before purchasing it, and the industrial fittings gave the feeling of a sanitary operation.[36] Hygiene was a critical concern for early twentieth-century diners and shoppers. People buying ground hamburger risked coming home with off-smelling beef mixed with chicken gizzards.[37] Hygienic concerns were particularly acute in the wake of Upton Sinclair's 1906 novel *The Jungle*. Born of intensive, undercover journalistic research in the "muckraker" tradition, the story was first published as a serial in a socialist journal called *Appeal to Reason*. A year later it appeared as a stand-alone work and sold twenty-five thousand copies within six weeks.[38] In Sinclair's vision of Chicago's stockyards, meatpacker to the nation, it was nothing short of a miracle if high-quality meat made its way to the market. The assembly-line slaughter of animals was mired in filth and disease, and the inspectors sent to mitigate against management's indifference were themselves corrupt. Sinclair's protagonist, Jurgis, learned "how the meat that was taken out of pickle would often be found sour, and how they would rub it up with soda to take away the smell, and sell it to be eaten on free-lunch counters."[39] Sinclair's narrative for the first third of the book is an almost continuous stream of nauseating prose. Canned products were a ghastly mix of biohazard and offal; cows were covered with boils that, once lanced, would splash workers with stinking liquids; and sausage was liable to be a dreadful slurry of beef gullets, rats and their feces, and borax. *The Jungle* suggested that the public (especially poor and immigrant residents) was at the mercy of a power structure that cared little for its welfare.

Sinclair's work ignited a firestorm of public outcry. Popular magazines such as *Collier's* published photos of slaughterhouse methods, and several widely read publications wrote about the terrible quality of U.S. meat. Industry executives reported that meat sales dropped by half in 1906. The public response to the issues raised in Sinclair's work led President Theodore Roosevelt to initiate an investigation of meatpacking practices, which quickly led to the passage of the Meat Inspection Act. For years afterward, the meat industry railed against *The Jungle* for its irrevocable effects on the market. During the 1920s, the industry engaged in aggressive advertising campaigns to emphasize how wholesome, healthy, and pure its products were. Still, "as late as 1940, meatpackers were still pointing to the lingering 'prejudice' against meat due to *The Jungle* as the main reason meat consumption had failed to keep pace with population growth."[40]

Around this time new burger chains tried to capitalize on the innovations bestowed by Automat service and benefit from a changing urban restaurant landscape, but were still tainted by the dodgy reputation of the meat they sold. The hamburger of the late nineteenth century was seen as food for the poor. These sandwiches were not offered at fine dining establishments, and in fact they rarely appeared on restaurant menus of any sort. Hamburgers were essentially an unadorned meatball served between two slices of white bread. A crude meal eaten at state and county fairs, it did not have much reach beyond these rural and small-town events. Much of Horn & Hardart's business model of cold, hard, clean food machines presaged the format of the burger restaurants that came to East Coast cities in the 1920s and 1930s. Cleanliness became a central selling point. Horn & Hardart had demonstrated that table service was not a prerequisite for an enjoyable dining experience; rather, it drew in patrons with fixed, affordable prices and consistency in product. Hamburger restaurants would use these same service methods to make their product the dominant fast food.

The threat of unclean dining establishments took shape in concerns not only about germs, but also about polluting bodies. White people were deeply affronted by social mixing with their Black counterparts, and they were determined that Black people would not share in the same pleasures they did. White mob violence in Chicago and across the nation revealed just how frequently Black patrons were subject to murderous attacks by self-appointed White gatekeepers at public leisure spaces, whether roller-skating rinks, amusement parks, or, most severely, swimming pools.[41] Black folks who attempted to partake of public leisure sites gambled with their lives. During the late nineteenth and early twentieth centuries, segregated amusement was seen as necessary because racial mixing rendered African Americans as social equals on the one hand and evoked perceptions of criminality, immorality, and disease on the other.[42] White citizens believed that a safe and virtuous space at private sites of leisure required Black exclusion, and the White media saw mob violence as a justifiable response to racial mixing.[43] Swimming pools involved the highest degree of racial risk, and violence at these spaces was routine.[44] A 1949 attack on a group of Black children in St. Louis by an angry mob of Whites turned into a daylong pogrom where any passing Black person was viciously assaulted. One man told a White child who was reticent to strike his Black counterpart, "Kill a nigger and you will make a name for yourself."[45]

Given that first-generation fast food emerged during an era when urban Black northerners could not expect to intermingle with White people in public or private leisure spaces, it is no surprise that when early fast food hamburger restaurants arrived they did so without any connection to urban Black space. While these outlets were not quite the leisure spaces that fast food restaurants became after World War II, they were a new convenience that Whites wanted to claim for themselves alone. The inexpensive, handheld meals on offer to workers and other pedestrians were humble, and the outlets were set in urban cores; yet the restaurants used imagery, names, and architectural design evoking shining castles and country estates. These burger "chateaux" were more than a convenience that Whites hoarded—the very constitution of the new burger chains relied on consumer appeals such as pristine cleanliness that were antithetical to accepted wisdom about Black bodies.

White Castle: The Birth of the Burger Joint

McDonald's is etched in the public's consciousness as the symbol for fast food, but White Castle preceded it by thirty-four years. Founded by Edgar W. "Billy" Ingram in 1921, it was the first fast food burger chain (though it, and the knockoffs to follow, did not franchise).[46] It entered the market as an eating place intimate in scale and focused on hygiene and cleanliness, like other burger contemporaries. For example, Krystal's, a chain based in Tennessee, promoted itself with the slogan "Clean as a whistle and clear as a crystal."[47] Though the brand is well-known, even at its height White Castle operated a relatively small roster of outlets—about three hundred restaurants mostly west of the Mississippi, a fraction of McDonald's holdings. Though characterized today as having "brought the hamburger sandwich to virtually every urban neighborhood and many rural communities,"[48] in fact, Black neighborhoods could not be counted among White Castle's clientele.

White Castle began when a Kansas short order cook named J. Walter Anderson experimented with different ways of grilling meat. After several restaurant stints, including briefly owning a restaurant his father had purchased for him, he ended up working in a Wichita diner. There, Anderson found that a flattened patty was easier to cook than the common meatball, and his customers enjoyed it served with onions on a bun instead of bread. His new concoction proved popular enough for him to launch his own business, where he put cleanliness on display, cooking in full view of the customers—including grinding the meat.[49]

Business boomed as Anderson served White, working-class locals who walked to the restaurant. Soon his new brand numbered several across the city, sporting the slogan "Buy 'em by the sack." Even as Anderson became a rich man, there remained some stigma against ground meat, and his elite peers did not dine at what were seen as poorly constructed street corner buildings. People also suspected that the unseemly stands were fronts for illicit activities. These beliefs brought Anderson's expansion plans to a halt. He was unable to obtain financing or secure leases for new locations and would have been at an impasse if Ingram, the real estate broker who had sold him his house, had not become his principal investor in 1921.[50]

As will be seen, Ingram was similar to founders of the other burger chateaux in that he was raised and worked in exclusively White communities where Black people were not accepted as social equals, and where racist violence was deployed to enforce those norms. Bill Marriott grew up in a context that would give birth to the Coon Chicken Inn, a restaurant that featured the racist caricature of a Black man with an open, gaping mouth as the front door. The kings of the burger chateaux also worked in professions that were deeply imbricated with the exclusion of Black Americans, such as real estate and leisure. Ingram was born in 1881 in Leadville, Colorado, and spent time as a child in Omaha and St. Joseph, Missouri. He moved to Wichita in 1907 upon securing a post as an agent for R. G. Dun and Company (later Dun and Bradstreet) and eventually opened his own insurance agency and real estate firm.[51] Wichita (and Kansas, more generally) was stained with racist violence. Lynch mobs in Kansas were frequent in the 1860s and 1870s, and sundown towns—where by local customs or laws Black persons who remained in town after dark met with arrest, violence, or death—enforced White racial boundaries, threatening Black migrants to Kansas with a climate of open hatred.[52] White men singled out for attack prosperous, successful Black people because "their achievements challenged the doctrine of natural white superiority, undermined white privilege, and under-scored the inadequacies of less successful white men."[53]

To begin his new venture, Ingram sold his share of his firm and, with an initial investment of $700, formed a partnership that resulted in White Castle. Modeled after Chicago's Water Tower, the only building to survive the Great Fire in 1871, the design was meant to evoke purity, cleanliness, sturdiness, and permanence. The restaurant took off by offering a spare menu comprising burgers, coffee, Coke, and pie. Ingram proclaimed that the days were over when the word "hamburger" would evoke dingy dives in lower-class sections of the city: "The day of the dirty, greasy

Figure 1.4. White Castle #16, 43 East Cermak Road (at 22nd Street) in Chicago, built in 1930. Photograph taken by author in November 2015. The plaque on the facade states, "This tiny white-glazed brick building remains the best-surviving example in Chicago of the buildings built by the White Castle System of Eating Houses, Inc." It is now a Famous Fried Chicken, which according to the marquee has been operating since 1972.

hamburger is past. No more shall we have to taste the hamburger at circuses or carnivals only."[54]

Reminiscent of *Super Size Me,* Morgan Spurlock's 2004 documentary, Ingram devised a stunt to prove his food's nutritional quality. He arranged for a University of Minnesota medical student to live on White Castle burgers and water for thirteen weeks. Toward the end, the student was eating about twenty to twenty-four burgers a day and purportedly remained in good health (unlike Spurlock).[55] Ingram's sponsored burger fest stood in contrast to the vegetarian and natural foods diets that saw many taking vitamins and eating Protose, a commercial meat substitute created by the Kellogg brothers, and such creations as nutburgers, served at Gates' Nut Kettle in Los Angeles.[56]

White Castle customers downed hamburgers by the sackful and the company's business grew throughout the mid-twenties. Its hamburgers became a staple lunch item for the White working class, and the restaurant was also appealing as a place of work, offering prized jobs that provided good wages, benefits, and a family atmosphere. Industry standards held that restaurant clerks required "a daily shave, well-trimmed hair, clean hands and fingernails, clean uniforms" and defined cleanliness as the result of "proper home training."[57] If management failed to monitor staff and prioritize desirable habits, the thinking went, workers would inevitably become unacceptably unkempt. White Castle followed this advice to the letter and required its employees to meet strict guidelines regarding hygiene, comportment, family background, and personal history.[58] In 1938, the company promoted the caliber of its food and its jobs by running print ads in Chicago in which its employees thanked the public. Sales of more than forty million burgers had apparently broken all sales records to date, and "we employes [*sic*] in the White Castles were given pay increases totaling nearly $50,000. In addition, we were given a special bonus at Christmas time, amounting to more than $33,000. Naturally we 620 employes [*sic*] are grateful to you for making these things possible."[59] The pay increases may have been the result of the Fair Labor Act, which required minimum wages and a forty-hour workweek, rather than White Castle's largesse. But these reports of record-breaking sales and employee bonuses would nudge curious potential consumers and workers alike to see what all the fuss was about.

First-generation burger joints therefore sold a consumable Whiteness in various forms. Early fast food was less openly racist than a restaurant like the Coon Chicken Inn, which sold Whiteness through the consumption, and indeed the domination and mockery, of Blackness.[60] But these small outlets were still premised on racial exclusion and sold Whiteness through the invisibility of Blackness. They sold Whiteness as consumable purity, cleanliness, and moral uprightness. They sold Whiteness through social standing and an honest day of working-class labor. And they sold the fuel that White men not so blessed as to work within its confines needed to sustain themselves wherever they toiled.

Immaculate White Work

If immaculate whiteness was required in uniforms, the same was true for skin color. White Castle's career opportunities extended only to White men. Since the restaurants were not located in Black neighborhoods, it was unlikely Black workers could find work there. For example, Black Chicagoans generally had difficulty finding work near their homes, and had to travel to factories, meatpacking houses, and steel mills, the last being the least hospitable.[61] Overall, Black workers were overwhelmingly restricted to domestic and personal service. In 1910, nearly half of employed Black men held one of just four jobs: porters, servants, waiters, and janitors. More than two-thirds of Black women were domestic servants or launderers. Professions, skilled trades, clerical work, and civil service—apart from postal workers—were essentially closed to Black workers.[62]

Accepted views of Black men as loathsome brutes ruled out their employment in the burger chateaux. In addition to a steadfast commitment to White space and White customers, fast food continued to keep a segregated service counter through the Great Depression and as the country approached World War II. What is striking about fast food's White labor force is that it ran contrary to social and labor norms that saw Black people as uniquely suited to service positions. Prior to World War I, Black men in Chicago were largely consigned to work in restaurants and railroad dining cars, where Black male servants were not only common but expected. In the late 1800s and early 1900s in New York, some commented in the popular press that "there are some occupations for which the negro has a natural born talent. As barbers, waiters, coachmen and janitors they are quite up to the mark of the proud Caucasian. In fact, I am not sure but that they are superior to the whites in the avocations I have mentioned." If any fault could be found with Black waiters, it was that their attentiveness bordered on obsequiousness, according to a 1912 article: "His principal failing . . . is the familiar fact that he errs by excess of zeal, as a general rule. He usually makes his services too obvious."[63]

But fast food saw things differently, and the perceived contagious threat of Black workers was again a key register. Even in the squalor of Chicago's meatpacking plants, industry leaders Swift and Armour both decreed that no finished products could pass through the hands of Black male employees, lest plant visitors see this and be put off buying or eating the products.[64] Horn & Hardart echoed this structure, sequestering its Black employees out of sight in back-of-house posi-tions.[65] Black workers were generally cooks, bussers, or dishwashers rather than servers or cashiers.[66] African American journalist Layle Lane was fascinated with Philadelphia's Automats, writing that "there is no color line with the mechanical de-vice." In fact, the mechanical device was central to keeping the color line. Even posi-tions behind the technological interface that delivered food were too visible. Black workers were segregated from White patrons and forbidden from loading food into the slots, lest the sight of Black hands offend customers.[67] The company's motto that it was "a good place to work" was not applicable to all.[68] By 1961, the Congress of Racial Equality picketed the Philadelphia Automats for sequestering Black em-ployees out of view.[69]

Black workers (and White immigrants, for that matter) were poorly paid at the Automats, and it was their cheap labor that allowed for its famously low prices. Hardart's great-granddaughter would later call the company's labor policies "be-nevolent despotism."[70] African Americans worked at Horn & Hardart for years, even decades, in precarious and underpaid jobs with little to show for their dedica-tion other than accolades in the company newsletter.[71] Black employees, regardless of whether they were consigned to monotonous jobs, were loath to take the risky step of unionizing. Members of the Colored Employees Relief Association (a segre-gated group to which workers contributed for health benefits) were told by manage-ment that any workers who voted to organize would be summarily dismissed and replaced with White workers.[72]

Horn & Hardart prided itself on a climate of inclusiveness; but given the com-pany's labor practices, it was a stretch even to call this an aspirational goal. And com-pany documents suggested there were additional racial problems hidden beneath the surface. In an undated annual report, Horn & Hardart president William J. Curtis argued that despite efforts to foster brotherhood among racial and religious groups, there were "times when we have failed to measure up to our democratic ideals and to the basic teaching of both Christians and Jews." What took place is unclear; but the tone suggested conflicts that undermined the company's purported ideals. If so, the company could not be surprised when its own organ published racist tropes; an anecdote about a Chinese restaurateur who had reportedly stolen Automat cutlery concluded, "Eating Slimp Slop Sluey, with Horn & Hardee Sliver, not velly healthy. Eh! Well, we'll be seeing you Wong—but not too Soon. Bletter watchee step next time Wong, or Soon gettem right back in cooler."[73]

Horn & Hardart's Automats wore an undeserved mantle of racial democracy, with notions of their egalitarianism quickly assimilated into public discourse about the chain, then and now. Even as it busied itself making reams of cash, the Automat, so it went, welcomed both Wall Street banker and newsboy, providing a unique setting for social mixing at tables.[74] In a 2007 report, New York City's Landmark Commission looked back at the Automats as a popular space, calling them "one of the city's cherished democratic institutions, appealing to a wide clientele."[75] David Freeland claimed that "the restaurant's managers proved extremely tolerant of those on society's outskirts," which included gay and lesbian New Yorkers. And yet, for Black customers, this tolerance was uncertain, Freeland qualified: "African Americans could, *for the most part,* dine without discrimination."[76] Indeed, the purported democracy of the Automat was not extended to all connected to it, and certainly not to its own employees.

At the burger chateaux, apart from racialized fears about hygiene, the subversion of a White public face and posture of superiority contraindicated hiring Black employees. In the postwar South, lunch counters were oriented toward quick and efficient service, usually run by White female servers. These women were a lunch counter's public face: while Black women prepared food in the back, White women took orders and served White diners who sat on stools out front.[77] But in northern burger joints, there was no back of house to which Black staff could be relegated. All the food was prepared and served up front, and large windows meant that the public face of the restaurant was visible even from the street. Black male employees would therefore have put Black masculinity on display as a representation of the business. From a White perspective, Black male waiters served platters to their racial betters in railroad dining rooms. As Malcolm X recalled of his work on the Yankee Clipper line to New York:

> I sold sandwiches, coffee, candy, cake, and ice cream as fast as the railroad's commissary department could supply them. It didn't take me a week to learn that all you had to do was give white people a show and they'd buy anything you offered them. It was like popping your shoeshine rag. The dining car waiters and Pullman porters knew it too, and they faked their Uncle Tomming to get bigger tips. We were in that world of Negroes who are both servants and psychologists, aware that white people are so obsessed with their own importance that they will pay liberally, even dearly, for the impression of being catered to and entertained.[78]

In contrast, burger chateaux countermen occupied a position of high visibility and responsibility as they took charge of a room full of White patrons. Moreover, they did so in a space where these patrons could not lay claim to social airs. Whereas fine dining restaurants could be expected to induce self-exclusion among potential

Black consumers by virtue of the price, the comportment of the elites who dined in them, or the style of service, burger joints erected no such barriers. A man clad in overalls could comfortably eat a ten-cent meal ordered from a limited menu that required few literacy skills. Little was required of patrons to dine at burger restaurants, and no pretense was made about the simple and humble quality of the meals served. The nature of the menu therefore precluded Black counter staff if racial hierarchies were to be maintained. Giving Black people the controls to technological advancements and showcasing them as master grill staff as they prepared new, modern meals would upend racial norms.

Countermen positions in the Northeast were often explicitly racialized as White. For example, in Baltimore, one employment agency sought "colored" busboys, waiters, and bellmen but "white" pantry- and countermen. In New York, among the individuals who listed "counterman" as an occupation in the 1940 census, White men outnumbered their Black counterparts by a factor of fifty. They also earned a higher weekly salary, with more variability in the range of earnings. Black men who worked in restaurants were generally kitchen attendants, kitchen helpers, cooks, dishwashers, waiters, and porters.[79]

As late as 1950, White Castle was not hiring Black workers, even in the face of labor shortages brought on by the Korean War. When a Louisville, Kentucky, executive observed throngs of work-seeking Black men gathering across the street, he did not think to hire any of them.[80] Black men certainly do not appear in any historical photos of the company's crews. Into the 1960s, White Castle employed no Black workers at all in several cities.[81] In 1963, CORE protested the chain's retention of only twenty-eight Black workers—all reportedly porters—out of a staff of five hundred in Bronx.[82]

World War II led the burger chateaux to hire White women for the first time, but they made no real changes in hiring Black folk, though some outlets in Kansas City resorted to hiring "colored girls" as servers.[83] In the fall of 1942, White Castle advertised in the Chicagoland *Southtown Economist* paper for counter and grill work for young women aged twenty or older. A year later, Little Tavern advertised in the *Washington Post* for counterwomen, marshalling a fair amount of chutzpah to describe a job serving burgers as essential to the war effort: "If you are interested in changing to an Essential Job get in touch with Little Tavern Shops, Inc." But by 1967 the company would be back to advertising for countermen alone. White Tower also brought women on board during the war; photos of "Towerettes" appeared as early as 1939, and more significant numbers came on after World War II. Though no large-scale changes in hiring practices for Black workers took place, Detroit's lone African American White Castle employee was a woman brought on to do janitorial work during the war.[84]

Neither did White Castle serve Black folk. Map 1.2 shows that in 1935, most of its Chicago locations were deep on the South Side—a time well before the area became home to large numbers of Black residents. None were in Bronzeville, at the time the heart of the Black community. In 1915, the neighborhood stretched approximately from 12th Street to the north, State Street to the west, 39th Street to the south, and Lake Michigan to the east.[85] The northernmost White Castle, at 22nd Street (Cermak Road) and Wabash (#16, shown in above in Figure 1.4), was on the cusp of the Black Belt. Using census statistics from 1940, the earliest year for which data are available at the tract level, Black Chicagoans resided in a staggered distribution: high in numbers west of State Street above 22nd Street, and also numerous below 22nd Street, mostly east of State. Thus, Cermak was the dividing line between an area that was 96 percent White and the beginnings of Bronzeville, which at its northernmost part was not as heavily Black (38 percent) compared to the rest of the neighborhood. The White Castle outlet at 63rd and Evans was another where the racial composition hung in the balance. By 1940, the census tract lying to the south side of 63rd was 92 percent Black; the tract across the street was 99.8 percent White. Note that because it is drawn from 1940, the census data indicate more Black residents than would have been the case five years prior. And, considering the overwhelming Whiteness of the remaining locations (the first of which to open was at 2501 East 79th Street in July 1929), these racially liminal spaces are not an indication of White Castle's seeking out Black customers; rather, the company found those neighbors increasingly proximal to its stores over time, a trend that would recur for McDonald's and other chains.

Interestingly, the chain also avoided the all-White areas west of Bronzeville, creating a visible gap between the more northern locations and those on the South Side. Most likely White Castle forwent this area because it housed the Union Stockyards made infamous by Upton Sinclair. Anything at all near the "Square Mile"—responsible for the slaughter of thousands of cattle, hogs, and sheep per day and the production of meat and by-products including glue and fertilizer—would be inhospitable to fast food. Even if White Castle sought out the enormous market of stockyard workers, slaughterhouse management would surely balk at restaurants selling meat to its staff.

White Castle was selling small, neat hamburgers in pristine conditions, so locating near the bloody chaos of slaughter would defeat the purpose entirely. Even with the abattoirs out of sight, the stockyards stank. The city's prevailing winds carried the stench across the South Side and as far as seven miles off to the Loop. In 1919, a city alderman argued that "when the wind is just right, the smell makes residents of Hyde Park and Englewood wish they had been born without olfactory nerves." Compounding the slaughterhouse operations were the noxious aspects of the site's

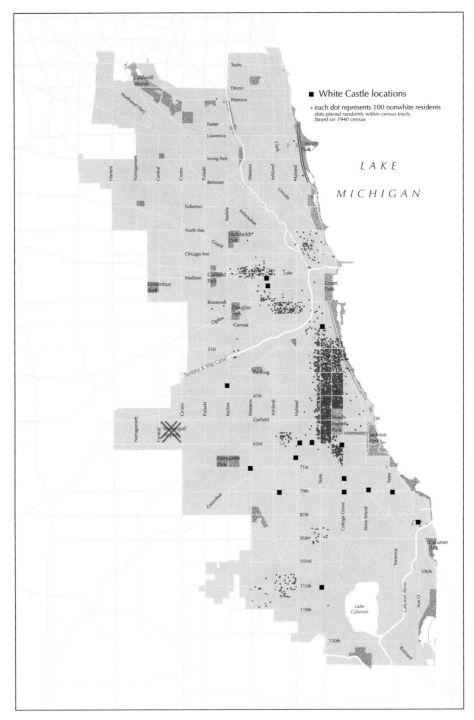

Map 1.2. White Castle locations in Chicago as of 1935 against the Black population in 1940. Today, these points largely describe the South Side's Black communities, ranging from 63rd to 127th Streets. In 1935, the populations in these areas were all White. Map by Dennis McClendon, CartoGraphics.

infrastructure. "Bubbly Creek," a mile-long open sewer that carried stockyard waste, chemicals, grease, and other toxins down 39th Street from Halsted to Racine, submerged a wide swath of the city in a continuous stink.[86] Sinclair detailed the smell as something "you could literally taste . . . you could take hold of it, almost, and examine it at your leisure." Real-life testimony affirmed this description. The *Chicago Tribune*'s "Inquiring Reporter" heard from Antoinette Arling, a stockyard visitor from the suburb of Downers Grove, who opined that "the smell is simply awful. It reminds one of a poison gas bombardment. The city should furnish gas masks at the main entrance."[87] In avoiding both the Square Mile and Bronzeville, White Castle showed that the Union Stockyards' nauseating mire and Black neighborhoods were equally off-putting.

White Castle Knockoffs

The other two restaurants that joined the ranks of the burger chateaux did so toward the end of the 1920s. White Tower and Little Tavern were led by White men from different regions of the country but similar backgrounds of privilege amid a terrain of White supremacy. There is little information on the racial views of these figures, but the worlds in which they lived are useful in triangulating how dominant attitudes about Black people animated their establishments.

White Tower was the brainchild of Thomas E. Saxe Jr., born in Milwaukee in 1903, and Thomas Sr., an Irish immigrant who arrived in 1900. With Thomas Jr. as the project lead, the two opened the first restaurant near Marquette University in Milwaukee, one year before Thomas Jr. graduated from the University of Minnesota in 1927. The Saxes owned a number of businesses together. As with Ingram, one of these was a real estate concern; and others were movie theaters and amusement parks, often in sundown towns.[88] In 1932, Thomas Saxe Jr. lived in Whitefish Bay, a town whose population has historically been so dominated by White residents that in contemporary parlance it is referred to as "Whiteface Bay" or "Whitefolk Bay."[89]

White Tower, in concept and design, was a clear copy of White Castle, a transgression for which the company would become locked in a protracted five-year legal battle that it lost in 1934. The ruling required White Tower to change almost everything about the company's business—its architecture, slogan, and any other features that were easily confused with White Castle. A name change would have been in order as well had Ingram not allowed White Tower to keep it in exchange for royalties.[90] Initially, the building design was a one-story edifice with a tower on one corner, minimal decoration, and small windows. Like White Castle, the white facade meant to evoke cleanliness and wholesomeness; indeed, the architecture itself enabled scrupulous cleaning routines. White Tower's architect, Frank B. Proctor, stated, "In Washington, D.C., I would go into the building with the plan examiners, and by the time I got finished with them they would say to me, 'This isn't a building, it's a machine.'"[91] More than that, the use of the color white and the castle imagery evoked racial purity and the strength of European culture.[92]

Open twenty-four hours a day, seven days a week, the restaurants had no use for standard front doors and disposed of anything in the entry beyond screen doors. White Tower's menu was dominated by a five-cent hamburger, which was served to the same kind of clientele as at White Castle—White, working-class men. The burgers were presented in rather austere fashion on a paper napkin, matching the spartan restaurant environment. Like White Castle, White Tower had to overcome customer wariness of hamburger meat. According to one employee, "At first, when the White Tower started, a lot of people were afraid of the hamburgers. That's why I prepared them in the window, so that people could actually see the product that they were getting. We're very quality conscious."[93] And, in line with White Castle and other restaurants that retained all-male kitchen, counter, and table help, White Tower did not hire women.[94] After a year of expansion in the Midwest, the company had made a name for itself, especially in Detroit, where it built over thirty stores in 1928, all within one block of automobile factories or busy intersections that served mass transit.

White Tower continued its growth in the early years of the Depression and expanded east to Philadelphia, New York, Pittsburgh, and Washington, D.C. As it did so, the outlets were enlarged and their interiors began to sport porcelain enamel wall coverings, more stools and, later, booths, to attract women. The company continued to prize corner locations near factories, transit lines, and major traffic interchanges.

Philadelphia's Broad Street subway line had a White Tower at more than half of its station entrances by 1932.[95] But because vacant land in the East was scarce (and therefore more expensive), restaurants often had to be retrofitted into existing storefronts or mid-block spaces.[96] Nevertheless, the outlets stood out because their compact, bright white facades contrasted with the stores around them, which were often dark, dirty, and busy with signage and text.

White Tower arrived in D.C. in the 1930s, unfettered by its nemesis White Castle. It chose downtown locations ideally suited to capture workers, shoppers, and other pedestrians. White Tower's first restaurant in the District landed at 631 F Street NW, near Judiciary Square and what is today the Gallery Place–Chinatown Metro station. Contemporary F Street is dominated by a wall of glass comprising the single address of the Verizon Convention Center. But in the early 1930s, the area was a busy, cast-iron commercial district with over one hundred

Figure 1.5. White Tower location at 740 Broadway in Brooklyn. The buildings were photographed by New York City as part of the Department of Finance's capturing images of all tax lots in the city for property tax appraisals, and as an employment program for the Works Progress Administration. The number in the photograph is the tax lot ID number. Photo print, 3_2276_0029, New York City tax lot photos. Courtesy Municipal Archives, City of New York.

businesses on the block. The chain's second, third, and fourth restaurants were close to the White House and a clutch of government buildings including the Bureau of Internal Revenue, the Agricultural Adjustment Administration, and the International Monetary Fund. All would have been a boon for lunchtime trade, and the vendors who set up carts in front of the Agriculture building to sell simple fare to government workers must have rued the burger chain's arrival. Nearby competitors included Chinese, Italian, and other restaurants, but there should have been ample foot traffic to share from neighboring auto-related businesses, several prominent hotels, and other establishments. Even White Towers in outlying residential areas, such as Store #5, a small building in the Columbia Heights neighborhood, were near community hubs including movie theaters, undertakers, churches, public schools, and post offices.[97]

Over time, the restaurant design changed. Initial stores had a medieval image that suggested "royalty and social and gastronomic prominence." For example, the New York City outlet at the corner of 138th and Broadway was a small, freestanding restaurant built in the original style with crenellation. Though located uptown, the restaurant was situated to the west of Black Central Harlem, in a community that was almost exclusively White. Soon, White Towers began to be built in a modern style that symbolized "luxury, cleanliness, speed, and efficiency."[98] The change was due in no small part to the White Castle lawsuit edict. The updated style was evident in buildings such as at 240 West 50th Street (Figure 1.6). By 1940, the Northeast was a hotbed of White Tower construction. They appeared in a wide variety of locations: little buildings on large lots surrounded by abundant empty space; stacked under taller buildings in busy commercial districts; or sandwiched between skyscrapers, lit up with gooseneck lamps. The unmistakable design rendered their prior function recognizable decades later when they were reused by independent restaurants.

The last of the prominent burger chateaux was Harry F. Duncan's Little Tavern, founded in Louisville. Born in 1899 in Missouri, Duncan grew up in Kentucky during a time of a racial terror for Black folks.[99] Black life in Kentucky was also devalued using racial caricature in cartoons, as it was elsewhere in the country. Connecting dim-wittedness to Black eating patterns, a newspaper cartoon printed in 1928 depicted a crudely drawn Black man named Hambone saying to himself, "Some folks selects what dey gwine eat fum dat bill, but I selects it fum mah pocket-book!!"[100] And like Ingram and the Saxes, Duncan came to his restaurant business from prior work in real estate, a profession deeply fraught by race in Louisville; in 1913, the city considered (and ultimately passed) racial zoning laws along the lines of those pioneered in Baltimore.[101]

Figure 1.6. White Tower at 240 West 50th Street, Manhattan. Photo print, 1_0121_0057, New York City tax lot photos. Courtesy Municipal Archives, City of New York.

Duncan set up shop in October 1928 in Washington, D.C., where a Little Tavern opened its doors at 814 E Street NW. Little Tavern kept to the castle theme, displaying crenellated cornices and white finishes to emphasize cleanliness. It offered a five-cent burger and employed a similar motto to White Castle's: "Buy 'em by the bag." Publicity on the East Coast made nary a mention of Duncan's having lifted the concept from White Castle. Instead, the dominant narrative was that of Duncan as hamburger pioneer. Media reports described his restaurant as distinct from "its slightly younger competitor, White Tower"; noted that his unique hamburger taste, flavored with onions, hadn't "changed since the mid-1920s"; and declared that he put cheeseburgers on the map "when the concept of marrying cheese to ground beef was unknown."[102]

Little Tavern eventually dispatched with its imitation of White Castle and created a new trademark image: a Tudor cottage style in porcelain enamel with a sloped, green, faux-shingled roof. The restaurant popped up all over D.C., often making the news when it did so. In 1939, there were twenty-one stores between the D.C. area and Baltimore; by 1949, there were forty-nine.[103] Little Taverns were erected in a variety of neighborhoods, ranging from busy, densely populated downtown business and commercial districts to quiet residential communities. The unifying characteristic was that when there were a significant number of residents nearby, they were sure to be White.

After taking his chain from Louisville to Washington, Duncan stayed on as a permanent resident. Both he and Ingram enjoyed their later years as rich men in exclusionary White settings.[104] Meanwhile, after ten years of selling burgers, White Castle determined that White men alone would not sustain the business. It began reaching out beyond this customer base in the 1930s, in large part because the Depression was depressing sales. White Castle began assuring women that its food was wholesome and should be part of a family's diet. A major tactic was to create the character Julia Joyce, a White Castle "hostess." She spread the good word about the restaurant, educating White, middle-class women in clubs, nonprofits, and other settings. Another new customer segment was college students, whom Ingram targeted by building outlets near campuses.[105] Promotional campaigns featuring reduced prices were common, albeit with copy that by today's standards was extremely verbose. In one newspaper promotion, White Castle offered a coupon special, five hamburgers for ten cents (carryout only): "This special offer is for the purpose of acquainting you with the superiority of White Castle Hamburgers. Incidentally, you will see how clean and elegant is the interior of a White Castle. Then you will continue to be a White Castle customer and that will repay us for making you this special inducement to once visit one of our

Figure 1.7. The intersection of Park Avenue and North Liberty Street near Baltimore's Inner Harbor. Little Tavern Shop #16 was located at 10 Park Avenue, a few stores down out of view, around the bend on the left side of the street. Source: Baltimore City Archives.

many White Castles, which you will find in 16 metropolitan centers throughout the country."[106]

After White women and college students, Ingram did not turn to Black customers, but instead to technological innovations. He created curb service in 1935, so that customers could eat in their cars, and introduced forty-foot billboards to entice motorists.[107] White Castle also began punching holes in its patties, purportedly a technological advancement to improve uniform cooking.[108] In fact, the company was responding to World War II–induced food price increases by reducing the patty size: first by thinning them down from 1.0 to 0.8 ounces, and second by punching those holes and using the extra meat to produce additional patties.[109]

The meat industry was also reaching out both to women and to those who ate less meat in the interwar years for reasons of nutrition. It also targeted the medical profession to sway their ideas about the healthfulness of a meat-centric diet. In the 1930s and 1940s, homemakers were also singled out in home economics materials aiming to convince women that abundant consumption of meat was not only healthful but beneficial for weight loss.[110] These forces helped propel higher consumption of meat, whether in grocery stores or at restaurants like White Castle. Taken together, hamburgers came to be widely "perceived as tasty, simple, cheap, and healthy."[111] Ingram's prediction that hamburgers would no longer be seen as suspect carnival food had come true. By the end of the 1940s, the negative connotations of the burger were gone; the National Restaurant Association proclaimed burgers to be a national food, along with apple pie and coffee.[112]

A national food would presumably include the entire nation, but the industry disavowed Black people. Since Black space was widely associated with disease and degradation, and the outlets' sine qua non was cleanliness, situating there would undo the work all that white tile was doing for racial purity. An association with Blackness was deeply incompatible for these literally white restaurants. Whiteness was an amenity that home builders could provide without cost; unlike blinds, tiles, or other home features, keeping a place segregated was free.[113] By analogy, the burger chateaux could provide a White dining experience, literally and figuratively fending off the perceived infectious immorality that Blackness brought.

Black communities were supposedly perilous to the health of White neighbors, but White residents illicitly enjoyed brothels, nightclubs, and other venues that provided a "primitive release and premodern pleasure."[114] Even as reformers castigated Black people as immoral and sexually lax, cities such as Chicago, New York, and Philadelphia founded vice commissions that ostensibly cracked down on gambling, prostitution, and other forms of social disorder, but in reality drove vice into Black districts.[115] It was profitable for politicians and police to do so, as they were paid off to forego surveillance in certain areas. Philadelphia police were willing to overlook anything White pimps did short of murder, and Chicago police tolerated prostitution if they kept to Black streets.[116] Black neighborhoods made to be coextensive with vice were inhospitable environments for early fast food.

Given that the founders of first-generation fast food came from social milieu and professional experiences that would render Black neighborhoods and customers invisible and even decidedly inferior, it further increased the likelihood that Black patrons would be excluded. These White men hailed from geographies where any indication of Black social mobility triggered the most severe racial sanctions. Their restaurants, in locating in White space alone and hiring and serving only White customers, adhered to the same social contract. The limited menus and dining styles available at the burger chateaux and the Automats did what homogeneous cuisine projects do: create a sense of order that minimized regional foodways and act as cipher for national virtues, which were then literally incorporated by citizens.[117] Early fast food's unifying virtue was to promote bonds of Whiteness across ethnic lines through the exclusion of people of color. Because these restaurants had national reach but were not franchised, they helped nationalize a brand of racial exclusivity that was not subject to the mediating forces of the individual owner/operators.

Fast food has long enjoyed a central place in the iconography of American culture, and popular discourse has seen these outlets as comfortable oases for average folk to enjoy a good meal. But Black people were always incompatible for one reason or another. Scholars have seen the burger chateaux as a unifying force in harmonizing the varied ethnicities that made up early twentieth-century America, one that forged a national identity that drew in diverse groups as they all shared their common meal of the hamburger.[118] In fact, these restaurants helped forge a national *White* identity. They made Black people invisible in new dining experiences, shunting them to the realm of unseen labor or excluding them from work and consumption entirely.

As the next chapter will show, a lack of neighborhood access to first-generation fast food outlets in no way prevented Black urbanites from eating out. They created their own casual dining establishments in Black Belts across the North and may not have even given much thought to the temples of Whiteness that served burgers across town. But the near total exclusion of Black people from the early chains was meaningful for Black life and for what fast food would continue to be over the course of the twentieth century. Whether drive-ins or walk-ups, regional chains or national brands, these establishments revealed that little is neutral about American food culture. Arising alongside of and dependent on the urban ghetto, early fast food quickly fell into (the color) line, reproducing not only a racialized geography of opportunity but also racial tropes that cast Black people to the fringes of decency. Fast food's first outlets would have the public believe that even the simplest of meals would be defiled by Blackness—that a plate of pie or a fried meat patty on bread could shore up a desperately needed premise of racial superiority. First-generation fast food embodied just how seductive Whiteness was to White people.

2

Inharmonious Food Groups

Burger Chateaux, Chicken Shacks, and
Urban Renewal's Attack on the Existential
Threat of Blackness

When in 1935 the Home Owners' Loan Corporation (HOLC) issued maps that graded neighborhoods on credit worthiness and risk, Black communities were uniformly marked red to indicate that they were "hazardous" and did not merit investment. A January 1940 assessment of an enormous section of Chicago's Black Belt—stretching from 35th Street to 67th Street north to south, and from Cottage Grove to State Street east to west—was unequivocal in its denouncement of Black space: "A blighted area, 100 per cent negro, predominantly apartment buildings. . . . Already Washington Park at the south, a very fine park, has been almost completely monopolized by the colored race." The assessment continued, suggesting that the pending construction of the Ida B. Wells public housing project, presumably a result of this "monopoly," foretold the inevitable: "the colored influence . . . further encroaching on park and lake water frontage . . . With approximately 6,500 colored people moving into this district, it is evident they cannot be closed in; they must have an outlet; and the problem of keeping park and water frontage close by reasonably free of them will be difficult to surmount."[1] It was as if Black people were a horde of rats.

HOLC's rhetoric concretized disgust in government policy. So, too, did the Federal Housing Administration, whose *Underwriting Manual* outlined a hierarchy of objectionable neighborhood characteristics that had bearing on lending decisions, with racial composition high in this hierarchy (but to be fair, in some instances, Black people were identified as but one among many material nuisances ranging from industrial uses, narrow streets, and "freakish architectural designs").[2] This was the tenor of racism that gave food retailing a particular taboo for White merchants. It meant that the rise of retail chains in the food arena worked at

Figure 2.1. This restaurant stood at the intersection of Bladensburg Road and Maryland Avenue NE (which Benning Road also passes through)—a White D.C. neighborhood in 1930. Like many of the burger chateaux, its hamburgers sold for a nickel. CHS 14859, DC History Center.

cross-purposes for White and Black consumers: the promise of standardized merchandise, service, and retail interiors for Whites, another layer of exclusion from the market for Blacks. Fast food, like other food retailers (e.g., groceries and supermarkets), would not be an equalizing force.

Contemporary public discourse sees Black people as somehow crazed for fast food, unable to exercise willpower and/or lacking the taste and good sense for healthy foods. This has never been the case, but it was especially evident in the early to mid-twentieth century, when first-generation fast food reigned. Black residents were excluded from these new chains, but went about their business eating in their own communities and showing minimal interest in hamburgers. Indeed, middle-class Black folks were inclined to look down on this kind of food and instead sought to engage in "respectable eating." First-generation restaurants were absent from Black communities, and those located elsewhere could not be counted on to serve

Black customers. Black folks did not accept such discrimination—in 1938, White Castle refused service to four Black diners in Whiting, Indiana, and found itself party to a lawsuit.[3] But neither were they unequivocally enthusiastic about fast food.

The 1930s and 1940s were a time of growth and challenge for early fast food. All the leading restaurants continued adding new locations to their rosters, brought in more and more customers, and made more and more money. They were able to do so within the same racial posture that launched these establishments—one in which Black customers and Black space were verboten. To use the language of the Federal Housing Administration, fast food willingly ceded the "inharmonious racial groups" in Black communities because they were incompatible with the industry's racial aims. Deciding to pass over Black consumer dollars, fast food embraced a stance of racial exclusion. Still, as urban policies changed the landscape around them, those sentiments came home to roost and first-generation fast food outlets found themselves on a trajectory that would ultimately render them obsolete. The broader racial politics that saw Blackness as an existential threat that needed to be spatially contained or eradicated altogether fueled slum clearance and urban renewal. Urban renewal did lasting damage to Black communities, hence the colloquial appellation "Negro removal" coined by James Baldwin. But these policies also upended urban-centered, first-generation fast food, setting the stage for the birth of second-generation fast food and the long demise of the early chains.

Food Retail in the Black Metropolis

In the late 1920s, a pair of Jewish real estate developers in Chicago surprised observers with the scale of their $1 million entertainment center, the Regal Theater and Savoy Ballroom. The complex was to house a deluxe theater, ballroom, department store, drugstore, bowling alleys, and dozens of other businesses. Equally surprising was the fact that Black workers would assume positions throughout. Noticing the Regal's potential, ambitious White business owners then began to seek out a larger share of the Black South Side market with new goods and services. These included Walgreen's (located within the Regal complex) and a number of other stores.[4] Perhaps these developers were personally motivated to provide commercial enterprises that served Black folks; perhaps they saw the potential profits to be made; or perhaps they figured that providing nearby retail would keep Black people from venturing to White space to meet their shopping needs. After all, Black folks who lived outside "[their] proper environment" (i.e., Black neighborhoods) became "a nuisance" obsessed with social equality, "overbearing, inflated, irascible . . . dangerous to all with whom [they come] in contact."[5]

White-owned food retail, however, maintained a posture of disinterest toward a Black consumer base. If White immigrants had to deal with high prices at small grocers, Black shoppers were doubly penalized at insular proprietorships often hostile to them as customers. African Americans therefore embraced packaged food and the emergence of chain stores, hoping that standardized pricing and packaging would mitigate against racial discrimination.[6] Chain stores such as the A&P (The Great Atlantic and Pacific Tea Company) began to compete in U.S. cities first with crowded and dingy outdoor markets, and then with the more orderly indoor markets that replaced them. With slogans such as "Quality you know by name" the A&P brought into focus the reliability and standardized merchandise that customers would find in the aisles. This was not to be realized for Black shoppers. They still lost out because chain grocers located in the immediate suburbs; in some instances, drive-in supermarkets were built as part of housing developments that had racially restrictive covenants. It was not until the onset of the Depression that grocers were incentivized to capture sales wherever they could and chains moved toward selling to Black customers.[7]

Black communities redressed inequalities in groceries by forming cooperative enterprises, which were attractive to those who rejected as insufficiently radical a Black capitalist posture. So popular were they in the 1930s that the *Atlanta Daily World* called them a fad. Veteran activist Ella Baker served as national director of the Young Negroes' Cooperative League and was an officer at Harlem's Own Cooperative before going on to become a staff member at the NAACP, executive director of the Southern Christian Leadership Conference, and founder of the Student Nonviolent Coordinating Committee.[8] Two of the largest co-ops in Chicago, born out of dissatisfaction with nearby low-quality food retail, were at the Ida B. Wells and Altgeld Gardens public housing projects. By 1947, Altgeld's more than three-thousand-square-foot store had the highest sale figures among all Chicago co-ops.[9]

Retail and groceries were not the only arenas in which food was a nexus for a conflicted consumer status. Restaurants emerged repeatedly during the 1940s as sites where consumerism and citizenship clashed. Black soldiers returned from World War II to heartbreak when they could not enjoy the same level of service that German prisoners of war did. Richard Wright was left to eat in his car at the D.C. opening of a stage adaption of his novel *Native Son*, barred from the restaurant at which the other producers dined. And the first lunch counter sit-in took place when three Black women enrolled at Howard could not get the hot chocolates they ordered at the United Cigar Store.[10] In New York City, Black diners could not count on acceptable service until after antidiscrimination laws arrived after World War II.[11] The Committee on Civil Rights in Manhattan studied sixty-two of East

Midtown's 771 restaurants and documented inferior service though not necessarily outright refusals. Black customers were met with surprise and dismay upon entry; were seated often with delays in undesirable locations; were either hurried or served excessively slowly; and were charged unreasonable prices for unpalatable food. Two years later, similar findings emerged in West Midtown.[12]

Fast food restaurants discriminated both through their avoidance of Black space and their refusal to serve Black customers. The high demand in Black neighborhoods for quick, inexpensive, ready-to-eat meals was clearly comparable to that among White ethnic immigrants. But first-generation fast food restaurants did not capitalize on that demand, as they were uninterested in interracial exchange.[13] Unlike in the realm of supermarkets, Black activists did not organize to create Black-owned entities until the 1960s, when fast food was a franchised business. Of course, this did not mean that there were no Black restaurants in Black communities or that Black communities were bereft of options simply because national chains rejected them. Black sole proprietorships decorated Black Belts with a variety of eating and drinking places selling prepared foods. In fact, in the 1920s and 1930s, Black entrepreneurs were heavily concentrated in the restaurant and grocery business, with Black women more likely to own restaurants than any other business. Drake and Cayton's investigation of Bronzeville businesses ranked groceries and restaurants as second and fifth in frequency owing to few requirements for specialized training or intensive capital.[14]

Across the urban North, restaurants were important sites for communal eating and socializing, especially for recently arrived residents.[15] They covered "the Stroll": State Street from 26th to 29th on Chicago's South Side, the place to see and be seen. Bustling theaters, restaurants, dance halls, and other businesses, particularly at the primary intersection of 35th and State, writ Black intellectual life in urban space.[16] The street was the best known in Black America, particularly due to the publicity it received from the *Chicago Defender*. It was rivaled only by Harlem's Seventh and Lenox Avenues. State Street stores did business twenty-four hours a day, and action on the street coursed alongside them. Jazz clubs, sports venues, pool halls, and other forms of entertainment were especially important because Black people were excluded from other commercial amusements in the city. In these establishments, residents spent as freely on necessities and luxuries as White counterparts did in theirs.[17]

In Harlem, fried fish joints, hamburger stands, and other outlets dotted uptown streets. Bon Goo Barbecue on St. Nicholas served a hearty menu to a mix of celebrities and working-class residents. Late-night spot the Metropolis welcomed musicians such as Ben Webster and Ornette Coleman after sets. The Cooper Rail at 120th and Lenox was a modest restaurant popular with single men who lived in rooming houses without kitchens. And Tillie's Chicken Shack at 227 Lenox was another venue that jumped, serving up fried chicken, yams, hot biscuits, and coffee for a dollar.[18] Tillie's appeared in the 1940 edition of *The Green Book,* an indispensable annual travel guide for African Americans. But hamburgers were scarce in that and other years of the publication. In the 1930s and 1940s, the restaurants listed in Chicago, D.C., and New York frequently used names that proudly displayed the owners' southern origins and advertising copy that evoked hearty, home-cooked meals. Fried chicken restaurants (some of which were explicitly "chicken shacks"), BBQs, and then cafeterias and luncheonettes appeared. Once the guide began categorizing restaurants, such sections as Seafood, Steaks, Chinese, and "American Specialties" graced its pages, but not hamburgers.[19] Overall, restaurants were fewer in number than other hospitality outlets like taverns and hotels. But notable is the relative absence of explicitly burger-focused establishments (presumably Hamburg Paradise at 377 West 125th Street was one?). To be sure, *The Green Book* did not comprise an exhaustive record of all Black-owned restaurants—even locally acclaimed outlets such as Harold's Chicken Shack in Chicago and Ben's Chili Bowl in D.C. were missing. So it is possible that hamburger outlets were simply overlooked. Alternatively, burgers may not have merited an entire restaurant to themselves— they were a pedestrian sandwich that could have appeared on broader menus at other establishments. In the South, they were often sold at the corner store and called meatballs.[20]

In any case, with an array of dining options, Black residents may not have been particularly concerned about the burgers that the chateaux had cordoned off from them. It was a basic working-class meal. Anyone could make a simple hamburger sandwich at home, and African Americans did so. Fast food was not yet an iconic symbol of American cultural life, and it was not yet the economic opportunity for which Black activists would clamor in the late 1960s. With no evidence that Black folks marshaled much social action to gain access to the first-generation restaurants with the broadest reach (the burger chateaux)—especially when considering that the 1930s embodied a new height of African American consumer activism[21]—it is unlikely that these restaurants or their racial exclusion took up much collective mental space.

African Americans were, however, very much concerned with what and how they ate, and under conditions of rank inequality, eating respectably was paramount for many. These concerns mirrored the social mores at the time. Cooking was a test of moral character for White women, and especially mothers, scored based on their willingness and ability to prepare meals for their families. Progressive reformers so emphasized the virtue of cooking that buying bread at the bakery or purchasing prepared foods from delis was seen as suspect.[22] Beyond the special scrutiny reserved for women, anyone who was working-class found their food choices deliberated and, more often than not, criticized. For African Americans in the early twentieth century, food choices would have been even more salient as barometers of respectability.

Respectable Eating

In a climate where Black people's rights were abrogated with impunity, African Americans employed respectability politics to reclaim their humanity and champion racial uplift. Historian Tanisha Ford shows that to disprove racist and sexist stereotypes, for example, Black women focused on clothing, hair styling, speaking Standard English, and refined comportment. Their colleges included these skills in the curriculum, hoping to propel students to middle-class society. Continuing into the 1950s civil rights struggle, respectability politics was a way for the middle class to distance themselves from poor and working-class African Americans, whose behavior was perceived as inappropriate and uncouth.[23]

These politics bore fruit in ideas about eating behaviors and restaurants that caused tension within the Black community. These establishments were intertwined with identity, adjustment to urban society, and respectability. Native Black Chicagoans in 1920 associated middle-class status primarily with behaviors (like attending a moderate church) rather than with socioeconomic resources; and eating habits were just the sort of behaviors that became important behavioral class markers. Those of means could not brook the "pig ankle joints," chicken shacks, and other dietary choices of their recently arrived southern brethren. Black elites promoted ideas about proper dining, emphasizing the fashionable European recipes and foodways that were popular in White women's magazines and decrying the familiar foods from the South.[24]

According to Grace Outlaw, who wrote for the Federal Writers' Project in Chicago, barbecue stands operating from old boxcars or discontinued streetcars were popular African American businesses. The streets of Bronzeville were home to many small lunch wagons, red-hot and hamburger stands, and doughnut shops—of which Lincoln Doughnut House at 30th and State was among the best in the neighborhood. Garfield Boulevard, heart of the "Negro Rialto district," hosted dozens of beer gardens and chicken shacks. Taverns were touch and go; Richard Wright saw them as dank and depressing, a stage on which inebriated patrons endlessly nursed soup, crackers, and beer. Some restaurants were reportedly worse than taverns, mere "shacks held together by rusty pieces of tin and old boards." Footes' Restaurant at 3032 South State Street fell into this category, but it was always busy, ringing up cheap bowls of soup for five cents or corned beef hash for a nickel more. A step up from Footes' was Bud's Eat Shop, which specialized in fish, tripe, and short orders.[25]

Chicken shacks and short order tripe clashed with the dictates of those whom historian Jennifer Jensen Wallach calls "respectable eaters," who served healthy and hygienic meals at home "even when no one was watching."[26] Because social reformers in the late 1800s saw food as a central axis for European immigrants' social transformation and assimilation, they sought to instill bland, staple-based diets that would make the people consuming them equally inoffensive. Respectable Black eaters engaged in similar practices, attempting to counteract stereotypes about gluttonous and uncivilized Black consumption, approaching cooking and eating intellectually and scientifically, and avoiding foods reminiscent of southern rural poverty and life under slavery.[27] The performative aspects of eating therefore figured prominently in demonstrating Black upward mobility and civility. Edward S. Green published in 1920 the National Capital Code of Etiquette to instruct Black people on proper behavior, cautioning against slippages between public and private and calling for careful eating and public comportment. Home meals were to be elegant, disciplined affairs, and eating on the street was to be avoided at all costs—messy at best, and reeking of an inability to delay gratification at worst.[28]

Respectable eaters did look beyond mere social graces; eating appropriately could also "discipline their bodies for political purposes."[29] W. E. B. Du Bois exhorted Black folks to avoid unhealthy foods, as he and others envisioned racial progress through dietary change. At the Tuskegee Institute, Booker T. Washington also cautioned against his students eating "knickknacks" (cheese, crackers, desserts) and pork, which he argued were contributors to African Americans' high mortality rate.[30] These arguments revealed a biopolitics of Black eating, wherein food was used to discipline the body to maintain the optimal health required for Black people's uplift.

Even so, respectable eaters knew their efforts might fall on deaf ears. Though Black folks might engage in sophisticated practices, "they could not ensure that White society would notice their efforts or, if they were indeed paying attention, interpret them in the manner intended."[31] White retailers and other industry commentators certainly glossed over Black eating habits. A 1944 report on the food preferences of varied ethnic groups in New York City saw Black people as mere consumers rather than producers of any particular gastronomic traditions. Worse, they were penurious, uninteresting consumers, even grotesque. In a dire economic climate, Harlemites were reportedly found to be buying dog food for themselves, a shocking detail offered in contrast to the affectionately portrayed traditions of Italians and other White New Yorkers.[32]

Indeed, White publics were more likely to make a mockery of Black persons they perceived to be putting on uppity airs via their dress or behaviors. Printed matter of all kinds disseminated images that American studies scholar Psyche Williams-Forson calls "symbolic slavery," in which Blackness outside servility was ridiculed.[33] As well, the urban Black working class knew full well that their behavior alone would not win their rightful claim to the country's resources. It was not necessarily in their interest to attempt to demonstrate their belonging and worthiness through eating, and indeed, foodways were in constant flux between attempts to demonstrate interest and inclusion in the body politic, rejecting it, or evincing competing national interests.[34]

Where did hamburgers fall in the spectrum between aspiration toward and rejection of the dominant culture? Burgers could have been seen as a respectable food inasmuch as beef and white bread held special allure for at least some segments of the Black population. Booker T. Washington served beef—not pork, with all its connotations of slavery—on Tuskegee's menus in the late 1890s and early 1900s. Doing so was a direct challenge to White supremacy when almost no rural, White southerners had the means to consume beef.[35] Meanwhile, Washington also eschewed cornbread and emphasized baked goods made from wheat (especially white) flour, for the same reasons. Hamburgers in theory should have been a win, combining beef with white buns. And since the modernity of the burger chateaux evoked the industrially produced foods encouraged by reformers, perhaps these restaurants nudged burgers into the province of the respectable.

On the other hand, burgers were of dubious nutritional quality. Would not they fall into the realm of knickknacks? Du Bois cautioned against the consumption of too much fat and starch—the two main components of hamburgers and buns. Worse, hamburgers presented outright health risks. One was potentially deadly "ptomaine poisoning." Nellie Walker, aged twenty-six, died in her South Side home reportedly due to ptomaine poisoning resulting from consuming a hamburger and ice cream. It was a fate that struck many in the late nineteenth century, confounding the medical profession.[36] Ptomaines, derived from the Greek word *ptōma* (corpse), were defined as a class of poisons animal in origin and activated through ingestion of food. Today, the etiology of those foodborne illnesses would be recognized as pathogens such as campylobacter, *E. coli,* or salmonella, but ptomaine theory was not discredited until the early 1940s.[37]

And if hamburger was not a source of ptomaine poisoning, it was potentially toxic from chemical adulterants. When *The Street*'s Lutie Johnson shopped at the butcher on Eighth Avenue, she balked at the "bright-red beef," which rumor had it was tainted with "embalming fluid . . . in order to give it a nice fresh color." Lutie considered the unnatural color long and hard before relenting and purchasing a half pound, because mixed with breadcrumbs it would go a long way and "Bub could have a sandwich of it when he came home for lunch."[38] Lutie's pragmatic purchase would have characterized those of real-life Harlemites; hamburger was basic fare, not an extravagance or delicacy. In these early years of fast food, then, Black folk were certainly not burger crazed; rather, they approached the industry's wares with a mix of attitudes ranging from indifference to enjoyment to hauteur.

Perhaps most telling is the contention Black-owned burger joints aroused. It was not Richard Wright alone who decried lunch wagons, the small outlets that served the customers ignored by the burger chateaux. Modest affairs that reused old vehicles, lunch wagons served hamburgers and other simple foods. In 1940, South Side residents in the vicinity of 55th Street and Calumet Avenue had reached the end of their rope when, despite repeated court orders to move, Jimmy Howard's hamburger lunch wagon remained in place. Judge Gibson Gorman had given the restaurateur three continuances to give him time to "move that atrocity" yet he had not done so, to the consternation of Carolyn Miles. As the *Chicago Defender* reported it, "the little meat-ball emporium" was "shame-facedly right next to the Miles' gorgeous gardens," and Howard's business was better suited "to a less classy neighborhood." Howard admitted that he had sunk the wheels of his establishment into three feet of concrete, making it quite a difficult proposition to relocate. One of the nearby property owners suggested he just take the hamburgers out first.[39]

So aggrieved by these kinds of establishments was A. N. Fields, a political writer, analyst, and one of the editorial staff of the *Chicago Defender,* that he wrote in favor of restrictive covenants. A scourge of Black home seeking, these addendums to residential property deeds were used to make the occupation of homes by Black persons in White neighborhoods illegal. Yet, Fields declared that Black folk needed the courage to implement these measures themselves. Doing so would win the respect of Whites, because "shiftless and vulgar" "parasite Negroes" who lacked control over their communities fueled White perceptions of Blackness as indecent. More specifically, he thought that restrictive covenants could tightly regulate land use and property, reigning in Black people who were wont to "build a $15,000 home and permit someone to move next door with a lunch wagon."[40] Fields's comments reveal that although mentions of hamburgers were scant in Black

Figure 2.2. A lunch wagon in Chicago's Black Belt. "Untitled photo" by Edwin Rosskam, April 1941. Library of Congress, Prints & Photographs Division, FSA/OWI Collection, LC-USF33-005181-M1.

media, these sandwiches and the kinds of places that served them bore enough ill repute to at least occasionally appear in public discourse.[41] They also reveal that burgers did not enjoy widespread appeal among Black consumers.

Meanwhile, White-owned fast food chains were of the same mind as Fields, unwilling to sell their wares to "vulgar, parasitic Negroes," even as they expanded across the country and into new markets within cities. Restaurant chain executives were bullish on an urban, White future, but could not have foreseen the massive changes that would take place across the nation's metropolitan areas. Central among them was slum clearance and urban renewal, policies that upended the streetscape. For African Americans, urban renewal pushed fast food even farther to the periphery and crushed existing Black food outlets. For White restaurateurs, first-generation fast food banked on urban Whiteness; when that project failed, cast aside for suburban landscapes, the outlets began to fail, too.

Urban Renewal Means Burger Removal

Slum clearance began via the New Deal's Housing Act of 1937. Buffeted among competing and varied interests, ranging from a governmental aim to eliminate poor housing stock and provide modern housing to businesses that wanted to get rid of "blight" to create more profitable land, slum clearance razed acres of substandard housing and surrounding businesses. The construction of public housing at its start held great promise; African Americans living in segregated city neighborhoods were consigned to woefully inadequate, dangerous, and unhealthy accommodations; for those who could gain access to public housing, it provided new, sound, spacious residences for Black urbanites delighted to be rid of their former, decrepit dwellings. And yet, it often meant homeowners became tenants. Moreover, the high-rise buildings isolated in the existing Black ghetto ended up creating a "second ghetto."[42] Slum clearance paused once the United States entered World War II but came back on steroids as part of the broader postwar urban renewal that continued for another three decades.[43] The term "urban renewal" was coined in the 1954 revision to the 1949 Housing Act. This project, which involved multiple strategies including eminent domain (the seizure of private property for public use), transformed cities and particularly downtowns to make them more attractive to the White middle class, to attract capital and reinvestment, and ultimately "to sweep away the nineteenth-century street grid."[44]

That grid was home to early fast food. And until urban renewal began taking the grid apart, fast food was well able to use it to define a spatial vocabulary of Whiteness as one of modernity and convenience, even if not steeped in wealth. Once fast food had been firmly racialized as the province of White people, it lent that construction of Whiteness back to urban populations as a housing amenity. In so doing, fast food helped catalyze White space as the exclusive repository of pleasurable urban living and constituted a modest building block of a segregated housing system. Like drive-in markets, which pursued affluent communities, some of which were housing developments bound by racially restrictive covenants,[45] first-generation fast food made Whiteness lucrative.

Horn & Hardart is instructive in how early fast food was a fulcrum for state and private practices of segregation, selling Whiteness both as image and financial instrument—an idea expressed in a *Chicago Tribune* classified advertisement for a restaurant business in May 1949 that lured potential owners with its location on an "ideal white neighborhood corner." The Automat buttressed its claim on Whiteness with a concerted effort to link the restaurant to White housing developments. Through the mid-1940s, anchored by its core constituency of lunchtime workers, the company's sales soared into the tens of millions. Horn & Hardart recognized the need for at least occasional forays to other consumer segments, including families. A 1937 newspaper advertisement depicting an affluent family encouraged readers to "Show Your Children THE AUTOMATS!"[46] Targeting city families increasingly meant marketing to new housing restricted to White tenants, among them developments like Montclair Gardens, built in 1941 in Jackson Heights, Queens. For New Yorkers weary of the city's rat race, the new real estate offering made a forceful pitch: "How can we escape the sour, million-throated discord that is New York? The jangling trolleys? . . . Honking horns and backfiring motors? . . . The clatter and patter of a million feet on the echoing pavement." Jackson Heights was the answer, and Horn & Hardart had enough brand recognition to be listed as a residential amenity in the new development, among other walkable retail conveniences such as Woolworth's, Kresge's, and Liggett's. Veiled references to racial exclusion made Whiteness a perk on par with the complex's quiet and privacy. "Great care will be taken in the choice of tenants," read the Montclair Gardens literature. "Suitable references will be required, assuring residents of an exclusive and selected tenancy." These allusions were prevalent in other Queens real estate brochures as well.[47] The Automat's presence in suburban Queens helped cement the pairing of retail amenities and White space.

Horn & Hardart also strove to create an atmosphere and reputation of exclusivity among White residents in middle-income housing closer to the city's core. The first Automat in Brooklyn opened at the corner of Willoughby and Fulton Streets, taking over the former site of the Bristol Restaurant and outfitting the posh new location with marble paneling, air conditioning, and bronze.[48] The company marketed this outlet to the Fort Greene Houses (today subdivided and renamed the Ingersoll Houses and the Walt Whitman Houses), originally designed for lower-income households in general, but shifting to become a housing project for defense workers in particular. The development took its first renters from the immediate vicinity in 1942, reifying the existing minimal presence of Black residents.[49]

Thus, when Horn & Hardart advertised in 1942 to Fort Greene Houses residents its Automat at 3 Willoughby Street, it was targeting White clientele alone.[50] Ironically, it is one of the few locations whose archival photos show Black patrons. The Willoughby Street area was 1.63 percent Black, a demographic pattern little changed for decades. Promoting the restaurant as an "appetizing jaunt" away, the restaurant took ownership of residential comfort in racially restricted housing.[51] Horn & Hardart also opened a retail store adjacent to the Peter Cooper Village apartment complex in Manhattan, the slightly more upscale neighbor to Stuyvesant Town. In this case, fast food benefited from urban renewal because the development arose from the rubble of the eighteen city blocks of tenement apartments, stores, and industrial uses that were cleared for its construction. Built by the large insurance firm Metropolitan Life in the early 1940s and aggressively backed by Robert Moses, the apartments intended to create a "suburb-within-the-city." Both complexes barred Black New Yorkers.[52] For renters who had not absconded the five boroughs for suburban, single-family idyll, Stuyvesant Town provided a high-rise facsimile of White, middle-class tranquility and consumer abundance.

Horn & Hardart may have been able to capitalize on the urban renewal version of White space, but for fast food to link itself to residential comfort in racially restricted urban housing became a less useful strategy over time since the suburbs were much better at both racial restriction and residential comfort. The HOLC showed how noxious was the idea of Black people existing in close proximity. And when slum clearance was designed to eliminate the menace of encroaching Blackness, it also meant a contravention of urban fast food's image. First-generation chains relied on a pristine and pure Whiteness, but that was now called into question by slum clearance policies: metaphorically, because slum clearance implied that the Whiteness fast food was selling was threatened; and literally, because slum clearance cleared away fast food's customers and even the outlets themselves.

New York's Robert Moses is infamous for his championing urban renewal in its most racist incarnation. He called for "courageous, clean-cut, surgical removal of all of our old slums," rather than a piecemeal rehabilitation that he perceived as inadequate. Slum clearance required "unflinching surgery which cuts out the whole cancer and leaves no part of it which can grow again, and spread and perpetuate old miseries." To call slums cancerous was not an indictment of the buildings—which do not grow by themselves, reproduce, or spread themselves across a neighborhood—but of Black and Brown people.[53] But Chicago is instructive as the first city to enact projects born out of the 1954 Housing Act, which included businesses in urban renewal for the first time. Urban renewal worked by allowing cities to condemn buildings, clear the land, and sell it to a private developer at a discount since the federal government made up most of the difference. Fast food was immediately vulnerable because one of urban renewal's first targets were spaces for food and drink. These businesses catered to "undesirables" and defiled the character of White space by creating rowdy sites of racial mixing.[54] The University of Chicago–backed South East Chicago Commission (SECC) forcefully championed renewal to keep the communities in question White. The SECC saw Black people as a sentient form of blight, creeping in from the periphery of the neighborhood and advancing contagious decline.[55] In 1953, aggressive urban renewal plans envisioned rehabilitation for physically deteriorating White space in Hyde Park but total demolition

Figure 2.3. Interior view of the Automat at 3 Willoughby Street in Brooklyn. Photograph by Drucker & Bates Co., Photographers. Manuscript and Archives Division, New York Public Library.

for Black spaces stretching from Cottage Grove to Woodlawn. Once cleared, the space would be acquired by the university.[56] Hyde Park's commercial corridors were strongly perceived as negative influences, and corridors like 55th Street were immediately targeted for action. Slum clearance produced a 57 percent decline in Hyde Park–Kenwood business between 1953 and 1966, an outcome that powerful community and political interests argued was preferable to the broader community decline that was inevitable had renewal never taken place. For those invested in Hyde Park and Kenwood's Whiteness, the potential for racial change had to be stopped at all costs.[57] Dozens of bars, lounges, and cafés in a four-block stretch described as a "skid row" were the first to go (along with their disorderly denizens). Forty-three

Figure 2.4. A store at 1417–1415 East 55th Street in Hyde Park closes due to land clearance. Photograph by Margaret Mead. Image apf2-09802, Hanna Holborn Gray Special Collections Research Center, University of Chicago Library.

taverns were banished from Hyde Park and Kenwood, and a preference emerged for contained shopping centers such as Harper Court at 53rd Street and the Hyde Park Shopping Center at 55th.[58]

Among the restaurants dashed to an uncertain future were the Woodlawn Chicken Inn on East 53rd Street, the C&J Chicken & Shrimp House on East 47th Street, and Darryl & Edwin's Snack Shop on Cottage Grove. Harold's Chicken Shack, which became a Chicago institution, was displaced as well. As will be discussed in chapter 9, owner Harold Pierce was a pioneer among Black fast food franchisors. He cooked chicken from scratch for each order, a move that quickly became popular. Though his Harold's Chicken Shack was primarily a local chain, Pierce's brand ultimately expanded elsewhere in the United States. It began at 1235 East 47th Street in 1950 or 1952.[59] Pierce migrated north from Midway, Alabama, and newspaper coverage is conflicted regarding his occupation before starting the

Chicken Shack. His obituary stated that he had worked as a chauffeur, and the Kenwood estate at which he was employed was a mere block away from his first location. Another report held that he and his wife, Hilda, ran a restaurant, H & H, on East 39th Street.[60] His outlet lasted more than a decade before the Hyde Park–Kenwood renewal program necessitated a move. Fortunately for Pierce, he was not moving far—just a few blocks over to 1106 East 47th Street. His second establishment, at 6419 South Cottage Grove, remained unmolested.[61]

When urban renewal razed existing establishments, it wiped out many Black businesses and wrecked economic and social engines on Chicago's South Side. Forty-Seventh Street, for example, lost a devastating number and diversity of businesses beginning in 1950 due to urban renewal. From Lake Michigan to State Street, corridors on 43rd, 47th, and the streets between were an epicenter of business, culture, and leisure for Chicago's Black Belt residents in the 1950s. A variety of goods and services met the needs of community residents, and entertainment was abundant in numerous blues clubs and spots like the Sutherland Lounge; together they hosted Muddy Waters, Thelonious Monk, Max Roach, and Miles Davis (with John Coltrane and Cannonball Adderley).[62] But bulldozers claimed a swath of shopping, leisure, and community sites. In the 1300 block of 47th Street alone, among those displaced were a barber shop, billiard room, shoe repair shop, beauty salon, tax consultant, optometrist, fishing bait store, TV and radio sales and repair shop, pool hall, men's clothing store, liquor store and lounge, and record shop. Businesses affected by renewal received variable assistance from the city. Valois Café survived renewal and went on to become a neighborhood institution.[63] Some establishments relocated by themselves without renewal leadership participation or support, and others faced a nebulous future of relocation "at some future date."[64]

Urban renewal cemented the connection between fast food and White space by virtue of the fact that it sequestered Black customers farther away from White-owned outlets. Black residents relegated to the "second ghetto" lived in public housing projects designed as vertical containers corralled within expressways, train tracks, and other barriers, and distal from existing fast food restaurants. It was no longer merely the case that the burger chateaux were socially inaccessible in White space, it was now physically difficult or even impossible to reach these establishments.

To be sure, difficulty accessing White-owned fast food was not the most serious consequence of urban renewal for Black communities. Apart from the obvious catastrophes in housing loss, a significant problem was the large-scale destruction of Black businesses, which had immediate and long-lasting effects. Legal scholar Cheryl Harris sees "the throwaway" as monetized and racially specific. In an interrogation of debt as central to Black subordination, she describes Black spaces as perpetually viewed as "subprime, unstable, and likely to be seen as waste."[65] In that formulation, the federal government razed Black businesses and gave them loans to start new ones. Nationally, business mortality from urban renewal was often highest among those that were Black-owned, and the ones that survived did so at heavy cost. Moreover, many businesses in Black neighborhoods lost to slum clearance—even if African Americans did not own them—provided essential goods and services to Black consumers. Clearly, Black residents were left with fewer eating places in their own neighborhoods, and the outlets that remained were often rickety. Thus, as fast food moved toward midcentury, Black agency was undermined in the realm of restaurants both as leisure and as an important gateway to community economic development and individual wealth. Ironically, by leaving Black neighborhoods in retail cinders, urban renewal catalyzed the agitation for franchise ownership that would seize Black communities in the 1960s. That is, having been stripped of their small businesses, it would become that much more imperative for African Americans to obtain franchises of the new national chains.

White-owned, first-generation fast food outlets that did not meet the fate of the bulldozer were still harmed by urban renewal. When apartment buildings were razed, existing customer bases were razed as well. As a result, White Castle found its sales falling.[66] Such was the cost of an urban empire. For first-generation fast food, a commitment to urban Whiteness did not pan out, and the policies that reconfigured city spaces were a large part of that. Urban change hobbled the burger chateaux and indirectly underwrote the rise of suburban fast food by eliminating older competitors. But because urban renewal didn't always renew—too often it left open wounds in streetscapes, clearing land never put to good use—it furthered the image of the failing city. Worse, the city was Black. The all-White facade in fast food crumbled despite the insistent marketing of racialized purity. When second-generation fast food ascended in the suburbs, it held up an even better version of Whiteness: one that was unsullied by the chaos of urbanity and the proximity of Black people. It was something new, in which urban Black residents could take no part. The early restaurants' commitment to the city first exposed them to existential threats from a rising tide of Black infiltration, and then to the threat of waves of White customers fleeing to the suburbs. First-generation fast food ended up saddled with the bad reputation of its locale. As second-generation fast food loomed on the horizon, Black, urban suffering haunted the rebirth of drive-in dining that was to come in the suburbs.

3

Suburbs and Sundown Towns

The Rise of Second-Generation Fast Food

"The battle of the itinerant, 15-cent hamburger has spread to Washington," proclaimed the *Washington Post* in the summer of 1959. Announcing plans by "the nation's three largest roadside hamburger chains" to open drive-in restaurants around the D.C. metropolitan area, the newspaper asserted that restaurant chains such as McDonald's, Burger Chef, and Golden Point were "revolutionizing food vending." To describe the outlets as roadside restaurants privileges a certain kind of road: wide, suburban arterials designed for and populated by motor vehicles rather than pedestrians or public transit. Elsewhere, different roads—narrow, busy thoroughfares that defined central city grids—were dotted with first-generation chains. The *Post* recognized this distinction, asserting that the new roadside drive-ins were revolutionary precisely because they were an update to the "downtown hamburger shop." Slotting into the lifestyle of a more mobile population, the new suburban restaurants, in comparison to their urban ancestors, "cut down the menu, added even more standardization and a good helping of automation, and [gave] it architectural class."[1]

These observations are debatable, but the revolutionary upstarts certainly differed from downtown hamburger shops in location and to some degree in menu. Golden Point Hamburgers, despite its accolades in the *Washington Post*, did not achieve the kind of renown to make it a household name. Born in the 1950s, as the majority of second-generation chains were, the chain tried several tactics to stand out. First was its attention-grabbing design: isosceles triangles–shaped buildings topped with a twenty-one-foot golden spire that resembled an enormous space-age antenna meant to symbolize "the world's most modern drive-ins." Second, the chain focused on promoting name brands such as "Wonder Bread buns, Maxwell House coffee, Kraft cheese, Hunt's catsup," and others—*"the same nationally known and respected brands you buy for your own kitchen."*[2] Golden Point was one of many new fast food concepts that departed from the austere fixtures of the burger chateaux. Located in the suburbs and making an explicit pitch to homemakers, the new chain epitomized the shift from first- to second-generation fast food.

Second-generation fast food's primary distinction from its forbears was its suburban location. It still constituted a consumable racial purity, but one to be enjoyed in suburban, single-family homes or in cars. These chains did open a few stores in urban centers, generally in neighborhoods that matched the racial demographics of their suburban counterparts, but occasionally making forays into Black communities as well. A second, and critical, distinction was a change in what the restaurants were selling. No longer were menu items primarily fuel for the working man (in environs of literally constructed Whiteness). Now, fast food symbolized leisure and the bliss of American family life. It invited children and moms rather than just male adults. The "national civil religion" of mass consumption reached its apogee in the suburbs and became the spatial locus of American households and their consumer dollars.[3] Fast food quickly slotted into this configuration and continued to exclude Black diners.

City versus Suburb

Between 1947 and 1953 the suburban population increased by 43 percent, and single-family homeownership grew more in the decade following World War II than in the 150 years that preceded it.[4] New homes prompted spending on household goods, and new department stores and shopping centers colonized arterials to serve these consumer desires. *Fortune* magazine called the suburbs "the frontier of American retailing," and it was clear that most stores could not resist the lure; news reports claimed that by the end of 1954, 50 percent of shopping centers in the country would be less than two years old.[5] Along with smaller stores, national retailers sought self-contained spaces where all the tenants were selected for their propensity to target White, suburban housewives.[6] In the D.C. area, Silver Spring, Maryland, saw a particular flurry of building and retail multiplying land prices by nearly a factor of fifteen.[7] Little Tavern kept the core of its business in the city, but it also financed a market and recreational center in the Silver Spring complex called the Duncan Building.

All the early burger outlets held onto their investments in city locations. Maps 3.1–3.3 reveal the burger chateaux's investment in New York's urban core. In Maps 3.1 and 3.2, displaying 1956 and 1960 respectively, the only national brand in the city was White Tower, and it was overwhelmingly situated within the five boroughs. Only two locations appeared in Westchester County (New Rochelle), and none in Nassau or Suffolk. It was not until 1964 (Map 3.3) that any other competitors

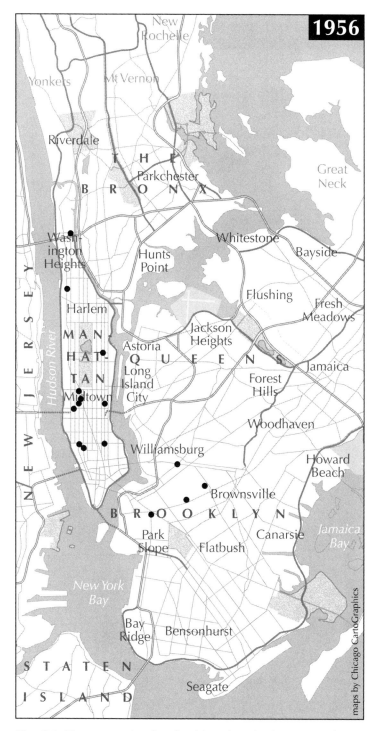

Map 3.1. First-generation fast food locations in the New York City metropolitan area, 1956. Locations were identified with Yellow Pages directories. Map by Dennis McClendon, CartoGraphics.

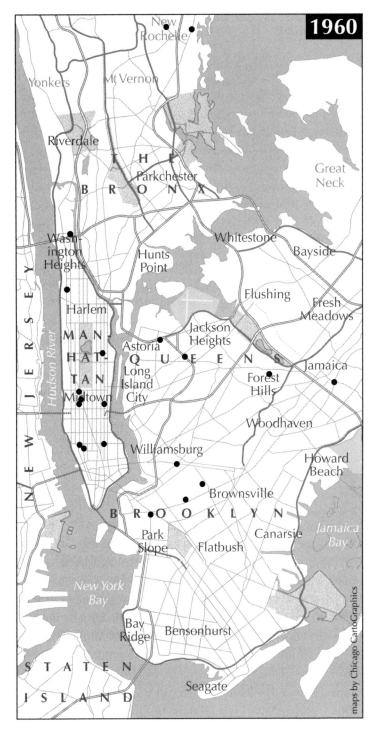

Map 3.2. First-generation fast food locations in the New York City metropolitan area, 1960. Map by Dennis McClendon, CartoGraphics.

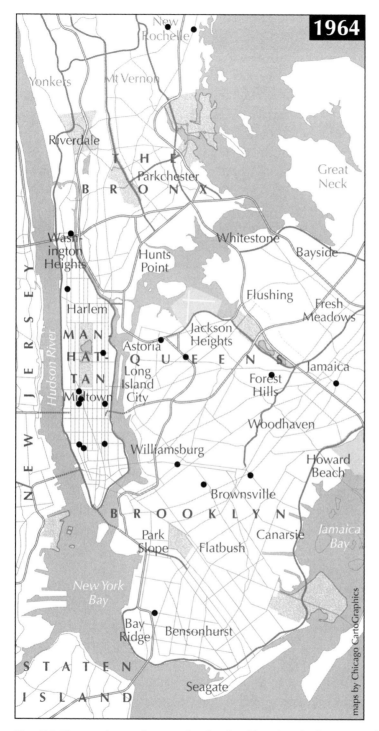

Map 3.3. First- and second-generation fast food locations in the New York City metropolitan area, 1964. Map by Dennis McClendon, CartoGraphics.

settled in city territory, and these were also primarily within the city limits (in Brooklyn, Burger Prince Drive-In in the Bay Ridge and East New York neighborhoods). The few suburban outlets were the new upstart McDonald's operating in Mamaroneck in Westchester and Merrick on Long Island, and a lone White Castle relatively close by in Lynbrook. The postwar retail exodus for the suburbs essentially left first-generation fast food in the dust, and owners began unloading their burger joints. One Chicagoan was ready to sell a "Hamburger hot spot" that was pulling down $80,000 per year ($682,000 in 2020 dollars); another sought to sell (or trade) a White Castle at 6740 South Halsted.[8]

For several reasons, the burger chateaux did not pick up and move to follow the action in the suburbs. In the case of White Castle, Bill Ingram had always expanded conservatively, and he remained committed to the large store base he had already established. His restaurants had long served urban clientele who arrived by foot or public transit, and Ingram wanted to continue that way. Furthermore, he rejected expansion unless the requisite capital was on hand—he foreswore debt of any kind, "not wanting to build his empire on credit."[9] Ingram bet instead on modernizing his fleet of existing outlets, sticking it out as he watched his customer base depart for the suburbs. Even after McDonald's, Burger King, and other chains burst onto the scene, White Castle remained confident it would endure with a high-quality product and reliable, no-frills service. Ingram hunkered down in places where his chain first started, perhaps "celebrat[ing] its own anachronism." Its decades-long practice of staying open twenty-four hours a day was now inviting assaults, drunkards, and "roving street gangs" that terrorized customers and staff alike. Dine-and-dash incidents also became a problem, as a result of which the company began requiring payment before eating. There were also many more cars on the road compared to White Castle's early history, so the chain's predilection for street corners made them frequent sites for accidents.[10]

White Tower maintained a similar path and found its allure evanesce. It remained an urban concern through the 1950s, increasingly stuck in defunct downtowns now largely devoid of its target patrons. The company's reputation became "tarnished by the unattractive context in which their shops now appeared and with which they began to be associated."[11] Little Tavern also struggled with disorder. It had contended with robberies in the late 1930s, but there were some indications that all the burger chateaux were beginning to struggle at a scale previously unseen.[12] For their part, cities used urban renewal to rid themselves of disorder, and early chains continued to disappear with the new municipal practices. For example, Baltimore's Highway 1 bulldozed sections of a community that had gone from ex-

Figure 3.1. A Little Tavern in Baltimore on Jordan Street, between Presstman Street and North Avenue, looking south, October 25, 1961. Source: Baltimore City Archives.

clusively White to predominantly Black by 1960. One of the casualties was a Little Tavern on Jordan Street, razed in 1961.[13]

It did not help that the features initially so attractive to customers were becoming less relevant. Concerns about food purity were less acute by midcentury, so the emphasis on hygiene was less compelling. White Tower's modern appearance was also no longer quite so modern; the visual and symbolic impact the restaurants had long claimed had begun to fade. And just as White Castle was synonymous with the sturdy fare that a workingman needed, White Tower was ill positioned to court the child and adolescent market that second-generation chains would make their raison d'être. According to White Tower brass, "In the outlying stores we did try to get family trade. At places like #23 we had coloring books to attract the kids to come in with their parents. If they colored the book, they'd get a free hamburger. We tried all sorts of stuff like that, but I don't think we were very successful with it."[14]

Hot Shoppes stood in contrast to its first-generation counterparts with a suburban drive-in presence since its inception that figured heavily in the lives of White teens in the D.C. metropolitan area. "Drive-ins" as a term was used to refer both to the self-service style that emerged in second-generation chains and to the more full-service concept that employed carhops, as Hot Shoppes did. Its main change in the 1950s was to reconfigure the menu to include more fast food rather than home cooking–style plates. It featured a triple-decker burger called the Mighty Mo, created to compete with the main feature at Bob's Big Boy, which was selling an eponymously named burger. Robert Wian, owner of a small burger restaurant in Glendale, California, developed the sandwich by splitting his hamburger bun twice rather than once and placing between them two meat patties garnished with mayonnaise, lettuce, cheese, and relish. His double-decker was borrowed (or stolen) not only by Hot Shoppes but decades later by McDonald's, which announced the Big Mac as an original creation by franchisee Jim Delligatti. Having worked in Southern California in the early 1950s, Delligatti learned of Wian's invention and duplicated it to create his new menu item for McDonald's. He admitted, "This wasn't like discovering the light bulb. The bulb was already there. All I did was screw it in the socket."[15]

Horn & Hardart, despite some suburban overtures, stayed resolutely a central city chain, still catering to individuals who worked or shopped in Manhattan's commercial core. The chain was prominent enough to appear in New York City's 1957 "Convention-Goer's Guide to Dining in the Coliseum Area," which lauded the chain for its "world famous" baked beans (White Tower was also noted in the guide, in the "eat and run" section: "Hamburgers are their specialty").[16] In 1955, 72 percent of the Automats were in Midtown or Lower Manhattan and new outlets were continually born, like the one in the 42nd Street Airline Terminal, across the street from Grand Central Station and featuring the largest seating capacity of any existing Automats. In 1952, the company opened a Brooklyn Automat at 427 Fulton Street, a corridor replete with glamorous department stores such as Abraham & Straus that drew a generation of White, working- and middle-class shoppers in the 1940s.[17] These new locations in Midtown and elsewhere in the city belied the new reality Horn & Hardart had to face—that the future lay in the suburbs. The company made deeper inroads into suburban sites in 1949, seeking out racially exclusionary developments such as Fresh Meadows in Queens.[18] But as major department stores and other retailers left the city, Horn & Hardart's overtures were simply too modest.

The mid-1950s had given Horn & Hardart its best years since opening, but the tides were turning. President E. K. Daly was wary of suburban shopping centers that had made "tremendous inroads" on downtown businesses. He argued, "These rapidly expanding suburban centers offer us a new and very real opportunity of which we should avail ourselves."[19] The chain began closing restaurants in downtown locations that were now assessed as too expensive. Toward that end, the company built a new restaurant and self-service retail store in the Cross County Shopping

Figure 3.2. Horn & Hardart's Automat at 427 Fulton Street, Brooklyn. Photograph by Drucker-Hilbert Co. Inc., Commercial Photography. Manuscript and Archives Division, New York Public Library.

Center in Yonkers, a new commercial space that attracted a variety of retailers and large departments stores including Wanamaker's and Gimbels. The shopping center, reportedly the largest in the East, was designed to accommodate twenty-five thousand cars per day.[20]

Horn & Hardart's new retail neighbors in Yonkers had themselves fled the city. Wanamaker's quit a location at Broadway and East Ninth Street that it had run for fifty-eight years in order to "concentrate its future operations in metropolitan suburbs." New York City lost several other retailers at this time. Eight landmark stores closed between 1952 and 1956, due in large part to the challenges posed by discount stores that targeted the lower-middle-class market to which these retail anchors had catered.[21] Brooklyn's Abraham & Straus was among the casualties, and Fulton Street declined as retailers fretted over declining numbers of White shoppers.[22]

First-generation fast food looked on warily from discredited urban retail corridors as the second generation reincarnated in the suburbs. And even though Black consumers, who resided in central cities, had been definitively segregated from the industry, some experts managed to equate fast food with the people it had studiously excluded. Morton Grodzins, a political science professor and former dean of the Division of Social Sciences at the University of Chicago, wrote in 1958 that as urban centers changed racially, one outcome would be that stores would begin selling merchandise of diminished quality. He claimed, "The main streets are becoming infested with sucker joints for tourists: all night jewelry auctions, bargain linens and cheap neckties, hamburger stands and jazz dives. The slums, in other words, are spreading to the central business district."[23] For Grodzins, fast food foretold not only a slide toward the tawdry, but one explicitly linked to Blackness. To equate burger joints with "jazz dives" renders them Black, a curious intersection given the vehement racial rejection the burger chateaux maintained. Somehow, the urban setting of early fast food contaminated it with Blackness, turning upside down the image it pursued. It was a mismatch that foreshadowed how suburban fast food's success could be predicated on the erasure of Black people.

Fast food did not begin as egalitarian or racially inclusive, and it would only worsen once the suburban version took root. When brands such as McDonald's and Burger King emerged in the 1950s, they added family fun to an emphasis on standardized food production and inexpensive prices. Black people, in the White imaginary, were neither fun nor human enough to constitute families. Pastoral suburbia became the setting for a modern, cleaner, and less pressured dining experience, and the burger chateaux were consigned to prehistory. Fast food was no longer just a place to go to fortify oneself for the battle of the urban rat race; it was a leisurely outing for wholesome (White) American families who enjoyed all the country had to offer.

Second-generation restaurants exploded in a slew of new brands, large and small, and too many to review comprehensively. Some were smaller chains, often local in reach. In Chicago, for example, the family behind the well-known Bresler Ice Cream Company launched the burger restaurant Henry's, copying a Los Angeles restaurant called Hamburger Handout, itself a copy of the original McDonald's in San Bernardino. Henry's served customers from thirty-five outlets in Chicagoland just two years after its start and grew to 138 in thirty-five states by 1965.[24] Meanwhile, the Chicago suburb of Forest Park was home to Brown's Fried Chicken, which began in 1951. Founded by John Brown, a chicken breeder who turned to selling fried birds when his farm went under, the carryout-only chain operated eleven stores by 1965. A group of young to middle-aged White men ran the outlets that served White suburbs and city communities.[25]

Chains achieving national prominence included Burger Chef, founded in 1958. It came close to McDonald's hold on the market in the early 1960s. One of the few that was not the brainchild of an individual entrepreneur, it entered the fast food market to further parent company General Equipment Manufacturing's food processing units (including broilers and shake machines). The chain thrived for many years and was just a few dozen short of McDonald's total by the close of the 1960s, when it was bought by General Foods.[26] Church's Chicken also began as a relatively small chain but quickly expanded and endured nationally. It launched in San Antonio in 1952 when George Church Sr., who had been selling chicken incubators, turned to a new business. George Jr. assumed the mantle in 1963, with an angle on quality—chickens came into the kitchen fresh, and the menu featured larger portions at prices lower than competitors. There is little available in archives to describe the chain's early years, but as it expanded in the 1960s Church's was unique in its explicit focus on central city, Black neighborhoods. Church's threw up prefab stores erected in as little as a month, harboring no compunction about building in inner cities because it knew residents would not be able to insist on edifices that matched existing frontages.[27]

The largest chains arose in quite disparate geographies: McDonald's in the Midwest, KFC in a border state, and Burger King in the South. All would find their largest markets in the segregated North. Indeed, two of the three arose in sundown towns—municipalities that forbade Black persons from remaining in town after dark under penalty of arrest, violence, or death. In doing so, they upped the ante on racial exclusion from early fast food, going from neighborhoods that were White-only to whole towns.

Kentucky Fried Chicken

Kentucky Fried Chicken was born in 1952 in Corbin, Kentucky, which claimed the ignominious distinction of qualifying as a sundown town in 1919.[28] Newspapers reported that just before Halloween of that year, "angered by a series of robberies and attacks on white men, a mob here last night rounded up virtually all negroes in Corbin, except the older residents, placed more than 200 on departing trains and forced the remainder to leave on foot." According to authorities, the "demonstration" resulted in several shots fired, one Black person killed, and two others wounded.[29] In fact, what drove the expulsion was two White switch operators who lost all their money to Black track layers in a poker game. The switch operators claimed the Black workers had robbed them, and the mob that formed pushed at gunpoint nearly every Black resident onto a train that would carry them to Knoxville.[30] Slightly more than ten years later, Harland Sanders, later given the honorific "Colonel" by the governor of Kentucky, began selling fried chicken at a Shell gas station and subsequently opened his own café.

Sanders was born in 1890 in Henryville, Indiana, twenty miles from the Kentucky border. He left home as an adolescent and led an itinerant lifestyle for several years. While in Jasper, Alabama, working on the railroad, he married, but it was short-lived. His wife left him and Sanders planned (but did not execute) kidnapping his children. A foul-mouthed and violent man, during a stint as a lawyer he physically fought his own client in the courtroom; and as a gas station owner, perturbed by a competitor who was painting over his signs, he shot him (the charges were dropped). At the age of forty, with a new wife and children, Sanders moved to Corbin, a town hard-hit by the Depression, and specifically to the neighborhood called Hell's Half-Acre, where residents were in dire straits.[31]

Switching from running a gas station to a café was a good move. First called the Harland Sanders Court and Café and later shortened to the Sanders Café, the informal eatery was quickly popular. Duncan Hines, before his days of cake mix fame, praised the Sanders Café in the travel guide he wrote for many years, *Adventures in Good Eating,* which enjoyed wide circulation across the country. Perhaps Hines was biased by the restaurant's locale in his home state, a place whose mint juleps, "lovely ladies," and state park (named My Old Kentucky Home after Stephen Foster's song) were dear to his heart. Foster's oeuvre was replete with references to "darkeys" content with their lives on the plantation, and Hines himself enjoyed dining at establishments where good darkeys were in service. About the Hotel Thomas in Gainesville, Georgia, he wrote, "Satisfying service by soft-footed Negro waiters under the guidance of a graying darkey who makes you feel he came out of a picture book." No darkeys were promised at the Sanders Court and Café in Corbin, but it did offer twenty-four-hour service, sizzling steaks, fried chicken, and more.[32]

Chicken became the focal point of Sanders' enterprise, founded on African American culinary traditions. When in the late 1970s Sanders was presented with McDonald's breakfast items, he scoffed at the poor quality. The egg in the Egg McMuffin came in for particular rebuke. Sanders explained the only correct way to prepare eggs, and stated, "An old darky cook in Georgetown, Kentucky, learnt me that years ago."[33] If the "darkies" had taught him how to cook eggs, it is logical to conclude they shaped his preparation of fried chicken as well. Once he became rich, Sanders was wont to drive around in a Cadillac accompanied by a pressure fryer he named Bessie.[34] That name could not be a better avatar for a Black woman. And yet he called his restaurant Kentucky Fried Chicken in order to distinguish it from "Southern fried chicken," which he thought lacked the requisite quality control.[35] Implicit here is an attempt to distance his enterprise from the Blackness he appropriated.

In 1951, Sanders modeled himself after cartoons of Kentucky colonels from his youth by growing a mustache and goatee. He then took on what became an iconic white suit after finding it made him stand out.[36] One year later, Sanders began selling to restaurants the right to cook and sell his recipe on their menus. Here, then, was an elderly, White, Southern man selling White-owned restaurants the right to cook Black-inspired fried chicken to White consumers in White-only geographies. In excluding Black customers, the chain seemed to forget pervasive stereotypes about Black people and their uncontrollable obsession with chicken, whether fried or stolen live from the coop.

The first restaurant to receive the franchised recipe was in South Salt Lake, Utah: Leon W. "Pete" Harman's Do Drop Inn, which he and his wife, Arline, opened in 1941. Primarily a burger shop, it served trademarked meals like the "Do-Drop's Double Header," the "Double Header Sandwich," and the "Pedigreed Hot Dog."[37] But Pete wanted a specialty item. He told Sanders as much when he met him at a National Restaurant Association convention in Chicago in 1951. Sanders showed up at Harman's home a year later with his herb and spice mixture, three chickens, and a pressure cooker and got to work preparing a meal. Once all the forks were laid to rest, Harman was in. He agreed to pay Sanders a nickel per chicken in order to become a franchisee.[38]

By 1963, six hundred KFC outlets dotted the country, run by an army of White franchisees (including Dave Thomas, who would go on to found Wendy's) eager to meet Sanders at annual meetings. John R. Neal, a former KFC vice president, saw the franchisees as "small, entrepreneurial American men and women who were trying to make a living in the restaurant business but didn't know how to fry chicken."[39] Excluded from this group were equally entrepreneurial Black restaurateurs who *did* know how to fry chicken. Sanders cashed out, selling the business to John Y. Brown and Jack Murphy in 1964.[40] Relieved of active franchisor duties, he transitioned to a "living mascot" for the chain, embodying a persona that romanticized the Old South: "His bleached white goatee signaled plantation rigueur. His mouth-full-of-gravel accent bespoke oak-shaded authenticity. That white jacket conjured mint julep–sodden afternoons on the veranda."[41] Despite hailing from Indiana, Sanders managed to monetize an image as a southern gentleman—or as KFC president John Y. Brown put it, a "lovable but gruff country boy." In this role

Figure 3.3. An advertisement for Kentucky Fried Chicken in the *Chicago Tribune,* December 12, 1965. Source: Newspapers.com.

he acted primarily as an ambassador, but he meted out critique as well. The battered chicken and goopy gravy the chain began serving in the mid-1960s repulsed him, it being a far cry from traditional (read: African American) cooking.[42]

By the time Kentucky Fried Chicken arrived in Chicago in the mid-1960s, it had gone public with a White-facing marketing strategy. In 1966, the company ran as an advertisement a full-page comic strip featuring a tidy White family who unequivocally enjoyed their fried chicken. In suit, hat, and dress coat, the father seemed a straitlaced executive, albeit one who exuded mirth and an inability to stop making puns, much to the consternation of his wife and two children.[43] The marketing could not have been further from the Black-centered imagery that would dominate decades later. The Chicago outlets numbered six in the metro area at that time, which were either in exclusively White space or in White neighborhoods that would soon transition to Black. The store at 2668 East 75th Street, for example, sat in a South Shore census tract that was home to six Black residents out of more than six thousand people in 1960, adjacent to another with only two out of more than eleven thousand—but this tract would be 61 percent Black by 1970. The same thing happened to competing brands—they eventually found themselves amid racial change they had not anticipated.

McDonald's

Although some scholars have described McDonald's as opening stores in Black communities in the late 1960s, most of those outlets had already been there—what was new were the Black neighbors who arrived as White people quit town. One of Ray Kroc's first restaurants landed in the sundown town of Torrance, California, where the first Black person to attempt to buy a home, attorney Otis B. Jackson, was thwarted by a builder who refused to accept his down payment.[44] But the start of the national franchise was in Illinois. Ray Kroc chose as his first location 400 Lee Street in Des Plaines, twenty miles from Chicago and close to the suburb he called home, Arlington Heights. There were twenty-eight thousand residents in the small town just north of O'Hare Airport, but home building rates were prodigious. Much had changed in Des Plaines from its days as a small, pious farming community that elected to go dry five years before the rest of the nation enacted Prohibition.[45] Des Plaines was also entirely White. In 1962, the mere formation of a Committee on Human Relation provoked anger and anxiety about the possibility of Black neighbors. The northwestern suburbs were so exclusively White that in the late 1960s, a program called Friendly Town sponsored visits by over two hundred "inner-city children." Black youth were invited into host homes for two weeks over the summer, as might be the case in a study-abroad program.[46]

Kroc came to McDonald's an affluent man, making $25,000 per year at his Malt-A-Mixer Company (nearly a quarter million in 2020 dollars) and a member of the Rolling Green Country Club in Arlington Heights. He observed the flight of businesses and people to the suburbs in the early 1950s, and after discovering the McDonald brothers' hamburger stand in San Bernardino, California, he anticipated that other food service establishments could follow the same model.[47] Once Kroc had bought the franchise from the McDonalds, he opened his first store on the outskirts of Des Plaines and it quickly became a favorite local spot.[48] The large arches dominated the low-lying landscape, but McDonald's was hardly the only drive-in game in town. A number of restaurants, including Howard Johnson, Dairy Queen, Kroc's own Prince Castles ice cream and hamburger shop (a White Castle knockoff that launched in sundown town Naperville in 1931 and encouraged customers to "Take a bagfull home" at twenty-four cents a burger), the Choo-Choo Hamburgers on Wheels, and Frejlach's Ice Cream ("Home of the Big Boy Original Double-Deck All Beef Hamburger") were all immediately adjacent or within a few blocks.[49]

Though McDonald's focused on suburbia, the chain's commitment was not total. The chain opened some stores in Chicago proper as early as 1956, one year after the franchise began in Des Plaines. Most outlets arrived in unequivocally White North Side neighborhoods—for example, Bill Barr opened his Chicago outlet at 4320 North Cicero on September 13, 1956—and stores opened over the next five years in other racially exclusionary spaces in and around the city limits.[50] But some locations were South Side outlets that opened when the neighborhood's racial compositions were unstable and heading toward fully Black. That meant the chain would find itself in Black neighborhoods when the areas it targeted changed due to White flight. For example, Morton Katznelson and Erwin L. Polakoff opened the McDonald's Jackson Park Drive-In at 6558 South Stony Island Avenue (later identified as 6560) on June 26, 1956. The Woodlawn community turned over in the 1950s from primarily older, long-term White renters and University of Chicago affiliates to Black renters.[51] The early years of the decade saw Black residents unevenly dispersed throughout the community, concentrated west of Cottage Grove, the racial dividing line. As the years passed, more and more residential space opened up in the White section. Throughout the month of November 1956, for example, the *Chicago Defender* advertised apartments in the East Sixties around Kenwood, Harper, Blackstone, and other streets. Attractive residences touted as amenity-rich and reasonably priced alternately welcomed poor Black people ("Children and A.D.C. accepted") or strove for a context of respectability ("Refined persons only").

Either way, these apartments were all near the new McDonald's drive-in, revealing the area's increasingly Black demographics. Southern Black migrants ar-

Figure 3.4. A replica of the original McDonald's in Des Plaines. The first franchised location was built at this site but was closed and demolished in 1984. This building was erected shortly thereafter to commemorate the restaurant. It was demolished in 2018. Photograph by author, March 2015.

rived at the 63rd Street train station and found themselves forced into dreadfully inadequate and crowded housing. The deteriorating stock was further pressured as urban renewal projects across the city shoehorned additional Black residents into the neighborhood. By 1958, the Woodlawn Block Club Council decried the streets from 61st to 63rd: "a clout era [*sic*], meaning crime, prostitution, and deterioration." Flashpoints for concern included vacant lots, illegally operated stores, and hotels that had devolved into a "burned out hull hiding place for thieves." As the magnitude of disinvestment in Black neighborhoods took hold, crime increasingly dominated community discussions and news accounts.[52]

The outlet at 6550 South Stony Island launched in a community undergoing substantial change; however, because the almost total inversion of White and

Black populations occurred between the 1950 and 1960 censuses, the store opening in 1956 targeted a racially ambiguous market. Hyde Park High School, a few
blocks from the restaurant on Stony Island between 62nd and 63rd had already enrolled substantial numbers of Black students by the time McDonald's opened, but
they came from a wide catchment area, not only Woodlawn.[53] Another McDonald's
outlet opened the same year in another racially changing South Side neighborhood, near the Dan Ryan Expressway. Fine Enterprises launched McDonald's
System Hamburgers at 7060 South Vincennes Avenue on July 1, 1956. Joseph R.
Fine and his brother Howard owned this outlet on the border of Englewood and
Greater Grand Crossing. Howard, previously a car salesman, ran Howard's Family
Shoe Store in the city's northern suburbs and enjoyed a semiprofessional golf ca-
reer, which was likely the brothers' entrée to McDonald's.[54] Joseph was, interest-
ingly, prominent in the local Black community. He belonged to the Cosmopolitan
Chamber of Commerce, formerly the Chicago Negro Chamber of Commerce, an
interracial chamber composed primarily of Black and White men from across the
Chicago metropolitan area.[55]

Did the Fines open the restaurant to target White or Black consumers? The
census tract was 2 percent Black in 1950 but 96 percent Black by 1960. Since
McDonald's locations were in exclusively White communities, one might assume
that at the launch date the neighborhood had not yet sustained substantial White
flight. In fact, Englewood seems to have been much further along in racial change
than Woodlawn. As evident in yearbook photographs, school population demographics suggest that the location at 7060 South Vincennes was primarily Black by
the time McDonald's opened. In concert with Joseph's activism, it would appear
that the Fines purposefully provided Black customers with this new dining experience that would otherwise be inaccessible. What remains unclear is how much oversight or input Kroc gave to the location selection. It may have been that although
corporate targeted White-only space, franchisees had some leeway if they were
interested in seeking out Black consumers; or perhaps Kroc simply was unaware of
the demographics where the Fines opened their franchise.

After Des Plaines, the Gee Gee Corporation—owned by John W. Gibson and
Oscar Goldstein—launched the second major regional McDonald's franchise following Kroc's in Chicago. Headquartered in Alexandria, their exclusive D.C. metro
franchise chose the exclusively White suburbs in Virginia and Maryland to begin
operations in 1957 and opened stores across the region.[56] The company would ultimately operate forty-three outlets across the District of Columbia, five counties
in Virginia, and three counties in Maryland before being bought back by corporate
in 1967 for $16.8 million.[57] Gee Gee's franchise would later turn out to be an in-

cubator for Black franchising, producing several staff who went on to managerial and executive positions across the country. Gibson came into the franchise as a beer distributor, and prior to that occupied varied posts in government and business, most prominently as assistant secretary of labor under President Truman.[58] As a beer distributor, he supplied Goldstein's tavern and deli. These men fit the model of Kroc's early franchisees—affluent and well-connected White entrepreneurs whose primary occupation lay in fields other than the restaurant industry, for whom McDonald's was a side venture.

Alexandria cast a wary eye in the 1950s to many of the new establishments that sought to set up shop on the city's major arterials, whether retail goods and services or social service institutions.[59] And yet, in a climate in which a variety of land uses were seen as incompatible with neighborhood character and detrimental to safety, traffic, and property values, Gee Gee's McDonald's launched with relatively little opposition.[60] Lilla Wood Daniels, of 3449 Duke Street, lodged a complaint about the new drive-in restaurant. Writing to the mayor and city council, she explained, "I am told there is to be a drive-in 'hotdog' stand built on property owned by Mr. C. N. Cockrell and situated directly opposite my home on Duke St. . . . I understand that permission was asked to have an over-size sign erected on the site but that the request was denied by the Planning Commission." She further argued that the new construction would lessen the value of her property and to a lesser degree, those of her neighbors.[61]

Not only did Gee Gee fail to attract community opprobrium, but the team also seemed to be well-known in at least some of areas it served. In June 1961, Oscar Goldstein wrote to corporate to celebrate a recent community event at the Spencerville Seventh-day Adventist Church, ten miles from his Alexandria store, where he helped with refreshments. Goldstein's initiatives epitomized the kind of community engagement corporate wanted from its operators: "It's McDonald's policy to support local causes and pitch in to help local charities and to participate in community activities in many varied ways, at many levels."[62] Corporate would take a different view eight years later when Black activists in Cleveland called for resources to be provided to the Black communities McDonald's served.

By 1962, Gee Gee's "small roadside drive-in restaurant" had sold almost two hundred million hamburgers, grossing $3 million per year (almost $26 million in 2020 dollars).[63] It did so primarily on the strength of White wallets. But two stores opened in Black space: 75 New York Avenue NE and 4950 South Dakota Avenue NE. 4950 opened in October 1961 in a neighborhood that was almost half Black in 1960 and undergoing dramatic change (it had been 1 percent Black in 1950). Given such demographic flux, Gee Gee surely opened to capture the newcomers. Indeed, Oscar

Goldstein brought in a Black man named Carl Osborne as a management trainee in
1963 because Gee Gee was serious about expanding into the District proper.[64] In
the 1960s, that necessitated including Black consumers, and there was no confusing
75 New York Avenue's base. It had been and would be going forward an unequivocally Black neighborhood.[65]

Taken together, the earliest McDonald's outlets had overwhelmingly sought
White customers, but the idiosyncratic decisions of certain franchises led a few
stores to an otherwise neglected Black market. A similar pattern emerged for competitor Burger King.

Burger King

Antebellum Florida "was another country, with its own laws and constitution."[66]
In Central Florida particularly, the repression and violence Whites inflicted on the
Black population in the 1920s and 1930s was grievous. The level of depravity that
witnessed the 1934 lynching of Claude Neal in the Panhandle drew more NAACP
files than any incident in American history, and during World War II and beyond
Black men were rounded up under vagrancy laws, fined for not working and either
imprisoned, or sent forcibly to plantations or turpentine camps to pay off the unjust debt.[67]

Burger King began in Miami—southern Florida—far from the poverty and brutality of citrus groves and turpentine camps. But Black Miamians were no less subject to an apartheid system that "made black people negligible."[68] McDonald's and
KFC originated in places where Black people were nowhere to be found; Burger King
was born in a place with a Black population but was no less hostile. Given the severity of the color line in Florida, it is surprising that the chain was the first of the "big
three" to serve Black customers.

Royal Castle, one of the burger chateaux, preceded Burger King in Miami. Some
described it as an egalitarian space where one might encounter "a derelict" nod-
ding off, a nurse having a pre-shift breakfast, or a cab driver who soothed himself
with a hamburger after a stressful night of work. But it was felled by the postindustrial hamburger in the form of James McLamore's Burger King.[69] In 1951, one sit-
down restaurant already in hand, McLamore started a second restaurant in one of
Miami's new commercial buildings. He did so before realizing that the surrounding
customer base was weak and that, as he put it, "Miami in the late forties and early
fifties was a seasonally oriented destination resort city, heavily trafficked during
the winter months and woefully quiet during the rest of the year."[70]

The shaky financial outlook of his two restaurants led McLamore to sell them both in 1954 in order to join with partner Dave Edgerton, a manager at a Howard Johnson restaurant in downtown Miami who wanted to try his hand at a new burger concept. Edgerton had encountered two restaurateurs in Jacksonville who were in the midst of construction for their new concept, Insta Burger, which would sell burgers, shakes, sodas, and French fries to patrons at a counter, rather than carhop-serviced restaurants. These owners, Keith G. Cramer and Matthew L. Burns, had been in food service for some time, and they too had witnessed the McDonald brothers' operation in San Bernardino. Cramer and Burns signed a license with the makers of the Insta Burger broiler and milkshake machines to develop Florida restaurants that would employ these appliances, paying a franchise fee to the developer of the Insta machines. Edgerton met them as they readied their first outlet in Jacksonville and contracted to build a second drive-in (in Miami), which opened in March 1954 at 3090 NW 36th Street. Lacking the capital to build the restaurant himself, he convinced the property owner to do so and lease it back to him. He also convinced Cramer and Burns to change the name from Insta Burger to Insta Burger King.[71] In one 1956 photo of a Miami outlet, the rooftop signage reads "BURGER INSTA KING," with "INSTA" encircled. The side of the building announced "INSTA BURGERS" and "INSTA SHAKES."[72]

It is interesting that Edgerton chose the edge of Brownsville, one of the few Black communities in Miami, to site his restaurant. There can be no doubt he was aware of the demographics. A suburb to the north and west of the central city, Brownsville was divided up into White and Black sections, the latter of which was populated by affluent Black people of varied ethnicity—those from the Anglophone and Spanish Caribbean as well as African Americans—who moved to the area seeking a suburban lifestyle far from the squalor that typified the congested neighborhoods downtown. When, in the early to mid-1940s, Black residents began taking up residences more widely throughout Brownsville, including spaces designated as White, they were met with cross burnings and other racial violence. Next came a 1945 Dade County ruling that Brownsville was for Whites only. Builders erected a concrete wall between the racially specified areas within the community and for good measure added a red stripe across the length of it.[73] The zoning ordinance was defeated in court in 1946, with local papers reporting on the "so-called 'red line'" that forbade individuals from buying or occupying property outside the neighborhood boundaries—a red line that was not only figurative but literal.[74] But by the time the ordinance was overturned, White people had already begun moving out.[75] The 1950 census reveals a dense population of Black residents around Edgerton's store. And by 1960, his outlet had immediate surroundings that were 89 percent Black. The community was recognized as such when Burger King opened; classified

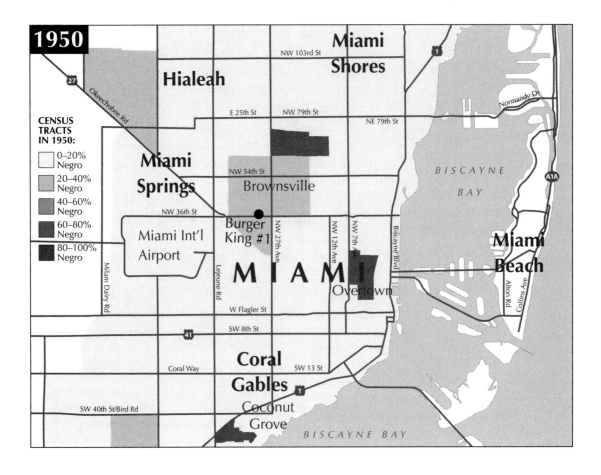

ads listed stores for sale "in colored neighborhood. Brownsville section," and apartments as "BROWNSVILLE. Colored sub-division."[76]

Because one does not stumble into a Black neighborhood in the Jim Crow South, and because there were wide expanses of White space in the city that Edgerton could have occupied, it stands to reason that he targeted Brownsville. According to historian N. D. B. Connolly, "the 1950s were also a period when white businesspeople outside of designated colored enclaves began appreciating the purchasing power of black locals, 'dark gentlemen from the South, the islands,' and what one white vendor called the 'rich Negroes' from Chicago and other points north."[77] Edgerton appears to fall in this camp, seeing the profitability of a location straddling the boundaries of White and Black suburban space. For reasons that McLamore left unstated in his autobiography, Edgerton apparently decided to try his hand at capturing consumer dollars that fast food peers were eager to ignore.

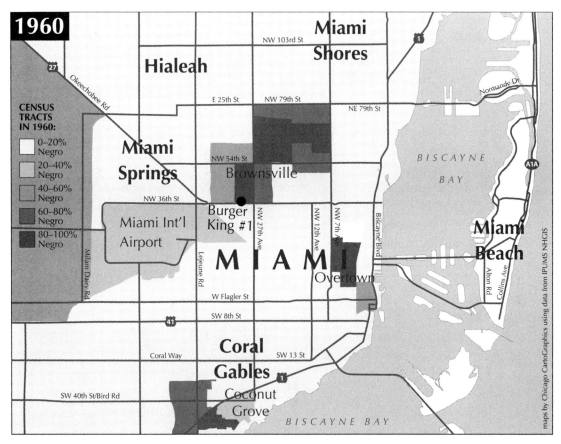

Map 3.4. Census demographics surrounding Miami's first Burger King outlet at 3090 NW 36th, Miami, in 1950 and 1960. Map by Dennis McClendon, CartoGraphics.

Leisure spots owned by diligent White investors drew crowds of affluent Black Miamians, and this may have been particularly motivating.[78]

Though Edgerton's business with the new burger restaurants proved slow, McLamore was willing to come in as a partner to develop the chain. The pair announced their venture in the *Miami Herald*, with a local column asking, "Did you know that Dave Edgerton and Jim McLamore are starting their own restaurant chain? They still haven't decided on the name of the organization."[79] Their next outlets were on Southwest Eighth Street, Northwest Seventh Avenue, and on the precipice of the Everglades, in Homestead, Florida (home to the Homestead Army Air Field). According to McLamore, "It was a long way from Miami, but the owner of this site was willing to have us build a Burger King store there." Interestingly, though the store was within White space, Homestead was home to one of the broader Miami metro's designated Black communities.[80] Those who made their homestead in Homestead, a dusty and desperate agricultural landscape in the late 1930s, were primarily poor migrant vegetable pickers from across the South and Midwest. By the 1950s, the conditions were perhaps not as dire, but agriculture was still dominant, migrant labor was still prevalent, and the laborers were still poor. It is hardly surprising that Burger King's relatively pricey fare drew little uptake in the area. Indeed, all four of McLamore and Edgerton's stores struggled, the initial outlets held by Cramer and Burns were in trouble as well, and other licensees decided to sell.[81] The unstable Insta machines broke down continuously and made for rocky service, and McLamore was pitching to a customer base that, despite Royal Castle's success, simply didn't believe inexpensive burgers could be wholesome. McLamore and Edgerton forged ahead nonetheless, opening three additional restaurants. Stores 6 and 7, in White neighborhoods, continued the trajectory of poor sales.[82]

The introduction of the Whopper and a rush of capital infusions from McLamore's family network eventually got the ball rolling. His wife's father invested $3,750 for stock in 1956 and followed up with a loan for an additional $10,000. As the duo continued to open struggling restaurants, McLamore's father-in-law introduced him to a retired businessman from Detroit who put in $65,000 and came in as partner with half interest. Within a few years, helped by its first television ads in 1958, the chain was on its way.[83] Critically, not all the initial stores fared badly. The fifth opened in the fall of 1956 at 7995 NW 27th Avenue. This store "gave us a badly needed boost in morale because the volume of business at that location was superior to any of the original four stores we had opened."[84] Though McLamore did not mention it, census demographics reveal that this store was in West Little River, a Black neighborhood on the other side of Brownsville. This would surely be a significant data point for Burger King's later decision-making. If Black communities could be counted on for robust sales, that made them a well to which the chain ought to return. But nowhere in McLamore's autobiography do African Americans appear: neither early store demographics, nor the crises and corporate policies related to minority franchise development (see chapter 8), nor the racial covenants the company signed with Black activist organizations (see chapter 11).

Although some of the Miami stores skirted Black space, Orlando stores were all in exclusively White communities, situated in languid and sparse landscapes in which burger outlets sprouted as oases for food and drink. The Pine Hills Burger King advertised its grand opening by making note of "an economical self service operation, no waiting" and "no tipping! you save 2 ways! see for yourself!" Again, self-service referred to the chain's shift from carhops; customers could walk

Figure 3.5. An advertisement for Orlando area Burger Kings. *Orlando Evening Star,* July 16, 1957. Source: Newspapers.com.

right up to the counter, order and pay in advance, and quickly receive their food. Photographs showcased White women employees working the Insta equipment. Orlando's Burger King employment ads did not specify race in seeking counter staff, perhaps leaving it as understood that these positions would not be open to Black applicants.[85] But in Fort Lauderdale, the outlet at 3291 West Broward explicitly sought White men over eighteen to work early nights, and White women (unlike McDonald's, which avoided hiring women) to work the lunch shift.

Around 1957, Edgerton and McLamore sold their fifth outlet to another entrepreneur, becoming franchisors. At that point, the two men decided to put their energies fully into franchising new units. Meanwhile, Cramer and Burns found themselves unable to pay off their loans and went asunder, leaving the company in the hands of their lender. By 1961, Edgerton and McLamore convinced the lender to sell the rights, title, and all aspects of the business to them. This national franchise for Burger King outlets comprised more than fifty stores across six states, and franchises were planned in D.C., Atlanta, Chicago, and elsewhere.[86] From then on, Burger King moved forward as a chain that sold licenses to franchisees across the country. Chicago-area outlets were realized in 1963 in the northwestern suburb of Skokie. Three more arrived within the city limits by 1965. Of these, two skirted the edge of existing or coming Black neighborhoods. Stores at 11201 South Halsted (at 65th) and 1539 W. Garfield (55th and Justine) bracketed a large cluster of Black residents in Englewood, just as the Florida stores bracketed Brownsville. Apparently learning from the Miami sales data, corporate again made overtures to Black customers, not locating squarely in longtime Black neighborhoods but confidently meeting the expansion of the Black Belt. As chapter 5 will show, at least one of those stores became the site of racial violence that took hold across several fast food establishments as White residents rejected breaking buns with Black customers. Fast food was still White, and apart from Burger King's early entrée, Blackness remained antithetical to the enterprise.

Taken together, the rise of second-generation fast food can be described as prepared with a base of Whiteness and just a splash of Blackness. Importantly, that White base was definitely suburban in focus, but a surprising number of city locations were included. Those early spots would become the initial foundation of fast food in Black, urban space. The tentative outreach to Black consumers made by Burger King was unique among chains of any size. While Burger King's founders located near Black space, only select individual McDonald's franchisees did so, and KFC avoided Black people altogether. For second-generation fast food, Blackness remained incompatible as the industry shifted from city to suburb, bringing with it a cure for White racial fears.

4

Freedom from Panic

American Myth and the Untenability of Black Space

It was not fast food alone that cast Black consumers as a peripheral market lacking spending power. Into the 1950s, retailers of all sorts ignored Black newspapers; only companies selling skin whiteners, hair straighteners, and patent medicine could be bothered to buy advertising space.[1] This despite several book-length studies on African American consumers. White corporate interests misconstrued Black consumer habits, ignoring the impact of life in a White supremacist society. *Time* reported that Black consumers would spend more proportionally than Whites because it gave them prestige among friends. Thus, historian Susannah Walker contends, "*Time*'s conflation of African Americans' desire for 'status' among peers and their demands for fair treatment in the marketplace is odd and analytically imprecise, but hardly unusual."[2]

Black radio, another major site for advertising, was ignored and subjected to racist stereotypes. WANN, which broadcast to D.C., much of Maryland, and counties in Delaware, Pennsylvania, and Virginia, enumerated its African American market as the largest outside of New York. But this audience was portrayed as bizarre and off-brand by mainstream media. *Broadcasting Magazine* described Black radio as unapologetically speaking to Black audiences that did not necessarily "use proper English"; and playing music "derived from soundtracks of old Tarzan movies" and "a lot of wild music with unintelligible lyrics."[3] Corporations did not begin spending in more significant amounts on Black radio until the mid-1960s—and *Broadcasting Magazine* listed among them Procter & Gamble, Coca-Cola, Pepsi, several alcoholic beverage companies, and Ford. Noticeably absent from this list was fast food.[4]

McDonald's implicitly dismissed Black radio as a marketing venue for operators. In 1962, having developed six new commercials, corporate enjoined franchisees to take advantage of local advertising and contract with radio stations for thirty- to sixty-second announcements. The company cautioned, "Do not discount any station in your market except those you definitely feel might attract the wrong type of audience for your McDonald's."[5] Although anyone who ate food should have been the "right" audience, Black people were the "wrong type," and with segregated airwaves it was easy to exclude them. The spending power of Black markets simply held no allure for White-owned corporations.

Because Black space was seen as untenable for fast food, into the 1960s Black print and broadcast media lacked fast food's advertising dollars and Black communities lacked fast food outlets—so much so that foreign countries won the spoils of new restaurant markets as corporations bypassed chocolate cities. All the major chains set up shop abroad before deciding to cater to Black consumers at home. International locations were reportedly attractive because capitalism's constant focus on larger markets made a relative lack of fast food outside the United States a critical opportunity.[6] In 1955, journalist Sylvia Porter wrote in the *Morning Call* of Allentown, Pennsylvania, that on a trip to Paris three years prior, her husband found himself craving a "good American hamburger," a dream that would finally be realized within a year when White Tower opened in the City of Light. The company planned to erect "an exact duplicate of the 225 White Towers which now dot our countryside from north to south—with the identical white walls, counters and stools." The food would also match as closely as possible what American consumers enjoyed at home. Porter queried company head Thomas E. Saxe Jr. about what motivated the move, and he explained, "'Common sense . . . with more and more tourists traveling abroad every year, with low-cost transportation sure to swell the number of American visitors, I don't see how we can miss." Saxe also noted that there were tens of thousands of American expatriates in Paris to boot, and thus "we'd open a stand to meet that demand alone even if we couldn't count on a single tourist, and we'll get plenty of tourists."[7] For Saxe, reaching Paris's expatriates made more sense than serving Black Americans at home. The same was true for other chains. In January 1969, when KFC had yet to market to African Americans, it was preparing to launch a franchise in Aruba and Curacao, at a time when it already ran outposts in Germany and Spain, six in Australia, and had contracts signed for hundreds more across the Philippines, Singapore, the Middle East, Europe, and Japan.[8]

The erasure of Black people and neighborhoods from most of the chains' franchising reflected more than the stereotyping of Black consumers as bizarre, peripheral, and unprofitable. Several forces were at play that made Black space untenable. First, fast food was a showcase for the purported moxie and capitalist mastery of (White) American businessmen. It promoted a narrative of the American restaurant frontier and pioneers who were able to tame it. Second, panics around gen-

Figure 4.1. Little Tavern restaurant #15 at 1200 Good Hope Road in Anacostia, Washington, D.C. Anacostia turned Black following White residents' departure after *Brown v. Board of Education.* Image PR 1435A, Emil A. Press slide collection, D.C. History Center.

der, sexuality, and adolescence threatened the idyll of White suburbia, and had fast food taken root in Black space a dangerous elision of racial boundaries would have occurred. Finally, amid the Cold War, fast food could not approach communities where American democracy clearly failed to live up to its promise.

American Moxie

Fast food cultivated an image of meritocracy and accessibility for customers and industry captains alike. In 1957, White Castle cofounder Bill Ingram was lauded as "Granddaddy of the Hamburger" on the cover of *Fast Food Magazine*. The trade magazine drew readers in with an appealing portrait of a self-made American man pictured alongside four White boys, burgers in hand. At that time, the chain was reportedly grossing $16 million annually (approximately $148 million in 2020 dollars), and through Ingram the halo of American ingenuity was narrated as the driving force. Workers from all sectors thronged to start restaurant franchises. In the mid-1960s, trade magazines listed a set of new franchisees (primarily Chicken Delight, Dog N Suds, Shakey's Pizza, and A&W Root Beer) as previously a realtor, musician, engineer, school teacher, CPA, meat cutter, druggist, advertising executive, lather, conductor (whether transit or orchestral was unclear), miner, and social worker.[9]

These were a diverse group of franchisees indeed. But fast food operators were almost all White men, and despite the prevailing discourse, anything but an open and meritocratic process gave them their start. When Ray Kroc began to expand his new company, he turned to social networks centered at his golf club Rolling Green, which "provided an enormous initial franchise base."[10] Like most private golf clubs, the membership was White-only. From Rolling Green Kroc brought in close friends, including Bob Dondanville, an advertising representative for *Ladies' Home Journal*.[11] Kroc's social networks were at play beyond Rolling Green as well. Sanford Agate became a franchisee when his wife, Betty, was selling Bibles door-to-door and called at Kroc's offices.[12] The Agates became millionaires. With franchisees coming from Kroc's personal and racially segregated spatial milieus, Black franchisees were an impossibility.[13]

Nor did the initial McDonald's crew include any Black men. Contemporary depictions portray something quite different, seeking to bring the staff into a blurred, multiracial past and present. For example, in the 2016 film *The Founder*, Michael Keaton, playing Kroc, supervises the crew of young men in his new restaurant, chiding those who could not keep up in his Fordist burger factory. The team includes two Black teenagers, but the first McDonald's was an entirely White affair in staff and customers. Field consultants hired by Kroc were also exclusively White men.[14] McDonald's also failed to include any more than a trivial number of Black workers (as well as White women) in its Hamburger University training facility, which opened in 1961 in Elk Grove Village, another Chicago suburb. This Basic Operating Course awarded a "Bachelor of Hamburgerology." The first two years produced twenty cohorts of trainees, variable in size, but increasing over time and often comprising dozens, all but a few of whom were White. Oscar Goldstein of the D.C. franchise raved about the Hamburgerology program, saying in 1962 that it was some of the most productive time he had spent with McDonald's and that it "is so important to me personally for my operation that I intended to come back periodically, possibly at least once a year to take the course again."[15] When Black operators finally came on board beginning in 1968, they would have missed out on several years of training and networking that White franchisees enjoyed.

Over the first twenty graduating classes, it appears only a few Black men enrolled as trainees though none were operators. Melvin Stepney, "a South Side

Chicago boy," was brought on as an assistant manager trainee to East 35th Street owing to his enthusiasm, and in 1963 Class XX (the twentieth cohort) featured one Black man, Bernie Payne, from Cleveland. Wallace Rogers, who worked as an assistant manager at 70th Street and Vincennes, had arrived from Mississippi in 1942 and was involved with several South Side restaurant ventures before taking up a position at McDonald's.[16] Rogers went on to be the manager of a new store at 17 East 35th Street, later reborn a few doors down at #25, between State and Wabash. Louis Rivkin was the White owner and a member of Class X (the tenth cohort).[17]

But a narrative of hard work and bootstraps earnestly lifted upward dominated the corporation's self-image. The early 1960s saw McDonald's internal newsletters profiling two brothers who had emigrated from rural Greece as children and worked in an Asheville, North Carolina, outlet after graduating high school. They went on to become comanagers and naturalized citizens. When asked what they liked most about the United States, they cheered, "Freedom! Freedom of movement, speech, religion, and, understandably, the unlimited opportunity for those willing to work!"[18] Of course, while fast food operators had to work hard, the very nature of franchised business involved a shortcut around the purported drive and independence in which industry captains reveled. Kroc spoke unreservedly about his success, attributing it to his own quality: "I have always believed that each man makes his own happiness and is responsible for his own problems. It is a simple philosophy. I think it must have been passed along to me in the peasant bones of my Bohemian ancestors."[19] Even as he handed out franchises to golfing buddies, he evinced little cognizance (or tolerance for discussion) of the deep inequalities that systematically blocked individuals who did not look like him from "making" their own happiness. Kroc spoke out vehemently against civil rights and antiwar movements, and cast any social critique as incompatible with patriotism.[20] His fans espoused the same decades later. A respondent named Glenn, when asked in 1998 about McDonald's business practices, sneered, "Why don't these critics of McDonald's go live in Russia or China? They don't want to see anybody succeed. They just want a big government to come in and tax away all profits and give the money to the minorities and other people who don't want to work . . . Kroc is an American hero."[21]

The decidedly unmeritocratic dealings that Kroc relied on to build his empire were swept under the rug. When Kroc sought new franchisees among his peer group, few had the requisite funds on hand or the ability to borrow them, affluent though they were. New restaurants required a half-acre site, which cost at least $30,000 (approximately $280,000 in 2020 dollars), and the building itself cost $40,000 (approximately $374,000 in 2020 dollars) to construct. To solve this problem Kroc formed a new company, the Franchise Realty Corporation, which retained a small army of real estate men, many of whom had been recruited from Standard Oil. They identified individuals who owned land in desirable locations and approached them with the following proposal: McDonald's would lease the land, and the landowner would build a McDonald's restaurant which the corporation would also rent on a twenty-year lease. McDonald's then re-rented the restaurant to new franchisees, with a profitable markup that started at 20 percent but later rose to 40 percent. In fact, the percentage surcharge was the minimum rent to be paid. Franchisees were charged whichever was higher of a 40 percent markup or a percentage of sales—beginning in the range of 5 percent and increasing over time.[22] By the early 1960s, McDonald's began purchasing the land from owners and financing the building with a mortgage. No McDonald's funds were used to finance its real estate purchases; all cash came from the franchisees (in the form of security deposits) and from bank loans.

The company quickly became known for an aggressive and combative stance as it acquired properties. When McDonald's planned to open a new outlet in Springfield, Ohio, area supervisor Ralph Lanphar introduced himself to a competing business across the street by saying "Hello, I'm the new McDonald's supervisor. We're going to run you out of business."[23] Lanphar's attitude is interesting because it speaks to not only the chain's ruthless orientation—which would become a problem later when dealing with Black and other minority franchisees—but also the extent to which Black communities were non grata at that time. The company was so competitive that it was ready to run its neighbors out of business, yet it continued to ignore Black folks both as potential franchisees and as customers.

McDonald's real estate juggernaut was foundational to the value of its portfolio and the company's overall financial position. But buying real estate was an expensive endeavor that soon ate up liquidity for future land purchases. The scheme was not attractive to bankers, who doubted the viability of a restaurant selling hamburgers for fifteen cents apiece. McDonald's needed a way to look richer than it was in order to secure investors. In 1958 it hired Richard J. Boylan, an accountant and lawyer who had worked for eight years at the IRS, to pull off the trick. He began counting future net rental income from franchisees as assets that were currently held. By 1960, assets were listed as $12.4 million, quadruple what they had been the year prior. The hugely inflated total was all due to "Unrealized Increment from Appraisal in Valuation of Assets."[24]

Boylan also used "innovative accounting" to increase reported earnings. His methods "worked magic on McDonald's income statement: they produced reported earnings where there were none before." Harry Sonneborn, a McDonald's executive from 1956 to 1966, said, "It was the greatest accounting gimmick ever devised."[25]

Without the strategy, the company would have posted a negative net worth. But magical money did not erase real-life constraints; McDonald's continued to face cash flow problems as more and more was needed to expand, to pay contractors, and indeed to keep the company out of bankruptcy. Corporate began to acquire major loans from willing lenders despite its minimal assets. Kroc also needed money to buy out the McDonald's brothers at a cost of $2.7 million so he could be free of their franchising contract rules. The company needed a loan, and fast. McDonald's executives went to John Bristol, a New York money manager who handled investments for large trusts and "was always on the lookout for somewhat riskier investments that would produce higher yields than triple-A bonds."[26] Bristol organized a loan backed by several of his clients. Foremost among them was Princeton University, which in the mid-1950s held a portfolio valued at more than $100 million. Bristol also managed the trust funds for Colby College, Howard University, Syracuse University, the Institute for Advanced Studies, and Swarthmore College as well as several charitable foundations. Princeton put up $1 million while the other eleven institutions put up the rest. Sonneborn was elated to obtain "old-line eastern money."[27] It was not moxie that set the chain alight, but privilege.

Kroc clearly meant for that privilege to seep into the look, dining experience, and operation of his restaurants. The food was cheap, but the restaurant itself could not be. McDonald's was one of the rewards for homeowners in suburban spaces free of Black people. Not only could fast food not enter Black space, but it also had to police any kind of untoward behavior that deviated from an ideal of White suburban domesticity or evoked the presumed disorderliness of Blackness.

Gender and Sexual Panics

If suburbia was the stage for the masculine expression of clever White capitalism, it was also a canvas for appropriately chaste White femininity. Architectural historian Diane Harris argues that in the new suburban landscape, houses were built to accommodate and promote traditional gender roles, self-contained leisure, and ultimately "a refuge against a chaotic world."[28] Postwar homes were not only brick and mortar exemplars of capitalist bounty, but also a cipher for Whiteness. Stable, clean, and spacious residences that housed individual nuclear families became iconographic for appropriate American domesticity. The houses' design, surfaces, fixtures, and goods therein all gave spatial and rhetorical expressions of race.[29] The suburban American home and its extensions in public space (e.g., family-centered fast food) coalesced around White women and their domestic responsibilities.

Toward that aim, fast food constructed women's bodies as antithetical to the dining experience. Kroc purposefully avoided women as servers, seeing them as catalysts for wanton sexual transgressions. He looked askance at carhops, believing them to have a bad reputation that would put off families. Kroc biographer John Love portrayed the climate as follows: "If the carhops were not having sexual encounters with the fry cooks, they were with the customers." The evidence for Love's assertion is unclear and likely exaggerated. But other restaurant chiefs were also reportedly afraid of sexual undertones at their establishments. Bob Wian of the Big Boy restaurant chain imported his staff from California when he opened in Dallas reportedly because the idea of the drive-in as a sex playground prevented his local hiring.[30] Why he perceived Texas women to be a risk is unclear. Other chains, including White Castle and Hot Shoppes (initially), also made it a policy not to hire women in the hopes that an all-male staff would prevent loitering by male customers, a discriminatory strategy of dubious merit.[31] If company leaders had their way, women would only appear on drive-in grounds as chaste and gender-conforming customers. But if the presence of any women, even those understood to be morally upright—White women—could provoke sexual digressions, then Black neighborhoods would be symbolically off-limits.

Fast food was already threading a thin line between acceptable and unacceptable gender roles. Food preparation was vexed with conflicted impulses—it was supposed to be a creative outlet for the average housewife, and yet she had to hew to precise recipes. It was really a chore, but she was supposed to do it bejeweled and bedecked in lovely outfits.[32] Sedate and secure suburban settings often produced frustrations for White women, who felt trapped in the monotonous and exhausting work of domestic chores and childrearing, and isolated by purely residential contexts.[33] But women could not express those feelings, else they be denigrated as terrible homemakers, wives, and mothers. Tricky, then, to have women derive pleasure from serving fast food to their husbands and children.

Historian Katherine Parkin holds that advertisers have long asserted that food is a vehicle for women to show and earn their love. Traditionally, the kitchen and the home was the centerpiece for this transaction, and so retailers had to straddle a line promoting their products' convenience without usurping women's proper role in domestic tasks. Advertisements carefully suggested that new products could help women work outside the home while simultaneously being attentive homemakers.[34] Ernest Dichter of the Institute for Motivational Research emphasized the importance of love in food advertising. In the late 1950s, he called for ads that felt like a "loving mother," eschewing a tone that was too assertive or insistent. Love themes were prominent in fast food advertising, particularly in the 1970s and 1980s. But in the 1950s and 1960s, dining out at McDonald's, Burger King, and other chains took place amid a swirl of conflicting messages. Women had to show love through food but were not to derive any pleasure from food themselves; food could bridge an idealized and constant past with a complicated and vexed present; women should fear failing at being a good wife, mother, and cook, but products were no armor because choosing the wrong one—or failing to use a particular one—was a failure itself.[35]

Fast food spoke to women by equipping them with the gendered rationales that made it a logical choice for forward-thinking mothers. As noted above, Golden Point stressed its focus on the name brands women would already have stocked in their kitchens, thereby reiterating that dining out at fast food restaurants was another way to demonstrate savvy homemaking. McDonald's advertising declared that "Mom likes McDonald's too . . . she says she can feed us for less there than she can at home. She likes the speedy service, no car hops, no tipping, plenty of parking space . . . and most of all no dishes to wash and no fussing in the kitchen."[36] Other ads reinforced the propriety of the restaurant for single women: "Before or after the game . . . or for a tasty snack anytime . . . bring your date to McDonald's. You'll be glad you did when you find out just *how good* a 15c Hamburger can be."[37]

Black women were, in the American imaginary, innately servile workhorses without any of the decorum or grace of White women. Black communities were therefore verboten for fast food, as they would taint the restaurants with perceived lifestyles seen as antagonistic to the enterprise. Fast food could not be a vehicle for women to show and receive love if the least lovable among them dined there, too.

Of course, women could not use any food—fast or otherwise—as a vehicle for love in excess, lest it lead to fatness. The 1950s emphasized bland cuisine partly in reaction to increased social tensions and partly due to a focus on slimness.[38] But some of those bland foods could translate into fat. Since the 1940s, psychiatric explanations of obesity had underscored moral and character flaws and a failure of willpower. Group therapy became popular in the 1950s, which gave both social support to address emotional problems and guidelines on diets that would help one reduce.[39] Organizations like Fatties Anonymous and later Overeaters Anonymous and Weight Watchers attempted to rein in undisciplined eating. By 1955, obesity took on additional weight in national discourse when President Eisenhower was presented with studies showing that American children lagged far behind Europeans in fitness. This meant both a compromised military force and a morally weak populace.[40]

Although broad public discourse about connections between fast food and body weight would not emerge for several decades, fast food still attended to the implications of selling food that could be seen as fattening. Already in the 1950s, the

Figure 4.2. A Little Tavern advertisement in the *Baltimore Sun,* September 3, 1950. Source: Newspapers.com.

restaurant industry kept an eye on the nation's weight. *Drive-In Magazine* reported in 1959 that "obesity is a major health problem in the United States. Most overweight people do not have glandular trouble—merely excessive appetites. Capitalize on this."[41] The text seems to suggest selling as many fattening items to those who could not control their intake, but in fact the magazine went on to promote advertising low-calorie menus. If overweight people could not control themselves, the thing to do was indulge them by encouraging them to eat in abundance lower-calorie fast food. Such a tactic would also be useful in targeting women, who would harbor concerns about eating and body image.

The pressure to maintain not only ideal homes but also ideal bodies stimulated anxiety among White women. In a context of unattainable gender expectations, the rise of the anti-anxiety drug Miltown, which along with McDonald's hit the market in 1955, surpassed that of any prior medication in U.S. history. Miltown was prescribed for myriad symptoms and conditions—and sometimes no stated reason at all. It had become a "virtual panacea, offered like patent medicines of old for nearly any ailment."[42] Driving the raucous demand were postwar gender roles that urged mothers to return to and stay at home, embrace maternal duties, and adhere to a particular set of expressions of femininity. In this frame, unmedicated women who did not adapt to these changes, including "frigid women" and those who insisted on working, were liable to pass loneliness and depression to the men in their lives. The confused gender roles of the times robbed white-collar men of their masculinity and their wives of appropriate feminine comportment. Tranquilizers like Miltown were positioned as interventions that could equip men and women alike to adjust.[43]

In that regard, the new hamburger drive-ins could potentially solve several conflicts. Mothers could serve their families a treat that while possibly fattening did not actually come from her hand, relieving her of culpability. She could catch a break from the drudgery of the kitchen. And the restaurants were an appealing, family-centered panacea for boredom and anxiety. It is striking that the all-white uniforms of burger chateaux and suburban-chain staff mimicked those worn by attendants in mental health facilities. In *One Flew over the Cuckoo's Nest,* the Black male orderlies who served as the muscle behind Nurse Ratched's directives donned the same short-sleeved white shirts and white pants as burger crews. Their uniforms telegraphed both control and support of hospital inpatients, an aesthetic meant to soothe and clarify social roles. By remaining in White space, fast food gave White women and their families a wholesome treat, free from any of the myriad anxieties that perturbed suburban psyches, not least of which was dining alongside Black customers. And yet, one of fast food's core demographics would start to become bothersome—teenagers. Just as women were necessary, desirable, but conflicted participants in the new suburban formulation of fast food, young people were a source of concerns about propriety and the incompatibility of Black neighborhoods.

Teenage Panics

Ernest Dichter argued that much of the appeal of fast food was its harking back to deep evolutionary drives to eat as our Stone Age forebears once had.[44] But the drive-in was not the place for teens to act out their unfettered impulses. The suburbs were manicured landscapes of White tranquility and social conformity; the city was the disordered and dangerous concrete jungle. Second-generation restaurants took pains not to open in Black neighborhoods, the perceived apotheosis of a lack of ego control; that even suburban outlets elicited wild adolescent behavior rendered the central city a nonstarter.

Fast food was almost immediately vexed by its immense popularity among youth, even though that was the demographic it courted the most. Children loved McDonald's and the company made it a point to attract them: "We have gone all out for the family trade; to make it a pleasure and very easy on the budget, to bring a whole carful of kids in."[45] The chain's public relations firm Cooper & Golin disseminated messages about children's seeming innate love of fast food—McDonald's especially. Franchisees were provided press kits with broadcast-ready material such as segments that claimed, "The average American boy under 10 easily eats his weight in hamburgers over the course of a year. At the most conservative estimate a 7-year-old boy weighing 55 pounds would put away a little more than a pound of hamburger a week"—and that was not counting the buns.[46] First-generation restaurant chains that had been happy to ignore children realized as the new chains took root that they, too, would need to court a young market. Horn & Hardart, for example, put a small boy on the cover of its 1963 annual report, suggesting that the automat was a child-friendly space, perhaps even one children eagerly sought out.

Teenage "hoodlums" were another matter; they were the bane of drive-in restaurants, a plague that warranted immediate action before it became unmanageable. Hot-rodding youth and their cronies occupied substantial real estate in the pages of restaurant periodicals. This new generation on wheels had unprecedented independence and perhaps less of the good judgment needed to exercise their mobility responsibly. Although even adolescents in the 1920s used automobiles to effect greater independence from their parents, teen car culture blossomed in the affluent 1950s and continued apace in the 1960s as car manufacturers proffered to teens vehicles ranging in price and muscle, from Corvette Stingrays to Ford Mustangs. Souped-up hot rods and motorcycles also fueled adolescent social life, though the average teen had to make do with unsexy cars borrowed from parents or bought used. Besides transportation, necessary in suburban communities, cars became places to listen to music, to date, to be free of adult supervision, and to enjoy privacy.[47] When all that teenage automobility collided with fast food, it provoked an outcry.

A *Drive-In Restaurant* article is worth quoting at length:

> This is an unhappy subject but it has to be met head-on. With balmy nights coming on, a small percentage of your people will attempt to make your life miserable . . . It's an unfortunate trend in our society that perhaps one percent of the teenagers are young misguided animals . . . You'll have to be firm right from the beginning. At the first sign of hoodlumism, *get tough* . . . The police will be most happy to cooperate if that becomes necessary. Again, don't be afraid to be firm with the hoodlums. If you're not, they can ruin your business.[48]

Striking in its severity, this owner's language invoked the potential for a police presence to manage "animals"—words not typically used to describe White youth. Such talk mirrored the sentiments typically roused by establishments that produce greater obvious harms or moral outrage, such as liquor stores and sex shops. Drive-in restaurants were disparaged with a vehemence that reflected urgent national concerns about American youth becoming juvenile delinquents. The early to mid-1950s saw marked concerns, even hysteria, about juvenile delinquency. Fast food got going at the height of such worries, when congressional hearings and a rush of publications by academics and journalists intruded on public consciousness. Youth culture came under intense scrutiny as comics, advertising, film, and rock and roll were theorized to cause delinquency. Immediately following World War II adults regarded adolescents with curiosity and amusement. But now, the prevailing wisdom (or fear) was that maybe a whole generation had gone wrong; teens were now a capricious, violence-prone group with time to waste and the freedom to travel.[49]

Aversion to youth culture was underlined by perceptions that it was working class in origin and a source of defilement for middle-class teens. Urban high schools often threw together adolescents from varied socioeconomic and ethnic backgrounds, and they became still more heterogeneous as the numbers of Black students rose. The perceived spread of delinquency from lower to middle classes was most often framed as one of "contagion, contamination, and infection." Political leaders located juvenile delinquency within young people, their families, and a troubled cultural fabric. FBI director J. Edgar Hoover attributed delinquency to American moral decline, calling the "juvenile jungle" a threat comparable with communism.[50]

Still, a national (White) youth culture based on consumption was of keen interest to retailers of all sorts. Programs such as *American Bandstand* played a major role by promoting numerous products—whether soda, snacks, hit records, or pimple cream—sometimes on the dance floor itself. The show advertised widely in print media, even to Black newspapers whose readers were barred from attending the show.[51] Fast food's dilemma was how to cash in on the spending power of a potentially problematic group (which it would later face again in seeking out the Black consumer market). Restaurateurs large and small struggled to reconcile adolescent disruption. In Des Plaines, Kroc attempted to stem the tide of problematic youth. Weekday lunchtimes always brought a crush of people—primarily construction and other area workers—making midday consistently busy but orderly. However, after 6:00 p.m., the demographic shifted to a younger crowd dominated by teens with hot rods. The restaurant stayed open late—10:00 or 11:30 p.m. depending on the day—and young drivers made a circuit of local restaurants, careening between Skip's on North Avenue, the Pie Room in Skokie, and other outlets in Niles and Park Ridge. Youth were often arrested en masse and clashed with McDonald's management for nearly a year.[52]

Al Olson, editor of the trade periodical *Fast Food*, wrote an acerbic column lambasting the drive-in across the street from his family's apartment. A burger joint that cooked over charcoal had been doing steady business from husbands in the residential complex, but adolescents quashed the men's enthusiasm for the restaurant. Olson asserted, "We're fed up with the drag races that start from the parking lot; with the yelling and screaming from animal-like teenagers as they fight on that lot." Adding insult to injury, the teens were considered weak spenders, averaging a fifth of what the family men typically spent.[53] Still, even if teens' average checks were modest, they came in number and came often, making them a lucrative customer segment that could not be banished altogether.

For otherwise wholesome, all-American White youth to symbolize disorder and disruption constituted a behavioral blurring of racial boundaries. In acting as "animals" White teens were acting Black, as far as drive-in owners were concerned. Fast food could not countenance the existential threat of Blackness, whether in person in Black neighborhoods or symbolically in unruly White teens. Burgers were supposed to assuage racial fears, not create them. For that reason, and as a representation of American ingenuity, abundance, and well-being, fast food dared not venture into communities that revealed how thinly those attributes were realized.

Cold War Burgers

From the mid-1940s to the mid-1950s, as suburbia became the center for a new consumer-oriented domestic life, Americans poured money into appliances and other home goods. National leaders took up these trends as "evidence of the superiority of the American way of life. Since much of the cold war was waged in propaganda battles, this vision of domesticity was a powerful weapon." Nixon told Khrushchev that the Soviet Union might have had *Sputnik,* but the United States had color televisions.[54] Free choice became synonymous with political freedom and abundant consumer goods as evidence that Americans were better than the Soviets at doing away with class divisions.[55]

Food retail hammered home the notion of freedom and choice as inherent to American society. Supermarkets and groceries in the 1950s and 1960s valorized abundant, anonymous, and beautiful spaces in which shopping was more of an exciting outing than a chore to meet basic necessities.[56] In doing so, food retail revealed the superiority of the American way of life; low prices "made customers feel that they were being treated equally"; and these stores "showcased the real value of American capitalism and free enterprise."[57]

Second-generation fast food, too, might have fostered a consumer environment that suggested equality by virtue of its prices. But it was also explicitly wedded to a Whites-only fever dream of suburbia. Because the restaurants were so deeply linked to state-supported residential exclusion, they were different from supermarkets. These restaurants showed the real value of Whiteness: not so much the comfort of equality within the confines of consumer abundance, but rather an experience that reified consumer pleasure as the domain of suburban, White families alone. Under those terms, consumers were meant to enjoy being the beneficiaries of racial exclusion—yet another of the conveniences wrought by the American way of life.

If fast food signaled to Cold War enemies the satisfaction to be found in consumerism, it could not be besmirched by racial contestations. The drive-in could hardly demonstrate the country's superiority over communist Russia if it were revealed as another beachhead on which the country's social divisions crashed. Springing up in a midcentury milieu that showcased the ease and pleasure of American life precluded siting in Black space. Drive-ins were new, modern eateries brimming with the confidence of a stable White future. They could not appear in ramshackle streetscapes that racist policies produced and left behind. Nor would it do to have Black people agitating for civil rights and making a scene. Fast food was a part of the consumer propaganda that convinced Americans that all was well on the home front.[58]

The hamburger, already becoming a symbol of comfortable American life, had the potential to soothe White racial anxieties in the face of social uncertainty, at least in the context of White space. A 1955 backyard gathering among White southerners discussing the slaying of Emmett Till—which occurred four months after McDonald's opened in Des Plaines—was one such setting. An Atlanta household played host to an impromptu cookout, bringing together locals and transplants from northern cities. The discussion at this "sensitive Southerner's" house ranged widely, touching on sore points for the homeowners; among them were a Kansas judge who had the temerity to call Robert E. Lee a traitor and, eventually, Till. The group found themselves "groping for a definition of lynching," but ultimately the debate was satisfactorily resolved.[59] The cookout brought together a diverse group of White neighbors—this one an advertising executive from New York City, that one an insurance adjuster from Alabama—who could be aggrieved together about racial politics. The meal, and specifically hamburgers, was the glue that held the convocation together. Home-cooked hamburgers served as an edible racial palliative, dissolving perseverations about the North's trampling of the hierarchies that defined southern life. In the North, over-the-counter equivalents served the same needs. The 1950s saw a strong imperative to mitigate social tension, and fast food's simple, bland fare fit perfectly.[60] It was the perfect medicament for White minds made anxious by Blackness. Kentucky Fried Chicken, Burger King, and McDonald's created empires meant to shield White people from the challenge of race, sex, and contested authority.

Second-generation fast food blocked out the intrusion of a reality-based assessment of America's social fabric. Just as the Atlanta cookout burgers melted away the idea of a country where the lives of Black boys were forfeited for speaking to White women, second-generation fast food fueled a fantasy of America where civil rights were not contested, and indeed where there was no need to. In so doing, much like Miltown, fast food acted as racial Xanax, assuaging fears of Black urbanity and mollifying a White suburban populace with simple, sensory-rich foods served at child-focused environments in racially pure suburbs. Fast food fed people determined to see their country as fair, safe, and fundamentally happy. The veneer of the drive-in seduced diners with a space that suggested there was no such thing as lynchings, a burgeoning civil rights movement, or even the urban districts they had left behind. Fast food not only was subject to racial notions but created them, by linking its products—symbolic of American ingenuity, modernity, and simple domestic pleasures—to White bodies and anti-Black geographies.

A possessive claim to fast food's Whiteness took on particular resonance in the 1960s as Black urbanites began to claim seats at fast food tables. Chicago was already a crucible of racial violence in the early years of second-generation fast food. Between 1956 and 1957 there were at least 127 attacks by Whites, who could clearly subject Black counterparts to violence with impunity.[61] The same kinds of violence turned to fast food outlets when Black would-be patrons dared visit them. Lizabeth Cohen points out that commercial settings had become focal points for public life following World War II, which made interracial fast food dining all the more incendiary.[62] City dwellers were determined to defend the bounds of Whiteness offered by fast food, and violence and even murder were to become fair game.

5

Delinquents, Disorder, and Death

Racial Violence and Fast Food's
Growing Disrepute at Midcentury

On June 5, 1968, the *New York Times'* arresting front page headline read, "Kennedy Shot and Gravely Wounded after Winning California Primary; Suspect Seized in Los Angeles Hotel." Robert Kennedy—senator, presidential hopeful, and brother of the slain president John F. Kennedy—had been assassinated that morning at the Ambassador Hotel, and the shooting was the lead story on papers across the country. The *Chicago Tribune* reported, "Bobby Shot in Head: Gunman Captured in L.A. Hotel." Immediately below that headline, sharing the front page and flanking a grim image of a prone and profusely bleeding Kennedy, was the story of another dramatic shooting: "Youth, 20, Slain by Cop in Chase at Restaurant." According to the report, the incident at the Franksville Drive-In Restaurant resulted from a police response to the proprietor's complaint that "youths congregating in the drive-in were creating a disturbance." The restaurant address places it steps from the Chicago Cubs' Wrigley Field, a busy commercial location on the city's North Side, a White area. When Officer Richard Nuccio and his partner Ronald Rothmund arrived on the scene, the proprietor pointed out two youths in particular, Steve Austil and Ronald Nelson. Rothmund apprehended Austil and charged him with disorderly conduct and criminal trespass, but Nelson ran. What followed was contested. Nuccio held that a third officer on the scene warned that Nelson was going to throw a knife; that the youth in fact did so; and that Nuccio fired at him in response, hitting him in the lower back. Witnesses on the scene denied seeing Nelson throw a knife, stating only that Rothmund shouted, "Stop him," and that Nuccio shot Nelson in the back as he fled.[1] Neighborhood teens held that Nuccio was a known bully who antagonized "street punks" like the White youth he had killed, and even that the officer took out on the boys his spurned advances on their female peers. He was sentenced to fourteen years in prison (but served only six).[2]

This incident was a particularly severe police altercation, resulting in the loss of life. Teens had already made drive-ins spectacles of social and physical disorder; now they were theaters of death. But conflict between youthful drive-in customers and authorities was commonplace. For example, Kirk Lawder, an eighteen-year-old from Bethesda, Maryland, was made to march in front of a Hot Shoppes restaurant, carrying a sign that read, "I WILL NOT USE FOUL LANGUAGE OR I GO TO JAIL." Having been found guilty by a local judge of assaulting "two hippies" alongside his friend, his sentence was to carry the sign around the eatery for two weekends. Following the 1950s' concerns about fast food's young crowds, sentiment in the 1960s turned to outrage. Teenagers were now a blight and a menace who could destroy unsuspecting owners' livelihoods. For community residents and municipal governments as well, drive-in restaurants had overstayed their welcome.

On top of battles among youth, restaurant owners, and authorities, new conflicts around fast food emerged as community protests linked disorder to the "ghetto"; and, most critically, as Black people found themselves subjected to racist violence for patronizing fast food. Changing neighborhoods increased the likelihood of Black people entering White space to access amenities. When the amenities were fast food it provoked violence from urban White residents. Across major chains and smaller establishments, territory, intimacy, and terror were recurring themes as fast food matured over the 1960s.

Bad Behavior in the 'Burbs

The adversarial relationships between youth and restaurant management that took place at drive-ins mysteriously disappeared from 1970s nostalgia for the 1950s. Producers of television and film who had lived through the era crafted a whitewashed cultural portrait of innocence and prosperity focused on a set of fads, cultural markers, and political events that White reporters wished to remember.[3] The film *American Graffiti* was released to critical acclaim in 1973, and *Happy Days* hit television airwaves in 1974. Drive-ins figured prominently in both as cornerstones of teens' social lives, depicted as wholesome spaces that magnanimously tolerated the mischievous behavior of young patrons. *Happy Days* centered on White teen boys, but unlike *American Graffiti*, these youths were shown at the center of secure, cozy, nuclear families that provided advice and benign authority when needed. Even "The Fonz," archetype of the 1950s hoodlum, was a mild example—not an "animal," as fast food restaurateurs labeled youth, but a cool young man in boots and a leather jacket who eschewed violence and kept company with cherubic middle-class counterparts at Arnold's Drive-In.[4]

Kroc sought out real-life versions of *Happy Days* when siting new outlets. In 1963, when McDonald's opened in Coral Hills, Maryland, Kroc described it as "a solid, substantial family community, the kind of city which seems almost made to order for a McDonald's restaurant." Kroc argued that success required careful investment in "the right kind of community."[5] For him and his contemporaries, family life was coextensive with Whiteness. Trade periodicals noted that families ate out and spent more, making them a prime market, in a framework where, "for most of the country, *selling to families and selling in the suburbs means the same thing*—a healthy market potential."[6] Since the suburbs were bastions of Whiteness, to argue that marketing to families and to the suburbs meant the same thing was to argue that family equals White. Individual restaurant owners saw White families as necessary for a generative business but continued to wrestle with teenagers sporting profane language and squealing cars.

By the late 1960s, the tenor had changed among restaurant owners about how to deal with youth, as they took a much harder line on juvenile delinquents than in the 1950s. Restaurant owners turned to police officers to discipline young customers, but the stamp of authority created a tense climate that could scare away the very families owners meant to assuage. Restaurateurs were deeply invested in tamping down any kind of perceived disorder, regardless of the source. Some businesses confronted "free parkers," people who parked their vehicles in restaurant spots but went elsewhere to conduct their shopping. One manager "on a friendly basis with the police" placed red tickets in car windows to warn such miscreants that their automobiles would be towed. He explained, "If somebody leaves his car on our lot, we inform the police and they keep an eye on him and tag him for an illegal turn, faulty tail light or other violation. We have found that such drivers get the hint and stop using our place for a free parking lot."[7]

That police could be conscripted to surveil and punish motorists offsite suggests that law enforcement was only too ready to participate in a project of making fast food into a territory of "law and order." Restaurateurs even gave officers free snacks to encourage their presence and obtain protection. Communities often pressured owners to resort to extreme methods of control and derided older guards "who had no authority"; they wanted men who could satisfactorily intimidate anyone who was out of line, especially by threat of firearms. One former drive-in owner went on to pursue a doctorate in sociology and completed a dissertation on the "teen problem" at Indiana drive-ins, concluding that managers ought to employ a "legitimate authority" such as off-duty police officers or private guards. Some drive-in owners minced no words in their need for cops: "We hire special private guards to control the teenagers, but we can't keep them because the kids keep beating them up . . . When there's a real policeman on the premises, the kids be-have." Another opined that he would pay police to eat in his restaurant if it were legal.[8] In fact, uniformed guards tended to amplify existing tensions and resorted to gunplay that in some instances proved fatal. In Bridgeton, Missouri, Willie Lee Stanton shot two teenagers in the arm while breaking up a fight; he was arraigned on the charge of "felonious wounding." Elsewhere, guards reportedly shot and killed at least three people at drive-in restaurants in 1967 alone.[9]

Whatever initiatives police and restaurant owners took, White youth did not simply fall in line. They saw fast food—and indeed anything in the built environ-ment leading to and from these outlets—as their territory, and they essentially dared authorities to take a different position. In one incident, young residents of Manchester, Connecticut, sent Officer Lawrence Smith on a wild goose chase in order to enjoy uninterrupted drag racing.[10] The frequency of these drag racing and similar incidents suggested that White youth were afforded significant leeway for disruptive behavior. In contrast, as will be seen below, Black youth who did nothing more than to try and buy hamburgers received no sympathy from police. Officers were content to stand idly by as White teens threatened and assaulted Black peers who dared to appear at fast food outlets.

As drive-in restaurants in White suburbs became synonymous with teenage "rowdyism," residents increasingly protested the issuance of restaurant permits and complained about the lack of control drive-in owners seemed to have over their young clientele. Industry leaders were of two minds. On the one hand, they did not want a heavy law enforcement presence to disrupt their profits. On the other, they were at their wits' end and ready to take whatever measures were necessary. Herbert B. Weingarden, president of a company that sold electronic ordering sys-tems to drive-in restaurants, wrote to *Fast Food Magazine* in May 1967 and claimed that Detroit's problems with littering, loitering, and cruising dissuaded "respectable families and individuals." He suggested that police forces deputize private guards and give them formal authority to act, and the magazine editors responded af-firmatively to his critique: "We know what you mean, Herb."[11] Weingarden wrote his letter just months before Black uprisings erupted in many U.S. cities, including Detroit. At a time of transformative unrest and heavily mediatized panic, flagrantly rebellious White youth who had raised public alarm at fast food restaurants since the late 1950s began to invite even more control. This time it took the form of mu-nicipal legislation.

After the calamitous unrest in Detroit, Wayne County debated measures that could quell restaurant disorder. On behalf of area restaurateurs, the Wayne County AFL-CIO asked the Common Council to act with haste. The group sought an ordinance that would require Detroit drive-in restaurants and theaters to hire police to control "hot-rodders, ruffians and troublemakers." While the outcome of this debate is unclear in the historical record, restaurant industry representatives, labor, and police all had conflicting ideas about how to achieve tranquility at eating establishments.[12] Did this call to arms reflect the racial panic of Detroit's White population? They had witnessed the 1967 upheaval and feared the lingering menace of unruly Negroes in the city. The threatening climate surrounding the rebellion led by Black residents seemed to foment a crackdown on disorderly customers even if they were White. For all restaurant owners knew, White hot-rodders might also erupt in the way Black Detroiters had. More directly, perhaps because disorder was seen as a product of Black people, White youth who were disorderly were "acting Black" and required police control. This is not to suggest that decision-makers made conscious connections between race and disorder and purposefully developed policies with that in mind. But the juxtaposition of urban rebellions and drive-in disorder likely coalesced in the minds of frightened Whites, even if they were not aware they were making those connections.

Soon, a flurry of local legislators and community groups began rolling back operations at drive-ins or even banning them altogether with zoning ordinances and laws. These targeted everything from littering, unchaperoned juveniles, "aimless driving" (defined as "passing one point more than once in ten minutes"), and loitering.[13] In Baltimore, the city council approved an anti-loitering bill that gave more power to police in controlling teens outside of shopping centers, bowling alleys, and drive-in restaurants.[14] Nearby, suburban D.C.'s Prince George's County ruled that teenagers under eighteen could not "roam the streets" between 10:00 p.m. and 5:00 a.m., and businesses were to be held responsible for infractions. However, McDonald's lobbied successfully for the stipulation that liability only applied when businesses "knowingly" allowed such behavior.[15] City council members in the small town of Gibbsboro, New Jersey, sought to prohibit drive-ins "because they [had] heard of problems in other towns where some drive-ins [were] a source of trouble." In Indianapolis, one restaurateur proclaimed in an advertisement that he would close on weekend evenings rather than suffer the "young rowdies." Nearby in Ohio, McDonald's briefly attempted to control loitering youth by charging a parking lot entrance fee, stopping traffic on a major arterial before motorists could enter the restaurant property—until the city ordered them to stop.[16]

The suburbs seemed to be on a slippery slope toward an inhospitable drive-in environment. Industry analysts worried as they saw the highly coveted sites second-generation outlets claimed colliding with opposition from community residents and a new, intensely regulated legislative landscape. Frank Thomas, president of Burger

Chef, complained, "One of the problems with the drive-in classification is you can't build them anymore. In many metropolitan areas, zoning laws are ruling out car service."[17] Indeed, local governments were less inclined to grant permits to establishments where patrons ate in cars, and overall the new regulatory climate meant franchising was stalling in White suburbs. Whither the drive-in burger stand, if not the suburbs? Second-generation fast food was designed for and pursued a community landscape that now felt ambivalent about its presence and was well able to erect roadblocks to its expansion. For some pundits, a "lack of available credit, up-tight landlords and soaring construction costs" suggested that the logical next step was "a profitable new frontier in ghetto markets."[18] This striking assertion, though not realized for many more years, suggested that the disrepute of drive-ins, in tandem with the looser regulatory climate of cities in general and the ghetto in particular, were tailor-made for a retreat to the urban spaces fast food had left behind in the 1950s.

Tiptoeing toward Tainted Territory

Thunderbird Chicken was one of the brands willing to try out an urban market. It moved into central St. Louis with walk-up and take-out stores rather than drive-ins, finding that "what with local restrictions and space restrictions, it became apparent that the Thunderbird unit would be the more salable franchise in the metropolitan area."[19] Marriott launched an offshoot of the Hot Shoppes restaurants in Washington, D.C., calling it Hot Shoppes Jr. Although *Nation's Restaurant News* described the move as a change from highway operation to in-city service, Hot Shoppes had long been planted throughout the District. The difference was that these were smaller-scale restaurants targeting pedestrian traffic rather than drive-in motorists on expansive corner lots. The first restaurant opened in affluent Georgetown, where it benefited from the foot traffic generated by the movie theater next door.[20]

McDonald's also modified its regular outlets in some urban contexts. Rather than the typical large-lot, freestanding units in suburban settings, the chain created a more restrained version called the Town House in the downtown areas of large cities like Boston, Pittsburgh, Los Angeles, New York, and Washington, D.C. In Boston and Madison, it targeted university students, and in Washington, government workers. The Town House name was coined by McDonald's D.C. regional manager Ken Fink "for lack of a better one."[21] Burger Chef's Frank P. Thomas wrote in to *Nation's Restaurant News* indignantly pointing out McDonald's was hardly an innovator because his restaurant had the foresight to target urban space years before: "To go to drive-ins now would be like taking a step backwards."[22]

Figure 5.1. An example of a McDonald's Townhouse outlet, at 6620 Bay Parkway in Bensonhurst, Brooklyn, in the 1980s. dof_3_05564_0049, New York City tax lot photos. Courtesy Municipal Archives, City of New York.

City locations were apparently the new frontier, but few chains rushed to seize them. The problem was that cities were the undoing of the market defined by second-generation fast food. Cities meant crime, crowding, dereliction, and disorder. Fast food was supposed to mean cleanliness, comfort, and child-friendly leisure. Cities should have been out of the question, but having left first-generation outlets behind in urban disorder, second-generation chains found themselves peeking into the city when pushed there by suburban attempts to regulate disorder. During the 1960s, the business community was preoccupied with disorder and its putative natural habitat, Black neighborhoods and the Black psyches resident there. The topic was raised repeatedly in issues of the U.S. Chamber of Commerce's periodical, the *Nation's Business*. In the October 1967 issue, Robert N. McMurry, "a psychologist with an international reputation," offered an analysis of Black people who had been involved in urban rebellions. He claimed, "From a psychological point of view, recent riots have tended to be marked by behavior which can only be described as berserk. At the height of these disorders many of those taking part have clearly cast aside all civilized restraints. In their activities they give free expression to the most primitive, atavistic impulses." McMurry rejected the idea that socioeconomic conditions or legitimate anger was the cause of the rebellions. Rather, he saw a lack of ego controls—the psychic structures responsible for managing impulses—as the critical factor. He contended that people who came from poverty had bad values and "psychopathic personalities—the people who hate." Ultimately, he claimed such persons "revert to a state in which they are enraged animals . . . immune to appeals to reason, to logic, or to their better natures. Actually, their consciences are so constituted that literally they have no better natures."[23]

Why then would fast food, with its consumable Whiteness, retreat to the province of the egoless? It was a particularly risky proposition since drive-in restaurants were now paradigmatic sites of disorder. To go where Black people lived was to forge by the transitive property a symbolic linkage between fast food and Blackness. Second-generation executives could see that even without serving Black people in appreciable numbers, first-generation fast food was growing more and more suspect. All-night and late-night restaurants, among which the burger chateaux were counted, had veered into theaters of the absurd and the eccentric. At a D.C. Little Tavern, a regular came in multiple times per night asking for bacon and eggs, persistent in the face of continual disappointment (bacon and eggs were not on the menu). At competitor White Tower, a young man from Harlem made the drive down to D.C. on amphetamines and was still high when he arrived at the company's Sixteenth and K Street NW location. Chain smoking, he paced back and forth outside the establishment and was soon joined by two more customers who were tripping on LSD. The three of them remained there until the sun came up in a vigil for sobriety.[24]

With such weirdos on the loose at first-generation outlets, second-generation chains, while lured by the looser regulatory climate, were reticent to take up urban clientele. The urban chains themselves saw their customers as marginal, and abundant revenues were cold comfort. Little Tavern had cornered the late-night market, but that brought its own challenges. The worst-case scenarios were robberies or other criminal activities. More routine were increasing cuts to the bottom line, either via the higher hourly rates the restaurant began to pay in the late 1960s or the need to pay workers overtime to stay in the shop until sunup (lest they come to grief outside the restaurant's confines). Horn & Hardart did not keep the same hours as Little Tavern and so did not contend as much with crime, but it negotiated its own concerns about reputation. In 1965, the company tried to eliminate less desirable customers. It hired a new ad agency, which developed the tagline "Horn and

Figure 5.2. Three former Little Tavern locations in contemporary Washington, D.C. *From left:* 655 Pennsylvania Avenue SE, 718 H Street NE, and 1301 Wisconsin Avenue NW. Photographs by author, 2016.

Hardart. It's not fancy. But it's good."[25] Focus groups in 1965 found that Horn & Hardart, while a fond memory from childhood, had veered into the lowbrow, with respondents remarking about seedy, creepy vibes, "cheap soup," "all sorts of bums going there," and staff who were "slightly oldish and vague looking."[26] In 1968, the company began to remodel several Automats in order to attract a more respectable clientele, as it harbored unease about patrons infamous for aimlessly nursing cups of coffee for hours on end. Management feared that the brand had become associated with "people who obviously had nothing to do and no place to go."[27] Corporate leadership therefore embarked on an extensive remodeling program throughout the system, updating the décor with more visual interest and piping music into the dining areas. The outlet at 59th Street underwent renovation costing over $300,000 (almost $2.3 million in 2020 dollars), and the Automat at East 86th Street received a complete makeover, complete with padded banquettes and brass chandeliers. Horn & Hardart's leadership perceived these changes to have met their aims, as a greater volume and cross-section of customers patronized the outlet, particularly executives. Concurrently, time-killing stragglers decreased in number and faded into the background.

If the outlets that had been rooted in urban core with an established customer base and knowledge of the terrain were having a rough go of it, the challenges would surely be acute for returning suburban chains. In fact, the city proper would bring little relief from the inhospitable climate brewing outside the city. Corporate brass worried about attracting unsavory characters, but so, too, did neighborhoods slated to host new fast food outlets. To wit, many urban neighborhoods, regardless of race, did not want fast food around. They may not have been able to initiate new ordinances, but there were plenty of community protests, which generated bad PR for the chains. In Chicago, the affluent, all-White community of Beverly worked for years (unsuccessfully) to prevent the opening of a McDonald's at the corner of 95th Street and Oakley Avenue. In 1967, groups in the community realized that the former parking facility for Mickleberry's Log Cabin Restaurant was to be sold, and rumor had it that one of the potential purchasers was McDonald's Systems. Residents were certain that McDonald's would "create serious problems in our residential community" and hoped that the company would be averse to conflict: "McDonald's is a larger chain and might well be interested in good 'Community Relations.'"[28]

Community groups led by the Beverly Area Planning Association and the Beverly Improvement Association worked together to undermine McDonald's siting, attacking the proposal on several fronts. Besides submitting petitions and writing to McDonald's, they enlisted the local police precinct, whose commander, Edward Sheehy, was opposed to the new outlet. Sheehy apparently sought to preclude disorder in the community, and yet, as will be seen, he allowed his officers to foment racial violence at other fast food restaurants in the area. Residents also entreated their alderman and the Department of Buildings to reject the proposal; attempted to change the zoning; and tried to change the street design. The residents argued that their opposition should not be taken as a slight on McDonald's; rather, they simply considered that the outlet would increase traffic, attract loiterers and litter, and generally be a nuisance for people who were "among the highest Real Estate tax payers of any single family residential area of the city, and whom own properties of considerable value." As an indication of both the community's racial politics and its concern about this restaurant, the president of the Beverly Area Planning Association wrote to another member about zoning changes on April 4, 1968—the day Martin Luther King Jr. was assassinated. Despite the group's high-powered nature, and the many lawyers who were working on its behalf, its efforts were ultimately in vain: McDonald's began construction on July 9, 1968.[29]

Beverly's contest left race unnamed, but concerns about disorder were invariably about race. Contemporary sociological research shows that all else being equal, the more Black people that live in an area, the more disorder that residents perceive.[30] At the center of White urbanites' concerns was an overlap between fast food's troublesome characteristics and invidious stereotypes of Black people—dirty, smelly, messy, greasy, noisy, polluting. Fast food's earliest apprehensions with racialized hygiene reared up again as community protests took root, mobilizing language more often used to decry commercialized vice. For example, denizens of San Francisco's Mission neighborhood described legalized sex businesses as "gaudy and ugly and vulgar . . . they attract the sort of people who enjoy that sort of thing."[31] In other words, the services provided by the businesses were repugnant, just like their morally dissolute clientele. Consumers of fast food elicited similarly forceful rebuke—their suspect behavior both suggested and reinforced by their ostensible taste for vulgarity. And the association went both ways, because individuals seen as harboring a propensity for illicit activity were also apparently attracted to fast food. As one respondent in Chicago's Woodlawn neighborhood put it, young people who sat about smoking marijuana "also litter the sidewalk with greasy fish bones and French fries and ketchup. Oh, it is terrible."[32]

Kentucky Fried Chicken faced sustained protests from Hyde Park residents when it angled for a new Chicago location in 1969. The company had chosen East 54th Street and Lake Park, a site made possible by urban renewal demolition. The Hyde Park–Kenwood Community Conference (HPKCC) immediately contested the plan, writing to the real estate firm brokering the deal, "The architecture, esthetics, the 'noise-type' commercial sign, is virtually unknown in this community. This is not happenstance, but by choice and design."[33] The controversy garnered attention in the local newspaper, the *Hyde Park Herald,* which reported that among the HPKCC's many objections was "the large yellow bucket revolving over the top of the building."[34] A protracted community struggle lasted until the winter, when the city finally allowed the new restaurant to set up shop. Leon Despres, alderman for the Fifth Ward, acted as the HPKCC's counsel. He warned the organization what it had to look forward to: "Incidentally, I spent some time on Sunday at a Kentucky Fried Chicken installation around the Southeast side, in South Shore, and found that the pollution from the cooking operation covered nearly a full block. It was unmistakable, disagreeable, and unavoidable. This was extremely distressing."[35]

South Shore flipped from White to Black in the late 1960s, and so KFC's perceived sullying of the neighborhood's streets hinted at a racial taint that was already taking place in area demographics. Given fried chicken's deep connections to Black foodways,[36] the objectionable nature of the food was surely due in part to the infiltration of symbolic Blackness. As discussed in chapter 2, Hyde Park, supported by the University of Chicago, marshaled considerable power to keep the community predominantly White. It must have rankled to allow the tawdry KFC to slip past its defenses.

Fried chicken was a ready cipher for connotations of undesirable Blackness, but other fast food items elicited the same response. Philadelphia's Fern Rock community battled McDonald's for more than a year when the company planned a drive-in. In this case, residents were explicit about fast food as a harbinger of a Black ghetto. A residential area in the Northwest section of the city, it had shifted from predominantly White to predominantly Black. In 1950, the two census tracts surrounding the intersection where McDonald's sought to open at the corner of North Broad and Green Lane collectively held nearly ten thousand residents, of which only twenty-three were Black (perhaps live-in domestic workers). In 1960, the west side of the intersection (at Broad Street) had gone up to 22 percent Black; by 1970, it had reached 73 percent. McDonald's had set its sights on the west side of the intersection at 6100 North Broad Street, previously home to a used car dealership. The location fell in the Sixth District, represented by Councilman David Cohen, who immediately protested both the zoning change that made the restaurant possible and the restaurant itself. He called out a number of issues, including possible damage to an adjacent colonial-era burial ground, the De Benneville Cemetery. The Philadelphia Historic Commission stated that the body "certainly doesn't look kindly on the building of a hamburger stand on top of an old cemetery."[37]

In truth, the community was much more worried about the threat of disorder. These Philadelphia residents read the writing on the wall and saw fast food as an immediate affront to, and harbinger of decline in, their middle-class community. This was true in other cities as well. For example, in Chicago's North Kenwood–Oakland neighborhood, Avis Green opined, "There's something about people who see a neighborhood like this with vacant lots who think that real people don't live in here, so that they drive by and throw trash in the street. You go out there, and somebody's been out there with McDonald's or Kentucky Fried or something, and boxes are all over the street and things like that."[38] Taking as evidence the nuisance of several similar restaurants near the proposed site, Councilman Cohen believed McDonald's portended "juvenile disturbances, gang wars and perhaps murders," falling property values, more noise, traffic and pollution, and a need for greater police presence. By February 1970, as the controversy continued to rage, the Ogontz Area Neighbors Association circulated handbills with statements such as "We do not want to see our area downgraded!" McDonald's offered to withhold construction until negotiations were complete but proceeded with excavation nonetheless in March. Picketers warned, "You're not wanted here, McDonald's" and "McDonald's will be a neighborhood nuisance." Mrs. Bertie Kaiser held that the neighborhood already had too many drive-ins, adding "I don't see why these business people who don't live here should keep coming into our neighborhood and destroying the residential nature of it."[39] Mrs. Kaiser's opinions were held by many. The City Council reported that communities routinely argued to the Zoning Board of Adjustment that "sandwich shops designed to lure motorists" ought to be categorized separately from other restaurants, since "drive-ins are no more restaurants than a corner grocery is a supermarket."[40]

Bob Beavers, an African American man from the D.C. metro who had moved up the McDonald's ranks from crew to manager and then on to the corporate office, was at this time the company's director of community action and development. He held fast, stating that despite the protest, the company still planned to open: "We want to upgrade the communities where we do business because that is good business. We want to be part of the community groups." Beavers went so far as to suggest the company might apply to join the Ogontz Area Neighbors Association. Beavers also argued that corporate had dealt with gangs before and was prepared to do so again. The outlet was planning to employ its own security force, would forbid loitering, would be meticulous about cleanliness and active in civic affairs and, in the end, would be "a fine restaurant . . . it will brighten up the block."[41]

Community residents were not convinced and saw the chain's plans as racist. Joseph Coleman, the only Black person on the planning commission, opined, "Whenever an area becomes black a business venture of this type comes in and destroys the community." Father Robert E. DuBose speculated that McDonald's believed the community's racial transition to mean that it was no longer a neighborhood whose views were worth reckoning. Doris Prosser complained that people had moved to the community to get away from the ghetto, but "now the commercial interests who don't care about the people are coming in here and trying to make this a ghetto, too."[42]

These residents were more explicit than other protestors in their assertion of fast food as a harbinger of ghetto pathology. While HPKCC ostensibly opposed fast food on the grounds that it was detrimental to the neighborhood's "character," implicating building designs and the like, the Ogontz residents made the racial undertones plain. Fast food did not originate in Black space and was still largely absent from it, yet this McDonald's would make the community Black. Fast food apparently had the power to transform a community into a ghetto, even one that had already seen an inversion of racial demographics. Perhaps it was because McDonald's was arriving concomitantly with Black neighbors that marked the chain Black as well. It is noteworthy that both Black and White Philadelphians saw fast food as an unsavory infiltration that insidiously and precisely targeted race in its location strategies. In other words, fast food was a nuisance, so it was delivered to people perceived to be a nuisance, too.

Quite in contrast, at least some White, working-class urbanites rejected entirely any notion of fast food as Black. Instead, they saw the outlets as part of defensible White space, a place where racial intermixing would not be tolerated and would be parried with brute force. It was bad enough that White people "lost" swimming pools when they desegregated and that the integration of urban parks prompted the construction of new theme parks far from city centers, leaving the originals neglected and cut off from public transit.[43] To the extent that fast food took the place of other racially exclusive leisure centers as they disappeared, either literally or figuratively, White residents would have been particularly sensitive to the threat of relinquishing these restaurants to Black patrons. For them, fast food was still White and they defended that idea with terror and deadly violence.

Fast Food's Dead Line

Chicago's Wentworth Avenue was the dividing line between Black space in Bronzeville and the White neighborhoods of Canaryville, Back of the Yards, and Packingtown. Crossing it meant physical violence and perhaps murder for Black transgressors, for which reason the street was known as the "dead line."[44] Beginning in the 1960s, fast food developed its own dead line.

Racist violence at fast food restaurants was part of a broader climate of enmity shown to African Americans who made incursions into sites of leisure. The anxieties provoked by intimacy with Black bodies in eating, dancing, or other activities resulted in heavy policing of interracial recreation.[45] Amusement parks, emblematic of youth culture, invalidated the innocence of Black teens through their exclusion. These parks were populated by a number of facilities and activities (e.g., dance halls) that were all deeply fraught with the possibility of interracial intimacy and provoked severe controversies around their integration. Because amusement parks were for the most part too large for Black communities to create for themselves, it meant Black pleasure seekers would have to visit those owned by Whites.[46] The D.C. community of Deanwood offered the only amusement park for Black patrons in the twentieth century.[47] For Black youth, showing up anywhere uninvited was a way to stick it to White crowds who resented seeing Black people in public. When they did so, the threat of Black contagion was operative: "For some white consumers African American teenagers embodied the poverty, crime, and dirt of cities and their presence in parks devalued urban leisure."[48]

Fast food restaurants had clearly become an important arena for urban leisure, and in White neighborhoods where residents were left behind by those who relocated to the suburbs, these outlets took on additional symbolic weight. They were exemplars of the good life led in the suburbs. They were something Whites had that Blacks did not. They were places to socialize and consume in contexts where retail outlets like department stores had dismissed White, urban consumer dollars for the future profits to be had outside the city. And if Black people could not move into public housing, private homes, or apartment buildings in White space, neither could they be allowed to sit down and enjoy burgers and fries. What was at stake was not an abstract Whiteness, but real social spaces and services—often the only ones available. That scarcity led White people to violence in one community after another.

Jamesburg, a small town in central New Jersey's Middlesex County, counted slightly more than 4,500 residents in 1969, and of these, census data suggest that nearly 12 percent were Black. Even with a relatively low percentage in comparison to large cities such as Trenton, Newark, and Camden, the small town was an island of relative diversity in a sea of whiteness; surrounding census tracts were between 4 and 5 percent Black. On July 13, racial violence catapulted the town into the national spotlight, appearing in restaurant industry periodicals and as a wire story in small community newspapers ranging from Bakersfield, California, to Brainerd, Minnesota, to Biloxi, Mississippi. The violence occurred just two years after widespread civil unrest hit more than a dozen New Jersey cities.[49]

Nation's Restaurant News described racial disturbances that lasted over a week, reportedly ignited at an ice cream restaurant where a White male owner was charged with "atrocious assault and battery" following an argument between his son and a Black youth over a spilled cone. A fight ensued in which "a Negro girl landed in the hospital"; however, the article failed to report why "a spilled cone" provoked a fight, who started it, whom the owner had attacked to receive the assault charge, what injuries the unnamed "Negro girl" sustained, and who inflicted them. Though it appeared as if the owner directly assaulted the girl, the news report downplayed a blatant act of violence against a Black child. Instead, the focus was on Black youth described as harassing and beating customers to the detriment of the business.

The owner, Charles DiBrizzi, a former marine, and his wife were shown as resolute in the face of Black wrath; she stated, "We will never close down," and a photograph showed a group of White men erecting an American flag on the restaurant rooftop with a caption that read, "Iwo Jima updated: Defending drive-in against black boycotters."[50] For the reporter, White men hoisting the flag may have evoked the image of the Marine Corps on Mount Suribachi, but that could not be based on visuals alone. The idea of war—of battling vicious enemy combatants in an engagement that would see the other side nearly decimated—undergirded this journalist's view of a struggle against Black youth.

In this telling, DiBrizzi was just another besieged White man trying to run a community business in the face of irrational Black demands, disorder, and violence. In fact, despite local journalism likewise failing to uncover the exact events that had transpired at the ice cream parlor, it was evident that much more was at stake than the industry story revealed. DiBrizzi (also spelled DiBrizze in several pieces), forty years old, was an "ex-convict." Conflict sparked at his Fancy Freeze Ice Cream and Sandwich Shop at the intersection of West Railroad Avenue and Forsgate Drive when DiBrizzi's son and a Black youth began throwing punches over who would buy an ice cream cone for Sonia Denise Gordon, a thirteen-year-old Black girl. According to DiBrizzi Sr., he intervened merely to break up the fight. But his intervention put Gordon in the hospital with head injuries. She entered the emergency room at St. Peter's General Hospital in fair condition and, once in intensive care, remained in the hospital approximately one week. Though the details of the incident were unclear, they suggested that an overture of friendship between DiBrizzi's son and a Black girl may have been the flashpoint. Had DiBrizzi struck her in outrage at the impropriety of his White son's offering of ice cream?

It is difficult to imagine a circumstance in which a thirteen-year-old girl could be "injured in a scuffle involving a white man" without his deliberately striking her with intent to harm. But news reports took pains to stress that the assault was alleged, and they were sure to use agentless or vague language to describe the events. Headlines such as "Girl Injured in Jamesburg" could have meant anything; perhaps Gordon fell down her front steps. Some accounts intimated that the entire uproar was the result of chicanery cooked up by Black "agitators" external to Jamesburg; others contested the severity of Sonia Gordon's injuries, reporting that she "had complained of nothing more than a headache." These articles sympathized with White residents' fears of what Black youth would do to "vent their anger"; and by declaring only that DiBrizzi had tangled with "Black teenagers," the media left it to the imaginary of its White readership to draw the logical conclusion: that criminally minded Black male youth had instigated violence at DiBrizzi's business. Indeed, Gordon herself was cast as the origin of the disorder: "The girl who claimed she was injured by DiBrizze [sic] . . . was recovering, while the 'spark she had helped to light' in the city was slowly being extinguished."[51]

News reports also characterized Black residents as embittered and volatile individuals who sought out racial conflict, picking up the kinds of discourse that typified urban rebellions. The Black population, comprising many second- and third-generation migrant workers from the South, were supposedly "angry youths who feel the town has treated them harshly and that they can't win for losing." Mayor Walter Mychalchyk declared that "plans for causing a disturbance were made a long time ago, they were just waiting for an incident to start it." DiBrizzi claimed that the town never had "a racial problem" and that what had erupted at his stand "was started by young hooligans. I was made a patsy, but I don't know the meaning of fear." The city enacted a curfew and arrested Black male youth for breaking it, but DiBrizzi incurred no penalties. He had assaulted a child on Sunday, and by Wednesday evening he was voluntarily presenting himself for arrest at police headquarters, chatting and smoking with police chief Peter Giacomozzi. He "offered to be locked up. DiBrizze [*sic*] said his offer to be jailed was designed to put on [*sic*] end to black and white reaction to the disturbances." Giacomozzi noted that because DiBrizzi had already posted $5,000 bail, there was no legal basis for his incarceration. Some Black residents likened DiBrizzi to Georgia governor Lester Maddox, elected in 1966 on a platform of arch segregation. Previously the owner of the Pickrick Restaurant, a cafeteria-style eatery that specialized in skillet-fried chicken, Maddox received national attention in 1964 after refusing to serve three Black men at his establishment, in violation of the new Civil Rights Act. Maddox confronted the would-be customers with a pistol, calling them "no good dirty devils" and "dirty Communists." The next month he sold his restaurant rather than capitulate to serving Black people. By 1967 it was reported that he had purchased two drive-in hamburger restaurants in Fulton and Cobb County in the Atlanta metro.[52]

The incidents in Jamesburg were not isolated, small-town anomalies. Racist violence was also frequent at national chains in major cities. White strongholds were prepared to use deadly force to keep these outlets within their exclusive remit. In Washington, D.C., Carl Eiland, thirty-five, was assaulted on May 11, 1963, in a Little Tavern restaurant at Georgia and New Hampshire Avenues NW. At approximately 3:00 a.m., a Black woman was served after a group of three White youths, despite having ordered before them. She complained, drawing a sharp rebuke from the youths, who boasted their entitlement to service as White people. Eiland reprimanded the boys and, after more words, the woman removed "something" from her purse (a knife, alleged the youths), and they exited the store. Soon, Eiland heard one of the youths shout, "Let's get that nigger," and the boys began chasing him, throwing rocks and beer bottles. Eiland sought help at a nearby residence, banging on the door and imploring the tenant to call the police, but the tenant refused and ordered him and the youths to "go away." At this point, Eiland was knocked down and kicked. Another Black man came to his assistance but was chased away by two White youths. Police later took Eiland into custody and charged both him and Douglas M. Jones, a twenty-year-old White youth from Hyattsville, with assault.[53]

In Chicago, assaults at fast food outlets could hardly be a surprise, given Chicago's dubious distinction of pervasive racist violence. The city became the first in the nation to establish a hate crime police unit in 1948, and mobs and days-long riots of Whites enraged by the presence of Black neighbors were painfully common.[54] Racial violence in Chicago was overwhelmingly perpetrated by young White men ranging from their mid-teens to early twenties. The same was true for fast food violence, which was visited on adult individuals, couples, and families.

Fast food violence took place in several communities, not all of which are well-known for move-in or other racial violence. The city's Southwest Side was one such hotspot.[55] At the White Castle at 79th and Pulaski, in December 1967, Floyd Joshua, a postal worker aged eighteen, was beaten directly in front of the store as he waited for a city bus. The location counted among its patrons a large number of students from the William J. Bogan High School and William J. Bogan Junior College across the street, as well as "truckers, city workers, and white collar business men." The White Castle had a reputation for warm, smiling service, which local media attributed to the company's code.[56] This work ethic apparently did not extend to assisting individuals under attack by restaurant customers. As Joshua and another Black man waited for the bus, a pair of White males emerged from the restaurant and set upon them. Joshua did not see them until hot coffee had been splashed in his eyes and his head was struck by a blunt object. He lost consciousness and fell to the ground; when he came to, his companion was under attack. Joshua was able to temporarily parry one of the assailants, and he explained that "at that point it appeared that other whites in the hamburger shop were going to come out and get into the fight. But just then the bus pulled up. Fortunately, the driver was a Negro. He jumped off the bus to help us and the white boys ran off." Joshua's mother was informed by another postal employee that this was not the first time racial violence had occurred in front of the fast food restaurant, for which reason Black people were discouraged from patronizing the outlet.[57]

Eight years later, Betty and Warren Freeman, residents of Missouri, drove from their hotel to the same White Castle at 79th and Pulaski. There they were accosted by two young White male customers who threatened that "niggers are not allowed in here." The Freemans left the restaurant and were followed by the two men. In the hotel parking lot, Warren approached the men, who continued to insult him with racial epithets and threats of violence, warning "You're a dead nigger." After the Freemans went into the hotel to call the police, the men smashed their car windows and slashed their tires; the bell captain who reported watching the car denied hearing or seeing anything.[58]

The community of Englewood also endured mob attacks at fast food outlets. The neighborhood was adjacent to the Irish Catholic community of Visitation Parish, where the arrival of African American Reginald Williams's family in July

1963 to a largely empty multifamily building drew a crowd of brick-throwing Whites almost immediately. While two dozen squads of police "observed," the violence escalated until the city, fearing a "full-scale race war," addressed the situation. When it did, Mayor Daley's call for law and order reified a standard narrative of Black perpetrators that warranted the swift intervention of law enforcement. Englewood, with its dramatic White flight, was no longer racially homogeneous, but racial turnover was spatially discontinuous: Whites staked out a position north of 59th Street and south of 71st. Black women motorists who violated these boundaries were attacked in street intersections by White men.[59]

The Kennedy family met the racist ire of area residents when they sought to spend their Friday night at the drive-in Burger King restaurant at 1539 West Garfield Boulevard. This being one of the two early outlets that Burger King opened when the chain arrived in Chicago, the bet corporate seemed to make on capturing customers on either side of the racial divide went bust. Just blocks from the community boundary of Visitation Parish, the Kennedys encountered a violent mob of ten to fifteen White youths and restaurant employees. The family noticed the large group of White boys outside the restaurant when they arrived, but they did not realize anything was amiss until a Black customer was attacked upon exiting the outlet. Mr. Kennedy was next. Mrs. Kennedy ran toward a parked patrol car for assistance, but it drove away; two other officers arrived on the scene, struck Mr. Kennedy with their clubs, and "grabbed Mr. Kennedy and pulled his coat over his head, while the white boys kicked him in the face." Mr. Kennedy recounted that "a short blond employee of the Burger King had a brick in his hand and was drawing back to hit her" (his wife); Kennedy brandished a hammer he had retrieved from his car and kept the employee at bay. In the words of Mr. Kennedy, as he and his wife made their escape, "whites ran alongside the car shouting, 'nigger, nigger.'" Mrs. Kennedy was hospitalized with internal injuries.[60]

The Dunlap siblings—Veronica, aged twenty, and William, aged nineteen—and their friend Leon Benford, nineteen, were Englewood residents who met with racist assault at a Burger King. They, along with Tyrone Therkield, sixteen, headed out on a late summer night to an area southwest of their homes, in what was still very much a White stronghold. It was on the wrong side of Ashland Avenue, the defensive perimeter that separated Black from White. Between 1960 and 1970, Whites had decamped from houses east of Ashland, leaving those to the west clinging desperately to the territory that remained. Bombings, fire, and vandalism awaited Black residents who attempted to cross Englewood's impermeable racial boundaries.[61] Burger King opened four blocks west of Ashland at 1814 West 87th between 1965 and 1967, one of only a few major commercial sites and the only restaurant. Situated

Figure 5.3. A hamburger restaurant sits on a corner in the Black section of Englewood at 63rd and Loomis. In 1956, the section was defined as stretching from 60th Street to 67th Street/ Marquette Road, and from Loomis to Carpenter. Chicago History Museum, ICHi-176483; Sam Kipnis, photographer.

on the same side of the street were several medical concerns (i.e., a doctor's office, pharmacy, and clinical lab) and an electric company. Across the street were two liquor stores and a beauty salon.[62] The outlet was the only place on that stretch where young White residents would hang out. And so, in mid-August 1968, between 9:30 and 10:00 p.m. when the four Englewood youths entered the Burger King hamburger stand, things turned bloody quickly. A mob of twenty to twenty-five White boys attacked the group, with William Dunlap sustaining the most visible injuries—a laceration on his forehead that required stitches. Veronica Dunlap and Leon Benford found a police officer and entreated him to help. He told Leon, "Get your black — out of here. You don't belong in this neighborhood anyway." Further, the officer drew his weapon and told Leon "that if he did not leave, he'd shoot him."[63] These officers would have belonged to the Gresham precinct—that overseen by Commander Edward Sheehy, who opposed McDonald's in affluent, White Beverly because it would generate and attract disorder.

Finally, fast food violence erupted farther south in Roseland, which was also intensely hostile to Black folks. When Ethel Scott purchased a small home in the 11300 block of South Indiana in 1971, she initially contended with rocks through the window, bullets, and the words "White Power" spray-painted on her garage door. Acts of intimidation proved to be a prelude to severe brutality. Eventually, at Scott's own home, an agitated White mob stabbed her son in the chest and neck. When she returned from the hospital, she "saw a mob in front of the house like there was going to be a lynching." An officer on the scene told her that someone had thrown a firebomb, and Mrs. Scott perceived that "he thought it was a big joke."[64] This deep enmity for Black neighbors had existed for years, and in 1966 a McDonald's at 550 East 103rd Street saw four unnamed Black people whose gender and age were not described narrowly escape gunfire from a White youth enlisted in the army. The shooter, identified as Alonzo Pope, was said to have fired on the Black patrons after an exchange of words with his group of four young men. Following the initial encounter, the four Black patrons left the restaurant but returned later, at which point Pope opened fire. Police tracked down and arrested three of the four in Pope's group who had fled the scene, and Pope turned himself in. However, police "were not certain who was to blame for starting the incident."[65]

Four years later, in 1970, at the same restaurant, Joseph Henson, aged twenty-one, was murdered by three White teens who fired on him and his brother-in-law Leotha Price.[66] Ethel Henson, Joseph's mother, returning home from the grim task of purchasing her son's casket, learned from relatives that just before her arrival a police car had been stationed in front of her house. Out of it emerged two officers who "let two white boys out of the car and then parked nearby and watched while the kids stood in front of my house and pointed at the house, laughing."

These stories are surely a small sample of racist attacks at fast food restaurants, most of which would not have been reported in the media. Critically, local law enforcement either turned a blind eye or joined in this violence, leaving Black patrons equally vulnerable from the wrath of White counterparts and police negligence. Fast food held special meanings for White, urban residents, who were willing to hold the color line at any cost. What were they, apart from the kinds of motivations that typically underlie anti-integrationist violence? Whites who brought violence on

Figure 5.4. The McDonald's restaurant at 550 East 103rd Street, where two incidents of racial violence took place. This photograph was taken in 1965, one year before the first shooting, likely soon after the restaurant opened. Chicago History Museum, ICHi-176463; Casey Prunchunas, photographer.

Black households attempted to keep social distance between themselves and minority neighbors, to fend off competitive socioeconomic threats, and to assuage fears of racial transition.[67] Fast food symbolized even more.

First, as previously seen, there was the matter of hygiene, a register that was especially salient in restaurant dining. Eating places have been focal points for White discomfort. In the South, Black people were seen as fit to cook food but unacceptable as fellow diners. And though Black customers were disrespected by restaurants that would serve them only at take-out windows, they were welcome to spend in other White businesses that did not involve food.[68] The corporeal intimacy of eating that has historically provoked racial anxieties among Whites continued in fast food, where particularly acute transgressions were provoked by the casual nature of the restaurants.[69] Despite their trading on racial segregation, chain restaurants, with their standardized prices, menus, and settings, set up the theoretical possibility of anonymous and accessible venues where anyone could eat and hierarchies would be dissolved.[70] Two generations of fast food promised White utopias that were never entirely achieved, and now the direct threat of competition with Black people hovered over these outlets. White residents in northern cities resisted this possibility with bitter violence.

Second, there was the issue of fast food's status as the national meal. Katharina Vester argues that "national cuisines consist of iconic dishes, methods of preparation, and culinary rules" that "represent the history, ambitions, and *terroir* (and thereby territorial claims) of a unified nation."[71] Further, she contends that eating the same food as others is a way of symbolically breaking bread with them and therefore of invoking unity among people, whether community or family. In the case of fast food, Whites eating the same meals in close proximity to Blacks suggested informal familial ties. At a moment when the country was riven by a White populace determined to hold on to the old racial order, fast food dining was an intimate dramaturgical reenactment of Black persons asserting their full citizenship and their fundamental sameness with White people.

Third, as Victoria Wolcott and Jeff Wiltse have shown with amusement parks and swimming pools, fast food posed the risk of interracial sex and intimacy. Black men in particular might attempt to consort with White women at fast food restaurants. The casual setting invited informal social interactions, and perhaps White residents felt that Black men would be emboldened to approach White women. Though social mores would not have made Black women a threat in terms of pursuing White men, neither would White women wish to see their men display sexual interest in Black women in these settings. Black women could not be trusted: as Mrs. Chandler remarked about Lutie Johnson, heroine of Ann Petry's novel *The Street,* as she worked in the kitchen, "That girl is unusually attractive and men are weak. Besides, she's colored and you know how they are."[72]

Fourth, Black patrons dining at fast food restaurants were an affront to the wages of Whiteness. If Black people dined where Whites did, that made them equals and called into question what Whiteness meant. How could White people eat at the same venues that Black people could afford? To do so would bring into sharp focus that these White residents were not dining at the fine establishments that would have been prohibitive to Black customers, either in cost or in custom. Violence was an easy remedy to make these outlets impossible for African American patronage.

The restaurants where hate crimes took place would have been particularly salient to White grievances because, with the exception of the Little Tavern where Eiland was attacked—which launched no later than 1930—most of the restaurants were fairly new at the time of the violence and were often one of only a few eating or drinking places in the immediate vicinity. White residents who thought it their mandate to defend public sites in White space would have been especially motivated by new establishments that they had only the opportunity to frequent for a short time. Moreover, these chains, which enjoyed significant popular discourse, advertising, and acclaim, came late to many of these communities, relative to their start in suburban space. Like the Burger King on 87th Street, the outlet at 1539 West Garfield stood alone amid residential space. It, too, opened either months or just one year before the violence, in late 1964 or early 1965. The White Castle at 79th and Pulaski was the only hospitality outlet, sharing the 7900 block with only two other businesses (builders); the rest of the block comprised residential addresses. This location opened between 1965 and 1966, and the first incident took place in 1967. Finally, the McDonald's at 550 East 103rd opened in 1962, four years before the racist attacks on its grounds. (In a sign of the racial change that continued in the community, the outlet would be Black-owned by 1974.) Taken together, all these restaurants where violence took place comprised new, scarce resources Whites were prepared to hoard at all costs. And at the end of the day, apart from the racial contest, the simple fact was that Whites did not want Black people having good things in life. In 1930s Florida, when a segregated housing project was proposed that would give Black residents access to a swimming pool, Whites were adamantly opposed because it was too much of an improvement in Black lives.[73]

There is no evidence that fast food corporations responded to the violent and even fatal incidents that erupted at their stores. Trade periodicals, national media, and first-person accounts by fast food operators and corporate executives were all absent any mention of companies attempting to redress these incidents by implementing policies to protect patrons and their right to safely enjoy a meal. Whereas juvenile delinquents were met with the heavy hand of police surveillance, there is little to suggest that perpetrators of hate crimes faced any punitive consequences. Juvenile delinquency was seen as a national issue, and local flare-ups at drive-ins as manifestations of a larger problem. In contrast, White people were in no way constructed as a national problem for inflicting racist violence on Black Americans.

Though, in the most cynical sense possible, routine racial violence would be bad for business, fast food seemed not to be terribly concerned. If anything, Black bodies were a clear and persistent danger, embodying the possibility of disorder although they were not the ones who instigated violence. It was a recapitulation of

White amusement park owners assuming that segregation was a precondition for peace, but failing to see violent Whites as the threat they clearly embodied.[74] Once urban unrest had struck several cities in the mid to late 1960s, business interests discussed at length the risk that Black people posed and the likelihood that business owners would have to deal with the threat themselves. For fast food operators, who worked in a business model that deliberately absolved corporate from managing any of the daily operations or concerns that emerged at franchised outlets, the menace of Blackness would have been felt front and center. Yet, it was Black customers who potentially risked life and limb by entering fast food establishments. If the incidents reviewed above were any indication of what transpired in other cities, Black ownership of fast food would be that much more appealing if it meant ensuring the safety of diners. For better or for worse, once neighborhood racial transitions were complete, White franchisees began abandoning their ghetto enterprises, making it possible for Black operators to run outlets that served Black communities.

Part II

Racial Turnover

If you'd like to sell us food and furniture and cars and beauty products and shaving stuff and whiskey and travel, try getting us where we live.

—*Ebony* advertisement in *Advertising Age,* July 22, 1968

6

How Does It Feel to Be a Problem?

(Mis)Managing Racial Change and
the Advent of Black Operators

The July 1966 issue of *Ebony* published photographs of James Meredith, the University of Mississippi student who in 1962 broke the institution's color line. In them he lay by a roadside, terrified, screaming, and crawling to safety under a hail of bullets. Meredith, then a law student at Columbia University, had embarked a month earlier on a 220-mile march from Memphis to Jackson. He meant to protest disenfranchisement in Mississippi and to show Black residents in the state that they had nothing to fear. On just the second day, Aubrey Norvell, an unemployed contractor, intended to show Meredith otherwise, firing at him repeatedly with a 16-gauge shotgun. He pled guilty to assault and battery with intent to kill and received a sentence of five to ten years with three of them suspended.[1]

The ghastly photo spread was adjacent to an article titled "A $65 Billion Gold Mine," which touted the promise of franchising for Black business. On the left, a symbol of the struggle for the Black franchise as civil rights; on the right, Black business franchising. In this juxtaposition the implicit premise of franchising was aptly realized: a form of business that could remediate the troubled citizenship Black people inhabited, one in which they could be shot by White bystanders for violating the racial order. Through this new form of capitalism, the market would save Black people.

Franchising's gold mine was explained thusly: "Suppose you could start a profitable business with little cash, no previous experience and lots of enthusiasm. Suppose your chances of failure were very low and national promotion and publicity were made available to you without your paying the heavy costs . . . would you?"[2] Certainly, the scenario *Ebony* proposed would be tempting to anyone who sought to go into business, were it true. In fact, too many companies were selling essentially worthless brands that were far from viable operations, pocketing franchisee money, and withholding support. An industry pundit admitted in 1968 that "the real estate and banking men will tell you that franchising is really just a way of raising money and expanding without capital. The sales experts will tell you that franchising is sometimes just a way of selling something that is otherwise unsaleable. Certainly there is something of the truth in both comments."[3]

Trade periodicals led readers to think fast food was an unequivocal money-maker. To hear it told by industry boosters, anyone willing to put in sweat equity would enjoy almost unlimited possibilities in fast food franchising. More than money alone, fast food put people on the fast track to realizing the American Dream of affluence, a home, independence, and happiness. The lede to *Fast Food Magazine*'s March 1969 cover story on franchising read, "Franchising is a system with sizzle . . . On one side of the contract stands the franchisor . . . on the other side, the franchisee, a man in search of every American's dream and goal—to be his own boss." Robert Walls, twenty-seven years old, owned four Der Wienerschnitzel restaurants in Tulsa. In 1969, he estimated that in a year or two his salary would reach $100,000 ($721,000 in 2020 dollars), and he enjoyed the use of a family car, a Jaguar XKE, and a '58 Cadillac Eldorado Brougham.[4]

When the *Ebony* spread was published, Black people had been shut out of the business end of fast food for more than forty years. First-generation fast food had not been franchised, but Black workers were overwhelmingly excluded from crew positions. Second-generation chains, which by this time had been operating for more than a decade, had not granted franchises to Black operators. Some stores may have been located in Black neighborhoods, but they were owned by White men. In the late 1960s, this finally began to change. Corporations began extending opportunities to Black men, and Black business entities began investigating and promoting franchising. The problem was that Black franchisees bore enormous risk, had little support, and ran a good risk of failure. They took up fast food ownership under terms that made it riskier than for White counterparts. They were redlined for loans and lucrative locations in White neighborhoods and saddled with high-cost / poor-performing stores. And they did so because fast food's corporate offices were worried about the long-term stability of running outlets in Black space.

Black franchisees (and as will be seen, franchisors) entered the industry in the late 1960s, a political climate in which Black Power bore down as "the manifestation of the brute force and physical rage of the African American underclass."[5] It was at Meredith's march that Stokely Carmichael, at the time the new chair of SNCC, was credited with coining the chant "Black Power!" He defined it as not only political power but also economic and cultural power, a project in which Black people would seize appropriate representation and control over their communities, organizations, and personal as well as political lives.[6] Establishment activist organizations also turned to Black Power. CORE, founded in 1942 to work toward nonviolent integration, took up the Black Power mantle in 1966 with Floyd McKissick at the helm, defining it as "effective control and self-determination by men of color in their own areas."[7] The explicit focus on men was not unique to CORE. The Black Panthers, too, stressed masculine uplift, locating Black liberation squarely within the confines of Black manhood and initially rejecting Black women who asserted independence and leadership, calling for their attention to domestic activities for the benefit of the Black community.[8]

When it came to opening up franchising opportunities, fast food corporations saw Black men as the rampart for maintaining a White-owned business structure in Black neighborhoods. Amid racial turnover, rebellion, and militant politics, restaurant chains began to see White franchisees as unsustainable. The industry extended access to Black owner-operators, and franchising as the metaphorical franchise took troubled shape. Black franchisees managed racialized risks for fast food corporations by putting a Black public face on ghetto stores—and bore the costs of doing so.

The Promise of Franchising

Ebony argued that a low-risk, high-reward business was hardly a pipe dream; that all of what it proposed could be had with franchising; and that being a franchisee was like being a "junior partner" in a multibillion-dollar corporation. Franchising, it was said, would train entrepreneurs and provide them with financing, field supervisors for daily troubleshooting, and assistance in location siting and negotiating leases. In effect, franchising "protect[s] you from yourself, that is, from your ignorance of business procedures."[9] Fast food was brought front and center in this formulation, described as the most sought-after sector among several. In fact, fast food was far from a reliable moneymaker. Black franchisees entered the arena as saturation and challenges around disorder were increasing in the suburbs, when fast food corporations were experiencing instability from a number of experimental (and mostly unsuccessful) ventures and from buyouts by conglomerates. And although *Ebony* suggested that fast food was the most desirable franchise category, Black people were more likely to be brought into brands that folded, such as Sea Host (whose Black franchising spokesperson was baseball star Jackie Robinson) and Chicken Delight. Moreover, the social climate was one that threatened businesses of all sorts in Black neighborhoods.

Ebony saw Roman Turmon, thirty-two-year-old owner with his wife, Carol, of a Chicken Delight restaurant in Harlem, as the consummate example of fast food's potential. With the help of eighteen employees, the couple had served more than one thousand customers each weekend since opening in 1964. A former Harlem Globetrotter, Turmon once earned $16,000 per year playing basketball, but he was grossing $35,000 per month at Chicken Delight and was planning to expand to Bedford-Stuyvesant, Brooklyn. Chicken Delight was struck by Turmon's success and enlisted market research to investigate why the chain wasn't doing as well in California's Black communities. Ernest Dichter hypothesized, "It could be that the typical Harlem resident has been out of the American South for many years and has been weaned away from a fondness for Southern style cooking—whereas the west coast Negro may be a recent emigrant from the American Southeast, still inclined to prefer the Southern fried chicken which Colonel Saunders [sic] sells in competition with Chicken Delight."[10]

Among the other franchise owners featured in *Ebony* were individuals and couples who owned car dealerships and gas stations. A group of brothers in Washington, D.C., owned a Gulf Oil franchise—and all of them were married, the article pointed out, highlighting not only their business acumen but their respectability. The text stressed the significant support these franchisees received from their corporate office and suggested that the same would be true for newcomers. Failure was unlikely because "a reputable franchising organization like Standard Oil will do everything within its power to prevent any one of its franchises from folding."[11] This turned out to be far from reality for Black fast food franchisees. *Ebony* did caution that franchisee mileage was likely to vary and that Black businesses often had difficulty obtaining loans, but the overall tone was very much a siren song. Notably, the only women depicted in the article were participating as joint partners with their husbands. *Ebony*'s framing of franchising as a Black man's world presaged the highly masculinized stance of Black franchisors that would develop years later and echoed Black Power's framing of revolution as the domain of men.

Black business associations in *Ebony*'s hometown of Chicago were also attuned to franchising's possibilities, and Black entrepreneurs did begin to participate in a range of sectors.[12] The Cosmopolitan Chamber of Commerce (CCC) organized action around neighborhood conditions that impeded business (e.g., crime and disorder), worked to promote business ownership among Black residents, and hosted social events such as summer bowling leagues for residents and business owners. Among the members was restaurateur Llewelyn Daniels, a banker who operated the Hamburger Hub on 47th Street. He and others in the CCC launched a new Restaurant Division in December 1960 to "improve service, stabilize prices, engage in joint promotion and insure better customer relations."[13] In 1967, the CCC launched a campaign intended to increase awareness of franchise business opportunities among minority groups. The U.S. secretary of commerce had identified barriers to franchise ownership, which the CCC sought to remediate. The campaign was led by a group including businessman Cirilo McSween, treasurer of the SCLC's Operation Breadbasket, an economic empowerment program (more on that in subsequent chapters). To increase franchise awareness, the CCC considered hosting trade shows and luring professional athletes, entertainers, and other affluent individuals to take up permanent residence in Chicago and engage in business.[14] The CCC was ahead of the curve, organizing the campaign two years before the Urban Research Corporation of Chicago, a research and publishing company focused on urban affairs, sponsored a national conference on minority franchising at the University of Chicago.[15] The several hundred participants were drawn from across the country, including franchisors, community development specialists, and government officials. Absent formal presentations, the conference was meant to "provide maximum opportunity for panelists and participants to talk together about the problems and benefits of franchising" through informal small group discussions.[16]

The most pointed statements came not from fast food entrepreneurs, though they did have a strong presence at the conference, but from Gordon Sherman, president of the auto repair shop franchise Midas International. He discussed at length the accommodations that franchisors ought to make for minority franchisees. Several of his ideas related to financing. Sherman claimed that minority franchisees should pursue franchise fee waivers from a franchisor's most senior executives; the fees were "a white man's luxury," and franchisors should be willing to offer a "ghetto discount" in pricing the business. Such a discount, Sherman conceded, would be illegal, but it was on the franchisor to take risks. This also held when siting businesses. One of his own shops would be erected in a vacant lot in "a typical Chicago ghetto," where he anticipated vandalism at best and destruction of the unit at worst. The building that previously occupied the site had burned down (whether this was purposeful was unstated), and Sherman's new outlet risked becoming another casualty of urban disorder. Were that to happen, his $100,000 investment would be lost in the face of insurance agencies that refused to cover ghetto enterprises. Sherman's final set of directives centered on hiring practices, where he suggested that Black franchisees should be situated in White communities to take up existing profitable shops, rather being assigned new and unproven ones. He also inferred that franchisors would benefit from hiring and promoting Black men because they could serve as cultural translators.[17]

Few of Sherman's ideas were implemented in fast food franchising. Black operators did receive financial accommodations in some cases, but as will be seen, these ended up causing more problems than they solved. And Black operators were very much frozen out of stores in White neighborhoods, instead being saddled with problem outlets in Black neighborhoods alone. Black operators therefore faced a far less certain pathway to wealth than did their White counterparts; and contrary to Sherman's suggestions, Black people carried the risk, not the parent companies.

Invading City Centers

The trend of second-generation fast food looking anew at urban markets as it encountered regulatory challenges and community pushback continued as the 1960s drew to a close. Experts were forecasting the inevitability of the ghetto as a primary siting strategy for fast food chains. For example, the Red Barn chain spun off a "new low-investment" version of the brand, called Chicken Pantry, which could "invade city centers" and move into "fringe communities." Locating solely in suburbia was a waste of resources because it meant advertising to entire metro areas but only serving those who lived beyond the city limits. With Chicken Pantry, President Richard Kearns argued, the chain could set up quintuple the number of outlets for every Red Barn site; and zoning approvals would be easier to get.[18] The dramatic population and infrastructural changes wrought by urban renewal were abating, and rising costs for highway frontage meant that city storefronts would soon become a better value. Moreover, with increasing suburban fast food chain saturation came pressure to create additional markets.

When it came to Black and Brown central cities, the editors of *Nation's Restaurant News* foretold, "Unless we accelerate our timetable to colonize the moon, those next-best markets are in cities—both in ghetto areas, where low-cost food is crucial, and in downtown cores which sadly lack high-speed food operations."[19] If the ghetto was the last stop before the moon, at least some White entrepreneurs had already made the expedition. Harry Phillips, a White Chicagoan who had moved to Los Angeles, ran BBQ rib takeout joints in South Central and West Hollywood, enjoying huge success in both communities. In 1969, Phillips expected his sales to reach $2 million (just over $14 million in 2020 dollars). He differentiated his services by area according to racial demographics, restricting Black customers in South Central to takeout while White West Hollywood patrons could dine in. On the other hand, he made it a point to hire Black managers and staff for his South Central establishments, calling it good business sense. But at the end of the day, industry journalists noted, "Phillips did not locate in the South-Central area to appeal to a Negro market. His prime motivation was the lower costs of real estate in the area. The heavy density of the population and the low real estate costs made the area a natural for a takeout operation."[20] White fast food restaurateurs were primarily motivated by the opportunities that racism and disinvestment provided, not any particular interest in serving a Black consumer segment.

In Chicago, Myron Kohn invested $100,000 in 1962 to open a new drive-in in Woodlawn, replacing the ruins of a condemned building. Holland's, located at 1347 East 63rd, was the third outlet in the city, following two others on the city's West Side. With plans to hire staff from the neighborhood, Kohn hoped that Holland's would "become an integral part of the Woodlawn community, and an asset in the conservation and rehabilitation of the area."[21]

Another such restaurant was Whoopee Burger, an independent fast food eatery that would later be supplanted by the Black-owned chain Afri-Kingdom. It opened in 1966 on Chicago's West Side, at 3545 West Roosevelt, managed by Jerry Needel, an alum of Henry's and McDonald's. Employing immense, histrionic signage scaled more for Times Square than a mixed-use street in Chicago, its food was outsize as well. One young Black male employee was pictured in the *Chicago Defender* eating the "tall burger," which was nearly half the size of his face.[22] Whoopee took out an equally exuberant full-page advertisement in the December 14 *Chicago Defender* to announce "FREE GIFTS! BALLOONS! RECORDS! EXCITEMENT!" There were raffles for a television (first prize) and twenty-five Christmas turkeys (second prize). Prizes or no, the extensive and relatively inexpensive menu offered something for everyone. Hamburgers and sundaes cost nineteen cents, fries and milkshakes each cost ten cents, and chicken, shrimp, and fish dinners, which came with French fries, sauce, a dinner roll, and coleslaw, were ninety-six cents. Also on offer (with no price advertised) were hot dogs, Polish sausage, fish sandwiches, and a deluxe hamburger. With that menu, the restaurant took off. It set out "with the dream of making it a million dollar business, and the dream is coming true," a trade magazine reported in 1967. "Opened a year ago, the drive-in hasn't seen a slow day . . . In choosing to locate where they did, the owners of Whoopee Burger have filled a need of the inner city community and expressed confidence in the area with their investment." Whoopee was open twenty-four hours a day, and busy crowds of Black patrons filled the burger joint for seemingly all of them.[23]

Whoopee was ideally located in a bustling mixed-use block that drew heavy pedestrian traffic on both sides of the street. Among them were storefront churches—the Lord's House of Prayer and the Burning Bush Pentecostal Church of Holiness—pharmacies and clinics, Soulville Record Shop, J&F Hardware, and Rothschild Liquor Mart.[24] Beyond the immediate neighbors, the community's economic challenges were in plain view. Closed businesses, vacant and decaying buildings (some

Figure 6.1. An advertisement for Holland's Drive-In published in the *Woodlawn Booster,* October 17, 1962. Source: Newspaperarchive.com.

Figure 6.2. 3050 West Roosevelt, Chicago. Photograph by Copelin Commercial Photographers, image #JPCC_01_0044_0456_015, Chicago Photographic Images of Change digital image collection, Special Collections and University Archives, University of Illinois Chicago.

of which were slated for demolition), and desolate retail corridors dotted the streetscape. Figure 6.2 depicts Roosevelt Road approximately two blocks east from Whoopee (a four-minute walk according to contemporary GPS apps), and Figure 6.3 shows the same street approximately eight blocks to the west (a thirteen-minute walk). The photographs portray the surrounding area in 1963 and 1964, respectively, two to three years before Whoopee opened.

Major chains including Kentucky Fried Chicken, Burger King, and McDonald's were largely absent from the kinds of communities in which Whoopee opened. And for the most part, when they were there, it was because they found themselves in a Black neighborhood after the area's demographics had shifted. However, as seen in chapter 3, McDonald's did launch a few stores in places that had been Black for decades. In Chicago, at least one was thanks to community activist Anthony

Figure 6.3. 3648 West Roosevelt, Chicago. Photograph by Copelin Commercial Photographers, image #JPCC_01_0044_0456_027, Chicago Photographic Images of Change digital image collection, Special Collections and University Archives, University of Illinois Chicago.

Stadeker. At a restaurant industry meeting, Stadeker described his square-mile Bronzeville district as a "concentration camp," where fifty-five thousand were forced to live in deplorable conditions without cooking facilities.[25] The fact was that Black residents in Bronzeville were very much imprisoned spatially. In the 1950s and 1960s, urban renewal under Mayor Daley's direction produced the Dan Ryan Expressway, a fourteen-lane highway with Chicago Transit Authority trains running down the middle. It was a concrete moat along the dead line of Wentworth Avenue separating the Black residents in the public housing projects that lined the State Street corridor from the communities beyond. Daley routed the expressway in this way not only to hem in Black people, but also to prevent it from cutting through his home community of Bridgeport. Robert Moses employed a similar tactic, sending the Triborough Bridge's exit ramp through East Harlem rather than the Upper East

Figure 6.4. 3505 South State, Chicago. Photograph by Copelin Commercial Photographers, image #JPCC_01_0052_0522_011, Chicago Photographic Images of Change digital image collection, Special Collections and University Archives, University of Illinois Chicago.

Side.[26] Urban renewal was "a form of warfare."[27] It ended up destroying more housing than it created and magnifying the city's apartheid structure.[28]

Streetscapes in Stadeker's community were indeed depressed. Figure 6.4 shows the States Theater at 3505–7 South State Street, at the corner of State and 35th Street, the intersection where a McDonald's outlet opened around 1961. The theater had once showcased a variety of entertainment, including films early in its history that debased Black people.[29] Where once a variety of local retail held sway, by the early 1960s all the stores and businesses were shuttered or had vacated the space. The States Theater itself had been condemned by 1963. The posting affixed to the boarded-up front door reads, "THIS BUILDING IS IN DANGEROUS CONDITION AND HAS BEEN CONDEMNED. The Department of Buildings."

Retail failures and turnover were evident farther down State Street, in the

Figure 6.5. 4662 South State, Chicago. Photograph by Copelin Commercial Photographers, image #JPCC_01_0052_0522_020, Chicago Photographic Images of Change digital image collection, Special Collections and University Archives, University of Illinois Chicago.

4600 block. In 1965 a strip that would have been adjacent to the recently completed Robert Taylor Homes public housing project underwent much change (Figure 6.5). Bowles Music House and Book Store was operating in a building that had been condemned. Retail turnover affected several eating establishments including Lou's Creole Kitchen, which was replaced by Jean's Snack Shop, which advertised "HAMBURGERS HOT DOGS CHICKEN TO GO."

The instability of retail on these corridors supports Stadeker's contention that the community's business infrastructure was troubled. He asserted, "There's money to be made in ghetto areas for chain restaurants, but operators are passing up the buck because of their attitude." Stadeker hinted at the scarcity of restaurants by characterizing the food environment as populated by "greasy spoons," which suggests that he saw these restaurants as unappealing. But those greasy spoons were some of the most popular haunts around. Soul legend Aretha Franklin asked for the Lord's mercy in recalling a humble food stand near Chicago's Regal Theater that served spicy sausage-based burgers topped with crispy fries.[30] But Stadeker was less enthusiastic about these kinds of local spots. He may have dismissed them for their modest operations, but they were common in Black communities in other cities. More than a stop for good food, they provided a refuge from racism.[31] Contrary to Stadeker's assertion that fast food was absent in Bronzeville, there were several such restaurants in and around the neighborhood at that time, some of which were popular franchises. Though the geographic boundaries Stadeker used to define his district are unclear, Map 6.1 displays the restaurants located on some of the major corridors in Bronzeville. Some were White-owned (e.g., Henry's), but many of these outlets were Black-owned, including Hamburger Hub, the Friendly Fried Chicken Shack chain, Harold's Chicken Shack, a King Kastle System restaurant at 211 East Pershing, and a White Owl Restaurant at 4302 South Cottage Grove (though the latter two may have opened the year after Stadeker spoke).[32]

Stadeker seemed to object less to an absolute lack of places where one could go out to eat, and more to the relative lack of franchising opportunities. He believed there were missed opportunities for fast food—operated by Black people—to make enormous profits. Stadeker had been successful in convincing McDonald's, and specifically VP of franchising Edward Bood, to open one or more outlets in his community. But he divulged little about the agreement other than that he had wanted the restaurant's decision-makers to be Black (excluding "house niggers"), and that McDonald's had been duplicitous in some way in building the unit. This would have been either 25 (later 17) East 35th Street, 635 East Pershing, or both. These Bronzeville locations, built by 1962, were the only Chicago McDonald's outlets that were newly constructed in Black areas, rather than in White neighborhoods that

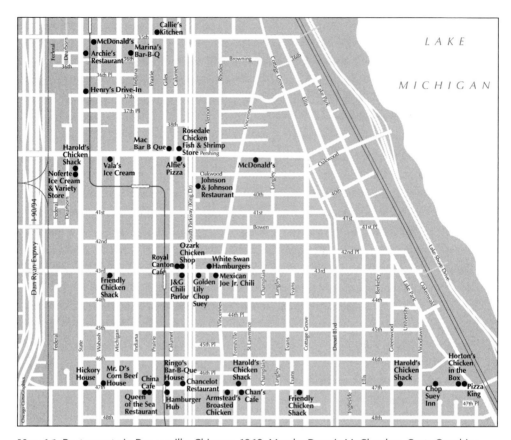

Map 6.1. Restaurants in Bronzeville, Chicago, 1968. Map by Dennis McClendon, CartoGraphics.

turned Black over time. Perhaps Stadeker balked at the new outlets because they were still White-owned.[33]

East 35th Street's 1961 opening had been reported with great fanfare in the *Chicago Defender*—though it misreported manager Wallace Rogers as the store operator—heralding the restaurant's "family trade" and instructing readers that McDonald's limited, inexpensive menu eliminated nuisances like tipping and waiting. Rogers opined that the Bronzeville location was chosen because it exemplified the McDonald's ethos: "a solid, growing family community with plenty of churches, schools and civic spirit." He also reinforced that the restaurant and the company sought to be an integral part of customers' lives: "a permanent community service just like the grocery or the neighborhood drug store."[34] Rogers's words were eerily prescient. Fast food would indeed become a fixture in Black communities (in Chicago and elsewhere), more prevalent than supermarkets or pharmacies.

A Call for a Black Public Face

Aside from the Bronzeville outlets, other McDonald's locations were found in Black space because White operators found their neighborhoods changing around them. Two members of the tenth graduating class of Hamburger University, Jerome G. Meyers and Peter Booras, opened restaurants on the South Side in the late 1950s and early 1960s. Meyers held 2425 East 79th Street, which opened when Grand Crossing was a White neighborhood. Situated on a triangular parcel at the corner of 79th between Yates and Phillips, the restaurant opened in 1960 in a community that was less than 1 percent Black.[35] By 1970, the census tract in which it was located had increased to 40 percent Black; and the three tracts abutting the intersection were higher still, at nearly 70 percent. The commerce surrounding the McDonald's changed as these demographic changes took place, but a relatively diverse mix of stores remained in 1968 (see Map 6.2).[36] Booras's franchise first launched in 1958 at 2040 West 79th Street, and subsequently moved a few doors down to 2048. At the time of the 1960 census, not a single one of the 5,380 residents were Black, and the proportion had only risen to 6 percent by 1970. Unlike many White neighborhoods, it would take until 1980 for the racial transition to take place—by that point it was 98 percent Black.[37]

Some operators were undeterred by the changing demographic landscape and continued to open outlets in neighborhoods that had become Black. The Fine brothers had been among the earliest McDonald's franchisees, and in August 1966 advertisements in the *Chicago Defender* and *The Bulletin* told of the grand opening of Howard and Joe's new location on 76th and Vincennes Avenue, moving from their original store on 71st. The grand opening—which promised "tempting cheeseburgers," "thirst quenching Coke," free "Bat Man rings" for children, and merrymaking for all—took place in the middle of the neighborhood's transition: in 1960, the surrounding census tract was 57 percent Black; by 1970, it had risen to 97 percent.[38]

The racial change engulfing U.S. cities had become a source of worry for fast food, and it reached a critical turning point when Martin Luther King Jr. was assassinated in 1968. Racialized divisions in staffing were now seen as too much of a liability. Franchisees like Meyers and others on the South Side perfectly exemplified the concerns that McDonald's began to harbor about outlets owned by White men but staffed and in some cases managed by Black employees. Roland Jones, who in the 1990s was a high-ranking African American McDonald's executive, was a new field consultant in 1969, and therefore responsible for assessing and grading stores' compliance with operating standards, evaluating owner eligibility for additional licenses, and ensuring that corporate met its responsibilities to franchisees. When

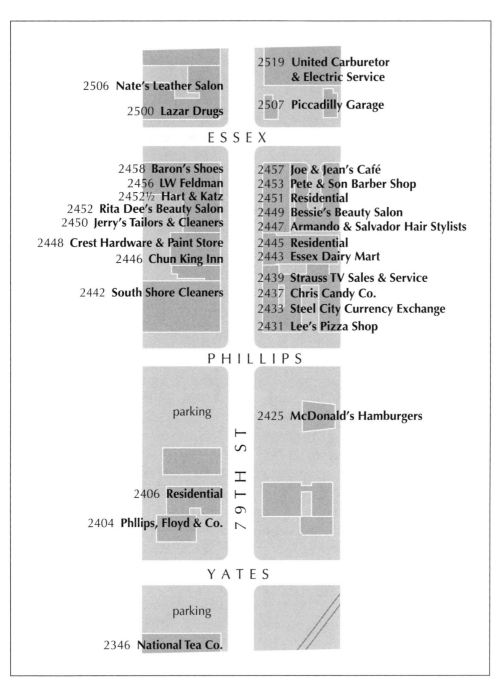

Map 6.2. Retail surrounding McDonald's outlet at 2425 East 79th Street, Chicago. Map by Dennis McClendon, CartoGraphics.

Jones assumed the position he was assigned twenty-three stores, nine of which were "troubled." As neighborhoods underwent racial turnover, the workplace became tense: White owners were reportedly "losing control." Did this mean tensions between owners and employees? Owners and customers? Owners and local gangs? All were possibilities, and as neighborhoods changed, White owners let their stores fall into decline or abandoned them altogether. Given that Ray Kroc's vision had centered on suburban families and "hadn't included decaying inner cities," a "bewildered" corporate headquarters had little help to offer White operators. Instead, fast food executives began seeking out Black franchisees who would buy the declining businesses.[39]

Jones began his work with the chain in 1965 as a crew member in the D.C. area, initially recruited to clean festering, unlined, outdoor garbage cans in the summer heat. His White manager in Alexandria was none too pleased to have a Black employee, but Jones began to move up the ranks, undergoing training that led him to another all-White site, Annapolis Road, in Landover, Maryland. He moved again to Good Hope Road, a site in Southeast that had once been White working-class but was nearly complete in its transition to a Black community. Finally, he received a managerial position at 3510 Duke Street in Alexandria, making him and Bob Beavers among the first to hold such a role. His mandate was to increase sales and remake an outlet where customer volume was low and patrons came only after exhausting other options. Jones started work the day after Dr. King was murdered. A single McDonald's in D.C. stayed open that night—one managed by Beavers.[40] But Jones's store closed early as the rebellion erupted; following the unrest, corporate decided it was too dangerous for White managers to run stores in Black neighborhoods. During the strife, some retail owners deliberately threw Black bodies in the line of fire; a D.C. liquor store proprietor, upon learning that his store window was broken, left his "colored boys" with guns and instructed them to "do what you can, not to get hurt" while the owners "ran for our lives, you might say."[41] Only two McDonald's outlets were damaged during the troubles, but corporate had seen enough. It determined that it had to get franchises into Black hands in order for them to remain sustainable.[42] The communities in which these stores were located would not forever brook White ownership and token positions for Black workers—a lesson McDonald's would learn in Cleveland a year later.

Other chains were learning this lesson, too. Sixteen years after Burger King began in Miami, Willie Taylor became the first Black Burger King franchisee in the city in 1970. Taylor and two partners received private funds and financing from the SBA. Taylor had joined Burger King in 1960, sweeping floors in the warehouse, and subsequently moved up incrementally in supervisory positions. He joined the ranks of franchisees in 1970, and in 1972 he remained one of very few Black operators. Jim McLamore contended that bringing in Black franchisees began as altruism but became a sound business practice. He explained of Taylor's first store, "Because this store is in the black community, we felt it should be owned by blacks." His self-assured and self-evident analysis here contrasted with the reality that he and the rest of Burger King's corporate leadership had never considered race prior to a 1969 protest in Houston, which led to the first Black franchisee a year before Taylor. Neither did McLamore expect the shift to bear out financially; when ownership transferred to Black hands, he was pleasantly surprised to find that sales continued to rise. Of the Houston conflict, he explained that partly because of an insufficient site analysis which did not reveal a Black population, "We had made a fatal mistake. We opened a Burger King in a black neighborhood in Houston with a white franchisee. The blacks let us know in a hurry they didn't like it one bit."[43]

Indeed, "the Blacks" made it clear in Houston and elsewhere that a Whites-only strategy was untenable. In 1968, a White McDonald's field consultant was shot at in the parking lot of 6560 South Stony, and headquarters frantically sought the expertise of people who understood "urban markets"—namely, Black people. Business interests in the country had come to believe that White employees were at special risk in Black neighborhoods, and that they ought to remain out of sight as much as possible. Black employees were now seen as important as fast food's public face in "sensitive areas," particularly because "one Detroit study under a U.S. Labor Department grant found that some Negroes have a pathological hatred of whites that they don't even know exists."[44] A month after Washington exploded in rebellion in April 1968, Senator Robert C. Byrd, in his role as the chair of the Senate Appropriations Subcommittee for D.C., held discussions with local business owners and first responders to assess their perceptions about the problems facing business in the District. He did so at night and in his office, to provide anonymity to those present.[45] The written transcripts masked the names of those who spoke. "Mr. P.," a store owner, feared for his safety because "these youngsters have too much hate . . . not personally me but they hate my race and it makes me the same thing."[46] While mainstream business discourse saw Black communities as pathological, those within them realistically outlined the need for Black retail management.

Landon Gerald Dowdey, attorney to George E. Storey, president of Build Black Inc., also spoke at Byrd's meeting, stating that in a city that was 70 percent Black, businesses were overwhelmingly owned by Whites, to the chagrin of Black shoppers: "When they go to a Safeway [grocery] store, for example, there is a white manager. They would like to see a black manager."[47] His testimony revealed, however, that a Black manager could not solve all community relations problems. One Black owner in D.C. was burned out because people thought he was just a front for a White-owned business. "Mr. Y.," a Black owner, believed his clientele were unlikely to object to White employees, "other than the fact that I think that they would question to find out why would you give this man a job when you know that someone else in the black community needs the job worse. I am sure that they would question that."[48]

Burger King's VP for marketing, John Hollingsworth, took Dowdey's viewpoint. Arguing that because its restaurants were many in Black communities, and because Black consumers were significant for the bottom line, it was "safer to have black managers run black-oriented stores." The chain may have been among the first to open in Black space, but it clearly had given no thought to the inclusion of Black operators.[49] Kentucky Fried Chicken, however, was conspicuously absent from the late 1960s race-related fast food landscape. It did not make any significant changes to incorporate African Americans. It did not participate in federal initiatives and did not appear in the media alongside other chains announcing their first Black franchisees. Indeed, it seemed too busy buying back its franchises to bother with instituting Black people as new operators. Starting in 1968—the year it debuted its "Finger Lickin' Good" campaign, at a cost of $9 million—it began acquiring eighty-three franchised outlets in major markets. In the spring of 1969, it acquired eight more licensees that were operating fifty-four stores grossing $12 million. Corporate assessed that buying them back from the franchisees would yield all the profits to corporate; why be limited to just franchise fees, leases, and royalties? Essentially, corporate could make more money if it ran the stores itself. The number of KFC's corporate-owned outlets grew from 228 in 1968 to 551 in April 1970 and yet again to 700 by July of that year. These locations were reportedly five to six times more profitable than franchised ones, and President John Y. Brown stated that going forward the company's focus would be to build new company-owned stores and continue buying up franchises.[50]

KFC was not the only chain to reacquire its outlets. The ratio of franchisee-operated to company-operated fell industrywide from 81:1 to 10:1 between 1960 and 1970. Though corporate brass made statements that company-owned stores were more profitable due to better management, others argued that the selective acquisition of profitable outlets in affluent locations was a better bet.[51] In June 1967, Pillsbury purchased Burger King after a year of negotiations, giving the conglomerate the opportunity to diversify and take advantage of a fast-growing food retail sector. Within a few years of coming under Pillsbury's wing, Burger King began buying back dozens of franchised outlets.[52]

McDonald's was the most explicit among the chains in articulating a racial risk management plan. Once it assessed Black space as too risky for White operators, it made these goals plain. Corporate bought back Gee Gee's D.C. territory in 1967. Once acquired, it mined the area's workers for candidates to take up higher-ranking positions. It promoted Carl Osborne, who would now serve as supervisor for the "inner city" Washington stores, the first such role anywhere in the system. He was directed to find new Black managers for White-owned outlets, making the business Black in its public face, if not in its ownership. A tokenizing approach meant that Black staff were likely to face racism in their new posts. Jones, for example, was successful in turning 3510 Duke Street around as store manager, but he received consistently poor evaluations from a supervisor who did not approve of having a Black manager in a White market. Once in the executive suite as a field consultant in Chicago, Jones was warned that White coworkers might harbor irrational fears that he would attempt to date White secretaries.

White business owners also distrusted the intentions of the Black public. As "Mr. U." asserted in Byrd's Senate office, "I don't think white people have demonstrated that they won't assist the well-intentioned Negro, and they have."[53] In other words, Black people were the problem. White businesses were doing all they could, but less well-behaved Black people were still wreaking havoc. McDonald's and other brands needed well-intentioned Negroes as the public face of franchised outlets if their marooned stores were to survive Black urbanity, and they turned to a number of dubious policies and strategies to do so.

How Does It Feel to Be a Problem?

W. E. B. Du Bois wrote eloquently about the question that hung unasked between him and "the other world." That other world tiptoed around him and studied him "curiously or compassionately," but refrained from asking what they really wanted to know: "How does it feel to be a problem?"[54] Fast food asked that question implicitly as it brought Black franchisees on board, seeing them as problem operators who, lacking the requisite skills and capital, necessitated special initiatives, and who served an illegible market. White men who were actual problems were little scrutinized as they jumped on the fast food bandwagon and garnered accolades while flailing in disastrous enterprises.

The spectacular rise and fall of the Minnie Pearl's chicken chain exemplified the worst of this bias. In 1969, the *Wall Street Journal* profiled John Jay Hooker, a Tennessee lawyer who had lost a bid for the state's governorship in 1966 and decided thereafter to seek his fortunes in fast food. At the time of the article, Hooker was a "hugely successful businessman" thanks to his brainchild, Minnie Pearl's Chicken Systems. Inspired by the success of Kentucky Fried Chicken, and believing fast food to be a get-rich quick scheme, he and his brother Henry borrowed $660,000 (approximately $4.7 million in 2020 dollars) from friends and banks and launched their chain in 1967. The name was the fictional incarnation of country music artist Minnie Cannon, who had campaigned for John Hooker in 1966, and whose employer the Grand Ole Opry was owned by an insurance firm the Hookers' family helped found. The men wanted a "country image" for the units and a name that customers would associate with home cooking. Rapid growth was immediate. By May 1969, the company had sold over 1,400 franchises, though only 120 of these were actually in operation. Industry commentators argued, "They laughed when Minnie Pearl's went public. But no one's laughing now. In less than two years, Minnie Pearl's . . . has achieved a growth rate that matches its stock performance."[55]

The chain registered with the Securities and Exchange Commission and sold out its public offering. The Hookers then branched out into other restaurant franchises, including buying half of the Black-targeted Mahalia Jackson's chain. The company was extending itself at a pace that looked to exceed its resources, human and financial, but the booming ventures completely remade John Hooker's image in the eyes of Nashville's business community. Hundreds of Tennessee residents were now holding securities worth one hundred times the purchase price, and John Hooker's viability as a political candidate shot up.[56] Money streamed in for Minnie Pearl's outlets, but their parent company, Performance Systems, could only survive if it sold enough franchises to generate revenue that would sustain the enterprise, so sell franchises it did. Hooker was unabashed in declaring to industry colleagues that his company made money using dubious methods. At a 1969 franchise conference he reveled blithely in the potential for riches in his unsustainable company. *Nation's Restaurant News* commented, "[He] had outlined to this audience exactly what he was up to—how, by copycatting Kentucky Fried Chicken and loading his balance sheet with dubious front-end income, he had managed to become one of Wall Street's all-time short-term darlings." Nonexistent only twenty-one months ago, it had already sold 1,700 franchises, though as Hooker professed, he was ignorant about fast food restaurant operations: "I can't tell you I know anything about the chicken business. But I'll sell you a franchise to compete with Kentucky Fried Chicken." *Nation's Restaurant News* reported that Hooker thoroughly charmed the audience with wit, candidness, and folksy southern humor. But one year later, when Minnie Pearl's was faltering, the paper critiqued these same remarks.[57] Cracks began to appear in the facade by July 1969, and they continued to grow as the company ran on anticipatory capital fumes rather than actual money.[58] Eventually it collapsed in losses totaling tens of millions. What began with an explosive rise ended in implosion within only four years.[59]

Driven by the hubris of White businessmen and financial actors who gave them the benefit of the doubt, Minnie Pearl's was buttressed by support that Black franchisees could never hope to receive. At McDonald's, a broad spectrum of Black applicants for McDonald's franchises had routinely been denied, not fitting the description of what a licensee should look like, figuratively or literally, in the minds of the White men in management.[60] This despite the fact that Black folks had been successfully running businesses in their communities for years, particularly restaurants. Even those who could appear to be well-intentioned Negroes and pass muster with corporate still faced financing obstacles. The high initial cost of purchasing an outlet and equipment was generally beyond the reach of potential Black franchisees, and banks refused to lend to Black businesses. As sociologist Robert Allen argued in 1969, "Blacks had no capital to speak of, and financiers, who after all are capable of recognizing a threat to their own interests, saw no reason to provide them any."[61]

McDonald's answered the question "How does it feel to be a problem?" by bringing Black operators in under problematic terms and giving them problem stores. In 1968, the company attempted to resolve racism in financing through the use of "zebra" or "salt and pepper" agreements, in which White owners fronted the start-up capital to launch the franchise, while Black owners were responsible for day-to-day operations. This arrangement violated core McDonald's franchising rules that operators had to have 100 percent ownership, and that owners had to live in the same market as their restaurants. Regardless, Chicago regional manager Ed Schmitt took the zebra idea to his corporate superiors, thinking the partnerships a safe way to bring in Black owners. Two White investors—Arthur Duplessie and Joseph Greenberg—entered zebra agreements with seven other operators across the country, and they would prove ruinous.[62]

At least four years after Roman Turmon became a Chicken Delight franchisee, Herman Petty became McDonald's first Black franchisee when he left behind a dual career as a barber by day and bus driver by night to take up ownership of the outlet at 6560 South Stony Island. A small plaque that remains on the outlet's facade memorializes his arrival on December 21, 1968.[63] Petty did so under a zebra agreement. Archives do not suggest how Duplessie or Greenberg came to be known by McDonald's executives. Duplessie was not a Chicago native, nor was he likely to have run in Kroc's circles. He earned a college degree in commerce, served three years as a U.S. Marine Corps officer, and before becoming involved in McDonald's franchising his first position in business was at the Olivetti typewriter company.[64]

Contemporary recollections of the partnership's genesis are mixed and contradictory. Executive Patricia Sowell Harris recounted the arrangement as initiated by Duplessie and Greenberg. The men reportedly approached Petty about running a McDonald's restaurant, and Petty then put in an application with Ed Schmitt, who headed franchising. If the men approached Petty, they may have been motivated by SBA programs that were available to minority entrepreneurs. McDonald's biographer John Love does not attribute the partnership initiation to either party, merely stating that McDonald's "allowed" it to happen. Roland Jones, for his part, recounted that Petty had told him he'd met the White partners at a franchise show—perhaps the one organized by the CCC?—and that the group planned for several months before moving ahead with the purchase. The two men pitched the plan to corporate in 1968 arguing that they would purchase the outlet, Petty would be the public face and day-to-day manager, and eventually Petty would buy the investors out. Whatever the genesis of the connection, Duplessie and Greenberg initially had the full support of Fred Turner, Kroc's right hand, and Ed Schmitt.[65]

In reality, the investors levied administrative fees at suspect rates and tied them to the store's sales. Just as troubling, the fees made little sense. For instance, Duplessie and Greenberg included "management fees" as part of their compensation—essentially demanding payment for managing their own store.[66] In effect, the restaurants were merely vehicles for the predatory investors to build their own wealth while they neglected major obligations like reinvestments and equipment.[67] For almost three years, corporate failed to recognize the warning signs in Chicago, and the same problems were occurring in other stores the partners held in St. Louis, Kansas City, and California. The new franchisees did not have the business experience to spot the accounting irregularities that were undermining their stores, and most had not participated in the Hamburger University training program at Elk Grove Village. Petty had, but he did so before ever stepping foot in his restaurant, making it difficult for him to fully assimilate the information he obtained.[68] Duplessie and Greenberg leveraged the restaurants for their own additional business ventures, ignored their promise to transfer equity to the Black owners, and failed to pay suppliers and others for months at a time. Eventually, each "hired his own bag man, who every day raced to the eight stores hoping to beat the other owner's revenue collector to the till."[69] Burt Cohen, McDonald's head of franchising, spent a year redressing the calamity of the zebra agreements, which ultimately cost the corporation $500,000. For whatever reason, although the two partners were forced out they did not face legal action, making the specifics of McDonald's half-million-dollar disbursement unclear.[70] In any case, the architects of the zebra partnerships went on with their careers. Duplessie moved to the Washington area in 1974 and held positions at two different businesses before becoming a vice president at Zenith Data Systems, a subsidiary of the consumer electronics company, in 1983. In 1985, he bought one of the most expensive homes in Bethesda, Maryland, but died of a heart attack a year later at age fifty-one.[71]

Ultimately, the cost of these disastrous arrangements was borne by the Black franchisees, evidence that these individuals were both "models of racial progress and victims of racial discrimination."[72] Because McDonald's would not assume debt on behalf of the zebra franchisees, their stores buckled under the liabilities incurred by Duplessie and Greenberg, even after being refranchised. Herman Petty was able to obtain a loan from the Hyde Park Bank and bought out his "investors," but of the eight zebra arrangements, only his and that of a Los Angeles operator survived.[73] Petty's difficulties would of course fade from official McDonald's history. Inflating the activity of the retail location and glossing entirely over Petty's struggles, a fact sheet from the 1990s lists one of the company's "Black Consumer Market Milestones" as simply "1968—Herman Petty buys a McDonald's restaurant on Chicago's popular Stoney [sic] Island strip, thus becoming the system's first Black franchisee."[74]

In fact, Petty made his debut as a McDonald's operator not only under a predatory investment scheme, but also in a decrepit store beset with problems. The restaurant at 6560 South Stony Island Avenue, like so many other urban McDonald's units, was situated in a neighborhood hobbled by White flight. The restaurant fronted the expansive Jackson Park, built in 1869 and designed by Central Park's Frederick Law Olmsted and Calvert Vaux. This verdant surround was atypical for site selection policies that called for high-traffic streets and retail anchors capable of bringing in customers.[75] These stipulations would become harder to meet as neighborhoods underwent the departure of White residents and businesses. But when Erwin Polakoff and Morton Katznelson opened their McDonald's Jackson Park Drive-In in 1956, it was situated in a residential section; much of the commerce on Stony Island was farther down the street. Four blocks up at 69th, for example, was a busy retail block including a snack shop selling "King Size Beefburgers" and jumbo red hots and a National Tea supermarket. The strip of Stony Island between 67th and 68th remained busy between the 1950s and 1960s, but changed a great deal as the neighborhood did. In 1953, two years before McDonald's opened, the strip was anchored by the Jackson Park Theater and the Jackson Park Hotel on the corner,

Figure 6.6. The east side of Stony Island Avenue in Chicago, June 1963. The Jackson Park Hotel is visible on the corner, but the Jackson Park Theater mid-block, with its defunct marquee, is no longer. Chicago History Museum, ICHi-176470; Tom H. Long, photographer.

flanked by a number of small businesses. By 1963 (Figure 6.6), the theater and per-haps the hotel were defunct, and several businesses had turned over.

Following the neighborhoods' racial transformation in the 1950s and 1960s, Woodlawn endured significant disinvestment and resulting decline into the 1970s. The "Blitz of Woodlawn," which occurred between 1967 and 1971, took shape in a raft of fires across the community. Nearly four hundred buildings were burned, abandoned or demolished. The peak of the fires in 1970 saw 1,600 flare in a one-square mile area in East and Central Woodlawn, displacement cut the population almost in half, and there was substantial evidence of profit-driven arson. Residents and the Woodlawn Organization saw the epidemic as a conspiracy to destroy Woodlawn.[76]

For quite some time 6560 South Stony had been a busy and successful location for Katznelson and Polakoff. In the early 1960s, the two expected to serve eighty thousand hamburgers during the month of August—typically their busiest month of the year "because it's when the family likes to get outdoors. They will usually grab a snack without any bother for mom." Indeed, Polakoff was profiled in the *Chicago Defender* as selling more hamburgers than anyone on the South Side.[77] And yet, contrary to McDonald's emphasis on franchisees working their way into the fabric of their communities, Polakoff, Katznelson, and their store were invisible in community discourse. No stories appeared about the two men, neither in community organization newsletters like United Woodlawn Inc.'s *Voice of Woodlawn,* nor in local papers such as *The Bulletin,* the *Woodlawn Booster,* or the *Woodlawn Observer.* Neither did the restaurant advertise in these newspapers, unlike other local establishments like Holland's.

Petty's store was in a precarious state when he took over. Late in the night of January 27, 1962, a grease fire broke out in the finishing French fry well, leaving the restaurant in shambles. Corporate's assessment of the extensive damage determined that "not a pane of glass remains." How well the store was renovated is unclear, though it is unlikely it remained fire-damaged for the six years before Petty's arrival.[78] The store was indeed open when Petty took over, but equipment was dysfunctional, broken, or altogether absent and the physical infrastructure of the building, both inside and out, was markedly decayed.[79] Petty also inherited food of poor quality; untrained staff; and rampant waste and theft of food, supplies, and money. Perhaps in response to the racial refabrication of the neighborhood, Polakoff and Katznelson fled Woodlawn and abandoned the business, leaving the restaurant to decline. Polakoff maintained a law office downtown and moved to a community in Franklin Park that was 99 percent White.[80]

Most other ventures in Woodlawn retreated as well. Competitor restaurants a few blocks over such as White Castle and White Corner vanished. Indeed, by the time Petty's franchise launched, there were only two businesses in the 6500 block of Stony Island: the W & T Sinclair service station at 6502 and the McDonald's.[81] The 6400 block was similarly anemic, and that condition would only grow as White flight increased. Figure 6.8 shows the decline of businesses from 1966 to 1974 in a nine-block stretch of the street. One-third of the businesses closed, leaving empty storefronts. Notably, while several independent restaurants closed, a Burger King and a Kentucky Fried Chicken acquired retail space. The City of Chicago exacerbated neighborhood decline by curtailing bus service as Whites moved out, cutting off access to the primary shopping area on 63rd Street.[82]

The gutting of area retail meant not only the depression of the community's

Figure 6.7. Chicago's Woodlawn neighborhood was devastated by disinvestment. Photograph taken from the seventh floor of 6327 South Dorchester, looking southeast, November 1973. Chicago History Museum, ICHi-176471; Gustav D. Frank, photographer.

overall economic well-being, but also the disruption of foot traffic on which the McDonald's outlet would rely. The demise of the Southmoor Hotel was a major loss. Occupying a full city block at 6646 South Stony when erected in 1924, the building housed hundreds of apartments and hotel rooms, whose residents were steps from "the Woodlawn business district with its shops, theatres, and amusement centers." Over the 1950s, the Southmoor hosted numerous social events, and its guests and employees would have constituted a plentiful client base for McDonald's. But by 1968 it had become headquarters to the notorious Blackstone Rangers gang.[83]

When Petty took over 6560 South Stony, he encountered an untrained "crew" comprising primarily Blackstone Rangers. But by relying on existing community-based relationships with many of the gang's members, and as a familiar figure and

Businesses Operating in 1966	Businesses Operating in 1974
WIRTH HF SERVICE STATION 6610	6610 NEELY STANDARD SERVICE
WALGREEN COMPANY 6658	
KOWALSKI STUDIO & SOUTHSIDE TV & RADIO 6700	
F&V ITALIAN & AMERICAN RESTAURANT 6705	
HOME WINE & LIQUOR 6706	**6706 HOME WINE & LIQUOR**
CAPRICORN LOUNGE 6713	
HATTON'S DOUGHNUT SHOP 6722	
EUCLID HOTEL 6733	
CHINA BOY RESTAURANT 6746	6746 STONY ISLAND MEDICAL CENTER
YOUNG, C., JR., OD 6800	6800 WATERGATE SHOE SHINE PARLOR
SEC-CESSFUL CLEANERS 6810	**6810 SEC-CESSFUL CLEANERS**
MANOR INC. 6832	6832 BURGER KING
STONY ISLAND & 69TH CURRENCY EXCHANGE 6851	6851 STONY ISLAND & 69TH CURRENCY EXCHANGE
SUN-RAY CLEANERS 6862	6862 PAUL'S GROCERY
METROPOLITAN DETECTIVE AGENCY 6906	**6906 METROPOLITAN DETECTIVE AGENCY**
CAIRO UNIFIED HATTERS 6910	6910 CAIRO UNIFIED HATTERS
CHICKEN COOP 6922	
REDS LIQUOR MART 6926	6926 REDS LIQUOR MART
BEST BEAUTY & BARBERSHOP 6942	6942 CITYWIDE PLUMBING AND SEWERAGE
	6958 CHEKER OIL COMPANY
COLUMBIA CAR WASH 7001	**7001 COLUMBIA CAR WASH**
GOLDCUP TRANSMISSION SUPPLIES 7004	
EATMORE RESTAURANT 7008	
	7018 SKYWAY LIQUORS
ABLE WINDOW SHADE WORKS 7028	
STONY CLUB 7056	7056 GLORIA'S LIQUORS
ED ERLICH VOLKSWAGON 7057	7057 BECKET & BEAN INSURANCE
READ BARBECUE RESTAURANT 7101	7101 THREE SISTERS SOUL FOOD CAFETERIA
HOLLANDER DENTAL LAB 7109	7109 COHEN, N., DDS
STONY ISLAND CHRYSTLER-PLYMOUTH 7137	
BILL'S TUCKPOINTING SERVICE 7202	
COMMUNITY SHOPPING CENTER 7203	7203 STONY ISLAND FOOD AND LIQUORS
SOUTH SHORE PRINTERS 7405	**7405 SOUTH SHORE PRINTERS**
SMITHEREEN EXTERMINATING & FUMIGATING CO. 7420	
	7451 KENTUCKY FRIED CHICKEN TAKE HOME
CHALT BROS. PAPER CUPS 7507	7507 ILLINOIS MENTAL HEALTH DEPT.
LUTHERAN WELFARE SERVICES OF ILLINOIS 7540	7540 AUGUSTANA HOME FOR THE AGED

Figure 6.8. Business change from 1966 to 1974 on Chicago's Stony Island Avenue. Some fast food restaurants emerged, while others closed over time. Businesses in bold were in operation across both time periods. Infographic by Kudos Design Collaboratory.

Figure 6.9. The Southmoor Hotel, southwest corner, at 67th Street, October 1961. Chicago History Museum, ICHi-176469; J. Sherwin Murphy, photographer.

a Black man, Petty was able to secure the staff's allegiance. In concert with other significant changes, such as breaking McDonald's code against hiring women, by the end of 1969 sales had increased by 75 percent. The turnaround of 6560 allowed Petty to acquire a second store shortly thereafter. This was 7601 South Vincennes Avenue, formerly owned by the Fines, whom Petty described as "the white franchisee just down the street."[84] Since Petty took over the store in the summer of 1969, the Fines' new outlet was theirs for a short three years only. Once again Petty would find himself reopening a store in a sparse retail corridor. His restaurant was one of only a few businesses on the block. Still, his new location thrived.[85]

In D.C., the McDonald's at 1164 Bladensburg Road NE, in the neighborhood of

Trinidad, was another "problem store."[86] There were financial shortfalls due to high costs for food, labor, and maintenance; losses incurred from wastage, pilferage, and robberies; and an untrained staff prone to high turnover and absenteeism. As was true of McDonald's generally at that time, the store did not feature inside seating or a drive-thru; people were served at walk-up windows and ate outside, either at benches or inside their automobiles. Trinidad sustained devastating damage during the rebellion, and a large proportion of the buildings destroyed were retail concerns owned by Whites. Roland Jones remembered the few businesses operating in the vicinity as a Sunoco service station; stores purveying home improvement goods, lumber, liquor, tires, and used cars; and a "mom and pop" grocery. Street directories largely corroborate this portrait (Map 6.3).

Contributing to 1164's poor state were the overall conditions of the neighborhood. The streets were dirty and litter-strewn, lacking the most basic sanitation services or infrastructure (including garbage cans).[87] Jones turned the Bladensburg store around by hiring new staff, retraining existing employees, and putting a new and intensive focus on improving and maintaining the physical appearance of the store and parking lot.

Thus, when McDonald's and other major chains turned more attention to urban areas in the late 1960s and early 1970s, it was not their first foray into cities, but perhaps their first purposeful one. McDonald's was in White urban space as early as 1956 and in Black Chicago and D.C. neighborhoods by 1961 or 1962. But racial change made the need for Black ownership acute, resulting in McDonald's issuing a directive to White operators to sell their franchises to Black people. Following corporate's injunction, at least twenty-one transfers were made to Black operators in Detroit, Oakland, Los Angeles, St. Louis, Denver, and Chicago. Bob Beavers oversaw the national minority effort, drawing as a Gee Gee alum on his connections to other Black McDonald's workers. Gee Gee was a catalyst for much of what took place with Black franchising across the country, and the connections between operators in different cities were many. One new franchise went to two women, Mrs. Iroma Porter and Mrs. Willie Glover, in Oakland. Others were the West Side Organization in Chicago, James Petty in Los Angeles, and Charles Petty in St. Louis (it is unclear whether these men were relatives of Herman).[88]

Mallory Jones was another St. Louis operator.[89] Originally from East St. Louis, Illinois, Jones's career path included stints as a Chicago school teacher and social worker and two years in the army before obtaining a master's degree in education. Later, he attended Kentucky Fried Chicken's manager training course and supervised the chain's operations in Chicago's Black neighborhoods. He left in 1968 for McDonald's, taking up a franchise on the Delmar Divide, St. Louis's infamous color

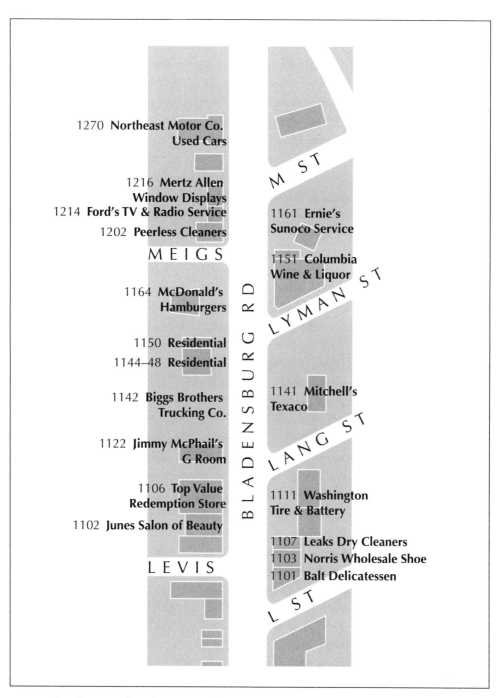

Map 6.3. Retail surrounding the McDonald's outlet at 1164 Bladensburg Road NE, Washington D.C. Map by Dennis McClendon, CartoGraphics.

line. Fifty-four percent of all commercial operations within a four-block radius had disappeared by the time Jones began operating the restaurant in September 1969. Jones remained determined to make a go of it, "because of the faith two white men had in me. They approved my bank loan so I could be the first black man in the St. Louis area to get a McDonald's franchise." The two men were none other than Duplessie and Greenberg.[90] His restaurant would not last, nor would that of Ken E. V. Ross, who purchased a store from Carl Osborne, nor several others.[91]

Racism pushed Black McDonald's franchisees out of the system. Field consultants wielded complete autonomy, which meant that prejudice affected their discretion in decision-making. An affirmative action executive at the corporate office, Mel Hopson, asserted that the corporation "did have some racists in key positions . . . We called them 'neanderthals' and we had to get rid of some of those people."[92] But this view makes racism the anachronistic view of a few bad apples, and not a structural problem that would shape company practices in the absence of individual antipathies. In the contemporary moment, corporate still averts an inward gaze to understand problems with the retention of Black franchisees. African American Patricia Sowell Harris contended in 2009 that Black operators who left the system had a "bad attitude" and that "prospects we brought into McDonald's did not understand what it took to succeed and be productive within a corporate culture, whether it was ours or anybody else's. And we did not understand how to manage people whose background and experience was so different from ours." Further, she asserted that new Black entrants lacked an understanding of corporate culture and how to operate successfully within it. As a result, "in many cases, what were perceived as 'racial' barriers were actually challenges that faced all employees, regardless of color."[93] In this view, the difficulties Black operators encountered were individual characterological deficits; these franchisees were saddled with a deficient cultural background, lacked business acumen, and were distracted by ill-founded racial concerns.

Of course, some Black McDonald's franchisees did find success. A group of four Chicagoans—Edward D. Wimp and his son Edward L. Wimp, Theodore Jones, and Cirilo McSween—purchased a set of stores at East 35th and Wabash, 635 East 39th Street, 6335 South Park Way (now Martin Luther King Drive), and 2425 East 79th Street. All of the stores were in poor condition. Little evidence is available to explain the declination of these outlets, but White franchisees may have abandoned them in the face of challenges such as rising crime.[94]

The Wimps and the other men managed to make the stores profitable. And despite a relatively hands-off approach, they came to fast food with a vision beyond profit, hoping to remake neighborhoods and catalyze commercial renewal. Franchis-

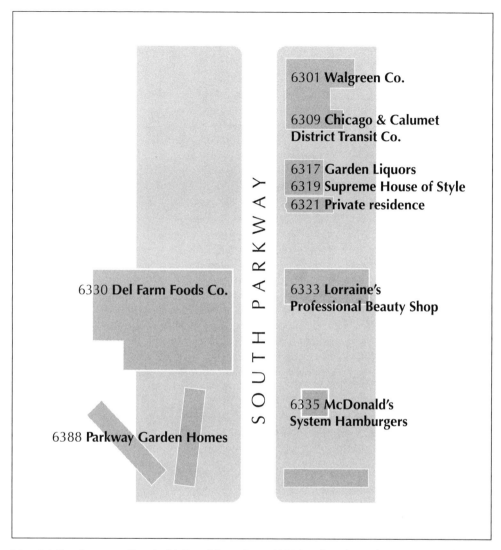

Map 6.4. Retail surrounding the McDonald's outlet at 6335 South Parkway (now Martin Luther King Drive), Chicago. Map by Dennis McClendon, CartoGraphics.

ing was part of community uplift as well as personal gain. Most White operators did not have the same motivations, and their inability to work within this social dynamic triggered serious backlash. Corporate assessments that a Black face at the counter would solve any and all problems gave short shrift to the urgent issues taking place around individual outlets and the nation as a whole. Fast food executives, like Whites across the political spectrum, had realized that "White administration of the black ghettos, at least in some instances, was no longer operating satisfactorily."[95] And yet they did not have a long-term solution that reflected real cognizance of what it meant to run fast food chains in a context of Black Power. The chains were ready to offload risk to Black operators, but they failed to realize that greater storms were brewing. They did not recognize that fast food would be at the forefront of Black activist struggle.

7

To Banish, Boycott, or Bash?

Moderates and Militants Clash in Cleveland

For African Americans challenging racial injustice, food was both sustenance and organizing tool. This was so in the well-known lunch counter sit-ins across the South, spaces that for White segregationists merited a virulently racial defense to restrict Black purchase on a fully American social life.[1] Ella Baker argued that the sit-ins "are concerned with something much bigger than a hamburger or even a giant-sized Coke . . . the Negro and White students, North and South, are seeking to rid America of the scourge of racial segregation and discrimination—not only at lunch counters, but in every aspect of life."[2] The burger itself was not the point. James Farmer, cofounder of CORE, warned that de facto segregation pushed Black people into a second-class citizenship where one was "able to eat a hamburger, but not to have a rewarding life."[3]

Both Baker and Farmer used hamburgers to refer to the literal product to be consumed at the lunch counter, but also as a symbol revelatory of American life writ large. Hamburgers came up again and again as Black people contested the country's durable racism. Muhammad Ali's telling of being spurned by a server in his hometown of Louisville while wearing his 1960 Olympic gold medal went as follows. Server: "We don't serve Negroes." Ali: "I don't eat them, either. Just give me a cup of coffee and a hamburger."[4] Across the country, food was a fulcrum around which racial inequities turned and were contested, whether in rural agriculture in the South or Black Panther urban meal programs.[5] In northern Black neighborhoods, moderate activists' work on grocery stores, addressing both food security and economic development, set the stage for militant contests around fast food and other restaurants. Where the former centered on better treatment in and access to food markets, the latter challenged White entrepreneurs' right to ownership (e.g., via fast food franchises) in Black communities in the first place. With fast food as the target, it's difficult to characterize the struggle as one that would address food security—the real prize was the possibility of economic and political spoils. At the end of the 1960s, CORE's national strategy turned ever more toward Black-owned business, making that the centerpiece of controlling Black destinies. Floyd McKissick began calling for White owners to relinquish ghetto businesses (as well as land and control of the education system) and transfer them to Black people individually or collectively. Some elected officials were skeptical of this approach; the Black mayor of Gary, Indiana, questioned whether, when he himself did not control the corporations, state agencies, and other actors in the city, simply making a pawn shop owner Black rather than White would make a difference.[6] In an explosive contest in Cleveland in 1969, Black activists answered in the affirmative, bringing a firestorm to McDonald's and producing an explosive upending of the racial status quo in franchising.

Black neighborhoods in the 1960s and 1970s saw dramatic losses of super-markets, and their shortage was compounded by subpar service.[7] The Southern Christian Leadership Conference fought for quality food and entrepreneurial access to retail markets controlled by Whites, particularly through its franchise program, Operation Breadbasket. It launched in 1966 in Chicago, led by Jesse Jackson, then a divinity student at the Chicago Theological Seminary. The program worked on several fronts to increase market access and employment for Black business-people.[8] Breadbasket also leveraged Black consumer power to create more opportunities through boycotts: "YOUR MINISTER SAYS: Don't buy Pepsi-Cola. PEPSI-COLA of Chicago keeps Negroes at the bottom in last hired, first fired jobs . . . We will stop drinking PEPSI-COLA, until Negroes can work in all jobs."[9] Breadbasket engaged in hard-fought negotiations with companies that often resisted making changes even after agreeing to sign covenants to support Black businesses.[10]

Breadbasket fought also for improved conditions for Black consumers. Shoppers faced difficulty meeting their basic grocery needs as poor-quality merchandise was rife in stores serving Black Chicagoans, particularly old and rotten meat, which organizers perceived as more acute following neighborhood racial transitions. In 1968, Jackson reported to other pastors in Chicago that Breadbasket had documented "bad meat, week old meat and rotten meat" on the city's South and West Sides.[11] City investigators arrested managers at the Big B Supermarket, which shared the block with Whoopee Burger at 3559 West Roosevelt Road, and the Wonder Food Supermarket at 1200 East 61st for shortchanging customers.[12] By 1974, when Jackson led his own organization, Operation PUSH, members were keeping a "vigilant watch" over food retailing in Black communities and boycotting businesses that endangered residents' health through such practices as selling rotten meat.[13]

Breadbasket's political and economic muscle had a significant impact on the growth of Black businesses, injecting thousands of jobs and millions of dollars into Black communities.[14] But the successes were not without some setbacks. Many small businesses closed and Breadbasket failed to adequately assist entrepreneurs with business fundamentals.[15] Despite its broad reach, the one domain Breadbasket did not seem to target was fast food. This may reflect the fact that Breadbasket served individuals who were already business owners, or that the more immediate needs of establishing food security, getting Black folks jobs, and ensuring the survival of existing Black businesses eclipsed plans for buying franchises. Still, those with ties to Breadbasket went on to become key players in fast food. For example, at the age of thirty-six, Breadbasket treasurer Cirilo McSween was a high-profile agent with New York Life Insurance Company and ran his own Chicago office in the Lake Meadows complex.[16] His company funded the multibuilding high-rise housing and business complex when Michael Reese Hospital and the Illinois Institute of Technology decided that the grim views of Black tenements were off-putting for patients and university members. Several acres of homes in good repair were razed in order to give Lake Meadows tenants an unobstructed view of Lake Michigan, and many displaced residents ended up in the State Street corridor of public housing.[17] McSween was one of the beneficiaries of the changes that swept the South Side, and he would become one of McDonald's top franchisees. When Black franchising entered the 1980s, he helped direct (and benefited from) Jesse Jackson's covenants with fast food companies. McSween's participation on both sides of the coin characterized most of the Black leaders engaged in the fast food industry.

Though Breadbasket did not challenge fast food, Black activists across the country did. A complex mix of issues were at stake. Like grocery stores, fast food's absence mattered because it left African Americans out of a consumer trend. In its presence, it buttressed racial hierarchies in White-only ownership. The more moderate tactics Breadbasket employed positioned it as a foil—an example of the stance more strident activists would eschew. In a context where, nationally, Black Power activists were calling for White to Black business transfers, the *Chicago Defender* had lauded Operation Breadbasket's approach as much as its outcome. Breadbasket used "a positive, peaceful approach to the economic and social ills of the Negro people," a moderate strategy that would be more effective than "furious agitations that stir hostility and increase frustrations."[18]

Activists elsewhere challenged White-owned restaurants with precisely the furious agitations the *Defender* viewed with caution, pushing the pace with increasingly aggressive methods. In Pittsburgh, Black "militants" pressured the owner of the Jolly Red Weiner to sell his twenty-four-hour hamburger restaurant in the pre-dominantly Black neighborhood of Homewood to his Black manager, Larry Gains.[19] In Seattle, more Black "militants" tangled with a White restaurateur, this time in a White neighborhood. The Beanery, a "landmark eatery" that for fifty years had been serving high school students, was, according to industry media, "forced to close be-cause, one of its co-owners stated, Black Panther Party (A Negro extremist group) members and black students have boycotted the restaurant, picketed it and intimi-dated its white customers." Black students complained of poor food and unsanitary conditions (the Board of Health failed to corroborate these complaints) and, remi-niscent of Buggin' Out's charge in the film *Do the Right Thing*, demanded that store owners buy and put up pictures of Black leaders. Students had "suggested" that the owner, Forrest Burke, should donate the restaurant to a new Black owner; he closed it and listed it for sale instead. Months later, the restaurant did change hands. A Black woman named Gladys Robertson came to the venture with fourteen years of food service experience as a caterer and a $5,000 loan from the Small Business Administration. The SBA was skittish about getting involved in a "racial dispute" but ultimately thought it better than leaving the restaurant fallow, particularly given that no White people wanted to buy it. Robertson enjoyed brisk business after she took the helm.[20]

It was clear that Black activists had taken it upon themselves to challenge the restricted entrée to fast food. In May 1969, months after Herman Petty obtained his franchise, a "group of militants" in Houston demanded ownership of a new Burger King unit that opened within the Black community. Protests led by Pluria Marshall of Black Concerned Citizens met an implacable Burger King, whose local represen-tatives had been dismissive, reminding Marshall and colleagues that it was "a free world" and that they might start their own business rather than bothering the cor-poration. This triggered pickets that elicited a heavy police response, and within ten days the transfer took place. This was the conflict that served as a wake-up call for Burger King president James McLamore, prompting him to say that "the blacks" did not appreciate outlets that operated under White ownership. After a Black owner was installed, McLamore argued that companies would need "to exercise more social responsibility" and Black franchisees like Willie Taylor entered the industry in Miami, Atlanta, and Detroit.[21]

McDonald's had not seen Black ownership as "social responsibility" so much as racial inoculation, replacing some White franchisees in settings where they were perceived as too visible and too risky to operations. Otherwise, the company was content to continue as it had been. It certainly did not see Black franchising from the lens that Black Power viewed businesses—as social property.[22] Therefore, when

Cleveland exploded in rebellion, the fast food chain was ill prepared for what was coming next.

Cleveland's Powder Keg

Civil disturbances tore through Cleveland on at least five different occurrences between 1964 and 1971, though three were relatively minor. That which devastated the Hough community on the city's East Side in mid-July 1966 was the most severe, with dozens of injuries, several fatalities, and extensive looting and arson.[23] While civil disturbances in cities such as Newark, D.C., and Watts have national prominence, those in Cleveland are less well-known but ended up setting the groundwork for national discourse about inclusion in fast food franchising.

Hough had been an affluent White neighborhood, built with 90 percent of its nearly eight thousand structures as residential, mostly single-family houses. But like many postwar urban communities, it was transformed into a working-class and poor Black neighborhood. The intensity of segregation in the city meant that more than 165,000 southern migrants as well as tens of thousands who were victims of the city's badly implemented urban renewal programs were crammed into East Side neighborhoods like Hough. They crowded into subdivided single-family homes, squalid but expensive apartments, and previously unused basements and attics. Wherever these Black residents went, White residents were determined to avoid them.[24]

Commercial and municipal services devolved into nonexistence as the Black population increased. Garbage lay strewn across streets and sidewalks and rats frolicked in backyard heaps. Merchants charged exploitative prices for food and other goods and services, and were just as negligent as landlords, failing to clean, update, or maintain their stores. The community contended with an anemic retail climate on commercial thoroughfares like Hough and Euclid Avenues, where 75 percent of the businesses were small and often "marginal operators." Several of these were taverns and pool halls that were sites of crime and disorder. Taken together, residential, commercial, and public spaces were substandard at best and appalling at worst. The conditions attracted national attention, and local media described the community as a "powder keg" set to ignite as Watts had the year prior.[25]

The prediction held in July 1966, when the community erupted after a Black patron at the Seventy-Niners' Cafe (79th Street and Hough Avenue) was refused a drink of water by the bar's White owners, who also posted a sign reading "No water for Niggers."[26] Dozens were injured in the unrest, with hundreds of incidents of arson, four persons killed, and extensively damaged businesses. The mayor called in National Guard troops, one of whom was quoted in the papers as stating "This is the Hough Insurrection and the animals are restless. Every type of deviate [sic] in the world can be found right here."[27] Two years later, in the adjacent Glenville community, another crisis flared when a city employee attempted to tow away an abandoned car and was shot. An intense shootout between police and residents described as Black Nationalists followed. Mayor Carl Stokes—who, following the Hough rebellion, had been elected the first Black mayor of a major U.S. city in November 1967—suffered politically. By this time his record of social programs and policies to redress inequality and resource deficits was little remembered. He was reelected in 1969, but many of his major plans for revitalizing Cleveland were scuttled and he was succeeded by Ralph Perk, a White "law-and-order candidate" whose administration lasted into the late 1970s.[28]

Damage from the civil disorders centered on Hough Avenue, affecting businesses for at least a dozen blocks, but some looting and arson extended to the neighboring communities of Kinsman and Glenville.[29] Groceries, drugstores, dry cleaners, liquor stores, and prepared food establishments were among those hit, such as Allen Drug, Union Center Supermarket, Al's Cut Rate Liquor Store, and the Starlite Delicatessen. Whether restaurants were affected is unclear, but major chains were few and far between. Hamburger spots such as Rhoton's Hamburgers and R&H Burgers imitated the burger chateaux in White space far from the East Side. But in Hough, restaurants tended to be small and somewhat rickety, such as Lovin's Grill and Kubby's Steakburger, which served burgers, hot dogs, barbecue, and the like.[30] Larger restaurants that had been in Hough left as the neighborhood changed. For example, Boukair's Beautiful Soda Grill served patrons at 7224 Hough Avenue until the late 1950s, when it moved downtown. The restaurant "served food and refreshments . . . in an atmosphere of beauty and color . . . open twenty-four hours a day for your convenience."[31] As a result, the only major fast food players on the East Side appear to be Burger Chef, at 8114 Euclid Avenue; and McDonald's, which held stores at 9101 Kinsman Road in Kinsman, 105th Street and St. Clair Avenue in Glenville, 142nd Street and Kinsman Road in Mount Pleasant, and 8320 Euclid Avenue in Hough.

In a weak retail climate, the Hough community was particularly sensitized to a national brand name like McDonald's operating in a paradigm of resource extraction. As with grocery stores, there was "resentment of white entrepreneurs who lived outside of black neighborhoods but did business within them. . . . African Americans' attempts to organize around the point of consumption illuminate the ways in which food stores became arenas for racial tensions and social change."[32]

Figure 7.1. Ohio National Guard protects the Starlite Delicatessen at 7224 Hough Avenue. Photograph by Jerry Horton, July 20, 1966. Cleveland Press Collection, Michael Schwartz Library at Cleveland State University.

White-owned fast food stuck out like a sore thumb and provoked a high-profile 1969 McDonald's boycott that shook the fast food and restaurant industry to its core.

The Cleveland McDonald's Boycott

One year after the unrest in Hough, the Cleveland Subcommittee of the Ohio State Advisory Committee to the United States Commission on Civil Rights issued a report asserting that little had changed in the area: "Now almost a year after the riot, the Hough area still bears the scars of battle. Store fronts are boarded up. Unoccupied houses have been vandalized. Stench rises from the debris-filled basements of burned-out buildings." Food security remained a problem, as poor Black households relied on merchants selling low-quality food at high prices.[33] The Democratic mayor Ralph Locher shrugged. A source within Locher's administration stated that in his reelection bid, he had "written off the Negro vote and intends to try to maintain the status quo." Martin Luther King Jr. had visited the city in May of that year and offered a nonviolent action program for the Hough community, but Locher refused to see him, stating that he would not meet with "an extremist."[34] The city administration was about to learn how to distinguish between moderate and militant protest action.

The scars of the Hough rebellion, the lack of progress, and a recalcitrant local government created a climate in which patience had run thin among Black Clevelanders. Operation Black Unity (OBU) was a Black Nationalist umbrella organization constituted in June 1969 in Cleveland comprising more than twenty local community groups. Organizations included the Hough Area Development Corporation, the local chapters of the NAACP and CORE, the House of Israel (led by a man known as Rabbi David Hill), and others. Before OBU's official assemblage, it was involved in racial disputes around the city such as an action to demand more Black firefighters in the Cleveland Fire Department and a rally to combat racial violence against Black high school students.[35] One month after OBU was born, it initiated a boycott against McDonald's, the kind of "furious agitation" against which the *Chicago Defender* cautioned.

In March 1969, the local SCLC—specifically Operation Breadbasket—reportedly asked McDonald's to sell its East Side franchises to Black operators.[36] It was also rumored that OBU went further than a request for sale, and in fact demanded that stores be granted outright, because McDonald's had been accruing wealth without reinvesting it in the community. Whereas Chicago's chapter prioritized other businesses, Cleveland's Operation Breadbasket zeroed in on fast food in its struggle for social justice. What prompted this action? The Black Panthers wanted to "build a well-fed well-cared for, healthy Black community."[37] Whether the same can be said of OBU's efforts is doubtful. Fast food's health risks were not well-known at that time, but it is unlikely anyone thought it particularly healthful or representative of real food security. Rather, the enticement was the money, specifically the possibility of owning a money-making entity that was heretofore controlled by White people outside of the community. Additionally, fast food held the allure of a food source far removed from the toil of agriculture. OBU members, their friends, or their family may have grown up in intimate attachment to the land, among those farmers who fled the South for the Midwest under cover of darkness and threat of death. And if so, they might have, as a respondent named Cliff in D.C.'s Deanwood opined, "started looking at some of the things like farming and they looked at that as associated with that feeling of 'Oh, we're not slaves.'" Pigs and a vegetable garden might have been a political weapon, but the modernity of the hamburger drive-in was seen as a better one.

McDonald's was a logical target. Apart from being a market leader, all the McDonald's stores in Cleveland's Black neighborhoods were highly profitable. The four outlets grossed more than $2 million per year, and 8230 Euclid Avenue had the second-largest volume in the nation. Bob Beavers, an intermediary in the Philadelphia protest and previously charged with identifying Black store managers, now worked in the corporate licensing office and was tasked with bringing on Black franchisees. He expressed that "the local management team just didn't get it and they were very insulting to customers."[38] What that meant exactly in terms of customer service was unclear, but there was no doubt that community residents bristled at enriching White operators.

McDonald's response to the mobilization was to refuse "the concept of reparations."[39] Working with Rabbi Hill, a minister named Ernest Hilliard applied to purchase a new McDonald's franchise to be located in the Black community. After he completed the training course, McDonald's found him unsuitable for ownership because he lacked the requisite capital. Hilliard pressed his case and was supported by Hill, who intimidated McDonald's executives by employing bodyguards, "shouting executives into silence," and other brash maneuvers. By April, prospects appeared slim. Hilliard and Hill learned that McDonald's was considering someone else to take up the first Black-owned McDonald's, at an existing, lucrative location.

Things took a turn for the worse in OBU's action when Hilliard was shot and killed in his suburban driveway. His dying words were his report that a White man shot him. Many believed it was the result of his negotiations with McDonald's because he had received several threats beforehand. Little progress was made on the investigation of his murder. The shock of the shooting and McDonald's frustration

Figure 7.2. *Cleveland Press* carriers eat at McDonald's at 5616 Memphis. Photograph by Bill Nehez, October 22, 1965. Cleveland Press Collection, Michael Schwartz Library at Cleveland State University.

with a bellicose Hill evaporated any further consideration for the proposed franchise. At this point, Hill turned to OBU for assistance and the group took action, contacting Edward A. Bood, McDonald's vice president for franchising, to demand a July meeting or else face a boycott. Bood refused. In a letter to OBU, he charged that Hill's tone and "unfamiliarity with sound business practices" precluded a productive meeting, and that he would not be subjected to threats, coercion, or violence. He characterized OBU member organizations' requests for donations to fund OBU's community programming as extortion, and he argued that McDonald's lack of Black franchisees was merely a reflection of the lack of business acumen in the Black community.[40] *Nation's Restaurant News* reported that McDonald's had eight Black-owned units in Chicago, Kansas City, and Los Angeles, though the publication neglected to mention that they were operating under zebra contracts as progressive fronts for White-dominated structures.

Despite the company's aversion to OBU's requests for additional funding, McDonald's had a reputation for valuing community engagement. A book about franchising cautioned, "If you're not a joiner, think twice about applying for a McDonald's franchise. It's McDonald's policy for its dealers to support local causes and participate in community activities."[41] Indeed, McDonald's was actively emphasizing outreach to its franchises and to the public with its slogan "Your kind of place." Corporate also extolled the virtues of franchisee involvement in their local communities.[42] One of Cleveland's very own McDonald's operators donated funds to support employees. In the summer of 1968 Bob Rhea, a franchisee who would go on to become head of McDonald's in Britain, paid for the textbooks of university students who had worked at his outlet for at least three months.[43] But to McDonald's corporate office, OBU's requests for donations seemed of a different character.

And so, on July 10, 1969, OBU launched a boycott and demonstration in front of McDonald's East Side outlets. *Nation's Restaurant News* called the situation a "black power protest" that had devolved into "one of the most terrifying entanglements ever to involve franchisors and their franchisees."[44] Exactly what was terrifying about people walking with picket signs the industry organ did not say. Perhaps, in linking the protest to Black Power, the periodical foresaw a contingent of black-clad, beret-sporting, rifle-toting Black men—the aesthetic that gave visual form to the Black Panthers' revolutionary rhetoric.[45] From the moment Stokely Carmichael called for Black Power, national media heard a proclamation of "reverse racism" that augured a frightening militancy that would endanger White people.[46]

If the protest was terrifying, it would be no more so than for the nineteen-year-old picketer who on July 12, 1969, was injured after Orvil Bensen, owner of two of the McDonald's, struck him with his car. The next day, one of the four managers received threatening phone calls.[47] By the end of the week, the restaurants were forced to close temporarily and negotiations between OBU and McDonald's began. But when OBU appointed Hill chair of the proceedings, McDonald's balked and refused to continue. Again OBU reinstated the picket line, and the battle was waged not only on the street but also in the press. On July 26, the *Cleveland Call and Post*, the local Black newspaper, reported verbatim text from letters by the parties involved. The Cleveland NAACP voiced their support for OBU and rebuked efforts "to divide the Negro community and those friends who support the Negro's participation in the mainstream of the American economy." CORE also released a statement. Charles Cook, project director and chair of CORE's Midwest Region, stated that McDonald's "must understand the rules of the new ball game. In this game whites no longer choose the blacks they prefer to negotiate with, nor dictate terms based upon racist attitudes." McDonald's held that Hill had tried to usurp control of the negotiations and when McDonald's insisted on working with all the member organizations of OBU, Hill terminated the negotiation and walked out with the rest of OBU.[48]

Nation's Restaurant News took a great deal of interest in the story, following up the initial report on August 4 with extended coverage for months afterward. On August 18, the newspaper's editors penned a long, above-the-fold article in which they outlined the most recent plot twists. Describing the boycott as an "anti-white campaign," they reported that McDonald's strategy had been to wait patiently for a rupture in the activist coalition, as a bridge to negotiating solely with the more conservative NAACP and Urban League. The paper reported that "the break McDonald's was seeking *might* have come this past fortnight. At least McDonald's thinks so."[49]

The break came in the form of a prominent local Black physician and NACCP and Urban League member, Dr. Kenneth Clement.[50] Clement reportedly declared that Hill was unqualified to lead the alliance and that the major civil rights organizations ought to be taking a more appropriate leadership role rather than colluding with an "unholy alliance." McDonald's perceived this as an opening to seek police protection from the mayor and reopen the four closed stores. Furthermore, the company launched a public relations campaign designed to push back the coalition's aims and draw customers in. The risk was that Dr. Clement being the only McDonald's advocate within the Black community would do little in the way of creating allies for the corporation. Dr. Clement called the OBU effort a "plain shakedown" and argued that though McDonald's shortsightedness was their own fault, many of OBU's demands were "nothing but blatant extortion." In a litany of denunciations,

Clement decried the NAACP and Urban League's association with Rabbi Hill: the organization was "bankrupt of courage," "bereft of reason" in their "inconceivable and unconscionable" dealings with an "uncontrite" man. Yet Clement seemed to have little to offer in the way of concrete suggestions. He made a vague assessment of the appropriate way to push for economic gains: "I obviously favor governmental subsidies and subsidies from private groups who evaluate the likelihood of success by a standard that can be judged."[51] Hill was unequivocal in his disdain for Clement's statement: "McDonald's has tried to buy every good nigger they can find, but they won't get anywhere that way."[52]

McDonald's found itself isolated when other restaurants that had been approached with similar demands eventually cooperated. Commentators thought a Burger Chef outlet would be targeted for protests next, but Hill claimed that he was not interested and instead would simply boycott the store until it went out of business. Local franchise operators believed that Hill's plan was to decimate the store's consumer traffic until the market value of the unit had collapsed, allowing Black owners to buy it and change it to a "Negro-named franchise" such as Willie Mays's or James Brown's.[53] In the end, two Burger Chef franchisees were convinced to sell, even as they enjoyed greater sales volume due to the closure of the boycotted McDonald's outlets. Wilbert Metz, one of the franchisees, did not expect to receive market value in the sale, and bitterly concluded, "I wouldn't operate a restaurant in a Negro neighborhood again if you gave me one free."

Campaigns were also launched against a Minnie Pearl's fried chicken restaurant, but these were staved off when the manager, an unnamed Black man, convinced "the militants" that he was the store owner. Hoping the true owner would come to his aid, this manager reported that the militants created disturbances and took food without paying for it. But the restaurant's corporate offices denied any knowledge of the situation and spokesperson Tom Seigenthaler in Memphis claimed, "Business is not appreciably down and Minnie Pearl is at peace with the blacks." Journalists reported that insider knowledge had it otherwise—sales at what was otherwise one of the strongest outlets in the company were down 40 percent. Reports also circulated that militants demanded the removal of Minnie Pearl from store edifices and the installation of Mahalia Jackson's signs.[54] After some internal dissension at the company, Minnie Pearl's agreed. Harold Jones, a Black man who was vice president at Mahalia Jackson's, also stated that he was willing to negotiate about possible royalties returns, wherein a portion of the unit's franchise royalties would go into a community trust, rather than to corporate.[55]

That some restaurateurs were amenable to the coalition's demands was unacceptable to Dr. Clement. He foretold that any financial support directed to Hill would be used to buy guns: "The white people will finance Hill's future terrorizing of themselves. If he pulls this deal off, every ex-con who knows Hill will be rushing to Cleveland for a piece of the action."[56] It is unclear but unlikely whether Clement's charges had any merit. The organization's Black Power agenda alone seemed to be enough to indicate a propensity to violence. Despite the hurling of recriminations, by mid-August picketing had been suspended while negotiations were hashed out.

Anticipating a settlement, McDonald's ordered the four restaurants to open for business; and took out full-page advertisements in Cleveland newspapers meant to portray the company as advocates for Black empowerment, downplaying the extent of the conflict and distancing corporate from the local controversy. McDonald's claimed in this advertising that it was "constantly seeking capable black licensees for its new restaurants" and was trying to "encourage the sale of existing McDonald's to black owners." OBU, feeling betrayed, resumed picketing, but its lawyers and the White franchise owners soon reached an agreement. Among the terms were the following: McDonald's was to make a $10,000 contribution to OBU "for the benefit and welfare of the black community"; McDonald's would make financial information available about the units so that fair market value could be assessed in their purchase; and OBU would be responsible for encouraging the Black community to resume patronage and for quashing the pickets as long as the terms of the agreement were maintained. McDonald's corporate office rejected the agreement over the $10,000 donation, which it could not "condone."[57]

Over the next several months, the contest continued to escalate. McDonald's and the franchisees squabbled publicly over who was responsible for the deal falling through. McDonald's argued that an agreement had not been reached because the franchisees backed out; they were independent businessmen, after all, and McDonald's could not coerce them to do anything. The franchisees argued that quite to the contrary, they were ready and willing to agree to the terms, including the donation, but "McDonald's pulled the rug from under us. They repudiated our agreement."[58] According to *Nation's Restaurant News,* the corporation's aim to create dissention within the coalition had failed, and had instead come home to roost within its own ranks. Meanwhile, OBU sought to take the campaign to a national stage. Roy Wilkins and Whitney Young, of the NAACP and Urban League, respectively, voiced disapproval. Roy Innis, previously director of CORE's Harlem chapter and national director since 1968, offered the organization's support. Innis "was pleased to note that in all the demands to McDonald's there was not one demand for a job. 'The demand,' he said with glee, 'is to take over the whole damned instruments.'"[59]

In mid-September 1969 an agreement was still unsigned, and proposals and counterproposals from both sides fell as water upon brick. OBU showed no signs of backing down, but McDonald's lawyer said his client would not negotiate "with what amounts to a gun at [our] head."[60] McDonald's castigated Black leaders and organizations it had perceived as moderate and thought likely to disavow Hill. An unnamed McDonald's spokesperson asserted that moderate groups had in fact "given Hill legitimacy. They are responsible for and have participated in his demand for money. They are damn reprehensible." The company doubled down on its "strategy of fragmenting the black community" though it had yet to produce results: "Reliable sources indicated the company will continue its efforts to cause a dispute among the blacks."[61]

Toward the end of September 1969, McDonald's learned that Rabbi Hill was likely to step down as chair of the negotiating committee, at the request of others within the coalition. For McDonald's, this foretold disunity among Operation Black Unity and in turn the demise of the boycott. McDonald's had agreed to four of the five demands, and progress was being made on the fifth. But when Hill stepped down, McDonald's quit the negotiations, thinking the matter moot.[62] In response, OBU, including Hill's House of Israel organization, planned to intensify the protest.

Mayor Stokes had intervened earlier in the dispute, and he did so again. Now it appeared an agreement would be reached for the franchises to be sold to Black owners.[63] Pressured by both sides, and with a primary election looming in five days, Stokes allocated a police officer at each location and entered the negotiations, helping OBU to outline its demands. These were as follows: McDonald's was to approve the sale of the four restaurants to Black owners, whether individual or institutional; all future outlets built in the Black community must be sold to Black owners; franchise royalties that owners would normally send to McDonald's corporate offices would instead be paid to OBU; McDonald's was to grant irrevocable franchise rights to purchasers; and OBU had the right to approve franchise buyers for Black ownership of the four outlets. McDonald's did not accept all these terms and submitted a counterproposal, which OBU rejected; the boycott continued. The picketing paralyzed sales at all of the restaurants and compromised the employment of over 150 Black employees, who largely supported the protest.

Just before an agreement was reached in the standoff, the Tenth Annual Conference of Multi-Unit Food Service Operators (MUFSO) welcomed more than three hundred attendees to Chicago. *Nation's Restaurant News* organized a seminar at the meeting, "Black Capitalism and the Restaurant Business," which was to include a McDonald's representative, someone from the Department of Commerce's Office of Minority Business Enterprise, and an individual from the Urban League. *Nation's Restaurant News* corresponded with the Urban League to query whether the organization knew anyone who could speak to a more "militant view," though not quite "burn the house down" in severity; in other words, someone who would be considered merely an "activist" by the White press.[64] Press releases about the event named the activist as Anthony Rodney Stadeker. It was here that Stadeker called his community a concentration camp. The *Nation's Restaurant News* representative, editor Michael Whiteman, wanted someone who would take Rabbi Hill's side, in counterpoint to that of McDonald's, represented by Edward Bood. Ashby Smith, director of economic development and employment at the Urban League, spoke at the event and called for full employment of Black people in the restaurant industry, including more Black restaurant owners.[65]

Bood no-showed, backing out of the conference and the *Nation's Restaurant News* invitation at the last minute. His views were therefore not directly represented in the paper's conference review. Using pointed language to characterize and perhaps exaggerate Smith's statements (e.g., calling White people "Whitey"), the paper gave a stark view of the proceedings. It described conference attendees as having come to the meeting curious in a distant way about McDonald's in Cleveland but leaving "with their collective guts churning—acutely aware, probably for the first time, that Negro demands for ownership of McD's ghetto franchises in Cleveland could also dramatically crumple their own P&Ls. And without any warning."[66]

The reporting suggested that few in the industry took racial concerns seriously, believing them to be McDonald's problem alone, unlike the perspicacious writers at *Nation's Restaurant News*. Yet the analysis tokenized the two Black spokespeople, and even used racial epithets to refer to them. Ashby Smith was portrayed as nonthreatening to an audience populated by men described as thinking "Yessir. Here's a nigger we can deal with." Stadeker (spelled Stadecker here), on the other hand, was depicted as barely contained fury. Simply put, "he wanted a fight."[67] This was a mendacious portrayal given that the outlet specifically sought out a "militant" from the Urban League to be a firebrand at the meeting. Stadeker played that role, and the periodical gave deadpan reporting on the incident as if it had merely bore witness to the inherent and problematic aggression of oppositional Black men. The paper summarized the discussion by querying why Stadeker "blew it" and what he might have had to gain from enraging the audience. For example, the climate devolved entirely after Stadeker used profanity for which he refused to apologize and he and a White attendee threatened to "settle it outside."[68]

In the end, formidable opposition from employees, customer, and community activists forced McDonald's to come to terms with the action.[69] In 1970, the boycott ended and the franchise ownership transferred hands to the Hough Area Development Corporation. *Nation's Restaurant News* reviewed what was at stake. McDonald's was cast as a rather hapless victim, unprepared for the coming carnage

Figure 7.3. Mayor Dennis Kucinich eats at McDonald's at East 105th Street and St. Clair Avenue. Photograph by Joseph E. Cole, November 5, 1979. Cleveland Press Collection, Michael Schwartz Library at Cleveland State University.

and, once confronted with it, handicapped by pursuing rational negotiations that relied on merit and sound financial principles—concepts lost on power-hungry and ignorant militants. According to the newspaper, the confrontation began when "one day, a militant black man walked in to McDonald's and said he wanted that store and five others."[70] Though caught off guard, McDonald's was amenable to working with responsible and qualified Black men; alas, the paper reported, such an approach was lost on these ill-tempered combatants.

McDonald's would not speak on the record afterward, but alleged that its executives were threatened and the whole process was essentially a shakedown.[71] Orvil Bensen contended that he was unaware of the proposal for McDonald's to contribute to a ghetto fund, and stated, "I wouldn't have had anything to sell if I had paid off. I'd have been selling a business that was making illegal-type payoffs to a Mafia-like organization." He also called the militants "stupid." He had bought the unit little more than a year before the confrontation began, sold by another White franchisee who fled the neighborhood's new racial demographics. Bensen stayed and had been grossing $500,000 per year. Now that he was selling, he "wouldn't take another ghetto unit at any price."[72]

Cleveland's Aftermath

The coverage in *Nation's Restaurant News* used language commensurate with war reporting. Headlines spoke of a "split Black front" and a "pledge to finish McDonald's" and warned that "Blacks cry war" and "clashes feared in battle." The paper was covering a military offensive waged by Black people against the all-American enterprise of McDonald's—and thus America itself. Despite the extensive reporting, the readership did not write in to comment. There were no letters to the editor during or after the disturbance, either from corporate brass or small business owners. It was an interesting silence when top executives and individuals from federal agencies wrote in regularly to discuss or contest a variety of issues, including those related to race and politics. Between August and November 1969, Jeff Tieger, director of advertising & public relations at Neba International Inc.; Fredrich H. Thomforde, vice president of Howard Johnson; Frank P. Thomas, former president of Burger Chef Systems Inc.; and African Americans Brady Keys, president of All-Pro Chicken, and Art McZier of the Small Business Administration, all wrote in to comment on or dispute the paper's reporting.[73] On Cleveland, however, they remained silent. Something about this contest was too hot to touch.

Even beneficiaries of the boycotts distanced themselves from the events. In 1976, looking back at the turmoil, some African American owners of McDonald's franchises gave full-throated support to the struggle that resulted in their becoming operators, but others were reticent to link themselves fully. Ceasar Burks, owner of two franchises, made it a point to distinguish himself from those who had participated in the boycotts: "When they had the boycott I wasn't involved, but as far as I'm concerned recognition should go to the efforts of Hill and Operation Black Unity." Narlie Roberts, owner of four outlets, would not speak at all: "I have mixed emotions, I'd just rather not comment."[74]

Operators like Roberts came in because Cleveland induced a special urgency in facilitating access. The frictions that coalesced around White-owned fast food outlets in Black communities revealed that the racial status quo could no longer hold. If they could not win full ownership, residents insisted on stewardship of the institutions in their communities, and rejected the idea that they could be shut out of wealth in their own neighborhoods, particularly when their consumer dollars generated that wealth in the first place. As a result, fast food corporations finally sat up and took notice of Black consumers—if indignantly and reluctantly.

For corporate executives and industry analysts, the troubles at McDonald's portended "black capitalism disputes" across the board. Hackles were raised when a "sympathy boycott" was staged by fifteen youths in Dayton, Ohio.[75] Demonstrating in front of a McDonald's restaurant, they admittedly had no beef with the outlet, but meant to show support for the Cleveland protestors. Also in Dayton, a group of Black organizations including Black Panthers and the Urban League initiated a boycott against four Church's Fried Chicken units. Church's franchising differed from McDonald's. It sold licenses only for geographic regions, not individual stores. However, after four years of ownership, managers were eligible to apply for individual restaurants using funds derived from the company's profit-sharing plan. Church's agreed to meet with the Black activists to discuss modifying the franchising policy by shortening the wait time to one year of ownership. The organizers demanded that Church's deliver other resources to serve the community as a whole. In response, the chain offered to donate food and furniture to local programs and parks. As a result of the chain's responsive cooperation, the boycott was halted.[76]

On the whole, industry analysis warned that Ohio was the harbinger of "a major storm yet to come," and the Cleveland situation "ought to scare the daylights out of any white restaurateur—whether he has a heavy black trade or not." White restaurant owners who dared to "tap the ghetto market" faced the risk of reprisals from militant Black residents who would demand ownership of neighborhood businesses. Hinting at the racial turnover that gripped urban cores, industry media asserted that "the way neighborhoods change these days, lots of white restaurateurs who think they're safe today could find themselves picketed into oblivion tomorrow."

Fast food corporations seemed as worried by the public shaming of picketing as they were of units being destroyed in uprisings. Indeed, the Cleveland boycott was described from the first as "terrifying." As a result, corporate boardrooms had to weigh the reality that "the Negro market is lucrative for low-priced food service" against the risk of militant protests. Black franchisees could act as a bulwark against the threat of unpredictable Black neighborhoods, but one narrative claimed that Black entrepreneurs with venture capital were actually uninterested in the "low status" restaurant industry.[77]

Clearly, boycotts could only happen when externally owned operations were situated in Black space. In the 1930s, boycotts were effective against food retailers who ran businesses in Black neighborhoods, but by the 1960s, this became challenging because national chains were absent.[78] Now, as previously White neighborhoods turned Black, and fast food was left behind, boycotts again became an option that hadn't existed before. Perhaps not recognizing the national urgency that undergirded Cleveland, industry media wondered whether McDonald's had been vulnerable to the Cleveland protests primarily because of its stature in the industry, or because it was tone-deaf to a new racial landscape in the restaurant business. Observers puzzled over the Cleveland disputes as indicative of broader racial strife with which restaurateurs would have to contend, and speculated that Black "agitators" would inevitably demand access to capital held by Whites regardless of whether businesses were located in the ghetto. The editors of *Nation's Restaurant News* sounded an alarm that "restaurant men doing business in fringe or mixed neighborhoods are uncomfortably vulnerable. And we wouldn't at all be surprised some day soon to hear of 'reprisals' against whites taking the form of picketing restaurants in *all-white* areas." While White owners were justifiably concerned about protecting the long-term investments they had made in their businesses, went the analysis, such considerations were meaningless to Black militants narrowly focused on accumulating profit.[79] If residents of America's apparently lawless, hate-filled ghettos weren't burning down your store, they were extorting you for the outlet and reparations.

News reports framed conflicts between White restaurateurs and Black residents as bewildering and threatening to industry actors, and White-owned business owners as resentful and anxious about these contests. When a Famous Recipe Fried Chicken restaurant in St. Louis was leveled after an explosion, the incident was attributed to a dispute with "black militants" over sponsorship of an athletic team, though Black activists denied involvement. Regardless of whether the allegations were true, the short newspaper account provided little conclusive evidence one way or another and left it to readers to decide—and readers were primed to interpret these news reports as evidence of the inherent danger posed by Black activists.

In the final analysis, for the mainstream industry media, the question was whether Black demands were in fact a call for equitable sharing of current profits, or a "demand for *reparations*—payments for what blacks see as past injustices by white businessmen." Here again pundits called OBU's action an attempt to obtain reparations. There is no evidence that activists were using the language of reparations to describe inclusive economic initiatives, nor were they asking for cash payments to redress unjust historical extraction of wealth. Indeed, McDonald's used the term itself, stating that it refused such demands. In deploying that word, the corporation inadvertently suggested that in fact the company's profits were ill-gotten. *Nation's Restaurant News* held that demands for reparations were coming, which would mean a new factor in figuring inner-city restaurants' profit and loss.[80]

On the other hand, for some, the ghetto now looked like an opportunity ripe for the taking. If Cleveland were sure to scare off operators who would reject potential market opportunities in Black neighborhoods, others would learn from the incident and capitalize on the ghetto's largely unclaimed profit potential.[81]

The McDonald's boycott brought seismic change to fast food, forcing the industry to begin thinking about African Americans as operators. The industry wrestled with the idea that franchise licenses would have to go to Black operators it deemed eminently unqualified. The view that Black people were not only indecent but undeserving of fast food emerged at the MUFSO conference. *Nation's Restaurant News* contended that conferencegoers were reticent to pose the questions that should have been asked of Stadeker. Namely, "What right have you to demand ownership of ghetto restaurants to which you have no financial or moral claim?" *Nation's Restaurant News* saw Stadeker as far from militant—indeed, a "Casper Milquetoast," to use his own words—compared to the "fuzzy-haired guys in the dashikis" that executives might face elsewhere. Stadeker, who sported a close-cropped haircut with a receding hairline and a conservative suit, did not conform (at least in appearance) to the notion of the riotous and angry Black people that had led the Cleveland campaign.

A few months after the event, Smith and Stadeker wrote letters to the editor taking issue with the paper's coverage of the event. Stadeker argued that his motives had been misconstrued. He meant "to awaken the entire audience" to the fact that Black communities would not countenance businesses that exploited them by failing to provide equitable economic opportunities and quality service at a fair price. He shrugged at his portrayal as "the *angry* black man"; for Stadeker, anger was a necessary part of instigating change. Moreover, he relayed that he came out of the meeting with productive contacts, some of whom indicated that they were planning ventures in the ghetto rather than shying away. Smith objected more strongly to the coverage. He argued that the article had failed to recount the solutions he offered, such as finding franchisees from among existing personnel; patronizing minority businesses; and retaining community-based consultants. Furthermore, Smith believed "there was a definite attitude problem at the meeting that did not come out in the report. Not so much that every mind was made up prior to the meeting, but more that most people just hadn't thought about minority groups at all."[82]

If *Nation's Restaurant News* had not previously thought much about fast food in relation to African Americans, it did now, and the view was not positive. It held that angry and "insultingly intransigent" Stadekers of the ghetto were the gatekeepers of commercial expansion into Black space. The alternative was for the industry to say "the hell with it and turn its collective back on the ghetto, the inner city and the problem of the Negro." McDonald's argued that the company's existing program to develop minority franchisees was sure to be affected by the disturbance: "[It] will have a great deal of bearing on where the hell we're going." And, *Nation's Restaurant News* hypothesized, based on overheard commentary about canceling city leases and abandoning plans for city units, that was what a number of attendees were going to do.[83]

In so doing, these restaurateurs used fast food punitively, withholding these outlets to chasten recalcitrant Negroes who could not manage to behave. In the *Nation's Restaurant News* framing, the imperative to make money was less important than putting Black people in their place. Cleveland rankled fast food executives because those activists refused to engage in the performative respectability that merited rewarding with franchises. More broadly, concern about urban uprisings touched all corners of American business. The Chamber of Commerce's magazine, the *Nation's Business*, ruminated about the specter of the ghetto, cautioning owners to prepare for an onslaught by erecting wood shutters and steel screens over plate glass windows to repel Molotov cocktails.[84] Architectural defense was the least of it. For fast food companies, the fear was that urban conflict would lead White diners to stay home or to go out in the suburbs rather than risk the peril of downtown. In May 1968, Taco Bell executive Glen W. Bell Jr. said, "We were caught in the middle of the Watts riots some time back—it temporarily set us back. We all hope the summer won't be as serious as they predict."[85] Others reported that each incident required a few days for things to return to normalcy, disrupting business.

Worse than White people staying away was Black people showing up. At Senator Byrd's hearings, the need to regulate Black conduct emerged repeatedly. Store owner Mr. "P." intimated that Black youth were animals: "They do run in whole bunches. . . . They are loose . . . if we leave them loose, these conditions get worse instead of better." He hoped that the law would intervene "to make them go to school or take them away somewhere."[86] Black people were outside the racial bounds of decency. Just as upsetting as smashed windows and merchandise losses were Black people swearing, calling White people "whitey" and other names, and generally failing to maintain a posture of subordination.[87]

If industry's immediate response was to punitively deny impolite Black communities fast food, within a few years the stance would flip. Fast food became a key means through which the federal government sought to ameliorate urban unrest. The next chapter shows that Presidents Johnson and Nixon saw elusive racial equality as a national security issue and a political threat, and believed that entrepreneurship through franchising could counter it.[88] Black Power, co-opted into Black capitalism by the federal government, infused federal funding to fast food in the ghetto, disbursing the outlets as a sedative to neighborhoods in rebellion.

8

Government Burgers

Federal Financing of Fast Food in the Ghetto

The five-pound blocks of processed cheese that the Reagan administration doled out to low-income families in the 1980s acquired the colloquial appellation "government cheese." "Government burgers" refers here to the many fast food franchises that in the late 1960s were funded with federal dollars. In tandem with the industry's turn to a Black public face, fast food restaurants began to proliferate in Black communities in the mid to late 1960s because the federal government put them there. Government burgers, like government cheese, went to communities in need; but unlike the dairy surplus compressed into bright orange rectangles, they were not meant to abate a biological hunger, but an economic one. Government burgers were part of federal initiatives to infuse capital into minority-owned businesses and spur Black entrepreneurship.

Conservatives, White and Black, decried a perceived lack of resourcefulness in Black communities, singling out for special condemnation welfare assistance. Black conservative ideologies expressed abhorrence for an "irrational" focus on injustice and the airing of grievances by Black folks, deep suspicion of the state, and an embrace of unfettered capitalism.[1] Among Chicago's Black business community, two prominent men gave voice to these ideas. Abraham Foote Jr., a colleague of Cirilo McSween's at New York Life, saw welfare as a problem of "people feeling sorry for themselves instead of pulling themselves up by their bootstraps," and he characterized the Black Power movement as "stupidity in its simplest form."[2] Similarly, fellow Chicagoan Richard McGuire, owner of what became the largest African American furniture business in the country, disparaged "government giveaway programs" that perpetuated a lapsed work ethic. McGuire asserted, "We've been crying so long that the foot of racism was on our necks that many of our people wouldn't know when it's taken off. They would just keep yelling."[3]

Conservative framing urged Black folks to mimic the purported initiative of

White business owners. Journalists saw franchisors in particular as "the new rich of American business . . . who had risen by their bootstraps after World War II, giving opportunity to thousands of little guys along the way."[4] Clearly, fast food's captains rose out of anything but a hardscrabble meritocracy, but their success was held out as the model to emulate. By the early 1960s, the federal government acknowledged to some extent that Black entrepreneurs lacked boots, or at best were issued deficient pairs without straps. As vice president to Lyndon Johnson, Hubert Humphrey ordered the Small Business Administration in 1964 to investigate its loan history with African Americans. The findings were stark: in ten years the agency had disbursed only seventeen loans (or was it actually seven? In *Dark Ghetto* Kenneth Clark quoted SBA director Eugene P. Foley as saying so). The remedy was a number of loan programs under the War on Poverty that would assist under-resourced entrepreneurs.[5]

The lending strategies, along with other minority enterprise initiatives, were narrow in focus and problematic in implementation. They were supposed to open up the world of American small business to African Americans and others who had historically been shut out. But federal small business programs did not target a wide range of business opportunities; instead, they focused heavily on franchised businesses. With fast food the most popular franchised operation, the result was that federal monies directly increased fast food prevalence in Black neighborhoods. And as historian Chin Jou has argued, even if federal actors pulled levers to assist Black entrepreneurs, it was not motivated by a desire to right long-standing inequalities so much as to intervene prophylactically to prevent outcomes that were unsustainable for the body politic (e.g., urban rebellions).

The small business programs advanced by an administration alarmed by Black, urban populations turned fast food franchises into a means to reform Black folks lacking in discipline. It was a reversal of the punitive project fast food corporations furthered; where the industry perceived Black folks as needing to settle down and sought to withhold fast food until they did so, federal programs made fast food precisely the means to achieve Black compliance. In the late nineteenth and early twentieth centuries, the provision of bland, simple, Anglo-American foods and cooking methods served as a vehicle to assimilate immigrants; but African Americans, seen as unassimilable, received no such attention from reformers.[6] Now, extending bland and simple fast food to Black entrepreneurs was both an indicator of their perceived assimilability and a means of imposing the necessary discipline for an otherwise defiant and impudent population.

The federal government's focus on fast food as economic salvation therefore made the body central to participation in the American marketplace for Black people. Legal scholar Cheryl Harris argues that Black people are excluded from markets and rejected as "proper economic subjects." When government initiatives began to consider Black persons as possibly proper economic subjects, it did so in a context that required them to literally consume to realize their credibility.[7] If fast food was to be the primary pathway to consumer citizenship, Black residents would need to eat their way out of the economic wastelands. The proper Black economic subject was one that relied on corporeality to participate in the market, literally embodying it.

The Task Force for Equal Opportunity

A primary catalyst of federal interest in fast food came from the Task Force for Equal Opportunity, initially chaired by Under Secretary of Commerce Franklin D. Roosevelt Jr. and then handed to LeRoy Collins, his successor and a longtime supporter of segregation.[8] Prior to this role, Collins served as chair of the Community Relations Service, an initiative within the Department of Commerce convened to work for the prevention and elimination of barriers in implementing the Civil Rights Act.[9] It was from this role that Collins came to the Task Force, appointed because he was thought to have the skills and gravitas to champion equal opportunities. He did not last long in this position, however, as he resigned to focus on an unsuccessful U.S. Senate bid.[10]

The Task Force sought to provide minority businesspeople with information about franchisors who "expressed their willingness to participate in encouraging minority groups to enter franchised businesses." It did so with the 1965 *Franchise Opportunity Handbook*, which listed brands across a variety of retail domains, from furniture to equipment rentals, all of which ostensibly did not "discriminate on the basis of race, color, religion or national origin in the availability, terms or conditions of their franchisees."[11] The evidence for nondiscriminatory practices was unclear; and if restaurant chains were committed to equitable treatment, it is logical to expect that that would extend to customers as well. But Denny's, despite its inclusion in 1965, would face a class action lawsuit in the 1990s for a pattern of racially discriminatory treatment of Black customers. What exactly was meant by "discrimination" was unclear when the 1985 edition of the handbook continued to describe its purpose as identifying nondiscriminatory franchises, notwithstanding that such policies had been illegal for decades.[12]

The *Handbook* was just one of the methods the federal government employed to increase awareness of business opportunities. But it was a key piece, and a primary reason it was dominated by fast food was because of who was invited to advise the government on minority business: A. L. Tunick, founder of the Chicken Delight chain. Anchored by familial wealth derived from a scrap metal business, he sought in the early 1950s to run his own venture and purchased a deep cooker business that had gone bankrupt. Tunick promptly lost $90,000 trying to sell the fryers at retail and staved off further losses by developing Chicken Delight as an enterprise where the cookers could be sold. His carryout chain had outlets in almost all states, but it was a middling player in the field with a minimal advertising presence. Still, it enjoyed a Hollywood product placement in *Play Misty for Me*, when Evelyn shows up at Dave's home unannounced and uninvited with groceries to prepare dinner. Though she brings steak, Dave's friend Al whispers that she is from Chicken Delight, presumably referring to the food being delivered.

Tunick is credited with producing the first Black fast food franchisee—that being a Mr. Bailey, whom *Jet* magazine reported as a former janitor, handyman, and painter. With private loans, savings, and the first minority-targeted SBA funds, he opened a Chicken Delight restaurant in New York.[13] His designation as "the first" appears to be inaccurate because his New York outlet opened a year after Roman Turmon's busy Harlem location. In any case, Tunick was active in bringing in Black franchisees; and as an appointee to the SBA's National Advisory Council, he was to advise the agency on effectively deploying its resources to address the problems franchisees encountered. He would go on to serve in this capacity for three consecutive presidential administrations, and did so even as Chicken Delight and its parent company (Consolidated Foods) were part of a $66 million class action lawsuit in the mid-1960s brought by eight hundred past and current franchisees forced to buy restaurant supplies at inflated prices from corporate. Tunick launched the chain to sell deep fryers and the company had banked on this model entirely, deriving its total income from supply sales to its franchisees. Operators were lured by the lack of franchise royalty fees, but they never achieved the profits the franchisor promised and found themselves without the support of the head office.[14] Many of the franchisees were Black, a reflection of Tunick's initiatives; but both they and White franchisees alleged negligible assistance. Courts ruled in 1970 that Chicken Delight violated antitrust laws, but this litigation victory brought little comfort to operators in New York City, particularly in communities of color. It was bad enough that they were operating at razor thin margins as the chain was torn asunder; but on top of that, franchisees were facing an incursion of Kentucky Fried Chicken outlets. Consolidated Foods shuttered its Chicken Delight chain in 1979.[15]

Tunick's influence on the Task Force for Equal Opportunity was surely responsible for the dominance of fast food over other business sectors in the franchise handbook. Among the promoted brands were A&W Root Beer, Chicken Delight, Dog 'n' Suds, Bresler's Ice Cream, Henry's Drive-In, and the Red Barn. Conspicuous in their absence were McDonald's, Burger King, and Kentucky Fried Chicken, leaving

potential Black fast food franchisees to infer that they were not welcome as operators for these corporations. In fact, their absence may have stemmed from the lack
of systematic sampling to survey of franchising restaurants. Al Tunick had simply
sampled people in his networks, including members of the International Franchise
Association, for which he served as president.[16] In Tunick's words, he had asked restaurant executives "whether the franchising company would be willing to grant a
franchise to a Negro, provided, of course, that the firm's other qualifications were
met by the applicant."[17] Tunick may have purposefully omitted "the big three"
brands from his queries because, as a fast food franchise owner, excluding competitors boosted his own odds of success and allowed him to corner the minority market.

Even if some companies answered affirmatively to Tunick's question, stating
that they were "willing" to recruit minority operators was different than actively
doing so. The federal government's initial forays into financing Black entrepreneurship made fast food the focal point, touting franchising as the optimal business
structure. But many fast food franchisors were marginal and suspect businesses
that weighed down operators with risk and brought few benefits. In shepherding
Black entrepreneurs to fast food, the federal government induced race-related precarity in their small businesses. A fast food–centric strategy for Black enterprise
heightened the likelihood of African Americans becoming ensnared in an industry
riven with poorly conceived chains meant to capitalize on hype. That strategy came
to life in funding from the Small Business Administration.

Loans and No Loans

The SBA was the agency responsible for most of the federal monies directed to Black
entrepreneurs. Born in 1953, it was meant to assist and protect small business, and
one way it did so was to guarantee loans issued by private banks. Its backing meant
that borrowers would receive better loan terms.[18]

SBA also made loans directly. In one early initiative, the SBA guaranteed rental
leases. Much as the FHA backed mortgage loans, lessening the risk to banks of default by home buyers, beginning in 1965 the SBA backed retail leases, insuring property owners against commercial tenant default. In 1967, the agency asked private
underwriters to take over as the primary guarantors, and the insurance program expanded rapidly; leases totaling nearly half a billion dollars were guaranteed by 1970.
Landlords who feared renting to risky or new entities were delighted to be covered
by insurance that lasted for the life of the lease. Insurance firms were equally enthusiastic about these contracts, anticipating that they would be highly profitable with
high, upfront premiums and little risk of losses.[19]

For franchised business, however, this new mechanism was not universally accessible. Fast food was largely shut out because the industry's outlook was seen as shaky. That Black franchised small businesses were largely in the domain of fast food meant they were disadvantaged in accessing new public–private financial supports. Compounding this exclusion was the fact that insurers also rejected policies on inner-city leases. An anonymous insurer stated, "The possibility of success for new inner-city businesses is slim indeed, and frankly, we're afraid we'd lose our shirts if we guaranteed many of them." Others held that since the SBA guaranteed ghetto leases, the private sector didn't have to.[20]

When it came to loans, in many instances SBA's interventions constituted golden handcuffs for Black borrowers, burdening them with policies that didn't actually work to their advantage. The 1965 Economic Opportunity Loan Program was one of the agency's early targeted programs, announced in the *Chicago Defender* as the "newest and most liberal" of SBA initiatives.[21] It was meant to provide up to $25,000 (approximately $204,000 in 2020 dollars) in capital to businesses that had difficulty obtaining conventional loans. The loan program could only enable mom-and-pop stores because the lending ceiling did not go far as the only means of startup funds. Tight margins meant that store owners quickly depleted working capital. Worse, additional financial assistance was impossible with business collateral already pledged to the federal government.[22]

A slate of other programs arrived in later years, which increased the amounts applicants could borrow. In 1968, the SBA announced a new loan program to "stimulate stagnant ghetto economies." Called Project Own, it was meant to provide seed money to thirty thousand new minority businesses over the following two years by channeling more private loans to minority businesses with the help of SBA guarantees. The SBA was slowly moving away from loaning directly to borrowers and toward backing more private loans instead; in other words, it wanted to "get out of the banking business." And in backing private loans, the SBA determined that franchising was ideal. The federal inclination was well aligned with that of restaurateurs, who believed that "franchising is about the only profitable way for restaurateurs to get on the ghetto's doorstep."[23]

In early 1969, the SBA brought on a new director, Hilary Sandoval, previously an El Paso magazine distributor who came on board as a lifelong Republican who fueled Mexican American support for Nixon's first presidential campaign in the Southwest.[24] Sandoval may not have been attuned to the needs of Black entrepreneurs. He spoke at congressional hearings in late 1969 stating that one of the main objectives of the SBA's minority enterprise program was to ensure that minorities were receiving their fair share of SBA lending. In the half year preceding his testimony, the agency was disbursing quantities of loans that met or exceeded the proportion of the country's population that was counted as "minority." But in dollar amounts, borrowers of color lagged.[25] Sandoval explained the disparity as borrowers being conservative in their requests, owing to their smaller, less capital-intensive ventures. He argued that SBA's primary focus—"in large part [due] to the applicants themselves—is toward smaller enterprises, retail and service oriented."[26]

Black business owners across the country expressed an opposing perspective. James E. Summers, publisher of the *Black Book Directory* in Chicago, contended that loans guaranteed by the SBA were often disbursed for a fraction of the application amount. As an example, an owner of a carpet store applied for $25,000 from a South Side bank but received only $5,000. Summers explained that loans were "far less than the absolute minimum needed to succeed—and just enough to convince you to give it a try." In the case of the carpet store, the low loan amount meant the owner would have to raise prices, limit merchandise, or reduce overhead costs by implementing a more austere retail environment, all of which would increase the probability of business failure.[27] Summers also charged that forthcoming loans were often months delayed between bank and subsequent SBA approval, and stores suffered significant losses, especially when they had already signed leases in the interim. Meanwhile, some of the SBA's regional directors were skeptical that minority businesses needed additional assistance at all.[28] And this was to say nothing of the outright racism many Black entrepreneurs faced. Field agents who were responsible for making SBA loans were lower- to middle-class White men who were resentful about Black people gaining assistance. One businessman who applied for a loan totaling $250,000 was met with the following rebuke: "No nigger got no business needing that kind of money."[29]

On paper, SBA initiatives allowed President Nixon to appear concerned with endemic racial inequities and redress them in a manner palatable to interests across the political spectrum.[30] But the grand plans did not bear out in practice. Loans and loan guarantees to minorities were robust from 1968 to 1970 but declined continuously for the next several years; minority lending comprised 19 percent of SBA funds in 1971 and fell to 13 percent in 1976.[31] The fact was that the SBA was not much more accessible to Black borrowers in the 1960s or 1970s than before Humphrey's study. Moreover, while Humphrey intended for SBA programs to redress the racial lending gap, in actual practice they were accessible to all, and White business owners obtaining SBA-related capital put Black entrepreneurs at a further disadvantage. Some White men paired with Black collaborators to obtain federal funds. In Harlem, an unlikely duo came together to open Soul Stop. Michael Schweitzer, a White restaurateur, and Cleveland Christophe, a Black man who worked in retail and banking, collaborated in order to target the untapped ghetto market: "The chicken and shrimp fast-serve market may be saturated in some places, but it's not saturated in the ghetto, because nobody wants to open a store there." Soul Stop, which strategically deployed itself as a minority-owned business to take advantage of the new capital being made available to Black entrepreneurs, exemplified how business could act as a liaison between the government and "the inscrutable ghetto life style."[32]

The restaurant also illustrated that when SBA funds were disbursed to the ghetto, they often wound up in fast food. Federal loans were certainly not flowing in large quantities to Black manufacturing concerns, arts businesses, technical services, construction, and historic preservation, or any number of other domains. Sandoval asserted in congressional hearings that "the greatest peril the average minority candidate faces in starting his own venture" was a lack of management skills, and that it had been difficult to bring those skills to the ghetto residents among whom they were seeking out potential business owners. Except, however, in the realm of franchising. Here, the SBA supported the Department of Commerce's franchising initiative because franchisors gave extensive training and supervision to their licensees, for the simple reason that they had to do so if they wanted to make money: "The franchisee requires overseeing. So he does it."[33] Setting aside the connotations of an overseer for Black workers, Sandoval's analysis made deficiency the centerpiece of Black exclusion from small business. Black people had not done better because they lacked management skills; therefore, if the government were going to infuse capital to bring them in, the most sensible way to do so was to give them franchises. Arthur McZier, the assistant administrator for minority business enterprise, also centered personality traits in evaluating business potential. If individual grit and temperament were the primary determinative factors in business success, their lack among Black entrepreneurs was the reason they lagged behind their White counterparts. McZier stated, "Basically we have to find someone who can cut it, someone who has a good attitude toward business. I think this is the biggest problem of failure in business of people who have the wrong attitude."[34] Regardless of whether McZier meant to do so, his statement suggested that Black business failures were due to "bad attitudes."

In practice, the SBA would clearly be no refuge for Black entrepreneurs. But the government was committed to making franchising, especially via restaurants, a direct solution to rebuilding in the wake of the country's civil disorders and preventing any new ones. Nixon's administration determined that a lack of jobs was the most critical determinant of urban unrest; once Black people had access to businesses, they would have economic resources that would negate any impulses to riot.[35] D.C.'s Council chair John W. Hechinger and David Rusk, associate director of the Washington chapter of the Urban League, argued that national chains and local retailers had to make Black residents a core part of rebuilding the capital, and that franchising would be critical to this effort. Rusk contended, "The franchise route may be the most effective way of expanding black ownership and black entrepreneurship . . . especially among the major retail and food chains."[36] This analysis did not consider that using franchising as a conduit for reconstructing the ghetto was of less benefit to Black entrepreneurs and communities than to the corporations behind them. Perhaps more metaphorically, it was striking that the government aimed to ply Black communities with businesses like fried chicken outlets. Cooking chicken had historically been a means for Black women to wield power.[37] But now White men had taken it up and were selling corporate fried chicken back to Black people. Initially, fast food was withheld to punish unruly Black subjects; now it was a way to tamp down their volatile behavior and instill discipline. Business franchising as a solution to urban unrest was as much a disciplinary project as a pathway to economic uplift.

The Office of Minority Business Enterprise

The Office of Minority Business Enterprise (OMBE) arose out of President Nixon's Executive Order 11458 in March 1969. Located in the Department of Commerce, OMBE did not itself have any project funds; rather, it provided information, acted as a clearinghouse for ideas and resources, and worked with the SBA and other partners to fund businesses. One of its products was the *OMBE Outlook,* a monthly newsletter published to communicate new developments to interested groups across the country.[38] Under Nixon the FBI widened COINTELPRO to eradicate Black Nationalist organizations at the same time that Commerce was stimulating Black, middle-class business through OMBE.[39] These financial programs were designed to depress real challenges to the economic status quo and the radical critiques of U.S. society offered by the Black Power movement. As Lizabeth Cohen has argued, "Articulating black discontent in the language of a liberal struggle to pursue individual rights in a free capitalist marketplace and then successfully securing those rights, moreover, only reinforced the legitimacy of the capitalist order as a way of organizing socioeconomic life."[40] In fact, OMBE's message of liberation through capitalism was half-hearted.

Many Black businesses felt that OMBE's programs were of little help. They saw OMBE as engaged primarily in talk but not in action, with little commitment to its own programs or the entrepreneurs they supported. Moreover, President Nixon's

PERIODICAL
OUTLOOK

News From the Office of Minority Business Enterprise / U.S. DEPARTMENT OF COMMERCE

D.C. Mayor Walter Washington and Secretary of Commerce Maurice Stans at the unveiling of new OMBE programs in Washington.

OMBE COMES TO WASHINGTON

ANNOUNCING MAJOR new programs and actions to aid minority business development in Washington, D.C., Secretary of Commerce Maurice H. Stans urged financial, business and minority leaders to join in exploiting to the fullest the opportunities created and developed by the Department's Office of Minority Business Enterprise (OMBE).

D.C. Mayor Walter Washington joined the Secretary as he made the announcements.

In an all-day series of meetings with Washington leaders Feb. 10, the following new programs for the D.C. area were described by the Secretary and government officials:

• 23 businesses and industries have made commitments which assure 89 minority business opportunities ranging from automobile dealerships through a wide variety of franchises, including food services, automobile parts and service centers, clothing and general merchandise stores, business services, lawn maintenance and swimming pool installations;

• A pilot program has been inaugurated to assist minority owned and operated national banks through deposits of Post Office Department receipts with the establishment of a bank account in the United Community National Bank of Washington.

turn page

Figure 8.1. The cover of the Office of Minority Business Enterprise's *OMBE Outlook,* February 1970. Source: HathiTrust.org.

Advisory Council eventually undid the mission of OMBE by arguing that all businesspeople had problems and challenges and that the government should be helping everyone, not just minorities.

In early 1970, OMBE and the SBA attempted to reduce business start-up barriers by issuing a three-day loan guarantee program. Tested in Chicago and then expanded nationally, the program stipulated that loan application processing time for minority franchises would be reduced to a maximum of three days; if the SBA had failed to reject it within that time, the loan would be automatically guaranteed. Administrators felt that decision times on loan applications, which averaged two to eight months, could fall drastically.[41] McDonald's took credit for the program's launch in Chicago, claiming that it stemmed from collaboration between Bob Beavers and Art McZier, and that it resulted in the company aggressively taking up minority franchisees.[42] In actuality, McDonald's had yet to amass a large number of Black operators, and the three-day loan guarantee program did not run as quickly or as seamlessly as described. Once loans had been screened and accepted by a bank, they went on to SBA for guaranteeing, a process that might take three days. But bank screening was a different matter, and often a lengthy process. Besides, Black businesses that sought direct loans from the SBA were routinely denied.[43]

Perhaps the most ambitious OMBE initiative was the 25 × 25 × 2 program, developed to increase the number of minority franchisees. The agency initially invited twenty-five franchisors (and immediately thereafter an additional fifty-three) to spur a minimum of twenty-five minority franchisees over two years.[44] Franchisors had little to lose because OMBE would sort out legal and technical logistics, franchisees received training that corporate didn't have to cover, and franchisees had SBA's backing. And franchisors were encouraged but not required to adjust their standard franchise packages to minority applicants.[45] Whatever assistance franchisors pledged—such as committing to screen potential franchisees and to assist them in completing lending applications—should have been taking place regardless.

A number of fast food franchisors signed on to participate in the program, including Burger Chef, Pizza Hut, McDonald's, Arby's, and Burger King. Of the major chains, only KFC was absent.[46] Burger Chef announced its first Black franchisee in May 1969, and President Frank P. Thomas hoped 25 × 25 × 2 would lure in more Black business owners.[47] Henry's launched a minority enterprise program in February 1969, planning for "units built by black firms in black neighborhoods to serve the black community, run by black operators and owned by black entrepreneurs." The chain held 148 national franchised units; it turned over two stores to Black owners in Chicago.[48]

It is unclear how much the 25 × 25 × 2 program assisted average Black entrepreneurs. At least one group of "regular" Black men were Ralph Kelly, Clayton Norman, and Bernard Price, who opened a Detroit McDonald's in early December 1970, seeking to make their store a social and economic community anchor.[49] But the OMBE did not keep track of how many franchisees actually benefited under the program. Corporations suggested that there had been significant gains, as minority franchisees quintupled between 1969 and 1971, but there was no way to independently verify this claim.[50] A year and a half after OMBE's "much-ballyhooed" minority franchising program, industry analysts pronounced that it amounted to a hill of beans: "OMBE proved a federal fraud. Many franchisors were blowing wind. Bankers agreed to participate only on the presumption that there'd never be a real program. And blacks with franchisee potential really weren't around."[51]

A franchisor who spoke on condition of anonymity to *Nation's Restaurant News* claimed that 25 × 25 × 2 had no teeth or federal commitment: "It was a lot of backslapping and talk." Franchisors offered limited training to low numbers of applicants and lackadaisically publicized programs in name only. Both franchisors and banks were reluctant to enter the ghetto.[52] In the final analysis, franchisors saw the creation of the OMBE as a concession to Nixon's campaign pledges, but one that was never meant to create lasting change. Garland Guice, executive director of the Chicago Economic Development Corporation, explained, "We are disillusioned. The Office of Minority Business Enterprise has not been given the weapons required to fight a winning battle. The ammunition has been shells of rhetoric."[53]

Nixon's already marginal and conflicted support of minority enterprise grew more lukewarm both in sentiment and dollars over time. He looked to the private sector rather than government to take control, perhaps harboring concerns about alienating White voters as he approached reelection.[54] Nixon's hedging was not lost on those who had a stake in minority business. By 1970, the Chamber of Commerce doubted Nixon's commitment to its minority enterprise programs and was reticent to expand its efforts.[55] But the Department of Commerce itself was making the same argument. Another of the bodies created by Executive Order 11458 was the President's Advisory Council on Minority Business Enterprise, whose task was to create a 1970s blueprint for a national strategy on minority-owned businesses.[56] Broadly, the Council turned to the private sector for solutions and deemphasized the unique barriers faced by Black entrepreneurs. Having moved from "Black capitalism" to "minority enterprise," the Council now recommended a transition to "expanded ownership." According to the Council report, "many of the economic problems of minority and non-minority small businessmen are essentially the same."[57]

The Council also argued a point that often came up in industry discourse: that the power structure bred frustration and anger among African Americans because television ads and other media bombarded them with images of wealth, and the discrepancy from their real lives was difficult to swallow. Naylor Fitzhugh, vice president of Pepsi-Cola, was quoted in *Advertising Age* advancing this argument: "Ghetto residents, through television, get to see, day after day, hour after hour, what life is like among the affluent. The stark contrasts with ghetto life certainly provoke deep feelings of frustration, resentment and animosity."[58] In this telling, Black communities were not so much seeking decent housing, gainful employment, functioning municipal services, and the like, as they were jealous about the trappings of White affluence. This framing was agnostic as to whether the inequities were unjust or whether Black people would perceive them as such if they didn't appear on television. The Council contended that were minority enterprises to flourish, it would boost community psychological well-being by reinforcing the possibility of success within the system. Put bluntly, "a class of capitalists and corporate managers within the black community . . . would ease ghetto tensions by providing living proof to black dissidents that they can assimilate into the system if only they discipline themselves and work at it tirelessly."[59]

A subgroup within the Council was the Task Force on Business Opportunities, chaired by Robert B. McKersie, an academic, and assisted by none other than militant firebrand Anthony Stadeker as associate director. Stadeker's community organizing and business activism and his connection to the University of Chicago in particular were likely the impetus for his participation. The group's focus was to assess where new or expanding markets poised for minority entrepreneurship existed. Once again franchising was offered as the solution. OMBE official Walter Sorg contended that fast food corporations found federal funds attractive because, "with the money market getting as tight as it is, for the most part these franchisors would prefer to go with the minorities. They can get support from the SBA in terms of 90% guarantee of the loan, and it's easier to expand under today's tight money market."[60] Therein lay the motivation behind franchisor interest in minority franchises. They represented a conduit to federal funding sources that could underwrite the chains' expansion.

At least some fast food executives were portrayed as motivated instead by social conscience. Al Lapin Jr., former president of the National Franchise Association, was reportedly such a man.[61] The *New York Times* reported on his 1969 program, "Two Plus You," designed to launch minority-owned franchises to be located in White neighborhoods. In so doing, Lapin hoped to cross the "Black Curtain" that sealed off such communities from the rest of society. Lapin charged that the federal government was too slow and bureaucratic to effectively assist Black entrepreneurs, and franchisors would have to do it themselves. In his program, the "two" referred to the 2 percent down payment that franchisees had to put up rather than the typical 50 percent for his company (a promissory note was signed to repay the rest over several years).[62] The "you" was an indication that the franchisee had to have emotional and psychological commitment to the endeavor.

Lapin's corporate management actually took a harder line than was reported in the *Times* in emphasizing the need for Black discipline and psychosocial remediation. On the one hand, Lapin's team doubted that "the placement of franchised businesses in the ghetto on a piecemeal, isolated basis will have any significant effect on the urban crisis. Trapping blacks and browns in marginal businesses in the ghetto in our judgment perpetuates the cycle of failure."[63] Such a view would suggest that the corporation recognized and sought to redress inequities in opportunity structures. But Lapin's program still saw Black people as the seat of pathology and the true cause for stunted opportunity. It required that a participant be willing to relocate (to use Lapin's gendered language) himself and his family and "to expose himself to deep probing of his feelings and attitudes toward himself, toward his peers, toward program management and toward the white community he must operate within."[64] He might need "remedial instruction in terms of basic language or mathematical skills." He almost certainly would require emotional and attitudinal work. The company felt that as a rule, minority franchisees were just as technically adept as their White counterparts, but what they really needed to work on was on "gaining insight into his apprehension, his anger, his suspicion—and how feelings like these affect his day-to-day relationships in the work setting."[65]

What was the payoff for this extensive soul searching and psychological and racial readjustment? After a weeklong orientation, the candidate would undergo a more extensive training than "ordinary" franchisees; supplemented with the remedial instruction, it would last thirteen weeks. After that, the candidate would be recommended either for further training or for an assistant manager position in a White-owned outlet. After that, at month nine, the trainee might be extended for another three months in that same position, or offered a (unspecified) position in a franchised or company-owned unit. In the end, it was hardly a foregone conclusion that the long process would culminate in franchise ownership.[66] Ultimately, Lapin's program was not at all oriented toward redressing structural barriers; rather, it was a scheme to activate latent Black discipline and transform otherwise psychologically unfit entrepreneurs into workers who would stop crying that the foot of racism was on their necks.

Minority Enterprise Small Business Investment Companies

One last federal initiative, formed in part because the SBA was perceived as failing to provide enough capital to Black businesses, was the Minority Enterprise Small Business Investment Companies (MESBICs).[67] Secretary of Commerce Maurice Stans (two years before he resigned to head the Nixon campaign's finance organization) announced the program in 1970 alongside D.C. mayor Walter Washington. The goal was the same as other programs. Stans declared, "We want to provide methods through which members of the nation's minorities will have an opportunity to participate productively in our American business and industrial economy."[68]

MESBICs were investment bodies that provided long-term venture capital and management advice to minority-owned small businesses. The minimum capitalization required was $150,000, and MESBICs theoretically had the capability of leveraging up to $2.5 million more from the SBA and private banks. Addressing Congress in March 1970, President Nixon outlined MESBIC's twofold government match: if an investor put in $150,000, the government matched with $300,000, and the investor could then apply for additional loans.[69] To minimize risk and make sure all those loans were repaid, MESBICs sought companies that could guarantee regular returns. They therefore tended to back small ventures rather than ambitious ones. And once again, fast food outlets particularly fit the bill because they had the security of a brand name, a steady customer base, and, theoretically, corporate support. The United Fund, a Chicago MESBIC, backed four McDonald's and two Chicken Unlimited restaurants.[70] Another apparent Chicago MESBIC, Urban Ventures Inc., provided capital to wide-ranging Black businesses including a truck hauling concern, a furrier, a shoe store, supermarkets, and a McDonald's outlet.[71]

Burger Kings began to proliferate in Black Chicago neighborhoods in the early 1970s, likely due to Burger King's initiation of a MESBIC in 1973. The chain created its own investment corporations and then received MESBIC funds directly, which was allowed and encouraged. It therefore double-dipped, receiving funds to fund itself to fund minority franchisees.[72] Burger King brought on Kelvin Wall, president of Kabon Consulting Inc., to consult on Black franchising and marketing to Black consumers. Burger King thought hiring Wall was "good business" because he would "keep Burger King in touch with happenings in the Black community." Wall exemplified the deeply intertwined relationships in fast food franchising among Black players. Just two years prior, while vice president of marketing development for Coca-Cola, he had been the beneficiary of SBA funding to buy Burger King outlets in Black neighborhoods in Atlanta. Wall and his associate Felker W. Ward purchased three outlets at a cost of $350,000, of which $290,000 came from an SBA-backed loan, the largest the agency had ever guaranteed in Georgia.[73] Wall had also been merchandise manager at *Ebony* and advertising director at the *New York Amsterdam News*.[74] After leaving Coca-Cola, he briefly joined Zebra Advertising, where in 1969 he argued that low-income families irrespective of race had a specific lifestyle— "need-oriented, peer-directed, income-limited, mobility-inhibited, and isolated." Repeating common narratives about the deficits of the poor, Wall's analysis suggested that Black consumers would not only accept but be positively inclined toward simple, rudimentary retail goods and services, as they lacked the taste or knowledge to demand otherwise.[75] Fast food's cheap, simplistic meals would therefore be ideally suited to Black, urban neighborhoods.

MESBIC investment partners came from a range of institutions including New York finance mainstays such as JPMorgan Chase, Chemical Bank, and Lehman Brothers.[76] A 1970 press release disguised as a news article, titled "Kentucky Fried Chicken Is Great," announced a partnership between Lehman Brothers and a franchise held by a Black-owned Chicago concern, USOMA Industries. Together, they would build and operate three KFC outlets in inner-city Chicago.[77] New York Life Insurance financed Soulville USA, a takeout BBQ restaurant headed by a Black celebrity athlete, William D. Naulls.[78] News reports did not name Cirilo McSween, but it is possible that he was behind the project, given his role at the insurance company. The store opened in Watts in 1970, five years after the uprising, and New York Life also financed a KFC outlet for Naulls. The insurance giant's capital infusion was part of a commitment of at least $1 billion to invest in central cities.[79] The Joint Committee on Urban Problems gathered hundreds of insurance companies that similarly pledged $1 billion to revitalize derelict areas. Although the focus was housing, it also financed a variety of small businesses in the hopes of stimulating job creation such as grocery stores and, apparently, fast food.[80]

Foundation monies were also prominent in MESBIC funding. By 1970, the Ford Foundation had made the largest single private contribution to the MESBIC program to date. Ford president McGeorge Bundy announced in 1966 that its primary domestic focus would be "Negro equality." Believing that Black people had to be assimilated in order for the "American system" to function—where the system referred to a benevolent "corporate capitalism"—the Foundation overlooked Black neighborhood isolation and systemic racism and sought instead to "fix" Black behavioral pathology.[81] Ford also provided funding to almost all the major protest groups, such as CORE, the SCLC, the Urban League, and the NAACP.[82] The Foundation's financial support could help CORE subdue the ghetto and potentiate corporate control of Black communities through Black elites.[83] This was evident in the

Figure 8.2. A KFC on North Capitol Street. The building's pointed-roof style reflected an older motif for the chain. Image PR 1814A, Emil A. Press Slide Collection, D.C. History Center.

MESBIC program, which set up franchises that could not really be expected to create radical change and were not fully owned by the Black operators who ran them.

Ford gave $2.5 million for six MESBICs supporting Black, Puerto Rican, and Native American communities, hoping to create ten thousand jobs. One of the recipients was the Interracial Council for Business Opportunity (ICBO), which gave services, technical support, and loans to minority businesses in several major cities.[84] Jack-of-all-trades Kelvin Wall sat on the board of directors.[85] ICBO's influence bore fruit in modest enterprises such as grocery stores and beauty parlors. The organization launched an initiative around 1969 in New York with the American Jewish Congress called Project Transfer, in which it oversaw the transfer from retiring Jewish owners of profitable concerns in "ghetto areas" to Black hands—the kinds of ownership transfers that OBU fought for in Cleveland.[86] Still, Darwin Bolden, ICBO executive director and member of the Council on Minority

Enterprise, recognized that "real economic development is not going to come through ownership of a few Chicken Delights and Dunkin' Donuts franchises."[87]

The Advisory Council on Minority Business Enterprise had made the same point in its report to President Nixon, but chicken joints were precisely the shape that Black businesses were taking under government initiatives. This strategy set in motion a theft of imagination that is only too prevalent under capitalism.[88] Fixating on franchising directed financial supports—however flawed—to fast food, and directed entrepreneurial energy away from the kinds of cooperative food retail enterprises so prevalent in the 1930s and 1940s. Instead, Black communities were positioned for a profit-focused enterprise that would be hard-pressed to meet needs for self-determination. The Cleveland boycotters repudiated the extraction of community wealth to White operators and a White corporate structure, but beyond that fast food was extracting the energy and resistance needed to bring into a being a different community retail structure. ICBO, despite its recognition that corner stores and restaurants were very much limited in what they could bring to Black communities, continued to back them. Jackie Robinson, who served as a franchising head of a seafood restaurant chain, said of the organization, "They had the money just for this kind of thing. They were interested in financing mom-and-pop stores, which is the way we are going."[89]

Everyone had the money for just this kind of thing. While the federal government financed new fast food outlets, a voracious appetite for them grew on Wall Street. Franchising was a hot commodity, and investors pursued companies that grew boundlessly and produced enormous returns. Food service was a $25 billion industry with stocks that rose at a breakneck pace. Tunick's International Industries rose from $25 a share to $250 in an eighteen-month period, while McDonald's shares grew from $28 in 1967 to more than $103 in 1968. And consolidation meant that fewer, larger corporate entities were dictating the product landscape.[90] Black neighborhoods were fertile ground for Wall Street speculation, and fast food corporate offices saw Black operators as ideal to take advantage of federal programs to manage the risks of an unruly ghetto.

African Americans who sought to enter the fast food arena did not all do so on the terms of White corporate actors. They, too, had agency and forged plans for building Black communities as well as their own wealth. Creating Black-owned franchisor companies was the means to do so. Led primarily by celebrities, African Americans began to launch their own corporations through which Black folks could bring the gospel of fast food franchising to their communities. It was a path equally fraught with the racism that franchisees encountered; but beginning in the late 1960s, it was one that Black franchisors were determined to tread.

9

You've Got to Be In

Black Franchisors and Black Economic Power

In 1970, the United States Congress investigated the possibility that celebrity-owned fast food restaurants such as singer Tony Bennett's Spaghetti House and athlete Joe Namath's Broadway Joe's were essentially grifts that made a quick buck at the expense of small businesses. A year prior, when Hilary Sandoval spoke before Congress, he noted that for the most part the SBA worked with well-known and reputable franchisors; but the agency had a whole office dedicated to verifying franchisor credibility, and about 75 percent of existing franchisors did not measure up.[1] The Senate's Small Business Committee convened a Subcommittee on Urban and Rural Economic Development to hear testimony. Celebrity franchisors were alleged to be selling their names and collecting royalties, and then failing to run legitimate businesses—or simply failing. When the government stepped in to investigate these claims, some of the biggest names in the business were called in to testify, including African American athletes like Jackie Robinson and Brady Keys. Keys, as will be seen, would prove to be one of few Black franchisors who were able to sustain a fast food brand for any appreciable amount of time. But when he spoke at the January hearings, he outlined his difficulties as a Black man in the business.[2]

In this he was not alone. Edward J. Dwight Jr., who had trained as the first Black astronaut in the early 1960s, turned to fast food when racial discrimination kept him from going into space.[3] In the fall of 1968 he launched the Rib Cage Bar-B-Q Drive-In restaurant in Denver and planned for a national franchise.[4] The company had difficulty getting off the ground as one of only three Black franchisors in the United States, and the inability to secure capital pushed it toward insolvency. With three existing outlets in 1969, Rib Cage sought funding from all kinds of institutions, from investment banks to religious groups, but was refused by all, until the First National Bank in Denver gave the company an SBA-guaranteed $200,000 loan.[5]

Dwight's experience shows that a distinguished reputation alone was not sufficient for Black franchisors to successfully start their own chains. But celebrity appeared to be necessary. Entertainers especially were safe for White audiences and calmed risk-averse financiers.[6] Celebrity franchisors were less likely to bring to mind the perceived threat of Black Power; and since entertainers were already rich, they modeled American ideals of hard work inevitably paying off. They were ideal figures to play the role of corporate manager that White America hoped would keep the ghetto quiet. As brokers between dominant power structures and poor Black communities, they could tamp down incipient unrest by serving as aspirational examples of how to fit into a capitalist society.[7] Robert Allen's analysis of Black America as a neocolonial nation saw Black elites (like franchisors) as complicit in conflating Black Power and Black capitalism. He argued that the message elites implicitly conveyed was "Give us a piece of the action and we will run the black communities and keep them quiet for you."[8]

It was a troubling reality, even for those franchisors who did not set out with an explicit project of inducing quiet in the ghetto. If the Cleveland boycotters were calling for a piece of the pie in franchise ownership, Black franchisors seemed to be after the whole pie, and on its face, this might be a sharper tactic. But there was no denying that putting even empowerment-minded Black folks at the head of fast food companies would ultimately provide little in the way of the radical change needed to truly improve Black lives.

Short-Lived Stardom

Some of the biggest names in entertainment and sports got into fast food and left not long after. Few could rival the star power of James Brown when he entered the world of fast food franchising, though his venture was relatively small in scope. Soul Brother No. 1 opened a restaurant in his hometown of Macon, Georgia, naming it Gold Platter after the hit records he had theretofore been churning out. With a menu offering standards such as fried chicken, fish, burgers, and hot dogs but also soul food—collard greens, black-eyed peas, and sweet potato pudding—the chain sought broad appeal among Black consumers. One company spokesperson claimed that ghetto residents spent proportionally more money on food and snacks, and that the ghetto was a fertile area for food franchising since most franchisors had avoided it.[9] It was the same argument that others in the business voiced, such as the Black–White partnership behind Harlem's Soul Stop. The ghetto was still a blank slate for fast food, so coming in now was a shrewd move for corporations seeking to capture Black spending. There was no mention of how the communities themselves might benefit. When asked whether he was worried about competition, James Brown replied, "This is pioneer, like Daniel Boone and Davy Crockett. And it's so big that you as an American can't be out of it. You've got to be in."[10]

The Hardest Working Man in Show Business surely could not be left out of restaurant franchising if multitudes of his peers were getting in. But his analogy to the frontier and conquest was an unfortunate one. Once Gold Platter got in, what was to follow in the communities in which it landed? Brown was in, but would the company open up the same opportunities for other Black entrepreneurs? Corporate planned to sell restaurants to Black operators or Whites who promised to train Whites who promised to train Black peers; it would be a nationwide chain that would make opportunities available to "members of minority races." The corporation itself was run by White businessmen, and the company's statements about its racial policies seemed to change depending on who gave them. Brown sought to stop any rumors before they started: "I have not sold out my name to a group of White businessmen. We are using primarily White capital to help Black people and I think that's a very good idea." It was a stance that would surely have made his venture palatable to corporate America.

When industry media reported that Gold Platter had been advertising in the *Wall Street Journal* to seek Black participants, questions emerged about whether the corporation had the savvy to partner with Black folks. The president, Herbert L. Parks, refuted these questions, claiming that the chain had targeted *Ebony*, the *Journal of the National Medical Association*, and other Black-centered periodicals. He asserted, "No one remotely responsible for Gold Platter advertising was under any delusion that an advertisement in the *Wall Street Journal* would attract many responses from black entrepreneurs."[11] Parks attempted to correct a misperception that Gold Platter brass had no clue how to find Black business partners by highlighting that they had targeted Black media. But in doing so, he effectively suggested that he thought Black executives unlikely to read the country's major financial paper. He also shot himself in the foot by pointing out that although most investor interest had been from White men, the company was clever enough to recognize that Black people would need to be involved. In other words, Black participants were primarily a front to gain credible access to the desired market.

Beyond James Brown, there was seemingly no end to the lineup of Black celebrities who sought to attach their names to restaurants. In Birmingham, baseball legend Willie Mays launched Willie Mays Foods Inc., a franchise that would sell fried chicken, hamburgers, fish sandwiches, fries, fried pies, shakes, and soft drinks. Initial costs to franchisees totaled $24,750 cash down, royalties of 5 percent of sales, and advertising at an additional 3 percent charge. These costs were relatively affordable compared to other small chains but still unlikely to be within reach for the average Black entrepreneur.

Jackie Robinson entered fast food after ending his pioneering Major League Baseball career with the Brooklyn Dodgers, first with a five-year executive position at the New York Chock Full o' Nuts chain.[12] He then joined a White-owned seafood chain, Sea Host, to manage its Black franchising program. A subsidiary of an industrial seafood packer and supplier, the new chain won federal funding for its plan of bringing "ghetto residents" into franchising. Robinson found that a friend at Standard and Poor's was enthusiastic about his venture; for his part, Robinson welcomed the collaboration because "we are ready to admit that the Negro community doesn't have the business expertise."[13]

In 1968, Sea Host franchise ads ran in the *New York Amsterdam News* notifying potential franchisees that "Jackie Robinson can show you how to earn big, year-round returns from a minimum investment with a Sea Host restaurant franchise." After a small standup counter prototype at 138th and Lenox, stores opened in Times Square and Bushwick (Brooklyn) in 1968, and four more grand openings were held in early August 1969 in Prospect and Crown Heights (Brooklyn), St. Albans (Queens), and East Harlem. The "locally owned, nationally franchised" restaurants offered shellfish, fish-and-chips, hush puppies, shakes, and soft drinks. Some industry pundits called Sea Host the "most exciting new, proven fast food business in the country" as it sought out Black and Puerto Rican entrepreneurs, reserving territory in Harlem, Bedford-Stuyvesant (Brooklyn), and the Bronx for that purpose.[14]

In only a year, Jackie Robinson graced the cover of *Fast Food Magazine* as an embodiment of racially integrated fast food ownership. He believed that the United States was "just a rumor away, just a toss of a brick away, from the worst confrontation this country has ever seen," and the Black/White business model behind Sea Host was couched as a salve to a tense social climate.[15] The role of Black corporate actors as intermediaries for Black communities who threatened to disrupt the social order was clear. It continued President Nixon's aim of quelling ghetto disorder with small business. For Robinson, fast food's promise extended beyond economic security. By his account, the Sea Host restaurant at 138th Street went untouched after the unrest in Harlem following Martin Luther King Jr.'s assassination because rumors had spread that the restaurant was owned by Robinson (once this was proved untrue, Robinson said, "we had some problems"). Robinson threw his support behind franchising but found his Sea Host project collapsing in the summer of 1970. The restaurant filed for involuntary bankruptcy, leaving franchisees in the lurch,

Enjoy these PENNANT WINNER SPECIALS at

EAT-IN OR TAKE-OUT SEAFOOD

Sea Host is a whole new thing in seafood restaurants. Come in and try our authentic English-style Fish 'n Chips, shrimp, clams, oysters and a variety of delicious Sea Host seafood specialties with that ocean-fresh flavor. All at budget-pleasing prices. Fast eat-in and take-out service.

One of our customers will win a
FREE PORTABLE TV
during our Pennant Winner Specials Days.

Nothing to buy. Fill out coupon and bring it to your nearest Sea Host Eat-In or Take-Out Seafood Restaurant.

Name _____

Address _____

Telephone _____

TV prize drawing December 15, 1969

You may also mail this coupon to Sea Host.

552 Lenox Avenue
at 138th Street New York, N.Y.

245 Flatbush Avenue
at Bergen Street Brooklyn, N.Y.

SEA HOST SEABURGER only 29¢
A delicious breaded seafood patty made with your favorite seafoods—shrimp, tuna, cod and clams on a fresh roll with tartar sauce.

SEA HOST FISH 'n CHIPS only 69¢
Authentic English-style fish fillets served with crisp French fries, tartar sauce and a wedge of lemon.

SEA HOST SHRIMP BOAT only $1 29
8 tasty shrimp in a special breading served with crisp French fries, hush puppies, cole slaw, tartar sauce and a wedge of lemon.

2310 Eighth Avenue
at 124th Street
New York, N.Y.

612 Nostrand Avenue
at Pacific Street Brooklyn, N.Y.
Phone 771-5185

172-02 Linden Blvd.
St. Albans, N.Y. (212) 291-6251

Figure 9.1. Advertisement for Sea Host chain in New York City. *New York Amsterdam News,* November 22, 1969. Source: ProQuest Historical Newspapers.

and Robinson contended that a lack of real resources from the parent company was the cause.[16]

As the congressional hearings showed, Sea Host was just one of many short-lived, White-owned franchisor companies. So, too, were the vast majority of new Black franchisors small in scale and short-lived. Boxer Muhammad Ali took on the burger business by starting a venture named ChampBurger, serving as vice president and director. No wonder, when he could not get Louisville waitstaff to serve him a burger. Ali's business began in December 1968, and the plan was to operate units only in Black communities and "run by franchisees indigenous to these communities." Concordant with the dietary proscriptions of the Nation of Islam, the restaurant would not sell products containing pork or shellfish. Other failed chains were fronted by entertainer Sammy Davis Jr. (Daniel Boone Fried Chicken—again with the "pioneers"), musician Fats Domino (another fried chicken restaurant), and comedian Moms Mabley (hamburgers). Mabley's ended before it started when the White nightclub owner who originated the idea claimed that her attorneys wanted more royalties than he thought reasonable.[17]

It is unclear the extent to which Black-named, White-operated franchisors engaged in unsavory business practices that took advantage of franchisees. What is clear is that they were short of capital and the requisite intentionality from parent companies and partners. And while the intent of Black franchisors may have been laudable, it was evident that the franchises would not benefit the average Black person. In fact, some companies, attuned to the sensibilities of White partners, would not cater specifically to Black entrepreneurs. Fats Domino's chain, for example, was going to give preference but not exclusive access to Black entrepreneurs. For all the chains, the franchisees were all men. For franchisors, the exception in the parade of Black male celebrity figureheads was gospel singer Mahalia Jackson, who lent her name to a chicken chain as the country rang in 1969.

Glori-Fried Chicken

A New Orleans native who migrated to Chicago in 1927, Jackson found stardom after her 1948 hit "Move on Up a Little Higher." Two years later she was the first gospel singer to perform at Carnegie Hall. But for Jackson, her music bore witness to injustice. She participated in civil rights rallies, sang at the March on Washington for Jobs and Freedom, and became a close confidant of Dr. King—apparently prodding him to "tell them about the dream" at the podium.[18]

Quite a different endeavor, then, to back a fried chicken chain. The *Chicago*

Defender reported on "the nation's first Negro-managed fast food franchise system," showcasing that the business was founded not only by a celebrity but by a Black woman.[19] From its Memphis headquarters, the operation intended for Black management to serve Black American consumers in their communities. A trade magazine advertisement for the franchise announced to potential new operators that new outlets could be had for $10,000 per unit (about $72,000 in 2020 dollars). In pointed language, the ad emphasized not only Jackson's celebrity but also the enterprise's unequivocal Blackness:

> Guess who's coming to dinner? Mahalia's Glori-Fried Chicken! Mahalia Jackson! The name and the fame of America's Queen of Gospel Singers are the success formula for a fabulous first in fast food franchising. The market: 22 million Black Americans . . . one out of four consumers in the nation's 78 largest cities! Mahalia Jackson's Chicken System, Inc. is ready to go with a unique Management, Menu and Marketing system specifically designed for Black America. MJCS licensees will be backed by a management team of successful Black businessmen plus experts in all phases of the franchised fast food industry. Continuous advertising and promotion based on the towering personality of Mahalia Jackson and her unique Soul Food menu are the keys to success for MJCS licensees.[20]

Like the other Black chains that eventually folded, Mahalia Jackson's was born out of a desire to reach Black people in an arena from which they had long been excluded. When the company debuted in Memphis, SCLC head Rev. Ralph D. Abernathy was on hand with local officials for the restaurant's groundbreaking.[21] The presence of the SCLC lent the brand and its message of Black empowerment the gravitas of a formidable civil rights organization. But at the end of the day, this Black-owned and -staffed franchise system was a for-profit business, not a social movement. Said board chairman A. W. Willis, "I don't think there is any other business philosophy than to make money."[22] His statement echoed John H. Johnson's candid declaration about starting *Ebony*: "I wasn't trying to make history—I was trying to make money."[23] Still, Black franchisors entered the fast food arena with racial inequity hovering in the background. For Willis, it was important that money generated by these restaurants circulated within the Black community, as this had not historically been the case with White-owned establishments. Nevertheless, the system could not afford to eschew White participation altogether. Most of the franchises had White partners, and their participation was publicized. The company also sold to investor groups, so that individuals could pool their resources to front the cash fee, which soon more than doubled to $25,000. The restaurant was both a realization of orthodox capitalist dreams and an emblem of Black mobility.

Mahalia's intended to confront the particularities of operating in Black neighborhoods, and addressed menu and pricing as foremost concerns. The chain would not make the same kind of amateurish mistakes that White-owned restaurants had made, claiming to "sell the ghetto areas" but discovering that the target community "couldn't relate" to a seventy-seven-cent roast beef sandwich when nineteen-cent hamburgers could be had across the street. Appealing to Black customers meant more than reducing absolute costs; good value for money was also critical. The restaurant served seventy-nine- to eighty-five-cent chicken snacks that included mashed potatoes and biscuits, and a "Soul Bowl" for sixty-five cents per pint, which included chicken giblets, rice, and gravy. These were hearty meals at a reasonable price, and the Soul Bowl was particularly popular as a late-night special. The chain challenged KFC, enjoining customers in advertisements for its first two South Side locations to "Stop Licking and Start Eating" its "Gloree-Fried Chicken." It also emphasized that Black patrons could look forward to an enjoyable dining experience, something that was not a given in White-owned establishments or restaurants in White space. Finally, as a Black-owned chain operating in Black neighborhoods, the aesthetics of the restaurant's architecture was another area in which the status quo was unacceptable. The chain used large picture windows on all storefronts, and was committed to doing so despite the social unrest in many cities. Willis insisted, "We don't screen the unit away from the community. After the riots in Chicago, some stores changed their whole architecture style by bricking up their windows. I saw some stores in Cleveland with no windows at all, just a front door. This is an effrontery to the community."[24]

Toward the end of 1969, half of the company had been bought by the Hooker's Performance Systems Inc. With its 50 percent stake in Mahalia Jackson's, Performance planned to open units that would allow Black entrepreneurs to "operate in the ghettos of America," although in ancillary roles for Black businesspeople. In any case, the enterprise began to falter in less than a year, as Performance Systems left ruined entrepreneurs in its wake. A. W. Willis resigned in the winter of 1970 and established Inner City Fast Food Corporation in Washington, D.C. He obtained the rights to develop Mahalia Jackson's Quick Diner, which was takeout only, and Mahalia Jackson's Kitchen, a full-service soul food restaurant. With a territory covering the entire Northeast, Willis planned for all units to be company-owned. Surprisingly, the soul food restaurants would not be in Black neighborhoods; instead, they would target downtown business and tourist traffic. Quick Diners, on the other

Figure 9.2. Yellow Pages listing for Mahalia Jackson's Chicken Restaurants in Chicago, 1971.

hand, were to be sited in Black neighborhoods in major cities, with a menu featuring burgers and prepackaged dinners. Industry observers viewed the Quick Diners as promising because they used Jackson's name, but were less sanguine about the Kitchens, perceiving less demand for soul food.[25]

The original Mahalia's forged ahead by entering into an agreement with Gulf Oil, in which it would cover the costs of converting existing and defunct service stations into chicken and catfish restaurants. Mahalia's would lease the service station from Gulf and, alongside the restaurant, operate one gasoline pump that would remain after the conversion. Mahalia's would then pay a percentage of food sales to Gulf, providing the energy company additional revenue beyond the wholesale profit on gas and oil.[26] The merged businesses took root in Detroit, Cleveland, and Chicago. Because the venture was not covered in mainstream business news, it is difficult to determine what besides the possibility to expand and revitalize central city business motivated Gulf Oil. It had been making overtures to Black communities to quell public critiques of its business practices, particularly in Africa.[27] A chicken chain would hardly erase these issues. In a very basic way, Black community outreach was a juggling act, because some Whites reacted negatively to overtures to Black communities. Indeed, Governor Lester Maddox of Georgia cancelled his Gulf Oil credit card in response to Gulf's advancing racially integrated advertising.[28]

For Mahalia Jackson's, the gas stations and the investment to refurbish them meant that the chicken chain could "move quickly into cities without having to expend capital on land and new buildings."[29] The next chapter will show that gas stations soon came into fast food's orbit more widely. But a Black consumer market was somewhat of a moving target. The neighborhoods the chain targeted had in some cases only recently become Black after undergoing racial transition. One such community was Chicago's South Shore. Beginning as marshy farmland outside Chicago's city limits in the 1850s, South Shore grew into a densely settled community home to a burgeoning White middle class that refused Black people admittance to the South Shore Country Club. African Americans did not begin to move in until the 1950s, in small numbers initially, and in much greater proportions in the 1960s. Though the South Shore Commission attempted to create "managed integration," the neighborhood turned over and rapidly became a middle-class, Black stronghold.[30] When that happened, White neighbors fled, in some cases literally taking their homes with them.[31]

South Shore did not necessarily want fast food outlets, backed by a Black celebrity or not. It already had the KFC that Alderman Leon Despres found disagreeable, and in February 1970, along with the neighboring community of Bryn Mawr West, residents ardently contested the proposed opening of a Mahalia Jackson's Chicken franchise: "We will not allow our community to be infested with stink, litter and excessive noises!" The carryout restaurant was to be sited as an addition to a Gulf Oil gas station at 75th and Euclid Avenue, and despite the vehement opposition of community residents, the franchise representative "arrogantly announced" that the "chicken shack" would be built regardless. The community sent telegrams and letters to Mayor Richard M. Daley, the local alderman, the Building and Zoning Commission, various city officials, and the president of the Gulf Oil companies. Unnamed residents argued that the restaurant would, in effect, be "an extension of the South Shore High School cafeteria," an assessment that harked back to the hot rod complaints and other concerns about drive-in restaurants' teenage clientele.[32] The restaurant was never built.

Mahalia Jackson's had two stores running in 1971, both on the South Side. One was in Chatham and the other was ensconced in the State Street corridor of public housing, adjacent to Stateway Gardens. If the goal were to bring fast food to Black communities that had heretofore been lacking, there could not have been a more appropriate location. Immediately before the store opened, there were fewer than ten intermittently spaced restaurants in the four-mile stretch of State Street from Cermak (22nd Street) to Garfield (55th Street). Among them were Fat Man's Golden Chicken, Harold's Chicken Shack No. 9, Burger King, and Prince & Joy's Drive-In. Apart from restaurants, residents had few retail options in general. Of the more than 160 businesses spanning more than thirty city blocks, the majority were doctor's offices and other sole proprietorships, community based organizations (particularly churches), municipal agencies, and health and social services. Few of the retail goods and services accessible to residents would constitute routine shopping and few were spaces where residents might window-shop, socialize, or make discretionary purchases. Moreover, many stores marked privation (e.g., check cashing) or created community risks (e.g., liquor stores).[33]

The resource deficits that characterized the communities where Mahalia's was opening shows that Willis's comments about the company's solely financial motivation was not entirely accurate. Willis seemed to dismiss any political aims. He did acknowledge that the chain would take special steps in developing the brand, such as avoiding highly securitized storefronts; but per his statement, this was primarily to assure that Mahalia's ran effectively and was appealing to the Black customers it sought. In other words, it would be unprofitable to produce outlets that were likely to cause offense. But surely these measures were also about an ethos of care for Black community residents. Customers could very well have bought their fried chicken from behind bulletproof partitions—indeed, they continue to do so today—but a carceral aesthetic was a nonstarter for this chain. Willis suggested that political mobilization and business were orthogonal when in fact they were very much entwined. The connection between the two was prominent in the case of All-Pro Chicken.

All-Pro Chicken

Mahalia Jackson's enterprise came on the heels of an operation that would become the largest Black-owned fast food concern: that of yet another athlete, NFL star Brady Keys. In 1967, the former All-Pro defensive linebacker for the Pittsburgh

Steelers founded All-Pro Chicken, a restaurant franchise targeted to "hard core inner cities." Unlike most of his celebrity fast food peers, Keys had no intention of being a titular figurehead; from the first he wanted direct involvement in the business operation. But there was no denying that his fame was the new chain's driving force. Indeed, All-Pro's executive vice president and director, Thomas M. Reich, a White man, wanted other athletes on board to capitalize on the public relations capital and market penetration they could bring. Because Reich recognized that Black business owners faced discrimination in securing financing and opportunities to be involved in business management, All-Pro would work closely with new franchisees to ensure they were adequately supported. However, Reich cautioned, they would do so without emasculating Black men with "handouts," the way he believed most American business enterprises did.[34]

Reich saw Black communities as a cash cow. A dearth of restaurants in Black communities made for "a bigger market for restaurant businesses in the hardcore inner cities than you can believe." Once again, the untapped frontier. He anticipated that All-Pro would be accepted in such communities because Black people were at the helm in management and ownership. If targeting Black consumers was a guaranteed moneymaker, it was despite the fact that they were foreign in behavior and values. Reich argued that "the black rank and file does not speak what you and I recognize as English. Instead of 'let's go downtown and do some shopping,' it's 'let's cut out and get us some rags.' And you hear this and think it's crazy. But this is the rank and file." From this perspective, it made sense to enlist Whites in the formation of the chain, because average Black folks were unlikely to have the sensibilities required for successful business.[35]

Keys came to the idea of a chicken chain after he had researched potential business ventures. Reading Harry Kursh's *The Franchising Boom* flipped a light switch, and he "decided that southern fried chicken was 'hot.'" He opened the first All-Pro Chicken restaurant in a racially mixed neighborhood in San Diego, though the company was headquartered in Pittsburgh. Offering a new "'Southern Crisp' taste in chicken," and making explicit use of a football theme wherein dishes included terms like "first down," "extra point," and "touchdown," Keys's new chain strove for novelty. Franchisees were sought in major newspapers with advertisements that continued the sports metaphors. The *New York Times* ran an ad in September 1968 calling for "Big League Investors" who were interested in "the big money fast-food franchise industry." On offer were six master franchise areas requiring an initial investment of $30,000, which could produce "highly leveraged profits." Ads made no mention of a career in the restaurant industry per se. Perhaps it was not seen as one.

All-Pro did not pretend to court those who dreamed of a career in food—it was after men who wanted to make plenty of money.

In 1968, Keys moved to play cornerback for the St. Louis Cardinals but continued to run All-Pro Chicken, relishing his potential to serve as a role model for Black youth in a domain beyond professional sports. In fact, he believed his business would "solve this whole damn problem" of U.S. racial divisions. Once again, Black capitalism as ghetto salve—the inclusion, finally, of Black people in the existing socioeconomic order would signal the end of racial strife. Keys had seven franchised outlets and wanted to license franchises to Black operators in Black ghettos, but after a few years of operation that hadn't "really worked out yet." The goal was to introduce two hundred franchises by the end of 1969. Perhaps in light of this goal, Keys gave a break to potential Black applicants: the initial capital requirements ($15,000) reported in the *Chicago Defender* were half what they were in the *New York Times*.[36]

By the summer of 1969, Keys had retired from the NFL to work full time on his chicken business. The summer also saw All-Pro's first stock offering.[37] There were approximately ten stores open at this time: four in Pittsburgh, three in Syracuse, two in San Diego, and a new unit at 780 Nostrand Avenue in Bedford-Stuyvesant, Brooklyn. Owned by Waldo Jeff, a counselor at Queens College and one of Keys's former college teammates, the restaurant—New York City's first All-Pro, and the first All-Pro anywhere to be owned and staffed by African Americans alone— was welcomed upon opening by Hilary Sandoval, executives from the Bedford-Stuyvesant Restoration Corporation, and other dignitaries. Jeff described the unit as an exemplar of "the proposition that a major business breakthrough by black men is essential to the ultimate resolution of the age-old black and white problem." Did Jeff mean that business would drive Black progress? Or that, as Booker T. Washington held, Black men who owned businesses were assured of the respect they deserved from Whites?[38] Keys, in any case, did not "believe in all Black." Reich had started out as the executive VP, and the company brass was integrated.

Conditions for prospective Black franchisees in the company worsened when the initial investment nearly tripled (though 100 percent financing was available); and Keys himself faced difficulties getting his company off the ground. Banks refused to lend to him, some bluntly expressing their prejudice: "You have an excellent franchising idea, but we're afraid to risk the money on a Negro management." Keys still managed to open six more units in New York's Black and Puerto Rican neighborhoods: Harlem, at 125th and Lenox, and 106th and Third Avenue; East New York, Brooklyn, at 1757 Pitkin Avenue; Bedford-Stuyvesant, Brooklyn, at 526 Nostrand Avenue; and Jamaica, Queens, at 88 Sutphin Boulevard. But Bob Browne, marketing director, said that the company had no plans to restrict their outlets to Black communities; they were also targeting sports fans in all-White neighborhoods and shopping centers. Growth continued in 1970 via another stock offering, the proceeds from which would go toward the building of thirteen new restaurants, about half company-owned, to join the twelve already operating in "inner-city areas."[39]

As the chain expanded, the company beefed up its advertising. Zebra Associates held the account. Caroline Jones, who would go on to become one of the most prominent names in advertising as an African American woman, recorded notes in her business notebooks about possible strategies and slogans for All-Pro advertising. A key theme was the idea of positioning All-Pro's chicken as of such high quality that it passed muster with Black women, and particularly mothers, who fried chicken in their own homes. A possible billboard campaign was "Ask your Mama. All-Pro Fried Chicken tastes so good even Mama buys it." Another possibility was to have nine Black women and one White woman pictured in an advertisement, with the copy reading "9 out of these 10 Mamas buy All-Pro Fried Chicken." And yet, Jones recognized that the agency would have to tread lightly with a "Mama" theme. She noted that the image could be perceived negatively, inasmuch as it called up tropes such as Aunt Jemima; any use would need to be careful and authentically positioned. Jones also toyed with the idea of emphasizing the frying oil as vegetable in origin (peanut), for the diet-conscious crowd, and mentioning that the menu contained no pork, perhaps both for cultural and health reasons. Regardless, quality was not the main theme to be stressed. Jones saw pricing as the main draw. Most of All-Pro's consumers were single and tended to buy the cheapest items, such as Snack Packs for $1.60. The store at 132nd and Lenox averaged purchases of just $1.75. These were not meals substituting for a whole family dinner but rather quick, affordable on-the-go snacks; Black people were buying "for convenience only." Jones thought that All-Pro should stress the pricing and the locations of the restaurants, to give the brand an identity that was lacking relative to its competitors.[40]

Keys focused on his brand's Black identity. But racism meant that the growth the company enjoyed and the exuberance Keys displayed did not always translate into success for Black franchisees. Keys fumed in a 1971 interview that only seventeen All-Pro outlets were operational, though hundreds had put in applications for a restaurant. These applicants—Black, with few resources or business experience—were denied bank financing. Each unit now cost $75,000 and banks required $11,000 as a down payment, far beyond the means of Keys's applicants. Even those with ample resources, such as the Harlem unit that, over a six-month period, had pulled in a $22,000 profit, could not obtain conventional bank funds. The SBA's promise to guarantee any bank loans seemed to be of no consequence in lenders' decision-making. Keys's explanation was simple: "The banks don't want to get involved with black people in the black community." One bank representative said of financing Keys' endeavors, "We're interested, but we're not sure whether Keys has really got a business going there, or he's just playing his blackness for all it's worth. What I mean is, are we talking about a 'good deed' that we just write off as community involvement if it goes sour, or is this a good investment."[41] The mere involvement of Black people in a business called into question its legitimacy as a for-profit enterprise—Blackness was equated with community-based charitable work. While banks dithered, All-Pro outlets were going belly-up. One short-lived New York unit held an auction in the Bronx in March 1974. Sold ignominiously were two Broasters, a Fryolator, a griddle, worktables, pots and pans, a refrigerator, office equipment, and the business itself.[42]

Keys nonetheless continued to search for potential Black franchisees, advertising in the Black press with language evoking both the potential for success and the necessity of a Protestant work ethic. A May 1971 advertisement in the *New York Amsterdam News* featured a sober portrait of Keys in a suit and tie, accompanied by the following text: "Brother—I want to hear from, and talk with 50 alert men, who want to own and operate their own All-Pro Fried Chicken and hamburger stores. Most of these new stores, maybe all, will be located in New York. There is no point in applying for this great opportunity, unless: 1. You have the skills to manage; 2. You are prepared to work hard; 3. You have $1,000 available as your personal investment in an All-Pro franchise."[43] All-Pro's franchise offering was cast in decidedly masculine terms that melded Black Power and conservative sensibilities. On the one hand, Keys was looking specifically for brothers—this business opportunity would be to the benefit of the potential Black franchisee and to his community, writ small and large. On the other, he exhorted would-be applicants to ensure they brought with them the requisite attitude of self-reliance, emphasizing the need for Black people to prove themselves worthy citizens.[44] Doing so gave government a pass on the conditions of Black citizens and made "moral fortitude a prerequisite for participating in civil society."[45]

Shortly after the ad ran, All-Pro finally saw an infusion of capital, this time from the federal government. The Department of Commerce's Economic Development Administration lent $2.2 million to the corporation to enable the construction of nineteen new stores. Additional monies came from Pittsburgh banks, local development groups in the three cities, and the All-Pro corporation itself. Despite Keys's purported reticence about "all-Black" businesses, he proclaimed that the new outlets would be "controlled by blacks, staffed by blacks and serve inner-city black communities and generate new income and jobs in these communities."[46] Furthermore, not content with the one fried chicken chain, All-Pro Chicken joined forces with John Y. Brown, president at KFC, to create Brady Keys' Kentucky Fried Chicken. Jointly owned by the two companies, the new partnership would develop Black-run chicken restaurants in dense, urban, Black neighborhoods, starting with fifty stores in the Midwest, and potentially expanding to the West and cities where neither KFC nor All-Pro had existing stores (therefore ruling out Baltimore, Pittsburgh, New York, and Washington, D.C.). Keys was named president and chief executive officer of the new company, and he envisioned employment opportunities in the range of one thousand positions. Industry observers saw this as a means to enter inner-city areas typically "shunned by white-run franchising companies."[47]

Marketing strategies for the venture centered on Keys entirely. He would replace Colonel Sanders in the design elements of all new outlets, including signs, packages, and advertisements (existing outlets would keep the original name and logo). Part of the rationale was that KFC believed the Black market was out of bounds with Colonel Sanders as the face of the company. According to one KFC spokesperson, "Black folks eat a lot of chicken," and therefore the inner-city market could be a new and lucrative one—but not with the Colonel as the brand image. Dick Beeson, an executive vice president at KFC, explained that Black consumers in central city communities would not buy chicken from a Kentucky colonel, the assumption apparently being that the Colonel would be too old-fashioned, out of step, or discordant for Black, urban customers, particularly those in northern cities. In fact, Sanders may have been a turnoff for Black audiences for reasons more explicitly about race. He had supported segregationist George Wallace's presidential bid and was reportedly pressured to resign from his post at the chicken chain as a result. KFC saw in Keys a cultural broker with an "ability to communicate with the black community," an intangible for which it was willing to lend resources. For his part, Keys was on board because he still needed capital for All-Pro, which was still in the red after three years. He also argued that the possibility existed for collaborative agreements to "develop inner-city areas usually shunned by white-run franchising companies."[48]

Industry pundits viewed the joint KFC–All-Pro venture with optimism and interest. *Nation's Restaurant News* commented that the collaboration would serve as a model for operating in inner cities. The editors argued that fast food had shunned urban spaces because downtown cores did not have a strong enough dinner trade, and ghetto markets were sown with "too much hostility, alienation and confusion." Now, KFC would "ride into the ghetto market on the husky shoulders" of

Brady Keys, a strategy that was sure to be profitable and for which the food service industry could be proud.[49] At least some Whites working in the industry did not agree. An anonymous Atlanta restaurateur wrote in to the magazine to voice his displeasure at the Keys–KFC venture. Stating that he was "dismayed enough" to read about the story at all, what he found particularly troubling was the newspaper's support: "It seems to me that with so many white franchisees struggling to hang on to businesses into which they've invested their life's savings, you should not be praising this deal which will only increase competition." The editors' acerbic reply was that White businessmen were not at risk, "for restaurateurs have studiously avoided the ghetto . . . this joint venture [is] really moving into a competitive vacuum."[50]

The editors were right. Fast food had yet to give Black neighborhoods a serious look, leaving unclaimed a significant customer base. The new Black franchisors were doing work that first- and second-generation chains largely would not. Despite Keys's partnerships, it was clear that fast food companies were reluctant to enter the inner city without Black chaperones who were perceived as mitigating risk. Keys continued to play chaperone as he expanded his fast food reach to hamburgers. In early 1970, he formed All-Pro Equities, which bought a Detroit Burger King outlet that had been planned to serve a "fringe neighborhood" that had become an all-Black community by the time the restaurant opened. The store enjoyed strong sales, but Burger King was reluctant to keep a White-managed and -owned unit in a Black location.[51] All-Pro Enterprises purchased the franchise hoping to capitalize on badly needed volume, and Burger King sought to make inroads into growth opportunities in the ghetto. Keys also saw the purchase as a conduit for his own professional development. He was learning extensively about law, operations, and restaurant management, and asserted, "Jim McLamore is honest about moving into the ghetto and he isn't out to exploit anyone." Burger King provided much of the financing for the project (neither party would divulge precise figures), and also appointed a manager of urban development. Keys's new Burger King outlets were quite successful, ranking among the top two nationally in sales. Between KFC and Burger King, All-Pro planned further expansion in Cleveland, Chicago, and D.C.[52]

All-Pro's last extension came in late 1973 in a venture that would develop as many as seventy franchised A&W restaurants targeting the same demographic across several large metropolitan areas, including St. Louis, Chicago, Detroit, Pittsburgh, New York, and Cleveland. A&W's traditional menu (primarily hamburgers) would be supplemented with Keys's chicken. Edward S. Weber Jr., president of A&W, was pleased to work with Keys "for our initial move into inner-city markets."[53]

Afri-Kingdom

Whereas Brady Keys had amassed a figurative fast food kingdom, Roger Brown, star lineman for the Los Angeles Rams, launched a literal one: Afri-Kingdom, which made its debut in 1970. Despite its seeming nod to the continent, the name was pronounced "A Fry Kingdom." The restaurant offered the "right applicants" a deferral in the $10,000 franchise fee, which the operator would pay back over five years. Although industry commentators stated that race was not a factor in considering franchise applicants, the *Chicago Defender* reported that the franchise was "a totally black owned and operated enterprise." Roger Brown declared that "Afri-Kingdom was set up to make black men businessmen, and to give them an opportunity that they would not otherwise have to go into business." Toward that end, he contracted with Black vendors and initiated a restaurant training school that taught young people not only to prepare and sell the menu items, but also how to keep books, manage inventory, and other skills that would set them on a trajectory to chain management.[54] Brown seemed to make it a point to bring in and elevate Black people from humble backgrounds, such as Vice President Alex Patterson, once a small-town boy from Greenville, Mississippi, who at twenty-seven became owner of the first Afri-Kingdom restaurant in Chicago.[55]

The chain launched in a "ghetto area"—210 East Pershing Road (at East 39th Street) in Chicago's Bronzeville neighborhood. Said Brown, "White areas are over saturated with fast food service restaurants, but they are really needed in the black community."[56] The outlet was a freestanding building that Brown believed resembled "a mini-colonial mansion from the Deep South." In fact, the modest building, despite its bright yellow–orange exterior siding, appeared rather marginal, with ill-fitting structural references to Georgian architecture on an otherwise nondescript one-story frame. Large freestanding signage displayed the logo and a basic description of what was offered within: "FRIED CHIK'N 59¢."[57] In Brown's view, Afri-Kingdom had placed something pretty—a reference to the building's aesthetic, which Brown himself had designed—"in the middle of a trash pile."[58] Hardly a ringing endorsement of the neighborhood in which Brown sited his new establishment. Besides, an architectural motif of slave-owning gentility could hardly have been compelling.

The restaurant's second location, at 3545 West Roosevelt, supplanted the popular Whoopee Burger, which had operated on Chicago's West Side for about five years. Apparently inheriting Whoopee's menu, Afri-Kingdom sold burgers, Polish sausage, and other items, though the outlet remained centered on fried chicken "cooked in an expensive and time consuming operation." Staff marinated the

Figure 9.3. An Afri-Kingdom Restaurant on the South Side of Chicago. A. Bernie Wood Papers, Archives Center, National Museum of American History, Smithsonian Institution, Washington, D.C.

chicken for twenty-four hours using a recipe from Brown's Virginia upbringing, and then battered and breaded it before deep frying. When *Quickservice Magazine* profiled the new chain, these cooking methods took center stage. Indeed, the report made no mention of the Black ownership, even as it featured photographs of Alex Patterson and other Black employees, some of whom were women.[59]

Brown, on the other hand, was vocal about the venture's emphasis on Black empowerment. He lauded the chain's hiring of a Black architect, in addition to the fact that "the sub-contractors are black, and we bank with a black bank—Independence National Bank." However, at least one contractor was not Black. A. Bernie Wood, president and creative director of Admart, was responsible for McDonald's corporate image and designed everything for the company from interiors to product merchandise. He worked on the design for other restaurants, including Afri-Kingdom. His logo immediately suggested a basic stick-figure person: a head, two arms raised as if cheering or in outreach, and two legs. Upon closer inspection, the torso and legs form the letter A, and the upper part mimics a crown with jewels at the top. Taken together, Wood's imagery suggested the royalty associated with this chicken

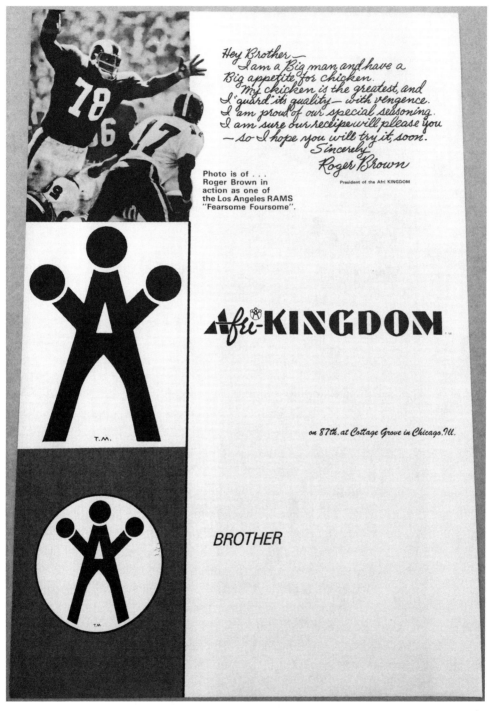

Figure 9.4. Promotional literature for Afri-Kingdom, 1970–72. A. Bernie Wood Papers, Archives Center, National Museum of American History, Smithsonian Institution, Washington, D.C.

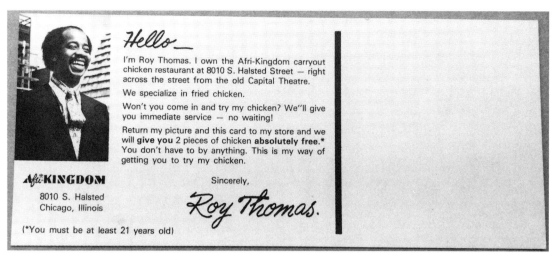

Figure 9.5. Promotional literature for Afri-Kingdom, 1970–72. A. Bernie Wood Papers, Archives Center, National Museum of American History, Smithsonian Institution, Washington, D.C.

kingdom. Rendered in striking black, white, and orange colors, the distinctive logo appeared throughout the restaurant's structures and materials, such as menus, paper carryout bags, and signage. Figure 9.4 shows the back side of a three-panel menu. The text reads, "Hey Brother—I am a Big man and have a Big appetite for chicken. My chicken is the greatest, and I 'guard' its quality—with vengeance. I am proud of our special seasoning. I am sure our recipe will please you—so I hope you will try it, soon. Sincerely Roger Brown."

A promotional coupon for the store at 8010 South Halstead made operator Roy Thomas the visual and topical focal point of the restaurant's reputation. In this appeal, Afri-Kingdom positioned its chicken as the stuff of manly Black men. Like Keys, Brown beckoned to his brethren. In this case it was to sample "his" chicken rather than to come on board as a franchisee. But both chains reveal that the gender politics of fast food in Black communities was one in which, appropriating the rhetoric of Black Power movements, empowering Black men with their own capitalist enterprises would replace racial justice as the means of achieving equity with Whites. If, as Nikol Alexander-Floyd argues, Black Power ideology framed Black liberation "as a quest to achieve manhood," Black franchisors wholeheartedly embraced that goal.[60] Fast food was the remedy to the kind of anguish a thirty-year-old respondent in Kenneth Clark's *Dark Ghetto* expressed: "A lot of times, when I'm working, I become despondent as hell and I feel like crying. I'm not a man, none of us are men! I don't own anything. I'm not a man enough to own a store; none of us are."[61] Black franchisors like Keys and Brown sought to alleviate the worries of Black men who feared they would never find themselves on the right side of capital.

In 1973, the company planned significant expansion in Chicago. Four new stores were to open, the first of which was on 87th Street, between the communities of Chatham and Auburn. Under construction were stores on 47th Street in Grand Boulevard, 43rd Street in Kenwood, and North Clybourn Avenue in the Cabrini-Green housing projects. McDonald's had tried and failed two years earlier to launch a restaurant in the Cabrini-Green community just two blocks away. Motivated by the fifteen-thousand-strong captive market and noticing that other low-income communities generated high sales and earnings, corporate assumed the same could be possible for Cabrini.[62] According to Roland Jones, the company badly misjudged the depth of poverty, isolation, and crime. Few locals and no one from outside the neighborhood patronized the store, and the store did not last long before it eventually closed.[63]

The idea of Black consumers as a captive market was one that resonated strongly with both Black- and White-owned corporate actors. Even if fast food were to serve as a pathway to collective economic empowerment, it could not erase the fact that the industry did so by exploiting a lack of residential mobility. The institutional practices that kept Black households restricted in space certainly created a ready-made market. In 1967, *Business Week* wrote that retailers in Black neighborhoods had it made: "Since many Negroes have no cars, they are prisoners of the ghetto and must shop there."[64] As late as 1980, Felix Burrows, head of Chicago-based Black marketing firm ViewPoint, argued on behalf of the Adolph Coors Company that the rising socioeconomic position of Black Americans, a "young, geographically concentrated market," made for an investment that was difficult to beat. He contended, "Earlier, we said that the Black consumer market is concentrated in the major metro areas of the country. If this is true, you have a virtually captive market if your business is located in the Black community. If your customers are going outside of your serving area to spend your money, then some consumer needs are not being met."[65] Burrows was frank in his assessment of the potential for retailers—in this case alcoholic beverages—to benefit from Black residential segregation.

Roger Brown also saw Afri-Kingdom as relying on the spatial constraints of race in urban America. Highlighting the deficits that characterized retail in poor Black communities, Brown pressed the need for fast food: "We are filling a basic need in providing quality, tasty food in ghetto neighborhoods too long neglected by white restaurant operators. Our success has proved beyond question that there is an excellent market for Afri-Kingdom Fried Chicken."[66] Both he and Keys overstated their contributions to local food environments by portraying Black communities as bereft of dining options. Keys claimed that before fast food, it was impossible to eat out cheaply in Black neighborhoods, and that go-to meals for community residents were beans, rice, and greens.[67] Setting aside that there would be nothing wrong with quick meals consisting of rice and beans, Keys dismissed all the small, independent restaurants run by Black owners in Bronzeville, Harlem, and elsewhere.

Brown was accurate in that White restaurateurs had foregone the ghetto. But Black-owned fast food chains had long been in the game. By 1965, after thirteen years in business, Harold's Chicken Shack operated several outlets, and owner Harold Pierce's franchise began informally through trademark agreements with friends and family members and royalties paid on each bird sold. He soon earned the nickname the "Fried Chicken King," and his logo was designed to match: a man in royal garb (coat and crown) chasing a chicken, hatchet in hand.[68] By 1975, he had twenty outlets around Chicago, though none in White neighborhoods. "They'd kick my ass out," Pierce mused.[69]

Meanwhile, Brown was busily expanding Afri-Kingdom. In addition to doubling the number of stores in Chicago, he sought to expand the burgeoning franchise nationally, with an eye toward starting in Detroit, his professional hometown. Notably, the chain would also be aiming for White suburbs as it grew. But like All-Pro Chicken, Afri-Kingdom had difficulty obtaining loans for its expansion plans. The company operated at a deficit in its first year but became profitable the year after, and by 1972 it was taking in sales of $2.3 million with profits of $90,000. In Brown's judgment, the obstacles to acquiring capital reflected lenders' lack of interest in funding new fast food franchises of any sort, but particularly "ghetto oriented" Black businesses. Brown lamented that he felt like a motel blanket, "having been turned down so many times."[70]

In the end, the kingdom was not to last. Brown thought his chain was on pace to enjoy nationwide recognition. Instead, the company was defunct within two years. When in 1976 Congress held hearings on the Fairness in Franchising Act, Brown testified. The proposed laws sought to protect operators from unfair franchisors, and Brown spoke in strong support. He was a franchisor, not a franchisee, so he had not experienced problems like arbitrary denials for license renewal or coercive practices. But having seen his hopes dashed, he argued that his "unfortunate history with Afri-Kingdom" showed that franchising was a risky proposition that hurt more entrepreneurs than it helped.

Brown told the Senate Committee on Commerce about his goal of building a nationwide fried chicken franchise in the Black community. He explained that like those of major chains such as McDonald's, his franchisees paid royalty fees and rent; but after his company began to founder following its expansion in Chicago,

Figure 9.6. Harold's Chicken Shack #1 at 1346 East 53rd Street, Chicago (Hyde Park), no date. Photograph by Adam Lisberg. Image apf7-05359. Courtesy of the *Chicago Maroon* and the Hanna Holborn Gray Special Collections Research Center, University of Chicago Library.

it was soon "unable to give any services to its franchisees." When Afri-Kingdom was declared bankrupt and sold, the unnamed individual who took over continued collecting payments from franchisees despite not providing any services from headquarters. Brown thought that the new owner might even evict the franchisees when their leases ended and take over the premises. Pointing to the many failed franchises that littered the landscape, Brown stated that legislation was needed to protect equally the relative investments of both franchisors and franchisees.[71]

In the final analysis, taking up the franchisor role did not appear to be the pathway to Black empowerment its proponents had hoped. Keys was the most successful of the Black franchisors by far, but even his path was hardly smooth. Yet, the allure of franchising, with its masculine sense of ownership and authority otherwise denied, was great for many prospective Black entrepreneurs; however, many who dove in despite the risks found themselves trod under foot by the fast food machine. The federal government made fast food the focus of funds and support; the flight of capital from America's ghettos left few other investments; and African Americans had been systematically denied access to building wealth. Black franchisors hoped to lead businesses that served as anchors for economic and community development. They would be part of a long history of African Americans finding the possibility of racial uplift through Black purchasing power—as Andrew Diamond put it, "businessmen as the quintessential 'race men.'"[72] For the most part, it didn't work. What it did seem to do was gin up interest among the major chains to pursue the Black frontier they had left unexplored. They heard the heads of Black franchisor operations say so many times that Black neighborhoods were waiting to be conquered that they finally took that advice. The work of Black franchisors showed that fast food outlets made sense in the ghetto and elsewhere in central cities. It could be more than a palliative for racial strife—it could make money.

Part III

Black Catastrophe

Yeah, they passed, they were going to the White neighborhoods, they ain't care about me. They were going somewhere else, I kept on trying to flag 'em down—man, we had lights, everything trying to stop them people. They did not come, they came here the fourth day. And gave me some water, I was in the boat. They dropped the water so hard they tried to sink my boat! I asked for some water, they gave it to me. Bet you I won't ask for no more.

—Michael Knight, resident of the Lower Ninth Ward, New Orleans,
When the Levees Broke: A Requiem in Four Acts

In my city we would keep the traffic in the dark people, the coloreds . . . they're animals anyway, so let them lose their souls.

—Philip Tattaglia, *The Godfather*

10

Blaxploitation

Fast Food Stokes a New Urban Logic

Priest—the slick, cocaine spoon–sporting, drug-dealing protagonist of the 1972 film *Superfly*—apparently eschewed fast food restaurants, eating and meeting with shady colleagues instead at sit-down restaurants, diners, cafés, or clubs. In one scene, he conducts an illicit business meeting at Mister B's, a restaurant on Lenox Avenue between 134th and 135th, across the street from CORE's Harlem office. Set in a brownstone's garden level, the interior design comprised wall-to-wall wood paneling, paintings of naked women, and a long bar with cushioned, vinyl, high-back chairs. According to his partner Eddie, Priest was living the American Dream; so it is notable that eating meals out at fast food outlets was not commensurate with a man of his stature.

To be sure, the major chains had yet to penetrate Harlem during Priest's time, but independent fast food restaurants dotted the neighborhood. Visible just up the block from Mister B.'s is a storefront whose "KFC" signage conveys to contemporary eyes a Kentucky Fried Chicken. But it must have indicated a Kansas Fried Chicken outlet. The local chain belonged to Horace Bullard, an East Harlem native and African American man whose string of chicken outlets made him a millionaire. Bullard launched his chain at the age of thirty in 1968 and had more than a dozen locations by the mid-1970s.[1] Despite appearing repeatedly throughout the 1970s in the *New York Daily News* among restaurants cited for health code violations, Kansas Fried Chicken received critical acclaim in the *New York Times* as a standout in the city's fast food scene. One reviewer declared its peppery "soul food" taste the victor over Kentucky Fried Chicken ("sloppy coating and unpleasant residue of grease"), Chicken Lickin ("no detectable taste"), and Chicken Delight ("dismal tired orange hue").[2]

Because *Superfly* was shot on location, Kansas Fried Chicken's cameo gives the viewer a peek into the physical consumer landscape of 1970s Harlem. After Bullard's outlets, there would follow a string of other fried chicken joints. The first of these appears to be Kennedy Fried Chicken, created by one Taeb Zia, an Afghan immigrant who, after finding work at Kansas Fried Chicken through an employment agency in 1972, worked as a crew member for three years before becoming a Bullard franchisee. After that he decided to strike out on his own and launched Kennedy Fried Chicken.[3] As will be seen, Zia spawned a legion of fried chicken establishments in Black and Brown neighborhoods, variously named with permutations of "Kennedy," "chicken," and other words; and with other monikers altogether such as Crown Fried Chicken.

Apart from the street appearance in Gordon Parks's film, a connection between fast food and works like *Superfly* exists symbolically as well, revealed in the motivational impulses that drove both industries. Blaxploitation films, as the genre came to be known, relied on a formula that typically portrayed pimps, gangsters, and other hard cases (including women) who battled "the Man" in tough Black neighborhoods. Arriving to screens in the late 1960s, these films saved Hollywood from economic collapse. Filmgoing audiences had been falling and becoming more fragmented for at least twenty years due to television, foreign films, and other competing media. When blockbuster films proved expensive but unprofitable and bankruptcy loomed on the horizon, Hollywood decided to capitalize on the fact that young, Black, urban residents were filling theaters abandoned by White people fleeing for the suburbs. Moreover, needing to reckon with increasing social critique over representation and labor discrimination, Hollywood was incentivized to create and distribute Black-focused films. Following back-to-back hits in *Sweet Sweetback's Baadasssss Song* and *Shaft*, the genre of Blaxploitation was born. The films drew huge crowds and made plenty of money, but they lowered artistic standards; also, by their sheer number they crowded out more socially and politically progressive representations of Black people on the big screen.[4] The moniker Blaxploitation therefore referred to both the problematic filmic portrayals of Black folks and the ways the genre fueled White corporate moneymaking with Black consumer dollars.

Fast food in the 1970s hewed a similar path, entering its own era of Blaxploitation. The industry found itself with a shrinking customer base in the suburbs that necessitated a move to the city. Fast food was not on the verge of collapse, but it certainly needed the urban market. Simply replacing White operators in racially changing neighborhoods with Black men was not enough—it was time for active construction of new outlets in the ghetto. Black customers were no longer a mere afterthought or a necessity wrought by social unrest; corporations now turned to actively exploiting Black communities for profit. While industry discourse in the 1960s was rife with hand-wringing about the "Negro problem" and how to assuage

Great Savings...
Great Eating...At...

Kansas Fried Chicken

...the Friendly Chicken Place

AS A SPECIAL OFFER FOR YOU . .

DAILY NEWS, WEDNESDAY, FEBRUARY 23, 1977

Figure 10.1. Kansas Fried Chicken advertisement in the *New York Daily News,* February 23, 1977. Source: Newspapers.com.

racial discord by doling out franchises, by the 1970s Black people occupied negligible space in trade periodicals. Fast food was no longer talking about Black people; it was simply determined to relieve them of their money as efficiently as possible. The banks that had created "minority loan pools" in the late 1960s under the guise of social responsibility closed out those special initiatives in the 1970s, believing that minority businesses were no different than any others.[5] Over the decade, fast food outlets would crowd out other dining options—and other businesses, for that matter. But unlike Blaxploitation films, the industry never deserted Black folks. Rather, the 1970s were just the start of a long trajectory of targeting Black communities.

The chains needed data to guide the new initiatives, so they embarked on market research to uncover how patrons used restaurants, down to which seats were occupied most often.[6] KFC worried that it had "made a few mistakes by not building in certain areas," and ad agency Leo Burnett completed an intensive, two-phased study to obtain a "clear and verifiable picture of KFCs empirical market position and potential within the Black communities of Chicago." McDonald's as well began to assess whether and where stores should be built to serve Black people and convened a Black Store Task Force that would "build more stores to serve black customers." Corporate determined that "cities were now essential to the company's continued growth, and winning over black and ethnic urban consumers was critical to the company's success in the cities."[7]

An Industry in Turmoil

The 1970s brought large-scale change to fast food, building on the late 1960s acquisition of chains by large food and beverage conglomerates. Processed food companies sought out fast food chains because restaurants were a primary reason why their sales were declining, and because they could sell their products to the acquired restaurant. By purchasing fast food brands, food-service companies would be ideally positioned to respond to the trend of Americans spending increasing time and money away from home.[8]

Burger King was purchased by Pillsbury in 1967, Burger Chef by General Foods in 1968, and Kentucky Fried Chicken by Heublein in 1971. Pillsbury wanted the burger chain but viewed its new franchisees with distrust and skepticism, thinking them minimally skilled and prone to lawsuits. It forged ahead with new initiatives, including a not especially imaginative animated spokesman—The Burger King—and a flurry of new products (such as onion rings). It soon launched the "Have It Your Way" campaign, the first single-theme approach across all media, which increased sales and consumer awareness.[9]

Meanwhile, the second-largest U.S. spirits company also entered fast food. Heublein anticipated that KFC would slot in easily with the conglomerate's broad variety of food and beverage products and quickly fatten corporate coffers. At the time of purchase, everyone associated with KFC seemed to be millionaires. President John Y. Brown had made himself and stockholders rich after buying and remaking Harland Sanders's franchise. He instituted a standard system where individuals obtained distinct outlets rather than the right to cook Harland's recipe at an existing restaurant. Many franchisees later got rich by selling profitable outlets back to corporate. And yet KFC was in trouble. Sales volume was decreasing, the economy was tight, store managers were leaving, store quality was declining, and the chain had overextended itself into money-losing ventures like roast beef, fish and chips, and even a series of Colonel Sanders Inns. Heublein took on the brand at a price of $200 million and promptly inherited a suite of problems.[10]

Fast food began to rethink its cruise control setting on the foundational consumer base of White, suburban families, particularly as fissures began to appear in the form of suburban saturation. McDonald's, Burger King, and Kentucky Fried Chicken had populated the suburbs to the point that they would soon be competing with themselves. They would need every means of differentiating which customers dined where, and differentiating their brands from one another. Psychographics emerged in the 1970s as a new way to characterize customers. It used demographic and psychological factors to create unique consumer segments more comprehensive than census data alone. The consumer clusters it constructed then targeted people with products thought to be the most appealing to those groups.[11] Inevitably, segments lacked complexity when it came to Black urbanites. Today, thanks to years of gentrification, Harlem carries a range of labels that a decade ago were the province of White space.[12] But in the early 1970s, psychographic analyses charted a one-note stereotype. In 1973, Kelvin Wall lambasted retailers for viewing Black people as a monolith. He contended, "Much of the advertising directed at blacks obviously is based on hunch and superficial assumptions."[13] When it came to fast food, this would mean a lack of attention to varied Black consumer needs and a blind rush to infiltrate the ghetto.

Fast food began trying to differentiate its brands through changes in style (e.g., more seating) and new, more diverse menu items. The design changes that began in the mid-1960s, such as McDonald's switch from red and white drive-ins to an earth-toned, brown mansard roof, had by the 1970s solidified the symbolism those changes meant to convey. McDonald's was now a "respite from the stresses of an impersonal society," a "field of care" that made it central to Americans' lives.[14] A sedate style signaled a restaurant that could credibly serve any food, and an atmosphere of comfort rather than ebullience. The new design epitomized White, middle-class family life.[15] In that vein, an important menu innovation was to offer new child-focused products. Burger Chef created the Funburger in 1973, a small sandwich for children presented in a colorful box with a prize. Then came the Funmeal, which contained a burger, fries, soda, and a dessert with games. McDonald's appropriated this to much success as the Happy Meal in 1978.[16]

But even as fast food companies made these changes, new competition arrived. One was Bojangles' Famous Chicken 'n Biscuits, named after Bill "Bojangles" Robinson, a Black tap dancer and entertainer of prodigious fame from the early twentieth century. After its 1977 launch, the restaurant transitioned into a regional chain.[17] Chicken George, named after the character in *Roots,* was introduced by an African American man named Theodore N. Holmes in 1979. Headquartered in Baltimore, the brand wanted to be "the gourmet chicken city slickers love."[18] Little is available to show how the chain advertised its arrival, but it did so to raucous demand. The Mondawmin store was expected to generate at most $15,000 a week in sales, but the registers overflowed with revenue totaling $46,000. The chain succeeded well into the 1980s before closing shop.

Two other chains had a more lasting impact. Wendy's brashly appeared on the scene in 1970. Launched by David Thomas, formerly a regional vice president at KFC, it offered only large burgers, ground and shaped in-store, along with fries. The chain began in small cities and towns in Ohio and Indiana, and sold regional franchises. By 1975, eighty licensees were slated to open approximately two thousand new outlets across the country. The décor hewed to its old-fashioned theme with Tiffany lamps, cane-back chairs, and tabletops that featured 1900s Sears catalog material.[19]

Al Copeland's Popeyes was the other major entrant to fast food in the 1970s, and one that set out from the start to tackle the chicken market in Black neighborhoods. Copeland (who was White) was born in Arabi, a working-class New Orleans suburb adjacent to the Lower Ninth Ward that maintained a paucity of Black residents. At midcentury, the population of twenty thousand was 1.23 percent Black, and by 1980 when the population had declined by almost two-thirds, there were no Black people at all.[20] Copeland, the product of a "broken marriage," was reared by his grandmother in public housing, and the family received welfare. He had a run-in with the law at age twelve after stealing a bicycle, but the officers let him go. Copeland later dropped out of high school.[21] He tried his hand at different quick service concepts, including a money-losing chicken restaurant called Chicken on the Run, in 1971. He tried again a year later and landed on the venture that would last—Popeyes—selling a Cajun heritage that wasn't his.[22] Franchising began in late

1976 or early 1977, targeting primarily the Black consumer market and selling the first northern outlet to yet another football player: African American Pittsburgh Steeler running back Franco Harris, a New Jersey native.[23]

Copeland named the chain not after the cartoon character (who did appear in early TV commercials), but after the nickname of a real person, NYPD officer Eddie Egan, portrayed as Popeye Doyle in the 1971 film *The French Connection*. Egan worked in Bedford-Stuyvesant's Eighty-First Precinct and said of himself, "They call me Archie Bunker with a badge." His colleagues agreed. Lieutenant Vincent Hawkes was Egan's commander during the bust depicted in the film. He disputed some cinematic representations, but said, "That guy Gene Hackman portrayed him perfectly. If you know Eddie Egan, that's the guy." Doyle (the film character) was a racist who took pleasure in violating the civil rights of Black citizens and proclaimed, "Never trust a nigger." The real Egan had apparently "started a riot" in Harlem as a rookie in the mid-1950s on account of his indiscriminate targeting of Black motorists. By 1971, when the movie was released, Egan had made more than eight thousand arrests in sixteen years on the force.[24] It took a particular kind of chutzpah to grow up in a New Orleans metro community that excluded Black people, appropriate African American cooking styles, and use them to develop a franchised chain named after an avowedly racist police officer who delighted in the subjugation of the Black people he was tasked to protect. A more apt expression of fast food's Blaxploitation is difficult to imagine.

In the early 1970s, McDonald's and Kentucky Fried Chicken had a significant lead in sales compared to Popeyes and the other chains. Table 1 shows sales in dollars for 1973. But in light of the new competition, all the brands fought vigorously for market share. They did so in a rush for cities, where high population density pulsed with unclaimed riches. New York, a late entrant to second-generation fast food, was the most fertile ground. Fast food had thrived in Chicago and Washington through the 1950s and 1960s, but New York only began to host major chains beyond White Tower and the Automat in the 1970s. Its dearth of outlets led the *Times* critic who raved about Kansas Fried Chicken to call the city a "benighted backwater" when it came to fast food.[25] Indeed, in 1974 only eighty of McDonald's 2,500 stores were in urban locations.[26] It along with KFC led the urban charge.

As chains rushed to populate Manhattan—specifically Midtown and other commercial districts—they called it the "inner city." The term was used interchangeably in industry discourse to refer both to downtowns and Black neighborhoods. Even when analysts meant the former, they were very much concerned about crime and approached with caution. Fast food outlets regularly appeared in newspapers as sites of robberies, shootings, and other offenses during the 1970s, with Little

Table 1. Leading fast food chains ranked by sales volume, 1973

Chain	Sales in 1972	Number of company-owned stores	Number of franchised stores
KFC	$1.147 billion	996	3,406
McDonald's	$1.033 billion	648	1,624
Burger King	$275 million	278	704
Burger Chef	$200 million	300	700
Gino's	$128 million	337	0
Church's	$100 million	360	66
White Castle	$57 million	126	0

Note: Data are drawn from "50 Leading Food Service Chains" (table), *Nation's Restaurant News,* August 6, 1973.

Tavern and Afri-Kingdom among the victims; and if an outlet was not hit itself, these acts were occurring in the immediate proximity, worrying franchisees and executives. But crime was no longer a deal breaker; it was now just a challenge to be overcome.[27] Whatever problems there were in 1970s urban America, fast food was determined to navigate them. Black communities were a key part of the calculus.

The focus on Black communities was not simply a reaction to suburban saturation or a side effect of generalized urban expansion. As shown in previous chapters, Black franchisors like Brady Keys modeled the possibility of money to be made in the ghetto, and the major chains could not leave that windfall uncontested. Potential profits in Black neighborhoods took on special resonance as shifting cultural terrains, oil crises, and economic and social shocks made Black communities ripe for extraction.[28]

A New Black, Urban Logic

Second-generation fast food's sustained push to the city was aided by the coming obsolescence of first-generation restaurants. White Castle was still planning new units in the cores of major metropolitan areas, but without the confident future it once had.[29] Many early chains had met their end altogether, such as Hot Shoppes. In 1974, Bill Marriott Jr. announced that his business would phase out the restaurants and focus on hotels. Stores were first scaled back to twenty locations, and then again to twelve. Eventually the flagship closed and was sold for $6.5 million to the National Bank of Washington, which promptly razed it.[30]

Horn & Hardart also fell into obsolescence, at which point it was reborn as second-generation fast food by becoming a Burger King franchisee, converting existing Automats in prime Manhattan real estate to do so. In Burger King, Horn & Hardart saw a fast-growing brand where youthful appetites and fun would carry it to the future. Horn & Hardart executives expressed growing consternation about the company's inability to compete. The head office was dismayed about every aspect of the operation, from low sales revenue to a substandard labor force (the latter included "an unkempt griddle man with wild hair and a largely-exposed hairy chest.") Partnering with Burger King was just the way to revive a struggling chain that had become old-fashioned and primitive.[31] After its transformation to Burger King, the company broke all sales records in its history, selling more than $100 million for the first time, mostly due to the new direction in fast food.[32] The company also bought Bojangles' to sell licenses, thereby becoming both franchisee and franchisor.

It was full steam ahead for the second generation's penetration of cities, but concerns about reputation remained. The disorder that drive-ins had provoked in the suburbs made for a stricter regulatory environment that hampered expansion. Such headaches were enough of a motivation to pursue the city, where local communities were less likely to be an impedance. But the second generation had to retain the aura of excitement that would make it attractive to downtowns and residential urban spaces. It could not be conflated with first-generation outlets whose familiarity bred contempt. Despite those chains' challenges with disorder, 1960s filmic portrayals of suburban fast food often set these outlets squarely within the realm of wholesome, normative Whiteness. For example, in the 1967 film *The Graduate*, the characters Ben and Elaine dine at a drive-in scintillating with the vibrancy of Southern California's glamour and its beautiful White youth. They might have been a bit rowdy—even Ben must roll up his window against the noise—but nothing is too out of hand, and he and Elaine with their burgers and fries remain charming, upper-middle-class young people. In contrast, urban fast food in 1970s cinema was portrayed as the province of the marginal, disreputable, and anachronistic. Second-generation fast food could be something the middle class ate abstractedly simply as a means to consume needed calories, as did journalists Woodward and Bernstein in the 1976 film *All the President's Men,* refueling late at night with McDonald's for the fortitude needed to strategize their next steps in investigating the Watergate scandal. But in new urban settings, second-generation restaurants might also be patronized by those who were apparently too troubled to make it to the suburbs. In the 1975 film *Dog Day Afternoon,* one of the two bank robbers, Sonny, is portrayed as doubly deviant because in addition to robbing a bank, he failed in a heterosexual

Figure 10.2. Former Horn & Hardart Automats transformed into Burger Kings and Bojangles' restaurants. (a) Automat location at 1177 Sixth Avenue in Manhattan in the 1940s (nynyma_rec0040_1_00998_0029). (b) (dof_1_00998_0029) and (d) (dof_1_00998_0030) depict two different sides of the building, where Bojangles' and Burger King were operating in the 1980s. (c) (dof_3_00150_0006) 427 Fulton Street location in Brooklyn (see also Figure 3.2) in the 1980s. All photographs from New York City tax lot photos. Courtesy Municipal Archives, City of New York.

Figure 10.3. Former Automat at 1557 Broadway in Manhattan in the 1940s and 1980s. dof_1_01018_0028 and nynyma_rec0040_1_01018_0028, New York City tax lot photos. Courtesy Municipal Archives, City of New York.

marriage and now has a male partner who is apparently transgender. His indigent, disheveled, and uncomfortably loquacious first wife is shown dining with their kids at a Queens McDonald's, a gritty urban setting that typified those Whites unfree of the urban crisis.

First-generation fast food in 1970s film was consumed by the weird, disorganized, and perhaps criminal. Tony Manero, the working-class Italian American protagonist of the 1977 film *Saturday Night Fever*, and his friends descend on the Bay Ridge White Castle at 92nd and Third Avenue, where they each order four burgers, fries, and a drink. The young men's racism and misogyny had already been on display earlier in the film, and Tony's family as well evinces retrograde ethnic ways— "vicious bigotry, charming tackiness, and old-fashioned loyalty."[33] At White Castle,

Tony is admonished for his eating style ("Hey don't you never chew, Tony? Don't you never chew?"), Double J makes a crude joke linking bisexuality and pedophilia, and Joey jumps up on a table and barks. Regardless of whether this crew can be seen as typical White Castle customers, at the very least the film suggests this is the kind of place that customers like Tony enjoy—people who express homophobia, an inability to deter gratification, narcissism, and aggressive hypermasculinity. Tony's crew and their eating choices reflected circulating ideas that working-class Whites were provincial and unable to assimilate into middle-class norms.[34]

It is difficult to assess the impact of these films on fast food corporations. But with these kinds of images in circulation, and to the extent that they reflected broader public sentiments about fast food, major chains seeking an urban presence would need to tread carefully to avoid sullying their reputation. Or would they? If fast food in city environs was already subject to a disreputable customer base, that would actually make the coupling of its products and pathologized Black, urban space more tolerable. In fact, there were tangible reasons for fast food to turn to Black communities. Socioeconomic and political conditions acted as catalysts for a Black, urban fast food offensive, and corporations saw the national oil crises in 1973 and 1979 as unique opportunities to exploit.

The Oil Crisis

The OPEC oil embargo began in October 1973, with the worst of it coming during the winter of 1973–74. Across the country but particularly in the Northeast, motorists faced acute gas shortages and waited in lines for hours, sometimes running out of gas while in the queue. People panic-bought gas, continually topping up their tanks, which only made things worse; and stations often closed after running out of gas before consumers could get to the pumps. In New York, where closures were often permanent, 25 percent of stations shuttered. Jesse Jackson at PUSH and Vernon Jordan at the Urban League foresaw disproportionate economic shocks for African Americans and even difficult living conditions as landlords dropped apartment heat levels.[35] What they did not anticipate was that fast food would strategize around the crisis by centering Black neighborhoods.

Fast food executives worried about the first oil crisis because higher utilities would eat away at profits, and because gas shortages could keep customers away (since most second-generation restaurant locations were on major arterials or in automobile-centric areas more generally). Furthermore, with expenses increasing, consumers would likely cut back on discretionary spending. When the second oil crisis of the decade struck in 1979, limited gasoline supplies were described as contributing to weak sales, with a dozen chains reporting that two-thirds of their locations were in areas affected by shortages.[36]

Still, the oil crisis presented an opportunity. At McDonald's, Fred Turner announced that "the company was preparing for such a contingency by strengthening its presence in 'walking' neighborhoods. That meant increasing and fortifying its city stores."[37] One way it would do this was to increase financing possibilities for minority-owned restaurants. Roland Jones argued to McDonald's board of directors that Black consumers were vital to the chain's future, with 75 percent of that population being younger and residing in cities.[38] Like the Black youth who remained in the city post–White flight and constituted the strategic audience for Blaxploitation films, young urban African Americans also were a natural target for fast food. "Walking neighborhoods"—areas with a tight, pedestrian-centered grid, where people walked or used public transit to meet routine needs, and where many residents did not have the means to own a car—were often Black neighborhoods.

Urban communities were a natural hedge against the risks of the energy crises. Fast food's relatively low price was a benefit when households were feeling the pinch; and as a treat it provided comfort food in stressful times. In the early 1970s, McDonald's had already been running a raft of commercials emphasizing the possibility of thrift at its restaurants. One asserted, "At McDonald's when you pay for two hamburgers, fries, and a Coke, you get change back from your dollar." It featured a portly, balding, white-haired, White man in a smoking gown whose McDonald's dinner arrived on a silver tray carried by a butler. The messages were clear: even the rich enjoyed McDonald's, and they were rich because they economized; if viewers ate at McDonald's they, too, might find themselves on the path to affluence.[39] So, as economic conditions further constrained spending during the oil crisis, the ability of fast food to serve as a luxury even on a frugal budget had been established.

Black neighborhoods were therefore an even better bet, as they were more likely to be suffering from the recession. Especially in a city like New York, Black residents did not generally own cars and could easily walk to fast food outlets in their communities, if more were opened there. African Americans contending with the difficult housing conditions endemic in segregated neighborhoods, whether a low thermostat in winter or crowded conditions and a lack of air conditioning in summer, could escape to the local fast food outlet. And with meat shortages, fast food could serve what consumers might otherwise struggle to purchase to cook themselves.

When the oil crisis left abandoned gas stations in its wake, this too facilitated fast food's penetrating Black neighborhoods. New restaurants repurposed the lots and their desirable corner locations. Mahalia Jackson's had made its deal with Gulf

Figure 10.4. An Esso gas station at 666 Bushwick Avenue in Brooklyn in the 1940s had become a KFC by the 1980s. nynyma_rec_0040_3_03194_0024 and dof_3_03194_0024, New York City tax lot photos. Courtesy Municipal Archives, City of New York.

to operate at functioning stations. Now the sites for a slew of failed gas stations—Gulf, Getty, Shell, Mobil, Texaco, Sunoco, and others—transitioned to fast food. New restaurants also replaced defunct industrial uses such as auto body repair shops and manufacturing businesses. Sometimes the fast food outlets that arrived themselves failed and were supplanted by yet another chain; sometimes nothing at all followed, leaving empty, impervious surfaces.

Beyond closed gas stations, the anemic retail corridors that too often characterized Black communities fomented fast food's urban offensive. Shopping stretches in Black space were either empty, blemished by weedy vacant lots—literally making it possible for fast food to take up space—or troubled, making it easier for these outlets to thrive. In Chicago's Beverly, fast food had already taken hold in the Black, eastern portion of the community by 1974.[40] Nationally, the infusion of federal capital in the 1960s and early 1970s had produced an imbalance in Black small businesses. They were still relatively low in proportion (e.g., 8.5 percent of D.C.'s twenty-eight thousand establishments in 1970) and more likely to fail. Stores also comprised a restricted set of retail categories such as liquor stores and beauty/barber shops.[41] Chicago's East 63rd Street was dominated by a few categories, led by beauty salons.[42] Throughout Black Chicago, the retail climate posed enough of a concern for the *Chicago Defender* to run an extensive series on the issue in 1973.[43] Several communities organized to reshape retail and bring in new businesses, but results were mixed.[44] If Black neighborhoods could not attract needed retail, what they would get was fast food—whether they wanted it or not.

Penetrating Weakened Defenses

Politically vulnerable Black communities would abet fast food's expansion goals in the ghetto. The industry could expect little in the way of resistance as it planted roots in communities lacking the political clout to give unwanted establishments the boot. Urban White communities of means looked askance at fast food—"In the minds of some, a meal-on-a-bun restaurant is a symbol of urban blight only slightly less repugnant than a porno store or a massage parlor"—and were willing to fight the chains tooth and nail.[45] A highly publicized 1974 conflict between McDonald's and potential Upper East Side neighbors drove the point home. With several outlets in Manhattan, McDonald's now targeted the corner of 66th and Lexington, realizing it was a "gold mine" of affluent residents that had not yet been plumbed. Corporate bought a funeral home and planned to build a small office building where the restaurant would be installed on the ground floor. In response, local architect David Beer organized the Friends of Sixty-Sixth to stop the outlet. The group gathered fifteen thousand signatures, among them some of the city's most powerful names. Soon negative press appeared in all sorts of media; a brokerage removed the chain from its list of recommended stocks and McDonald's stock value fell. McDonald's soon quit and ended up owning an office building with regular retail.[46]

McDonald's relied on local real estate agents with intimate knowledge of the community, suggesting that Black neighborhoods were selected with precision. They constituted attractive repositories for profit, and McDonald's ad agency Needham, Harper & Steers recognized that segregation made for efficient targeting of Black consumers. And yet the captive nature of the market was working against McDonald's. Black residents rated outlets in Black neighborhoods as worse than White counterparts, particularly because Black operators were seen as essentially fronts for a White-owned corporation. Black women in Atlanta saw outlets in Black neighborhoods as inferior, and resentful community members felt they had been "exploited and betrayed by their 'own.'"[47]

If fast food were to capture the sales it desired, it would need to convince Black communities that the company was an ally—a hard sell, when many neighborhoods rose up against the new influx of outlets.[48] Brady Keys attempted to head off racial criticism by running ads showcasing the Blackness of his Burger Kings. Some used photos of Black employees with copy that read more like a corporate annual report than a burger advertisement: "Having it your way in Brownsville means black enterprise on the move . . . it means a spanking new Burger King restaurant has opened and is boosting the community's renewal efforts."[49] In other ads the company seemed to be responding to a public relations crisis, with multiple ads offering a defense of company operations and benefit to Black people. The text made entreaties such as "FACT: The Burger King in Harlem is owned by a Black Company, All-Pro Enterprises" and "What MORE can a struggling Black Company do for its employees?" The ads were signed by Keys himself as president.[50]

Other Black franchisees sought to reinforce their embeddedness in their communities with tactics such as food donation. In one instance, in response to an environmental disaster, local Black McDonald's operators gave free food to the community. The *Chicago Defender* reported in 1974 that residents in the Altgeld Gardens public housing project outside of Chicago were evacuated due to a leak of silicon tetrachloride fumes at a nearby factory. Glossing over the health threat's severity, the *Defender* made no mention of the miles-long chemical cloud that triggered the evacuation of about fourteen thousand residents. Dozens were hospitalized and there was a further risk that the chemical cloud would turn into hydrochloric acid, inhalation of which would be fatal. But despite their distress, residents were at least privy to a hamburger meal.[51]

Time and again, Black residents protested the arrival of fast food, contrary to contemporary popular notions that fast food density is best explained by community demand. A mass rally erupted about a mile away from Altgeld Gardens to protest a proposed Burger King at 95th Street and Michigan Avenue.[52] That battle was lost, and as a result, a South Side coalition said to represent Black property owners some 150,000 strong bonded together against the unwanted entry of a Burger King and a Chicken Delight, both on 95th Street. The coalition announced their dedication "to the demise of Burger King" and managed to block a Church's at 87th and Wabash.[53]

Another skirmish resulted in the involvement of the Department of Justice's Community Relations Service. The agency, created in 1964 to work toward racial conciliation and mediation, was called into Chicago in 1975 over a McDonald's dispute at 96th and Halsted, where the chain was planning to open across the street from a forthcoming $5 million regional library.[54] Community residents from an area nearly forty blocks long demonstrated for six hours at the groundbreaking. An agreement was eventually reached, with Roland Jones among those representing McDonald's.[55]

In New York, fast food outlets slowly multiplied in the wake of social catastrophe. The Bronx and other Black and Puerto Rican communities were devastated by the city's implementation of "planned shrinkage."[56] Planned shrinkage eviscerated critical municipal services in predominantly Black and Puerto Rican neighborhoods with the intention of stimulating the departure of residents so as to reclaim land for industrial renewal.[57] The policy closed fire stations, cut sanitation, and made building inspections infrequent. It produced a calamitous epidemic of fires in the South Bronx, East and Central Harlem, Bushwick, Brownsville, the Lower East Side, and East New York; and in turn, the destruction of as much as 80 percent of the housing in those communities and a raft of disease epidemics including tuberculosis, substance abuse, and HIV infection.[58] These were among the New York communities that fast food penetrated over the 1970s (Map 10.1).

Even as fast food set its sights on Black neighborhoods, there was little evidence that residents were more likely to consume fast food or to view it more positively. Afropessimism scholar Frank Wilderson reports that his partner Stella "thought of White Castle as a temple where Satan killed you with sodium and trans fats."[59] What was clear was that fast food's core consumers were growing increasingly wary of these restaurants' nutritional profiles, a trend that would continue into the 1980s. A 1971 research study found middle-class, White homemakers to be "heavy fried chicken users."[60] To be sure, there were a substantial number of diners in this demographic who did not count themselves among KFC's faithful. Ernest Dichter had completed a study of the chain's lunchtime trade in 1972, but he himself had yet

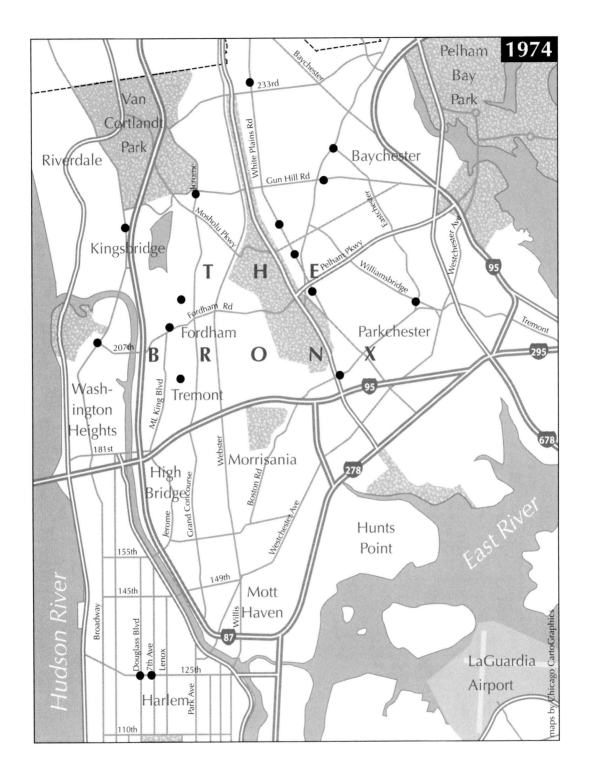

1974

Pelham
Bay
Park

Van
Cortlandt
Park

Riverdale

Baychester

233rd

White Plains Rd

Gun Hill Rd

Baychester

Jerome

Eastchester

Mosholu Pkwy

Westchester Ave

Kingsbridge

THE

Pelham Pkwy

95

Williamsbridge

Fordham Rd

Fordham

Parkchester

Tremont

BRONX

207th

295

ML King Blvd

95

Washington
Heights

181st

Webster

678

High
Bridge

Jerome

Grand Concourse

Boston Rd

Morrisania

Westchester Ave

278

155th

Hunts
Point

East River

145th

Broadway

149th

Mott
Haven

Douglass Blvd

7th Ave

Lenox

125th

Willis

87

LaGuardia
Airport

Harlem

Park Ave

110th

Hudson River

maps by Chicago CartoGraphics

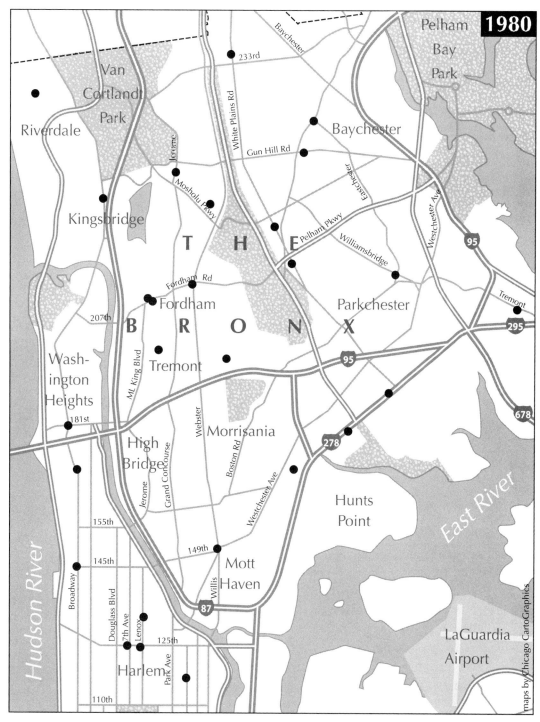

Map 10.1. Fast food locations in the Bronx and Upper Manhattan in 1974 and 1980. Source: New York phone directories, New York Public Library. Map by Dennis McClendon, CartoGraphics.

to venture to a KFC. Dichter was pleasantly surprised by the food and suspected that other middle- and upper-middle-class people might harbor prejudices or other subconscious resistance to eating there.[61] While Dichter may have simply had a passing indifference to his client, other White middle-class consumers were actively growing wary of fast food owing to its nutritional character. Fast food was not just cheap and tawdry, it was also increasingly seen as unhealthy. Changing sentiments among Whites was yet another reason for fast food to turn strongly to Black neighborhoods.

Industry commentators argued, not surprisingly, that fast food could be consumed without detriment to health as long as it was not to excess. Pillsbury told shareholders that Burger King met nutritional guidelines because it offered items from all food groups. A Whopper, fries, and milkshake, apparently, was a well-balanced meal because it contained plenty of minerals—and as much vitamin A as one and a half ears of sweet corn.[62] But the industry was concerned that the public and even the U.S. government had begun to question the nutritional value of fast food. *Good Housekeeping* and *Consumer Reports,* for example, pointed out that fast food was high in calories and sugar but lacked many essential nutrients. *Nation's Restaurant News* complained that such analyses overlooked the high protein content in fast food, which it saw as beneficial. But most Americans would not parse nutritional information so closely. A small university study in Texas showed that respondents gave seemingly arbitrary rankings of nutritional quality for dishes such as a three-piece chicken meal with sides at KFC or a Whopper-centered option at Burger King. Some were reluctant to speak ill of the food out of loyalty to chains: "I really don't think they're that good for you but I want to be fair to McDonald's."[63]

That reluctance to criticize fast food was not shared across American society. The late 1960s through the 1970s was the era of "health food nuts" lauding boring but wholesome vegetarian food. Fervent attention to healthful foods grew and new contrasts came to the fore: brown versus white (e.g., rice, bread), processed versus natural, slow versus fast, and animal versus vegetable.[64] Fast food was chided for being junk food. As the organic foods business raked in hundreds of millions of dollars, conventional food companies and their collaborators pushed back aggressively.[65] Advertising buys were a key way to control messaging both directly and indirectly. For the popular Black press, where ad revenues were harder to come by, critiquing companies whose expenditures supported the magazine would be an uncomfortable proposition. *Ebony* published no articles on "health food" or "natural food" during the decade, and the only items including those words were advertisements for baby food and prune juice. Neither did critiques of fast food appear. The only food whose nutritional value was questioned was soul food. Health resort chef Harmony McCoy proclaimed that though he prepared diet food for spa guests, he

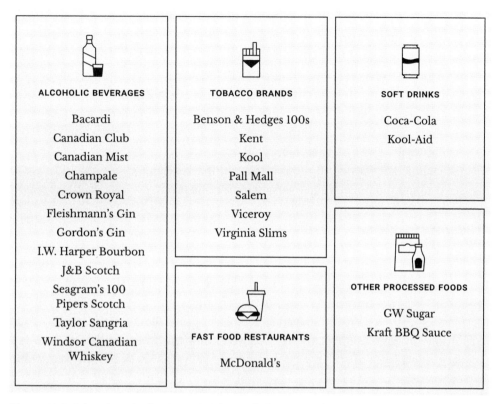

Figure 10.5. Advertisers in the June 1973 issue of *Ebony*. Fast food's advertising presence would not pick up until the late 1970s and 1980s. But the abundance of alcohol and tobacco was consistent across issues. Infographic by Kudos Design Collaboratory.

didn't consume it; he was raised on soul food, and that was what he ate. The article made a point to mention his weight as 260 pounds, suggesting that his soul food diet was to blame.[66] Dr. Elijah Saunders, chief cardiologist at Provident Hospital in Baltimore, noted the important link between obesity and salt intake, and between salt and soul food. *Ebony* warned that "a heavy or exclusive diet of soul food with its high salt content may be literally suicidal." Dr. Saunders advised strongly reducing consumption of such foods as "heavily salted greens, bacon, salt pork and ham hocks, all of which are soul-food specialties."[67] No mention was made of fast food, alcohol, tobacco, sugary drinks, or processed foods, which increase obesity and hypertension risk. The reason was most likely because those were advertisers *Ebony* could not afford to antagonize. Figure 10.5 shows the advertisers in the June 1973 issue. Fast food's problematic health profile received a pass in the largest and most prominent African American magazine.

Changing public sentiment about dietary behavior and nutrition meant that fast food had a potentially narrow window to establish itself in urban markets. Perhaps Black communities were not yet as preoccupied with fast food's nutritional content, or could be otherwise appeased given all the energy activists put into acquiring existing outlets from White interlopers. Perhaps communities would welcome the coming cascade despite their qualms about the health implications of fast food menus. The battles Black communities waged against new outlets tended to focus on social disorder more so than nutrition, but those concerns might arise as well. Clearly, chains that wanted to acquire space in Black neighborhoods would have to disregard community needs and focus on extracting profit.

Predatory Inclusion

Fast food board rooms alluded to colonial plunder by frequently referring to gold. Industry pundits held that some brands "have edged into that gabled 'ghetto goldmine'—and are turning their new frontier efforts into positive profit sheets."[68] McDonald's, one such brand, also couched its foray into Black neighborhoods as an expedition relying on natives to produce wealth for the company. It saw the need for Black franchisees to stay put "in those confined areas" because "there's gold in them there ghettoes, and we need some folks who can bring it out."[69] In fact, fast food could extract gold not only from cash register transactions, but from the real estate that hosted the outlets as well.

Historian Keeanga-Yamahtta Taylor shows that in the 1970s the real estate industry began selling and lending to Black people. Central cities were a "new frontier" for financial extraction, and African Americans were brought in under what Taylor defines as "predatory inclusion": no longer excluded, but included on terms favorable to the industry. Speculators preyed particularly on Black women, capitalizing on their motivation to escape tenuous and often deplorable conditions as tenants, selling them money pits at inflated prices, and pocketing the insurance provided by the FHA.[70] After decades of redlining in various forms, funds now flowed to investors essentially risk-free.[71]

Fast food's expansion, particularly in the case of McDonald's, relied on the racial inequities that underlay the real estate market. Real estate was always central to McDonald's operations, which was brought into sharp relief in a context of Blaxploitation. When the company began in the suburbs, it paid landlords a flat rate, regardless of how much it was taking in from franchisees' rent payments. Landlords often tried to negotiate for rent to be based on a percentage of sales volume, or for an escalation clause that would allow rent to increase over time based on store sales, but McDonald's refused. So, although it required such contract terms with their franchisees, the corporation did not bear that burden. Landlords still found McDonald's proposals attractive, a primary reason for which was that the suburbs were heavily residential and commercial development was scant, other than gas stations. McDonald's offered better terms than oil companies, and in any case the sites proposed for its restaurants were generally those that oil companies rejected.[72] McDonald's therefore benefited on the landlord side of real estate transactions, and also had better terms in relation to its franchisees. Operators paid the corporation a security deposit that was not sequestered in an interest-bearing account, but instead was used to fund McDonald's growth. Half of the deposit was returned to the franchisee after fifteen years, and the remainder in year twenty. Franchisees also had to pay property taxes, insurance, and maintenance costs.[73]

The strategy had been devised by Harry J. Sonneborn, McDonald's early financial wizard. His ideas drove McDonald's highly profitable growth, and he was indifferent to the concept of drive-ins or the burgers and fries the company was selling; according to Sonneborn, he "didn't even eat hamburgers."[74] He came from an apparel background and could have applied the strategy to any business. For Sonneborn, McDonald's was primarily a real estate company that happened to sell hamburgers. This framing would later come into conflict with Kroc, because Sonneborn passed up sites that had strong sales potential for burgers but were less attractive for potential real estate appreciation. However, overall, Sonneborn's strategy positioned McDonald's to be able to reap essentially all the profit it received from franchised restaurants in the form of real estate.[75]

McDonald's scored when it got into suburbs early, a time when purchase prices were low. Now, it was building in Black neighborhoods that had sustained flights of commerce and capital. Land owners would be incentivized to take in stable revenue from fast food outlets, especially those that were sitting on what would otherwise be vacant lots and defunct land uses. Of course, it made sense for McDonald's to buy property anywhere it could be had at low cost, and then profit from a rise in value over time. But in the context of the ghetto, this was acutely important. The systemic racism that hollowed out the property values where Black people lived allowed the corporation to maximize its real estate operations. If McDonald's was actually a real estate company that sold hamburgers, it is logical that it entered Black space in the 1970s alongside all the other real estate speculators. Whereas Black women were targeted with suspect homes, Black men were bestowed with problematic fast food franchises.

Apart from the profits to be made, predatory inclusion in real estate helped keep African Americans in urban centers. Nixon had run for reelection with a campaign that hinged on White racial resentment and the reassurance that White suburbs would remain as such. Now that the 1968 Housing Act theoretically made it possible for Black people to live wherever they wished, opening up homeownership to Black people in cities might keep them away from prized White suburbs.[76] The same could be said for fast food. A raft of outlets in the ghetto would keep Black people from making forays to the suburbs to dine out. Ghetto stores may not have been desirable locations, and franchisees may not have succeeded at them, but in the meantime they would serve the targeted customer base where they lived. If in the end the outlet failed, it could be resold to the long queue of would-be franchisees expectantly biding their time on company waitlists. Indeed, David Bradwell, a franchise consultant, described at a 1976 congressional hearing on franchising the practice of "churning," in which a franchisor profited from repeated sales of the same unit. A franchisee might purchase a unit and find after a few months that it could not be run profitably. The franchisee would cut his losses and sell it back to the company at a fraction of the original investment, allowing the franchisor to sell it again and collect additional franchise fees and possibly rent.[77] What Bradwell called churning sounded very much like contract selling, the unregulated market into which Black homebuyers were thrust, and which in Chicago alone extracted Black wealth to the tune of $3.2 billion to $4 billion between 1950 and 1960.[78]

Black franchisees were just as exploited as the communities they served. In the late 1960s, Black operators generally took over existing restaurants previously owned by White peers. Now, new outlets were being constructed for them. These establishments often failed, or at least suffered setbacks that undermined their success and the operators' financial health. They did not have a smooth entry to the industry, but as more of them entered in the 1970s they were met with increasingly exploitative terms. Well into the decade, minority franchising participation remained negligible, constituting 1.5 percent of operators. Thirteen Burger King outlets out of 880 were owned by Black franchisees, and this figure did not even represent unique individuals—a few people owned several restaurants.[79] In the late 1970s, Black McDonald's franchisees held 31 percent of franchised restaurants in Chicago, but these were owned by only eight people, including relative veterans McSween and Petty. Newcomers brought on during the 1970s like Lee Dunham, a former NYPD officer whose McDonald's opened on 125th Street in 1972, started out in troubled locations beset with operational barriers that corporate seemed little motivated to redress. Dunham was the first Black franchisee in New York City,

and his store contended with youth violence and other issues like employee pilferage, especially of uncooked burgers, toted home to feed hungry family members.
Dunham tried security guards, but conditions worsened as they provoked hostility.[80] Burger King was nonetheless emboldened to enter Harlem once McDonald's
had. With Brady Keys, it set up an outlet at 125th and Eighth Avenue in a previously
burned-out storefront.[81]

Around the same time, Philadelphia's first Black McDonald's franchisees took
on their operation in Germantown, a new market for the company. Things began in-
auspiciously for Matthew Mitchell and Anthony De Luz when a construction strike
delayed the opening by months, and soon the pair was nearly $200,000 in debt.
Years later, Mitchell, then vice president of the National Black McDonald's Association, had still not fully recovered from his initial undercapitalization. Mitchell also
failed to attract strong customer traffic, in part because residents assumed he was
just a Black public face managing a White-owned business. In a way, he was, though
perhaps not in the manner that neighbors perceived. Mitchell could find no support
from corporate.[82]

Black franchisees' tales of woe—bankruptcy, discriminatory corporate practices, and dashed dreams—were scattered across chains. Black Burger King franchisees charged that the company exploited them with inflated sales prices, excessive
construction costs, and other fraudulent practices. In one dispute, a former franchisee said, on the condition of anonymity, "Burger King put the Blacks into sites
they had chosen for themselves, and then didn't want. In my case, I had several
sites I wanted to go into, but they said, 'That's for white franchisees.'" Operators
in Detroit sued Burger King for millions, embittered by the profits Pillsbury extracted while the franchisees faced financial ruin.[83] Franchisee Albert Harris eventually settled with corporate after six months of negotiations but said bluntly,
"I think it is a racist, and most deceiving organization—the American dream that's
really not there."[84]

If fast food were to proliferate in Black neighborhoods, it could not have Black
operators speaking out about racism. Some Black franchisees were more generous
in their assessment of the chains to which they belonged. John Perry, now owner
of two Chicago stores, including the Roseland location on 103rd that was a site of
racial violence, spoke effusively about McDonald's support for its Black operators.
He argued that "the beautiful thing about McDonald's is the fact that they give us
all the help we need; they support us."[85] Perry seemed to have forgotten telling the
same newspaper three years prior that when he was just starting out and saw the
condition of his new business, "I'll never forget how disappointed I was."[86]

Figure 10.6. This McDonald's, at 29 East Chelten Avenue in Germantown, Philadelphia, was likely relocated from Mitchell and De Luz's original store at the end of the block. Photograph by author, July 2019.

An extensive charm campaign was necessary to smooth entry into Black gold mines, showcasing intermediaries who would collaborate with chains to promote the brand by vouching for its commitment to Black communities. As early as 1973, Black advertising shop Kabon had been highlighting the need to feature actual Black employees in marketing to "close this suspicion gap" that Black residents had regarding the outlets in their communities.[87] Perhaps fast food had moved past trying to solve "the Negro problem" of the 1960s, but it remained ready to offer franchising as a solution to the entrenched racial inequality of the 1970s. Difficult economic conditions hit Black communities especially hard; Black unemployment skyrocketed across the 1970s, rising from 9.6 percent in 1974 to 25.4 percent in 1976, and for teens the figure stood at 65 percent.[88] In such circumstances, individuals of all ages might turn to fast food for relief—whether as comfort food or as a job—and the industry could play up its support for Black communities, however illusory. Walt Simon, a former New York Knick turned KFC executive, encouraged African Americans to enter fast food, claiming myriad opportunities. Speaking at a Harlem YMCA All-Stars competition that KFC sponsored, Simon asserted, "Maybe three or four years, you can be a very high management person earning a great deal of money." He helped recruit Black employees by collaborating with organizations like the Urban League.[89]

As the 1970s drew to a close, Burger King began advertising much more frequently in *Ebony*. But instead of centering burgers and fries, the ads promoted franchisees and staff from Los Angeles, Detroit, New York, and other cities. Willie Taylor, Miami's first Black franchisee, testified that his customers and staff were in fact friends, and that he found it rewarding to be able to sponsor youth groups and otherwise contribute to the community. He acknowledged, "Sure I like all the other good things that have happened to me since I got my own Burger King restaurants—the proud feelings of achievement, the financial security—that means a lot to a black man from Georgia." Other featured Black franchisees, including Pettis Norman, yet another former NFL player, took pride in their customers enjoying Burger King meals. But the food was almost an afterthought in a campaign instead focused on the civilizing influence the chain had on Black youth, who learned the meaning of honest work within the franchise confines. The operators were depicted as instilling in their crew an ethic of diligence, hard work, and ambition, and their efforts reportedly translated into better customer service. For Black consumers who viewed Black-owned fast food outlets negatively, these ads reassured them that eating there would be a pleasant experience and contribute to the uplift of their neighbors. Burger King's *Ebony* campaign suggested that Black Burger King operators enjoyed financial success, the adulation of Black neighbors and employees and,

Figure 10.7. Advertisement in *Ebony,* July 1979, featuring Willie Taylor, Burger King franchisee. Source: *Ebony* Archives, Google.

more broadly, the recognition as decent and productive people that was sorely lacking for Black people in America. Burger King's pitch to *Ebony* readers was not only to promote the restaurant as a place to dine out, but also to entice those who had the means to consider taking up franchises.

Once the 1970s turned to the 1980s, Black activists began working on the other end of the franchise ownership pipeline, enjoining fast food companies to bring franchises to Black neighborhoods. The pressure civil rights groups had previously brought to bear on various corporations to use Black services had died down considerably by the mid-1970s; Jesse Jackson's Operation PUSH was essentially the only such advocate.[90] Jackson instituted a covenant with General Foods in 1972, which was a "mutual commitment to expand the relationship" between the company and Black communities "in order to build economic solutions for a developing people."[91]

Operation PUSH would make a sustained effort to acquire cooperative agreements with fast food corporations in the 1980s. An initial foray began in the late 1970s. Jesse Jackson argued at Operation Breadbasket's Commercial Association 1977 annual banquet that "the Black business community is a threshold and beleaguered body of outcasts, facing a bleak and uncertain future unless we can turn the corner soon." Remedy came in the form of a slew of Church's Fried Chicken outlets for Noah Robinson, Jackson's half brother and Breadbasket's national director. Under the agreement, Church's would open between sixty and eighty outlets in the Chicago metro area—presumably in Black neighborhoods. Robinson called it a momentous deal, the fruit of six months of negotiations, and one that he and Church's director of Midwest operations, Milton D. Sanders, believed would produce thousands of jobs and millions in salaries and construction. Robinson hoped it would spur other corporations to engage in "similar affirmative action planning."[92] This intervention was the beginning of actions that would open the dike to Black neighborhoods.

Operation PUSH put forth several requests for formalized support from Burger King, including the idea that student scholarships should be funded by the corporation and its twenty minority franchises, and the creation of Burger King PUSH Day, wherein restaurants that served minority communities would donate 10 percent of their receipts to the civil rights organization. With his large afro, casual shirt, and black leather jacket, Jesse Jackson was the antithesis of the Burger King franchisee with whom he posed for a photo op—Glenn L. Glass, a White man with a conservative haircut and an ill-fitting suit.[93] It was perhaps an appropriately awkward representation of the collaborations that were to follow between Operation PUSH and

Church's® Fried Chicken is looking for talented people like Milt Sanders. People willing to make a strong commitment to themselves and to us. We're a rapidly growing national company with an impressive record of success. For the past two years, we've been ranked the number one growth company in the U.S. by Financial World magazine. In just twenty-five years, we've grown from one little chicken restaurant into the second largest chicken operation in the country with over 700 company-owned stores in 35 states.

As we continue to grow, the need for strong management grows with us. We recognize this demand, and already we are a leader in the development of progressive management training and incentive programs. At Church's, the work is challenging but the rewards are great.

Right now, we're looking for store management and executive candidates. If you're interested in a career with a rewarding future, Church's is interested in you. For more information, mail this coupon or call 312-640-0885. You could be doing us both a favor.

Please send me career information on Church's.

Name _____

Address _____

City _____ State _____ Zip _____

Mail to: Mike Blackmon, Division Manager, Church's Fried Chicken, 1445 Brummel, Elk Grove Village, Ill. 60007

CHURCH'S FRIED CHICKEN®

MS-1

"WE'RE HIRING."

"At Church's, the opportunity is here, the growth is here, and if you have the desire, you can go a long way. I'm a living witness to that."

Milton D. Sanders

Milt Sanders
Director of Operations
Midwest Division
CHURCH'S FRIED CHICKEN

Figure 10.8. Advertisement in *Ebony,* February 1978, featuring Milton Sanders, executive at Church's Fried Chicken. Source: *Ebony* Archives, Google.

fast food. The major chains, having already embarked during the 1970s on a path of Blaxploitation, entered the 1980s with a view toward continuing ghetto growth. Fast food was willing to make financial and other investments if it meant it could more fully capture the untapped Black, urban market. And Black activists were willing to cultivate that growth if it meant increased economic opportunities—in theory for average Black citizens, but in practice for Black elites who dominated as beneficiaries.

11

PUSH and Pull

Black Advertising and Racial Covenants
Fuel Fast Food Growth

When fast food embarked on its gold rush in Black neighborhoods, residents' actual consumption seemed a nonfactor. Black folks remained casual fast food consumers into the 1970s. They tended to purchase fast food as individuals rather than families, in snack portions rather than as large meals, with less adherence to traditional mealtimes. For example, customers at Herman Petty's first store were under age thirty-five, primarily men who visited alone, especially in the early morning and late at night.[1] Many Black customers did not even see burger outlets as proper restaurants; rather, they were "just a sandwich type place—just something to eat and carry with you and keep on trucking." They lacked privacy and intimacy; "Burger King is not what you call a restaurant." Women rarely planned trips to fast food outlets, instead adding on a visit as part of shopping or other activities with children.[2] The onslaught of new outlets was not in response to rapidly rising Black consumer demand, but rather fast food's demand for more markets, specifically that which retailers called "the last virgin market in the U.S."[3] Once fast food corporations realized they had a stake in Black urban space and began pushing into these unchartered territories, they recognized they would need advertising campaigns to attract Black consumers. And they would need Black ad shops to make them. As fast food's Blaxploitation thrust to extract untapped profits ignited, so too did advertising, after two decades of silence.

Two mutually reinforcing streams collided to intensify the proliferation of fast food in Black neighborhoods through the 1970s and the early to mid-1980s. One, exemplified by new Black advertising, was pushing fast food as a concept to Black consumers, selling a product that had yet to become a staple in Black lives. Black neighborhoods were brimming with geographically concentrated consumers who could be reached efficiently by targeted store openings and by advertising. The other, exemplified by new activist action, was a pull factor dragging fast food into greater occupation of Black space. Foremost among these was the Reverend Jesse Jackson's Operation PUSH, which enacted racial covenants with fast food in order to increase minority business access and employment, following the model of the SCLC's earlier work with Operation Breadbasket. PUSH and other activist organizations made the argument that Black communities merited particular investment from fast food corporations on the basis of their significant contribution to corporate profits, and secured monies for new franchises and related suppliers. PUSH was successful in developing agreements that brought corporate dollars and new franchises into Black hands, but it could not foresee that these initiatives ultimately contributed to a climate of excessive fast food density that would be to the detriment of Black neighborhoods decades later.

Fast Food's Incursion to Black Consumer Market Advertising

If new stores were to open apace in Black neighborhoods, targeted marketing would need to go along with them. This shift began at the outset of Blaxploitation and requires looking back to 1971, when the shop that would become the dominant force in Black advertising began. African American Tom Burrell had been a copy supervisor at Needham, Harper & Steers, the firm that created McDonald's well-known "You deserve a break today" campaign. In 1971, Burrell left Needham to start his own firm. Joining him was Emmett McBain, a designer at the first Black agency, Vince Cullers Advertising. The Chicago firm, affiliated with Operation Breadbasket, held several advertising accounts including Newport and Afro Sheen. The two men founded Burrell McBain Advertising, whose first major client was McDonald's.[4]

The firm's campaign featured Black youth and adults interacting in convivial and comfortable settings. The first in the series, "Get Down with Something Good at McDonald's," appeared in *Ebony* in 1973. The ad featured a boy nattily dressed in a brown and white striped sweater eating a hamburger with his father, a mustached man in a hat and jacket, also brown. The interior of the car was brown, too—dark leather seats and beige upholstered roof—steeping the image in the earth tones that evoked the skin color of the consumers the ad was meant to reach. The copy read, "Daddy and Junior Gettin' Down. Daddy and Junior really dig doing things together . . . going to a game or just ridin' 'n rappin'. But, the biggest treat is stopping for something good at McDonald's." Others in the series featured a father and daughter, and schoolchildren in an exuberant extracurricular scene. McDonald's initially required Burrell McBain to work with Needham as the general market shop, and Needham thought this campaign, designed for Black consumers, was "too

Black." The series did not continue beyond 1973.[5] Eventually, Burrell's team was able to report directly to corporate rather than going through Needham, and they created "McDonald's sure is good to have around."[6] The 1974–75 campaign positioned the company as part of the Black quotidian. *Ebony* ads emphasized that the chain was literally around—in the neighborhood, an outlet bound to be nearby as residents went about their daily lives, serving good, affordable food quickly. And in a marked departure from the constant pathologizing and erasure of Black families from White corporate fast food, these images allowed Black people to see themselves in the simple act of enjoying a meal out at a fast food restaurant.

Burger King responded with its own Black marketing campaign, attempting to counter McDonald's new thrust. Kabon Consulting, under president Kelvin A. Wall and creative director Caroline Jones, developed promotional plans intended to increase sales and generate goodwill. Among the strategies they considered were health promotion (e.g., sickle cell and blood pressure testing in Burger King parking lots); targeted urban amenities (e.g., logoed trash receptacles and a bus that would ferry people to shopping centers or to and from Burger King outlets); and an unfortunately named "Gang Bang" in which customers who arrived with friends received premiums such as a Burger King portable pik "for natural hair wearing customers." The creative plan adapted the "Have it your way" theme for a Black audience, as Kabon believed the general market tagline lacked credibility. But any adaption could not simply place Black actors in general market commercials without addressing Black consumers' unique motivations and idiom. More than any other medium, Black radio disseminated fast food advertising, and Kabon developed commercials featuring a "very happy Black family" in an awkward, heavy-handed soap-opera format. In one sketch, the Leroy family returned home after church and listeners were told that "Mama Leroy may be fast in the house, but she's slow getting the news about Burger King. Burger King, home of the biggest, hottest burgers in town. . . . Will Mama Leroy find out about Burger King in time for tomorrow night's dinner? Will she discover that you can eat in or take out a Yumbo, french fries and coffee for very little bread?"[7]

These radio spots, meant to reach the Black masses, differed from the messaging that Burger King deployed in *Ebony* in 1979, which positioned the chain as both economic repair and civilizing mission. The radio ads focused on the food, not the franchising. They meant to convince Black households that Burger King's menu was not to be missed. And the ads delivered the message, not only in content but in the mode of dissemination, that the brand's products were for ordinary Black families. Burger King did not pursue advertising in the more expensive print medium until 1976, when Caroline Jones held a vice presidency at BBDO. She created campaigns

Join the punch bunch for a free meal.

At Burger King.®

Buy any sandwich and you get one punch. Ten punches get you a free meal. Whopper,® fries (or onion rings) and a regular soft drink.

Everybody loves a free meal. And that's what you get if you join the punch bunch.

All you have to do is stop in and ask for your Burger King® punch card. Then every time you buy any sandwich on our menu, we'll punch your card for you. Ten punches earn you a complete meal, free: A Whopper,® fries (or onion rings) and a regular soft drink.

So come in soon. And join the punch bunch for a free meal. At Burger King.

And to get you started, here's a special bargain:

MANHATTAN
118 W. 125th Street (between 6th & 7th Ave.)   2331 Eighth Avenue (at 125th Street)   **BROOKLYN** 1630 Bushwick Avenue

Figure 11.1. Advertisement in the *New York Amsterdam News,* September 1976.

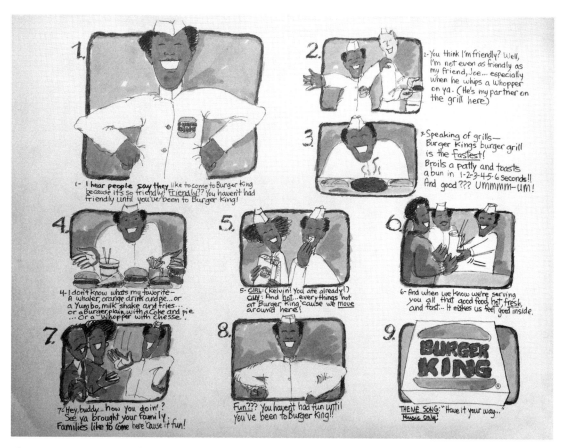

Figure 11.2. Creative work in progress for Burger King at Kabon Consulting Inc., 1973–74. Caroline P. Jones Papers, Archives Center, National Museum of American History, Smithsonian Institution, Washington, D.C.

for Black audiences under the national umbrella of "Have it your way," but her tenure was short-lived, as BBDO lost the account one year later and Jones herself soon departed as well. Her drafts depicted happy Black families—two parents, one boy, one girl—in all-American settings such as a children's baseball game. In addition to the national tagline, these print ads featured sub-taglines such as "We'll make it special" and "It's the only way."[8]

Upon leaving BBDO Jones founded a new firm with Frank Mingo—Mingo-Jones—designed to wield a depth of knowledge about Black consumers that general agencies lacked. Here Jones was responsible for spearheading KFC's new Black-targeted campaigns. She depicted Black family life and showcased "KFC as part of the Black community," breaking from Young & Rubicam's general market slogans

Figure 11.3. Creative work in progress for Burger King at Kabon Consulting Inc., 1973–74. Caroline P. Jones Papers, Archives Center, National Museum of American History, Smithsonian Institution, Washington, D.C.

(e.g., "It's so nice to feel so good about a meal—so good about KFC").[9] Mingo–Jones was tasked with the New York City metro's Black advertising strategy. According to Jones, sales there had been declining, the corporate image was unclear, and there was poor morale and turnover among staff. The chain needed a "rallying cry" that credibly promised great food and service, could elicit crew pride, and would connect well to community relations efforts. That cry was realized in "We do chicken right," a campaign that was disseminated primarily on radio and in outdoor advertising. It was successful, increasing sales by 25 percent in the first year and by 100 percent three years later. The theme soon was expanded to Black consumers in nearly a dozen other markets, and then became the national slogan.[10]

The push to Black Consumer Market advertising grew rapidly across the 1970s, and Black firms evinced the psychographic segmentation that retailers and advertisers in the general market tended to gloss over. A range of new marketing tactics emerged in the late 1970s as competition intensified. Beyond corporate competitors, McDonald's worried that it might be losing Black consumer dollars to "more ethnic ('soul') food penetration" and plain indifference.[11] No strategies could go unexamined, and Burrell Advertising put it bluntly: "We're at war—perimeters will be attacked."[12] The assault came in the form of methods like programming around Dr. Martin Luther King Jr.'s birthday and Black History Month, but it also considered sickle cell anemia drives and promoting "to black children through local schools."[13] The Black consumer media plan that Burrell developed in 1979 aimed to bolster McDonald's growing position among African Americans, especially among adolescents and young adults.[14] McDonald's was to advertise "as continuously as possible," particularly with the use of Black media outlets that allowed "optimum intrusiveness." Radio continued to be the most efficient outlet to that end, but print was also important. A twelve-month plan was articulated for *Ebony, Jet, Essence,* and *Black Enterprise. Ebony* would receive the lion's share—one per month, more than a doubling of what ran in 1978.

The published ads showcased warm, inviting images of McDonald's as an integral part of diverse Black lives. There were smartly dressed adult couples laughing over a game of backgammon, embodying the middle-class comfort suggested by the tagline "McDonald's hamburgers: It's a matter of taste." There were working-class Black men who gained sustenance from McDonald's breakfasts. In one ad, a hairy-armed man sporting a blue work shirt and yellow hard hat lay smiling in his sleep, apparently dreaming of eating an Egg McMuffin, his hands dwarfing the sandwich that was the focus of his reverie. And as always, there were families. In some, McDonald's appealed to mothers with didactic text about McDonald's service goals and accountability; in others, McDonald's showcased parents and children walking hand-in-hand toward a McDonald's restaurant at dusk, the golden arches looming as beacons above a mansard-roofed outlet.

McDonald's Black market research had shown that its restaurants were perceived as pleasantly informal, so Burrell's work highlighted the outlets as oases of comfort and symbols of home. The research suggested that at least for some African Americans, the strategy of flooding Black neighborhoods with new outlets was beginning to pay off. Some respondents described McDonald's stores as inviting spaces for children and adults, even those with limited resources. One research interviewee explained, "I don't go in there dressed up. If McDonald's is good enough for me, it sure ought to be good enough for her"; "I go in when I'm working and my clothes are dirty and greasy because I do repair work. Sometimes I sit down, but if the place is crowded, I just go on out because I don't want the other people to feel bad because of me being in there. When I am dirty like that, I only go into a greasy spoon place or a fast food place."[15] That feeling was true not only for working-class Black men. For anyone intimidated by formal restaurants, what with the attendant "discomfort over which fork to use," fast food was the regular place next door, with the easygoing atmosphere and the teenage workers shown on TV.[16]

Toward the end of the decade, chains ramped up their advertising, trying out multiple campaigns, goals, and moods. Whereas McDonald's print ads tended toward the earnest and determined, with restorative portrayals of domesticity, KFC was willing to veer toward goofiness in TV spots in 1980: a Black Aladdin ad featured a beefy, lamp-rubbing genie and wishes for buckets of KFC chicken.[17] The chains even began switching between ad agencies, a trend that accelerated in the 1980s with the advent of the burger wars.[18] But even as Black advertising campaigns drilled down to multiple consumer segments, industry discourse suggested that advertising to Black people was a waste of time. One report by an unnamed author held that Black consumers were a monolith, undifferentiated in taste by age or class distinction. They spent freely without saving and gravitated toward conspicuous consumption, but did so as "very unsophisticated shoppers; they may have problems with the language; they may not take time to read. They may have trouble making the buying decision, so they usually buy the top of the line."[19]

Prominent Black creatives such as Caroline Jones stressed Black people's brand loyalty. If that were true, the point was not that Black consumers had not the cognitive capacity or inclination to be receptive to ads—it was that companies that managed to create appealing campaigns might win those customers for life. In that light, Black agencies were incentivized to bring in previously elusive accounts with the promise of dedicated sales. And the received wisdom among Black industry observers was that there plenty of sales to be had. Wildly overstated estimates of Black "buying power" circulated among Black media and business leaders, who believed that retailers seemed not to see Black consumers at all, or at least not in a manner commensurate with their spending power. Figures in the hundreds of billions were put forth as indicators of Black consumer earning and spending. African American marketing guru D. Parke Gibson argued in 1979 that by 1987 Black Americans would be earning $210 billion and therefore would constitute the difference between profit and loss for many companies. Miraculously, *Ebony* reported almost the same number Gibson predicted that very year: "FACT . . . Blacks now control $218 billion in buying power."[20] Black buying power as a construct worked to support Black media, which needed to convince White advertisers that their readers and viewers could afford to buy the products depicted in those ads. It relied on figures that had no basis in fact and continue to lack credibility today. Black buying power was reported as more than $1 trillion in 2019 when Black workers collectively only earned approximately $740 billion. The figures in any case conflated "generating wealth for others . . . into a concept of individual and collective political, economic, or social power."[21]

But the notion of Black consumer power was central to the strategies Black activists used to engage with fast food corporations. Black ad agencies were perhaps both push and pull, in that their work on the industry side pushed fast food; but their members were largely Black, so they were pulling fast food into their own communities. Activists, who operated within communities to bring sorely needed resources and political mobilization, were squarely on the pull side. The covenants Operation PUSH enacted with Heublein (owner of Kentucky Fried Chicken) and Burger King, for better or worse, were integral to the centrifuge that spun fast food deeper into Black social and economic life in the 1980s.

The Heublein Covenant

Operation PUSH began its "racial covenants" or "trade agreements" with Kentucky Fried Chicken's parent company at the end of 1981 or beginning of 1982. Milton Greaves, director of information for the PUSH International Trade Bureau (PITB), the economic arm of Operation PUSH, charged that since Black consumers spent billions of dollars, "these companies have a moral obligation to return some of this money to the community."[22] The structure of that return was realized in the covenant, over which executives at Heublein and KFC expressed pleasure for the hard work that had produced it and its potential to attract positive national attention for all involved. It might even model for other companies that they needn't believe the rumor that "Operation PUSH's only posture is confrontation."[23] Walter J. Simon, vice president for business and resources development, argued, "We recognize that the minority community is a good market, and it makes sense to support people who support us." And PUSH was pleased because its goals were met without having to resort to a "withdrawal of enthusiasm," otherwise known as a boycott.[24]

The final terms of the agreement were announced in February 1982, in a press release jointly released by Heublein and Operation PUSH. Reverend Jackson anticipated that the five-year program would generate more than $360 million in economic activity in the Black community, through franchising and new contracts with Black suppliers. More than one hundred Black-owned stores were planned, with estimated annual sales of more than $50 million and payrolls greater than $7 million per year.[25] The Heublein covenant pertained to the corporation's entire business, of which Kentucky Fried Chicken was just one part. The fast food chain would ramp up efforts to enable "qualified Black candidates who lack sufficient capital or credit to enter this business," to be reviewed during the first year by a joint KFC–PUSH task force to ensure program implementation.

To start, Heublein planned to make available eight franchised stores to Black investor groups with special financing, and eight additional franchisees in each of the following two years. Candidates would be required to invest $20,000 at the minimum, and those with previous fast food experience were preferred. The covenant stipulated that KFC would assist potential Black franchisees by providing a computerized trade area model to identify sites that were likely to be profitable; assist with leasing, guaranteeing them where required; and providing equipment financing. Further, KFC agreed to buy back any stores that failed to break even. KFC would make additional stores available to financially able Black franchisees who wished to own and operate a store personally. With an increasing number of such stores each year over the next three years, culminating in twenty per year in the later stages, the corporation would work with PUSH to identify potential Black franchisees "in geographic areas where stores are to be built." In other words, it was a top-down process where KFC would choose the sites it wanted and assign operators to them. Franchisees had no say in the locations for new outlets, a sticking point that would emerge years later in claims of redlining.[26]

Interest from Black entrepreneurs was high and immediate. Jackson began meeting with existing KFC franchisees in Chicago as applications and requests for franchise information kits poured in by the hundreds. For all the hoopla and envisioned capital infusion, the total amount Heublein would spend ($180 million) constituted a fraction of the corporation's total budget ($3.4 billion).[27] Heublein gained the veneer of a commitment to Black communities with little real risk or investment. *Fortune* evaluated the agreement as simply good business sense. Heublein chair Hicks

Waldron was quoted as saying "When you see a black go into a chicken store, you see on average a person who will eat twice as much chicken as a white person."[28] Fast food had come to its senses and remembered American racial tropes about Black people's apparent natural affinity for chicken, which had disappeared from consciousness when second-generation restaurants were born and exclusively catered to White people.

The Burger King Covenant

Garland Guice, head of Inner City Foods Inc., acquired fifteen Burger King restaurants in 1976. The primary franchise operator, Chart House, had decided that its locations on Chicago's South and West Sides should be operated by Black franchisees, and it yielded to the "tremendous pressure put on companies operating in inner-city areas to bring blacks into ownership." But as years passed and Guice failed to receive the support he needed from corporate—as was true for other minority operators—he turned to Jesse Jackson for assistance, aware of PUSH's agitation for food and beverage corporations to invest in Black communities. Burger King CEO Jeffrey Campbell admitted that minority franchisees like Guice were undercapitalized and undersupported compared to their White peers. District managers especially were loath to visit Black outlets "once the sun goes down."[29]

To remediate the concerns of Black Burger King franchisees, corporate entered into a covenant with PUSH. This agreement, initially dated from 1983 to 1987 but subject to possible extension, was heralded as particularly momentous because it totaled more in dollar value than PUSH's covenants with Coca-Cola, Heublein, and 7 Up combined.[30] Interestingly, Operation PUSH did not target McDonald's. Ray Kroc's third wife, Joan, donated to Democratic causes—quite opposite from her husband's staunchly Republican politics—and one such recipient was Jesse Jackson, perhaps one reason for PUSH's avoidance. Jesse Jackson announced to PUSH International Trade Bureau members the Burger King covenant as "another significant victory for reciprocal trade with corporate America." The official signing took place the day after the fifteenth anniversary of Dr. Martin Luther King Jr.'s assassination, for which PUSH planned a candlelight memorial.[31]

The covenant clarified that the agreement was "not to be construed as a formal legal document," but that it expressed "a firm moral commitment by Burger King Corporation to continue the expansion of meaningful opportunities for Black franchisees, employees, suppliers, professionals and entrepreneurs." Citing Federal Reserve Board data that indicated Black consumers injected $175 billion into the economy, the covenant contended that Black Americans should receive a fair share of jobs and other economic benefits for that spending, and that Burger King would "trade with those who trade with it."[32] African American marketing firm ViewPoint served as consultants in Burger King's implementation of the agreement, drawing on identical experience with 7 Up. ViewPoint would develop, monitor, and execute Burger King's covenant, which might include supporting Burger King's efforts to market the program to African Americans, conducting needs assessments to identify gaps and opportunities in the company's extant marketing strategies, and conducting psychographic analyses of Black consumers.[33]

Operation PUSH sought twenty new Black Burger King franchisees per year over the life of the covenant; if that proved easily attainable, then the numbers were to increase to thirty-five per year. Further, PUSH called for a minimum of 15 percent of expenditures to Black firms because Black consumers represented 15 percent of the corporation's annual volume. The percentage was a national benchmark that would be adjusted accordingly as a function of geography, market data, and availability of Black suppliers.[34] To maximize access to suppliers, Burger King was to use lists provided by PITB. The vendors of course included purveyors of restaurant equipment and supplies, but extended to a wide spectrum of business services. Advertising was at the top of the list, but it also included construction, trucking and hauling, real estate brokering, and waste removal. Legal services, banking, and accounting received detailed treatment in the trade agreement, and even preemployment physicals would take place on a proportional basis with Black physicians and dentists.

Burger King also agreed to increase corporate contributions to relevant organizations; 35 percent of its donations would go to organizations such as the United Negro College Fund, the NAACP, the Urban League, and the Liberty City Revitalization Program.[35] But franchise opportunities remained the critical focus of the covenant. The trade agreement formally recognized the importance of African Americans as fast food consumers and concretized the company's social responsibilities. Burger King claimed a commitment "to assisting Black people and other minorities to move into the economic mainstream through the sales of restaurant franchises." The agreement stipulated that Burger King aspired to Black operators making up 15 percent of all franchisees by the end of fiscal year 1987. Hard-set requirements did not exist; were the goal not met within that time frame, the corporation would simply try again. Franchisees could receive assistance in different aspects of restaurant operations, and those who met expansion criteria and took advantage of the support would become eligible to acquire an additional restaurant. Like KFC, Burger King also committed to buy back underperforming outlets. Taken together, the plan was for Burger King to "try" bringing Black entrepreneurs into the system in a way that should not have necessitated a covenant, and with no real consequences if it did not.

Burger King president Jeffrey Campbell gave an extensive interview a few months after the covenant was signed to *Dollars & Sense,* a Black magazine focused on finance and business. He expressed high regard for Jesse Jackson—"I think he is super-sharp, honorable and lives up to his word"—perhaps compelled to do so because Jackson was being skewered by White corporate America. *Fortune* reported that "to listen to Jesse Jackson, the flamboyant black preacher who has become a scourge to American business, is to enter a world of oddly distorted contours and imagery." The article cast Jackson's ideas about Black America as a nation within a nation as outlandish rhetorical excess, and it scoffed at critiques of other inequities such as police occupation of Black neighborhoods. *Fortune* called Jackson a self-appointed, albeit popular, ambassador for Black communities and described PUSH's boycotts in language that suggested extortion.[36] Other media evinced skepticism of the covenant agreements, if somewhat less acerbically, calling it a "voluntaristic affirmative action" program, superficial and self-serving. Some food executives deflected credit for the program from Jackson, stating that they were already planning such initiatives and that talking to PUSH merely "accelerated what we were going to do." But corporate brass admitted concern about what lay in store if they rejected these agreements. An executive at Anheuser-Busch explained that corporations were fearful that Jackson "will cause consumers to react and the black employees to demonstrate."[37]

For his part, Campbell argued that even if Burger King had not been especially focused on attracting Black customers, the company had changed its stance not only because of PUSH's influence but also because of a change of leadership at corporate and "enlightened self-interest." That is, Campbell recognized that Black people constituted a market the corporation had overlooked; he was not motivated by social responsibility. He also reiterated that the covenant was not a legal document that could be challenged in court. Rather, it was "a gentleman's agreement."[38] Media buys in *Ebony* played up the amicable and collegial basis of this arrangement. A 1983 Burger King ad, rendered visually arresting through black-and-white photography, centered a portrait of Jesse Jackson with the tagline "Burger King Is Helping Business Take on a New Complexion." Quotes from Jackson and Campbell stood side by side. Jackson's read "They're doing it with one of the largest financial commitments ever made by a major corporation to Black America. By opening over 500 new restaurants which will be owned by Blacks and built by Blacks. By using Black financial institutions and other Black suppliers. They're setting down roots in inner-city communities and succeeding where no one else has. They're recognizing the value and potential of Black America. Burger King Corporation has chosen trade beyond aid."

The Covenants' Consequences

Had Burger King—or Heublein for that matter—made trade with Black constituents a central part of their operations? Did the initiatives leave Black communities in the black? PUSH benefited from the compacts, particularly in name recognition and influence. Myriad small connections with fast food were angled toward PUSH. For example, a Chicago Chicken George outlet at 62nd and Halsted advertised a 50 percent off promotion, of which a small portion would go to back to PUSH. The covenants were also high-profile initiatives that fostered Jackson's national reputation as he moved toward a presidential run in 1984.

It is less clear that the covenants bore out Black finance media's arguments that such agreements could ensure the economic reciprocity needed to reach "total liberation and parity if the quality of life is to be improved for America's black population."[39] It does appear that the numbers of Black franchisees increased, and suppliers such as Black-owned banks enjoyed more deposits. However, all these ostensibly positive changes were fraught. The numbers of Black operators remained small in the overall share. Moreover, many of those who gained access to new franchisees were well-connected players already in the industry. Herman Cain, who would go on to run for president of the United States in 2012, entered Burger King's rapid management development program and at the age of thirty-six was a regional vice president and general manager of the Philadelphia region, responsible for more than four hundred restaurants. Despite his turn to conservative politics in later years, in the 1980s he was a beneficiary of Operation PUSH's Black empowerment actions.[40] Milt Sanders was the first inheritor of the PUSH covenant with Heublein. He had been at General Foods, Burger Chef, and Keebler Cookies before becoming "overseer" of 250 Church's stores. Once he left, his serving as the liaison between Church's and PUSH put him top of mind when the civil rights organization sought out Black talent for KFC franchises. In turn, Sanders obtained a franchise in Georgia. One of the few new operators featured in trade media who had come from outside elite circles was Lois Foust, a Black woman. She opened a KFC in Long Beach, California, under the terms of the covenant by moving up the ranks from crew to management.[41]

Caroline Jones worked to funnel funding to Black fast food franchising. She wrote to TWA Airlines about investment possibilities, and first among them was Walt Simon at Kentucky Fried Chicken: "Walt has a new $10 million budget to develop new minority franchises, $50–$75,000 needed if no prior food experience,

Figure 11.4. Bojangles' and Wendy's share a block on Adam Clayton Powell Boulevard, 1980s. Might they have belonged to Noah Robinson? He owned a busy Wendy's in Harlem and embarked on a plan in 1984 to open a dozen or more Wendy's and Bojangles' across Chicago's South Side (Herb Greenberg, "Noah of Fast Food: Too Much to Swallow," *Chicago Tribune,* February 12, 1984). dof_1_02008_0061, New York City tax lot photographs. Courtesy Municipal Archives, City of New York.

$30–$35,000 if this money cannot be borrowed."[42] Jones also made use of her connections to attempt to purchase a KFC franchise for herself. She completed operator training, suggesting she was serious about the endeavor, but Walt Simon regretfully informed her in the winter of 1986 that her application for a Miami metro outlet had been rejected. Corporate would not provide a release for the proposed site in Coconut Grove, and Simon noted that the company's new policy to avoid infringing on existing franchisees "makes it very tough to get new people into franchising with KFC." He suggested that Jones be open to other areas of Florida since she wouldn't be actively involved in running the business anyway.[43]

Whether Jones ended up obtaining a different outlet is unknown, but what is clear is that she was more representative of those who reaped benefits from covenants than ordinary Black small businesspeople. By 1987, between McDonald's, Burger King, and Kentucky Fried Chicken, Black franchisees totaled only 350 out of 15,000.

The covenants also had limited reach for Black suppliers, and here again, the most elite firms received the lion's share. It was not until 1988 that Burger King made its first deposit with a Black bank. A total of $1.6 million, in deposits of around $90,000 each, went to banks in Chicago, including Seaway National and Independence Bank. Independence was also the beneficiary of a separate pilot program for short-term receipt of Burger King's FICA and other federal withholding taxes.[44] It was not due to chance that Independence received such largesse. The vice chair of the board was Cirilo A. McSween, whose connection to Jesse Jackson went back to his days as treasurer of Operation Breadbasket. Independence, banker for Burrell, also backed McSween's outlets.[45]

Other key suppliers were advertising and marketing firms. Burger King's first order of business in working with Black advertising suppliers was to hire the ad shop UniWorld Group as part of its Minority Tactical Action Plan. Burger King would continue to create Black-oriented radio commercials and use more Black talent in its casting. But there were fewer Black firms in existence by the time PUSH executed its covenants. By the mid-1970s, Black ad shops were collapsing in large numbers.[46] Some attributed the decline to a lack of knowledge about business administration; Black ad folks tended to come from creative or production. Byron Lewis, president of UniWorld Inc., contended that to lure staff away from general market firms, Black agencies had to pay higher salaries, which left them vulnerable. He also held that it was institutional pressure from the NAACP, the federal government, and others that led advertisers to bring on Black agencies, not real interest; in other words, it was simply tokenism. Adding insult to injury, retailers began to think that general agencies could reach Black consumers just as effectively, especially as they hired more Black staff.[47] Under such circumstances, Black advertising agencies faced dwindling revenue despite racial covenants funneling money their way.[48]

KFC's investment in more Black advertising called on Mingo–Jones to create a slate of campaigns, some of which honed rather cynically on African American vulnerabilities. For example, sickle cell occupied prominent positioning in community-based marketing. Mingo–Jones created a sweepstakes with the Sickle Cell Disease Foundation of Greater New York. The event's catering featured Kentucky Fried Chicken and Coors, and sweepstakes entrants could win a grand prize of a trip for two to Trinidad and Tobago.[49] The brand also contributed nearly three hundred dinners to the foundation's annual meeting in 1988 and sponsored research grants on sickle cell that went to major universities. Said Don Solomon, chair of the Kentucky Fried Chicken National Advertising Co-op, "Sickle cell anemia is a serious hereditary disorder. It was always the Colonel's dream and it remains the dream of the Kentucky Fried Chicken family, to help give every baby a healthy start in life."[50]

KFC would reap not only enhanced sales but also an enhanced corporate image.

Figure 11.5. This creative work in progress appears never to have run. While Mingo–Jones went out on a limb in making fried chicken a cure for sickle cell disease, it also developed several radio spots in 1986 meant to show how KFC could help take the edge off life's minor frustrations. In one, for which the firm imagined hiring Flip Wilson or Scatman Crothers, a man complained about the high prices of cars, real estate, and his lady "eyeballin a diamond that could balance a national budget." Caroline P. Jones Papers, Archives Center, National Museum of American History, Smithsonian Institution, Washington, D.C.

Print ads highlighted community-based organizations and emphasized that the company's efforts toward social responsibility were due to its strong moral compass. One ad read, "You worked hard to get off the old block. Now you work even harder so your baby has it easier than you did. Kentucky Fried Chicken wants to support your efforts." Another asked "What does your neighborhood need most?" prodding readers to respond with issues such as housing or street repair; KFC would then purportedly donate to relevant organizations.[51] These ads sought to change perceptions that KFC's community involvement was negligible, and possibly to assuage consumer concerns about the Colonel, "a symbol of Southern gentility and Black oppression so widely promoted."[52]

The advertising made possible by the covenants, then, was often self-serving for corporate interests, limited proportionally in expenditures, and sometimes problematic in its racial messaging. The covenants did not usher innovation in Black Consumer Market creative, and Black ad spending was but a trickle compared to general market accounts. In 1986, R. J. Reynolds (which owned Heublein) spent nearly $43 million at Young & Rubicam, while Mingo–Jones received almost $3 million.[53] And Black ad firms had to do a dance that was not required of their general market peers, creating campaigns (and pitches to win said campaigns) that uniquely targeted Black psychographics and demographics and still mirrored the national marketing plan. Fast food corporations did not want to stray too far from the general market messaging just for Black consumers. Even by 1988, when Brady Keys deployed radio spots in Detroit for his Burger Kings to much success, to his mind, corporate "did not believe in black advertising."[54]

In the final analysis, the covenants did not live up to their promise. They reportedly produced many new franchisees and brought millions of dollars to advertising firms and goods and service providers who obtained valuable contracts.[55] But the beneficiaries were largely elites who were already well connected to either the fast food industry or to PUSH. Unless those entities went on to disperse funds to the community (e.g., through home lending), average African Americans would not feel the effects of the covenants other than through low-wage employment in fast food outlets.[56] The full impact of the covenants is difficult to assess because corporations were signing covenants but deploying them and reporting on them in a haphazard manner.

But to say the covenants were less effective than they could have been misses the mark. The greatest weakness of the covenants was the underlying rationale, not the execution. The assertion that Black people's substantial consumer expenditures merited corporate investment seems plausible on its face. The NAACP had instituted a Fair Share program with McDonald's, Wendy's, Hardee's, and Church's premised and buttressed by Black people's constituting a large share of those chains' profits.[57] Upon closer inspection, these agreements do not hold water as an empowerment strategy. It was deeply problematic to yoke Black consumer spending patterns to corporate investment. Those businesses should have already been engaging with Black contractors as a matter of course, if accounts were merit- and expertise-based. To connect Black consumption with corporate contracts and franchise opportunities suggested that if Black people spent less, Black-owned businesses would also receive less or perhaps nothing.

The covenants intimated that Black vendors were not warranted in the absence of a specified level of Black spending. Once again, this would put Black communities in the position of needing to eat their way to economic standing, as they did in the 1960s franchise push. Black consumers would end up risking their health for gains that would in the end benefit only a few. When PUSH re-signed its agreements with explicit plans for five hundred more Black Burger King stores over the next five years, it meant Black bodies would have to carry the weight of all those fast food outlets.

PUSH meant well, but the terms on which the covenants rested were untenable. What if the covenants had exceeded the originators' wildest expectations and many thousands of fast food outlets washed over Black neighborhoods? Could that really be seen as liberatory? Would desperately needed living wages, healthful living conditions, or real wealth follow the crest of the wave? Black communities protested the arrival of fast food in the 1970s, so explosively successful covenants would just bring into fruition more of what residents saw as a disamenity. In the 1980s, most Black communities remained unreceptive to fast food crash landing in commercial space. When Church's opened in D.C.'s Shaw neighborhood in 1983, it was the first "major private business" to open on that stretch of Seventh Street NW since the rebellion in 1968. And it was not welcome. Ibrahim Mumin, executive director of the Shaw Project Area Committee, argued, "We don't need another fast-food store." He called for bowling alleys, movie theaters, or hardware stores, but not "10 more liquor stores or fast-food shops."[58] Nearby, in multiethnic Mount Pleasant, the fried chicken restaurant Holly Farms had secured a lease for an outlet in a previously abandoned corner store on a block home to a small grocery, a liquor store, and a collection of abandoned and burned-out storefronts. Community members expressed the usual concerns about neighborhood disorder were the restaurant to open. More pointedly, resident Gerald Green was angered because Safeway, which was a major stockholder in Holly Farms, had pulled out of leasing the same location. Green charged, "We'll pay for groceries, but not for trash food. If they don't want our money, leave us alone."[59]

But fast food would not leave Black communities alone. And the pull of activist action would soon weaken under an intensified push from the fast food industry. Burrell Advertising had declared that all perimeters would be attacked, and now fast food embarked on what pundits called the "burger wars" and "chicken wars." Black neighborhoods became vital battlegrounds. As social, economic, and public health crises weakened Black communities in the 1980s, fast food multiplied aggressively. And so, in a context of Black suffering, fast food wars became ghetto wars.

12

Ghetto Wars

Fast Food Tussles for Profits amid Sufferation

Mingo–Jones's sixty-second spot for KFC's new chicken livers opened with singers who crooned, "They're tender on the inside, golden brown and crispy too; they're our brand new chicken livers fresh made just for you." The 1985 commercial continued with an announcer who cautioned, "For all of you out there who hate liver—we understand. And this announcement is NOT FOR YOU. But for those of you liver lovers (yeah) who appreciate fresh chicken livers, golden brown and crispy on the outside (yeah), tender and moist on the inside (uh huh), liver up!"[1] Chicken livers are hardly a typical fast food menu item, and both the new product and its advertising pitch were a bit of a reach. Whether or not they sold, their creation is indicative of the fever pitch that characterized fast food competition across the 1980s, but particularly in the middle of the decade. Mingo–Jones's commercial was just one of many attempts to increase spending in the Black Consumer Market as the turn to Black-centered advertising initiated in the 1970s solidified into accepted practice.

The media, investment analysts, and other commentators called the crush of marketing campaigns, product introductions, and brand-to-brand combat the "burger wars" and the "chicken wars." Fast food corporations were drawn into keen competition with one another over declining market shares, saturation in the suburbs, and changing dietary trends. What pundits failed to discuss was the extent to which the fast food wars were buoyed by, and magnified, racial inequalities. Fast food wars fueled central city expansion, and Black communities became ever more logical repositories for a product that was becoming harder to sell. Fast food therefore began its final, and most substantive, infiltration of Black space in the 1980s, enriching corporate coffers but doing little for operators or the communities in which they lived.

For Black communities, the fast food wars were waged on many more fronts than brand competition and dubious ads for poultry livers. For Black franchisees,

Operation PUSH and other activist actions had accelerated the proliferation of Black-owned franchises, but they remained a minuscule proportion of all franchisees, and the discriminatory treatment they faced now pushed them into lawsuits with head-quarters. Black neighborhoods continued to battle fast food as more outlets took hold of the street, and in most cases they did not emerge the victor. But even as unwanted restaurants multiplied, the industry called Black neighborhoods "waste-lands" that held the capacity for ever more fast food and made explicit the possi-bility of capitalizing on disinvestment, targeting communities on that basis. The restaurants that were built evinced an aesthetics of war—fortified, bunker-like outposts—that made the streetscapes in Black communities less attractive. The intertwining of fast food and vice products (liquor and tobacco) revealed fast food as combat medicaments to deal with conditions of sufferation, particularly acute under the Reagan administration. Taken together, the broad context of the fast food wars was better characterized as ghetto wars, an environment in which fast food became entrenched in the ghetto. Fast food may have been at war with itself, but Black urbanites were the casualties.

Burger and Chicken Wars

Whereas in 1965 the *Franchise Opportunities Handbook* listed thirty-four fast food chains, by 1985 that number soared to 278. Alongside the leading brands, new ven-tures opened their doors, ranging from national chains like Fuddruckers to ran-dom outlets such as Watta Ethnic Food Delight. By this point, fast food had real-ized that Black neighborhoods were critical to the bottom line. Financial analyst Bernard Addo commented, "There's a McDonald's restaurant in almost every Black neighborhood. Without the Black community, you would see McDonald's revenues diminishing."[2] For that reason, all the corporations mounted intense offensives to capture and retain Black customers as part of their overall growth strategies. But the broader strategies were implemented to varying degrees of success—and the more they failed, the more chains would need Black customers to shore up revenues.

Among the second-generation chains, Burger King's marketing mishaps were the most pronounced and publicly observed. The chain floundered across the en-tire decade. A revolving door of executive brass produced short-term initiatives, confused messaging, and rising prices, all of which perpetuated a decline in cus-tomers. Struggles in head-to-head burger contests lead to other product types. A new roast beef sandwich arrived in 1980 ("there's a lot of meat here, and it tastes great!"), and Burger King later developed a steak sandwich to rival McDonald's. The industry leader remained unbothered, confident that Burger King's sandwich would not be competitive since it used "the flap"—a cut of meat with a seam down the middle.[3]

J. Walter Thompson had served as Burger King's advertising firm since 1976, but over the 1980s it cycled through myriad taglines, muddling the corporate message, confusing or even alienating customers, and losing market share.[4] Early Thompson taglines included "Make it special, make it Burger King" and "Have it your way." "Aren't you hungry for Burger King now?" showcased such products as the Croissan'wich and operational features like late-night drive-thrus. Herb the Nerd, a man who had never eaten a Whopper, appeared in 1986 and was quickly dropped after three months of ridicule. After that came "This is a Burger King town," commercials that were heavy on images of good old boys and so-called heartland Americana. Finally, "The best food for fast times" prompted Burger King to show Thompson the door; in one of the biggest account switches in advertising history, N. W. Ayer won the $200 million Burger King account in 1987 (roughly $450 million in 2020 dollars).[5]

Ayer created "We do it like you do it when we do it like we do it at Burger King." It was not a compelling slogan, and the campaign was panned on the front page of *Ad Age* even before the spots had run. Within a year of winning the account, now billing at $215 million, Ayer found its creative under review, prompted by yet another corporate buyout—this time Pillsbury was purchased by British conglomerate Grand Metropolitan. Ayer lost the account, which was split between two shops: national strategy went to D'Arcy Masius Benton & Bowles and retail promotions, events, and product introductions went to Saatchi & Saatchi. D'Arcy's first campaign was "Sometimes you've gotta break the rules," an attempt to show that Burger King would go to necessary extremes to deliver what customers wanted. But it was confusing and even angering to many customers, who chastised the company for telling children to defy authority. Operators also disparaged Ayer's work, charging that not only were sales flat but that promotional giveaways were costing them money.[6]

While Burger King endured public trials and tribulations, Wendy's, in contrast, born as a late 1970s upstart, continued to thrive and keep its competitors off-balance. The hugely successful "Where's the beef?" campaign of 1984 attracted customers and brand recognition. Wendy's trajectory warned McDonald's that it could not rest on its laurels. The latter, too, put forth multiple campaigns, messages, and products. Among the slogans it disseminated over the 1980s were "Nobody can do it like McDonald's can," "You deserve a break today," "It's a good time for the great taste of McDonald's," and "McDonald's and you." It issued the McDLT, the chopped beefsteak sandwich (served after 4:00 pm), and Chicken McNuggets. The fast food

Figure 12.1. A McDonald's townhouse in Upper Manhattan. The wallscape advertises the new McDLT sandwich. dof_1_02092_0026, New York City tax lot photos. Courtesy Municipal Archives, City of New York.

wars prompted most burger chains to begin selling chicken. McDonald's released its "boneless clumps of the meat" in 1983, prompting KFC's retaliation with Kentucky Nuggets and later Chicken Little sandwiches for as little as thirty-nine cents.[7] Neither would Wendy's be left out, creating Crispy Chicken Nuggets, for which Kool & the Gang sang a jingle covering their own hit song "Celebration."

While the other chains scrambled for chicken products, Church's struggled to diverge from its tried-and-true formulas, leaving it vulnerable to KFC, which attempted to co-opt crispy chicken, spicy chicken, and anything else that competitors brought to the market. Church's stuck to its bland chicken (though the company preferred the word mild) in homage to European foodways it thought would appeal to the broadest possible market.[8] Church's plowed through one ad agency after another, casting aside six in ten years, landing on Grey Advertising in 1983. Church's had long been skeptical of advertising, only initiating a national campaign in 1973. It was also perhaps unrealistic in its expectations of what advertising could do. When BBDO could not produce a 20 percent return on investment, Church's scuppered the firm's tagline "We make chicken a juicy deal" and the nondescript commercials that accompanied it.⁹ Grey produced "The Bucketheads," TV spots styled as a White family sitcom meant to mock KFC. The husband wore a bucket upside down over his head and his wife confessed that yet again she would be serving "the bucket" for dinner. The announcer chided, "Don't be a bucket head. Head to Church's Fried Chicken and get bigger chicken that's crispy and juicy, at a lower Church's price. You won't get that in a bucket."¹⁰

A flurry of ad campaigns was the most prominent manifestation of the burger and chicken wars, but advertising could not distinguish brands if focused solely on products, price, or promotions. McDonald's was particularly successful in the fast food wars because it created a symbolic persona beyond the products it served, one in which McDonald's lay claim to critical rites of passage for (White) Americans across the lifecourse. In the "Back Home Again" television spot, a White family traveled in their station wagon to Dad's hometown, called Fenton Falls, where he eagerly anticipated sharing his youth with the family. But his old house has been replaced by condos, and his best friend Shorty's house by a gas station. All that remains of the life he once knew is the neighborhood McDonald's—where, lo and behold, the family encounters none other than a grown-up Shorty dining at the next table. McDonald's was the lighthouse in a changing world, a place where heartwarming experiences were realized and remembered. It could do so even for the most privileged. The Academy Award–winning 1980 film *Ordinary People* portrayed the Jarrett family, an affluent White household ensconced in the tony suburbs of Chicago's North Shore, but rent asunder by the death of elder son Buck in a boating accident and younger brother Conrad's ensuing attempted suicide. Even wealthy Conrad (played by Timothy Hutton) had his first date with a new love interest at McDonald's. The chain reconstituted the White, American family within its outlets, centering happiness and love and selling community, intergenerational bonding, and stability.¹¹

First-generation chains lacked the wherewithal to actively compete in the fast food wars. White Castle was fading into obscurity, unable to muster the requisite marketing ammunition. It could only manage lackluster ads with tired taglines like "Without White Castle, every hamburger tastes the same." Early peer Little Tavern clung to survival in Black neighborhoods, motivated by "prime inner city real estate." News media described Little Tavern as a D.C. institution that, into the 1980s, continued to welcome all sorts of patrons: "Everyone from congressmen to high-priced lobbyists seemed to have a secret weakness for the chain's 'death balls' (the greasy, cholesterol-laden hamburgers), and they could be seen ponied up to the counters late at night next to homeless people nursing cups of coffee and trying to

Figure 12.2. A White Castle on Queens Boulevard in the 1980s. dof_4_00168_0026, New York City tax lot photos. Courtesy Municipal Archives, City of New York.

stay warm."[12] But its reign as a member of the burger chateaux was nearing an end. Despite its history as a scrappy business persevering in a fierce market, by 1981 the chain was down to approximately thirty-five shops and eighty-two-year-old Harry Duncan sold it to an Ohio lawyer named Gerald E. Wedren and retired to Florida. Wedren, who had no restaurant experience, set about refurbishing all the shops "to a state of near beatific whiteness," the metaphorical racial purity at the foundation of the burger chateaux. Many outlets received full makeovers, including one where Black patrons had been spurned for service decades earlier. But neither the renovations nor Wedren's new Club LT, an upscale version of the chain, lasted, eventually being sold to a corporate group that owned Hardee's and Fuddruckers restaurants.[13]

Fomenting the burger and chicken wars were changing dietary mores that shunted fast food to the realm of junk food and embraced trends around gourmet dining. Consumers worried about fat, salt, cholesterol, red meat, and butter (opting instead for margarine, only to produce cardiovascular disease from trans fats decades later). Fast food had come to be seen as a "heart-attack special with a side order of coronary-bypass fries."[14] The industry responded actively to try and incorporate foods that health-focused Americans might want to eat.

It was in this context that Kentucky Fried Chicken became KFC. Four years after the tobacco company R. J. Reynolds purchased Heublein in 1982, it was sold again to PepsiCo; key among the changes it made was abbreviating the name of the Heublein brand. The new name sought to circumvent the worrisome word "fried." Urban rumors circulated that the word corporate was in fact trying to dodge was "chicken," because the chain was using fake or abnormal birds.[15] At least KFC was spared rumors that their product caused cancer or sterility as part of a nefarious plan by the Ku Klux Klan—an urban legend that dogged Church's.[16]

Renaming was a singular move; much more common were new nutrition-conscious menus. Americans were reportedly counting calories, exercising, and becoming less likely to identify as "pro meat."[17] As a result, fast food chains began to issue a slate of items that could be perceived as healthier, regardless of whether they actually were. New chains like D'Lites entirely dedicated the menu to "healthy" fast food, even if it was standard fare allegedly with lower fat and calories.[18] Wendy's created a salad bar called the Superbar, which included calorie-light lettuce and other raw vegetables, but also featured cheese, meat, and other energy-dense items, the latter compounded by unlimited servings. Wendy's also released stuffed baked potatoes, hardly a departure from calorie-rich foods and animal proteins. The offering came in choices such as bacon and cheese, broccoli and cheese, chili and cheese, and sour cream and chives. Salad bars proved unprofitable in the end and were seen as unsanitary. McDonald's led with prepackaged salads but those too struggled to gain consumer confidence.[19]

Advertising was of course central to fast food's healthy makeover. In the most basic implementations, brands simply stuck in signals of reduced risk, such as Church's "100% Vegetable Oil" icons in television commercials. More comprehensive approaches framed the brand as part of a healthful and wholesome family and reinforced the compatibility of fast food with the preferences of health-conscious, typically White mothers. A KFC television spot featured an apron-clad mom whose presentation suggested she had prepared a home-cooked meal. Actually, she was serving boxes of takeout chicken to her children. She claimed, "You know, I used to serve fast food as a treat. But now fast food is more than a once in a while thing. That's why I serve Kentucky Fried Chicken more and more. The kids love it and I know they're eating well. It's made from the highest-quality chicken cooked with the Colonel's finger lickin' recipe of eleven herbs and spices."

The commercial shifted KFC from something one grabbed and consumed on the go to a sit-down meal supervised (though not cooked) by Mom. It was a shrewd move at a time when Americans were not only shying away from perceived junk food but were also enamored with gourmet food and cooking. Before the 1960s, when Julia Child arrived on television, gourmet food culture was an elite activity. French food and cooking methods epitomized high-status cuisine. Child made French food accessible to White, middle-class America, and food took on increasing weight as a marker of a stylish lifestyle. The 1980s brought a widespread embrace of gourmet cooking and eating, as part of a national cultural imperative of conspicuous consumption.[20] Specialty food writing and food stores blossomed and new cooking shows like Jeff Smith's *The Frugal Gourmet* brought an emphasis on ingredients, expertise, and equipment into American homes.

Concerns about salt and cholesterol and infatuation with gourmet food meant White, middle-class America was turning away from fast food. If so, fast food outlets needed Black urban neighborhoods more than ever. Not that Black people welcomed fast food unreservedly; but the industry routinely turned to Blackness to solve crises it encountered with Whiteness. In that vein, it turned to Black media to assuage health concerns about fast food. While *Ebony* failed to critique fast food, *Jet* was actively championing it. The American Council on Science and Health was founded in 1978 ostensibly as a consumer organization focused on scientific evidence, but generally promoted or defended a range of corporate products such as processed food, sugar, food additives, and even Agent Orange. The group was cited in *Jet* in 1982 under the headline "Value of Fast Foods Upheld by Health Group." The "health group" claimed that fast food could be enjoyed even by individuals fanatical about healthy foods. It simply needed to be part of a varied diet: "Many people think that fast foods are distinctly different from other foods in nutritional value. In fact, it's only the speed and style of service not the food itself, which distinguishes fast food from others."[21] Such a claim was not backed by scientific evidence and was out of step with public sentiment. The Council was attempting to convince Black readers that nutritional concerns about fast food were unfounded in a moment where their White counterparts were increasingly concerned about the industry's staples.

Positioning fast food widely to Black audiences as part of a healthful diet had the potential to affect the behavior of many as new outlets sprang up in Black neighborhoods. As will be seen, sales took off among Black consumers in the 1980s, particularly in neighborhoods where these restaurants had become prevalent but other choices were limited, and where individuals had limited means for discretionary spending. To be sure, members of the Black middle class also consumed fast food, and racism meant that communities better off economically were not necessarily blessed with a surfeit of retail options. But upwardly striving Black urbanites also valued the gourmet food that was captivating White people. And fast food presented a vexed dining choice—acceptable as a convenient lunch option while working downtown or as a treat for the kids, but not necessarily what residents wanted in their own backyards. *Ebony*'s editor and publisher John H. Johnson wrote in 1987 that the new Black middle class was distinguished by its participation in the mainstream American economy, and though fast food was mainstream, it was ordinary— cheap burgers and fries were hardly fitting for a group that had risen through "the power of excellence and sweat and determination."[22] Tom Burrell, head of the firm that held McDonald's Black Consumer Market account and resident of Chicago's exclusive Gold Coast, was inclined to opt for soul food more than haute cuisine, but there was no indication that he ate the food he pitched.[23]

The pressures that motivated White, corporate fast food to shy away from White consumers were not entirely relieved by entrenchment in Black space, because Black-owned establishments were capturing fast food dollars there. Smaller Black chains both fomented and benefited from the burger wars, spurring intense competition among major chains that could ill afford to lose sales to small operations and enticing investor interest in a booming industry. Harold Pierce of Harold's Chicken Shack passed away in 1988 but left behind a thriving business.[24] After Chicken George catapulted into thunderous sales upon opening in the late 1970s, it intended to sustain high traffic among Black, middle-class households in central cities, aiming to "draw off black pride to attract inner-city, middle-class chicken eaters. . . . The black community was just waiting for a business that wouldn't take them, their tastes, or their dollars for granted."[25] In fact, Chicken George attracted a multiracial customer base that drove local sales totals to levels reportedly triple that of KFC and McDonald's. Johnnie Ponzie, vice president from 1981 to 1985, gloated that they were putting nearby competitors out of business: "We were so proud because we were black and making money like the white guys did it."[26] Still, the "we" was an executive team, not exclusively Black, which Ponzie described as a frat house.

Eventually, the chain's internal management problems and weak marketing were its downfall. Mingo–Jones produced Chicken George commercials that tread a well-worn path of Black celebrities ranging from Patti LaBelle to Ben Vereen, and the major chains couponed the company into oblivion.[27] Franchising plans for hundreds of outlets never bore fruit, in large part because there was no formal franchise division within the disorganized company. Worse, franchisees weren't paying fees, leaving insufficient revenue to support operations nationally. By 1986, Chicken George went bankrupt and closed.[28] While it collapsed, a small fried fish chain in

Chicago flourished. Dock's began as a burger shop in an abandoned gas station in 1973, saving on building costs and taking up attractive corner locations. Owner Eugene Qahaar sold franchises that blossomed in the 1980s, showing "how fledgling franchise companies can build a niche by targeting low-rent, hand-me-down locations in black neighborhoods."[29] The chain rose from the ashes not only of defunct gas stations but also of failed Wendy's, KFC, and Burger King outlets, surprising pundits who believed that Black neighborhoods lacked disposable income. One such person was Dennis Robertson, a part owner of Sizzler restaurants. Qahaar's landlord introduced his tenant to Robertson, thinking him a source of investment capital and credibility—either because of his Whiteness, restaurant experience, or both. Robertson was skeptical and lacked any "desire to get involved in an inner-city business" but changed his mind when he learned the true potential for profit in Black neighborhoods, given their high population density, minimal competition, and cheaper properties.[30]

Black entrepreneurs who knew all along that their communities were profitable continued to pursue careers in fast food and were more likely to seek out franchises of the major chains than to try starting their own. Their numbers remained small. Despite all the minority franchising programs that arose in the 1960s, Black operators were still few and far between, and split into a minority that accrued high revenues and a majority that found themselves on a treadmill that more often than not threw them off. Even the high earners found their tenure cut short by corporate indifference. While fast food chains went to war with one another, Black franchisees warred with company headquarters.

What Happens to a Franchise Dream Deferred?

Fast food in the eyes of Black boosters was first and foremost a financial instrument, and it was failing. PUSH's covenants, agitation by Black franchisees, and community activism to obtain access to restaurants were about accumulating wealth. Fast food stood out as a lucrative arena from which African Americans had been excluded. Those who fought for franchises did not do so because fast food beckoned with gastronomic delights. The word "delicious" never appeared in Black activist discourse about these outlets. The quality of the food was also absent from articles in which the Black press beat a steady drum for fast food franchising. *Dollars & Sense* argued that "franchising is perhaps the most lucrative and practical vehicle for the enterprising business person interested in cashing in on the American dream behind a fast food cash register." It was an awkwardly written statement that could either mean fast food was the way to cash in on the American Dream, or that franchising was the way to cash in on fast food (as opposed to being an independent restaurateur). The latter was the more likely meaning, because the article went on to say that "the beauty of the franchising system is that it has a safety net of protection." *Dollars & Sense* maintained the party line on franchising: that it gave the benefits of corporate muscle in advertising, brand name, trade secrets, public relations, and other business networks, all while lowering risk. It noted that while the Small Business Administration estimated that 65 percent of new businesses failed, the rate was only 4 percent for all franchises (across business sectors). But those figures were not specific to fast food, nor to Black franchisees, which failed at a higher rate.[31]

To be fair, it was not the Black press alone that touted franchising. The United States Chamber of Commerce's periodical *The Nation's Business* published articles throughout the 1980s arguing that franchising, especially in fast food, was lucrative and growing and did not require the slightest expertise. Charlotta Stephens, an attorney who left a career in the Department of Commerce to become a McDonald's operator in Baltimore, was profiled in one issue as an example of the many women who had successfully entered franchising.[32] Fred Snowden, another African American business owner, worked as vice president of Urban Development for Baskin Robbins. With responsibilities that sounded very much like contemporary schemes to dragoon Black homeowners to subprime lending, Snowden explained, "Basically, we enlist the support of the urban community—the local government, school system, churches and civic groups—to help the company find franchisees."[33] Whether the franchisees benefited from that arrangement was another question.

In fact, by 1987, Tracy Powell, director of PUSH's International Trade Bureau, worried that franchising would be saturated before Black operators could obtain their fair share.[34] But *Ebony* was still arguing that "fast-food franchising offers the best business opportunities for Blacks and other minorities who want to go into business for themselves but lack the background, the exposure, or the financial backing."[35] Featuring Brady Keys, Cirilo McSween, Noah Robinson, and others, the article held that fast food was still king—and that civil rights and business groups were continuing the fight to increase participation in "this lucrative sector." *Black Enterprise*'s "Franchise 50" ranked companies by the number of Black-owned units and fast food was at the top. In fact, many of those chains had Black multi-unit owners, which artificially increased the totals. McDonald's and Burger King were ranked first and second in Black franchising, but the appropriate inter-chain measure would have been the percentage of Black franchisees, not the absolute number. Those at the top of the chart had percentages hovering at 4 percent, while Popeyes had a much higher proportion at 15 to 20 percent. Neither did the total number of franchisees address whether those numbers were in decline, nor the qualitative experience of Black franchisees. Moreover, franchising could not be said to have a major impact on Black participation in the economy or on individual or community economic resources.[36]

The reality was that the spoils of the fast food wars went to corporate head-quarters, not to Black franchisees. Burger King faced a class action lawsuit in 1988 from Black and other operators of color who alleged redlining, delays in approval for licenses, and fraudulent representations of sales potential. Seeking $500 million in damages, the operators felt that franchisors had only turned to Black space after having saturated the most desirable locations.[37] It was a rude awakening for those who believed in the premise of the franchise model. Black operators had gone on the record championing fast food and its potential for Black entrepreneurs, only to do an about-turn soon after. Pettis Norman, featured in Burger King advertising in 1979, still held in 1983, despite concerns, that he was "encouraged by the corporation's sincerity."[38] At that time he owned three restaurants in Dallas. But a year later he stated, "We feel the system is designed to keep us in set neighborhoods. We feel we have been locked into less-than-successful operations."[39] Norman became president of the Burger King Black Franchising Association in 1980 and was responsible for developing a team that took concerns to Operation PUSH, many of which were concretized in the covenant.[40] According to the covenant, Burger King agreed to move minority operators in failing stores to company-owned locations in White space, with corporate taking over the failing stores and either trying to make successes out of them or simply writing them off as business losses; but it appears that did not come to pass.

Among McDonald's operators, it was more of the same. A Charles Griffiths claimed that McDonald's kept separate Black and White lists for new stores; his own outlets turned out to be "hellholes." Operators in Philadelphia were burdened by debt and forced into bankruptcy.[41] In Baltimore, Osborne Payne, a latecomer to fast food franchising who entered the McDonald's system at age forty-nine, owned the most outlets in the city and was frequently profiled in local newspapers.[42] Payne strongly advocated for franchising (though as a diabetic he could not eat his own food) and called McDonald's "one of the best franchise companies in the business. . . . You get all types of assistance." Payne's enthusiasm was a public relations benefit for McDonald's, as he embodied the chain's supposed commitment to community partnerships.[43] However, it all came asunder for Payne in the late 1990s. He sued McDonald's alleging that corporate was opening stores too close to his own and cannibalizing his business. Corporate settled for $1.7 million.[44]

Black franchisees were in the difficult position of obtaining their businesses largely in a framework where corporate hired them as miners to extract ghetto gold; and they were restricted from accessing stores in White communities that would be lucrative for them as operators. Indeed, potential Black operators might not receive locations at all, and instead company-owned stores were opened on sites with high anticipated volumes. Either way, fast food sought out Black residents, the poorer the seemingly better. It did so with the knowledge that urban disinvestment made its businesses more attractive than might otherwise be the case.

Retail Deaths, Fast Food Births

In New York, city administrators welcomed new fast food restaurants, as many were erected on vacant—and therefore tax unproductive—lots. Restaurant supervisors for Bojangles' in Harlem saw how the economy could suppress customer counts but nevertheless remained bullish on fast food's prospects in the community, calling for more and more outlets.[45] KFC had already committed to extensive growth in Black neighborhoods. In 1984, it announced a spending plan of nearly $30 million to open almost five dozen new stores in Baltimore, which it saw as "underdeveloped." KFC divided Chicago into five quadrants, of which four were categorized "Inner City"— and those areas contained nearly four dozen restaurants. Popeyes, too, operated nearly two dozen outlets in the city in 1982, almost all in Black neighborhoods, and it intended to expand to more than sixty.[46]

Remarkably, Black neighborhoods were portrayed as virtually devoid of fast food during the 1980s, even as outlets multiplied rapidly. Perhaps in a context where the industry measured new store openings literally on a scale of hours, corporate headquarters perceived infinite capacity for more restaurants.

KFC's fifty-five stores in New York City, all but five of which were in Black neighborhoods, drew in revenue that smaller chains like Bojangles' could only dream of.[47] Harlem's sales for the first quarter of 1982 totaled $704 million across the six stores located in the neighborhood. And yet, corporate headquarters could not be sated. KFC marketing executive Marvin Winkfield believed the totals should have been higher and speculated the restaurant facilities were to blame; they were commensurate with other local chicken takeout outlets such as Kansas Fried Chicken, but worse than national chains such as Church's.[48] Church's, for its part, had decided that "selling fried chicken, mostly in inner-city, blue-collar markets, proved immensely profitable," and continued to focus on these communities. The chain had been aggressively opening stores in Harlem. A location at 140th and Adam Clayton Powell Boulevard was meant to challenge the KFCs at 135th and 145th and Lexington Avenue. KFC's Winkfield warned his colleagues, "As you know, Church's

Figure 12.3. Storefront signage for a Little Tavern in Old Town, Baltimore, 1984. Source: Baltimore City Archives.

market entry strategy is to build a base in the 'seat' of the black community then expand into other fringe areas. Thus, they intend to establish a loyal hardcore following of black [*sic*] in this important 'seat' of the black community. The 'Harlemites" influence not only permeates throughout the other black communities in NYC but other areas in the country."[49] Church's was happy to serve its chicken behind bulletproof glass to capitalize on these inner-city communities.[50]

In D.C., the 1980s saw an unprecedented boom in ghetto fast food. When Chicken George opened on Minnesota Avenue NE, it joined a crowded corridor of almost a dozen other fast food chicken outlets. The District had become a "fried chicken capital," with most of the establishments having opened within the past five to ten years. In the Black strongholds of the Southeast and Northeast, it was "almost impossible to make it down a mile or so of any major commercial street without encountering some kind of chicken outlet."[51]

D.C.'s fried chicken deluge mirrored nationwide trends. Fast food was one of the few things opening in Black urban neighborhoods. A swath of other retail and in-

Figure 12.4. A Bojangles' at Fulton Street and Nostrand Avenue in Brooklyn. It was one of three locations participating in a kids-eat-free deal in April 1986; children also received a free Mr. T sticker. dof_3_01849_0055, New York City tax lot photos. Courtesy Municipal Archives, City of New York.

dustry had quit Black territories, making disproportionate the presence of fast food (and other ghetto merchants like liquor stores and check cashing outlets). Between 1967 and 1987, Philadelphia lost 64 percent of its manufacturing jobs, Chicago lost 60 percent, New York 58 percent, and Detroit 51 percent.[52] When manufacturing plants closed, it meant not only the loss of millions of jobs within those factories but also the upending of small businesses that relied on employees spending their salaries locally. Chicago's North Lawndale lost 75 percent of its businesses between 1960 and 1970 due to manufacturing decline or the loss of insurance subsequent to urban rebellions, abandonment, or being burned out. Mostly what remained were liquor stores and bars.[53]

If not alcohol, it was fast food that settled into withered and marginal retail corridors. Chicago's South and West Sides are a case in point, where few businesses opened and where new restaurants meant fast food. Black neighborhoods like

Figure 12.5. Mama's Fried Chicken, a chain owned by a White family, started in 1977, photographed in the 1980s. An example of the fried chicken deluge, this outlet at the corner of Liberty and Pennsylvania Avenues in Brooklyn in 1970 had been a Burger Prince Drive-In, which closed around 1981. dof_3_03704_0016, New York City tax lot photos. Courtesy Municipal Archives, City of New York.

Austin, West Garfield Park, Englewood, South Shore, Chatham, and others had a paucity of retail and numerous vacancies, which forced residents to travel out of their communities to shop. Existing businesses were often deteriorating, dirty, or unattractive, as were the streets and sidewalks around them.[54] Between 1987 and 1990, Austin's only new retail apart from a Walgreens were a McDonald's and a White Castle; West Garfield Park received a Wendy's but nothing else; Chatham's new retail comprised a Dunkin' Donuts, a check cashing outlet, and a Dock's Fish Restaurant; Roseland was crowded with Wendy's, Wally's Fast Food, Dock's, and White Castle; and South Shore, harboring a "middling mix of stores," heavy on liquor stores, bars, and fast food chains, quashed a proposal for a Burger King by Guice's Inner City Foods franchise group.[55]

Fast food's physical appearance in Black neighborhoods added insult to injury. The architecture embodied the message that these outlets were first and foremost

Figure 12.6. A KFC at 458 Utica Avenue, Brooklyn, in the 1980s. dof_3_04588_0086, New York City tax lot photos, Courtesy Municipal Archives, City of New York.

vehicles for corporate profit, and that the merchandise within was nothing more than a basic source for caloric intake. Clearly they were not gourmet restaurants, but neither were they even humble establishments that could nourish in the many ways local eateries can. They were not designed for children's' play, nor were they extensions of domestic space. KFC embarked on a refurbishing program in 1977, yet it continued to operate shoddy and unattractive outlets through the 1980s. Executives at parent companies Heublein and R. J. Reynolds realized that KFC could not be managed like all their other brands. If a customer encountered a dirty store when buying a pack of Camels, they'd simply shop at another store, leaving the brand itself untarnished. But a patron who was met with a dirty KFC would switch to Popeyes.[56] Still, the chain was content to build dismal ghetto outlets and leave them in a state of disrepair. Figures 12.6–12.8 depict KFCs in central Brooklyn during the 1980s. The buildings lack coherence in design, varying from a rectangular bunker to an outdated style using a rooftop cupola; and all present a mishmash of

Figure 12.7. A KFC at the corner of Bedford and Lafayette Avenues, Brooklyn, in the 1980s. dof_3_01950_0031, New York City tax lot photos. Courtesy Municipal Archives, City of New York.

signage. Most were deficient in windows, taking a hostile stance to the communities they served, denying customers and passersby the ability to look in or out. The impenetrable facades are siege-ready, anticipating and defending against an inevitable Black criminality.[57] Two of the restaurants are topped with razor wire, intensifying that defense with threatened fatality or grievous injury. All the restaurants are planted in cold and impervious surfaces devoid of plants, floral landscaping, or other architectural elements that warmly welcome patrons. The surroundings—vacant lots, industrial uses, abandoned cars—further deaden the dining atmosphere. While Mahalia Jackson's saw the bunker aesthetic as an affront, the major chains were unconcerned.

Fast food's ghetto aesthetic was a world apart from the safe, fun-loving environs of White, suburban outlets where teenagers—whether fictional in the case of Conrad Jarrett or real—engaged in developmental milestones. They were also far removed from the tone of fast food advertising, which was replete with whimsy, ex-

Figure 12.8. A KFC at the corner of Atlantic Avenue and Ralph Avenue, Brooklyn, in the 1980s. dof_3_01339_0049, New York City tax lot photos. Courtesy Municipal Archives, City of New York.

citement, and conviviality; television commercials were more likely to depict people breaking into exuberant dances and unrestrained laughter than to actually eat the food being promoted. But ghetto fast food was a sullen affair, the buildings a cipher for the industry's disrespect for the community.

To be sure, advertised images are hardly a faithful representation of the true dining experience anywhere. But in Black communities, the disparity was marked. Far from the homey familiarity advertised on television, Black outlets were spartan and unkempt. In contrast to the consumable mirth and merriment fast food offered White families, Black consumers received something in their neighborhoods closer to an analgesic. Fast food outlets and liquor stores, which dominated postindustrial retail strips in Black neighborhoods, both seemed to offer respite from the trouble that might be on Black minds. They were also similar in aesthetics, and today they remain clustered in close proximity in Chicago's Black communities.[58] The two products also shared similar messaging and the same outdoor media. Fast food, like the vice products of tobacco and alcohol, took note of the difficult conditions in Black urban neighborhoods and cynically exploited them. Fast food's deepening entrenchment was evident not only in its sheer numbers of outlets, but also in its racially pinpointed advertising strategies.

The 1980s saw a strong ramping up of selling tobacco and alcohol to Black communities, especially those for whom the products could serve as an escape from the misery of dire living conditions.[59] Real consumer segmentation, previously underutilized for Black consumers, now emerged in a clear way during the 1980s, with vice targeting low-income consumers (though not to the exclusion of affluent Black people) and the travel, financial services, automobile and other industries enticing the middle class in magazines like *Dollars & Sense* and *Black Enterprise*. The terms "buppie" and "underclass" that circulated in public discourse revealed the chasm between the African American haves and have-nots. Retailers pursued this stratification, making it "the best of times and worst of times" for Black consumers.[60] The worst of times was a context of sufferation in which Black communities were hobbled by the hostile policies of the Reagan administration and the incursion of crack cocaine.[61] These injuries weakened Black communities' resistance and created a damaged landscape in which fast food arose ever more frequently not as domestic beacons but as liabilities.

Exploiting Sufferation

It was the worst of times. In 1980, Black unemployment was at 13 percent, compared to the national figure of 8 percent. By 1982, the Black rate had increased to 20 percent, and that was a conservative measure that did not include those who had stopped looking. Among Black men aged eighteen to thirty-four, the rate was a staggering 33 percent. The poverty rate was also grim, with 36 percent of Black households falling below the threshold, three times that of their White counterparts.[62] In communities where more than 40 percent of the population were poor, only one in three residents over the age of sixteen had a job in a typical week. The loss of manufacturing jobs was a key precipitant of unemployment.[63]

Unemployment rates that high had not been seen since the Great Depression; and it was at that moment that President Reagan cut all but 30 percent of the nation's training and labor budget. It was an enormous blow of nearly $4 billion. Indeed, Reagan slashed almost every federal program except for highways. The cuts spurred layoffs from government jobs and induced cities into austerity measures as they were forced to subsist on 6 percent of their budgets coming from federal funding (rather than 22 percent).[64] In the wake of widespread suffering, Reagan's Black corporate supporters looked on with indifference or active support of policies that would harm Black masses because they remained enriched.[65]

Fast food therefore thrived as one of the few occupational opportunities in communities that had sustained massive job losses. Even in the absence of racial targeting, fast food was likely to proliferate in Black neighborhoods because egregious unemployment levels provided a labor pool that did not exist in White space.[66] Jobs had departed to the suburbs, and those seeking work confronted a lack of reliable transit, on the one hand, and hostile White suburbanites and police who were wont to surveil and harass Black people, on the other.[67] Close to home, jobs "flipping burgers" were relatively plentiful. By the early to mid-1990s, the ratio of applicants to fast food jobs in Harlem was fourteen to one; the population submitting for those positions comprised primarily men, an inversion of national gender trends and an indication of the widespread lack of work.[68] For some, the low-wage, high-stress work of fast food was seen as a poor bet compared to the remuneration available through the drug trade. Worse, taking a job like that threatened a worker's self-assessment as desperately lacking in skills.[69] For others, the drug economy was no lure at all; many worked resolutely at fast food restaurants, often on punishing schedules. For this they endured ridicule for holding a low-status job, ameliorated at least in part by guaranteed meals and a safe space from the bullying and the drug use among peers.[70]

It was the worst of times. While Black communities were devastated by increasing poverty and joblessness, cocaine took hold, following directly from the Reagan administration's drug policies. Cocaine imports increased at least 50 percent as the price of a kilo dropped fivefold over the first few years of the 1980s, resulting in abundant, less expensive cocaine on the market. Crack gained a real presence in 1984 before exploding in 1985–86. In East Harlem, few people even knew what crack was in the spring of 1985; by the end of the year, it had created a "cyclone" of sales, usage, and collateral damage.[71] The punishing crack cocaine epidemic and the neighborhood disorder left in its wake fit fast food perfectly. Plentiful, dingy fast food outlets signaled to onlookers that the host community was devalued by public and private actors and offered a consumable reprieve from stress—a vehicle to escape, however tenuously, conditions of privation and stigma. And if crack addicts in particular required cheap, easily digestible food,[72] what could beat fast food?

It was the worst of times. Retailers organized a concerted push of health-damaging vice products to Black people, often the most toxic among them such as malt liquor and menthol cigarettes. Advertising often suggested that individuals could drink or smoke their way to social mobility; while most Black consumers did not have the trappings of wealth like stocks or real estate, "[they] can certainly demonstrate that [they have] good taste by ordering premium liquor."[73] Those messages have persisted into the 2000s in Central Harlem's outdoor advertising.[74] Brown & Williamson recognized that in a depressed economy, it could position Kool as a way to enjoy otherwise elusive freedom, independence, and control. Black men were seen as "looking for a way out of the ghetto, if not economically or physically, out of the ghetto mentally"; smoking could be a way to achieve that escape.[75]

Outdoor advertising was a mainstay for vice products; an upswing in racially targeted neighborhood placements in the late 1970s and into the 1980s caused a renaissance for outdoor media companies, in some cases saving smaller vendors from extinction. R. J. Reynolds was the largest outdoor advertiser in the United States by 1990. Vice primarily used eight-sheet posters, which were understood across the industry to target pedestrian traffic and "ethnic populations" in the "inner city." Yet, these businesses were "somewhat reluctant to talk too loudly about their presence in minority markets."[76] They knew there was profit to be made in targeting Black neighborhoods but did not want to admit they were capitalizing on the cordons of segregation. Outdoor executives argued that liquor advertisers were the first to recognize the potential of Black space. An example was Private Stock, a new malt liquor that in the late 1980s graced Harlem billboards with scantily clad Black women "to attract a fresh generation of young, inner-city street alcoholics."[77] Cigarette companies, especially motivated by the ban on broadcast advertising for tobacco, followed suit. Brown & Williamson's Kool and R. J. Reynolds's brands topped the list.[78]

Fast food came on the heels of Big Tobacco, capturing Black audiences with multiple outdoor formats. For example, Mingo–Jones skewed its ad buys for the KFC "We do chicken right" campaign to New York subway lines that would target African American riders.[79] Tobacco research determined that self-indulgence was a critical itch that tobacco could scratch because "there are few large scale luxuries or ways to pamper oneself in the inner city."[80] R. J. Reynolds also believed that Black youth lived in "an extremely negative and boring environment where no one / nothing stands out." If fast food relied on the same kinds of negative assessments that Big Tobacco made, it might deploy the same marketing strategies. In fact, fast food did not take as aggressively cynical an approach as tobacco and alcohol, even if some ads today are seen as racist or facile, as with "Dinnertimin' at McDonald's."[81] But fast food was connected to tobacco and its messaging in the form of intertwined promotions. For example, Newport created a tie-in between its cigarettes and breakfast at Burger King.[82]

Marketing that sought to maximize synergy across brands was especially important for KFC, a subsidiary of a tobacco company. Connections between chicken

Figure 12.9. Outdoor advertising hawking KFC and Tanqueray gin, on the corner of West North Avenue and St. Paul Street, Baltimore, photographed between 1975 and 1988. Source: Baltimore City Archives.

and cigarettes were forged in a number of promotional contexts. R. J. Reynolds proposed promotional strategies for a major national convention of the Black press including gift baskets containing cigarettes for registrants and a picnic dinner at a music festival catered by KFC.[83] R. J. Reynolds also planned in 1984 to increase sales volumes of Salem menthol cigarettes by distributing flyers (the "Salem Spirit Street Sheet") at "high traffic locations in the Black community (i.e., fast food restaurants, night clubs, check cashing services, etc.)."[84] Brown & Williamson achieved a triptych of Black consumer targeting in melding fried chicken, jazz, and menthol cigarettes. A June 1982 advertisement invited viewers to "Enjoy 'finger lickin good': Chicken & Kool Jazz," displaying a KFC bucket, emblazoned with the Kool Jazz logo and the Colonel's face, filled with musical instruments.[85] Brown & Williamson had sponsored Kool music festivals all over the country for years. The two-night affair at Cincinnati's Riverfront Stadium in 1987 was sure to draw a big crowd with headliners including New Edition, Cherelle and Alexander O'Neal, Zapp, Luther Vandross, Natalie Cole, Maze featuring Frankie Beverly, Midnight Star, Klymaxx, and the S.O.S. Band.[86]

It is unclear whether companies specifically targeted Black neighborhoods with another fast food–tobacco initiative, that of including cigarette vending machines in restaurants. It is possible they would have done so, given the other synergistic marketing tactics in use at the time. Some chains (e.g., Burger King) included cigarette vending machines for customer convenience; McDonald's wanted nothing to do with them; and KFC lacked a company-wide policy, leaving those decisions to area managers.[87] R. J. Reynolds considered installing the machines in its company-owned KFC outlets with the obvious goal of stocking them primarily with its own brands. The potential for more than $100,000 per year in cigarette revenue was attractive, but beyond logistical disadvantages (e.g., machine malfunction, vandalism, and theft) the biggest concern was a tarnished image. "We do chicken right," a family theme, was simply not compatible with cigarette vending. Moreover, Colonel Sanders was strongly opposed to having his name associated with alcohol or tobacco, and a written agreement had been signed in 1975 to forbid it. Corporate instructed operators who had independently installed cigarette vending machines to remove them.[88]

Even if the literal mixing of chicken and cigarettes was relatively rare in the grand scheme of fast food marketing in the 1980s, the attraction to Black communities—spaces that retained a reputation as reservoirs of vice—was marked. And fast food took advantage of the vulnerable state of Black communities, garnering high sales volumes in the midst of much destabilization. Fast food served as a source of (precarious) employment for communities in need and occupied land made available by structural racism. It also offered its products as an inchoate solution to socioeconomic, social, and psychological crises. Even if the outlets themselves were dour and decrepit, fast food invited Black people to use it as a way to reassert participation in American social life. Just as Ella Baker had asserted in the 1960s, fast food was still bigger than a burger. All foods embody social identities and serve as markers of cultural distinction, and fast food is no exception.[89] While gourmet food may have captivated Americans during the 1980s, something as simple as fast food consumption could amplify perceived social status, something particularly important for marginalized groups.[90]

But Black folks are not afforded the right to participate without restriction or critique in whatever American society might offer. Certainly they could not work in fast food jobs and count on respect. No longer a workplace for young, upstanding, White men, fast food labor had solidified as a contemptuous occupation held by Black and Brown people perceived as unable to compete in American society. And as the 1980s came to a close, the fast food blitz had produced a surfeit of restaurants that dominated dining options in Black neighborhoods. That did not mean residents could patronize them without opprobrium. Slotting into endemic racial tropes about Black deviance, fast food customers were stigmatized as grotesque. As the symbolic meanings of fast food shifted over its long history from all-American treat to fattening pollutant, Black people who consumed its meals became the face of moral turpitude.

13

Criminal Chicken

Perceptions of Deviant Black Consumption

Television in the 1990s exploded with programs targeted to Black audiences. Appearing on new networks—Fox, UPN, and the WB—most of these shows define what media scholar Robin Means Coleman calls a period of "Neo-Minstrelsy." They were an unremittingly denigrating catalog of Black people and culture, trafficking in base stereotypes: in the case of men, simple, brutish coons; and in the case of women, sassy, bellicose, emasculating loudmouths. Means Coleman pointedly asserts that these shows presented Black culture "in a hyper-racialized manner through gross lampooning. Black characters break out in frenzied dancing more often and with greater intensity. The blackvoice has remained, laden with gross malapropisms. . . . Dialogue is often accentuated by ample finger snaps, eye rolling, neck swaying and tongue clucking. . . . Characters literally scoot face down across floors, fight with objects such as food, mops, wigs, clothes and nail buffers (and often lose)."[1]

Characteristic of the era were *Martin, In Living Color, Malcolm and Eddie, Sparks, Homeboys in Outer Space, The Wayans Brothers, The Jamie Foxx Show,* and *Goode Behavior.* In the last show in that list, Sherman Hemsley played a father recently paroled and living with his adult son; he often brought "stolen goods into the home, and is ever eager to burst into a foolish dance, literally shuffling his way out of tight spots."[2]

In an episode of *The Fresh Prince of Bel-Air,* preppy, affluent Carlton dares to go to the 'hood, where he encounters an environment rife with standard tropes of Black deviance ranging from a marked criminal element to "a conspicuously placed large bucket of fried chicken."[3] The chicken could have stood alone as a prop in a set design meant to connote a troubled Black neighborhood because, by the 1990s, fast food had lost its Whiteness and, importantly, had moved to a downscale socioeconomic position. If the 1998 Spike Lee film *School Daze* is any indication, fast food was at the very least liminally situated between clashing social classes. Dap (played by Laurence Fishburne) and his revolutionary friends, militant students at fictional Mission College, meet their comeuppance at a Kentucky Fried Chicken. Da Fella Booker T (Eric Payne) offers a bit of product placement to viewers by prominently handling a table card for Chicken Littles; and as the young men eat, they are subjected to heckles from a nearby table. Older locals, led by a tough with a Jheri curl (Samuel L. Jackson), resent the college students for their perceived arrogance and elite status. The Mission men are forced to leave their meals behind, suggesting that perhaps fast food was not for upwardly striving Black men after all, but rather for the "country 'bama ass" whose insecurities provoked a fight.

By the 1990s, fast food was entrenched in Blackness not only in space, but also in symbol. That fast food was becoming Black in the 1980s was evident in the emergence in White space of national chains like Johnny Rockets (which opened in malls, amusement parks, boardwalks, small towns, and suburbs) and local establishments like Chicago-based Ed Debevic's. These brands attempted to restart the genre, taking up retro 1950s aesthetics in order to cloak themselves in the lost Whiteness of second-generation fast food's early days. While this restart insisted on its Whiteness and nostalgia for all-White past, "regular" fast food became one of many popular conceptions of Black deviance. It was acutely on display in Neo-Minstrelsy shows and widespread elsewhere in popular culture (e.g., talk programs like *The Ricki Lake Show*, *The Jerry Springer Show*, and *The Maury Povich Show*) and in politics. Again, Means Coleman: "The message of the early 1990s about Black America was clear, African Americans in their 'Black world' was sufficiently deficient—culturally, familially, economically, socially, and criminally."[4] That message makes moving through the world while also Black a dare.

Sociologist Elijah Anderson argues that people who occupy White space "typically look on with disgust, pity, judgment, and fear" at Black persons.[5] White observers perceive nearly all Black people as emerging from the crime-ridden and degenerate ghetto, and see their presence in White space as an unwarrantable intrusion. Anderson argues that when within the White space, Black people are forced to be "'on,' performing before a highly judgmental but socially distant audience."[6] Critically, that judgment extends also to Black space, where behaviors thought to reflect Black depravity—among which consumption looms large—are also distantly observed and graded. Black people in Black space are not free from the White gaze. In the case of fast food, that gaze was penetrating and highly critical. What the fast food industry deemed a success—ever increasing consumption by Black urban residents—the rest of America deemed criminal. Once fast food was abundant in Black neighborhoods, Black people were rebuked for actually eating it, especially because by now the product was tarnished. Diners who patronized fast food outlets were wholly lowbrow. To the *New York Times,* New York's storied Gage & Tollner stood alone as an outpost of civility among a tawdry landscape of retail despair in Downtown Brooklyn. In the fall of 1993, the newspaper noted that the historic restaurant still epitomized dignified dining despite floating in "a field of fast-food restaurants, with stores and offices seemingly just filling the spaces between hamburger stands, pizza places and fried chicken joints."[7]

Vilified as the foodstuffs of the poor, ignorant, and gluttonous, fast food, now racialized as Black, fell neatly into broader narratives of characterological deficits purportedly rife in Black communities. Like the welfare recipients that President Clinton sought to banish from the rolls, Black fast food consumers in the 1990s were cast as morally unfit, lacking discipline and self-control. For anthropologist Ashanté Reese, the emphasis on lack that undergirds terms like "food desert" becomes inscribed in Black bodies. Lack leads policymakers and other actors who seek to improve food environments to presuppose a lack of knowledge, lack of will, and lack of efficaciousness among Black residents, and to make this lack the focus of their efforts.[8] For fast food, too, the concept of lack is relevant because the dietary behavior of Black urbanites was read definitively as a moral lack that (deservedly) hobbled Black lives far beyond the impact of structural racism. And yet a process opposite in valence to lack was more salient. As will be seen, the dominance of fast food outlets in Black neighborhoods became inscribed in Black bodies as an assumption of excess—indeed criminally excessive—appetite, body size, and behavior.

Discourse about the excess of Black consumption was widespread, especially in terms of what Elizabeth Chin calls "combat consumerism," the notion that Black people go to desperate, criminal, and violent ends to satisfy consumer needs. News reports in the 1990s of people being beaten or killed over a pair of Air Jordan sneakers or other high-status apparel were readily reported, and the narrative of combat consumerism was that "the nature of materialism among the urban poor, is quite simply sick": the (Black) poor engage in irrational and unbridled consumption to a degree that makes them a danger to themselves and others.[9]

Eating Themselves to Death

It was nothing new for the media to disparage imagined dietary practices of marginalized people.[10] But Black poor people always came in for special critique: for what they ate, how they looked, and for being sick. In 1990, the *Wall Street Journal* published a series of articles about the food environment using the euphemism "inner cities." In the first article, without naming "Black" or "African American" people and instead focusing on the "ghetto" and "low income" residents, the newspaper portrayed Black urbanites in New York and Chicago as disgusting, anachronistic, and, owing to their defiance of dietary norms, deserving of the suffering brought by chronic illnesses.

At Harlem Hospital, Dr. Harold P. Freeman, former president of the American Cancer Society, visited during rounds a fifty-nine-year-old female patient whose legs the reporter described as "so grotesquely swollen they may have to be amputated." The patient, Ms. Williams, had learned to reject pigs' feet and chitterlings on Sundays but, despite her high blood pressure, continued to fry her food and use table salt. Another woman of the same age, diagnosed with colon cancer, confessed her daily consumption of soul food, the meals she grew up on. Dr. Freeman sighed at the repetition of the same story across the hospital.[11]

When in the 1970s Americans shuddered at the hunger experienced by the poor, legislators created the food stamp program, which quickly enrolled millions, along with school breakfast and lunch programs. But in the 1980s Reagan repeatedly portrayed welfare recipients living in luxury off White taxpayer dollars, so he cut food stamps during a recession. The *Wall Street Journal* mirrored contempt for the poor, disputing the idea that Harlemites were consigned to a Dickensian poverty felt as hunger; instead, they ate too much and the wrong things: "A great many residents are seriously overweight, their hunger sated by a damaging smorgasbord of high-sugar, high-salt, high-fat food. . . . The problem raises troubling issues relating to class, race and culture. Many of the badly nourished are victims of their own cultural traditions and notions."[12]

What exactly were the troubling issues? What cultural traditions hamstrung Black folks and consigned them to pitiable lives? The *Wall Street Journal* answered that question in multiple ways, indicting junk/processed food, fast food, and soul food. The last, with African American cultural roots, suggested that there was something intrinsically deviant about Black self-regulation, which explained why Black folks also ate too much fast food. Dr. Freeman asserted, "Poor blacks have one of the worst diets in America, but this isn't a popular thing for black officials to talk about."[13] Soul food was always already defective, lacking in nutrients and an indicator of Black people's lack of good sense. Labeling a food as traditional normally indicates approval, but soul food—a fraught cuisine for White critics of Black behavior, and within Black communities as well—had long been (and continues to be) a conflicted source of comfort and harm.[14] Soul food as the construct we know today emerged in the 1960s as the dietary axis of Black Power politics. Arising in the endpoints of the Great Migrations—the North and West—soul food characterized Black foodways that had once been shamed by respectable eaters, circulating

Figure 13.1. Ellyn's Soul Food Restaurant at Livernois Avenue and Ellsworth Street in Detroit, 2013. The establishment's architecture and gooseneck lamps reveal it as a prior White Tower location. Ellyn's was abandoned a few months after the photograph was taken. Photograph by Camilo J. Vergara, additional information from Vergara's *Detroit Is No Dry Bones* (Ann Arbor: University of Michigan Press, 2016).

not only as a food preference, but as an expression of allegiance to Black social and cultural commitments.[15] Restaurants like Tillie's in Harlem had been serving dishes that became exemplars of the cuisine since the 1930s, but no one called them soul food until the 1960s.[16] That appellation has carried much ambivalence to the present day.

Filmmaker Byron Hurt's *Soul Food Junkies* asked the question the *Wall Street Journal* answered—whether soul food was essentially killing African Americans. Hurt lauded his sister's switch to a plant-based diet and recounted that his mother was learning healthier ways to prepare soul food. As evidence, the viewer sees her pour a can of chicken broth into a pot of black-eyed peas, foregoing a chunk of meat as seasoning. The scene echoed social reformers bringing the untutored into modernity with canned food and other cooking practices, but left unstated that the canned broth is essentially salt water. Professor and political commentator Marc

Lamont Hill, looking back to a childhood that included Kool-Aid and plenty of hot sauce, now recognized that "I have to make a choice and say okay today I have to make a different choice because yesterday I made a bad choice. And I try to regulate myself but it's a work in progress. It's like somebody who's trying to get off crack or heroin or something, I'm trying to wean myself off fried chicken, man."

Hill is obviously speaking tongue-in-cheek here, but his take resonates with the abiding message of the film—that individuals consume at their own risk and based on their own choices. That logic underlay Hurt's framing of African American morbidity from diabetes, cancer, high blood pressure, and other chronic illness as "soul sickness," without mention of socioeconomic position, environmental toxins, racism, or health care. Similarly, the viewer learns that Mississippi was the state with the highest rate of obesity, but not that it also had the highest rate of poverty.[17] In the film, poet Sonia Sanchez bemoaned supermarket vegetables that looked like "they were having a nervous breakdown." But an interrogation of these, and other aspects of Black food environments, not least of which was the high density of fast food outlets, was missing.

Structural factors also went unexamined in the *Wall Street Journal*'s report, which relegated Harlem Hospital patients to a purgatory of indolence. Social conditions that exerted constraints on what people ate were ignored, and consumption was chalked up to long-standing problematic cultural traditions. Thirty-seven-year-old Ricky Louallen ate fast food for all his meals because he did not have his own place and so split his time among friends and family across New York City. In the wake of the catastrophic housing loss from planned shrinkage policies, the economic devastation of the 1980s, and other constraints, it was hardly surprising that Black New Yorkers frequently ate outside the home. Inevitably, that meant fast food. In addition to national chains, a swath of "X-Fried Chicken" restaurants— where X comprised Cincinnati, Famous, Southern, Mama's, Kansas, and others— inundated Harlem, but the fact that residents actually ate at these neighborhood outlets was interpreted as a behavioral failing.[18] Even the Reverend Jesse Jackson, whose activism brought large numbers of new outlets to Black communities, said, "Low-income Americans, with a certain desperation that there might not be any more food tomorrow, are eating themselves to death." The senior vice president at PUSH, the Reverend George Riddick, claimed the organization would be paying increased attention to nutrition. But surely it was too late to consider the nutritional profile after agitating for as many restaurants as possible.[19] Without attention to context, the *Wall Street Journal* led its readers to ask of Black urbanites the age-old question: how does it feel to be a problem?[20]

White people eating gourmet meals equally energy-dense as fast food were not subject to the same kind of critique. "New American" cuisine arrived in the 1980s, defined as a reinterpretation of French nouvelle cuisine with fresh local produce, new flavor combinations, and plentiful butter and cream. At the same time that the *Wall Street Journal* pilloried the calorie and fat-filled dietary choices of Black people in Harlem, *New York Times* restaurant reviews glowed about dishes including grilled sirloin garnished with herb butter and served with French fries; chilled sweetbreads (lamb thymus/pancreas) in a mayonnaise dressing; brandy- and butter-flavored foie gras encircled by gelatin; and a potato nest filled with caviar-topped scrambled eggs.[21] These dishes were laden with sodium, fat, and animal protein, but their refined provenance distinguished them from those deserving of opprobrium. Steak frites was cosmopolitan; burgers and fries, the poor man's version, was unacceptable.

Acclaimed White male chefs also appropriated the foods and cooking styles that, when practiced by those from whom the dishes originated, connoted poor dietary choices and slavish adherence to tradition. "New World Cuisine," which was just Latin American and Afro Caribbean cuisine "discovered" and repackaged by influential White men, took South Florida by storm in the 1990s. Norman Van Aken, one of the "Mango Gang," who took for himself the mantle of father of New World Cuisine, ate at modest Cuban restaurants and wondered, "Why are there bananas on my dinner plate?" (they were plantains).[22] Bereft of the civilizing influence of Whiteness that men like Van Aken could impart, poor Black individuals and families could only remain grotesque. They occupied both ends of nutritional disorder: obesity and malnutrition. And, the *Wall Street Journal* emphasized, they were unapologetic. A twenty-one-year-old in Harlem had been diagnosed in early adolescence with beriberi, a disease defined by a lack of thiamine, a vitamin present in vegetables. She lived in one of the most cosmopolitan global capitals, and yet she developed a "debilitating Third World disease" and continued to eschew vegetables: "We don't pay any attention. We're going to eat what we're going to eat."[23]

These individuals lived in a puzzling, disgusting state of horror unknown to rational persons, as in the kinds of narratives that dog representations of African persons and countries. Okwui Enwezor has argued that photographic images of Africa construe "an atlas of disorder," rendering African bodies "defamiliarized if not altogether monstrous."[24] His analysis is worth quoting at length: "Every photograph of Africa . . . repeats the same appropriation of singular scenes as stand-ins for a larger collective scene, turning the practice of photography into a mythology factory. Every image exists under the aegis of a particular typology: there is the grotesque, the despot; the fetid shantytown that is the very picture of disorganized geometry; the dank, frightful hospital scene crowded with patients dying from diseases not yet known to science; the wild undisturbed beauty of primeval forests full of animals. All of which signify and represent one and the same thing: Africa."[25] In fast food discourse, the same tropes imbue the one-note characterization of Black people in the United States: the neighborhoods a place of squalor, the inhabitants the embodiment of dangerous and morally bankrupt excess. Even worse, drug dealers who both garnered high wages in their trade and avidly consumed fast food merged illicit work with illegitimate dietary choices.[26] Fast food was not simply one of the choices some consumers made; rather, it inhered in those of questionable behavior and judgment. Drug dealers used tainted money to buy tainted food, and the assumption was that all their neighbors failed to exercise appropriate responsibility for their health or that of their community. In those bodies, multiple forms of deviance—whether drug-selling, violence, or gluttony—were ferociously enmeshed.

The second article in the *Wall Street Journal*'s series now reported that fast food had pervaded the inner city in the 1980s, but the underlying critique remained the same: Black people were at fault for eating so often at the establishments in their communities. The real problem was that inner city residents could not control their frequency of visits. An occasional trip would cause no harm, but African Americans failed to exercise appropriate restraint. The article reinforced a portrait of deviance by calling fast food outlets a "surrogate for home and hearth." In this reporting, even fast food operators saw Black clientele as bizarre and debased consumers from whom they bemusedly collected their money. Georgi Olivero, manager of a Harlem KFC, marveled at the outlet having won the status of a "million dollar store," despite the fact that it was "dealing with poor people—it's great!" A Burger King manager claimed, without evidence, that Black customers were two and a half times as likely as Whites to buy a Double Whopper with Cheese; a corporate spokesperson rejected that assertion, stating that no such data were available to confirm it.[27] The manager could say such things because Black proclivity to excess seemed common sense.

For White observers, fast food consumers and Black people in general embodied a lack of resolve for resisting the products that surrounded them. Geographer Julie Guthman writes that her students' discussions of obesity centered responsibility to make appropriate choices and were laced with revulsion for those who did not: "I think the people who eat the fast food are to blame. It is *their* choice to pull up to the drive-through. . . . It basically comes down to will power."[28] Guthman argues that in the neoliberal frame of "healthism," health responsibility falls solely to individuals, who are expected to avoid contributing to health care costs and to forego pleasure; healthism equates goodness with denial.[29] This is a particularly dangerous equation in a society that would deny Black people joy by fiat. Black women also compute badly under this equation, mothers even more so. Sociologist Sabrina Strings shows that Black women have repeatedly been constructed as a singular burden on public resources, as "social dead weight." She argues that Black women are seen as "endangering not only their own health with their high-risk practices but the health of their families and the public health. They are figured as a heavy burden on self, family, and society."[30] The *Wall Street Journal*'s report evinces the discourse that Strings finds dominant in race science from the early nineteenth century, wherein Black people were not just different from White counterparts but "deemed culturally inclined to an uninhibited indulgence in their animal appetites."[31]

Under healthism, those presumed animal appetites meant that ignorant and recalcitrant Black consumers had only themselves to blame for any negative outcomes. Tom Burrell disavowed responsibility for his role as an ad man promoting McDonald's: "People have free will to order what they want to eat. It isn't up to me or anyone else to determine what people do with their money." Caroline Jones, who by this time had left Mingo–Jones to start her own agency, argued, "The tobacco and liquor companies are going to continue advertising their products so we may as well extract as much as we can and put that to good use. The alternative is to be angry—and broke." For Jones, the bottom line was clear: "It's all big business and it's all tainted money."[32] The stance these advertising executives took saw markets as something that merely existed, rather than something made (in part by advertising). And whether it was fast food or vice, Black ad agencies fought for access to retailer ad spending, often in a conflicted context where it meant selling products and messages that were harmful to Black communities.

Second Chance

Fast food at the close of the 1980s was finally considered saturated and mature, stabilized rather than growing. Heading into the 1990s, that meant chains would need to poach market share from one another in order to increase sales. Again, Black consumers were central to the strategy to capture and strengthen selling niches, and corporate headquarters began formalizing their racial targeting. For example, Burger King created a position for director of ethnic marketing.[33] Corporate America was continually rediscovering the necessity of marketing to Black consumers. It would realize that Black people bought things and made up a lucrative consumer segment, then would forget and find itself at a loss as to how to speak to Black people. Interest in Black consumers came and went; whenever it was on an upswing, advertisers turned to Black agencies.[34] And Black agencies wanted the money, tainted or not. They were already at a disadvantage because a firm's largest source of compensation was typically commissions from media buys, and those commissions depended on firm size. Small shops received as much as 25 percent less than their larger peers; with Black firms being smaller, they would accrue less revenue. Moreover, commissions were only paid after ads were "conceived, produced, approved, run and collected for."[35] If Black firms had difficulty obtaining buy-in from their clients, this would be a further obstacle to financial solvency. Black shops encountered significant constraints within an already pigeonholed position. Advertisers, leery about race, did not encourage the innovation and boundary-pushing they sought from White firms. Instead, they tended toward anodyne campaigns that bored even the agencies making them. Keith Lockhart of Lockhart & Pettus also felt constrained by the preferences of Black consumers. His firm took over KFC's Black Consumer Market from the Mingo Group (after Caroline Jones's departure) and won the same market for Wendy's. He asserted that Black firms could not take risks with portraying Black people in a negative light; roles that called for slapstick comedy from actors, for example, risked devolving into Neo-Minstrelsy. What's more, a cultural zeitgeist around Afrocentricity often meant showcasing role models, family, success stories, and social mobility—themes that tended toward the banal in creative execution.[36]

Further complicating the development of creative for fast food's Black Consumer Market in the 1990s were contestations around racism in food and beverage retailing. Some companies came under fire for racist remarks by corporate heads (e.g., CEO William K. Coors stating that Black people were intellectually inferior and benefited from slavery) and systemic racism in restaurant service (e.g., Denny's). Controversies about the volume and racial targeting of ads for liquor and tobacco also roiled Black communities. Focus groups in New York, Atlanta, Chicago, and San Francisco found Black residents angered by excessive marketing for tobacco or junk food paired with sexualized imagery. Participants averred: "Every Black neighborhood is full of signs for liquor and cigarettes. Partly our fault. Whites protest those signs and we don't"; "Liquor and greasy foods and cigarettes is all you see"; "The billboards are mostly beer and cigarettes. I think we're being exploited"; "A lot of alcohol too. We get all the ads for anything that sounds like they might kill you."[37]

Black ad agencies also expressed their reliance on, and willingness to accept, accounts from deadly products.[38] Keith Lockhart argued, "There's no reason not to accept these dollars. . . . If they kill off cigarette and alcohol advertising, black papers may as well stop printing."[39] Caroline Jones held that the 1990s were a dangerous time for Black ad agencies because advertisers might decide that if Black people didn't want to be targeted, they ought to stop advertising altogether.[40] Fast food did not carry the same threat as tobacco and didn't face the same severity of critique as alcohol and cigarettes, but at least some Black urban residents took umbrage at the greasy food staining the outdoor ad panels in their communities. And debacles around targeted cigarette marketing kicked off the 1990s with an important lesson—whatever racially targeted campaigns advertisers developed could not be brazenly stated as such, and could not appear to actively induce self-deleterious behaviors. Fast food shared a negatively trending reputation with tobacco that behooved its paying attention to advertising trends. As fewer and fewer Americans smoked, R. J. Reynolds worried that the public had come to see the practice as a "messy, indulgent, down-scale, non-family oriented, non-fashionable habit" that was "alien to contemporary lifestyles."[41] Fast food had the same problem. It was twenty years past fashionableness and White, middle-class, domestic sensibilities. It was now a downscale product; for the industry to survive, it needed to continue attracting the very customers that spoiled its reputation.

The industry continued to display ambivalence and confusion about how central Black people should be as a market segment, and analysts became entangled in a dance of approach and avoidance. John C. Melaniphy was a marketing expert who had started at a restaurant site selection firm before a stint as a vice president responsible for real estate and construction at Kentucky Fried Chicken. There he oversaw site selection, market strategy, and construction of hundreds of units. He left KFC when it was acquired by Heublein and went on to his own firm. In 1992, he published a book on restaurant site selection in which he vacillated between lauding and devaluing Black space for fast food. On the one hand, Melaniphy saw "ethnic characteristics" as a potential barrier to attracting customers and noted Skokie, Illinois, with a 1.7 percent Black population, as an ideal site for fast food. He implied in tortured language that fast food restaurateurs ought to avoid poor people and people of color: "Consider factors such as physical and psychological barriers, road patterns, and ethnic characteristics. Do they affect the areas of income concentration within your city? Almost certainly they do. Furthermore, if you begin to record these various characteristics, the structure becomes quite obvious. More importantly, you should now understand why those patterns exist."[42] On the other hand, he fostered stereotypes of Black people as the truest market for fast food: "Chicken and fish quick service food operations usually capture higher sales in black neighborhoods."[43]

Covertly, fast food was willing to exploit the privation that gripped many of its Black customers. Check cashing outlets exploded following the deregulation of the banking industry that began in 1980, which led banks to abandon Black neighborhoods. In New York, Bedford-Stuyvesant, Crown Heights, and Prospect Heights lost

30 percent of their banks between 1978 and 1990, and Central Brooklyn was left with one bank per twenty-three thousand residents, nearly quintuple the national average. The void in banking services was filled by check cashing, lucrative businesses that increased 538 percent over the same period. Cashland Check Cashing Centers, typically outfitted with "bulletproof windows and a security system," charged customers fees of 1.75 to 1.95 percent per transaction, making money for the operators; and the operators paid 9 percent royalties on gross revenue, making money for the franchisor. The individuals who had to rely on check cashing, payday lenders, and other banking alternatives wasted at least 10 percent of their income accessing these services.[44]

KFC thought check cashing outlets to be fruitful grounds for targeting economically precarious Black folks. Most Distribution Services ran an advertising program at 1,500 check cashing outlets across the country with monthly traffic of approximately seven million that provided everything from in-store displays and product samples to "coupons and flyers handed directly to consumers cashing checks on payday." It was able to reach urban communities via "targeting on an ethnic and language specific basis."[45] Newport cigarettes had made use of the program to give customers a special envelope into which they placed cigarette pack bottoms in order to win a prize. KFC initiated a scheme to "increase volume in inner city KFC stores" by giving out coupons at check cashing stores in close proximity to its chicken outlets. The idea was that heavy pedestrian traffic at check cashing locations allowed the chain to capture a ready audience of people with "cash in their hands."[46] Over a two-month period, the program was deemed a success.

Overtly, fast food could not in broad daylight be seen targeting the most precarious Black populations, nor making overtures that deployed obviously racially segregated messaging (as with reviled cigarette brand Uptown).[47] If fried chicken and burgers were now racialized as Black, corporate boardrooms would need to seek out customers either quietly and without fanfare, or else shrouded in a halo of respectability and an embrace of Black culture. Black-targeted advertising in the 1990s often made by Black agencies, positioned fast food as an authentic part of the African American experience, and indeed one that made Black lives better.

Getting racialized targeting right was important for KFC because it wasn't anyone's favorite fast food chain. When asked, only 2 percent of consumers offered the chicken chain as tops, compared to 23 percent for McDonald's and 13 percent for Wendy's. Among Black customers, some estimates showed that KFC indexed at about the national average while competitors like Popeyes and Church's ran as much as two and a half times as high.[48] KFC worried that it had lost relevance among African Americans, and it was clear that Black targeting would "help the system to achieve its overall long and short term business objectives." To wit, Black people needed to eat more chicken to shore up corporate's bottom line. In New York, Black customers felt they "grew up with Kentucky Fried" and continued to like the food and pricing, but they found service in the area rude and the vibe cold and uncaring, particularly when ensconced in bulletproof glass.[49] Believing that a new product called Honey Barbecue Chicken would be of particular appeal to Black people, the chain invited agencies to compete for the Black Consumer Market account by developing ads, promotions, and merchandising that could redefine KFC to Black audiences and increase consumption over a twelve-month period.[50] Caroline Jones Advertising pitched a campaign that deployed television commercials in markets with high proportions of Black households and on programs with many Black viewers; these would surely have included the Neo-Minstrelsy lineup.[51] The pitch made outdoor advertising a centerpiece: "Key market billboards and subway posters in Black communities with a consistent presence could prove extremely beneficial to our total awareness effort."[52] Just as Mingo–Jones linked "We do chicken right" to particular subway lines, outdoor ads could hone in on Black space for the new chicken product.[53] Jones suggested promotional strategies like KFC's sponsorship of events (e.g., the Black Family Reunion) in order to "generate a lot of goodwill within the community and increase their overall image," and a focus on children via "Storytellers Storytime" where once per month children could pay a "nominal fee" to be served KFC lunches at school and be told stories sponsored by the chain.[54] In the end, Lockhart & Pettus won the account.

Caroline Jones Advertising succeeded in winning the Black Consumer Market communications strategy for the New York City metro McDonald's advertising co-op. Quite in contrast to the portrayal in the *Wall Street Journal,* local data showed that Black people spent less per visit than did the general market consumer. Black children strongly patronized McDonald's, but they were medium consumers at best for fast food overall. Burrell Advertising believed, "There's still plenty of hamburger business to take."[55] Jones's firm was asked to increase order totals and stimulate more repeat visits. Her plan again emphasized outdoor media with eight-sheets and transit ads and targeted community events, particularly churches, schools, and health-related programs.[56] The strategy comprised a yearlong suite of marketing possibilities: in May, McMother's Day; in the summer, sponsorship of a Twilight Summer Basketball League; in the fall, the West Indian Labor Day parade. All were meant to reinforce the company's commitment to Black people and activities that would meet the marketing goals.

In a trite attempt to capitalize on the 1990s turn to Afrocentricity, Jones created a Black History Month promotion featuring Kente Kups. These plastic freebies were printed with a series of patterns that the agency thought would showcase "their relations to the various countries in Africa." Kente is a fabric and design tradition from the Ashanti region of Ghana, specifically Kumasi. But Jones's firm attributed it to "various countries" and gave the vaguest possible lineage, collapsing the continent to a region: "a kind of African fabric." With that in mind, Jones's initial creative design envisioned school tie-ins like audio cassettes that discussed "the African countries and significance of the various types of fabrics"; and the chance to win trips to (irrelevant) countries such as a photo safari in Kenya or a historical tour of Senegal. A sixty-second radio commercial for the promotion, "Surprise/Kente," announced a twenty-two-ounce Kente Kup with every Extra Value Meal: "Three authentic patterns—each one a work of art . . . Get yours and raise your Kup to celebrate Black History Month."[57] Kwanzaa, too, fed into McDonald's Afrocentric posture. The annual Kwanzaa Holiday Expo in New York asked McDonald's to underwrite the cost of producing "The Rappin' Fireman's show," tray liners, and a magazine that would be distributed as a Sunday supplement in six cities.[58] The *New York Carib News,* one of the official newspapers of the Expo, also hoped that McDonald's would sponsor its own supplement. For a cost of $12,000 (about 20,000 in 2020 dollars), the company would receive prominent acknowledgment and advertising space and an "Editorial on McDonald's various involvement in Black culture and commerce, featuring some of your African American store owners . . . very much in keeping with the spirit of the Kwanzaa Holidays." The paper reassured McDonald's that its participation would translate into increased Black market penetration.[59]

Kente Kups offered superficial and inaccurate engagement with African culture, but it was the kind of saccharine overture McDonald's thought it needed to woo Black customers. More sober and cynical messages also emerged in McDonald's 1990s advertising, reverting to fast food's 1960s disciplinary project, though under a friendly veneer. The market research that revealed how negatively African Americans saw alcohol and tobacco advertising also found that "the most popular execution of all is that of a McDonald's TV commercial showing a young boy's coming of age as he moves up the ranks and succeeds."[60] The commercial in question was McDonald's "Second Chance" spot, developed by Burrell and better known by the name of its protagonist as the "Calvin commercials." What set the campaign apart from the Kente Kups and Kwanzaa promotions was that it did more than sell fast food to African Americans under the guise of cultural authenticity. Rather, it sold fast food to the American public as an antidote to Black deviance—which, ironically, the dominant society saw as the impetus for Black folks eating fast food in the first place.

In the spot, young Calvin emerges from a New York brownstone and makes his way down the street with his cap on backwards. He passes what must be a group of gang members, but shrugs them off with a smile. His approach frightens an elderly woman, but she is cowed when he helps her with a grocery cart. Meanwhile, two unseen women onlookers wonder where Calvin has been, narrating that the rumor was he had a new job—a good idea, as he was finally learning the responsibility he needs. In the end, we find that he works at McDonald's, where he turns his hat brim from back to front. When Calvin turns his hat around, he signifies that McDonald's has given him "the fortitude to reject the criminal life of the black street gang. . . . The McDonald's job can produce miracles."[61] A job at McDonald's had turned Calvin around, or at least acted as a much needed prophylactic against the pernicious threat posed by young Black men and the deviance apparently endemic in their urban neighborhoods. Moreover, the job was a miracle for the community; the chain's civilizing influence had given the neighborhood a second chance. Robert Jackson, a consultant on the Calvin ads, asserted that they were designed in part to counter the stigma of a McDonald's job.[62] In doing so, the commercial may have given fast food a second chance among skeptical potential employees who looked down on the industry. Mingo–Jones created a similar commercial for KFC. In "Going to Work," a young man named Eddie is eagerly greeted by mothers and girls on a brownstone New York Street, as he proclaims he does one thing as a KFC employee: he concentrates on "making it great. . . . I do it just for you."[63] Eddie has easy camaraderie with the mothers of the neighborhood, and it's clear that his job has raised him right.

The civilizing power of McDonald's was evident in "Brother Knows Best," a commercial depicting two Black boys perched on their brownstone stoop, their father in the background. The brownstone setting evokes the middle-class comfort of *The Cosby Show*'s Huxtable family. The older brother cautions, "Hey little brother, you gotta get wise to money," while the announcer intones that burgers are only fifty-nine cents. "A penny saved is a penny earned," the elder brother continues, "that's why you have to pinch 'em." Again, the announcer speaks up to support the sage advice, stating "Get good stuff at a great price. 'Cause money doesn't grow on trees." It remains unclear whether the younger brother is internalizing any of this information, as he stares off into space, enjoying his McDonald's. Eventually, the older brother concludes, "When you get to be my age you'll understand." The two boys laugh together, their grownup play and wholesome enjoyment of McDonald's evidence of their assimilation to mainstream society. These are not the typically frightening Black youth of urban America. They are docile, oriented toward thrift and responsibility, and under parental supervision. For good measure, the scene

"GOING TO WORK"

MUSIC.

EDDIE: I do one thing....
MOTHER: Morning, Eddie.

EDDIE: Like no one else can do....
MAN: Hey, my man!

EDDIE: I concentrate on making it
great....
TEEN GIRL: Mom, it's Eddie!
EDDIE: I do it just for you....

2ND MOTHER: See ya at noon.

EDDIE: Just one thing... doin' it right.

EDDIE: I do it fresh. Juicy. "It's finger-
lickin' good." And just for you.
SINGERS: KENTUCKY FRIED
CHICKEN....

EDDIE: And Ed Cooper!

EDDIE AND SINGERS: WE DO
CHICKEN RIGHT!

Figure 13.2. Mingo–Jones created this commercial storyboard in 1985. Source: Caroline P. Jones Papers, Archives Center, National Museum of American History, Smithsonian Institution, Washington, D.C.

closes with a blonde, White woman walking past, reinforcing the safety of this Black space and solidifying the middle-class belonging of both the family and the fast food they consume.

McDonald's seemed to believe its own press in seeing itself as a beacon of civility, community stability, and even of America itself. McDonald's adamantly proclaimed to all that its restaurants were spared in the 1992 Los Angeles uprising because it was an anchor in South LA, owned by and serving Black constituents. It "proudly proclaimed" that it was the chain's centrality to Black communities that had saved it. Some reports suggested minor damage at stores, while others asserted no damage at all.[64] In fact, at least one McDonald's outlet is described as having burned down to the ground. Artist Mark Bradford created his storefront project at Philadelphia's Fabric Workshop after visiting a vacant lot in Los Angeles at Western and 54th Street, where a friend told him that they used to work at a McDonald's that stood on the corner before the uprising.[65] McDonald's fable about its untouchability reflected the corporation's self-perception as a representation of America itself. An anonymous McDonald's executive contended that after planes struck the World Trade Center and Pentagon on September 11, 2001, all McDonald's regional offices were closed and evacuated; the terrorists were attacking America, and McDonald's represented America.[66]

Dollars & Sense's 1983 profile of McDonald's—which read essentially as an extended press release for the company—argued that the corporation was a good neighbor with an unassailable record of commitment: "McDonald's currently does more for the black community than any of the other burger chains and practically all of the other segments of the fast-food industry."[67] Black financial periodicals had never subjected fast food corporations to much critique, and the same message was carried through in television commercials like "Second Chance," telling the Black community (and nervous White observers) how much McDonald's had done for it, reforming constituents who otherwise had little to show for themselves. While McDonald's adopted the mantle of benefactor for the Black community, the rest of the industry had yet to achieve equity in its franchising and continued to spark controversies in communities.

Small Business as Savior—Again

Even if some Black folks were fond of "Second Chance," fast food restaurants remained a LULU—locally unwanted land use. In D.C.'s upscale Black suburb of Lake Arbor in Prince George's County, Applebee's arrived in the mid-1990s. Though the town objected to the proposed signage, the arrival of the restaurant itself was welcome, as the only places nearby to eat were fast food restaurants. Sit-down eateries populated predominantly White areas like Bowie, Greenbelt, and Laurel, while Lake Arbor struggled to cast off an image of being a "low rent" district, despite its being the most prominent and affluent of the newer developments in the county. The community voiced its opposition to fast food and liquor stores, calling for sit down restaurants, bookstores, and upscale boutiques.[68] Sociologist Karyn Lacy's ethnographic research in Prince George's shows that retail was a flashpoint for Black homeowner concerns. A resident of one of the most affluent subdivisions questioned the idea of a true Black upper class because there were no suitable restaurants nearby. Indeed, fast food bracketed both ends of the major collector road: at the more elite end one found Subway, KFC, and a gas station; at the other end, where income was lower, a McDonald's and a dollar store. Fast food did not differentiate among Black communities, even as Black middle-class people engaged in what Lacy describes as "boundary work" to distinguish themselves from their poor Black counterparts. In her sample, fast food existed only as cautionary example, representing the kind of future they warned their children awaited them if they did not apply themselves.[69]

Contestations around fast food arose repeatedly in middle-class, Black communities because fast food's use values and exchange values were misaligned. David Harvey argues that when these two values are at odds with each other, they create a contradiction, or even a crisis.[70] Use values describe the immediate, human-centered benefits that people take from a commodity. For example, a house provides use values such as shelter and a private place to raise families. In contrast, exchange values describe the monetary worth associated with a commodity. For houses, that may mean the speculative value an investor anticipates when constructing it or that a homeowner can realize from selling or refinancing it.[71] For fast food in Black communities, there was a constant tension between the exchange values that corporate entities and franchisees sought (and these were not necessarily concordant) and the use values—often negative—to which communities attended. Where blight, disorder, or depreciation of status were concerns for community residents, operators were obviously focused on the potential for a profitable enterprise. The fact that the restaurant served meals was, as is true for all such exchange value–focused endeavors, ancillary: "The aim of producers is to procure exchange values not use values. The creation of use values for others is a means to that end."[72] In other words, Black franchisees for the most part sold burgers and fried chicken because it was a means by which to accrue profit. Or as Harry Sonneborn saw it, fast food was a real estate enterprise that sold burgers. And yet Black franchisees were in a double bind because their pursuit of exchange values was in most cases poorly realized. At the conclusion of the 1990s, franchising for Black and other restaurateurs of color revealed itself once and for all as a failed experiment.

Some forty years after the emergence of second-generation fast food, Black and other operators of color had yet to claim en masse the riches eternally promised by franchise boosters. Black franchisees were still few and far between, the enterprise still cost more, and they were still earning less.[73] The Los Angeles uprising, like those of the late 1960s, stimulated talk of corporate solutions; perhaps franchising could assuage Black America—again. According to *Restaurant Business,* White America worried about "looting and lawlessness throughout the land"; and with a short memory of fast food's inefficaciousness as a social cure-all decades prior, the industry periodical suggested that fast food held the key to social unrest: "Out of the fear grew new buzz words of the day: Entrepreneurship. Enterprise. Growing small businesses." Ron Johnson, former footballer and a KFC operator, asserted that the country was increasingly bifurcated into haves and have-nots, an incendiary condition that risked America's survival. As a fast food franchisee, Johnson was presumably arguing that his restaurant foray was precisely the means by which to undo entrenched inequality.

Restaurant Business saw the many Black franchisees who managed to enter the industry only to founder as victims of "cultural isolation" that sheltered them from "the rules of the capitalist game, rules promulgated by the dominant White majority against whom these newest players must complete." It was an interesting take to claim that Black people in the United States were anything but intimately familiar with the crush of capitalism. But the periodical had no explanation for why Black people were still a negligible proportion of fast food operators. At Burger King, operators categorized as Black, Hispanic, and Asian added up to only 12 percent all together; at KFC, these groups totaled 7 percent. Yet, Commerce chief Richard Stevens stated that if a "minority American" wanted to start a business, a restaurant was the best way.[74]

By design, franchising simply could not serve as a liberatory economic strategy. To argue otherwise was to misconstrue not only a business model that placed the risk on franchisees and directed most of the reward to corporations, but also the additional barriers Black participants faced in a racist society. A 1993 congressional hearing entered a time machine and once again grappled with the concerns that arose in hearings in the 1960s. Once again Congress acknowledged the barriers that undermined franchising, including lack of capital, lack of franchisor interest in minority markets, redlining, steering, bait and switch tactics, and arbitrary evaluations. Committee chair John J. LaFalce of New York introduced three bills on franchising, each submitted twice, in the 103rd Congress (1993–94); all were referred to subcommittees but went no further.[75] Yet LaFalce remained steadfast in his faith in small business. He opened the hearings with the claim that "franchising is gaining increasing attention as a means to facilitate new small business growth and minority business ownership." But franchising was far from a novel concept and had done little to facilitate business growth for average African Americans.

Anthony W. Robinson, president of the Minority Business Enterprise Legal Defense and Education Fund, testified about his organization's work with plaintiffs in a Burger King class action lawsuit filed in 1988. The suit outlined a litany of by now familiar complaints, including underperforming stores, higher costs, and depressed sales. What had not been widely publicized in the Black franchising experience was the "vicious retaliation" headquarters dealt to those who fought corporate's practices. Litigants were forced into bankruptcy as they amassed legal fees in the hundreds of thousands before cases ever went to trial; at the time of Robinson's testimony, most of the litigants had gone out of business.[76] Rep. Kwesi Mfume of Maryland, head of the Congressional Black Caucus, summed up franchising thusly: "In many respects it is the old master/slave relationship."[77]

At the time of the hearings, Mfume served as representative to the district where Joseph E. Sanchez Jr., who identified as a Hispanic man, formerly held a McDonald's franchise. Echoing Mfume's remarks, Sanchez declared his tenure with the company "designed and calculated indentured servitude."[78] He was embroiled in a lawsuit against McDonald's that was on appeal in the Fourth Circuit Court of Appeals after a previous dismissal in the U.S. District Court in Baltimore. Sanchez's counsel argued that his case brought under scrutiny what they described as a pattern of corporate mendacity and raised "extremely important legal questions" about racial discrimination in franchising.[79] Sanchez's experience echoed those of Black operators that preceded him and those that would follow, and were as much a reflection of discrimination against him as for the customers he served. Sanchez's lawsuit and congressional testimony alleged systematic subordination based on race and ethnicity. Originally from the D.C. metro area, he began his career as an operator in Houston in 1985. Immediately he collided with a bait and switch when corporate announced upon his arrival that a planned site on Gessner Road was "not good for him." McDonald's instead gave him a store on Kuykendahl Road on an interim basis that lasted sixteen months, irreparably damaging Sanchez's finances. Once installed on Gessner, Sanchez won the Outstanding Store award for two years running, but McDonald's repeatedly denied him the possibility of expansion.[80] According to Sanchez, McDonald's charged that expansion was impossible because there were "too many Blacks in your staff."[81] After years of racist abuse, Sanchez fled Houston. He attempted to sell his outlet to his father, who preceded him in McDonald's franchising, but corporate rejected the transaction, reprimanding him by saying "You have to know how to operate in this White man's company."[82]

Sanchez also alleged that he had been charged rent more than twice that of the White operator who took over the Gessner store; and that once he moved east, he was redlined from outlets in predominantly White Baltimore County. Sanchez acquired a store in Park Heights, a Black Baltimore neighborhood, ignorant of the fact that crime was a challenge at what corporate labeled a "major problem restaurant." It was an outlet at 4400 Reisterstown Road, where a series of Black franchisees had been installed and ejected. Mfume had led a boycott against it twelve years prior and was threatened with arrest by McDonald's for his trouble. At the hearings, Mfume described Sanchez's experience as a replication of what had befallen several others; once forced out, McDonald's took over the store. Sanchez claimed that corporate misrepresentations of sales figures had sunk him deeply into debt, and he was told not to complain "because Hispanics in McDonald's had to be subservient to succeed."[83] McDonald's denied Sanchez's allegations and argued that, in any case, his contract stipulated that nothing was promised, including profitability. Ultimately, the Fourth Circuit upheld the summary judgment, ruling that Sanchez's appeal had no merit.

Certain Congresspeople spoke strongly on behalf of McDonald's. Jan Meyers of Kansas warned that the whole franchise system ought not be condemned over a few bad apples, and took exception to the fact that Sanchez was allowed to testify: "We reviewed the testimony by Mr. Sanchez, and it seemed to us that there were some things that he was saying that were undocumented and defamatory, and we asked him to withdraw his testimony." James M. Talent of Missouri said that more "perspective" was needed: "Do you know the employer who has the most successful Black entrepreneurs in the system in the country? It is McDonald's. Do you know who the largest employer of Black employees in the country is? You can probably guess. It is McDonald's." He questioned Sanchez's judgment, stating that he appeared to believe that "Everybody is either afraid to say anything or they have been bought off." Whether this was a Freudian slip is an open question—Talent himself received political donations from McDonald's.[84] Talent entered into the record a statement that read as though it came straight from McDonald's corporate offices. It recounted the company's success with minority communities, vendors, franchisees, and the like. The statement concluded by insinuating that the real problem was Black people who could not simply get over their racial grievances: "The people of our country are growing farther apart. Few people from any of the racial or ethnic communities feel that we are making progress. . . . It is very clear that both sides have to be careful to move strongly against racism where it does exist and to be careful about alleging racism where it does not exist. People and companies who do have a record of credibility should be encouraged rather than attacked."[85]

Talent's statement suggested that challenges to racial discrimination in the fast food arena were not only illegitimate, but also indicative of undue racial slights in the broader society. The same ideas would be turned against Black communities that sought to intervene in local food environments in the 2000s. Fast food's long history ended in the contemporary moment with a consistently disproportionate density in Black space. Activists used new tools to combat unjust retail siting, researchers and communities made clear that food environments and other social determinants were at the root of health inequities, and critics rushed to levy specious arguments against grassroots action, calling community-initiated and supported interventions "paternalism." Once Black neighborhoods were saturated, public authorities and private citizens coalesced around a rallying cry for "personal responsibility" being the only legitimate analytic framework for health. Fast food in the 2000s, its racial transformation complete, embodied and reproduced the glaring inequities and tropes that shadow Black people in America.

14

365 Black

A Racial Transformation Complete

In late September 2021, news outlets cheerily announced that to celebrate the fortieth anniversary of the McRib sandwich, McDonald's was bringing back the menu item later that fall. Described as a cult favorite, the sandwich appears on select menus annually; but for this anniversary, it would be available nationwide. The McRib, "a boneless pork patty shaped like a rack of ribs and smothered in barbecue sauce," looked every bit of its forty years in promotional photos. The fatty gray meat languished beneath a red coating of sauce, both of which rested on desiccated white buns; and the pieces of onion and/or pickles clinging haphazardly to the sandwich components did little to enliven the portrait.[1] Perhaps the McRib had seen better days, but credit is due to its longevity. When it was born in 1981, it came into a fast food world entirely different from that in 2021. Louis Malle's 1986 documentary *. . . and the Pursuit of Happiness* depicted an English-language class for new immigrants to the United States, in which the British instructor used a mock visit to Wendy's to typify the discourse Cambodian adults could expect to encounter in their new country. She is shocked when one of the pupils is unfamiliar with the chain.[2] Because the instructor herself is not American, her attention to fast food underscored the iconography of hamburgers in American culture, whereby Wendy's (or any other brand) could serve to teach English to future citizens. It is an implicit lesson on attaining a credible American lifestyle.

By the time the McRib celebrated its fortieth anniversary, fast food had become synonymous with a growing public health crisis (obesity), with industrial methods that ran counter to growing attention to food production, and with taste profiles that were antithetical to an emphasis on local, artisanal, and fresh. Fast food had traveled 180 degrees from origins that rejected Black people entirely, gathering White communities ranging from trolley-riding laborers to ruddy-cheeked children ensconced in suburban manors. Now it was synonymous with Black urbanity, way finder for the American ghetto, a racial symbology expressed as Black.

For the first time, significant concerns about the health impact for Black communities emerged as the concept of food environments swirled in public discourse: a focal point for some in understanding population health, discounted by others as an excuse for lacking personal resolve. Lee Dunham claimed in the 1990s that the food environment paled in comparison to the other social conditions Black neighborhoods needed to confront—"drugs are the problem, not beef"—and the journalist who interviewed him also argued that the health hazards posed by fast food were negligible compared to crime and crack.[3] To be sure, it is unsurprising that a McDonald's operator like Lee Dunham was disinclined to lay an obesity epidemic at his doorstep, but crime and crack were differentiated from fast food in health risk only by a factor of time. Taking a position contrary to Dunham's, Los Angeles–based food activist Ron Finley held that the drive-thru was worse for Black communities than the drive-by.[4]

Harlem in the 2000s was more likely to be beset by burger joints than high crime rates. It was a different place than the one that received Manhattan's first McDonald's. Lee Dunham's outlet was still implanted on 125th, but many of its early competitors, like All-Pro Chicken, were long gone. New restaurant chains that once would have never set foot above 96th Street, like IHOP, Applebee's, and Chuck E. Cheese, had made themselves at home among a slate of restaurants representing cuisine from around the world: Jamaican (including vegan establishments such as Strictly Roots and Uptown Juice Bar), Mexican, Japanese, Italian, Pakistani, Senegalese, Ethiopian, and many more. And several chic, full-service restaurants like Red Rooster and Ristorante Settepani stood alongside soul food stalwart Sylvia's.[5] Even with increasing restaurant diversity over the 2000s, which quickened alongside gentrification, fast food still took up much of the oxygen in the retail food landscape. Of the at least 430 restaurants in Central Harlem, fast food made up approximately 10 percent. Some were the multinational chains, others were of the motley assortment of X-Fried Chicken outlets.

Brooklyn's Black communities were replete with smaller chains and independents, often small, rickety, and encased in Plexiglas, sporting windows festooned with posters meant to diminish visibility or to entice passersby with unnecessary pictures of the kinds of meals served within. Newspapers reported on them as sites of despair and belligerent customers but these outlets were also putting their owners' children through college.[6] Hardly restricted by name to fried chicken, if signage is to be believed, outlets like Kennedy Fried Chicken and Crown Fried Chicken served burgers, steak and other sandwiches, gyros, ice cream, donuts, sea-

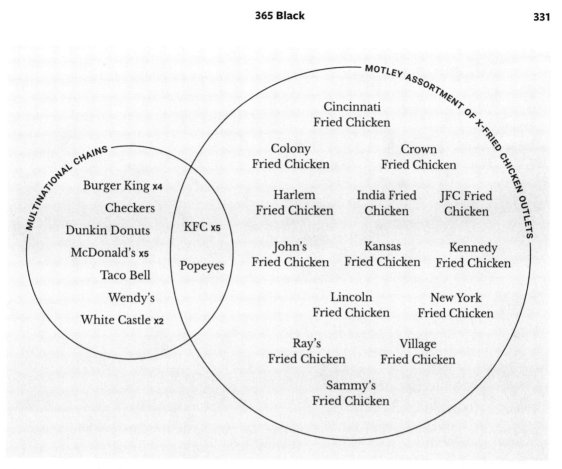

Figure 14.1. Fast food outlets in Harlem, New York City, 2011. Source: National Establishment Time-Series Database (Oakland, Calif.: Walls & Associates, 2011). Infographic by Kudos Design Collaboratory.

food, hot wings, hot dogs, coffee, pizza, and even salads. The dense saturation of fast food across New York's Black neighborhoods played out across the Northeast, the Midwest, and in communities around the country. As will be seen below, Los Angeles became a battleground for fast food in 2008. What was variable across cities was how stable restaurants were over time. In some instances, fast food that had operated for decades eventually succumbed in the 2000s. For example, in Baltimore, the KFC at the corner of East North Avenue (shown operating in the 1980s in Figure 12.9) was still there in 2011.[7] The restaurant closed and was reincarnated as a City Subs Cheese Steak, which itself was for sale by 2014. In 2017, the building had become a NextCar auto rental outlet.[8] In other instances, changing retail environments brought in fast food that endured. In the Bronx, the corner of East 149th Street and Prospect Avenue went from a Citibank in 1980 to Off Beat Video in 1989,

Figure 14.2. These former Little Taverns in Baltimore have been repurposed to new fast food uses. Photographs by author, December 2018.

to Falcon Discount $0.99 store in 1994, to a Popeyes in 2004. It remained in business as late as 2019, though in 2013 it changed the name from Popeyes Chicken and Biscuits to Popeyes Louisiana Kitchen as part of a nationwide brand transition.[9] Capital (in the form of banking) fleeing Black and Brown communities only to be replaced with fried chicken is a too-real metaphor for the intertwining of fast food, racism, and urban divestment.

Storefronts in Brooklyn cycled through small retail establishments, vacancies, and fast food throughout the 2000s, a process dating back decades. At some addresses, food had always been served in some form. Once a restaurant is in place, retail spaces tend to remain as such because they are already configured for food service needs (e.g., venting from stoves and ovens, refrigeration).[10] 255 Kingston Avenue went from a bakery in the 1980s to a Kennedy Fried Chicken in 2010; 399 Mother Gaston Boulevard had a deli in the 1980s, a pizza and pasta restaurant in 2008, and a Crown Fried Chicken in 2017; and 411 Utica Avenue changed from a US

Figure 14.3. Berry in front of his business, Berry's Grill, at Woodward Avenue and West Dakota Avenue in Highland Park, outside Detroit, in 2001. The architecture reveals this was previously a White Tower restaurant. By 2007, Berry's was shuttered. Photograph by Camilo J. Vergara, additional information from Vergara's *Detroit Is No Dry Bones* (Ann Arbor: University of Michigan Press, 2016).

Fried Chicken in 2007 to Kennedy Fried Chicken in 2015.[11] Precarity and frequent turnover in the retail landscape fertilizes fast food. Predominantly Black neighborhoods tend to have small stores, which are less well able to withstand changing retail conditions, and they have fewer stores topping $1 million in revenue.[12] Predominantly Black New York neighborhoods have more retail churn than their White counterparts, higher retail mortality, and a lower likelihood of stores staying in place.[13] All small businesses face challenges in longevity, but they are amplified in a context where discriminatory institutional policies and practices foment business failure. What was clear was that the instability of retail corridors did not affect the overall density of fast food in Black space. Such enduring saturation posed challenges for business and economic development. It also undermined the health and well-being of community residents.

A Public Health Crisis

Black neighborhoods awash in fast food prompted public health and social science researchers to investigate in earnest racial patterning in fast food exposure and the consequences for health. The CDC published maps showing the prevalence of obesity (defined as a body mass index of thirty and above, measured by weight in kilograms over the square of height in meters) by state, and the results were a subject of concern and debate. Racial differences in obesity prevalence were marked, which also stimulated the interest of medical and public health researchers.[14] Black Americans had a higher prevalence of obesity, though much of that was carried by gender. Tables 2 and 3 show that Black women had higher rates than either White women or Black men, a pattern that was not eliminated when stratifying by income.

The food environment came to the fore as an important social determinant of health in the early 2000s, as studies investigated associations with various health outcomes and health disparities.[15] Fast food seemed the only retail sector that Black neighborhoods could count on having nearby. Black communities are systematically underserviced for retail in general—an inequity that is not simply about poverty[16]—and supermarkets and other venues for fresh produce were especially scarce. But fast food was ubiquitous in Black space, and again this was not attributable to income or demand.[17] Income did not protect African Americans in California from fast food exposure, particularly as such restaurants increased in availability.[18] Studies documented these patterns in suburban settings as well.[19] In many cities, the overall impact of fast food prevalence was heightened by the fact that fast food restaurants tend to cluster spatially around one another and also around other health-deleterious resources such as liquor stores.[20] In addition to high absolute levels of fast food, researchers found that Black communities had unequal balances between food retail types, such as between supermarkets and fast food.[21]

The implication of this body of research was that Black communities faced racially patterned risks for obesity and other health conditions. Studies began to mount during the 2000s showing that residential proximity to fast food mattered for health. The most immediate connection is to frequency of consumption: living near fast food increases the likelihood of visiting these outlets and eating the food.[22] Apart from outlet density, fast food price also affects consumption: the lower the price, the greater the consumption.[23] When it came to health outcomes, researchers found fast food density to have consequences for cardiovascular disease, stroke, and blood pressure.[24] Findings for weight are mixed, with some studies of both children and adults failing to detect an association between fast food exposure and weight, obesity, or change in BMI over time.[25] Others showed that fast food, whether alone

Table 2. Prevalence (%) of obesity, by age, gender, and race, 2005–2008

Age	White women	White men	Black women	Black men
12–19	14%	16%	31%	19%
20–39	29%	26%	47%	37%
40–59	37%	36%	52%	37%
≥ 60	32%	35%	55%	37%

Note: Table adapted from "Table 1. Prevalence of Obesity, by Age and Race/Ethnicity—National Health and Nutrition Examination Survey, United States, 2005–2008," *MMWR* 60, suppl. (January 14, 2011): 75.

Table 3. Prevalence (%) of obesity, by income, gender, and race, 2005–2008

Poverty–income ratio	White women	White men	Black women	Black men
< 1.30	39%	30%	53%	29%
1.30–3.49	36%	34%	51%	35%
≥3.5	29%	33%	48%	45%

Note: Table adapted from "Table 2. Prevalence of Obesity, by Sex and PIR—National Health and Nutrition Examination Survey, United States, 2005–2008," *MMWR* 60, suppl. (January 14, 2011): 76.

or in contexts of "food swamps" (areas dense in fast food but also other high-calorie junk food), was associated with obesity for individuals across the developmental spectrum.[26] Among children and adolescents, in general, proximity to fast food near schools is associated with higher weight, with potentially larger effects for younger children. Individual studies also documented age-dependent effects.[27]

If exposure near schools was a health threat, Black youth were especially at risk. As early as 1973, market research showed that fast food sought to capitalize on high school students' desire to eat off campus by opening restaurants near schools: "Site planners for such companies are fully aware of those dynamics, for a concerted effort seems to have been made to locate fast food establishments near a high school building."[28] The same trends held into the 2000s, with the additional reality that all schoolchildren were not equally affected. Multiple studies showed not only that fast food clustered around schools, but that clustering was much more likely near schools with high proportions of Black students and in Black neighborhoods—even after accounting for the higher densities of fast food in those communities.[29] Other research completed the loop by documenting how fast food proximity was associated with more consumption, at least for boys.[30]

The picture that emerged from studies of food environments was of Black communities burdened disproportionately by fast food and paying for it with their health. It was a long trajectory that finally racialized fast food as Black.

Racialized Marketing in the 2000s

Once entirely excluded from print and television advertising, Black people now appeared as the face of fast food. The racial trope that makes Blackness the natural embodiment for serving and selling food is a long one. Those ideas were put on display in Popeyes television and radio commercials in 2009 featuring a new spokesperson, a Black woman named Annie. *Adweek* reported that Annie was a "feisty, truth-talking character" who offered a "no-nonsense approach" in exhorting customers to buy Popeyes. Meant to highlight the brand's personality and authenticity, in one of the spots she made note of an affordable $1.99 chicken and biscuit offer. Annie declared ruefully, "I work my fanny off making this chicken perfect, and they practically give it away."[31] In another, she invited prospective customers to "come on over to my world, honey!"—a phrase redolent with the language used in the 1893 tagline on R. T. Davis's Aunt Jemima pancake mix promotions: "I'se in town, honey!"[32]

Fast food consistently spent on Black-targeted advertising, constituting 37 percent of all food-related ads in 2015 on programs geared to Black viewers. Black youth were targeted anywhere from 50 to 100 percent more than their White counterparts, and by 2019, the ratio had increased, so that double the targeting was the baseline.[33] The large chains created African American–specific platforms in other media. New websites merged advertising, promotions, and the halo of corporate responsibility. KFC launched its Pride 360 site, featuring events such as an HBCU homecoming, family reunions, a Black College Expo, and a Hitmaker contest, in which contestants were to create songs that "express the signature themes of KFC's Pride 360 initiatives as expressed in the Pride 360 keywords: Individual, Family, Community, and Heritage" and "may, but [are] not required to, make reference to KFC, its heritage and food."[34] KFC saw sponsorship of community programs centering core African American values (e.g., education as means to social mobility) as a means to build consumer loyalty, enhance corporate image, and increase brand awareness.

KFC's approach surely borrowed from McDonald's, which created My InspirAsian, Me Encanta, and 365 Black to target Asian, Latino and Black populations, respectively. The purpose of 365 Black was elaborated as follows:

> At McDonald's®, we believe that African-American culture and achievement should be celebrated 365 days a year—not just during Black History Month. That's the idea behind 365Black.com. It's a place where you can learn more about education, employment, career advancement and entrepreneurship oppor-

tunities, and meet real people whose lives have been touched by McDonald's. Plus, you can also have a chance to win exciting once-in-a-lifetime opportunities. So make sure you visit often—you just might get inspired. Like the unique African Baobab tree, which nourishes its community with its leaves and fruit, McDonald's has branched out to the African-American community nourishing it with valuable programs and opportunities.[35]

McDonald's sought African American identification by preying on long-standing (and as yet unrealized) struggles for racial equity and opportunity, constructing McDonald's as pivotal in an authentic African American experience. It is ironic that the *food* is not described as nourishing the African American community, but rather the company's support of programs and provision of opportunities. Among them were a DJ Flavor battle, a Men of McCafé casting call, an HBCU classics celebration, and a gospel tour. McDonald's hoped that such strategies would lead viewers to see the company as more than a fast food brand, but a modern, trustworthy, community-involved entity that offered opportunities and culturally relevant dialogue.[36] Advertising is the most visible of marketing strategies but only a part of the overall picture, as sales promotions, food sampling, product placement, and corporate sponsorship make up a significant portion of marketing efforts—and particularly as it concerns African American consumers.[37]

Though 365 Black invited viewers to the site to learn about career advancement and entrepreneurship, McDonald's had never been a source for the kind of economic transformation the site trumpeted, neither for communities as a whole nor individual franchisees. The charges of discrimination that emerged over and over again for Black franchisees arose once more in 2020. Black McDonald's franchisees filed a class-action lawsuit contending they were misled and experienced racial discrimination. The lawsuit alleged the same kinds of complaints that have dogged McDonald's (and other chains') franchising history: for example, "McDonald's proclaims a commitment to racial equality, profits from its Black customers, yet places Black franchisees in locations that are destined to fail, with low-volume sales and high operating costs." The lawsuit notes that the highest number of Black franchisees in the system was 377 in 1998; that number has fallen steadily since, with only 186 counted within the ranks by 2020, even as the number of franchised restaurants more than doubled over that same time period. Many of the plaintiffs owned and lost multiple McDonald's outlets.[38]

The chains also capitalized on Blackness by using hip-hop music, imagery, and sensibilities in its advertising. White youth took up the perceived Blackness of fast food with "drive-thru raps," in which teens rapped their orders from car windows and recorded the transaction for upload to YouTube. One example was "the funk rapper Mr. B., a white college kid" who rapped his order at Wendy's and ended up a viral sensation. The activity, popular among adolescents in the 2000s, was meant to be goofy and fun, but in some instances youth were met with harsh consequences. Four Utah teens (race unstated) were arrested at McDonald's for their rapping visit and cited for disorderly conduct—a contemporary version of problematic hot-rodding teens frequenting second-generation fast food outlets. But the chains immediately saw the potential of these activities and sought to cash in on the trend. Taco Bell "capitalized on this youth-based, home-grown creative production and produced its own 'drive-through rap' commercial to promote its eighty-nine-cent chicken burrito," evidence of "the all-too-common commercial appropriation of youth culture for market ends."[39] In fact, in hip-hop, Taco Bell was appropriating *Black* youth culture and capitalizing on *Black* creative production. It did so not only because of hip-hop's "global appeal" but because the genre was a natural fit for fast food now racialized as Black. Unfortunately for the chains, racial connotations led at least some affluent White youth to dismiss fast food as a choice of last resort, more appropriate for the poor. Fast food, which was seen as "dirty" and unhealthy, invited disdain among some "upper income" teens (race unstated); one girl explained that "sushi or a Panera salad will sound more appealing."[40] Black critics of Black behavior seemed to agree. Despite the aggressively racialized marketing and the saturation of Black neighborhoods, observers continued to castigate Black people for consuming the fast food that surrounded them.

Chewicide

Bill Cosby attacked the Black poor, speaking at a 2004 dinner in honor of *Brown v. Board of Education*'s fiftieth anniversary. In a widely publicized tirade, he lambasted Black people and families for their moral turpitude. At one point he declared, "These people are going around stealing Coca Cola. People getting shot in the back of the head over a piece of pound cake!"[41] It is unclear to what Cosby referred here, but the effect was to make Black people out as crazed animals inciting violence over junk food. The same discourse that made the news in the 1990s about Black people's purported inability to control their behavior and appetites for unhealthy food continued to circulate in the 2000s.

Tom Burrell left advertising in 2004 and published a book meant to show that Black people had been brainwashed and how to reverse its effects. He grew up in a community that he believed was "indoctrinated with the idea that we were unable to take care of ourselves, and that we needed help and handouts from Mr. Charlie in the form of government programs, including public assistance, food stamps, and any other 'gifts' the government bestowed."[42] Burrell argued that his many years in advertising revealed that Black people purchased to compensate for low self-esteem and to meet needs for immediate gratification. With such chapter titles as "Why Do We Perpetuate Black Sexual Stereotypes?," "Why Are We Killing Ourselves?," "Why Do We Give Up Our Power So Willingly?," and "Why Can't We Stop Shopping?," the book read as an extended shaming of Black people for myriad character failings. Burrell said of the portrayals of Black sexual deviance on the talk shows of Maury Povich and his ilk, where paternity was always a mystery, that one could not blame the producers: "These situations aren't fabricated; they're just carefully picked realities of black life." Even the foreclosure crisis that ravaged Black households was apparently because of "undisciplined, indiscriminate buying habits."[43]

Burrell railed against Black health behaviors, interpreting a significant burden of preventable deaths to mean that Black people weren't doing enough individually to prevent them. He clucked his tongue at apocryphal church services that called out the names of sick constituents and then served up pork chops and fried chicken. For Burrell, Black food traditions and cherished dishes were particularly troublesome, what with their high fat and salt content; but Black people remained in denial and relied on the crutch of "culture" to justify their consumption. Burrell called it "chewicide"—eating food low in nutritional value because of "untreated trauma and depression."[44] Remarkably, Burrell made these assertions as if he had not worked for forty years promoting McDonald's to Black communities, perhaps because he saw his advertising firm as a purveyor of "positive propaganda." In fact, he argued, "we aren't deaf or blind to media messages specifically created to prod us into consuming bad food and addictive products, such as malt liquor and menthol cigarettes."[45]

In 2008, even presidential candidate Barack Obama used fast food to shame, reprimand, and single out Black constituents for their laxity and impropriety in child rearing. As political scientist Frederick Harris recounts, Obama scolded a Black audience, telling them they could not feed children junk all day and fail to involve them in exercise. "I know how hard it is to get kids to eat properly," Obama said. "But I also know that if folks [are] letting our children drink eight sodas a day, which some parents do, or, you know, eat a bag of potato chips for lunch, or Popeyes for breakfast . . . Y'all have Popcyc's out in Beaumont? I know some of y'all you got that cold Popeye's out for breakfast. I know. That's why y'all laughing. . . . You can't do that. Children have to have proper nutrition. That affects also how they study, how they learn in school."[46]

Setting aside whether Black families were actually eating Popeyes for breakfast, what exactly was the nature of Obama's folksy critique? It's unlikely that he faulted them primarily for having a heavy breakfast; it is hard to imagine him scolding small-town, White Midwesterners for eating steak and eggs for breakfast—or a Jamaican audience for eating ackee and saltfish, for that matter. Perhaps he would have been less inclined to look askance at fried chicken for breakfast were it home-cooked, though this remains unclear. What is true is that Obama frowns on eating fast food, and by situating the hypothetical meals at breakfast time he makes a bad situation worse. These are parents who would not only feed their children nonnutritious food, they also lack sense about the times and places when such meals might be appropriate.

Obama's critique of Black parenting elides the real barriers that Black households, particularly poor households, faced in providing health-supportive meals for their children, particularly amid the deluge of fast food that researchers had documented. Once he was president, the food stamp program underwent a name change to SNAP (Supplemental Nutrition Assistance Program), a moniker that emphasized nutrition and public health. But new vocabulary did not undo "the power of a loosely regulated food industry to flood consumer markets with unhealthy foods."[47] As sociologists Bruce Link and Jo Phelan articulate in their explication of fundamental causes, a state of health should be contextualized by looking at what puts people at risk of health risks.[48] Obama's critique also did not consider that eating fried chicken for breakfast might in fact suggest a resourceful family making the most out of meager means. Indeed, in 1985, marketing firm Tri-Ad Research Services conducted focus groups with Black respondents in Detroit, Chicago, Philadelphia, Atlanta, and Houston, and reported a recurring theme of appreciation for the ability to eat fried chicken cold, therefore expanding the utility of meals purchased away from home.[49] Though Obama's comments suggest something intrinsic about Black predilection for fast food, African Americans, of course aware of the dietary proscriptions health authorities make about healthful foods and nutritional intake, attempt to meet them. And, unsurprisingly, White people consume fast food, too. More than a quarter of White adults surveyed in one Wisconsin study reported eating fast food at least one or two times per week, and more frequent fast food dining was associated with higher BMI.[50]

President Obama was aghast at the *idea* of eating Popeyes for breakfast, but in 2005 Burger King advertised in a store window in Brooklyn's Fulton Mall, "Burgers for Breakfast: Beginning at 8 am."[51] These kinds of posters are unlikely to appear in outlets in White space. Research finds more child-directed marketing in fast food restaurant windows and on outlet facades in Black neighborhoods. In a national analysis of hundreds of communities, researchers examined the presence of indoor play areas, displays of toys as part of kids' meals, cartoons, children's events (e.g., birthday parties), and other marketing ploys. Lower-income and Black neighborhoods were more likely to display any form of child-targeted marketing, and in particular, Black neighborhoods were almost twice as likely as their White counterparts to display kids' meal toys.[52] In 2007, fast food outlets across Upper Manhattan displayed advertisements at child-eye level of varied promotions: sweepstakes (e.g., a chance to win backstage access to a Jonas Brothers concert), giveaways (e.g., tickets to a Six Flags theme park), events (e.g., Family Nights), and more. Kennedy Fried Chicken had a school special from 2:00 p.m. to 4:00 p.m. that offered items with widely varying value for money. For example, eight onion rings, twelve pieces of popcorn chicken, or three "munchers" (whatever those might be)— each could be had for a dollar.[53] In 2019, a McDonald's adjacent to Temple University on Philadelphia's Broad Street sported large posters in the window at child height advertising sugary drinks, such as the apparently clear-colored "Mix by Sprite" and flavors of "Minute Maid Slushie" drinks. The latter, colored turquoise, orange, and red, featured the flavors "blue raspberry," "sweet peach," and "fruit punch," respectively.[54]

Ironically, it is worth noting that although Obama admonished Black families for eating junk food, his inaugural luncheon served the very same to child guests. While the adults enjoyed a first course of seafood stew and a second course of a brace of American birds (pheasant and duck) with sides of sour cherry chutney and molasses sweet potatoes, young attendees were offered an entirely different menu, one that was thought to cater to their tastes. They received "hot dogs, cheeseburgers, macaroni and cheese, french fries, grilled cheese sandwiches, cheese pizza, chocolate chip cookies, apple and orange juices and soft drinks."[55]

Meanwhile, First Lady Michelle Obama also criticized Black families for their eating habits. Sabrina Strings contends that her "Let's move" campaign "also fingers black culture as somewhat wrong-headed, and its translational medium, black mothers, as enablers of disease."[56] Michelle Obama gave a speech in 2010 where she acknowledged environmental barriers to health-related behavior, like lack of parks, safe streets, or grocery stores. But she then said that at the end of the day, the most important explanatory factor was what Black Americans did at home: "We all need to start making some changes to how our families eat. Now, everyone loves a good Sunday dinner . . . [the] problem is when we eat Sunday dinner Monday through Saturday."[57] Is, then, junk food for breakfast the source of health concerns? Or are home-cooked meals for dinner problematic? What exactly should Black people be eating?[58]

No one seemed particularly concerned about the fact that a "sport" comprising predominantly White participants made eating into actual spectacle. The professional league of eating contests, administered by Major League Eating and its governing body the International Federation of Competitive Eating, hosts nearly six dozen events per year. As of this writing, its website MajorLeagueEating.com features the current top-ranked eater as Joey Chestnut, age thirty-seven, from San Jose, California. He holds the world hot dogs record, having consumed seventy-four Nathan's Famous dogs and buns in ten minutes; he also has eaten fifty-five glazed donuts in eight minutes, among several other records. Records held by persons other than Chestnut include burritos (Eric "Badlands" Booker ate fifteen in eight minutes), Chinese dumplings (Cookie Jarvis ate ninety-one in eight minutes), and Hooters chicken wings, 281 of which Geoffrey Esper consumed in ten minutes.

Instead, critiques by Black elites and the public at large were focused on Black people, charged by stereotypes about excessive and inappropriate Black appetites and mixed with the country's pervading healthism. Mike Bloomberg's tenure as mayor of New York epitomized the notion of healthism and a neoliberal approach to health. He advocated for several public health initiatives, some successful (indoor smoking bans in 2002 and 2011) and some not (limiting the size of soft drink portions and prohibiting any soda sales to SNAP recipients). Bloomberg understood food insecurity and diet-related disease as a market problem that hurt the city's bottom line. Chronic illness—and the socioeconomic fallout for the city—reflected poor lifestyle choices that merited tighter controls. His administration constructed citizenship as something only for those who could responsibly support the city as business. Others "could be abandoned by the state and left to rely on charity or to eat at the whim of the grocery store."[59]

An emphasis on individual personal responsibility was taken to an extreme in proposed congressional legislation. In 2003, a Florida representative proposed H.R. 339 in response to litigation against the food industry that held companies responsible for selling products that contributed to obesity and chronic illness. The bill would hold "that a seller of food shall not be subject to civil liability where the claim is premised upon on individual's weight gain resulting from the long-term consumption of food or nonalcoholic beverages."[60] Chris Cannon of Utah saw lawsuits against the food industry as frivolous and sympathized with Big Tobacco, for whom the lawsuits under the 1998 Master Settlement Agreement represented "cost prohibitive and potentially bankrupting cases." Cannon warned that corporate lawsuits would tumble down a slippery slope that would end in ordinary citizens being hauled before civil courts: "Some say these lawsuits will soon reach your own backyard barbecue unless Congress acts." He surmised that since physical inactivity was also a cause of obesity, perhaps next on the docket were TV manufacturers or those that made comfortable couches.[61] The bill's supporters expressed views that could be summarized in a statement by Todd G. Buchholz, an economic adviser to the George H. W. Bush administration: "Swallowing food is very much an individual act."[62] John Banzhaf, a professor of law at George Washington University who fought Big Tobacco for years, called H.R. 339 "an industry-sponsored bailout and protection bill" and argued that in proposing the legislation Congress was essentially predetermining that there were no circumstances or set of facts for which a company could be held liable, precluding both states' and individuals' rights.[63] In the end, the bill passed the House in a largely partisan vote with all but one Republican in favor and fifty-five Democrats signing on. It was sent to the Senate, where it was placed on the legislative calendar but never got to the floor for a vote.

Shortly afterward, in July 2003, Mitch McConnell introduced a bill—the Common Sense Consumption Act—that went no further than initial hearings. This legislation would "limit the liability of food retailers where the underlying premise for the litigation is not that the food was defective or prepared unlawfully."[64] Essentially, the bill would prohibit state or federal lawsuits against food sellers when the stated outcome was weight gain, obesity, or any related health condition. McConnell sought to protect corporations from "abusive suits by people seeking to blame someone else for their poor eating habits."[65] Hearing chair Jeff Sessions argued, "We need to think really hard before we hold sellers of food responsible because consumers eat too much. We need to address how far the pendulum should swing. . . . Is your mom liable for her good cooking? I hope not. Or are parents liable for not making their children exercise?"[66]

The hearings underscored that those lawmakers were more concerned with protecting corporations than with the health of Americans. And for Black people especially, it appeared that the only acceptable behavior was to regulate individual diet within an inch of their lives. Attempts to engage in structural interventions to change the contexts in which Black people made food choices were met with consternation and even outrage. This was brought into bold relief when the city of Los Angeles sought to initiate a moratorium on fast food. The same year soon-to-be President Obama scolded Black people for eating too much fast food, they were busy trying to repel these outlets from their communities.

The Los Angeles Fast Food Ban

Black and Brown communities in Los Angeles such as Crenshaw / Leimert Park encountered more fast food restaurants, less diversity of dining options, and outlets that were less likely to have a pleasant dining environment (e.g., cleanliness) than predominantly White West Los Angeles—which also had more options with healthier cooking methods and nutritional content.[67] Sociologist Joshua Sbicca describes the vigorous organizing and activism that took place around food and retail in Los Angeles in the 2000s, including the largest protest against Walmart in history in 2012. A Blue Ribbon Commission had determined that "food deserts" were spreading and supermarket redlining was a primary cause. The city tried to stimulate store siting with redevelopment funds, but it took years (or rather gentrification) for results to materialize. Typically pressured to accept nonunionized retailers, South Los Angeles's food justice activists worked successfully to bring a grocery that adhered to a Community Benefits Agreement in 2014.[68]

It was therefore in a context of robust food justice work that the city council, led by Councilperson Jan Perry, developed in 2008 an ordinance that would forbid additional fast food outlets in already saturated communities. Coming out of prior work focused on Central Avenue alone, ordinance 180103 imposed restrictions lasting one year on new, standalone fast food restaurants on Major Highways (Class I and Class II) and Secondary Highways in South LA, West Adams–Baldwin Hills–Leimert, and Southeast LA. In addition to forbidding the erection of new outlets, existing restaurants would not be allowed to expand their floor area nor add a drive-thru window. The ordinance was meant to "provide a strong and competitive commercial sector which best serves the needs of the community, attract uses which strengthen the economic base and expand market opportunities for existing and new businesses, enhance the appearance of commercial districts, and identify and address the over-concentration of uses which are detrimental to the health and welfare of the people of the community." The legislation also pointed out that fast food land use affected pedestrian activity and the environment through heat release and air pollution. For that reason, any permits issued (as there could be hardship or other exemptions) would require a minimum of 7 percent of outdoor space that was landscaped with plants and would require the number of driveways to be minimized.[69]

As a whole, the ordinance was comprehensive in scope, seeking to shape the built environment and quality of life, targeting health from multiple vantage points, and recognizing retail diversity and strength as critical in community well-being. Community-based organizations such as Strategic Actions for a Just Economy, which worked on tenant rights and employment opportunities, and the Community Coalition, which focused on the conditions that fostered addiction and violence, wrote in to express strong support for the measure. They urged its passage, contending that healthy food was scarce, that fast food and liquor stores were crowding out alternatives, and that "the residents of South L.A. merit more than being a dumping ground for nuisance sites and unhealthy food options."[70]

Several years later, health researchers followed up with studies of whether obesity had declined in South Los Angeles—excluding the other two communities and assessing a target that had never been stipulated as a particular or singular goal—and also investigated whether the composition of food retail and restaurants changed.[71] The analysis looked at changes between 2007 and 2009/2011–12 for health outcomes and 2013 for restaurant and retail differences.[72] A comparison of relatively small samples of South LA residents to the rest of the city found that seventeen new fast food outlets from larger chains opened in the community but, meeting the terms of the ordinance, were not freestanding. Overall, new businesses in the area were most likely to be small food stores, while comparison areas were most likely to receive large independent restaurants. Regarding obesity, overall BMI increased across the city; but so, too, did the gap with South LA. Fast food consumption also went up, and soda consumption dropped, across the city. The authors argued that in targeting only freestanding locations, "there was a complete disconnect between the justification and the policy."[73]

To be sure, the specification of standalone restaurants, likely a concession to fend off claims of governmental overreach, limited the scope of what was possible. But journalists took up the charge that the ban was merely a symbolic gesture, and a dangerous one to boot. Some argued that the philosophy behind the ban was similar to that regulating school lunches. How this was so was not stated explicitly; but having built this straw man, the argument to attack it went as follows: "More troubling yet is the subtext . . . that policy should be dictated for poor people the way it is for children. Unless the tenor of the conversation about obesity gets a little less paternalistic, it is going to be a challenge to get anyone to the table."[74] A second-year law student published a journal article also arguing that the moratorium was "an eye-opening act of government paternalism"; that "opponents" to the ban saw it as "racially-motivated and an act of paternalism"; and that the ordinance had "been met with equally notable opposition, both among industry leaders and the public."[75] It turned out that the "public" cited in the article were national media pundits rather than the residents of the actual communities where the legislation took effect.

None who spoke out against the ban could explain why self-determined action that was desired by and enacted by a community was paternalism. The initiative had not originated from an external, top-down, forced directive, and had not attempted to dictate what people ate. Those who were offended by a perceived abrogation of choice could not explain how choice was impeded when dozens of existing restaurants continued to operate. The problem was not that there was *any* fast food, it was that there was too much of it. Who, other than the affected community, should determine how much was desirable? Critics of the ban were oddly silent on other municipalities that banned fast food. Elsewhere in California, Berkeley and Arcata regulated the siting of fast food, while the city of Calistoga banned fast food altogether, categorizing it as a disamenity that defamed neighborhood character and prestige.[76] So, too, did Concord, Massachusetts, and Port Jefferson, New York. These predominantly White communities were apparently seen to be exercising legitimate control over the built environment; but given the (lack of) value accorded to Black space, critics were unwilling to allow Black communities to make similar claims.

White paternalistic food action was, however, very much in evidence in Black and Brown Los Angeles. In 2010, anthropologist Hannah Garth found that individuals working at an organization that sought to increase healthy food access in South and East Los Angeles felt comfortable reprimanding her for telling teens that her favorite food was mac and cheese rather than something from the brassica family. Garth argues, "In this context, 'healthy eating' took on an aura of 'punitive justice'" intended to prevail over Blackness. Garth's research also revealed that other White-led organizations took umbrage at even framing the issue as "food justice," seeing the term as unduly critical of innocent White people.[77]

The *Los Angeles Times* reported on the post-ban food landscape and pointed out that the problem was a lack of the new, healthier, full-service restaurants envisioned to take fast food's place. Between 2009 and 2014, nearly ninety restaurants opened in the area (and some fast food locations closed), but more than half of those were on or near the University of Southern California campus. The remainder were fast food outlets such as Jack in the Box and Taco Bell. Organizers had conceived the ban as a stopgap measure that could stem the tide until desirable restaurants moved in, but they recognized, too, that redlining was the underlying issue, something the ban could not fix on its own. The *Los Angeles Times* lay partial blame on Governor Jerry Brown's shuttering of redevelopment agencies in 2012, which was thought to undo the possibility of tax or other incentives that could have attracted restaurants.[78] In fact, the real barrier was the retail redlining of Black space, incentives notwithstanding. When a controversial Church's Chicken opening was slated for D.C.'s Seventh Street NW in 1983, city officials hoped that a simultaneous new supermarket project would lure developers, but it did not.[79] Black communities cannot count on retailers evaluating their consumer base as viable, regardless of the enticements city governments might extend.

Redlining persists because Black space is stereotyped and stigmatized as a consumer desert poorly matched for upscale shopping.[80] In the restaurant industry, researchers have documented pervasive beliefs that Black persons are poor tippers and also difficult to wait on more generally. Anti-Black attitudes translate to poor service and avoidance of Black patrons—in some cases with the explicit encouragement of management, as in the case of Denny's.[81] Trade media described Black non-tipping as a reality that required "a brutally honest look" and quoted restaurant wait staff who believed that Black people were mad about slavery and took it out on White people.[82] Individuals wrote letters to the editor, and one pizza delivery driver stated, "The education mentioned to get minorities to tip better will probably be a long time coming, and it will probably do little good. These people simply don't care." If restaurants shunned a population perceived as unskilled eaters, the question remains what final trajectory fast food will traverse as neighborhoods change and gentrify. Black neighborhoods remade to suit the tastes of affluent White newcomers may push fast food out—especially the shabby outlets that are often more numerous than national chains. Or, as fast food reinvents itself, new, chic iterations like Shake Shack may arrive. However, because Black neighborhoods continue to be starved of resources and development when only Black residents remain, it is possible that many communities won't see either outcome.

The Final Frontier

Apart from seeking desirable consumers, retailers also seek desirable retailers. Stores can be desirable for many reasons: they may sell expensive goods and bask their neighbors in reflected glory; they may be synergistic with the products incoming stores sell (e.g., a hardware store would benefit from locating next to a home décor store); they may draw heavy traffic. Corridors with plentiful stores and brisk retail activity suggest to potential establishments that the business environment is conducive to operation, thereby lowering perceived risk.[83] By the same token, anemic retail, and particular retail uses like liquor stores, rebuff other stores.[84]

Some evidence is emerging to reveal how fast food has fared in the 2000s as Black neighborhoods have gentrified and the retail corridors in which they have been seated have changed around them. As noted at the outset of the chapter, the dining landscape in Harlem has changed dramatically over time, and continues to do so. The corner of Adam Clayton Powell Jr. Boulevard and 140th Street, previously home to a Bojangles' and a Wendy's in the 1980s (see chapter 12), sustained new eateries in the early 2000s. Bojangles' became the Sea & Sea Seafood Market, which sold both fresh and fried fish, and the Wendy's became a McDonald's in 2004, shown in Figure 14.4. By 2017, the seafood outlet had been replaced by an enormous crater surrounded by wooden fencing—an indication of impending construction. Indeed, a generic residential building with ground floor retail space available for

Figure 14.4. McDonald's at 140th Street and Adam Clayton Powell Jr. Boulevard, Harlem, New York. Photograph by author, December 2005.

lease came into being by November 2019. It dwarfed the neighboring McDonald's, which had changed its architecture entirely, no longer the homey mansard-roofed building that the brand has employed for so long, and instead a squat cube with smooth paneling and brightly colored, square-shaped outdoor seating.[85]

Media covering the city's inflated real estate market thought the McDonald's, despite its makeover, not long for this world. The generic building, at 2389 Adam Clayton Powell, was in fact a new "luxury" development that arrived, journalists mocked, "to the dismay of the anti-gentrification crowd." The developers betrayed their aspiration for who would occupy the building by rendering site images with DKNY, Gucci, Burberry, Prada, and Cartier as commercial lessees. Residents who might otherwise be priced out of such a building could find their fortune in an affordable housing lottery, if they earned no more than 130 percent of the area median income. For an "affordably-priced" $1,850 per month one-bedroom, that meant a potential tenant could earn no more than $97,110—and no less than $63,429.[86]

Meanwhile, a couple of blocks away on Adam Clayton Powell rose the Rennie, a condo development whose fact sheet told prospective buyers, "The Manhattan you didn't know you could have. A medley of new condos in the heart of Harlem. Eco efficient. Tech smart. Style flows from every block. The mood, the blues, the buzz. The Rennie." Touting the slate of amenities the building offered, the text told of a rooftop lounge, party and fitness rooms, bike storage, a pet spa, and a twenty-five-year tax abatement. As of January 2021, among the available apartments listed on TheRennie.com was #217, a studio measuring 573 square feet and listed at $598,000. The Rennie was named for the Renaissance Ballroom and Casino, the 1924 landmark it replaced. Once a Black-owned social hall, the venue hosted events including Horn & Hardart's Colored Employees Relief Association ball in 1939.[87] By the 1980s it had been abandoned for many years and was eventually sold to developers. A former patron, Adrian Irene Allen, commented, "Those wood floor[s] were once gleaming, the box seats upstairs gave a [bird's-eye] view of all the happenings on the dance floor. You were able to dance in the space between the box seats and the windows that were opened during the summer months as the music flowed out onto 7th Ave."[88]

In this new "renaissance" Harlem, "old school" fast food may soon seem anachronistic and out of step if it is not already. In gentrified neighborhoods, what could be called third-generation fast food—burger and other outlets mirroring earlier generations but remade to serve wealthy Whites repatriating to urban space—is the norm. Restaurants like Shake Shack have enjoyed success casting themselves as more clever versions of the national cuisine now widely derided by foodies. Fast food may be unable to survive as neighborhoods grow Whiter and chicer, though this did not bear out in Chicago, where population changes suggestive of gentrification had little impact on the likelihood of fast food or liquor stores turning over into a different retail sector.[89] Chicago might be a special case, however. Gentrification has proceeded at a slower pace in Chicago communities that are more than 40 percent Black.[90] Indeed, in contrast to certain strongholds in New York and D.C., where Black people now make up less than half the population, in Chicago, between 1960 and 2000, not a single Black neighborhood changed from Black to White.[91]

Chicago's durable inequalities have meant that over a decades-long trajectory, fast food outlets are perhaps just as likely to devolve into palimpsest as to turnover into another fried chicken or burger joint. As Black communities remain divested of capital and other resources, and long stretches of street walls endure only as urban prairies, the restaurants that once stood on them have also disappeared. Nearly three dozen Black-owned restaurants such as the King Kastle System, the Friendly Chicken Shack, and Ward's Snack Shop (and others that were not fast

Figure 14.5. A prior Automat building on Chestnut Street in Center City Philadelphia that still retains its signage. Elsewhere, an Automat near the 69th Street Transportation Center has been repurposed into a Crown Fried Chicken. Photograph by author, January 2019.

food) advertised in Chicago's Black Business Directory in 1969 were, by 2018, primarily vacant lots. They had also been replaced by shuttered buildings, nonprofit uses such as community centers or senior homes, the occasional liquor store or takeout eatery, and parking lots. Few of the fast food restaurants encountered in earlier chapters persisted. Of course, chains and individual establishments such as Afri-Kingdom, All-Pro Chicken, Mahalia's, Whoopee Burger, Holland's Drive-In, and White Corner Hamburgers had long ago ceased operations. In their stead are institutional uses (most commonly churches), vacant lots, small retail stores, and other fast food restaurants, often in fortified, bunker-like buildings with impenetrable glass block windows or sometimes no windows at all.

For fast food to be marketed with a tagline of 365 Black is evocative of how pervasively fast food is linked to Blackness, and of the circle of change that characterizes its racial embodiment. The industry began with a position of market exclusion and ended in one of market exploitation—the same trajectory African Americans encountered with bank lending and subprime mortgages.[92] Not quite boom and bust, because there was little boom for Black neighborhoods, fast food certainly never lived up to the promise of socioeconomic mobility, and it brought a slow subsidence of health in its wake. Fast food's racial future remains to be seen. But the 2000s, the closing bookend of a nearly 110-year history, consolidated the arc in how fast food became Black.

Conclusion

The Racial Costs

Julius Motal's project "First Meals: This Is What Freedom Tastes Like" depicted the first thing formerly incarcerated individuals ate upon their release.[1] Offerings from fast food chains dominated. People eat fast food because salty, fattening, and sugary things taste good. "First Meals" reveals that especially when juxtaposed against the sensory deprivation of prison, fast food can not only be deeply pleasurable, but can constitute an edible form of freedom itself. On the other end of the carceral spectrum, fast food also shows up as the final meal of persons condemned to death. Because prison food is monotonous, often cold, and of variable quality, fast food, with the intensity of its flavors and its connotations of America, tops the list as the most requested last meal among Texas death row prisoners.[2] In some instances, prison administration have taken the liberty of substituting fast food when requested items are unavailable; Pedro Muniz asked for salad and shrimp, but received a burger, fries, and cola instead. These meals are not the same. But prison staff saw burgers and fries as vested with enough value to serve as the last bodily experience Muniz would have before departing the world of the living. That fast food permeates all corners of American life, even death row, speaks to its centrality in the nation's collective consciousness.

The competing tensions between taste, pleasure, power, and peril that govern fast food in carceral settings also extend to the heart of everyday society. As a cultural product with iconic status, the workings of the fast food industry intersect with national concerns and struggles around everything from housing to policing; and fast food shows up in pop culture and public discourse in ways that other everyday retail sectors—say, laundromats—don't. Fast food intrudes substantially on myriad social domains, a position that perhaps only the national food (at least, a proxy for it) could occupy. But that cultural badge as national food is now quite vexed. Fast food's long racial transformation begs the question, could this story have gone any other way? The answer seems to be no, but of course everything looks inevitable in retrospect. The players involved in producing the contemporary fast food landscape were many, and they were hardly organized under a single set of aims or strategies. And yet it is painfully logical that Black communities would first be excluded from a neighborhood resource when it was desirable and then become a repository once it was shunned. If the outcome was inevitable, it's because fast food embodies the deeply entrenched racial inequities that, in one form or another, have always existed.

Sociologist Victor Ray sees organizations as critical to understanding racial structures in the United States, and fast food's history clearly reveals it to be an organization that is deeply racialized. Ray argues that organizations' very development is contingent on racial schemas linked to social and material resources, and those linkages perpetuate relations that are predicated on inequality. Indeed, he defines race as "a relationship between persons mediated through things."[3] Fast food, the thing you eat; and fast food, the corporations (organizations) that sell the thing, bring these ideas into sharp relief. Over the course of the twentieth century, fast food has always been racialized, shifting from Whiteness to Blackness, differentially allocating access to itself—as social resource for consumers, as material resources for franchisees—and to other resources. Each generation of the product has relied on and deployed racial schemas, always anti-Black though varying in form. In doing so, fast food made existing racial tropes part and parcel of its relationship to American consumers and communities, perpetuated racialized labor hierarchies within its organizations, and capitalized on and reproduced urban disinvestment.

How then should we interpret the cost of fast food's pervasive reach? Its most perilous consequences have been articulated by journalists as fomenting industrial food production, undermining sustainable and just labor conditions, and harming the environment.[4] For Black folks, in whose communities these outlets have proliferated most densely, disproportionate burdens of chronic illness clearly must figure here. But fast food's costs include so much more. For Black folk, they are deeply racial. Fast food restaurants are in fact places to eat. So their impact necessarily is of interest to those who are concerned with food environments. But the legacy of this industry extends far beyond what people might be able to buy for lunch, because fast food has been instigator and indicator of racial inequities for Black communities across time and place. The ways fast food operates—controlling territory, running product to segregated markets, and extracting resources—has required local and national infrastructures of racial catastrophe. That catastrophe includes but is not limited to an American imaginary that holds Blackness as a contaminant that despoils the sanctity of White life; continual turning to market-based solutions for apartheid; racial narratives about deviant Black consumption; and social structures that sort Black people into an America distinct from their White counterparts at every turn.

Fast food also has racial costs because it has been a cipher for the ideals in which the country is most invested and the psychological conflicts it has yet to master. From the business side, fast food has been constructed as an honest get-rich quick scheme of sorts, an example of the fundamental promise of American business enterprise. The allure for Black entrepreneurs extended beyond individual wealth; it was a chance to empower Black communities, to make something in spaces where the country deemed nothing shall prosper. But for the most part, the American Dream through franchising remained inchoate aspiration and even outright fantasy. It turned out that fast food could not actually confer twice the business benefit with half the required know-how or purported risk. The winners in a rigged game were largely elites whose social networks spanned related industries and whose financial fortunes did not depend on a sustainable restaurant operation. So many of the Black entrepreneurs who put everything on the line were ruined by a racial project that happened to sell fried food.

But what about the Black people who made millions off of fast food? They do exist. Isn't the entry of Black businesspeople into the industry—however late—and their piece of a lucrative pie a cause for celebration? James Baldwin argued, "There is so much that's more important than Cadillacs, Frigidaires, and IBM machines. No. And precisely one of the things wrong with this country is this notion that IBM machines and Cadillacs *prove* something. People always tell me how many Negroes bought Cadillacs last year. This *terrifies* me. I always wonder: Do you think this is what the country is for? Do you really think this is why I came here, this is why I suffered, this is what I would die for? A lousy Cadillac?"[5]

No. And neither for a hamburger.

Franchising is a vehicle perfectly suited to carrying the myth of meritocracy, a fallacy that is deeply allergic to the country's racial realities. Americans want to believe that theirs is a country where success is equitably distributed to those who evince hard work, pluck, and perseverance, and that the country runs on the dogged pursuit of professional success that only comes from delayed gratification. Fast food's unmeritocratic system was a barrier for all franchisees, but especially for Black laypeople. Fast food's outlook has always been forward, to the future, to a self-concept unweighted by history, much as America has done. In 2016, when the Ray Kroc biopic *The Founder* was released in theaters, it advertised on Instagram with a post featuring its lead actor, Michael Keaton. One user, @_soulsnatcher_2, commented, "So we gone sit here and act like those ain't start off as whites only burgers," laughing heartily at this denial (with emojis). Fast food, like America—as America—has had little patience for looking to the past, much less to an unvarnished one with visible racial scars. Fast food's promise was always to the America that America thinks it is.

And if fast food has embodied the idea of a life made better by retail goods, then Black exclusion matters even for a product that few would argue is a necessity, or its lack a state of deprivation. In this highly consumerist society, fast food has symbolized a mythical American quality of life attributable to the panoply of goods available for purchase. Fast food actively excluded Black people from participating in this exercise, until it had reoriented entirely to exploit the population's consumer dollars instead. Black people never looked for salvation in however many billions of ground beef patties, buns, or fried chicken parts sold. But it mattered that they were excluded because it was an exclusion from convenience, an occasional place to dine and hang out, and sometimes something more profound than that.

James Baldwin walked into a diner named after America and ordered a burger, because what else ought someone to order in such a setting? But he was denied his meal and sent into a rage, about which he wrote, "There is not a Negro alive who does not have this rage in his blood—one has the choice, merely, of living with it consciously or surrendering to it."[6] Baldwin raged because he could not procure the all-American meal at a diner named after America, but what else ought to happen in such a setting? And yet both ends of fast food's racial spectrum—exclusion and exploitation—can incite that blood-borne rage, because both evoke casual dismissal from organized American society. Both evoke contempt for Blackness, rendered outside the bounds of legible humanity. Fast food's relationship to Black folks is particular but also rooted in the racial impulses in which the rest of America steeps. The story of fast food's relationship to Black folks is a story about America itself.

Acknowledgments

As I write these acknowledgments, 2021 is coming to a close. That means this book has been five years in the making in the short run, and thirteen over the long haul. The idea was a seed first planted around 2008–9 when I published a couple of articles in public health journals on fast food. I worked in fits and starts, doing some initial research here, taking photos there; and the project was never far from my mind while I ran other projects and lived my daily life in New York City—Bed-Stuy, Brooklyn, in particular. The seed germinated more fully in 2016 with fellowships at the Smithsonian Institution (National Museum of American History) and the Black Metropolis Research Consortium at the University of Chicago. Those allowed me to dedicate protected time in a real way, and from there the ball kept rolling. A full record of thirteen years' worth of acknowledgments of everyone and everything that made this book happen is impossible, and despite the weight of this tome I do have a word limit, which is bearing down on me like a ceiling built abnormally low (like the one in *Being John Malkovich*, where the offices were on the 7½th floor). So this is my best effort to parsimoniously recognize the forces that brought this book into being.

The research and writing for this project spans two institutions. I was at Columbia University when I wrote my first two public health articles about fast food. The first was a conceptual article that came about because I was writing an R03 grant proposal to the NIH to empirically study fast food density in New York City. The grant went unfunded, but I was able to complete the analyses with colleagues anyway, and that was my second article. While writing the grant, my colleague and mentor Ilan H. Meyer read drafts of the proposal along the way. On successive drafts he kept telling me to shorten the "Background and Significance" section. Eventually he had to tell me, "Okay, clearly you have something to say, but it doesn't belong in the grant—save it for an article." I followed his advice and went on to write "Fried Chicken and Fresh Apples: Racial Segregation as a Fundamental Cause of Fast Food Density in Black Neighborhoods" (the first article), which lay a critical foundation for this book. So I thank Ilan, still a mentor, but also a friend, for his initial feedback on that grant; and then for his unflagging support over my academic career. Other colleagues at Columbia, such as Kim Hopper, Ana Abraido-Lanza, and Bruce Link, were also instrumental in my finding success in the unorthodox career path that led to this book.

While I remain solely responsible for the contents of this book, I benefited tremendously from the insights of several stellar historians, directly and indirectly, on different aspects of the project. Andrew Diamond and Julia Katz read early drafts of a few chapters, and Minkah Makalani read substantially more; all gave invaluable feedback. Mia Bay and Keith Wailoo were sounding boards, encouraged me as the research progressed, and were instrumental in my receipt of the NIH grant that funded most of the research, writing, and production of the manuscript. Regarding the specifics of that grant: research reported in this publication was supported by the National Library of Medicine of the National Institutes of Health under Award Number G13LM012463. The content is solely the responsibility of the author and does not necessarily represent the official views of the National Institutes of Health. David Herzberg and James Colgrove graciously sent a copy of their prior applications for this mechanism (and Herzberg sent his to a total stranger); I appreciate their generosity. And when I wrote my own application, Jesse Bayker, then a graduate student in history at Rutgers, gave me excellent feedback on the proposal.

Other funding support came from the Black Metropolis Research Consortium, where the administrative leadership, Camille Brewer and Anita Mechler, made for an amazing fellowship. Shout-out to fellow fellow William Horatio Adams, who turned me on to the ViewPoint files at Vivian Harsh. As I noted, I had the privilege of being a fellow at the Smithsonian's National Museum of American History. Many thanks to senior archivist Vanessa Broussard for her expertise and assistance as my project adviser, and to Omar Martinez, the fellowship director. I also received funding for preliminary research from the New Jersey Agricultural Experiment Station and from the Rutgers University Research Council. And when I spent a wonderful year as senior fellow at the Institute for Advanced Studies in Marseille at Aix-Marseille Université, I was able to continue my research and wrote *Burgers in Blackface: Anti-Black Restaurants Then and Now,* published by the University of Minnesota Press in the Forerunners series in 2019. Thanks to Rutgers University for being generous with leave time to accept these fellowships and for sabbatical leave.

A few other colleagues I'll mention include Fred Harris, for telling me way back when that this project had the potential to be the go-to book on the topic. That remains to be seen, but his early interest and support, and his reading a very early draft of the proposal before I had any clue of how to write a book proposal, were a critical early spark to move this project forward. Psyche Williams-Forson's brilliant work on food and African American culture, sharing of her Smithsonian application, and consultation and collaboration have been an absolute boon. Shiriki Kumanyika has my thanks for mentoring, letter writing, career advice, and encouragement. I will acknowledge as a group the brilliance and commitment of the faculty of Africana Studies at Rutgers, who provided inspiration over the long course of this project.

There are about a trillion archivists and librarians to thank, and I apologize for any I've left out. Here they are, in alphabetical order: Lucas Clawson at the Hagley Library, Ken Cobb at the New York City Municipal Archives, Tracey Drake at the Vivian G. Harsh Research Collection (Chicago Public Library), Andrea Felder at the New York Public Library, Saul B. Gibusiwa and Robert Schoeberlein at the Baltimore City Archives, Jessica Hopkins at the National Archives in Kansas City, Edward Luthy at the D.C. Office of Planning, Philip Mohr at the Des Plaines History Center, Tal Nadal at the New York Public Library, Kay Peterson at the Smithsonian's National Museum of American History, Kimmi Ramnine at the D.C. History Center, Morag Walsh and others at the Special Collections at the Chicago Public Library, staff at the City of Alexandria Archives, and staff at the Research Center at the Chicago History Museum and the Newberry Library.

I also owe thanks to research assistants. Larry Traylor, RA extraordinaire, leapt over EndNote references in a single bound and helped with so much more. Keon Dillon lent a much-needed hand, and the students who took the Capstone in Environmental Policy, Institutions, and Behavior class with me in the spring of 2015 conducted research activities that led me to key sources. Members of the Black LIFE Study team also helped gather early data. Other important collaborators helped with spatial analyses, cartography, and graphic design: Mapping Analytics, Dennis McClendon of CartoGraphics, and Kudos Design Collaboratory.

I could not be happier that this book found a home at the University of Minnesota Press. Those books and webinars and blog posts and everything else that says you should choose a press based on having an editor who gets and loves your project, who advocates for it and actively helps you craft and think through it, are correct. When I began the project, as a psychologist who had only ever published journal articles, I was pretty clueless about writing a book. Jason Weidemann reached out to me and took a chance on a manuscript that even I wasn't sure I would be able to pull off. He stuck with me for the three years it took to get a proposal together and has continued to shepherd it all the way through. I am grateful for such a wonderful experience publishing my first monograph. Editorial assistant Zenyse Miller has also been a constant support in the nuts and bolts of getting this manuscript together from start to finish. And, formerly at the press, Danielle Kasprzak was the humanities editor who published *Burgers in Blackface,* so thanks are due to her for getting me started at Minnesota. Many thanks are also due to the anonymous peer reviewers who gave so generously in their feedback, and Nicholas Taylor for exceptionally careful copyediting, which has helped the book become its best self.

I have lived in three different cities and one town in the time I've been writing this book, making my way down the Northeast Corridor from NYC to Philly (with a year in D.C. in between). Across them all I've had the fortune of having in my life incredible Black women who are also academics. They contributed love, strategy, and scholarly ideas. Misogynoir is very real in academia and I wouldn't have made it this far without these women. The late Cheryl Wall provided much needed informal mentoring and career advice. Shatema Threadcraft is always ready for my mad scientist schemes, introduced me to the world of fellowships, and indulged my real estate fantasies the world over. Janice Johnson Dias is a troublemaker of the best sort and had the needed impatience for me to write something that could reach a larger audience. She sees our adventures as akin to those of Harold and Kumar, which I guess is appropriate since they went to White Castle. Stacey Sutton knows everything there is to know about cities and an unusual number of other things; also, despite becoming a cyclist after me, she is way faster. Sonya Grier, Tené Lewis, Melody Goodman, Deidre Anglin, Carla Shedd, Zaire Dinzey-Flores, and Tracy McFarlane span different disciplines, different times, and even different countries, and have been excellent partners in academic crime and friends in good times and bad.

Then there are friends who aren't academics, who have, apart from humoring or even actively supporting my research, just been great people to have in my life. Again, I can't thank each and every one, but I'll single out a few here. Some go way back—to a time when I couldn't have dreamed I would be writing the acknowledgments for a book, like John Thurston; others not quite as far, but have been my East Coast family for many years, like L. Michelle Williams and Senaka Peter. They have all kept me in stitches, helped me out when I had procedures requiring stitches, and were an all-around source of love and support that thrummed beneath the writing of this book the whole way. Still other friends are brand-new but already feel like old ones. When I moved to Philly a few years ago, Cobbina and Roberta Frempong welcomed me like a long-lost sibling. And Joseph Johnson read and commented on a couple of chapters without passing out from boredom, so I took that as a hopeful sign for the book.

Finally, more thanks than I can express go to my family. My kin extend from the States to Ghana to the UK and elsewhere, and trying to acknowledge any substantive portion of them is an impossibility, so I will avoid trouble by sticking with just my immediate family in Chicagoland. They gave me a loving base to come back to whenever I did, and cheered me on and enjoyed my exploits vicariously whenever I was somewhere else. So, thanks to my older brother, Fred Nii Kwatei Eddie-Quartey, with whom I still have vivid memories from our childhood—how are we both middle-aged now? Thanks to my father, A. C. Eddie-Quartey, who has been a continual source of support and love, has delighted in my career achievements, and always told me I could do anything I set my mind to. Daddy, you were right! And last but not least, thanks to my mother, Alice L. Eddie-Quartey. I left writing the acknowledgments for last not only because completion of the manuscript is a logical time to do them, but because I couldn't face having to write about my mother passing away when the work was about 75 percent completed. I am heartbroken that she didn't get to read this book before departing. She taught me to read, fostered my love of writing and creative production, and was so dear to me and the rest of our family. Mommy, I wrote through my grief because I had to finish this for you. I still have yet to come to terms with the fact that you are now one of the Ancestors, but I know you know I only managed to get this book done because you all had my back. I only want to make you proud.

Notes

Abbreviations

ABWP A. Bernie Wood Papers, Archives Center, National Museum of American History, Smithsonian Institution, Washington, D.C.

CCIR Coon Chicken Inn Records and Graham Family Papers, 1913–1973, Archives Center, National Museum of American History, Smithsonian Institution, Washington, D.C.

CRJP Caroline R. Jones Papers, Archives Center, National Museum of American History, Smithsonian Institution, Washington, D.C.

CULR Chicago Urban League Records, Special Collections and University Archives, University of Illinois Chicago

DIR *Drive-In Restaurant*

EDP Ernest Dichter Papers, Hagley Museum and Library, Wilmington, Delaware

FFM *Fast Food Magazine*

H&HR Horn & Hardart Records, Archives Center, National Museum of American History, Smithsonian Institution, Washington, D.C.

HPKCC Hyde Park–Kenwood Community Conference Records, Hanna Holborn Special Collection Research Center, University of Chicago

MCDDP McDonald's Archives, Des Plaines History Center, Des Plaines, Illinois

NRN *Nation's Restaurant News*

NYT *New York Times*

RFBC Robert F. Byrnes Collection of Automat Memorabilia, Manuscripts and Archives Division, New York Public Library

TTID Truth Tobacco Industry Documents, UCSF Library, San Francisco

VPIA ViewPoint Inc. Archives, Vivian G. Harsh Research Collection of Afro-American History and Literature, Chicago Public Library

WANN WANN Radio Archive, Archives Center, National Museum of American History, Smithsonian Institution, Washington, D.C.

WAPP W. Alvin Pitcher Papers, Hanna Holborn Special Collection Research Center, University of Chicago

WSJ *Wall Street Journal*

Introduction

1. James Baldwin, *Notes of a Native Son* (New York: Dial Press, 1963), 85.

2. John Eligon, "Minneapolis's Less Visible, and More Troubled Side," *New York Times,* January 10, 2016.

3. Bruce G. Link and Jo Phelan, "Social Conditions as Fundamental Causes of Disease," *Journal of Health and Social Behavior* 36 (1995): 80–94; David R. Williams and Chiquita Collins, "Racial Residential Segregation: A Fundamental Cause of Racial Disparities in Health," *Public Health Reports* 116 (2001): 404–16.

4. Naa Oyo A. Kwate, Chun Yip Yau, Ji Meng Loh, and Donya Williams, "Inequality in Obesigenic Environments: Fast Food Density in New York City," *Health & Place* 15 (2009): 364–73.

5. Because I discuss these studies in detail in chapter 14, I do not include the citations here.

6. Gregory Sharp and Matthew Hall, "Emerging Forms of Racial Inequality in Homeownership Exit, 1968–2009," *Social Problems* 61, no. 3 (2014): 427–47.

7. Douglas S. Massey and Nancy A. Denton, *American Apartheid: Segregation and the Making of the Underclass* (Cambridge, Mass.: Harvard University Press, 1993).

8. Michael Omi and Howard Winant, *Racial Formation in the United States: From the 1960s to the 1990s,* 2nd ed. (New York: Routledge, 1994).

9. Sidney Mintz, *Tasting Food, Tasting Freedom: Excursions into Eating, Culture, and the Past* (Boston: Beacon Press, 1996).

10. "Radio a Leading Force in Negro Progress," *Broadcasting Magazine,* November 7, 1966, box 7, folder 20, WANN.

1. A Fortress of Whiteness

1. John DeFerrari, *Historic Restaurants of Washington, D.C.: Capital Eats* (Charleston, S.C.: American Palate, 2013).

2. Sanborn Map Company, *Sanborn Fire Insurance Maps of District of Columbia, 1927–1960.*

3. I borrow here from the title of Robert V. Guthrie's landmark 1976 text on the history of psychology in the United States, one that revealed the discipline's research and methods throughout the nineteenth and twentieth centuries to be replete with notions of White superiority. To underscore the discipline's racist epistemology and the singular lack of racial and ethnic diversity among its practitioners, he named the book *Even the Rat Was White.*

4. John DeFerrari, "The Hot Shoppes: Teen Twists, Mighty Mo's, and Pappy Parker's Fried Chicken," *Streets of Washington* (blog), April 22, 2013, http://www.streetsofwashington.com/.

5. Jean Jones, "Negro Eating Ban Is Checked," *Washington Post and Times Herald,* August 26, 1957.

6. "Restaurants Have Right to Refuse Service to Negroes, Almond Says," *Washington Post, Times Herald,* April 6, 1960; "Negro Reporter Loses Suit." *NYT,* February 17, 1960.

7. James W. Loewen, *Sundown Towns: A Hidden Dimension of Segregation in America* (New York: The New Press, 2005).

8. Loewen.

9. James N. Gregory, "The Second Great Migration: A Historical Overview," in *African American Urban History since World War II,* ed. Kenneth L. Kusmer and Joe W. Trotter (Chicago: University of Chicago Press, 2009).

10. David F. Krugler, *1919, the Year of Racial Violence* (New York: Cambridge University Press, 2015), 10–11.

11. Krugler.

12. Krugler.

13. Douglas S. Massey and Nancy A. Denton, *American Apartheid: Segregation and the Making of the Underclass* (Cambridge, Mass.: Harvard University Press, 1993).

14. Katherine Leonard Turner, *How the Other Half Ate: A History of Working-Class Meals at the Turn of the Century* (Berkeley: University of California Press, 2014).

15. Lizabeth Cohen, *Making a New Deal: Industrial Workers in Chicago, 1919–1939* (New York: Cambridge University Press, 2008).

16. John A. Jakle and Keith A Skulle, *Fast Food: Roadside Restaurants in the Automobile Age* (Baltimore: Johns Hopkins University Press, 1999).

17. Turner, *How the Other Half Ate*.

18. Douglas J. Flowe, "'Fighting and Cutting and Shooting, and Carrying On': Saloons, Dives, and the Black 'Tough' in Manhattan's Tenderloin, 1890–1917," *Journal of Urban History* 45, no. 5 (2019): 925–40.

19. Turner, *How the Other Half Ate*.

20. F. Scott. Fitzgerald, *The Great Gatsby* (New York: Charles Scribner's Sons, 1925), 4.

21. Franklin W. Dixon, *What Happened at Midnight* (New York: Grosset & Dunlap, 1931), 1.

22. Dixon, 3.

23. Andrew P. Haley, *Turning the Tables: Restaurants and the Rise of the American Middle Class, 1880–1920* (Chapel Hill: University of North Carolina Press, 2011).

24. Mark Kurlansky, *The Food of a Younger Land: A Portrait of American Food from the Lost WPA Files* (New York: Riverhead Books, 2009); Carolyn Hughes Crowley, "Meet Me at the Automat," *Smithsonian Magazine*, August 2001.

25. Hughes Crowley.

26. Angelika Epple, "The 'Automat': A History of Technological Transfer and the Process of Global Standardization in Modern Fast Food around 1900," *Food and History* 7, no. 2 (2009): 97–118.

27. Kurlansky, *Food of a Younger Land*, 42–43.

28. Robert G. Benchley, "The Automat of the Luncheon Table," *New York Tribune*, January 14, 1917.

29. Nicolas Bromell, "The Automat: Preparing the Way for Fast Food," *Periodicals Archive Online* 81, no. 3 (2000): 300–312.

30. Bromell.

31. David Freeland, *Automats, Taxi Dances, and Vaudeville: Excavating Manhattan's Lost Places of Leisure* (New York: New York University Press, 2009).

32. Institute for Motivational Research Inc., "Public Attitudes toward Horn & Hardart Company Operations: A Motivational Research Study," May 1965, Market Research and American Business Reports, 1935–1965, EDP.

33. Turner, *How the Other Half Ate*, 83.

34. Turner.

35. Advertisement, *New York Herald*, September 7, 1929.

36. Hughes Crowley, "Meet Me at the Automat."

37. "Gives His Hamburger Steak to Health Department," *Chicago Defender,* September 11, 1920.

38. Wilson J. Warren, *Tied to the Great Packing Machine: The Midwest and Meatpacking* (Iowa City: University of Iowa Press, 2006).

39. Upton Sinclair, *The Jungle* (1906; repr., New York: Bantam Dell, 2003), 142.

40. Warren, *Tied to the Great Packing Machine,* 146.

41. See, for example, the recounting by Livingston Johnson, a Pittsburgh activist in the 1960s, of his experience attempting to enter a roller-skating rink in the 1930s: "The ticket collector told me, 'get out of here; these people will kill you.' I got out." Victoria W. Wolcott, *Race, Riots, and Roller Coasters: The Struggle over Segregated Recreation in America* (Philadelphia: University of Pennsylvania Press, 2012), 13.

42. Wolcott.

43. Wolcott; Michael Eric Dyson, Alfred L. Brophy, and Randall Kennedy, *Reconstructing the Dreamland: The Tulsa Riot of 1921—Race, Reparation, and Reconciliation* (New York: Oxford University Press, 2003); Charles E. Coulter, *Take Up the Black Man's Burden: Kansas City's African American Communities, 1865–1939* (Columbia: University of Missouri Press, 2006).

44. Jeff Wiltse's history of swimming pools reveals the first officially segregated pool (Fairgrounds Park in St. Louis) as the first gender-integrated one as well, and this was no coincidence; Whites (primarily men, but speaking for all) did not want Black men near White women. Black residents who attempted to participate in the community-building taking place at swimming pools were often repelled by officers and pool staff, and if not, by White pool-goers' brutal and potentially fatal attacks. Time and again, officials left it to White swimmers to enforce the color line. Jeff Wiltse, *Contested Waters: A Social History of Swimming Pools in America* (Chapel Hill: University of North Carolina Press, 2007).

45. Wiltse.

46. In the mid-1980s, Illinois congressman Henry J. Hyde had to remind the city of Des Plaines's public relations office of that fact. The city wanted to designate Ray Kroc's first McDonald's, located in Des Plaines, a national landmark. Hyde replied that apart from the designation being out of his office's jurisdiction, "There was a feeling, also that McDonald's overstated the role of its corporation in the fast food business. While it is by far the largest, other smaller companies had been serving fast food for 30 or 40 years before. White Castle is but one example of these older companies." Henry J. Hyde, House of Representatives, Congress of the United States, Washington, D.C., to Karen M. Hendrikson, Public Relations, City of Des Plaines, Illinois, September 5, 1986, MCDDP.

47. Jakle and Skulle, *Fast Food.*

48. David G. Hogan, *Selling 'em by the Sack* (New York: New York University Press, 1997), 49.

49. Hogan.

50. Hogan; Marilyn Nierenberg, "Hamburger's 1st Stand a Castle," *Chicago Tribune,* July 15, 1978.

51. According to 1920 census data and city directories available on the Ancestry historical records database (http://www.ancestry.com/), Ingram lived at that time on Carter St. in Riverside, a centrally located, amenity-rich, leafy residential neighborhood between the city's two rivers.

52. Loewen, *Sundown Town*; Brent M. S. Campney, *This Is Not Dixie: Racist Violence in Kansas, 1861–1972* (Urbana: University of Illinois Press, 2015).

53. Campney, 107.

54. Hogan, *Selling 'em by the Sack,* 31.

55. Hogan.

56. Laura J. Miller, *Building Nature's Market: The Business and Politics of Natural Foods* (Chicago: University of Chicago Press, 2017); Richard Longstreth, *The Drive-In, the Supermarket, and the Transformation of Commercial Space in Los Angeles, 1914–1941* (Cambridge, Mass.: The MIT Press, 1999).

57. Ernest Fleischman, *The Modern Luncheonette: Planning, Layout, Construction, Operation: A Practical Guide to Success in the Luncheonette and Restaurant Business* (Stamford, Conn.: Dahl, 1947).

58. Hogan, *Selling 'em by the Sack.*

59. Advertisement, *Chicago Tribune,* January 16, 1938.

60. Naa Oyo A. Kwate, *Burgers in Blackface: Anti-Black Restaurants Then and Now* (Minneapolis: University of Minnesota Press, 2019).

61. Cohen, *Making a New Deal.*

62. Allan H. Spear, *Black Chicago: The Making of a Negro Ghetto* (Chicago: University of Chicago Press, 1967).

63. "The Colored Waiter," *The Inter Ocean,* June 18, 1912; Archibald H. Grimke, "Survival of the Fittest Servants," *New York Age,* October 5, 1905; Alex E. Sweet, "The Negro in Gotham: He Is Numerous and Fills Many Public Places," *Onaga Herald,* June 20, 1895.

64. Cohen, *Making a New Deal.*

65. Alberta Baylor was one exception, having started as a floor worker before a promotion to "silver girl" and finally to the sandwich table at an Automat on Philadelphia's Market Street. *Horn & Hardart Highlights* 6, no. 2 (Fall 1961): 43, H&HR.

66. Alec Tristin Shuldiner, "Trapped behind the Automat: Technological Systems and the American Restaurant, 1902–1991" (Ph.D. diss., Cornell University, 2001). One such employee was Gladys Richardson, featured in the *Saturday Evening Post* for having worked as an onion peeler for twenty-five years. Jack Alexander, "The Restaurants That Nickels Built," *Saturday Evening Post,* December 22–23, 1954.

67. Melvin S. Barasch, "Good Riddance," *NYT,* April 26, 1991.

68. Making Black labor invisible was not unique to Horn & Hardart. Sociologist Ester Reiter recalled her experience working as a teenager in a New York restaurant chain in the 1950s: "There were no black waitresses. In sub-basement B, where food preparation took place, about half the workforce were visible minorities who worked as kitchen 'aids.'" Ester Reiter, *Making Fast Food: From the Frying Pan into the Fryer* (Montreal: McGill University Press, 1991).

69. "CORE Pickets Resume Action, Talks Ignored," *Chicago Daily Defender,* December 11, 1961.

70. New York City Landmarks Preservation Commission, Horn & Hardart Automat—Cafeteria Building, January 30, 2007, Designation List 385, LP-2192.

71. Howard Fauntleroy had been employed for fifteen years; he was outdone by Callie Tomlin's thirty-seven years and the forty-plus years served by Earl Wilson, Norwood Henson, Edgar Searles, and Charles Church. Their history was celebrated in the company's newsletters

(available at H&HR), which made note of entrants to the "25-Year Club" and other such commendations. Nonetheless, five minutes of fame in print did not undo the harsh reality of these positions.

72. Freeland, *Automats, Taxi Dances, and Vaudeville*.

73. *Horn & Hardart Herald* 3, no. 1 (January–February 1955), H&HR.

74. Hughes Crowley, "Meet Me at the Automat"; Epple, "The 'Automat.'" Regarding the reams of cash, in 1932, for example, it netted over $2.7 million (more than $50 million in today's dollars).

75. New York City Landmarks Preservation Commission, Horn & Hardart Automat—Cafeteria Building, January 30, 2007, Designation List 385, LP-2192.

76. Freeland, *Automats, Taxi Dances, and Vaudeville*, 174; emphasis added.

77. Angela Jill Cooley, *To Live and Dine in Dixie: The Evolution of Urban Food Culture in the Jim Crow South* (Athens: University of Georgia Press, 2015).

78. Alex Haley and Malcolm X, *The Autobiography of Malcolm X: As Told to Alex Haley* (New York: Ballantine, 1989), 85.

79. The following search on the Ancestry 1940 census database (http://www.ancestry.com/) yields 1,676 hits: lived in New York, N.Y.; occupation = counterman (exact); keyword = restaurant (exact); gender = male; and race = white (exact). Several of these men lived outside of New York at the time of the census, but the interface does not allow specification of current residence. Running the same search with race = negro produces only thirty-three hits. I examined a sample of thirty-two pairs of these men's salaries.

80. Hogan, *Selling 'em by the Sack*.

81. Hogan.

82. "Riot Trained Police Keep Vigil at Bronx Restaurant," *Chicago Daily Defender*, July 9, 1963.

83. Hogan, *Selling 'em by the Sack*.

84. Hogan.

85. Elizabeth Schroeder Schlabach, *Along the Streets of Bronzeville: Black Chicago's Literary Landscape* (Urbana: University of Illinois Press, 2012).

86. "Another Attempt to Make Big Biz Fill 'Bubbly Creek,'" *Day Book*, October 10, 1916; "Stockyards Smell Better Than That, Expert Sniffer Says," *Freeport Journal-Standard*, August 13, 1947; "Aldermen Plan to Abate Odor of Stockyards," *Chicago Tribune*, November 14, 1919; "Desire for Economy Causes the Stockyards Smell," *Day Book*, December 15, 1913; "New Lake to Zoo Street to Bury 'Bubbly Creek,'" *Chicago Tribune*, April 25, 1920.

87. "The Inquiring Reporter: Every Day He Asks Five Persons, Picked at Random, a Question," *Chicago Tribune*, September 30, 1920.

88. Minnesota saw its share of racist violence and lynchings (Ralph Ginzburg, *100 Years of Lynchings*. [Baltimore: Black Classic Press, 1988]). Thomas Sr. and Jr. together were the principals of Saxe Realty Corp. in Milwaukee. Thomas Sr. and his brother John also ran Saxe Amusement Enterprises, a company that operated movie theaters and amusement parks at a time when they were hostile to Black visitors. The Saxes' theaters numbered in the dozens across the state of Wisconsin, many of which were located in confirmed sundown towns (e.g., Janesville, Appleton), probable sundown towns (e.g., Marinette, Wausau, Menasha, Stevens Point), or possible sundown towns (Oshkosh, Whitefish Bay). (Loewen, *Sundown Towns*; "Sundown Towns," His-

tory and Social Justice, n.d., http://sundown.tougaloo.edu/sundowntowns.php.) In Oshkosh, constituents saw the Reverend Daniel Woodward, great titan of the Ku Klux Klan, run (unsuccessfully) for the U.S. Senate. Klan activity was normative enough that Woodward wrote into local newspapers to clarify the group's finances related to a tabernacle campaign (*Journal Times,* December 4, 1926; *Oshkosh Northwestern,* January 4, 1927). Indeed, just two years prior, the Klan staged a march there numbering at least fifteen thousand, welcomed by the town's vice mayor. The day also included weddings of Klan couples from Milwaukee and Madison. ("Big Ku Klux Klan Demonstration Is Staged at Oshkosh," *Green Bay Gazette,* July 6, 1925).

89. "Sundown Towns," History and Social Justice, n.d., http://sundown.tougaloo.edu /sundowntowns.php. By 1947 Saxe Jr. had moved to the East Coast, to another exclusively White and wealthy enclave, New Canaan, Connecticut (city directories and ship passenger lists, Ancestry, http://www.ancestry.com/).

90. Hogan, *Selling 'em by the Sack.*

91. The architecture facilitated cleaning because white tile, metal, and the like were easy to wash and scrub, and did not retain stains as wood surfaces might. Paul Hirshorn and Steven Izenour, *White Towers* (Cambridge, Mass.: The MIT Press, 2008), 120.

92. Cooley, *To Live and Dine in Dixie.*

93. Hirshorn and Izenour, *White Towers,* 57.

94. Jakle and Skulle, *Fast Food.*

95. Hirshorn and Izenour, *White Towers.*

96. Hirshorn and Izenour.

97. Sanborn Map Company, *Sanborn Fire Insurance Maps of District of Columbia,* 1927–1960; Hirshorn and Izenour.

98. Hirshorn and Izenour, *White Towers,* 9.

99. In September 1913, Henry Crosby was lynched in Louisville for asking a White woman at a farmhouse an "impertinent question" (that being whether her husband was home). Officers searching for him found him hanging from a tree the next day. In March 1921, Richard James was hanged in Versailles, sixty-one miles from Louisville, charged with murdering two guards at a local distillery. Ginzburg, *100 Years of Lynchings.*

100. Standalone comic (no title), *Courier-Journal,* November 10, 1928.

101. W. D. Binford, superintendent of the *Courier-Journal* mechanical department, spoke at a meeting of the city's real estate exchange: "There is no problem so grave, nor one fraught with so much danger to property values, as the gradual influx of the negro into blocks or squares where none but whites resides." Binford warned that some White Baltimoreans felt immune to the threat, having not yet experienced any Black neighbors. But they would learn their lesson when a Black family disrupted their lives for profit: "The negro doesn't always attempt to purchase and locate in an exclusively White section of his own volition, nor does he expect to be welcomed as a neighbor. His purpose is purely mercenary." "Segregation of Races Is Urged. W. D. Binford Asks Enactment of Ordinance. Addresses Real Estate Exchange at Luncheon. Explains Measure in Force in Baltimore. Tells of Negro Invasion," *Courier-Journal,* November 15, 1913.

102. Claudia Levy, "A Rich Life of Burgers: Business Also a Hobby," *Washington Post, Times Herald,* May 30, 1973.

103. DeFerrari, *Historic Restaurants of Washington, D.C.*

104. In 1940 Duncan was drawing a salary at the highest end of the census taker's scale (above $5,000, or about $100,000 today). Divorced, Duncan lived on Connecticut Avenue NW, between Cleveland Park and Woodley Park, paying seventy-three dollars per month for the privilege of renting at the Kennedy-Warren, a towering art deco luxury residence built only nine years prior and designed to be ultramodern. Excluding individuals perceived as downscale, especially Black people, would have been central to the building's goals. The *Washington Post* said as much in veiled language describing the tenants' exclusivity: "To this end it was necessary that the management observe the highest standards in the selection of tenants who will aid in maintaining the character of the property." "Attractive Service Management's Aim. Owners of Kennedy-Warren Want Tenants Who Will Be Permanent," *Washington Post*, September 13, 1931. The Kennedy-Warren claimed residents working in a variety of high-prestige jobs. The only Black residents in the building were live-in cleaning staff, chauffeurs, and the building janitor (1940 census archives, Ancestry, http://www.ancestry.com/). By 1940, Ingram was enjoying a life of affluence as president of White Castle Systems. He had remarried and occupied a $35,000 house on Roxbury Road in Columbus, Ohio, with a live-in staff. Edgar Jr., now twenty-nine, worked as a purchasing agent for White Castle, drawing a salary of $2,500 per year. By the mid-1950s, he was assistant vice president of White Castle System Inc. and lived just outside Columbus in Worthington, where his children attended school with only a handful of Black classmates (1920 and 1940 census data and school directory/yearbook information, Ancestry, http://www.ancestry.com/).

105. Hogan, *Selling 'em by the Sack.*

106. Advertisement, *Chicago Tribune*, November 11, 1934.

107. Hogan, *Selling 'em by the Sack.*

108. "Grandaddy of the Hamburger," *Fast Food Magazine*, March 1957.

109. Hogan, *Selling 'em by the Sack.*

110. Warren, *Tied to the Great Packing Machine.*

111. Jakle and Skulle, *Fast Food.*

112. Hogan, *Selling 'em by the Sack.*

113. Matthew Delmont, *The Nicest Kids in Town: American Bandstand, Rock 'n' Roll, and the Struggle for Civil Rights in 1950s Philadelphia* (Berkeley: University of California Press, 2012).

114. Davarian L. Baldwin, *Chicago's New Negroes: Modernity, the Great Migration, and Black Urban Life* (Chapel Hill: University of North Carolina Press, 2007), 31.

115. Khalil Gibran Muhammad, *The Condemnation of Blackness: Race, Crime, and the Making of Modern America* (Cambridge, Mass.: Harvard University Press, 2010).

116. Spear, *Black Chicago*; Muhammad.

117. Katharina Vester, *A Taste of Power: Food and American Identities* (Berkeley: University of California Press, 2015).

118. Hogan, *Selling 'em by the Sack*; Elizabeth Abel, *Signs of the Times: The Visual Politics of Jim Crow* (Berkeley: University of California Press, 2010).

2. Inharmonious Food Groups

1. Robert K. Nelson, LaDale Winling, Richard Marciano, et al. "Mapping Inequality," *American Panorama*, 2015, https://dsl.richmond.edu/panorama/redlining.

2. David M. P. Freund, *Colored Property: State Policy and White Racial Politics in Suburban America* (Chicago: University of Chicago Press, 2007), 158.

3. "Await Judge's Decision in Discrimination Cases," *Chicago Defender,* October 15, 1938. At the time of the article's publication, the case, filed by Mr. John F. Potts and his wife and Benjamin Wilson, an attorney, and his wife, was being considered by Judge B. C. Jenkins. White Castle had filed a demurrer to the action.

4. Christopher Robert Reed, *The Rise of Chicago's Black Metropolis, 1920–1929* (Urbana: University of Illinois Press, 2011); Elizabeth Schroeder Schlabach, *Along the Streets of Bronzeville: Black Chicago's Literary Landscape* (Urbana: University of Illinois Press, 2012).

5. Freund, *Colored Property,* 14. This statement was made by the Property Owners Association in Kenwood and Hyde Park in 1920.

6. Katherine Leonard Turner, *How the Other Half Ate: A History of Working-Class Meals at the Turn of the Century* (Berkeley: University of California Press, 2014).

7. Turner; Tracey N. Poe, "The Origins of Soul Food in Black Urban Identity: Chicago, 1915–1947," *American Studies International* 37 (1999): 4–33; Lizabeth Cohen, *Making a New Deal: Industrial Workers in Chicago, 1919–1939* (New York: Cambridge University Press, 2008); Richard Longstreth, *The Drive-in, the Supermarket, and the Transformation of Commercial Space in Los Angeles, 1914–1941* (Cambridge, Mass.: MIT Press, 1999).

8. Lizabeth Cohen, *A Consumers' Republic: The Politics of Mass Consumption in Postwar America* (New York: Knopf, 2003); Tanisha C. Ford, *Liberated Threads: Black Women, Style, and the Global Politics of Soul* (Chapel Hill: University of North Carolina Press, 2015); Jennifer Jensen Wallach, *Every Nation Has Its Dish: Black Bodies and Black Food in Twentieth-Century America* (Chapel Hill: University of North Carolina Press, 2019).

9. Wallach.

10. Cohen, *Consumer's Republic.*

11. Black New Yorkers dealt with retail discrimination in many ways at this time. During World War II, rationing systems meant to prevent hoarding and inequalities in food distribution functioned rather loosely in stores where Black Americans shopped, and customers could not count on price controls. For example, the NAACP found that Black residents paid 6 percent more for food of inferior quality, and complaints to the Office of Price Administration (OPA) did nothing. Eventually, in August 1943, a "commodity riot" broke out in Harlem, and White-owned stores guilty of overcharging were destroyed while Black-owned stores were spared. Damage on 125th Street totaled between $3 million and $5 million. Whereas unrest during the Great Depression centered on merchants' refusals to hire Black employees, in this case "African American wrath targeted those who brought undue suffering to consumers." Within a week of the disorder, the OPA opened a local office, but President Roosevelt's administration continued to avoid dealing with Black community's grievances. Retail was brought into bold relief as a site where the government was unwilling to extend the full protections due to all Americans, and where local operators were committed to upholding the color line. Lizzie Collingham, *The Taste of War: World War II and the Battle for Food* (New York: Penguin, 2012), 11, 96; Cohen, *Consumers' Republic,* 426.

12. Chin Jou, "Neither Welcomed, Nor Refused: Race and Restaurants in Postwar New York City," *Journal of Urban History* 40, no. 2 (2014): 232–51.

13. In small local restaurants, for example, Black New Yorkers learned to eat the foods of their White ethnic counterparts, such as knishes and Italian sausages. Turner, *How the Other Half Ate.*

14. St. Clair Drake and Horace R. Cayton, *Black Metropolis: A Study of Negro Life in a Northern City* (1945; repr., New York: Harper Torchbooks, 1962).

15. Poe, "Origins of Soul Food."

16. Davarian L. Baldwin, *Chicago's New Negroes, Modernity, the Great Migration and Black Urban Life* (Chapel Hill: University of North Carolina Press, 2007).

17. Reed, *Rise of Chicago's Black Metropolis*; Schlabach, *Along the Streets of Bronzeville.*

18. Frederick Opie, *Hog and Hominy: Soul Food from Africa to America* (New York: Columbia University Press, 2010).

19. Alma D. Green, ed., *The Negro Travelers' Green Book: Guide for Travel and Vacations* (New York: Victor H. Green & Co., 1962).

20. Thanks to Psyche Williams-Forson for this insight.

21. Cohen, *Consumer's Republic.*

22. Turner, *How the Other Half Ate.*

23. Wallach, *Every Nation Has Its Dish.*

24. Poe, "Origins of Soul Food."

25. Maren Stange, *Bronzeville: Black Chicago in Pictures, 1941–1943* (New York: New Press, 2003).

26. Wallach, *Every Nation Has Its Dish*, 39.

27. Wallach.

28. Wallach.

29. Wallach, 14.

30. Wallach.

31. Wallach, 26.

32. Paul Sayres, *Food Facts to Help Sell Grocery Products in the Greater New York Market* (New York: Paul Sayres Company, 1944).

33. Psyche A. Williams-Forson, *Building Houses Out of Chicken Legs: Black Women, Food, and Power* (Chapel Hill: University of North Carolina Press, 2006).

34. Wallach, *Every Nation Has Its Dish.*

35. Wallach.

36. "Hamburger and Ice Cream Prove Fatal," *Chicago Defender*, August 8, 1936.

37. John William Severin Gouley, *Diseases of Man* (New York: J. H. Vall & Co., 1888); Edward Geist, "When Ice Cream Was Poisonous: Adulteration, Ptomaines, and Bacteriology in the United States, 1850–1910," *Bulletin of the History of Medicine* 86, no. 3 (2012): 333–60. And even still, on the twenty-first-century television show *Mad Men*, set in the 1960s, one character jokes that another risks ptomaine poisoning from the office food cart.

38. Ann Petry, *The Street* (New York: Houghton Mifflin, 1946), 61–62.

39. David H. Orro, "Says Neighborhood Too Classy for Hamburgers," *Chicago Defender*, February 10, 1940.

40. A. N. Fields, "There's a Need for Restrictive Covenants," *Chicago Defender*, November 20, 1948.

41. The *Chicago Defender* published 778,192 articles between 1910 and 1949; of these, 190, or

0.02 percent, mentioned the word "hamburger." In contrast, between 1860 and 1949, 0.5 percent of the *Philadelphia Inquirer*'s 766,320 articles mentioned the word, and a similar 0.4 percent of the *Pittsburgh Post-Gazette*'s 532,659 between 1840 and 1949.

42. Arnold R. Hirsch, *Making the Second Ghetto: Race and Housing in Chicago, 1940–1960* (Cambridge: Cambridge University Press, 1983); Dorceta E. Taylor, *Toxic Communities: Environmental Racism, Industrial Pollution, and Residential Mobility* (New York: New York University Press, 2014).

43. Samuel Zipp, *Manhattan Projects: The Rise and Fall of Urban Renewal in Cold War New York* (New York: Oxford University Press, 2010).

44. Zipp, 8.

45. Longstreth, *Drive-In.*

46. Newspaper clipping, *North Jersey Edition*, March 27, 1937, H&HR.

47. Montclair Gardens, 35-35 75th Street, YR.0656.QNS, http://nyre.cul.columbia.edu/projects /view/YR.0656.QNS. Elsewhere in Jackson Heights, the Elbertson boasted that management would make "careful and restricted selection of tenants" and that appropriate references were required. Elbertson, 35th Avenue and 80th Street, YR.0407.QNS, http://nyre.cul.columbia.edu /projects/view/YR.0407.QNS. The same language appeared in the offering for the Leslie in Forest Hills, which "caters strictly to a restricted clientele." The Leslie, 150 Greenay Terrace, YR.0130.QNS, http://nyre.cul.columbia.edu/projects/view/YR.0130.QNS. All in New York Real Estate Brochure Collection, Avery Architectural and Fine Arts Library, Columbia University.

48. "First Automat Restaurant Here to Open in Boro Hall Section," *Brooklyn Daily Eagle*, June 28, 1936.

49. Nicholas Dagen Bloom, *Public Housing That Worked: New York in the Twentieth Century* (Philadelphia: University of Pennsylvania Press, 2008).

50. Advertisement, *Brooklyn Daily Eagle*, August 16, 1942.

51. Social Explorer, "Census Tract Data," n.d., https://www.socialexplorer.com/.

52. Zipp, *Manhattan Projects.* Robert Moses, New York City's Parks Department commissioner, expressed unabashedly racist views about African Americans, which were codified in the planning initiatives that reshaped the physical works in every corner of the five boroughs. For example, he used his power to keep Black beachgoers away from Long Island's Jones Beach by a number of measures, including building bridges low enough over roadways to preclude passage by buses (given that Black New Yorkers were less likely to own cars). Robert A. Caro, *The Power Broker: Robert Moses and the Fall of New York* (New York: Vintage, 1975).

53. "Texts of Eisenhower, Baruch, and Moses Talks at Housing Project," *NYT*, August 20, 1953. Paul Holland, commissioner of the Community Conservation Board of Chicago, used the same language of medical pathology in his assessment of urban renewal in Northeast and Midwest cities at the close of the 1950s. For him, urban renewal tackled the "malignant disease" of "urban blight." Holland saw the citizenry as having tried to amputate a gangrenous limb by fleeing to the suburbs and turning their backs "on the sorry mess behind them." But that was not successful, and so "whole neighborhoods, whole communities, whole areas have had to be cut out with the dull, plodding heartless, and relentless bulldozers." Woodlawn Block Club Council, Special Collections Division, box 1, folder 3, Harold Washington Library Center, Chicago Public Library.

54. Davarian L. Baldwin, "The '800-Pound Gargoyle': The Long History of Higher Education and Urban Development on Chicago's South Side," *American Quarterly* 67, no. 1 (2015): 81–103; Brian J. L. Berry, Sandra J. Parsons, and Rutherford H. Platt, *The Impact of Urban Renewal on Small Business: The Hyde Park–Kenwood Case* (Chicago: Center for Urban Studies, University of Chicago, 1968).

55. Baldwin, "800-Pound Gargoyle."

56. Baldwin.

57. Berry, Parsons, and Platt, *Impact of Urban Renewal*.

58. Berry, Parsons, and Platt; Muriel Beadle, *The Hyde Park Kenwood Urban Renewal Years: A History to Date* (n.p., 1967), Hanna Holborn Special Collections Research Center, University of Chicago. Beadle was the wife of University of Chicago president George W. Beadle, and she herself served as president of the Harper Court Foundation.

59. The Humpty Dumpty Snack Shop was for sale at this location in 1952. Pierce may have started his restaurant there since the site was already set up for food service, but newspaper accounts state that Harold's launched in 1950, which would be impossible if Humpty Dumpty was still active in 1952, unless both outlets shared an address. *Chicago Tribune*, July 27, 1952.

60. Another Black-owned H & H Cafe operated on the South Side, at 125 East 51st Street. Mr. and Mrs. Hubert Maybell owned the restaurant, which was open at least as early as 1959 and was still in business in 1971. At that time, the owners advertised it as a place "for the finest experiences in up-to-date soul food." "Chamber Forms Cafe Division," *Chicago Defender*, December 10, 1960; Women's Auxiliary Chicago Southside Branch Thirty-First Anniversary Tea, 1971, program book, E. Winston and Ina D. Williams NAACP Papers, box 2, folder 32, Newberry Library, Chicago.

61. "Southside Man Opens New Shop," *Chicago Defender*, May 8, 1965; classified advertisement, *Chicago Tribune*, January 29, 1942; "Chicken King Harold P. Pierce, 70, Obituary," *Chicago Tribune*, March 11, 1988; "Harold's Chicken Shack to Move," *Chicago Defender*, July 21, 1962; "The First Family of Fried Chicken," *Chicago Reader*, April 14, 2006.

62. Mary Pattillo, *Black on the Block: The Politics of Race and Class in the City* (Chicago: University of Chicago Press, 2007).

63. Mitchell Duneier, *Slim's Table: Race, Respectability, and Masculinity* (Chicago: University of Chicago Press, 1992).

64. "Appendix B, photocopies of 'Commercial Establishments in the Hyde Park–S. Kenwood Urban Renewal Area,' lists of relocated and vacated businesses and properties, ca. 1960s," Hyde Park–Kenwood Razed Buildings Collection, box 5, folder 42, Hanna Holborn Special Collections Research Center, University of Chicago.

65. Cheryl I. Harris, "The Afterlife of Slavery: Markets, Property and Race," Artists Space, New York, January 17, 2016, https://youtu.be/dQQGndN3BvY.

66. David G. Hogan, *Selling 'em by the Sack* (New York: New York University Press, 1997).

3. Suburbs and Sundown Towns

1. Frank C. Porter, "Hamburger Chains Vie for Area Trade," *Washington Post and Times Herald*, July 14, 1959.

2. "Display Ad 70: No Title," *Washington Post*, May 27, 1960; "Display Ad 202: No Title," *NYT*,

November 15, 1959; advertisement, *Arlington Heights Herald,* September 4, 1958; "Golden Point Hamburgers Same Size Coast to Coast," *Arlington Heights Herald,* May 7, 1959.

3. Lizabeth Cohen, *A Consumers' Republic: The Politics of Mass Consumption in Postwar America* (New York: Knopf, 2003).

4. Cohen.

5. Lizzie Collingham, *The Taste of War: World War II and the Battle for Food* (New York: Penguin, 2012); Vicki Howard, *From Main Street to Mall: The Rise and Fall of the American Department Store* (Philadelphia: University of Pennsylvania Press, 2015).

6. Howard.

7. "Free Parking Big Factor in Silver Spring Success Story: Silver Spring Lures Business," *Washington Post,* November 27, 1949.

8. "Classified Ads," *Chicago Tribune,* February 14, 1958.

9. David G. Hogan, *Selling 'em by the Sack* (New York: New York University Press, 1997), 124.

10. Hogan, 146–47.

11. Paul Hirshorn and Steven Izenour, *White Towers* (Cambridge, Mass.: MIT Press, 2008), 22.

12. "Four Boys Seized in Little Tavern Holdup on E St.," *Washington Post,* January 6, 1938; "Youthful Bandits Rob Restaurant," *Washington Post,* February 11, 1937.

13. As noted previously, Black-owned businesses suffered nationwide from the urban renewal wrecking ball. In Detroit, Nelson Cloud, a candy store and restaurant owner, lost one thousand dollars per month while waiting to settle with the city, which was an early entrant to urban renewal. "Can Subsidies Solve America's Problems? A University's Answer," *Nation's Business,* August 1965, 34.

14. Hirshorn and Izenour, *White Towers,* 181.

15. John F. Love, *McDonald's: Behind the Arches* (New York: Bantam, 1995), 294.

16. "Convention-Goers Guide to Dining in the Coliseum Area," 1957, Robert Twain Publishing Co. Road Map and Travel Ephemera Collection record group Z: United States, Series 25: New York, box 47, folder—NY Places, NYC, General Visitor Information 1938–ca. 2010, Newberry Library, Chicago.

17. Horn & Hardart Company, Annual Report Year Ending December 31, 1949, box 1, RFBC.

18. Horn & Hardart Company, Annual Report Year Ending December 31, 1953, box 1, RFBC.

19. Horn & Hardart 1953 Annual Report, 2.

20. Horn & Hardart 1953 Annual Report.

21. Howard, *From Main Street to Mall;* Gene Boyo, "Wanamaker to Close Main Store after 58 Years on Broadway Site," *NYT,* October 26, 1954.

22. Howard; Rosten Woo, Meredith TenHoor, and Damon Rich, *Street Value: Shopping, Planning, and Politics at Fulton Mall* (New York: Princeton Architectural Press, 2010).

23. Morton Grodzins, *The Metropolitan Area as a Racial Problem,* 7th ed. (Pittsburgh: University of Pittsburgh Press, 1966), 12.

24. John A. Jakle and Keith A Skulle, *Fast Food: Roadside Restaurants in the Automobile Age* (Baltimore: Johns Hopkins University Press, 1999); Love, *Behind the Arches.*

25. "John Brown and His Ever-Growing Family Invite You to Try Their Very Tasty (and

Remarkably Low Priced) Fried Chicken," *Chicago Tribune*, August 14, 1965; "The Story of Brown's Chicken," *Berwyn Life*, June 18, 1965.

26. Jakle and Skulle, *Fast Food*; Love, *Behind the Arches*.

27. Jakle and Skulle; Love; Philip Langdon, *Orange Roofs, Golden Arches: The Architecture of American Chain Restaurants* (New York: Random House, 1986).

28. James W. Loewen, *Sundown Towns: A Hidden Dimension of Segregation in America* (New York: The New Press, 2005).

29. "Kentucky Town Expels Negroes," *Reading Times*, November 1, 1919.

30. Loewen, *Sundown Towns*.

31. Jack Perkins, host, *Colonel Sanders: America's Chicken King* (New York: A&E Television Networks, 1998).

32. Duncan Hines, *Adventures in Good Eating: Good Eating Places along the Highways of America* (Bowling Green, Ky.: Adventures in Good Eating Inc., 1940), https://www.hathitrust.org/. Stephen C. Foster, Walter Kittredge, et al., *The Old Plantation Melodies*, illus. Charles Copeland and Mary H. Foote (New York: H. M. Caldwell Co., 1890), https://www.hathitrust.org/.

33. John T. Edge, *The Potlikker Papers: A Food History of the Modern South* (New York: Penguin, 2017), 111.

34. Edge.

35. Robert Metz, *Franchising: How to Select a Business of Your Own* (New York: Hawthorn Books, 1969).

36. Perkins, *Colonel Sanders*.

37. "Legal Notices," *Murray Eagle*, February 4, 1949.

38. Jakle and Skulle, *Fast Food*; "Business Notes along State Street," *Murray Eagle*, June 15, 1951.

39. Perkins, *Colonel Sanders*.

40. The chain only adopted the abbreviated KFC in 1986, but given contemporary parlance and variation in naming across different citations I use both the names Kentucky Fried Chicken and KFC interchangeably throughout the book.

41. Edge, *Potlikker Papers*, 111.

42. Edge.

43. "The Colonel and the Kids," *Chicago Tribune*, March 6, 1966.

44. "Negro Buys Tract House," *Valley Times Today*, July 13, 1963; Paul Weeks, "Builder in Torrance Rejects Negro's Offer," *Los Angeles Times*, July 25, 1963.

45. David Whittingham with the Des Plaines Public Library and Des Plaines History Center, *Des Plaines: Images of America* (Charleston, S.C.: Arcadia, 2012); "Niles Retains Home Building Permits Lead," *Chicago Tribune*, July 3, 1955.

46. "New Committee Not Paving Ground for Race Integration," *Des Plaines Suburban Times*, May 13, 1962; "Howard Goes Home, but Asks to Come Back," *Des Plaines Day*, September 11, 1968. In Arlington Heights, seven-year-old African American Howard Settle befriended agemate Bob Nelson; reticent at first, Howard eventually opened up, and it was "just like adding any extra child to the family" averred Mrs. Nelson. Jan Bone, "Suburb, City Play Together in Friendly Town," *Des Plaines Day*, September 6, 1968.

47. Love, *Behind the Arches*.

48. Interview with Jim McGovern, one of the original crew at the Des Plaines McDonald's. He started his first job as a teenager at the new restaurant in the summer of 1956, one of the younger employees among a staff comprising mostly twentysomething Air Force recruits stationed at O'Hare Airport. McGovern, in discussion with the author, March 17, 2015, Des Plaines History Center, Des Plaines, Illinois.

49. Jakle and Skulle, *Fast Food;* Whittingham, *Des Plaines;* advertisement, *Des Plaines Suburban Times,* June 2, 1955; photograph of the intersection at Lee Street and Des Plaines Avenue, MCDDP; advertisement, *Des Plaines Suburban Times,* April 14, 1955.

50. "Display Ad," *Chicago Daily Tribune,* Nov. 17, 1960; Illinois Bell Telephone Company, *Chicago Telephone Numbers, June 1959* (Chicago: Illinois Bell Telephone Company, 1958–59). The restaurant on Cicero is identified in the McDonald's archives (MCDDP) as 4820 North Cicero, but this is likely a typo. There was a 4830 South Cicero some years later, but consumer phone books, street address directories, and newspaper advertisements show only 4320 North Cicero.

51. Brian J. L. Berry, Sandra J. Parsons, and Rutherford H. Platt, *The Impact of Urban Renewal on Small Business: The Hyde Park–Kenwood Case* (Chicago: Center for Urban Studies, University of Chicago, 1968).

52. "Minutes from the December 14, 1958, Meeting," Woodlawn Block Club Council Inc. Records, box 1, folder 3, Special Collections, Chicago Public Library; "Area Buildings Demolished as Part of Beautification Program," *Woodlawn Booster,* August 1, 1967; "Despres Seeks Better Deal for Community," *Woodlawn Booster,* August 1, 1967; John Hall Fish, *Black Power / White Control: The Struggle of the Woodlawn Organization in Chicago* (Princeton, N.J.: Princeton University Press, 1973); "Area Buildings Demolished as Part of Beautification Program: Hazards, Eyesores Removed," *Woodlawn Booster,* August 1, 1967.

53. Hyde Park High School Yearbook, 1955, Chicago, https://www.ancestry.com/.

54. "Cross Country Shopper," *Arlington Heights Herald,* May 5, 1960; "Consumer Needs Got Top Plaza Priority," *Daily Herald,* July 21, 1960.

55. "Other People's Business," *Chicago Defender,* November 16, 1963; A. L. Foster, "Other People's Business," *Chicago Defender,* May 17, 1958.

56. *Washington, DC, White Pages Covering Lentz through Z for Areas Ashton, MD, Bowie, MD, Brandywine, MD, Damascus, MD, Engleside, VA, Fairfax County, VA, Gaithersburg, MD, Herndon, VA, Laurel, MD, Poolesville, MD, Waldorf, MD, and Washington, DC,* 1958.

57. Patricia Sowell Harris, *None of Us Is as Good as All of Us: How McDonald's Prospers by Embracing Inclusion and Diversity* (New York: Wiley, 2009).

58. "John Gibson, Businessman, Labor Official under Truman," *Washington Post,* October 24, 1976, obituaries; United Press, *Washington Post,* July 4, 1948.

59. City of Alexandria Planning Commission Minutes, April 1, 1958, and May 6, 1958, p. 721; "Petition" City Clerk's Office, September 5, 1958; Edith P. Cazenove to the City Council, September 4, 1958; Special Use Permit No. 442, George P. Kettle, Enterprises, May 23, 1961, City Council Minutes; City of Alexandria Planning Commission Minutes, May 10, 1961, all in the City of Alexandria Archives, Alexandria, Virginia.

60. The Alexandria Planning Commission considered and initially denied Gee Gee's application for a special use permit for outdoor signage at 3510 Duke Street. The property abutted residentially zoned and occupied property, and as such "the installation of an oversize neon lighted

sign at this location would have an adverse effect upon and be detrimental to the nearby property owners." The McDonald's restaurant and accompanying fifty-seven parking spaces were eventually built at a cost of $36,000, on August 5, 1960. City of Alexandria Planning Commission Minutes, November 3, 1959, p. 798; and Application for Permit to Build, City of Alexandria, Permit No. 7174, both in City of Alexandria Archives, Alexandria, Virginia.

61. Letter from Lilla Wood Daniels, November 5, 1959, City Council Minutes, November 10, 1959, City of Alexandria Archives, Alexandria, Virginia.

62. "What McDonald's Means to the Local Community," McDonald's press kits, 1964, box 5, folder 9, ABWP; McDonald's employee newsletters, June 1961, box 5, folder 13, ABWP.

63. Edward S. Cohen, "Mcdonald's Hamburger Chain Expands to 14 in D.C. Area," *Washington Post and Times Herald*, September 2, 1962.

64. Roland Jones, *Standing Up and Standing Out: How I Teamed with a Few Black Men, Changed the Face of McDonald's, and Shook Up Corporate America* (Nashville, Tenn.: World Solutions, 2000).

65. 4950 South Dakota was in census tract 952000, which was 44 percent Black; neighboring 953000 was 45 percent. In 1950 the area had been at 1 percent. In contrast, 75 New York Avenue in census tract 860000 was 95 percent Black in 1960, neighboring 460000 was 98 percent, and 470000 was 88 percent. It was essentially the same in 1950.

66. Isabel Wilkerson, *The Warmth of Other Suns: The Epic Story of America's Great Migration* (New York: Random House, 2010), 59.

67. Wilkerson.

68. N. D. B. Connolly, *A World More Concrete: Real Estate and the Remaking of Jim Crow South Florida* (Chicago: University of Chicago Press, 2014), 57.

69. Bruce Lohof, "Hamburger Stand: Industrialization and the American Fast Food Phenomenon," *Industrial Archaeology Review* 2, no. 3 (1978): 265–76.

70. James W. McLamore, *The Burger King: Jim McLamore and the Building of an Empire* (New York: McGraw Hill, 1998), 3.

71. McLamore.

72. "The Insta-Burger-King Success Story," *FFM*, April 1956.

73. Connolly, *World More Concrete*.

74. "Negroes Win Dade Fight on Restrictive Zoning," *Miami Herald*, November 1, 1946.

75. Connolly, *World More Concrete*.

76. "Classified Ads," *Miami Herald*, February 5, April 5, 1954.

77. Connolly, *World More Concrete*, 204–5. White business owners had long sold to segregated Black markets, though not in all domains, forsaking "body-oriented services" such as beauty shops and funeral parlors. Bobby M. Wilson, "Captial's Need to Sell and Black Economic Development," *Urban Geography* 33, no. 7 (2012): 961–74.

78. Connolly.

79. "Two Partners in Search of a Name May Stage a Contest," *Miami Herald*, March 12, 1956.

80. Connolly, *World More Concrete*.

81. Classified ad, *Fort Lauderdale News*, August 23, 1958; classified ad, *Palm Beach Post*, February 19, 1958.

82. McLamore, *Burger King*.

83. Lohof, "Hamburger Stand;" McLamore, *Burger King*.

84. McLamore, 40.

85. Classified ads, *Fort Lauderdale News*, September 12, November 25, 1958.

86. "Pair Buy All Burger Kings," *Miami News*, April 16, 1961.

4. Freedom from Panic

1. Susannah Walker, "Black Dollar Power: Assessing African American Consumerism since 1945," in *African American Urban History since World War II*, ed. K. L. Kusmer and J. W. Trotter (Chicago: University of Chicago Press, 2009), 386; Robert E. Weems, *Desegregating the Dollar: African American Consumerism in the Twentieth Century* (New York: New York University Press, 1998).

2. Walker, 386.

3. "Radio a Leading Force in Negro Progress," *Broadcasting Magazine*, November 7, 1966, box 7, folder 20, WANN.

4. Though not representative of corporations' attempt to reach the Black Consumer Market, the advertising buys the day after President John F. Kennedy was assassinated is interesting anecdotally regarding which product sectors appeared. The WANN archives include the ad schedule for November 23, 1963 ("Program Log, 11/23/63," box 24, folder 1, WANN). That day, the WANN airwaves were generally free of commercial advertising, with most spots comprising public service announcements like "Hire the Handicapped," "Social Security," "Savings Bonds," "Fire Prevention," and "Boy Scouts of America." But a few retail brands did advertise; perhaps they could not resist the size of the Black audience that would surely be glued to the radio that day. Among them were Coca-Cola, Wonder Bread, Colt 45 Malt Liquor, Camel Cigarettes, Carling Beer, and Navy Recruiting. These brands and product categories reflect those noted by *Broadcasting Magazine* (i.e., Coca-Cola and alcoholic beverages).

5. "Good Weather Advertising," *McDonald's Newsletter*, April 1962, box 5, folder 14, ABWP.

6. John A. Jakle and Keith A. Skulle, *Fast Food: Roadside Restaurants in the Automobile Age* (Baltimore: Johns Hopkins University Press, 1999).

7. Sylvia Porter, "Hamburger in Paris," *Morning Call*, October 14, 1955.

8. Rod Wenz, "Kentucky Fried Chicken Franchises Going to Caribbean, Europe, Japan," *Courier-Journal and Times*, January 12, 1969.

9. *Modern Franchising Magazine*, January–February and September–October, 1965, box 2, folder 1, ABWP.

10. John F. Love, *McDonald's: Behind the Arches* (New York: Bantam, 1995), 74.

11. Reid Hanley, Ed Sherman, and Joseph Tybor, "Integrated Private Clubs Few, If Not So Far Between," *Chicago Tribune*, May 5, 1991. As late as 1991, private Chicago area golf clubs remained highly segregated with few women or Black members; Rolling Green refused to comment on the club's demographics. Dondanville's name was spelled Robert Dondenville in McDonald's archival materials.

12. Love, *Behind the Arches*.

13. Love; McDonald's Corporation, "McDonald's History," n.d., MCDDP.

14. Photographs of field consultants, box 5, folder 15, MCDDP.

15. *McDonald's Newsletter*, June 1962, box 5, folder 14, MCDDP.

16. A. L. Foster, "Other People's Business," *Chicago Defender,* June 6, 1959.

17. Hamburger University files, box 5, folder 14, ABWP.

18. "Success Story, Horatio Alger Style," *McDonald's Newsletter,* January 1962, box 5, folder 14, ABWP.

19. Ray Kroc and Robert Anderson, "Grinding It Out (Excerpt)," *Saturday Evening Post,* March 1978, 52.

20. Joe L. Kincheloe, *The Sign of the Burger: McDonald's and the Culture of Power* (Philadelphia: Temple University Press, 2002).

21. Kincheloe, 30.

22. Love, *Behind the Arches.*

23. Love, 113.

24. Love, 173.

25. Love, 174.

26. Love, 95.

27. Love.

28. Diane Harris, *Little White Houses: How the Postwar Home Constructed Race in America* (Minneapolis: University of Minnesota Press, 2013), 164.

29. Harris.

30. Love, *Behind the Arches.*

31. Love.

32. Tracey Deutsch, *Building a Housewife's Paradise: Gender, Politics, and American Grocery Stores in the Twentieth Century* (Chapel Hill: University of North Carolina Press, 2010).

33. Elaine Tyler May, *Homeward Bound: American Families in the Cold War Era* (New York: Basic Books, 2008).

34. Katherine J. Parkin, *Food Is Love: Advertising and Gender Roles in Modern America* (Philadelphia: University of Pennsylvania Press, 2006).

35. Parkin.

36. Display advertisement 172, *Chicago Daily Tribune,* September 23, 1956, MCDDP; display ad 126, *Chicago Daily Tribune,* October 25, 1959, MCDDP.

37. Display advertisement 37, *Chicago Daily Tribune,* February 3, 1960, MCDPP.

38. Margaret J. King, "Empires of Popular Culture: McDonald's and Disney," in "The World of Ronald McDonald," ed. Marshall Fishwick, special issue, *Journal of American Culture* 1 (1978): 424–37.

39. Particular foods that were singled out tended to be those high in sugar. For example, insurance company Metropolitan Life put out an educational filmstrip called *Cheers for Chubby* in which Mr. and Mrs. Chubby learned to avoid cakes and syrup.

40. Nicolas Rasmussen, *Fat in the Fifties: America's First Obesity Crisis* (Baltimore: Johns Hopkins University Press, 2019).

41. "Drive-In Newsletter," *DIR,* January 1959.

42. Jonathan M. Metzl, "'Mother's Little Helper': The Crisis of Psychoanalysis and the Miltown Resolution," *Gender & History* 15, no. 2 (2003): 240–67; David Herzberg, *Happy Pills in America: From Miltown to Prozac* (Baltimore: Johns Hopkins University Press, 2010), 38.

43. Herzberg.

44. Dr. Ernest Dichter, "Fun Food-Not Just Fast Food," article slated to appear in *FFM*, October 1966, box 168, EDP.

45. "Meals to Go in a Minute or Less," *FFM*, March 1960, 54.

46. "How to Use Your New McDonald's Press Kit" and "Speech on the 'Lighter Side,'" Cooper & Golin Inc. Public Relations, Chicago, McDonald's Press Kits, 1964, box 5, folder 9, ABWP.

47. Victor Brooks, *Last Season of Innocence: The Teen Experience in the 1960s* (New York: Rowman & Littlefield, 2012).

48. "Newsletter: A Digest of Events Which Are of Personal Interest to You," *DIR*, April 7, 1958, 5–7.

49. Victoria W. Wolcott, "Recreation and Race in the Postwar City: Buffalo's 1956 Crystal Beach Riot," *Journal of American History* 93, no. 1 (June 2006): 63–90; James Burkhart Gilbert, *A Cycle of Outrage: America's Reaction to the Juvenile Delinquent in the 1950s* (New York: Oxford University Press, 1988).

50. Gilbert; Ramona Caponegro, "Where the 'Bad' Girls Are (Contained): Representations of the 1950s Female Juvenile Delinquent in Children's Literature and Ladies Home Journal," *Children's Literature Association Quarterly* 34, no. 4 (2009): 312–29.

51. Matthew Delmont, *The Nicest Kids in Town: American Bandstand, Rock 'n' Roll, and the Struggle for Civil Rights in 1950s Philadelphia* (Berkeley: University of California Press, 2012).

52. Jim McGovern, in conversation with the author, March 17, 2015. Des Plaines History Center, Des Plaines, Illinois.

53. Al Olson, "Nuts to the Noise!," *FFM*, September 1960, 7; Fred C. Matthews, "Nuts to Noise Solution," *FFM*, November 1960, 8.

54. May, *Homeward Bound*, 159.

55. Lizabeth Cohen, *A Consumers' Republic: The Politics of Mass Consumption in Postwar America* (New York: Knopf, 2003).

56. Deutsch, *Building a Housewife's Paradise*.

57. Deutsch, 192.

58. Historian Mary Dudziak argues that racial discrimination in the United States posed a real problem for the country's prestige, international perceptions of its leadership, and the integrity of democracy in general. She contends that part of what drove civil rights reform was in fact the United States needing to address the hypocrisy of engrained racism at home as it sought to promote democracy internationally. Mary L. Dudziak, *Cold War Civil Rights: Race and the Image of American Democracy* (Princeton, N.J.: Princeton University Press, 2002). Fast food obviously did not rise to a tangible level of reputational threat on the world stage, but it did have symbolic value that would be defaced by putting inequality on display.

59. Robert H. Denley, "Harmony in Hambergers; or Let's Get Acquainted," *Clarion Ledger Sun*, September 11, 1955.

60. King, "Empires of Popular Culture."

61. Many involved police who were present—even on detail to protect Black subjects—but who did nothing. A conflagration in Calumet Park laid bare the city's dire racial climate. Sociologist St. Clair Drake, renowned co-author with Horace Cayton of *Black Metropolis*, recounted that a "well-dressed and well-behaved group of Negroes" who had had the temerity to picnic in the park were attacked by a mob, and for the rest of the week residents threw rocks at any car

thought to contain Black occupants (Whites flew white flags on their vehicles to identify themselves). Few were arrested, and those who were received either no sentences or light ones. "A Working Paper on Reported Incidents of Racial Violence in Chicago: 1956 and 1957," preface by Dr. St. Clair Drake, chair of the Research Committee, Chicago Urban League, compiled and analyzed by Research Department of the Chicago Urban League, November 1958, *African American Communities*, https://www.libraries.rutgers.edu/databases/aac.

62. Cohen, *Consumer's Republic*.

5. Delinquents, Disorder, and Death

1. William Granger, "Youth, 20, Slain by Cop in Chase at Restaurant." *Chicago Tribune*, June 5, 1968.

2. John Kass, "From Another Time, a Kid Murdered by Chicago Cop," *Chicago Tribune*, January 29, 2016; Bill Granger, "One Turbulent Night in Turbulent Times Stands Out," *Daily Herald*, June 4, 1998.

3. Daniel Marcus, *Wonder Years: The Fifties and Sixties in Contemporary Cultural Politics* (New Brunswick, N.J.: Rutgers University Press, 2004).

4. Marcus.

5. "Mcdonald's Adds 3 New Drive-Ins," *Washington Post and Times Herald*, April 14, 1963.

6. "Executive Outlook," *FFM*, October, 1967, 37; emphasis added.

7. Publishers of Drive-In Management, *Drive-in Operators Handbook* (Duluth, Minn.: Ojibway Press, 1964), 237.

8. "No Title," *DIR*, January 1967. Some police department heads thought special favors to be inappropriate. At Tops Drive-Inn in Fairfax County, Virginia, police had been enjoying a half-price discount for hamburgers and coffee, but it came to a halt when Tops asked officers to sign a register for bookkeeping purposes. The police chief forbade the discount, saying it was "out of hand," should not be formalized in writing, and that officers should pay what regular patrons did.

9. "Residents Stiffening Opposition to Drive-Ins," *NRN*, September 29, 1969; "Wound Two in Row at Steak N Shake," *NRN*, September 29, 1969; "Backlash," *FFM*, March 1968; "Keep Kids Cool at Drive-Ins: Fire Your Female Carhops, Hire a Cop," *NRN*, July 5, 1971.

10. The officer sped to the scene of a reported fight at the Center Street Drive-In—a site where police had reportedly been "attacked by a mob of teenagers several weeks ago"—but his trajectory took him down a stretch of new highway in a nearby town, and there he encountered a group of drag-racing teens and spectators. Smith managed to apprehend Roberta L. Ginsberg, aged nineteen. She was "racing for fun after having been challenged earlier at the Center Street drive-in restaurant." "Phony Complaint Leads Police to Drag Race," *Hartford Courant*, September 12, 1964.

11. "Can't Help but Wonder 'Where Are We Heading?," *FFM*, May 1967.

12. "Ordinance Round-Up," *DIR*, July 1967, 59. While the Drive-Restaurant Owner Association fought the measure, arguing that such an ordinance would violate their constitutional rights, the Hotel, Motel, and Restaurant Employees Union, Local 705, charged that the proposed ordinance was in fact not tough enough. They looked askance at the proposal to install licensed, private guards on weekends. Myra Wolfgang, secretary-treasurer for the union, claimed that such guards

should be on duty seven days per week. Police were not in favor of armed guards but otherwise supported the measure.

13. "Ordinance Roundup," *DIR*, July 1967; "Ordinance Roundup," *Drive-In Magazine*, February 1967.

14. "Local Legislation," *DIR*, November 1967.

15. "Ordinance Roundup," *DIR*, July 1967.

16. "Ordinance Roundup," *DIR*, August 1967.

17. "Executive Outlook," *FFM*, October 1967, 37.

18. "Despite Fed'l Support Minority Franchising Fizzles," *NRN*, August 31, 1970; Howard Cooper and Irma R. Lobe, "Special Report: The Franchise Challenge of the '70s," *FFM*, December 1968.

19. "New Chicken Chain Taps Urban Mart," *NRN*, September 29, 1969.

20. "Marriott Adapts Highway Jr. to D.C. Storefront," *NRN*, October 27, 1969.

21. "McD Tests Townhouse Concept for City Areas," *NRN*, October 26, 1970.

22. Frank Thomas, "Letter to the Editor," *NRN*, May 12, 1969.

23. Robert N. McMurry, "Who Riots and Why," *Nation's Business*, October 1967, 75.

24. Ivan Brandon, "All Night Long," *Washington Post and Times Herald*, September 3, 1972.

25. Corporate's annual report showcased slightly different wording: "It's not dandy, but it's good."

26. "Horn & Hardart Progress Report," May 1965, Institute for Motivational Research Inc., Croton-on-Hudson, New York, Ernest Dichter, Ph.D., president, *Market Research and American Business Reports, 1935–1965*, https://www.libraries.rutgers.edu/databases/amdigital-market-research.

27. Horn & Hardart, Annual Report, 1969, in *Robert F. Byrnes Collection of Automat Memorabilia*, New York Public Library Manuscripts and Archives Division; "Horn & Hardart Starts Multi-Million Dollar Renovation Program," *FFM*, November 1968, 112.

28. Letters, 95th Street Beverly Hills Business Association, University of Illinois at Chicago Special Collections.

29. Nelson C. Blackford, Executive Secretary, Beverly Area Planning Association, to Thomas Haney, McDonald's, 221 North LaSalle Street, January 22, 1968, Correspondence—General (Folder 9), box 5, folder 71; Correspondence—General (Folder 10), box 5, folder 72; Executive Secretary's Reports, 1968, box 6, folder 103; McDonald's Proposed Construction, box 8, folder 130, all in Beverly Area Planning Association Records, 1947–1975, University of Illinois at Chicago, Special Collections.

30. R. J. Sampson and S. W. Raudenbush, "Seeing Disorder: Neighborhood Stigma and the Social Construction of 'Broken Windows,'" *Social Psychology Quarterly* 67, no. 4 (2004): 319–42.

31. Wesley G. Skogan, *Disorder and Decline: Crime and the Spiral of Decay in American Neighborhoods* (Berkeley: University of California Press, 1990), 35.

32. Skogan, 33.

33. Donald B. Clapp, Executive Director, to Frank Shaeffer, Arthur Rubloff Co., July 30, 1969, box 89, folder 15, HPKCC.

34. "Co-Op Says No to Col. Sanders," *Hyde Park Herald*, November 19, 1969.

35. Leon Despres, to Mr. Zundel, Department of Urban Renewal, February 25, 1970, box 89, folder 15, HPKCC.

36. Psyche A. Williams-Forson, *Building Houses Out of Chicken Legs: Black Women, Food, and Power* (Chapel Hill: University of North Carolina Press, 2006).

37. "Cohen Maneuvering Fails to Block Fern Rock Hamburger Restaurant," *Philadelphia Inquirer,* July 6, 1969; "Councilman Spins Spider's Web to Block Hamburger Stand in Fern Rock," *Philadelphia Inquirer,* September 4, 1969; Robert Fensterer, "Commission Joins Hamburger vs. History Spat," *Philadelphia Inquirer,* July 10, 1969.

38. Mary Pattillo, *Black on the Block: The Politics of Race and Class in the City* (Chicago: University of Chicago Press, 2007), 70.

39. "Neighbors to Picket Drive-In," *Philadelphia Inquirer,* February 19, 1970; "Residents' Outcry: 'Too Many Drive-Ins,'" *NRN,* June 8, 1970.

40. "Separate Law Gets Support for Drive-Ins," *Philadelphia Inquirer,* July 2, 1970.

41. Robert Fensterer, "Drive-in Planning to Join Opposition," *Philadelphia Inquirer,* July 2, 1970. The article reports his name as "Beaver" but it is in fact "Beavers."

42. "Cohen Maneuvering Fails to Block Fern Rock Hamburger Restaurant," *Philadelphia Inquirer,* July 6, 1969; "Residents' Outcry: 'Too Many Drive-Ins,'" *NRN,* June 8, 1970.

43. Victoria W. Wolcott, "Recreation and Race in the Postwar City: Buffalo's 1956 Crystal Beach Riot," *Journal of American History* 93, no. 1 (June 2006): 63–90; Jeff Wiltse, *Contested Waters: A Social History of Swimming Pools in America* (Chapel Hill: University of North Carolina Press, 2007).

44. Andrew Diamond, *Mean Streets: Chicago Youths and the Everyday Struggle for Empowerment in the Multiracial City, 1908–1969* (Berkeley: University of California Press, 2009).

45. Matthew Delmont, *The Nicest Kids in Town: American Bandstand, Rock 'n' Roll, and the Struggle for Civil Rights in 1950s Philadelphia* (Berkeley: University of California Press, 2012). *Bandstand* kept its studio segregated using covert and explicit methods to ensure exclusively White adolescent attendees. What began as a regional television show recorded at WFIL's West Philadelphia studio in 1952 became a national broadcast in 1957 and was at the center of broader racial clashes by White homeowners in the surrounding community. Young Black Philadelphians were therefore excluded from a national centerpiece of youth culture taking place in their own backyards.

46. Wolcott, "Recreation and Race in the Postwar City."

47. Ashanté M. Reese, *Black Food Geographies: Race, Self-Reliance, and Food Access in Washington, D.C.* (Chapel Hill: University of North Carolina Press, 2019).

48. Wolcott, "Recreation and Race in the Postwar City," 89.

49. Robert Shellow, ed., *The Harvest of American Racism: The Political Meaning of Violence in the Summer of 1967* (Ann Arbor: University of Michigan Press, 2018).

50. "Raises Flag in Defiance of Boycott," *NRN,* August 18, 1969.

51. "Jamesburg Calm during the Night," *Asbury Park Evening Press,* July 22, 1969; "Girl Injured in Jamesburg," *Central New Jersey Home News,* July 14, 1969; "Curfew Lifted in Jamesburg," *Courier News,* July 16, 1969; Gordon Sharp, "Was Jamesburg Flim-Flammed?," *Central New Jersey Home News,* July 20, 1969; Richard Gorman, "Police in Full Riot Gear Keep Jamesburg Peace," *Central New Jersey Home News,* July 15, 1969; Gordon Sharp, "Curfew Continues in Jittery Jamesburg," *Central New Jersey Home News,* July 18, 1969.

52. "From Ice Cream Cone to Race Riot," *Courier News,* July 24, 1969; Richard Severo, "Lester

Maddox, Whites-Only Restaurateur and Georgia Governor, Dies at 87," *NYT*, June 26, 2003; "Police, Curfew Impose Calm as Jamesburg Seeks Peace," *Central New Jersey Home News*, July 17, 1969; "Town Bias Riot Stems from Ice Cream Cone," *Bakersfield Californian*, August 4, 1969; "Clips and Quotes: Gov. Lester Maddox Is Going into the Hamburger Business," *DIR*, March 1967, 14; Kevin M. Kruse, *White Flight: Atlanta and the Making of Modern Conservatism* (Princeton, N.J.: Princeton University Press, 2005).

53. Ernest A. Lotito, "Settlement Sought in Negro's Beating," *Washington Post and Times Herald*, May 22, 1963. Arresting Eiland, the victim rather than the perpetrator, paralleled the arrests of Black pool-goers who were attacked by White residents. See Wiltse, *Contested Waters*, for incidents at pools. Eiland did not seek legal redress. U.S. Attorney Paul A. Renne argued that the case presented legal challenges; because "the white youths had no prior records and their parents were willing to 'impose appropriate restrictions, the best interests of the community would be served by not going through with the prosecution.'" Surely, Renne's view would have discouraged Eiland, and it is unclear to what extent he may have been pressured to drop the charges. It would also seem that the press coverage of the case put Eiland and others like him at further risk and retaliatory violence for having spoken out. The *Post* reported that Eiland received a cash civil settlement, though witnesses were equivocal as to what exactly had transpired in the attack. Lotito, "Settlement Sought."

54. Janine Bell, *Hate Thy Neighbor: Move-In Violence and the Persistence of Racial Segregation in American Housing* (New York: New York University Press, 2013). An example of this violence occurred in 1953 when Donald and Betty Howard endured months of sustained and violent protest from Whites when they moved into the Trumbull Park Homes in Chicago's South Deering neighborhood, located in the Southeast section of the city. A. R. Hirsch, "Massive Resistance in the Urban North: Trumbull Park, Chicago, 1953–1966," *Journal of American History*, September 1995. Segregationist tracts in the community railed against *Brown v. Board of Education* five years later, warning of latent "savagery, immorality, and brutality" that would be awakened in the context of integrated schools. See Hirsch; and "What about Mixed Schools?," *South Deering Bulletin*, October 30, 1958, Segregationist Material, 1958–1961, Kenan Research Center, Atlanta, *African American Communities*, https://www.libraries.rutgers.edu/databases/aac.

55. Some neighborhoods, such as Cicero and Bridgeport (home to five Chicago mayors), are infamous for racial hate crimes. However, other parts of the city have been equally treacherous for Black folk, such as the Southwest Side. The neighborhood's racial hostility led to its selection as one of the areas in which the SCLC and other civil rights activists marched in August 1966 to demand desegregated housing; they were met by open hostility and lackadaisical police—though perhaps not at the same scale of virulence as the mobs that turned out to meet Dr. King. Memo from Bennett Hymer to Pat Fitzgerald, "March in the Bogan Area—Friday, August 12, 4:00 p.m.," August 18, 1966; and memo from Sanford Sherizen to Pat Fitzgerals, August 24, 1966, "Re: Demonstration in South Deering, Sunday, August 21, 1966," both in CULR; and Sheila Curran Bernard and Samuel D. Pollard, dirs., "Two Societies, 1965–68," episode 8 of *Eyes on the Prize: America's Civil Rights Movement* (Arlington, Va.: PBS, 1990). In 2007, the Bradshaw family moved to that area and found their garage door defaced with the words "Niggers Beware." Bell, *Hate Thy Neighbor*.

56. "Hamburgers Sell Like Hotcakes Where Castles Are for Real," *Chicago Tribune*, November 13, 1969.

57. "College Student Tells How He Was Attacked by Whites," *Chicago Defender*, December 5, 1967; "Southside Boy Accosted, Beaten by White Youths," *Chicago Defender*, December 4, 1967.

58. In the years that preceded and followed the two attacks at White Castle, residents protested school integration of students or staff at Bogan High School. In 1977, three hundred students at the high school were suspended and thirty-three arrested (on minor charges including failure to disperse and disorderly conduct) following days of violence to protest a busing program. The chaos was sparked when two women attempted to block Black students from entering nearby Stevenson Elementary School. Bogan High School seniors walked out in sympathy, and the protest escalated to days of bedlam. Leslie Palmer, "Hunt Two Whites in Race Incident," *Chicago Defender*, August 19, 1975.

59. Lennie Robinson evaded being struck, but her passenger, James Solomon, was punched in the face and his glasses were smashed. Driving with her infant child, Marie Sweatt was attacked by nearly a dozen White men when her car stalled at 57th and Halsted. The windshield was smashed, and her baby's face was cut from the broken glass. Police were nonresponsive. Sweatt reported the incident at the local precinct, but the desk sergeant found it funny and another officer "told me to get my car out of the parking lot or he'd give me a ticket." "Racial Clashes Stir Fears of Another Hot Summer," *Chicago Bulletin*, May 1964.

60. "Cops Didn't Protect Us, Family Charges," *Chicago Defender*, August 24, 1965.

61. James Stampley, board chairman and co-organizer of the United Block Clubs of Englewood, an interracial group, wrote in 1979 about racist violence in the area. Nearby communities were virulently hostile places where racism was on stark display. Approximately three miles west in Chicago Lawn, the American Nazi Party had its headquarters on West 71st Street; painted in large type on the whitewashed side of a building that was highly visible to passing motorists and pedestrians was the phrase "STOP THE NIGGERS!" James D. Stampley, *Challenges with Changes: A Documentary of Englewood, Illustrated* (n.p., 1979).

62. *Chicago Street Address Directory*, September (Chicago: Reuben H. Donnelley Corporation, 1968).

63. "Black Youths Say White Hoodlums Attacked Them as Cops Looked On," *Chicago Defender*, August 13, 1968.

64. "Powerless Black Woman, Family Suffer as Hatred Grows in White Area," *Chicago Daily News*, July 8, 1971.

65. "Arvia 'Satisfactory' after Shooting," *South End Reporter*, August 10, 1966.

66. "Arrest 3 White Youths in Slaying of Black, 21," *Chicago Defender*, June 17, 1970.

67. Bell, *Hate Thy Neighbor*.

68. Angela Jill Cooley, *To Live and Dine in Dixie: The Evolution of Urban Food Culture in the Jim Crow South* (Athens: University of Georgia Press, 2015); Robert E. Weems Jr., "African-American Consumer Boycotts during the Civil Rights Era," *Western Journal of Black Studies* 19, no. 1 (1995): 75–79.

69. Cooley, *To Live and Dine in Dixie*.

70. Elizabeth Abel, *Signs of the Times: The Visual Politics of Jim Crow* (Berkeley: University of California Press, 2010).

71. Katharina Vester, *A Taste of Power: Food and American Identities* (Berkeley: University of California Press, 2015), 17.

72. Ann Petry, *The Street* (New York: Houghton Mifflin, 1946), 45.

73. Wiltse, *Contested Waters*.

74. Victoria W. Wolcott, *Race, Riots, and Roller Coasters: The Struggle over Segregated Recreation in America* (Philadelphia: University of Pennsylvania Press, 2012).

6. How Does It Feel to Be a Problem?

1. "Suspect Admits He Shot Meredith," *NYT,* November 22, 1966; Peniel E. Joseph, *Waiting 'til the Midnight Hour: A Narrative History of Black Power in America* (New York: Henry Holt, 2006).

2. "A $65 Billion Gold Mine," *Ebony,* July 1966, 88.

3. "Minnie Pearl Gets Smaller Day by Day," *NRN,* September 14, 1970, 1; "Franchising . . . the State of the Art," *FFM,* 1968, 80.

4. "The New Independents," *FFM,* March 1969.

5. Robert Allen, *Black Awakening in Capitalist America: An Analytic History* (New York: Anchor Books, 1969), 12.

6. Allen.

7. Allen, 55.

8. Ashley D. Farmer, *Remaking Black Power: How Black Women Transformed an Era* (Chapel Hill: University of North Carolina Press, 2017).

9. "A $65 Billion Gold Mine," *Ebony,* July 1966, 88.

10. "Proposal for a Motivational Research Study on the Sales and Advertising Opportunities of Chicken Delight," Institute for Motivational Research Inc., Croton-on-Hudson, New York, Ernest Dichter, Ph.D., president, *Market Research and American Business Reports, 1935–1965,* https://www.libraries.rutgers.edu/databases/amdigital-market-research.

11. "A $65 Billion Gold Mine," *Ebony,* July 1966, 90.

12. Mr. and Mrs. Don Rivers in Chicago were the first Black Montgomery Ward catalog franchisees in the country. They opened a store in a shopping center at 55th and Martin Luther King Drive to sell appliances and home entertainment. Also on the South Side, Leslie N. Bland opened the first Black-owned Lincoln–Mercury dealership, at 27th and State.

13. A. L. Foster, "Other People's Business," *Chicago Defender,* May 17, 1958; A. L. Foster, "Other People's Business," *Chicago Defender,* November 16, 1963; "Restaurant Owners Close Ranks, Defender's Candid Camera," *Chicago Defender,* January 7, 1961; "Chamber Forms Cafe Division," *Chicago Defender,* December 10, 1960.

14. "CCC Launches Drive to Spur Businesses through Franchises," *Chicago Defender,* March 4, 1967.

15. "Defender Conference on Black Franchising," *Urban Enterprise: A Bi-Weekly Newsletter on Minority Economic Development,* October 24, 1969.

16. "Defender Conference on Black Franchising."

17. "Defender Conference on Black Franchising," 8.

18. Michael Whiteman, "Red Barn's 2-Chain Strategy: Deeper Penetration of Market," *NRN,* August 12, 1968, 1.

19. "Urban Prospects," *NRN*, October 27, 1969, 7.

20. "White Operator in Black Area: A Portrait in Green (Cash)," *NRN*, April 14, 1969, 36.

21. "New Drive-In Snack Shop Shows Faith in Woodlawn's Future," *Woodlawn Booster*, October 3, 1962.

22. "Photo Standalone 1: No Title," *Chicago Defender*, December 31, 1966.

23. "Ideas from Whoopee Burger," *FFM*, October 1967.

24. *Chicago Street Address Directory*, September (Chicago: Reuben H. Donnelley Corporation, 1968).

25. Stadeker's incendiary language had been used by other Black Chicagoans, as when the dispossession of thousands of Black residents to build Lake Meadows was compared to the Jewish experience in Nazi Germany. Andrew Diamond, *Mean Streets: Chicago Youths and the Everyday Struggle for Empowerment in the Multiracial City, 1908–1969* (Berkeley: University of California Press, 2009).

26. Sarah Schindler, "Architectural Exclusion: Discrimination and Segregation through Physical Design of the Built Environment," *Yale Law Journal* 124 (2015): 1934–2024.

27. Diamond, *Mean Streets,* 151.

28. Arnold R. Hirsch, *Making the Second Ghetto: Race and Housing in Chicago, 1940–1960* (Cambridge: Cambridge University Press, 1983); Preston H. Smith, *Racial Democracy and the Black Metropolis: Housing Policy in Postwar Chicago* (Minneapolis: University of Minnesota Press, 2012); D. Bradford Hunt, *Blueprint for Disaster: The Unraveling of Chicago Public Housing* (Chicago: University of Chicago Press, 2009).

29. *Tale of the Chicken* portrayed a Black chicken thief who had a love affair, while *Mother of Men* depicted an enslaved person stealing a White child and the hunt that ensued. The *Chicago Defender* chastised, "This picture is foolish. Slaves do not steal white children, and if they did they could not find a place to hide them." "States Theater Shows Colored Men Stealing Chickens," *Chicago Defender,* May 30, 1914. In the ensuing decades, the theater became a hotspot for jazz, but by 1963 it had been abandoned. Robert Cross, "Evanston Music Buff Writes Book on 'Golden Era' of Jazz," *Chicago Daily Tribune*, January 17, 1963.

30. Frederick Opie, *Hog and Hominy: Soul Food from Africa to America* (New York: Columbia University Press, 2010).

31. "Hot Sauce" Williams ran a barbecue stand in Cleveland in the 1950s. A migrant from New Orleans, he borrowed fifty-eight dollars from the city's "barbecue czar," cajoled a hometown chef into tutoring him on preparing ribs, and ended up with a business that grossed $100,000 a year in 1950 (more than $1 million today). In Richmond, Virginia, Johnnie B's made bologna burgers, topped with fried onions, lettuce, tomato, and optional cheese, on large buns, and served alongside wide variety of milkshakes. According to Yemaja Jubilee, a Virginia Union student in the 1960s, "It was the kind of place where there were often lines going out the door to order food" (Opie, 104).

32. Black Owned Business Directory, 1971, Operation PUSH Collection, box 105, folder 1188, Special Collections and University Archives, University of Illinois Chicago.

33. "Review of Mufso/69, Undercurrents and Countertrends," *NRN*, September 29, 1969; "Bad Small Business Loans Lower Than Officials Expected," *Chicago Tribune*, October 2, 1966.

34. "McDonald's Restaurant Opens on 35th St," *Chicago Defender*, September 16, 1961.

35. Sanborn Map Company, *Sanborn Fire Insurance Maps of Chicago, Illinois*, 1927–1960.

36. *Chicago Street Address Directory.*

37. January 1962 McDonald's newsletter, box 5, folder 14, ABWP; Social Explorer, "Census Tract Data," n.d., https://www.socialexplorer.com/.

38. "Display Ad 8," *Chicago Defender*, August 16, 1966; "Advertisement," *The Bulletin*, August 11, 1966; Social Explorer, "U.S. Demography, 1790 to Present," n.d., https://www.socialexplorer.com/.

39. Roland L. Jones, *Standing Up and Standing Out: How I Teamed with a Few Black Men, Changed the Face of McDonald's, and Shook Up Corporate America* (Nashville, Tenn.: World Solutions, 2006), 118.

40. Peter Binzen, "McDonald's Pioneer Battles Economic Racism," *Philadelphia Inquirer*, May 29, 1989.

41. 114 Cong. Rec. S30508 (1968), *HeinOnline.*

42. Jones, *Standing Up and Standing Out.*

43. "Miami Gets First Black Restaurant Franchise," *Baltimore Afro-American*, May 30, 1970; "Burger King Corp Is Making More Franchises with Blacks," *Miami News*, October 13, 1973.

44. "If Riots Erupt Again . . . ," *Nation's Business*, March 1968, 66.

45. J. Samuel Walker, *Most of 14th Street Is Gone: The Washington, D.C., Riots of 1968* (New York: Oxford University Press, 2018).

46. 114 Cong. Rec. S30498 (1968), *HeinOnline.*

47. 114 Cong. Rec. S31966 (1968), *HeinOnline.*

48. 114 Cong. Rec. S31934 (1968), *HeinOnline.*

49. Alan Gersten, "Black Owns Burger King Units," *Miami News*, November 13, 1972.

50. John T. Edge, *The Potlikker Papers: A Food History of the Modern South* (New York: Penguin 2017); Phil Norman, "Kentucky Fried Chicken Merger: New Spirit and Money," *Courier Journal*, July 18, 1971; Dan Dorfman, "Heard on the Street," *WSJ*, April 13, 1970; "Kentucky Fried Chicken Buys Some Franchisees," *WSJ*, April 11, 1969; "Kentucky Fried Chicken Buys Nine Retail Chains," *WSJ*, July 10, 1968; John Getze, "Franchising: It Must Adapt If It Is to Survive," *Los Angeles Times*, July 26, 1970.

51. *Fairness in Franchising Act: Hearings before the Committee on Commerce, United States Senate, on S. 2335*, 94th Cong. 80–90 (1976) (statement of David Bradwell, David Bradwell & Associates).

52. In contrast to KFC, Burger King was also attuned to the promise of Black franchisees. Pillsbury showcased Black crews and its initiatives in urban franchise development in its 1970 annual report. However, the need for Black participation to insure outlets against racial antagonisms was not stated. Pillsbury Company annual reports, 1967, 1969, 1970, Library of Congress, Washington, D.C.

53. 114 Cong. Rec. S31921, S31929 (1968), *HeinOnline.*

54. W. E. B. Du Bois, *The Souls of Black Folk* (1903; repr., New York: Penguin, 2018), 5–6.

55. Richard Lifschutz, "Renamed Minnie Starts Diversifying, Buys Chain," *NRN*, March 3, 1969; Lee Berton, "How a Tennessean Pins His Gubernatorial Hope on Fried Chicken Stands: John Jay Hooker, '66 Loser, Rebounds as Voters Profit by His Minnie Pearl Firm," *WSJ*, June 2, 1969.

56. Berton; "Leroy Collins Succeeds Lawrence E. Singer as Head of Royal Castle," *WSJ*, February 26, 1969; "Performance Systems Offering," *WSJ*, May 5, 1969; "Performance Systems Purchases for Cash 64% of Royal Castle," *WSJ*, February 17, 1969; "Holders of Minnie Pearl's Vote Name Change, Split," *WSJ*, February 11, 1969; "Minnie Pearl's 391,694 Shares Are Sold at $20 Apiece," *WSJ*, May 2, 1968; "Minnie Pearl's Chicken System," *WSJ*, March 4, 1968.

57. "How Minnie Found Pearl of Success," *NRN*, May 12, 1969, 16; "Massive Debt, No Income Strangle Minnie Pearl Chain," *NRN*, September 28, 1970.

58. "Performance Systems Agrees to Sell Interest to National General," *WSJ*, July 2, 1969; "Performance Systems Expects to Post Loss for First Fiscal Half," *WSJ*, November 5, 1969.

59. "Massive Debt, No Income Strangle Minnie Pearl Chain," *NRN*, September 28, 1970; "Performance Systems Asks Dismissal of Suits Alleging False Report," *WSJ*, August 4, 1971; "Performance Systems Had 1969 1st Half Loss; SEC Inquiry Disclosed," *WSJ*, July 31, 1970; "Performance Systems Revises Report, Shows $1,270,000 Loss in 1968," *WSJ*, December 23, 1971; "Performance Systems Tells SEC 28 Weeks Showed $5 Million Loss," *WSJ*, September 11, 1970; "SEC Reschedules Hearing on Performance Systems," *WSJ*, April 20, 1971; "Studebaker Taps H. Hooker of Performance Systems," *WSJ*, January 27, 1971; "Minnie Pearl Gets Smaller Day by Day," *NRN*, September 14, 1970.

60. John F. Love, *McDonald's: Behind the Arches* (New York: Bantam, 1995).

61. Allen, *Black Awakening in Capitalist America*, 81.

62. Love, *Behind the Arches*.

63. Marcia Chatelain, "Fast Food, Civil Rights: McDonald's and Black America in the Post-King Years," Washington History Seminar, January 30, 2017, Woodrow Wilson International Center for Scholars, Washington, D.C.

64. "Arthur T. Duplessie," *Washington Post*, October 15, 1986.

65. Jones, *Standing Up and Standing Out*.

66. Jones.

67. Patricia Sowell Harris, *None of Us Is as Good as All of Us: How McDonald's Prospers by Embracing Inclusion and Diversity* (New York: Wiley, 2009).

68. Jones, *Standing Up and Standing Out*.

69. Love, *Behind the Arches*.

70. In other words, it is unclear on what the $500,000 was spent; no lawsuits were initiated and Black owners were responsible for their stores' financial insolvency.

71. "Duplessie Obituary," *Washington Post*, October 15, 1986; "Home Sales," *Washington Post*, September 19, 1985.

72. Marcia Chatelain, "The Miracle of the Golden Arches: Race and Fast Food in Los Angeles," *Pacific History Review* 85, no. 3 (2016): 352–53, 327.

73. Love, *Behind the Arches*. Love describes the owner as Lonear Heard, but Jones names the franchisee as Jim Heard. Jones reports that Jim Heard died in 1981 and turned over ownership to his wife, Lonear. He also states that both Jim Heard and Petty became millionaires.

74. McDonald's Corporation, "Black Consumer Market Milestones," box 50, folder 11, CRJP.

75. Love, *Behind the Arches*.

76. John Hall Fish, *Black Power / White Control: The Struggle of the Woodlawn Organization in Chicago* (Princeton, N.J.: Princeton University Press, 1973).

77. "Burger Sellers Tell History since Earl of Sandwich Days," *The Bulletin,* August 25, 1960; "15¢ Hamburger Spells $ales," *Chicago Defender,* April 8, 1961.

78. "Extensive Fire Damage at 65th & Stony." McDonald's employee newsletters, January 1962, box 5, folder 14, ABWP. A little over a year before the Woodlawn store burned, a Flint store was ravaged by a basement fire resulting from a discarded cigarette, with damage in the range of $10,000. In that case, an insurance adjuster was on-site the next day and the store was back in operation two days later. The same rapidity of repair may have taken place in Woodlawn, and if so, the fire could not have been the reason the unit was in a state of total disrepair when Petty came to it. But again, it hardly seems likely it was in a decimated state for six years.

79. Jones, *Standing Up and Standing Out.*

80. *Chicago White Pages,* 1968, microfilm, Library of Congress, Washington, D.C.; *Chicago White Pages,* 1970, http://www.newspaperarchive.com/.

81. *Chicago Street Address Directory.*

82. Rashad Shabazz, *Spatializing Blackness: Architectures of Confinement and Black Masculinity in Chicago* (Urbana: University of Illinois Press, 2015).

83. Jones, *Standing Up and Standing Out;* "The Southmoor," *Chicago Daily Tribune,* September 14, 1924; "Southmoor Hotel Is Sold to Dewoskin," *Chicago Daily Tribune,* August 8, 1956.

84. Jones, *Standing Up and Standing Out,* 371.

85. Within two years of opening Petty had taken out a program advertisement at a local NAACP event for the outlet promoting "plenty of parking . . . no tipping . . . instant service" and naming three managers. Petty took out other ads in the program, showcasing by name the crew that worked at his stores. "Women's Auxiliary Chicago Southside Branch, 1971," Williams NAACP Collection, series 2, box 2, folder 32, Newberry Library, Chicago.

86. Jones, *Standing Up and Standing Out.*

87. D.C.'s city services were scant in neighborhoods populated by poor Black citizens, a problem compounded by external control of the city by Congress; D.C. would not obtain its own mayor and city council until 1974.

88. Since 1955 Charles Petty had been the owner of an exterminating company on the West Side at 1515 South Pulaski Road, and in 1959 he organized a unit of the CCC in the same community. Raised in Chicago and St. Louis, he was a prominent figure in the Black business and activist communities, a member of the SCLC's Operation Breadbasket and of the Urban League, and in 1974 was an officer of Operation PUSH's new commercial division. Charles Petty's McDonald's endeavor apparently did not last, as he went on to work with Burger King in 1975 (either contracted to perform pest extermination or as a franchisee; the newspaper report was unclear). His firm obtained other contracts thanks to Breadbasket's work, such as an $11,000 extermination agreement for United Airlines at O'Hare Airport, part of the airline's pledge to increase minority vendors. "Blacks in Hamburgers," *Chicago Defender,* October 13, 1973; "Minority Purchases Up," *Chicago Defender,* June 7, 1975; "PUSH Honors Petty," *Chicago Defender,* March 6, 1974; "Photo Standalone," *Chicago Defender,* April 10, 1958; A. L. Foster, "Other People's Business," September 12, 1959; "Exterminating Firm Here in Fifteenth Year: Black Business of the Day," *Chicago Defender,* February 24, 1970.

89. "McDonald's Moves Franchises as Fast as Hamburgers," *Urban Enterprise: A Bi-Weekly Newsletter on Minority Economic Development,* March 6, 1970, 2.

90. D. D. Obika, "A Black Businessman's Fight against Crime in the Inner City," *St. Louis Post-Dispatch*, August 22, 1971.

91. Binzen, "McDonald's Pioneer Battles Economic Racism."

92. Sowell Harris, *None of Us Is as Good as All of Us*, 60.

93. Harris, 74.

94. "Two Sought in $1,000 McDonald's Robbery," *Chicago Defender*, October 9, 1967, 3.

95. Allen, *Black Awakening in Capitalist America*, 59.

7. To Banish, Boycott, or Bash?

1. Alondra Nelson, *Body and Soul: The Black Panther Party and the Fight against Medical Discrimination* (Minneapolis: University of Minnesota Press, 2011); Robert Self, *American Babylon: Race and the Struggle for Postwar Oakland* (Princeton, N.J.: Princeton University Press, 2005); Elizabeth Abel, *Signs of the Times: The Visual Politics of Jim Crow* (Berkeley: University of California Press, 2010).

2. Ella J. Baker, "Bigger Than a Hamburger," in *The Eyes on the Prize Civil Rights Reader: Documents, Speeches, and Firsthand Accounts from the Black Freedom Struggle, 1954–1990*, ed. Clayborne Carson, David J. Garrow, Gill Gerald, Harding Vincent, and Darlene Clark Hine (New York: Penguin, 1960), 120.

3. Speech by James Farmer, CORE Twenty-Third Annual Convention, July 1, 1965, Annual Report to the CORE National Convention, Special Collections and University Archives, University of Illinois Chicago.

4. Jennifer Jensen Wallach, *Every Nation Has Its Dish: Black Bodies and Black Food in Twentieth-Century America* (Chapel Hill: University of North Carolina Press, 2019), 159.

5. Nelson, *Body and Soul*; Monica M. White, *Freedom Farmers: Agricultural Resistance and the Black Freedom Movement* (Chapel Hill: University of North Carolina Press, 2018).

6. Robert Allen, *Black Awakening in Capitalist America: An Analytic History* (New York: Anchor Books, 1969).

7. Tracey Deutsch, *Building a Housewife's Paradise: Gender, Politics, and American Grocery Stores in the Twentieth Century* (Chapel Hill: University of North Carolina Press, 2010); Ashanté M. Reese, *Black Food Geographies: Race, Self-Reliance, and Food Access in Washington, D.C* (Chapel Hill: University of North Carolina Press, 2019).

8. Robert B. McKersie, *A Decisive Decade: An Insider's View of the Chicago Civil Rights Movement during the 1960s* (Carbondale: Southern Illinois University Press, 2013).

9. McKersie, 155. The threatened boycott may have reflected the greater difficulty in getting Black men into bottling operations in the North compared to the South. And since Pepsi had dominated Coca-Cola in market share among African Americans into the 1950s, Breadbasket would have capitalized on Pepsi's motivation to keep Black consumers happy.

10. Flyer, n.d., box 3, folder 7, WAPP; covenant between SCLC and A&P, October 5, 1968, box 3, folder 6, WAPP.

11. Jackson sought the pastors' cooperation, hoping they would spread the word to congregations and networks. Rev. Ma Houston noted that the Jewel supermarket on 39th Street continued to sell "bad meat" despite an earlier closure by the Health Department for "filth," and the

Organization of Southwest Communities picketed the National Tea store at 75th and Racine for uncleanliness. The Garfield Organization also worked on this issue, collaborating with residents and Chicago's Department of Consumer Weights and Measures to quash the operations of merchants dealing in shady meat sales. Marcelline Jackson, chair of the Organization's meat committee, reported, "Since the change in the racial makeup of Garfield there has been a drastic cutback in the quality of foods sold by area merchants." Stores were reportedly rigging scales for greater profit, dying meat, and engaging in other deceptive practices. See Jesse Jackson to "Fellow Pastor," February 23, 1968, box 3, folder 4, WAPP.

12. "Westsiders Start All-Out Meat Cheating Crackdown," *Chicago Defender*, September 26, 1967. Even in 2017 they were still dealing with the issues of poor quality that Chicagoans faced in 1968. That year, a Safeway was cited for selling expired meat (Reese, *Black Food Geographies*, 51). The challenges Black Chicagoans faced in retail were not unique to recent generations. As early as the 1930s, Black shoppers were cheated by scales with weights hidden underneath, "tricky math" that resulted in higher sales taxes, and grocers who switched fresh meat for old (Deutsch, *Building a Housewife's Paradise*). Nor was all of this limited to Chicago. D.C.'s Deanwood residents experienced the same. Emily Marin recalled one store owner rigging a scale, "marking up somebody's by putting a piece of meat and putting it on the scale and making it heavy. So I never bought anything from him but bread and milk" (Reese, *Black Food Geographies*, 33). Even when using a scale—the literal instantiation of equality and standardization—Black shoppers could not count on fair treatment.

13. "What Is This Idea Called PUSH?," September 1974, box 96, folder 1064, CULR.

14. Robert B. McKersie, *A Decisive Decade: An Insider's View of the Chicago Civil Rights Movement during the 1960s* (Carbondale: Southern Illinois University Press, 2013).

15. Each of Breadbasket's negotiations with local businesses revealed a much broader web of deficits: "White scavengers picked up all of the garbage in the ghetto; white exterminators killed all of the rats in the ghetto, white construction companies built all of the stores in the ghetto, in fact with the exception of a few Negro employees white people did everything in the ghetto except eat and pay for groceries." Alvin Pitcher, "Operation Breadbasket," box 2, folder 5, WAPP. And even when stores agreed to carry Black products, they often left them in stockrooms and warehouses, or displayed them ineffectively. President's Advisory Council on Minority Business Enterprise, *Minority Enterprise and Expanded Ownership: Blueprint for the 70s* (prepared for President Richard Nixon and Secretary of Commerce Maurice H. Stans, Washington, D.C., 1971).

16. McSween was one of three Black men inducted into the Million Dollar Round Table, which comprised insurance agents who wrote a minimum of $1 million in new business each year; the Panamanian native had been doing so since he joined the company in 1956. "Million Dollar Men of Insurance" (New York Life advertisement), *Ebony*, May 1965, 207.

17. Dorceta E. Taylor, *Toxic Communities: Environmental Racism, Industrial Pollution, and Residential Mobility* (New York: New York University Press, 2014); Thomas Buck, "Chicago Spirit Meets a Challenge: Lifts Near South Side out of Slums," *Chicago Tribune*, November 9, 1958; Michelle Boyd, *Jim Crow Nostalgia: Reconstructing Race in Bronzeville* (Minneapolis: University of Minnesota Press, 2008).

18. "Good Work, Dr. King," *Chicago Defender*, May 9, 1967, box 1, folder 2, WAPP.

19. "Black Press White Owner to Sell Eatery," *NRN*, May 20, 1968; "Black Takeover in Pitt," *NRN*, October 21, 1968.

20. "Militants' Pressure Closes Restaurant," *NRN*, October 21, 1968; "Negro Takes Over Seattle Restaurant," *NRN*, December 16, 1968.

21. Joyce Wadler, "Burger King War Never Really Began," *NRN*, November 10, 1969.

22. Allen, *Black Awakening in Capitalist America*.

23. William J. Collins and Fred H. Smith, "A Neighborhood-Level View of Riots, Property Values, and Population Loss: Cleveland, 1950–1980," *Explorations in Economic History* 44 (2007): 365–86.

24. Todd M. Michney, "Race, Violence, and Urban Territoriality: Cleveland's Little Italy and the 1966 Hough Uprising," *Journal of Urban History* 32, no. 3 (2006): 404–28; David Stradling and Richard Stradling, *Where the River Burned: Carl Stokes and the Struggle to Save Cleveland* (Ithaca, N.Y.: Cornell University Press, 2015); Marvin B. Sussman, R. Clyde White, and Eleanor K. Caplan, *Hough, Cleveland, Ohio: A Study of the Social Life and Change* (Cleveland: Case Western Reserve University, 1959).

25. Stradling and Stradling; Sussman, White, and Caplan; "Confiscate Weapons," *Salem News*, December 27, 1963.

26. Collins and Smith, "Neighborhood-Level View of Riots"; Michney, "Race, Violence, and Urban Territoriality"; Stradling and Stradling, *Where the River Burned*.

27. Ken Rosenbaum, "Rioting Continues in Hough Area," *Medina County Gazette*, July 22, 1966.

28. Collins and Smith, "Neighborhood-Level View of Riots."

29. Michney, "Race, Violence, and Urban Territoriality."

30. Ohio Bell Telephone Co., *Cleveland Metropolitan Area Street Address Telephone Directory*, April 1967; Cleveland Press Photograph Collection: Photograph Subjects, 1920–1982, Special Collections in the Michael Schwartz Library, Cleveland State University.

31. Cleveland Press Photograph Collection.

32. Deutsch, *Building a Housewife's Paradise*, 37.

33. United States Commission on Civil Rights, *Cleveland Still Has Unfinished Business in Its Inner City: Final Report of the Cleveland Subcommittee of the Ohio State Advisory Committee to the United States Commission on Civil Rights* (Cleveland: Subcommittee of the Ohio State Advisory Committee to the United States Commission on Civil Rights, 1967), 11, *HathiTrust*.

34. "Fear-Filled Hough: Delicate Balance of Hope, Hostility," *Akron Beacon Journal*, June 4, 1967.

35. Nishani Frazier, "A McDonald's That Reflects the Soul of a People: Hough Area Development Corporation and Community Development in Cleveland," in *The Business of Black Power: Community Development, Capitalism, and Corporate Responsibility in Postwar America*, ed. L. W. Hill and J. Rabig (Rochester, N.Y.: University of Rochester Press, 2012), 68–92.

36. Marcia Chatelain, *Franchise: The Golden Arches in Black America* (New York: Liveright, 2020); "Operation Black Unity Boycotts McDonald's," *Urban Enterprise: A Bi-Weekly Newsletter on Minority Economic Development*, October 10, 1969.

37. White, *Freedom Farmers*.

38. Patricia Sowell Harris, *None of Us Is as Good as All of Us: How McDonald's Prospers by Embracing Inclusion and Diversity* (New York: Wiley, 2009), 42.

39. "Operation Black Unity Boycotts McDonald's," *Urban Enterprise: A Bi-Weekly Newsletter on Minority Economic Development*, October 10, 1969.

40. Frazier, "McDonald's That Reflects the Soul of a People"; "Operation Black Unity Boycotts McDonald's," Urban Enterprise: *A Bi-Weekly Newsletter on Minority Economic Development*, October 10, 1969; advance copy of *NRN* article "Black Power Battles Close 3 McDonald's" by Ken Sandler and Noel Wical, box 69, folder 773, CULR.

41. Robert Metz, *Franchising: How to Select a Business of Your Own* (New York: Hawthorn Books, 1969).

42. In an ironic twist on the conflicts with juvenile delinquents, a police chief in small-town Upper Pottsgrove, Pennsylvania, gave "tickets" to motorists for good driving that were redeemable at McDonald's for burgers and fries. "McD Units Put Accent on 'Good Citizen' Role," *NRN*, July 20, 1970.

43. "Standalone Photo: 'Booking up Staff,'" *NRN*, July 1, 1968; "God Save the Onion Rings," *Cincinnati Enquirer*, March 10, 1976.

44. Advance copy of *NRN* article "Burger Chef Selling Out; Minnie Pearl Hanging On," box 69, folder 773, CULR.

45. Ashley D. Farmer, *Remaking Black Power: How Black Women Transformed an Era* (Chapel Hill: University of North Carolina Press, 2017).

46. Peniel Joseph, *Dark Days, Bright Nights: From Black Power to Barack Obama* (New York: Basic Books, 2010).

47. "Operation Black Unity Boycotts McDonald's," *Urban Enterprise: A Bi-Weekly Newsletter on Minority Economic Development*, October 10, 1969.

48. "Unity Groups State Positions on McDonald's, House of Israel," *Cleveland Call and Post*, July 26, 1969.

49. Michael Whiteman and Ken Sandler, "Reopen McD; Aim to Split Black Front," *NRN*, August 18, 1969.

50. In *Behind the Arches*, John Love gives a one-sided and overly optimistic account of Clement's role in the process. He states that after Clement's intervention, the tide turned in McDonald's favor: "Not long after Clement spoke out, the boycott of the McDonald's units ended and black franchisees were soon found for all six restaurants" (360). This ignores the significant negotiations and the many parties and processes involved. Clement appears to have played a minimal role.

51. Woody Taylor, "Unholy Alliance: Clement, Jackson Chide Urban League, NAACP," *Cleveland Call and Post*, August 9, 1969.

52. Advance copy of *NRN* article "Black Power Battles Close 3 McDonald's" by Ken Sandler and Noel Wical, box 69, folder 773, CULR.

53. Advance copy of *NRN* article "Burger Chef Selling Out; Minnie Pearl Hanging On," box 69, folder 773, CULR.

54. Advance copy of *NRN* article "Burger Chef Selling Out; Minnie Pearl Hanging On."

55. Michael Whiteman and Ken Sandler, "Reopen McD; Aim to Split Black Front," *NRN*, August 18, 1969.

56. Whiteman and Sandler, 18.

57. "Operation Black Unity Boycotts McDonald's," *Urban Enterprise: A Bi-Weekly Newsletter on Minority Economic Development,* October 10, 1969.

58. "McD Rejects Payoff; Blacks Cry War," *NRN,* September 1, 1969.

59. "500 at Antioch Meet, Black Unity to Expand Boycott of McDonald's," *Cleveland Call and Post,* August 30, 1969.

60. "Operation Black Unity Boycotts McDonald's," *Urban Enterprise: A Bi-Weekly Newsletter on Minority Economic Development,* October 10, 1969; "Police-Picket Clashes Feared in McD Battle," *NRN,* September 15, 1969, 1.

61. "Police-Picket Clashes Feared in McD Battle," *NRN,* September 15, 1969.

62. "McDonald's Breaks Off Negotiations; Picketing Resumed at Four Outlets," *Cleveland Call and Post,* September 20, 1969; Ken Sandler, "Blacks Split, Reunite; Pledge to Finish McD," *NRN,* September 29, 1969.

63. Frazier, "McDonald's That Reflects the Soul of a People."

64. Michael J. Whiteman to Joanna Martin, July 30, 1969, box 69, folder 69-773, CULR.

65. Press release, September 5, 1969, Community Education Department, Chicago Urban League, to City Editors; and press release, September 9, 1969, Community Education Department, Chicago Urban League, to City Editors, both in box 69, folder 69-773, CULR.

66. "Review of MUFSO '69: Undercurrents and Countertrends," *NRN,* September 29, 1969, 8.

67. "Review of MUFSO '69."

68. "Review of MUFSO '69."

69. Frazier, "McDonald's That Reflects the Soul of a People."

70. "For the Mighty McD: Costly Lesson in Bargaining with Black Power," *NRN,* March 2, 1970.

71. "Costly Lesson in Bargaining with Black Power," *NRN,* March 2, 1970.

72. "White Franchisee: 'Stupid' Militants Forced His Exit," *NRN,* March 2, 1970.

73. Jeff Tieger, "Letter to Editor: 'Kiddie Dog,'" *NRN,* August 18, 1969; Fredrich H. Thomforde, "Letter to Editor: 'The Real Beal,'" *NRN,* October 27, 1969; Fredrich H. Thomforde, "Letter to Editor: 'Up, Not Out,'" *NRN,* November 24, 1969; Brady Keys, "Letter to Editor: 'Slight Slip,'" *NRN,* October 26, 1970; Arthur McZier, "Letter to Editor: 'Mixed Reactions,'" *NRN,* October 12, 1970.

74. "McDonald's Black Owners Grateful to 'Rabbi Hill': Nurlie Roberts, Owner of Four Units Only Exception," *Cleveland Call and Post,* July 10, 1976.

75. "New Rules for Ghetto Franchising," *NRN,* August 18, 1969.

76. Fred Germain, "Church's Franchise Policies Challenged by Dayton Blacks," *NRN,* August 31, 1970.

77. "New Rules for Ghetto Franchising," *NRN,* August 18, 1969; Germain.

78. Deutsch, *Building a Housewife's Paradise.*

79. "The Ghetto Equation," *NRN,* September 1, 1969; "Pre-Dawn Blast Wrecks Ghetto Chicken Walk-Up," *NRN,* December 22, 1969.

80. "Ghetto Equation."

81. "Lessons in Ghetto Franchising," *NRN,* October 1, 1969. Perhaps it was that kind of thinking that produced another Black-owned McDonald's franchise in Ohio. In Toledo, the Christian Brothers Development Corp. took over ownership of an existing unit in the "inner city" starting

in May 1970. The group had been contacting franchisors as early as June 1969, and McDonald's was among those unwilling to consider their candidacy. But the company reversed course and in October provided the group with a large below-market loan to finance the unit. "McDonald's Tranquility Transfers Toledo Unit to Black Businessmen," *NRN*, June 22, 1970.

82. "'Anger Explained': Letter to the Editor by Tony Stadeker '. . . and Attitudes Clarified' by Ashby Smith," *NRN*, December 8, 1969, 7.

83. "Review of MUFSO '69: Undercurrents and Countertrends," *NRN*, September 29, 1969.

84. "If Riots Erupt Again . . . ," *Nation's Business*, March 1968.

85. "Mid-Year Assessment: Labor Shortage Is Still the Biggest Barrier," *NRN*, May 20, 1968, 22.

86. 114 Cong. Rec. S30498 (1968), *HeinOnline*.

87. Police officer "No. 36" confessed that morale was low among the D.C. force because officers were often subject to abuse from Black residents: "They can stand on the street and call you white honkey or white—or a no good this or a no good that. They can walk right up to your face and call you this and there is nothing you can do about it" (31940). A bus driver reported that while White passengers did on occasion swear, it was generally restricted to men drinking during wartime but "never filthy names like the colored people use" (31949). Store owner "Mr. I" refused to recount the language used by some who came into his establishment: "I am not going to repeat the profanity because it would be ridiculous . . . I do not even know some of these profane words that they use" (30526).

88. Chin Jou, *Supersizing Urban America: How Inner Cities Got Fast Food with Government Help* (Chicago: University of Chicago Press, 2017).

8. Government Burgers

1. Michael C. Dawson, *Black Visions: The Roots of Contemporary African-American Political Ideologies* (Chicago: University of Chicago Press, 2001).

2. Stanford S. Sesser, "Nimble Negro: Hard Work and Confidence Pave Way to Middle Class Life," *WSJ*, March 13, 1967, 12.

3. Robert McClory, "Claim Businessmen Soft," *Chicago Defender*, March 31, 1973. McGuire had worked for twenty-two years with S. B. Fuller, one of the most successful Black businessmen of the twentieth century, and his views were concordant with his employer's. Fuller came from a childhood of poverty in Louisiana and built up a multimillion-dollar beauty and personal care concern that employed a sales force of thousands and could reward top workers with Cadillacs. In the early 1960s he purchased the expansive commercial center that housed the Regal Theater and the Savoy. Dismissing the impact of racism on Black life, he argued that it was only a lack of hard work and motivation that impeded Black businesses. Ironically, racism was the undoing of his own business. Once White, southern customers realized that their favorite products came from a Black-owned business, they boycotted it, and discrimination from lenders pushed him to use unorthodox means of raising capital. His company went bankrupt in 1968, and he was indicted by the Securities and Exchange Commission for fraudulent sales of promissory notes. Clovis E. Semmes, "King of Selling: The Rise and Fall of S. B. Fuller," in Building the Black Metropolis: African American Entrepreneurship in Chicago, ed. Robert E. Weems Jr. and Jason P. Chambers (Urbana: University of Illinois Press, 2017), 92–110.

4. Robert Metz, "Franchiser Aids Store Operators from Minorities: Franchiser Promotes Ghetto Aid," *NYT*, April 20, 1969.

5. Chin Jou, *Supersizing Urban America: How Inner Cities Got Fast Food with Government Help* (Chicago: University of Chicago Press, 2017); Task Force for Equal Opportunity in Business, *Franchise Company Data* (prepared by the U.S. Department of Commerce, Washington, D.C., 1965), *HathiTrust*; Kenneth B. Clark, *Dark Ghetto: Dilemmas of Social Power*, 2nd ed. (Middletown, Conn.: Wesleyan University Press, 1965).

6. Jennifer Jensen Wallach, *Every Nation Has Its Dish: Black Bodies and Black Food in Twentieth-Century America* (Chapel Hill: University of North Carolina Press, 2019).

7. Post–World War II America centered mass consumption, but an enormous range of retail goods, large and small, were off-limits to Black consumers. The largest and most conspicuous goods were houses, which were conspicuously absent from *Ebony*. Because the magazine sought to promote a positive image of Black lifestyles and to showcase Black achievements, housing basically had to be ignored. Susannah Walker, "Black Dollar Power: Assessing African American Consumerism since 1945," in *African American Urban History since World War II*, ed. K. L. Kusmer and J. W. Trotter (Chicago: University of Chicago Press, 2009), 376–403; Diane Harris, *Little White Houses: How the Postwar Home Constructed Race in America* (Minneapolis: University of Minnesota Press, 2013); Lizabeth Cohen, *A Consumers' Republic: The Politics of Mass Consumption in Postwar America* (New York: Knopf, 2003).

8. During a six-year term as governor of Florida, he supported segregation in his election campaigns after the *Brown v. Board of Education* ruling. For Collins, segregation was simply "the way it was supposed to be," though he reportedly changed his views as the civil rights movement progressed. Glenn Fowler, "Ex-Gov. Leroy Collins Dies at 82; Floridian Led Way in 'New South,'" *NYT*, March 13, 1991.

9. Morton Mintz, "LBJ Picks Collins to Fill No. 2 Post in Commerce," *Washington Post*, June 22, 1965; "Collins to Leave U.S. Post to Seek Smathers Seat," *NYT*, June 30, 1966; "U.S. Commerce Secretary Raps Dr. King Alabama Boycott Plan," *Chicago Defender*, April 7, 1965; James T. Wooten, "Republican Is Elected New Senator in Florida," *NYT*, November 6, 1968.

10. LeRoy Collins stepped down from his Commerce position in the summer of 1966 to prepare for his 1968 Democratic U.S. Senate seat run in Florida, then left politics for fast food. James T. Wooten, "Republican Is Elected New Senator in Florida," *NYT*, November 6, 1968, 4. He was appointed interim president of Royal Castle Systems Inc., the burger chain that began in 1930s Miami as one of the burger chateaux but was on its last legs. Collins did not resuscitate the company, but rather departed as quickly as he came in. After less than a year he departed to practice law in Tallahassee, and the chain eventually closed in 1975. "Collins New Head of Royal Castle," *Miami News*, February 26, 1969; "Collins Quits Royal Castle," *Miami News*, December 24, 1969; "Once Best, Royal Castle Food Chain Bows Out," *Des Moines Tribune*, April 25, 1975. Coming from a Task Force that recommended franchises—and fast food in particular—Collins's abrupt departure was hardly a ringing endorsement for the industry.

11. Task Force for Equal Opportunity in Business, *Franchise Opportunities Handbook* (prepared for the U.S. Department of Commerce, Washington, D.C., 1965), *HathiTrust*.

12. Task Force for Equal Opportunity in Business, *Franchise Opportunities Handbook* (prepared for the U.S. Department of Commerce, Washington, D.C., 1985), *HathiTrust*.

13. "New York Man First Negro to Win New SBA Loan," *Jet*, May 13, 1965.

14. Ken Sandler, "Franchisee Suit May Mean the End of Chicken Delight," *NRN*, December 8, 1969.

15. Elizabeth Brenner, "Father of Franchising Profited from Failure," *Chicago Tribune*, July 23, 1980; "Chicken Delight Case: Franchisees Find Victory Has Bitter Aftertaste," *NRN*, May 11, 1970.

16. "U.S. Commerce Secretary Hodges Announces 'Task Force for Equal Opportunities,'" *Modern Franchising*, January–February 1965, 14, box 2, folder 1, ABWP.

17. "U.S. Commerce Secretary Hodges Announces 'Task Force for Equal Opportunities.'"

18. Jou, *Supersizing Urban America*.

19. Timothy D. Schellhardt, "Insurance That Guarantees Rent Payments Is Helping Many Small Businessmen Survive," *WSJ*, February 25, 1971.

20. Schellhardt.

21. "5 Here Gets $25,000 in Loan from SBA," *Chicago Defender*, May 8, 1965.

22. 114 Cong. Rec. S31921, S31929 (1968), *HeinOnline*.

23. Jou, *Supersizing Urban America*; Mark O. Thompson, "U.S. Loan Plan Opens Ghettos to Restaurants," *NRN*, September 9, 1968.

24. "Hilary Sandoval Dead at Age 43," *Del Rio News Herald*, June 12, 1973; "Despite Fed'l Support Minority Franchising Fizzles," *NRN*, August 31, 1970.

25. *Federal Minority Assistance Program: Hearings before the Subcommittee on Small Business of the Committee on Banking and Currency*, 91st Cong. (1969) (hereafter cited as *Federal Minority Assistance Program*). Hilary Sandoval abruptly resigned from the SBA directorship in 1970, to the bewilderment and dismay of many. He retired at his physician's advice, undergoing brain surgery in 1971 and 1972 before dying in 1973. Industry rumors circulated that Sandoval's health was not the impetus for his resignation, and instead that he was forced out for poor administrative skills and engaging in "reverse racism" against White entrepreneurs. "Hilary Sandoval Dead at Age 43," *Del Rio News Herald*, June 12, 1973; "SBA Chief, Force in Fed'l Minority Franchise Program, Resigns Post," *NRN*, December 21, 1970; *Urban Enterprise*, August 14, 1970.

26. *Federal Minority Assistance Program*, 29.

27. Robert McClory, "Red Tape Snarls Black Business," *Chicago Defender*, March 28, 1973.

28. Ken Sandler, "Franchise Conference Glow and Gloom," *NRN*, May 12, 1969.

29. "Despite Fed'l Support Minority Franchising Fizzles," *NRN*, August 31, 1970.

30. Jou, *Supersizing Urban America*.

31. Jou.

32. Thompson, "U.S. Loan Plan."

33. *Federal Minority Assistance Program*, 31.

34. *Federal Minority Assistance Program*, 33.

35. Robert Allen, *Black Awakening in Capitalist America: An Analytic History* (New York: Anchor Books, 1969).

36. *Hearing before the Subcommittee on the Judiciary of the Committee on the District of Columbia*, 90th Cong. 352 (1968).

37. Psyche A. Williams-Forson, *Building Houses Out of Chicken Legs: Black Women, Food, and Power* (Chapel Hill: University of North Carolina Press, 2006).

38. Jou, *Supersizing Urban America; Federal Minority Assistance Program.*

39. Ashley D. Farmer, *Remaking Black Power: How Black Women Transformed an Era* (Chapel Hill: University of North Carolina Press, 2017).

40. Cohen, *Consumers' Republic,* 189.

41. "Despite Fed'l Support Minority Franchising Fizzles," *NRN,* August 31, 1970; "Sandoval Testifies at House Hearings," *Urban Enterprise: A Bi-Weekly Newsletter on Minority Economic Development,* January 9, 1970, 6.

42. Patricia Sowell Harris, *None of Us Is as Good as All of Us: How McDonald's Prospers by Embracing Inclusion and Diversity* (New York: Wiley 2009).

43. *Federal Minority Enterprise Program.*

44. "25 × 25 × 2 = Minority Franchising," *Urban Enterprise: A Bi-Weekly Newsletter on Minority Economic Development,* January 9, 1970.

45. Jou, *Supersizing Urban America.*

46. *Federal Minority Enterprise Program;* "Feds Push Big Chains to Draft More Blacks," *NRN,* August 18, 1969.

47. At that time, the brand held nine hundred "family drive-to" restaurants. Financing for the venture came from Burger Chef, the Small Business Administration, and a local bank.

48. "Sandoval Testifies at House Hearings," *Urban Enterprise: A Bi-Weekly Newsletter on Minority Economic Development,* January 9, 1970, 6; "Henry's Out to Grab Share of Ghetto Biz," *NRN,* May 11, 1970.

49. "New Restaurant Opens in Detroit," *OMBE Outlook,* December 1970 / January 1971.

50. Jou, *Supersizing Urban America.*

51. "Despite Fed'l Support Minority Franchising Fizzles," *NRN,* August 31, 1970.

52. "Despite Fed'l Support Minority Franchising Fizzles."

53. *Federal Minority Enterprise Program;* "Black Business Still Struggles Here, but . . . ," *Chicago Defender,* September 6, 1972.

54. Jou, *Supersizing Urban America.*

55. "Franchise Industry Stumbles," *Urban Enterprise: A Bi-Weekly Newsletter on Minority Economic Development,* August 14, 1970.

56. President's Advisory Council on Minority Business Enterprise, *Minority Enterprise and Expanded Ownership: Blueprint for the 70s* (prepared for President Richard Nixon and Secretary of Commerce Maurice H. Stans, Washington, D.C., 1971).

57. President's Advisory Council on Minority Business Enterprise.

58. "Business Must Promptly Meet Rising Minorities' Expecations, Ana Told," *Advertising Age,* May 6, 1968.

59. Allen, *Black Awakening,* 178.

60. President's Advisory Council on Minority Business Enterprise, *Minority Enterprise and Expanded Ownership,* B25.

61. He was also president of International Industries Inc., parent company to International House of Pancakes, Orange Julius, Ramada Inns, and others.

62. Metz, "Franchiser Aids Store Operators"; President's Advisory Council on Minority Business Enterprise, *Minority Enterprise and Expanded Ownership.*

63. Leonard Korot and Thomas W. Bell, "Two Plus You: A Case Study of Minority Business Development," *FFM*, July 1970.

64. Korot and Bell.

65. Korot and Bell.

66. Korot and Bell.

67. Jou, *Supersizing Urban America*; President's Advisory Council on Minority Business Enterprise, *Minority Enterprise and Expanded Ownership*.

68. "President Nixon Unwraps Small Business Package," *OMBE Outlook*, April 1970, 2.

69. "President Nixon Unwraps Small Business Package."

70. "Art Mczier Is Captain of SBA's Minority Enterprise Team," *OMBE Outlook*, August 1970, 4.

71. "Fund for Black Business 200 New Jobs Created," *Chicago Defender*, April 29, 1974.

72. Jou, *Supersizing Urban America*; "Blacks in Hamburgers," *Chicago Defender*, October 13, 1973.

73. "Burger King Sets Up Minority Business Enterprise Company," *New York Amsterdam News*, February 10, 1973; "New Minority Investment Firm Formed," *Baltimore Afro-American*, February 10, 1973; "Ex-Ad Mgr. Buys into Burger Stores," *New York Amsterdam News*, November 6, 1971; "Chain Hires Black Franchise Expert," *NRN*, March 19, 1973; "Executive Outlook," *FFM*, September 1971.

74. "Miami Gets First Black Restaurant Franchise," *Baltimore Afro-American*, May 30, 1970.

75. Kelvin A. Wall, "Marketing to Low-Income Neighborhoods: A Systems Approach," *University of Washington Business Review*, Autumn 1969, 23, box 26, folder 4, CRJP.

76. "New York Banks Sponsor Largest Mesbic," *OMBE Outlook*, April/May 1971.

77. "Kentucky Fried Chicken Is Great," *Chicago Defender*, June 13, 1970.

78. Naulls was a former NBA star with the St. Louis Hawks, New York Knicks, and Boston Celtics.

79. "Loans for $875,000 Made for Investments in Watts," *NYT*, February 16, 1968; "New Ghetto Soul Food Unit Financed by Insurance Co," *NRN*, September 14, 1970.

80. Keeanga-Yamahtta Taylor, *Race for Profit: How Banks and the Real Estate Industry Undermined Black Homeownership* (Chapel Hill: University of North Carolina Press, 2019).

81. Karen Ferguson, *Top Down: The Ford Foundation, Black Power, and the Reinvention of Racial Liberalism* (Philadelphia: University of Pennsylvania Press, 2013); Karen Ferguson, "The Perils of Liberal Philanthropy," *Jacobin Magazine*, November 2018.

82. CORE received funds beginning in 1967 for training community workers, voter registration, economic development, and more. The organization needed the money, as it carried debt in the hundreds of thousands and saw potential donors running scared from McKissick's Black Power rhetoric. But that same rhetoric was ideal for Ford: ambiguous enough in its call for Black control of Black communities, and revolutionary enough to appeal to more volatile elements within the Black community.

83. Allen, *Black Awakening*.

84. Formed in 1963 under the aegis of the Urban League and the Metropolitan Council of the American Jewish Council, ICBO was a national, nonprofit consulting organization designed to assist minority businesses, either to start new ones or improve existing ones. By 1972, it had

assisted more than 7,500 minority firms. "Ford Foundation Provides $2.5 Million for MESBICs," *OMBE Outlook*, December 1970 / January 1971, 3.

85. "ICBO Pioneer in Minority Business Assistance Programs," *OMBE Outlook*, January 1970, 4; "ICBO Dinner Marks Ninth Year," *OMBE Outlook*, May 1972, 4.

86. "ICBO–Jewish Congress Form Minority Partnership," *OMBE Outlook*, March 1970, 11.

87. "ICBO Dinner Marks Ninth Year," *OMBE Outlook*, May 1972, 4.

88. Ashanté M. Reese, "Preserving the Legacy of Black Farming" (lecture, Black Urban Farmers and Gardeners Conference, New York, October 26, 2019).

89. "Toward a Black Middle Class: Sea Host, Inc., New York, New York," *FFM*, November 1969, 120–21.

90. Burger Chef was purchased by General Foods for $15 million; Pillsbury purchased Burger King, with its more than 225 restaurants; and Hot Shoppes purchased the corporation that franchised Bob's Big Boy drive-ins. "Shop Talk: '67 Pace Already Is Faster," *DIR*, January 1967; "General Foods Acquires Burger Chef Systems," *DIR*, November 1967; "Pillsbury to Acquire Burger King Drive-Ins," *DIR*, February 1967.

9. You've Got to Be In

1. *Federal Minority Assistance Program: Hearings before the Subcommittee on Small Business of the Committee on Banking and Currency*, 91st Cong. (1969).

2. "It's the Same Old Story: Celeb Chain Bites the Dust," *NRN*, December 21, 1970; "Namath Sells Out His Stock in Eateries," *NRN*, October 26, 1970; Paul Delaney, "Namath Tells Franchise Inquiry Business Isn't a Passing Fancy," *NYT*, January 23, 1970.

3. "Ed Dwight Interview," n.d., accessed January 5, 2019, http://www.thehistorymakers.com/biography/ed-dwight-39.

4. "Executive Outlook," *FFM*, March 1969.

5. *Urban Enterprise: A Bi-Weekly Newsletter on Minority Economic Development*, November 7, 1969.

6. Coca-Cola's first ad with a Black model appeared in *Ebony* in 1953, featuring Harlem Globetrotter Reece "Goose" Tatum. Celebrities went on to rule Coke's Black advertisements for the next two years. Brenna Wynn Greer, *Represented: The Black Imagemakers Who Reimagined African American Citizenship* (Philadelphia: University of Pennsylvania Press, 2019).

7. Robert Allen, *Black Awakening in Capitalist America: An Analytic History* (New York: Anchor Books, 1969).

8. Allen, 16.

9. "Executive Outlook," *FFM*, November 1969.

10. "Executive Outlook," 36.

11. "James Brown," *NRN*, May 26, 1969.

12. "Chock Full O' Nuts Adds Robinson to Directorate," *NYT*, December 13, 1961.

13. "Toward a Black Middle Class: Sea Host Inc., New York, New York," *FFM*, November 1969, 120; "Sea Chef Fishing Ghettoes with New Franchise Lure," *NRN*, March 25, 1968.

14. "Toward a Black Middle Class"; "Display Ad 2," *New York Amsterdam News*, September 21, 1968; "Display Ad 68," *New York Amsterdam News*, August 2, 1969; "Expanding Sea Host Adds New Restaurants," *New York Amsterdam News*, October 5, 1968.

15. "Toward a Black Middle Class."

16. "Franchisees Left Hanging as Sea Host Takes a Dive," *NRN*, August 17, 1970.

17. "What's Happening: The Celebrity Game," *FFM*, March 1969, 66; "'Fats' Chain Features Chicken, 'Dirty Rice,'" *NRN*, July 7, 1969; "Moms Bids Bye-Bye to Quick-Serve Food Chain That Never Was," *NRN*, May 25, 1970.

18. Emily J. Lordi, *Black Resonance: Iconic Women Singers and African American Literature* (New Brunswick, N.J.: Rutgers University Press, 2013); W. Ralph Eubanks, "I Will Move on Up a Little Higher: Mahalia Jackson's Power to Witness through Music," in *Can I Get a Witness? Thirteen Peacemakers, Community-Builders, and Agitators for Faith and Justice*, ed. Charles Marsha, Shea Tuttle, and Daniel P. Rhodes (Grand Rapids, Mich.: Eerdmans Publishing, 2019), 124–40.

19. "Photo Standalone 1," *Chicago Defender*, June 27, 1968.

20. "Mahalia Jackson's Chicken System Advertisement," *FFM*, January 1969.

21. Al Duckett, "Mahalia Had the Whole World in Her Hands: Mahalia Jackson at the Peak of Her Career," *Chicago Defender*, January 29, 1972.

22. "Toward a Black Middle Class: Mahalia Jackson," *FFM*, November 1969, 132.

23. Greer, *Represented*, 196.

24. "Toward a Black Middle Class: Mahalia Jackson," *FFM*, November 1969.

25. "Mahalia Jackson Moving into New Concepts for Urban Area Eateries," *NRN*, February 16, 1970.

26. "Gulf Oil Gives Boost to Mahalia Jackson," *NRN*, August 3, 1970.

27. In the late 1960s, the company came under fire for developing a new oil field off the coast of Angola, which was still in the grip of Portuguese colonial power, and activists such as Jesse Jackson rebuked Gulf's practices. "Gulf Oil to Spend in '68 $76 Million to Develop Oil Find off Africa," *WSJ*, September 20, 1967.

28. "The Big Companies Venture Their Help in the Civil Rights Effort," *WSJ*, June 14, 1968.

29. "2d Mahalia Jackson Chicken Shack Opens," *Chicago Defender*, October 31, 1970.

30. Charles Celander, *Chicago's South Shore: Images of America* (Charleston, S.C.: Arcadia Publishing. 1999); Ann Durkin Keating, *Chicago Neighborhoods and Suburbs: A Historical Guide* (Chicago: University of Chicago Press, 2004).

31. It was in South Shore that in 1967 Ida Mae Gladney, a Chicago resident who had migrated north from Mississippi, bought her first home. She and her family purchased a three-flat from an Italian homeowner and delighted in the quiet, tree-lined block. Within a few weeks, the neighbors across the street moved. Not merely their belongings; they detached the house itself from the lot where it used to stand, leaving a crater behind. Isabel Wilkerson, *The Warmth of Other Suns: The Epic Story of America's Great Migration* (New York: Random House, 2010).

32. "Residents Organize Opposition to Chicken Carry-Out Franchise," *South Shore Scene*, February 1970, 2, clipping sent from Leon Despres to the Hyde Park-Kenwood Community Conference, box 89, folder 15, HPKCC.

33. *Haines Criss Cross Directory, Chicago* (North Canton, Ohio: Haines & Company, 1971).

34. "Toward a Black Middle Class: All-Pro Chicken," *FFM*, November 1969, 127.

35. "Toward a Black Middle Class."

36. "Keys Turns Chicken—into Profits," *Washington Post and Times Herald*, August 20, 1967; Robert Lipsyte, "Sports of the Times: All-Pro Chicken," *NYT*, August 26, 1968; "Display Ad 128,"

NYT, September 5, 1968; Larry Casey, "Sports Ledger," *Chicago Defender*, September 10, 1968; Robert A. Wright, "Family Recipe Pays Off for a Negro Athlete: Brooklyn Outlet Is Opened by Keys's All-Pro Chicken," *NYT*, June 7, 1969.

37. "Display Ad 3," *NYT*, July 25, 1969.

38. Allen, *Black Awakening in Capitalist America*; Michael C. Dawson, *Black Visions: The Roots of Contemporary African-American Political Ideologies* (Chicago: University of Chicago Press, 2001).

39. Robert A. Wright, "Family Recipe Pays Off for a Negro Athlete: Brooklyn Outlet Is Opened by Keys's All-Pro Chicken," *NYT*, June 7, 1969; "Keys Quits NFL to Sell Chicken," *Washington Post and Times Herald*, July 8, 1969; "Franchise Units Will Be Opened," *NYT*, December 7, 1969; "All-Pro Picking Up Big Yardage," *NRN*, May 12, 1969; "Sports Star Succeeds as Businessman, Too," *Chicago Defender*, June 11, 1969; "Display Ad 99," *WSJ*, June 9, 1970; "All-Pro Chicken Stock, Notes," *WSJ*, May 26, 1970; "Photo Standalone 29," *New York Amsterdam News*, September 12, 1970.

40. Caroline Jones business journals, October 12, 13, 15, 16, 22, 27, 28, 1970, CRJP.

41. Fred Germain, "All-Pro Prexy Charges: Blacks Can't Find Unit Financing," *NRN*, May 24, 1971.

42. "Display Ad 635," *NYT*, March 3, 1974.

43. "Display Ad 106," *New York Amsterdam News*, May 1, 1971.

44. Dawson, *Black Visions*.

45. Nikol G. Alexander-Floyd, *Gender, Race, and Nationalism in Contemporary Black Politics* (New York: Palgrave Macmillan, 2007), 23, 24.

46. "All-Pro Chain to Double Size with Uncle Sam on the Line," *NRN*, September 27, 1971.

47. "All-Pro, KFC in Joint Minority Venture," *NRN*, September 28, 1970; "All-Pro, Kentucky Fried in Venture," *New York Amsterdam News*, October 24, 1970.

48. Germain, "All-Pro Prexy Charges"; "Hands across the Line," *Bay State Banner*, October 1, 1970; "Begins KFC Venture," *Urban Enterprise: A Bi-Weekly Newsletter on Minority Economic Development*, October 2, 1970, 1.

49. "The Market in Town," *NRN*, September 28, 1970.

50. "Avoid Competition," *NRN*, October 26, 1970.

51. "Bi-Racial Food Company Opens 13 New Stores," *Chicago Defender*, June 4, 1970.

52. "Burger King, Black Franchisor Joining Hands in Ghetto Unit," *NRN*, March 30, 1970.

53. "Brady Keys Scoring in Food Industry," *New York Amsterdam News*, August 4, 1973.

54. Toni Anthony, "Football, Food Passions for Roger Brown," *Chicago Defender*, September 14, 1970; Sallie Anne Neblett, "Greenvillian Tries Hand as Restauranteur," *Delta Democrat-Times*, October 5, 1970; "New Chain Defers Unit Cost for Minority Franchisees," *NRN*, October 12, 1970; "Chicken Chain Expansion Set," *Chicago Defender*, February 20, 1973; Dick Yerg, "A Big Business Man with a Big Business," *Journal News*, November 11, 1973.

55. Patterson had left behind a life in the South chopping cotton for twenty-five cents per hour; at Afri-Kingdom, he worked his way up from a crew member earning one dollar per hour to assistant manager and then to owner. His success allowed him to send half his pay to his family down south; as a result, his father was "only working one and a half jobs a day." Neblett, "Greenvillian Tries Hand as Restauranteur," *Delta Democrat-Times*, October 5, 1970.

56. Anthony, "Football, Food Passions."

57. "Afri-Kingdom, a Pre-Blanching System for Chicken." *Quickservice Magazine,* November/December 1971, box 5, folder 2, ABWP.

58. Yerg, "Big Business Man."

59. Anthony, "Football, Food Passions"; "Afri-Kingdom, a Pre-Blanching System for Chicken."

60. Alexander-Floyd, *Gender, Race, and Nationalism,* 57.

61. Kenneth B. Clark, *Dark Ghetto: Dilemmas of Social Power,* 2nd ed. (Middletown, Conn.: Wesleyan University Press, 1965), 1.

62. Roland L. Jones, *Standing Up and Standing Out: How I Teamed with a Few Black Men, Changed the Face of McDonald's, and Shook Up Corporate America* (Nashville, Tenn.: World Solutions, 2006). The winning bid for the construction of the outlet (to be located at 1425 North Clybourn) went to the H. Kent Hopkins Construction company and Arnold Armstrong, a Black-owned, South Side business that worked in residential, commercial, and industrial settings. "Blacks to Open New McDonald's Drive-In," *Chicago Defender,* June 22, 1971; Black Owned Business Directory, 1971, Operation PUSH Collection, box 105, folder 1188, Special Collections and University Archives, University of Illinois Chicago. McDonald's real estate agent proposed a Black-managed and -constructed store staffed by forty to fifty employees from Cabrini–Green.

63. Jones, *Standing Up and Standing Out.*

64. "Why the Negro Market Counts," *Business Week,* September 2, 1967, 68.

65. Felix Burrows, "Black Consumers: A Distinctive and Flourishing Market," address given on behalf of the Adolph Coors Company to the National United Affiliated Beverage Association, New Orleans, September 22, 1980, box 35, folder 10, VPIA.

66. "Chicken Chain Expansion Set," *Chicago Defender,* February 20, 1973.

67. Chin Jou, *Supersizing Urban America: How Inner Cities Got Fast Food with Government Help* (Chicago: University of Chicago Press, 2017).

68. Mike Sula, "The First Family of Fried Chicken," *Chicago Reader,* April 14, 2006.

69. In fact, just four years prior, Pierce and his family had been burned out of their home in South Shore. In July 1971, while Harold was working at the main restaurant, his wife, Hilda, awoke at 2:00 a.m. to an explosion and fire in a house they had purchased just seven years before. She and relatives managed to get out in time. Pierce suspected a bomb, but that had yet to be confirmed by the fire department at the time he spoke to reporters. Robert McClory, "Chicken Shack King's South Shore Home Ripped by Blast," *Chicago Defender,* July 8, 1971.

70. Yerg, "Big Business Man"; James Mateja, "Blocked in Business," *Chicago Tribune,* October 3, 1972.

71. *Fairness in Franchising Act: Hearings before the Committee on Commerce,* 94th Cong. (1976).

72. Andrew Diamond, *Chicago on the Make: Power and Inequality in a Modern City* (Berkeley: University of California Press, 2017), 61.

10. Blaxploitation

1. "Coney Island Dreamer Taken for a Roller Coaster Ride," *Daily News,* September 6, 1992; "Big Plan for Coney Island, Baby," *Daily News,* August 6, 1985.

2. "24 Food Spots Cited for Code Violations," *Daily News,* November 8, 1979; Raymond A. Sokolov, "Take-Out Chicken Stores Are Taking Firmer Hold Here," *NYT,* December 7, 1972.

3. Marvine Howe, "Afghans Get a Slice of the Fast-Food Business," *NYT,* October 7, 1984;

Tim Carman, "The Terrific Uncle C's Tells a Little Known Story about Fried Chicken in America," *Washington Post*, September 27, 2021.

4. Blaxploitation's demise came once Hollywood realized Black people would also go to major features featuring few (if any) African Americans (e.g., *The Godfather*). Ed Guerrero, *Framing Blackness: The African American Image in Film* (Philadelphia: Temple University Press, 1993).

5. Michele Gaspar, "Hyde Park Bank Still Makes Minority Loans," *Chicago Tribune*, February 1, 1978.

6. "Seating Utilization," n.d., box 27, folder 1, VPIA.

7. Roland L. Jones, *Standing Up and Standing Out: How I Teamed with a Few Black Men, Changed the Face of McDonald's, and Shook Up Corporate America* (Nashville, Tenn.: World Solutions, 2006), 247; "Black Customers and Black Stores," McDonald's internal memo, May 11, 1976, box 90, folder 5, VPIA.

8. "Fast Food's Restaurant Growth Index," *FFM*, January 1968, 25.

9. James W. McLamore, *The Burger King: Jim McLamore and the Building of an Empire* (New York: McGraw Hill, 1998); Pillsbury Company, *Annual Report for Year Ended May 31, 1973* (Minneapolis: Pillsbury Company, 1974).

10. Phil Norman, "Kentucky Fried Chicken Merger: New Spirit and Money," *Courier Journal*, July 18, 1971; Dan Dorfman, "Heard on the Street," *WSJ*, April 13, 1970; Jim Thompson, "Colonel Sanders Inns in 3 Cities to Be Sold," *Courier Journal*, December 24, 1971; "Heublein Bids $240 Million for Kentucky Fried Chicken," *Los Angeles Times*, January 22, 1971.

11. Lizabeth Cohen, *A Consumers' Republic: The Politics of Mass Consumption in Postwar America* (New York: Knopf: 2003).

12. For example, some areas of Harlem are designated "Trendsetters," a group illustrated in industry documentation with a photograph of two young, White women. These single renters reportedly "live life to its full potential," spending freely on socially and environmentally conscious goods, travel, and technology. This designation reflects new retailer attitudes about a gentrified Harlem. In contrast, "Family Foundation," illustrated with a Black family, characterizes stereotypical profiles of Black communities. This segment is home to people focused on religion, urban format radio, big box shopping, and dollar stores. Esri, "'Family Foundations' and 'Trendsetters' Market Profiles," n.d., accessed July 24, 2020, http://www.esri.com/tapestry.

13. Kelvin A. Wall, "Positioning Your Brand in the Black Market," *Advertising Age*, June 18, 1973, 71, box 10, folder 3, CRJP.

14. Margaret J. King, "Empires of Popular Culture: McDonald's and Disney," 424–37; Conrad P. Kottak, "Rituals at McDonald's," 370–76; and Marshall Fishwick, "Special Section of *Journal of American Culture*," 339–47, all in "The World of Ronald McDonald," ed. Marshall Fishwick, special issue, *Journal of American Culture* 1 (1978).

15. Joe L. Kincheloe, *The Sign of the Burger: McDonald's and the Culture of Power* (Philadelphia: Temple University Press, 2002); "McD Quarter Pounder to Hit Nationwide Market," *NRN*, January 22, 1973; "Drive-Ins Are Taking on Coffee Shop Look; Now What'll Coffee Shops Do?," *NRN*, January 19, 1970.

16. Andrew F. Smith, *Fast Food: The Good, the Bad and the Hungry* (London: Reaktion Books, 2016).

17. Bojangles' was founded by a former Hardee's franchisee by the name of Jack Fulk and his

partner Richard Thomas, who had been president of Kentucky Fried Chicken Operating Companies. John T. Edge, *The Potlikker Papers: A Food History of the Modern South* (New York: Penguin, 2017).

18. Caroline Jones business journals, June 1979, CRJP.

19. "A to Z: A Profile and Analysis of the 50 Top Food Operators," *NRN*, August 4, 1975; "Wendy's Sold on Old-Fashioned Way," *NRN*, May 28, 1973.

20. Edge, *Potlikker Papers*; Social Explorer, "U.S. Demography, 1790 to Present," n.d., https://www.socialexplorer.com/.

21. Michael Barrier, "Chicken That Packs a Punch," *Nation's Business*, July 1989, 52.

22. "Popeyes Thrives on Spicy Chicken," *Chicago Tribune*, June 18, 1979. Copeland's first wife's family was Cajun. Edge, *Potlikker Papers*.

23. "Popeyes Thrives on Spicy Chicken"; "Popeyes Spreads North to Cities via Franchising," *NRN*, August 2, 1976.

24. Andee Beck, "Television: Week of July 8–14," *Pacific Daily News*, July 8, 1979; Stewart Rouse, "Eddie Egan: On Narc Squad by Coin's Flip," *Central New Jersey Home News*, June 9, 1972.

25. Sokolov, "Chicken Chains Come to Roost."

26. Donald R. Case, "Food Service Site Selection," *Cornell Hotel and Restaurant Administration Quarterly*, November 1968.

27. Bill Mulligan, "Fast Feeders Create Downtown Pile-Up," *NRN*, May 27, 1974; "McDonald's Employee Shot after Fracas," *Evening Sun*, May 27, 1977; "Guard Shot outside West Side Restaurant." *Chicago Tribune*, May 5, 1975; "Two Wounded during Holdup," *Washington Post*, May 8, 1974; "Two Slain at Carryout: Man Held," *Washington Post*, November 10, 1977; "Four Youths Rob Little Tavern Diner in NE," *Washington Post*, April 21, 1970.

28. Sam Fullwood III, "Chicken George: Triumph and Disappointment," *Baltimore Sun*, March 1, 1987.

29. "White Castle Stays Downtown," *NRN*, August 6, 1973.

30. John DeFerrari, *Historic Restaurants of Washington, D.C.: Capital Eats* (Charleston, S.C.: American Palate, 2013); John DeFerrari, "The Hot Shoppes: Teen Twists, Mighty Mo's, and Pappy Parker's Fried Chicken," *Streets of Washington* (blog), April 22, 2013, http://www.streetsofwashington.com/.

31. Memoranda, F. H. Guterman to T. R. Hardart, January 24, 1973, and January 29, 1974, box 1, unprocessed, H&HR; "One Automat Left in N.Y. after Today," *Washington Post*, January 1, 1978; Matthew L. Wald, "Automat, a Down-to-Earth Windows on the World, a Shadow of Old Self," *NYT*, March 20, 1978; "Whopper Marches into Gotham as H&H's Fast Food Beachhead," *NRN*, December 18, 1974.

32. Burger King alone was not responsible—the company established a new Arby's franchise with exclusive rights in New York City and some Florida counties. Embarking on the Arby's venture resulted in extensive litigation with Burger King and Pillsbury, which settled in 1980 and allowed Horn & Hardart to retain the fourteen most profitable Burger King locations. Pillsbury Company, *Annual Report for Year Ended May 31, 1973* (Minneapolis: Pillsbury Company, 1973).

33. Derek Nystrom, *Hard Hats, Rednecks, and Macho Men: Class in 1970s American Cinema* (New York: Oxford University Press, 2009), 118.

34. Nystrom.

35. Meg Jacobs, *Panic at the Pump: The Energy Crisis and the Transformation of American Politics in the 1970s* (New York: Hill and Wang, 2016).

36. Charles J. Elia, "Gasoline Pinch Blamed for Further Weakness in Fast-Food Outlets' Already Faltering Sales," *WSJ*, July 17, 1979.

37. Jones, *Standing Up and Standing Out*, 262.

38. Joseph M. Winski, "Economy Restaurant and Take-Out Chains Worry about Effects of Energy Shortage," *WSJ*, November 21, 1973.

39. McDonald's TV commercials, 1970–73, U.S. National News Broadcasts, Vanderbilt Television News Archive, Vanderbilt University, Nashville.

40. "The Study of Economic Development Potential of the Beverly Area of Chicago" (prepared for the Beverly Area Planning Association by the Real Estate Research Corporation, Chicago, December 1974), Special Collections and University Archives, University of Illinois Chicago.

41. "Black Businesses Rise in D.C," *OMBE Outlook*, March 1970, 12.

42. Retail sectors were categorized using the North American Industry Classification System codes. Out of 336 total addresses listed in the *Chicago Street Address Directory*, published by the Reuben H. Donnelley Corporation, there were 111 establishments to which I could not assign codes. These were institutions, individual names (e.g., "Clara Waynard," which could be a residence or a sole proprietorship), and a few retail stores that either did not belong to an obvious sector or were ambiguous and for which different codes could apply. For example, Visual Aids Inc. could be related to optometry, office supplies, or manufacturing. Among the notable institutions were the United Auto Workers of America; the Railroad Food Workers Union Local 1460; several city agencies including Chicago Urban Renewal, Chicago Commission on Urban Opportunities, and the Cook County Departments of Welfare; the Chicago Conference for Brotherhood, the Woodlawn Organization, Planned Parenthood, the Chicago Urban League, Jehovah's Witnesses, and the YWCA. Though the sectors were imbalanced, there was greater breadth in comparison to the same corridor today.

43. Robert McClory, "Black Business Failures on Increase," *Chicago Defender*, March 24, 1973.

44. Morgan Park's Development Committee tried to no avail to bring in a dime store, and clashed with owners who left their storefronts in disarray—some of which were fast food establishments. Morgan Park Files, Morgan Park Development Committee, Standards Committee Report March 9, 1971, and June 8, 1971, Special Collections and University Archives, University of Illinois Chicago.

45. Paul Gapp, "Big Mac: Fresh Fare for Magnificent Mile," *Chicago Tribune*, December 31, 1978.

46. John F. Love, *McDonald's: Behind the Arches* (New York: Bantam, 1995).

47. "Designated Regional and Ethnic Exploration of Factors Affecting Present and Potential Consumer Attitudes and Appeal toward Burger King Restaurants" (prepared by J. Greene Associates–Qualitative Research Services for Kabon Consulting Inc., November 1973), box 26, folder 9, CRJP.

48. Needham, Harper & Steers, "The State of the Black Market," October 1977, 3, box 87, folder 17, VPIA.

49. "Display Ad 32," *New York Amsterdam News*, February 21, 1976.

50. "Display Ad 32 and Display Ad 30," *New York Amsterdam News*, July 21, 1973.

51. "Thousands Flee Leak of Deadly Chemical: Silicon Tetrachloride Escapes in Chicago," *Herald-Press*, April 27, 1974; "'Big Mac' Helped Big Leak Victims," *Chicago Defender*, June 1, 1974.

52. "Fight over Business Site," *Chicago Defender*, July 17, 1973.

53. Emmett George, "Alliance Fights Food Drive-Ins," *Chicago Tribune*, January 3, 1974.

54. The Community Relations Service, which offered guidance on how racial problems could be avoided or solved, was the only one of its kind in the federal government. It was a non-litigative, non–law enforcement arm of Justice, providing free services for a host of issues like housing, policing, and employment. The regional library was the Woodson branch, now home to the Vivian Harsh Collection, the largest African American archive outside of the Schomburg Center for Research in Black Culture in Harlem.

55. Community Relations Service, *Cooperation in Racial Conflict: CRS and the Business Community*, no. 1 (November 1975), no. 2 (December 1975), *HathiTrust*.

56. Deborah Wallace and Rodrick Wallace, "Consequences of Massive Housing Destruction: The New York City Fire Epidemic," *Building Research and Information* 39, no. 4 (2011): 395–411. The authors describe planned shrinkage as emanating from Nixon administration adviser Daniel Patrick Moynihan's recommended policy of "benign neglect." Moynihan wrote to Nixon in 1970 that his administration and Americans in general should take a stance of benign neglect of racial issues (essentially, stop talking about them, because that was the cause of racial discord). His phrase eventually spawned policies that actively neglected Black communities. Daniel Geary, *Beyond Civil Rights: The Moynihan Report and Its Legacy* (Philadelphia: University of Pennsylvania Press, 2015).

57. Deborah Wallace and Rodrick Wallace, *A Plague on Your Houses: How New York Was Burned Down and National Public Health Crumbled* (New York: Verso, 1998). Roger Starr, formerly at the city's Housing and Development Administration and later a professor at NYU, argued that "large parts of the Bronx south of the Cross Bronx Expressway are virtually dead. . . . Yet the city must still supply services to the few survivors. . . . If the city is to survive with a smaller population, the population must be encouraged to concentrate itself in the sections that remain alive. This sort of internal resettlement—the natural flow out of the areas that have lost general attraction—must be encouraged." Roger Starr, "Making New York Smaller: The City's Economic Outlook Remains Grim," *NYT*, November 14, 1976. The city did not hide its devaluation of these communities or the people who inhabited them, noting in 1969's *Plan for New York City* (Cambridge, Mass.: The MIT Press, 1969) that it could prove difficult to reconcile increased economic opportunities for Black and Puerto Rican residents and White flight in a context where "middle-class neighborhoods" felt "that blacks and Puerto Ricans are having too much done for them as it is."

58. Wallace and Wallace.

59. Frank B. Wilderson III, *Afropessimism* (New York: Liveright, 2020), 79.

60. Douglas J. Tigert, Richard Lathrope, and Michael Bleeg, "The Fast Food Franchise: Psychographic and Demographic Segmentation Analysis," *Journal of Retailing* 47, no. 1 (1971): 88.

61. Ernest Dichter to Barry M. Rowles, president, KFC, August 31, 1973, Kentucky Fried Chicken, 1972–73, box 194, EDP.

62. Pillsbury Company, *Annual Report for Year Ended May 31, 1969* (Minneapolis: Pillsbury Company, 1970).

63. James U. McNeal, Donald E. Stem, and Carol S. Nelson, "Consumers' Nutritional Ratings of Fast Food Meals," *Journal of Consumer Affairs* 14, no. 1 (1980): 165–79.

64. Warren J. Belasco, *Appetite for Change: How the Counterculture Took on the Food Industry* (Ithaca, N.Y.: Cornell University Press, 2006).

65. Belasco. Dr. Frederick Stare, founder and chair of Harvard's Department of Nutrition, defended processed foods, writing with another nutritionist that people should eat additives because they were good for them, and that the "back to nature" movement was a hoax.

66. "How to Eat Everything and Lose Weight," *Ebony*, July 1973, 74.

67. Jack Slater, "Hypertension: Biggest Killer of Blacks," *Ebony*, June 1973, 75, 80.

68. Fred Germain, "Restaurateurs Plan Bigger Ad Budgets, More and Better Publicity Drives in '73," *NRN*, January 22, 1973.

69. Patricia Sowell Harris, *None of Us Is as Good as All of Us: How McDonald's Prospers by Embracing Inclusion and Diversity* (New York: Wiley, 2009), 65. Other institutions saw and used the ghetto as gold mines. The NYPD called Harlem, a high-income district for police graft, "The Gold Coast." Graft in Harlem yielded one officer his down payment, and a Black peer complained to Congressman Charles Rangel that White officers were getting all the opportunities. Eric C. Schneider, *Smack: Heroin and the American City* (Philadelphia: University of Pennsylvania Press, 2011). New York's law enforcement was a model for extracting resources from Black communities. The Knapp Commission, which investigated corruption in the NYPD and released its findings in 1972, found that at least half of the force was guilty in some fashion. Apart from being paid off by offenders, the NYPD's Special Investigations Unit was the second-largest wholesaler of heroin in the city, behind the Lucchese crime family. The sources of graft were almost too many to name, extending far beyond vice and narcotics to construction, parking and traffic, gratuities (free meals, goods, and cash payments), and much more. Plainclothes officers' salaries were augmented by hundreds, while those in narcotics scored $3,000 per month (over $18,000 in 2020 dollars). *The Knapp Commission Report on Police Corruption* (New York: George Braziller, 1972). Officer Frank Serpico, played on the big screen by Al Pacino, articulated in his biography, "If the cops wanted to, they could eliminate a great deal of the narcotics business almost overnight." Instead, they kept the traffic running because payoffs from robbing bag men could be enormous—as big as $30,000 per man. Peter Maas, *Serpico* (New York: Viking Press, 1973), 271.

70. Keeanga-Yamahtta Taylor, *Race for Profit: How Banks and the Real Estate Industry Undermined Black Homeownership* (Chapel Hill: University of North Carolina Press, 2019).

71. James Stampley explained that in Chicago's Englewood community, lenders deliberately made payments too difficult for Black homeowners and could then procure "30 years' worth of profit in 1 year" from FHA insurance. James D. Stampley, *Challenges with Changes: A Documentary of Englewood, Illustrated* (n.p., 1979). The 1970s also saw investors enriched by unfair property tax laws that stripped African American Chicagoans of money and in some cases their homes. Andrew W. Kahrl, "Capitalizing on the Urban Fiscal Crisis: Predatory Tax Buyers in 1970s Chicago," *Journal of Urban History* 44, no. 3 (2018): 382–401.

72. Love, *Behind the Arches*.

73. Love.

74. Love, 253.

75. Love. By 1996, the net property value for land alone under franchise agreements totaled $2.5 billion (more than $4.5 billion today). *The Annual: McDonald's Corporation 1996 Annual Report*, 41, ProQuest.

76. Taylor, *Race for Profit*.

77. *Fairness in Franchising Act: Hearings before the Committee on Commerce*, 94th Cong. (1976).

78. Samuel George, Amber Hendley, Jack Macnamara, Jasson Perez, and Alfonso Vaca-Loyola, "The Plunder of Black Wealth in Chicago: New Findings on the Lasting Toll of Predatory Housing Contracts" (prepared by the Samuel DuBois Cook Center on Social Equity, Duke University, Durham, N.C., 2019).

79. "Standalone Photo," *Chicago Metro News*, June 18, 1977, 8.

80. C. Gerald Fraser, "Burger Shop in Harlem Shows It Can Cut the Mustard," *NYT*, November 11, 1972.

81. "Burger King Making It in Harlem," *New York Amsterdam News*, July 28, 1973.

82. Mary Larkin, "First Black-Owned McDonald's Fulfills Dream of Two," *Philadelphia Inquirer*, October 24, 1971; Dominic Sama, "The Road to Success Is Rocky for Black McDonald's Owner," *Philadelphia Inquirer*, November 14, 1976.

83. Barry Rohan and Allan Sloan, "Burger King 'Aid' Fund Aids the Chain's Profits," *Detroit Free Press*, October 3, 1976.

84. Angela D. Chatman, "Black Franchisees Charge Burger King with Racism," *New York Amsterdam News*, June 11, 1977.

85. Chatman.

86. "No Easy Money, but Lots of Work in Franchising," *Chicago Tribune*, July 26, 1974.

87. Report, Kabon Consulting Inc., 3, Burger King Black Consumer Market Research, 1973–74, box 26, folder 10, CRJP.

88. Taylor, *Race for Profit*.

89. Wista Johnson, "Demand for Blacks Great in Fast Food Biz," *New York Amsterdam News*, September 22, 1979.

90. Jason Chambers, *Madison Avenue and the Color Line: African Americans in the Advertising Industry* (Philadelphia: University of Pennsylvania Press, 2009).

91. The goal was to achieve at least a 10 percent share from General Foods across a range of employment and economic goals such as advertising, insurance, and supplies. "Covenant Between General Foods Corporation, White Plains, New York and People United to Save Humanity, Chicago, Illinois," n.d., Special Collections and University Archives, University of Illinois Chicago.

92. David Axelrod, "Black Business Needs Boost, Jackson Says," *Chicago Tribune*, May 21, 1977.

93. "Burger King Aiding Push," *Chicago Defender*, October 11, 1975; "Photo Standalone 23: 'Sealing a Deal . . . ,'" *Chicago Defender*, October 11, 1975; "Photo Standalone 3: 'For Push Projects . . . ,'" *Chicago Defender*, October 29, 1975.

11. PUSH and Pull

1. Burrell Advertising, "Analysis of McDonald's National Baseline Study for 1974 and for 1977 as It Relates to Black Consumers," June 2, 1978, box 62, folder 3, VPIA; "Marketing to the Black Consumer: A Motivational and Behavioral Study of Black Consumers of Convenience Foods"

(report prepared for Central City Marketing Inc. on behalf of Leo Burnett Company, Inc., submitted by Behavioral Systems Inc., February 1974), box 87, folder 13, VPIA.

2. Burrell Advertising.

3. "All Negro Davidson Hardy Agency Creates 'Multi-Ethnic' Advertising," *Advertising Age,* May 20, 1968.

4. "Black Ad Agency Leads Way to Sales for Negro Market," *Chicago Defender,* November 11, 1969; Emmett McBain Design Papers, Special Collections and University Archives, University of Illinois Chicago; Roland L. Jones, *Standing Up and Standing Out: How I Teamed with a Few Black Men, Changed the Face of McDonald's, and Shook Up Corporate America* (Nashville, Tenn.: World Solutions, 2006).

5. Jones.

6. Jones.

7. Kabon Consulting Inc., "Burger King Suggestions for Promotions for the Black Consumer," March 16, 1973, box 26, folder 9, CRJP.

8. Burger King / BCM, 1973–74, box 26, folder 9, CRJP.

9. Caroline Jones business journals, January 1978, May 10, 1979, October 1977, box 78, CRJP.

10. "Marketing Success," box 28, folder 19, CRJP.

11. "Black Customer Analysis," McDonald's internal memo, September 6, 1977, box 90, folder 5, VPIA.

12. "BCM Market Plan, 1979," Burrell Advertising, box 62, folder 4, VPIA.

13. "Black Customers and Black Stores," McDonald's internal memo, May 11, 1976, box 90, folder 5, VPIA.

14. "McDonald's 1979 Recommended Black Consumer Market Media Plan," Burrell Advertising, box 62, folder 4, VPIA.

15. Burrell Advertising, "Analysis of McDonald's National Baseline Study"; "Designated Regional and Ethnic Exploration of Factors Affecting Present and Potential Consumer Attitudes and Appeal toward Burger King Restaurants" (prepared by J. Greene Associates–Qualitative Research Services for Kabon Consulting Inc., November 1973), box 26, folder 9, CRJP; "Selected Menu Item Preferences Among Black McDonald's Customers: An Eight-City Study" (prepared by Audits & Surveys Inc., New York, for Burrell Advertising, July 1978), box 62, folder 1, VPIA.

16. Marshall Fishwick, "Special Section of *Journal of American Culture,*" in "The World of Ronald McDonald," ed. Marshall Fishwick, special issue, *Journal of American Culture* 1 (1978): 339–47.

17. This video was playing in an exhibit at the Smithsonian Institution's National Museum of American History, Washington, D.C., on April 3, 2017.

18. Robert L. Emerson, *Fast Food: The Endless Shakeout* (New York: Chain Store Publishing, 1979); Roman/Visschers Inc., "Market Analysis: The Fast Food Industry," March 1978, box 63, folder 13, VPIA; George Lazarus, "The Colonel's Out Shopping for New Advertising Agency," *Chicago Tribune,* July 4, 1977.

19. "Advertising to Blacks," n.d., box 7, folder 25, WANN.

20. Roger M. Kirk Jr., vice chairman, Brown & Williamson Tobacco Corporation, "Minority Marketing: A Continuing Challenge" (address, Twenty-Sixth Annual Conference of the National

Association of Market Developers, Washington, D.C., May 22, 1979). TTID; Johnson Publishing Company Inc., Research Department, "Facts about the Black Consumer," September 1987, TTID.

21. Jared A. Ball, *The Myth and Propaganda of Black Buying Power* (Cham, Switzerland: Palgrave Macmillan, 2020), 14.

22. Cheryl D. Cato, "Moral Covenants: How They're Faring," *Dollars & Sense*, August 1983, 81, TTID.

23. "Bob and Ed's Copy," letter to Jackson from Edward M. Byrd, director, Affirmative Action at Heublein, February 2, 1982, box 95, folder 29, VPIA.

24. "Franchising: New Opportunities for Black Business," *Ebony*, October 1984, 116; "PUSHing Ahead: Heublein's Pact with Blacks," *Fortune*, April 19, 1982, TTID.

25. Press release, jointly released by Heublein and Operation PUSH, March 17 (no year), box 95, folder 29, VPIA.

26. Covenant between Operation PUSH–Heublein, box 95, folder 29, VPIA.

27. Irwin Ross, "PUSH Collides with Busch," *Fortune*, November 15, 1982, TTID.

28. Ross, 92.

29. Carmichael, Carole A., "Burger King Opens Doors to Minority Owners," *Chicago Tribune*, May 29, 1983; Carole A. Carmichael and Herb Greenberg, "PUSH Opening 'Trade Routes' to Blacks: Prodding by Jesse Jackson Brings 'Minority Participation' Pacts," *Chicago Tribune*, May 29, 1983.

30. The reality of the Coke covenant, however, was that while it made a splash, the corporation essentially reneged on the terms by making its efforts so minimal as to be nonexistent, painfully illustrating the limits of Black capitalistic approaches. See Manning Marable, *How Capitalism Underdeveloped Black America*, rev. ed. (Boston: South End Press, 2000).

31. Jesse Jackson to PITB, March 24, 1983, box 95, folder 25, VPIA.

32. Covenant among Operation PUSH, Burger King Corporation, and the Minority Franchise Association, April 18, 1983, box 95, folder 25, VPIA.

33. Felix Burrows, president of ViewPoint, to J. Jeffrey Campbell, president of Burger King, June 16, 1983, box 95, folder 25, VPIA.

34. Covenant among Operation PUSH, Burger King Corporation, and the Minority Franchise Association, April 18, 1983, box 95, folder 25, VPIA.

35. Covenant among Operation PUSH; Barbara C. Hopkins, "An Interview with J. Jeffrey Campbell, chairman and chief executive officer Burger King Corporation," *Dollars & Sense*, August 1983, 26, TTID.

36. Ross, "PUSH Collides with Busch"; Hopkins, 26.

37. Carmichael and Greenberg, "PUSH Opening 'Trade Routes'"; Iver Peterson, "Making Big Business a Threat It Can't Refuse," *NYT*, December 2, 1984.

38. Hopkins, "An Interview with J. Jeffrey Campbell."

39. Donald C. Walker, "Moral Covenants: Good Business Sense," *Dollars & Sense*, August 1983, 9, TTID.

40. Burger King Corporation, *Dollars & Sense*, August 1983, 25, TTID.

41. "Fast Food Franchising," *Dollars & Sense*, August–September 1983, 138.

42. Outgoing correspondence, August–December 1985, box 30, folder 1, CRJP.

43. Walter J. Simon, Kentucky Fried Chicken, to Caroline Jones, February 21, 1986, box 33, folder 2, CRJP.

44. Susan Crandler, "Black Banks Get Burger King Aid," *Chicago Sun Times*, May 21, 1988.

45. "McSween Opens First McDonald's Featuring Jazz," *South End Citizen*, January 1, 1991; Thomas Olson, "After King: Black Business Earns Its Bread by Olson," *Crain's Chicago Business*, January 20, 1986.

46. Jason Chambers, *Madison Avenue and the Color Line: African Americans in the Advertising Industry* (Philadelphia: University of Pennsylvania Press, 2009).

47. Lammy Johnstone, "Black Agencies: Their Quiet Demise," *anny*, June 18, 1976, 16, box 6, folder 7, CRJP; "1986 RJRN U.S. Advertising Agencies Billings/Compensation," TTID.

48. "Black Business: A Status Report," 1987, box 47, folder 1, WAPP.

49. "Sickle Cell Sweepstakes on June 16," *New York Amsterdam News*, August 20, 1988.

50. "Colonel's Fund to Help Find Cure for Sickle Cell," *New York Amsterdam News*, August 20, 1988; "Flake to Guest Speak at Sickle Cell Meeting," *New York Amsterdam News*, June 11, 1988.

51. "Kentucky Fried Chicken Black Consumer Market, Corporate: 'Old Block' and 'Neighborhood,'" December 11, 1985, box 32, folder 17, CRJP.

52. "Final Report on Exploratory Attitude and Usage Study to Assess the Marketplace Dynamics Facing Kentucky Fried Chicken in Select Black Communities" (prepared for Mingo–Jones Advertising Inc. by Tri-Ad Research Services, August 1985), box 32, folder 16, CRJP.

53. "1986 RJRN U.S. Advertising Agencies Billings/Compensation," TTID.

54. Trudy Gallant-Stokes, "Brady Keys Does Franchising Right," *Black Enterprise*, September 1988, 56.

55. Cato, "Moral Covenants."

56. Heublein covenant, first quarter report, June 24, 1982, box 95, folder 29, VPIA.

57. Michael King, "Finding the Franchise Formula for Success," *Black Enterprise*, September 1987, 50.

58. Lyle Harris, "Seventh St. Corridor Gets a Fast-Food Restaurant," *Washington Post*, September 29, 1983.

59. Sharon Conway, "Holly Farms Stopped from Opening a Store in Mount Pleasant," *Washington Post*, April 7, 1977.

12. Ghetto Wars

1. "Kentucky Fried Chicken Black Consumer Market, 'Chicken Livers,'" December 16, 1985, box 32, folder 17, CRJP.

2. Frederick H. Lowe, "Black Owner Pushes Beef at McDonald's," *Philadelphia Daily News*, February 24, 1987.

3. Robert L. Emerson, *Fast Food: The Endless Shakeout* (New York: Chain Store Publishing, 1979).

4. Randall Rothenberg, "Burger King Ads: Which Way Now?," *NYT*, December 21, 1988; James W. McLamore, *The Burger King: Jim McLamore and the Building of an Empire* (New York: McGraw Hill, 1988).

5. "Ayer Wins Burger King Ads," *NYT*, September 29, 1987.

6. McLamore, *Burger King*; Eric N. Berg, "Burger King's Angry Franchisees," *NYT*, Novem-

ber 14, 1988; Randall Rothenberg, "Burger King Campaign: 'Break Rules,'" *NYT*, September 28, 1989; Randall Rothenberg, "Burger King in Account Shift," *NYT*, May 19, 1989.

7. R. J. Reynolds Industries Inc., "Management Presentations," November 1, 1984, New York (Richard P. Mayer, chairman and chief executive officer, Kentucky Fried Chicken Corporation, Presenting), TTID; Sid Smith, "On the Frying Line of the Great Chicken Wars," *Chicago Tribune*, September 15, 1982.

8. Smith; Caroline Jones business journals, August 9, 1982, and February 1981, box 78, CRJP.

9. Tom Bayer, "Can Grey Shake Church's Awake?," *Advertising Age*, January 31, 1983, TTID.

10. "Radio TV Reports" (Product: Church's Fried Chicken, Program: *Beverly Hillbillies*), April 1, 1986, WGN-TV, Chicago, box 32, folder 17, CRJP.

11. James Helmer, "Love on a Bun: How McDonald's Won the Burger Wars," *Journal of Popular Culture* 26, no. 2 (1992): 85–97.

12. Emerson, *Fast Food*, 135; John DeFerrari, *Historic Restaurants of Washington, D.C.: Capital Eats* (Charleston, S.C.: American Palate, 2013).

13. DeFerrari; "Bids and Proposals, Classified Ads," *Washington Post*, November 7, 1983; Benjamin Forgery, "Defying the Times: Old Sparkle Restored at the Little Taverns," *Washington Post*, December 24, 1983; Nancy L. Ross, "'Club LT' Beware: Little Tavern Bought, to Spruce Up Image," *Washington Post*, February 13, 1981; Tom Sietsema, "'Club LT' (District Dining)," *Washington Post*, February 19, 1987; Clay Chandler, "Little Tavern Shops Are Sold," *Washington Post*, August 19, 1988.

14. Michael Moss, *Salt Sugar Fat: How the Food Giants Hooked Us* (New York: Random House, 2013); Colman McCarthy, "Really Greasy Spoons," *Washington Post*, April 12, 1986.

15. John A. Jakle and Keith A. Skulle, *Fast Food: Roadside Restaurants in the Automobile Age* (Baltimore: Johns Hopkins University Press, 1999).

16. Betty Pleasant, "No Truth to Fried Chicken Story," *Los Angeles Sentinel*, July 5, 1984; Gary Alan Fine, "The Kentucky Fried Rat: Legends and Modern Society," *Journal of the Folklore Institute* 17, no. 2 (1980): 222–43.

17. Rona Gindin, "The Healthy Food Phenomenon," *Restaurant Business*, February 10, 1986, 125.

18. "Fast Food for the Diet-Conscious," *Nation's Business*, July 1983, 69.

19. Bozell, Jacobs, Kenon & Eckhardt Research, "Kentucky Fried Chicken Situation Analysis," December 1988, box 48, folder 8, CRJP.

20. Josée Johnston and Shyon Baumann, *Foodies: Democracy and Distinction in the Gourmet Foodscape* (New York: Taylor & Francis, 2009).

21. "Value of Fast Foods Upheld by Health Group," *Jet*, January 28, 1982, 25.

22. John H. Johnson, "Editor's Column," *Ebony*, August 22, 1987.

23. Robert E. Weems, *Desegregating the Dollar: African American Consumerism in the Twentieth Century* (New York: New York University Press, 1998).

24. Kenan Heise, "Chicken King Harold P. Pierce, 70," *Chicago Tribune*, March 11, 1988.

25. Sam Fullwood III, "Chicken George: Triumph and Disappointment," *Baltimore Sun*, March 1, 1987.

26. Fullwood.

27. Caroline Jones business journals, June 22 and June 24, 1981, box 78, CRJP.

28. Sam Fullwood III, "Running Off Power of One Man's Charisma, Food Empire Falters," *Baltimore Sun*, March 2, 1987; Fullwood, "Chicken George."

29. Barbara Marsh, "Fast-Food Firm Finds a Niche in Black Neighborhoods," *WSJ*, August 2, 1989.

30. Marsh; "Inner-City Restaurant's Success a Fish Story," *Pentagraph*, July 9, 1989.

31. "Fast Food Franchising," *Dollars & Sense*, August–September 1983, 138.

32. Nancy L. Croft and Meg Whittemore, "Finding the Right Franchise," *Nation's Business*, February 1988; Meg Whittemore, "The Great Franchise Boom," *Nation's Business*, September 1984; Nancy Anne Rathburn, "The Franchising Wave of the 80s," *Nation's Business*, March 1982. The article did not mention that Charlotta was married to Rufus Stephens, another McDonald's franchisee. In 1981, there was a confrontation in Baltimore between a Black McDonald's operator and corporate that gave him his store. The company evicted another African American franchisee, Ronald Thomas, allegedly for nonpayment of rent, and installed Rufus Stephens. Thomas, who bought the store in 1970, fought the proceedings, claiming that corporate said it would remodel his store but then started a year late, did not follow the specifications, yet still charged him higher rent. His eviction prompted a boycott supported by leaders such as City Councilman Kwesi Mfume and State Senator Clarence M. Mitchell.

33. Meg Whittemore, "Franchising's Future," *Nation's Business*, February 1986, 53.

34. Michael King, "Finding the Franchise Formula for Success," *Black Enterprise*, September 1987.

35. "Franchising: New Opportunities for Black Business," *Ebony*, October 1984, 116.

36. Matthew C. Sonfield, "Progress and Success in the Development of Black-Owned Franchise Units," *Review of Black Political Economy* 22, no. 2 (1993): 73–87; "Eye on the Future," *Black Enterprise*, September 1988, 45; Buck Brown, "Minority Franchisees Allege Redlining by the Big Chains," *WSJ*, October 26, 1988.

37. Brown.

38. "Fast Food Franchising," *Dollars & Sense*, August–September 1983, 142.

39. Andrew Geller, "$50M Suit Challenges Big Mac Black Franchisee: I Was Kept from White Areas," *Philadelphia Daily News*, March 8, 1984.

40. "Fast Food Franchising," 142.

41. Andrew Geller, "Mac Attacked by Minorities," *Philadelphia Daily News*, March 6, 1984; Tamar Lewin, "McDonald's Is Battling with Black Franchisee," *NYT*, March 12, 1984.

42. Stacie Knable, "Five Big Winners in the Business Game," *Baltimore Sun*, January 8, 1984.

43. Wanda L. Dobson, "Franchising Happy Alternative for the Ownership," *Baltimore Sun*, November 20, 1985; Dudley C. Snyder, "Golden Arches Deliver for Franchisee," *Baltimore Evening Sun*, January 26, 1987; Nancy Kercheval, "A Quick Rise in the Fast-Food Biz," *Baltimore Sun Magazine*, April 9, 1989, 10.

44. Liz Bowle, "McDonald's Settlement Reported," *Baltimore Sun*, February 26, 1987.

45. Angela Jones, "Fast Food Is a Boomer," *New York Amsterdam News*, April 12, 1980; J. Zamgba Browne, "Bojangles' Booming on Famed 125th Street," *New York Amsterdam News*, October 26, 1985.

46. Smith, "On the Frying Line."

47. Caroline Jones business journals, April 3 and April 16, 1981, box 78, CRJP.

48. Memorandum, Marvin Winkfield to Dick Sivewright, October 14, 1981, box 32, folder 18, CRJP.

49. Memorandum, Winkfield to Sivewright.

50. Paulette Thomas, "Going Out for Church's Fried Chicken," *WSJ*, May 12, 1987.

51. Courtland Milloy, "Washington's Fried Chicken Wars," *Washington Post*, September 7, 1981. Corroborating extant reports, I met a D.C. native in 2016 while doing research in the city; when I asked him when he thought fast food became a major presence in the District, he replied without hesitation or equivocation, "The eighties."

52. William J. Wilson, *When Work Disappears: The World of the New Urban Poor* (New York: Knopf, 1996).

53. Wilson.

54. Melaniphy & Associates Inc., *Chicago Comprehensive Neighborhood Needs Analysis* (n.p., 1982).

55. Melaniphy & Associates Inc.

56. Memorandum, David Fishel to John Cox at Heublein and Greg Reynolds at KFC, January 14, 1983, TTID.

57. Carolyn C. Cannuscio, Eve E. Weiss, Hannah Frunchtman, Jeannette Schroeder, Janet Weiner, and David A. Asch, "Visual Epidemiology: Photographs as Tools for Probing Street-Level Etiologies," *Social Science and Medicine* 69 (2009): 553–64.

58. Naa Oyo A. Kwate and Ji Meng Loh, "Fast Food and Liquor Store Density, Co-Tenancy, and Turnover: Vice Store Operations in Chicago 1995–2008," *Applied Geography* 67 (2016): 1–13.

59. Weems, *Desegregating the Dollar.*

60. Weems.

61. Jovan Scott Lewis's concept of sufferation is central to his study of the Jamaican lottery scam in Montego Bay. He follows several young Jamaican men engaged in the fraud, for whom the notion of sufferation was deeply embedded in their experience of the world. Intergenerational, immutable poverty was central to this experience. Sufferation means the routine, systematic exclusion from productive life, such that it "is understood within the cosmological and ontological senses Jamaicans use to understand and organize their world." Lewis, *Scammer's Yard: The Crime of Black Repair in Jamaica* (Minneapolis: University of Minnesota Press, 2020), 53. My use of the word is not to the level of the ontological, but still something more than regular "suffering." The harms Black communities sustained across socioeconomic, social, and health conditions were serious, intersecting, and precipitated and maintained by state actions.

62. Weems, *Desegregating the Dollar.*

63. Wilson, *When Work Disappears.*

64. Carol Anderson, *White Rage: The Unspoken Truth of Our Racial Divide* (New York: Bloomsbury, 2017).

65. Manning Marable, *How Capitalism Underdeveloped Black America*, rev. ed. (Boston: South End Press, 2000).

66. Naa Oyo A. Kwate, "Fried Chicken and Fresh Apples: Racial Segregation as a Fundamental Cause of Fast Food Density in Black Neighborhoods," *Health & Place* 14, no. 1 (2008): 32–44.

67. Wilson, *When Work Disappears.*

68. Katherine S. Newman, *No Shame in My Game: The Working Poor in the Inner City* (New York: Vintage, 1999).

69. Elijah Anderson, *Streetwise: Race, Class, and Change in an Urban Community* (Chicago: University of Chicago Press, 1990); Philippe Bourgois, *In Search of Respect: Selling Crack in El Barrio* (Cambridge: Cambridge University Press, 1995).

70. Newman, *No Shame in My Game*.

71. Anderson, *White Rage*; Bourgois, *In Search of Respect*; Elizabeth Hinton, *From the War on Poverty to the War on Crime: The Making of Mass Incarceration in America* (Cambridge, Mass.: Harvard University Press, 2017).

72. Elijah Anderson, *Streetwise: Race, Class and Change in an Urban Community* (Chicago: University of Chicago Press, 1990).

73. Weems, *Desegregating the Dollar*, 110.

74. Naa Oyo A. Kwate, "Take One Down, Pass It Around, 98 Alcohol Ads on the Wall: Outdoor Advertising in New York City's Black Neighbourhoods," *International Journal of Epidemiology* 36 (2007): 988–90; Naa Oyo A. Kwate, "Racial Segregation and the Marketing of Health Inequality," in *Beyond Discrimination: Racial Inequality in a Postracist Era*, ed. Fredrick C. Harris and Robert C. Lieberman (New York: Russell Sage, 2013), 317–48.

75. Eaton & Associates, "Kool Inner-City Research Project," Cincinnati, Ohio, January 6, 1986, TTID.

76. "Planning Tactical Usage: Out of Home," 1990, TTID.

77. Bourgois, *In Search of Respect*.

78. Alan Radding, "Outdoor Revival," in *Minority Marketing* (Chicago: Crain Books, 1980). For a comprehensive history of menthol cigarette marketing to African Americans, see Keith Wailoo's *Pushing Cool: Big Tobacco, Racial Marketing, and the Untold Story of the Menthol Cigarette* (Chicago: University of Chicago Press, 2021).

79. Audio recording, interview with Caroline Jones, tape 1, side 1, box 9, Campbell "Red & White" Soups Advertising History Collection, circa 1904–90, Archives Center, Smithsonian Institution, National Museum of American History, Washington, D.C.

80. Eaton & Associates, "Kool Inner-City Research Project."

81. Marcia Chatelain, *Franchise: The Golden Arches in Black America* (New York: Liveright, 2020).

82. "Black YAS Initiative," 1989, TTID.

83. "Present RJR Commitments to NNPA Convention," 1986, TTID.

84. "Salem Brand Black Market Promotion Plan," March 9, 1984, 10, TTID.

85. Advertisement, June 1982, TTID.

86. Press release, TTID.

87. "BK Weighs Pros and Cons of Vending Machines," *Nation's Restaurant News*, November 7, 1974.

88. Memorandum, Ed Dudley to Dick Mayer, March 8, 1983, R. J. Reynolds Collection; Sidney Morris, St. Louis, to John J. Sept, R. J. Reynolds, February 21, 1983; memorandum, Richard P. Mayer to Hicks B. Waldron, March 8, 1983; John J. Sept to W. Bill Reece, March 23, 1983, R. J. Reynolds Collection; W. M. "Bill" Reece, to R. D. "Bob" Sherrod, April 13, 1983; memorandum, R. D. "Bob" Sherrod to Ralph Angiuoli, April 19, 1983, all in TTID.

89. Deborah Lupton, *Food, the Body and the Self* (Thousand Oaks, Calif.: Sage, 1996).

90. Yunxiang Yan, "McDonald's in Beijing: The Localization of Americana," in *Golden Arches East: McDonald's in East Asia,* ed. James L. Watson (Stanford, Calif.: Stanford University Press, 1997); Rafi Grosglik and Uri Ram, "Authentic, Speedy and Hybrid: Representations of Chinese Food and Cultural Globalization in Israel," *Food, Culture & Society* 16, no. 2 (2013): 223–43; Joe L. Kincheloe, *The Sign of the Burger: McDonald's and the Culture of Power* (Philadelphia: Temple University Press, 2002); Deborah Lupton, "Consumerism, Commodity Culture and Health Promotion," *Health Promotion International* 9 (1994): 111–18.

13. Criminal Chicken

1. Robin R. Means Coleman, *African American Viewers and the Black Situation Comedy: Situating Racial Humor* (New York: Garland, 1998), 107.

2. Means Coleman, 121.

3. Means Coleman, 108.

4. Means Coleman, 106.

5. Elijah Anderson, "The White Space," *Sociology of Race and Ethnicity* 1, no. 1 (2015): 13.

6. Anderson, 14.

7. Rosten Woo, Meredith TenHoor, and Damon Rich, *Street Value: Shopping, Planning, and Politics at Fulton Mall* (New York: Princeton Architectural Press, 2010), 91.

8. Ashanté M. Reese, 2019. *Black Food Geographies: Race, Self-Reliance, and Food Access in Washington, D.C.* (Chapel Hill: University of North Carolina Press, 2019).

9. Elizabeth Chin, *Purchasing Power: Black Kids and American Consumer Culture* (Minneapolis: University of Minnesota Press, 2001), 49.

10. In 1977, *Time,* in a piece that otherwise railed against the depravity of the "underclass," characterized this group's typical consumption as "hot dogs, Twinkies, fritos, soda pop and, in rare cases, whatever can be fished out of the garbage can." Keeanga-Yamahtta Taylor, *Race for Profit: How Banks and the Real Estate Industry Undermined Black Homeownership* (Chapel Hill: University of North Carolina Press, 2019), 231.

11. Alix M. Freedman, "Amid Ghetto Hunger, Many More Suffer Eating Wrong Foods," *WSJ,* December 18, 1990.

12. Freedman.

13. Freedman.

14. Sheila Bock, "I Know You Got Soul: Traditionalizing a Contested Cuisine," in *Comfort Food: Meanings and Memories,* ed. Michael Owen Jones and Lucy Long (Oxford: University Press of Mississippi, 2017), 163-181.

15. Bock; Jennifer Jensen Wallach, *Every Nation Has Its Dish: Black Bodies and Black Food in Twentieth-Century America* (Chapel Hill: University of North Carolina Press, 2019).

16. Frederick Opie, *Hog and Hominy: Soul Food from Africa to America* (New York: Columbia University Press, 2010).

17. Byron Hurt, dir., *Soul Food Junkies* (coproduced by God Bless the Child Productions and the Independent Television Service and the National Black Programming Consortium, 2012).

18. Freedman, "Amid Ghetto Hunger"; Alix M. Freedman, "Habit Forming: Fast-Food Chains Play Central Role in Diet of the Inner-City Poor," *WSJ,* December 19, 1990.

19. Freedman, "Habit Forming."

20. W. E. B. Du Bois, *The Souls of Black Folk* (1903; repr., New York: Penguin, 2018).

21. Florence Fabricant, "Enter the 'New American Cuisine,'" *NYT*, September 25, 1983; Bryan Miller, "Restaurants," *NYT*, April 5, 1991; Bryan Miller, "Restaurants," *NYT*, June 7, 1991.

22. Judith Williams, "The Mango Gang and New World Cuisine: White Privilege in the Commodification of Latin American and Afro-Caribbean Foods," in *Black Food Matters: Racial Justice in the Wake of Food Justice*, ed. Ashanté M. Reese and Hannah Garth (Minneapolis: University of Minnesota Press, 2020), 251-278.

23. Freedman, "Amid Ghetto Hunger." Also recounted in the article, the *Wall Street Journal*'s intrepid journalist shadowed a social worker who had to traverse urine-smelling hallways and pass bullet-ridden doors to visit Black households where some adults were addicted to crack and others to soda, dwellings that emitted "a foul stench" and housed residents like "a ragged woman, surrounded by a brood of children."

24. Okwui Enwezor, "The Uses of Afro-Pessimism," in *Snap Judgments: New Positions in Contemporary African Photography* (New York: International Center of Photography, 2006), 12.

25. Enwezor, 15.

26. Freedman, "Habit Forming."

27. Freedman.

28. Julie Guthman, *Weighing In: Obesity, Food Justice, and the Limits of Capitalism* (Berkeley: University of California Press, 2011), 50–51.

29. Guthman, 56.

30. Sabrina Strings, "Obese Black Women as 'Social Dead Weight': Reinventing the 'Diseased Black Woman,'" *Signs: Journal of Women in Culture and Society* 41, no. 1 (2015): 107–30.

31. Strings, 109.

32. "To the Roundtable," June 26, 1990, box 3, folder 3, CRJP.

33. Victor Wishna, 2000. "Getting with the Program: As Minority Populations Grow Nationally, Restaurants Are Scrambling for More—and More Focused—Ways to Make Them Customers," *Restaurant Business*, March 1, 2000.

34. Audio recording, interview with Caroline Jones, tape 1, side 1, box 9, Campbell "Red & White" Soups Advertising History Collection, circa 1904–90, Archives Center, Smithsonian Institution, National Museum of American History, Washington, D.C.; Carolyn Phillips, "Data Gap: When It Comes to Understanding Black Consumers, Most Companies Are Surprisingly Ignorant," *WSJ*, February 19, 1993.

35. "Advertising Agencies: What They Are, What They Do, and How They Do It" (published by the American Association of Advertising Agencies, New York, 1976), box 31, folder 1, CRJP.

36. Audio recording, interview with Caroline Jones; Warren Berger, "A Different World," *Advertising Age*, July 6, 1992.

37. Advertising Inc., "A Summary of Fourteen Focus Groups among African Americans to Identify Major Problems and Challengers [*sic*] in the Black Community" (prepared by Thorne Creative Research Services for Caroline Jones, August 1994), box 6, folder 23, CRJP.

38. "Conference Report, Secret," June 5, 1989, TTID. Black shops did not necessarily hold the accounts for Black-targeted brands or brands that had a high market share. Uptown, for example, was developed by FCB / Leber Katz.

39. Allan M. Brandt, *The Cigarette Century: The Rise, Fall, and Deadly Persistence of the Product That Defined America* (New York: Basic, 2007); Shaun Assael, "The Uptown Fiasco: Why Big Tobacco Woos Minorities," *Adweek*, January 29, 1990, TTID; Marcus Mabry, Daniel Glick, and Shawn D. Lewis, "Fighting Ads in the Inner City," *Newsweek*, February 5, 1990, TTID.

40. Randall Rothenberg, "The Stresses in Marketing to Minorities," *NYT*, March 9, 1990. Described as "animated and angry" by the *Times*, Jones resented the implication that Black shops bore a duty to eschew marketing troublesome products like cigarettes. She held that even though her father was dying from emphysema, she would not necessarily turn down a tobacco account. Jones claimed the country's ability to adequately educate its children was more important to worry about.

41. Brandt, *Cigarette Century*, 314.

42. J. C. Melaniphy, *Restaurant and Fast Food Site Selection* (New York: John Wiley & Sons, 1992), 64.

43. Melaniphy, 64.

44. Nancy L. Croft and Meg Whittemore, "Finding the Right Franchise," *Nation's Business*, February 1988, 53; Mehrsa Baradaran, *How the Other Half Banks: Exclusion, Exploitation, and the Threat to Democracy* (Cambridge, Mass.: Harvard University Press, 2015); *Check Cashing Stores: Necessary Service or Excessive Profit? Hearing before the Human Resources and Intergovernmental Relations Subcommittee of the Committee on Government Operations*, 103rd Cong. (1993). Predatory financing was compounded at check cashing by criminal activity. Swift, a robber on Chicago's South Side, identified currency exchanges as ideal for robberies, and Icepick stated that the corner of East 43rd Street and Cottage Grove Avenue was a particularly fruitful location—it thronged with people, what with it hosting a Western Union check cashing outlet, a grocery store, a liquor store, and a takeout restaurant called Tasty Beef. Peter K. B. St. Jean, *Pockets of Crime: Broken Windows, Collective Efficacy, and the Criminal Point of View* (Chicago: University of Chicago Press, 2007).

45. Joseph Mastrocovi, Most Distribution Services Inc., to Diedre Thompkins, R. J. Reynolds, March 13, 1996, 2, TTID.

46. Mastrocovi to Thompkins, 4.

47. Keith Wailoo, *Pushing Cool: Big Tobacco, Racial Marketing, and the Untold Story of the Menthol Cigarette* (Chicago: University of Chicago Press, 2021).

48. Bozell, Jacobs, Kenon & Eckhardt Research, "Kentucky Fried Chicken Situation Analysis," December 1988, box 48, folder 8, CRJP.

49. Caroline Jones Advertising Inc., "Successful Marketing of KFC to Black Consumers," January 22, 1992, box 48, folder 12, CRJP.

50. Letter from WilCom Associates, St. Paul, Minnesota, December 26, 1991, inviting Caroline Jones Advertising to present to KFC in Louisville, box 48, folder 9, CRJP.

51. Indeed, a study conducted in the fall of 1999 examined food messaging on "Black prime time shows" such as *Malcolm and Eddie*, finding that these programs had more advertisements for candy and soda than did general audience shows. Fast food constituted the same proportion (31 percent versus 30 percent) across both markets, but it is a certainty that the racial makeup of those ads would have differed. Manasi A. Tirodkar and Anjali Jain, "Food Messages on African American Television Shows," *American Journal of Public Health* 93 (2003): 439–41.

52. "Creative Promotions and Rationale for Kentucky Fried Chicken, January 22, 1992," box 48, folder 11, CRJP.

53. Audio recording, interview with Caroline Jones, tape 1, side 1, box 9, Campbell "Red & White" Soups Advertising History Collection, circa 1904–90, Archives Center, Smithsonian Institution, National Museum of American History, Washington, D.C.

54. "Creative Promotions and Rationale for Kentucky Fried Chicken, January 22, 1992," box 48, folder 11, CRJP.

55. Burrell Advertising, "The Black Consumer Market MIR," 1993, box 50, folder 2, CRJP.

56. "Presentation to McDonald's and McCann–Erickson, Caroline Jones Advertising Inc.," November 20, 1992, box 50, folder 1, CRJP.

57. "Presentation to McDonald's and McCann–Erickson."

58. At the Expo, there was to be a Children's Village, and one of the featured events was a fire prevention and safety program. A New York City firefighter named John Ruiz ("The Rappin' Fireman") who used rap music to teach fire safety, was slated to perform. McDonald's would underwrite the costs of twelve shows, three daily. "Presentation to McDonald's and McCann–Erickson."

59. Cynthia Franklin, Marketing Consultant, Kwanzaa Holiday Expo, Bronx, New York, to Patrick Buddington, October 20, 1994, box 49, folder 8, CRJP; Faye A. Rodney, president, *New York Carib News*, to Caroline Jones, president, Caroline Jones Agency, October 21, 1994, box 49, folder 8, CRJP.

60. Advertising Inc., "A Summary of Fourteen Focus Groups among African Americans to Identify Major Problems and Challengers [*sic*] in the Black Community" (prepared by Thorne Creative Research Services for Caroline Jones, August 1994), box 6, folder 23, CRJP.

61. Joe L. Kincheloe, *The Sign of the Burger: McDonald's and the Culture of Power* (Philadelphia: Temple University Press, 2002), 59.

62. Marcia Chatelain, *Franchise: The Golden Arches in Black America* (New York: Liveright, 2020).

63. "Going to Work" commercial storyboard, box 32, folder 16, CRJP.

64. Chatelain, *Franchise*.

65. Fabric Workshop, *Mark Bradford* (DVD; Philadelphia: Fabric Workshop, 2007).

66. Kincheloe, *Sign of the Burger*.

67. "McDonald's Corporation," *Dollars & Sense*, August 1983, 64, TTID.

68. Terry M. Neal, "In Sign Debate, a Suburban Dilemma," *Washington Post*, March 9, 1996.

69. Karyn R. Lacy, *Blue-Chip Black: Race, Class and Status in the New Black Middle Class* (Berkeley: University of California Press, 2007).

70. David Harvey, *Seventeen Contradictions and the End of Capitalism* (New York: Oxford University Press, 2014).

71. Harvey.

72. Harvey, 17.

73. Jeffrey Tannenbaum, "All That Glitters: For Many Blacks, Purchasing a Franchise Hasn't Lived Up to Its Bright Promise," *WSJ*, April 3, 1992.

74. Joan Oleck, "Move Over: Challenging White America's Rules—and Sometimes Winning," *Restaurant Business*, July 1, 1992.

75. *Hearings before the Committee on Small Business,* 103rd Cong. (1993–94). The proposed bills were the Federal Franchise Disclosure and Consumer Protection Act, the Federal Franchise Data and Public Information Act, and the Federal Fair Franchise Practices Act.

76. *Hearings before the Committee on Small Business,* 103rd Cong. (1993–94).

77. *Hearings before the Committee on Small Business,* 103rd Cong. 9 (1993–94).

78. *Hearings before the Committee on Small Business,* 103rd Cong. (1993–94).

79. Brief of Appellant, accession 276-96-0004, Brief of Appellee, and Reply Brief of Appellant, 2, *Joseph E. Sanchez v. McDonald's Corporation,* August 23, 1993, U.S. Court of Appeals for the Fourth Circuit, National Archives, Kansas City, Missouri (hereafter cited as *Sanchez v. McDonald's*).

80. *Hearings before the Committee on Small Business,* 103rd Cong. 18 (1993–94).

81. *Sanchez v. McDonald's,* 11.

82. *Hearings before the Committee on Small Business,* 103rd Cong. 21 (1993–94).

83. *Hearings before the Committee on Small Business,* 103rd Cong. (1993–94); *Sanchez v. McDonald's.*

84. In fact, both Talent *and* Meyers received political contributions from fast food. Talent was still in Congress in the 2000 election year, at which time he received two contributions of $1,500 from McDonald's operators (https://www.followthemoney.org), though he had not received such donations in 1992 (https://www.opensecrets.org/). If not from operators, did Talent receive money from the McDonald's PAC before the 1993 hearings? This is unclear, because the earliest year for which PAC donations data are available at opensecrets.org is 1998. By that year he received $5,500, more than any other House member. Across Congress, in 1998, McDonald's PAC gave 24 percent to Democrats and 76 percent to Republicans. Meyers's last year in Congress was 1997, so her PAC contributions are also unavailable. In 1990, she received two $1,000 contributions from Gene Bicknell of the National Pizza Company in Pittsburg, Kansas. This was the largest Pizza Hut franchise in the country. In 1990 and 1992, McDonald's executives such as Ed Rensi donated to the McDonald's PAC, and McDonald's affiliates donated relatively small sums to a number of politicians, including John Boehner, Mike Pence, Mitch McConnell, and Sherrod Brown. African American operators also donated to their representatives and local officials and activists. In 1990, Lee Dunham gave $500 to Charles Rangel and $500 to Al Sharpton in 1992. Rufus Stephens, apparently taking heed of the circumstances under which he acquired his restaurant, donated $900 to Kwesi Mfume in 1992 (https://www.opensecrets.org/). Individuals associated with McDonald's had a long history of contributing to politics. In 1972, Kroc donated $255,000 to Nixon's reelection campaign, an amount well above contemporaries such as Joseph Coors, executive vice president at his brewery ($3,000) or David Rockefeller, chair of Chase Manhattan Bank ($32,000). Kroc denied that the donation was meant to influence any federal policies. He just wanted "some insurance in the free enterprise system in which I strongly believe" ("Names of Contributors of $2,000 or More to the Nixon and McGovern Campaigns," *NYT,* September 25, 1972; Jack Anderson, "Burger Tycoon Aids Nixon Campaign," *Washington Post and Times Herald,* September 27, 1972). To hear Kroc's biographer tell it, Kroc was but a simple man uninvolved in politics—though he did have concerns about "what he perceived as the country's drift toward a social welfare state"—and in no way attempted to direct Nixon's policies to benefit McDonald's. John F. Love, *McDonald's: Behind the Arches* (New York: Bantam, 1995). In

2018, PACs for other brands included the Association of KFC franchisees, Wendy's Co., White Castle System, and YUM! Brands.

85. *Hearings before the Committee on Small Business,* 103rd Cong. 64 (1993–94).

14. 365 Black

1. Jordan Valinsky, "Here's When McDonald's Is Bringing Back the McRib," *CNN Business,* September 30, 2021, https://www.cnn.com/2021/09/30/business/mcrib-mcdonalds-return-date-2021/index.html.

2. Louis Malle, dir., *. . . and the Pursuit of Happiness* (New York: Pretty Mouse Films, 1986). In halting English, the class repeats the following exchange: "You must be short of money if you only worked three days a week. Let's go to Wendy's and have a hamburger." "Sorry, I'm out of money." "I'll treat you this time. Next month you can treat me." The exercise concludes with one of the students expressing uncertainty regarding this purported "Wendy's," prompting the instructor to exclaim, "Wendy's? Where you buy the hamburgers! You can go to McDonald's or Burger King, anywhere!"

3. Alix M. Freedman, "Habit Forming: Fast-Food Chains Play Central Role in Diet of the Inner-City Poor," *WSJ,* December 19, 1980.

4. Michael W. Twitty, *The Cooking Gene: A Journey through African American Culinary History in the Old South* (New York: Amistad, 2017).

5. *National Establishment Time-Series Database* (Oakland, Calif.: Walls & Associates, 2011).

6. Steven Kurutz, "Chicken Little," *NYT,* August 15, 2004; Dan Bilefsky, "A Chicken War in New York, Where Afghans Rule the Roost," *NYT,* February 14, 2011.

7. In the 1980s photograph, the thirty-sheet ad panel showcased Tanqueray gin. In 2011 (according to historical images from Google Street View), the two panels featured one advertisement stating "You don't have to be a perfect parent" (for a nonprofit website about adopting children) and another for 7-Eleven that featured a picture of a sandwich that might be tuna or chicken salad on toasted bread with visible lettuce and a plastic container of salad. The taglines read "Not so fast food" and "More in store."

8. Google Maps Street View, accessed November 2017, https://www.google.com/maps.

9. Camilo J. Vergara, "Time-Lapse Series, Camilo J. Vergara Collection, Library of Congress," 2021, http://hdl.loc.gov/loc.pnp/vrg.00056.series.

10. Jenny Schuetz, Jed Kolko, and Rachel Meltzer, "Are Poor Neighborhoods 'Retail Deserts'?," *Regional Science and Urban Economics* 42 (2012): 269–85.

11. Collections, New York City Municipal Archives, "New York City Tax Photos," accessed June 20, 2020, http://nycma.lunaimaging.com/luna/servlet/nycma~7~7; PropertyShark, accessed June 20, 2020, https://www.propertyshark.com/. Retail turnover is also evident in changes in ownership. City records (accessed from PropertyShark) show, for example, that 83 Livonia Avenue was held sequentially by 779 Grocery, Brooklyn's Finest Barbershop, Crown Fried Chicken, Fatawani Market, Stumpys Spot, 79 Livonia Food Corp., Alex Deli and Grocery Inc., Fatawa Mini-Market Inc., and finally a Crown Fried Chicken. 357 Nostrand Avenue changed hands from Kennedy Fried Chicken to Mr. Gate Deli & Grill, Prince Deli Corp., Kamaran Deli and Grocery Corp, Gates Deli & Grocery, Nostrand Deli Grocery, to Crown Grill Halal Chicken.

12. William K. Bellinger and Jue Wang, "Poverty, Place or Race: Causes of the Retail Gap in Smaller U.S. Cities," *Review of Black Political Economy* 38 (2011): 253–70.

13. Rachel Meltzer and Sean Capperis, "Neighbourhood Differences in Retail Turnover: Evidence from New York City," *Urban Studies* 54, no. 13 (2017): 3022–57.

14. J. Guthman, *Obesity, Food Justice, and the Limits of Capitalism* (Berkeley: University of California Press, 2011). Guthman points out that the NIH lowered the BMI threshold for overweight from twenty-seven to twenty-five in 1998, instantly creating a whole new population of people classed as such.

15. Chelsea R. Singleton, Olivia Affuso, and Bisakha Sen, "Decomposing Racial Disparities in Obesity Prevalence: Variations in Retail Food Environment," *American Journal of Preventive Medicine* 50, no. 3 (2016): 365–72.

16. William K. Bellinger and Jue Wang, "Poverty, Place or Race: Causes of the Retail Gap in Smaller U.S. Cities," *Review of Black Political Economy* 38 (2011): 253–70; Mario L. Small and Monica McDermott, "The Presence of Organizational Resources in Poor Urban Neighborhoods: An Analysis of Average and Contextual Effects," *Social Forces* 84, no. 3 (2006): 1697–24; Naa Oyo A. Kwate, Ji Meng Loh, Kellee White, and Nelson T. Saldana, "Retail Redlining in New York City: Racialized Access to Day-to-Day Retail Resources," *Journal of Urban Health* 90, no. 4 (2013): 632–52.

17. Naa Oyo A. Kwate, Chun Yip Yau, Ji Meng Loh, and Donya Williams, "Inequality in Obesigenic Environments: Fast Food Density in New York City," *Health & Place* 15 (2009): 364–73; J. P. Block, R. A. Scribner, and K. B. DeSalvo, "Fast Food, Race/Ethnicity, and Income: A Geographic Analysis," *American Journal of Preventive Medicine* 27, no. 3 (2004): 211–17; Philip M. Hurvitz, Anne V. Moudon, Colin D. Rehm, Laura C. Streichert, and Adam Drewnowski, "Arterial Roads and Area Socioeconomic Status Are Predictors of Fast Food Restaurant Density in King County, WA," *International Journal of Behavioral Nutrition and Physical Activity* 6, no. 46 (2009), https://www.doi.org/10.1186/1479-5868-6-46; S. E. Fleischhacker, K. R. Evenson, D. A. Rodriguez, and A. S. Ammerman, "A Systematic Review of Fast Food Access Studies," *Obesity Reviews* 12 (2010): e460–e471; Peter James, Mariana C. Arcaya, Devin M. Parker, Reginald D. Tucker-Seeley, and S. V. Subramanian, "Do Minority and Poor Neighborhoods Have Higher Access to Fast-Food Restaurants in the United States?," *Health & Place* 29 (2014): 10–17; R. Meltzer and J. Schuetz, "Bodegas or Bagel Shops? Neighborhood Differences in Retail and Household Services," *Economic Development Quarterly* 26, no. 1 (2012): 73–94.

18. Emma V. Sanchez-Vaznaugh, Aiko Weverka, Mika Matsuzaki, and Brisa N. Sanchez, "Changes in Fast Food Outlet Availability near Schools: Unequal Patterns by Income, Race/Ethnicity, and Urbanicity," *American Journal of Preventive Medicine* 57, no. 3 (2019): 338–45.

19. A. S. Richardson, J. Boone-Heinonen, B. M. Popkin, and P. Gordon-Larsen, "Are Neighborhood Food Resources Distributed Inequitably by Income and Race in the USA? Epidemiological Findings across the Urban Spectrum," *BMJ Open* 2 (2012), https://www.doi.org/10.1136/bmjopen-2011-000698.

20. Naa Oyo A. Kwate and Ji Meng Loh, "Fast Food and Liquor Store Density, Co-Tenancy, and Turnover: Vice Store Operations in Chicago, 1995–2008," *Applied Geography* 67 (2016): 1–13; Timothy F. Leslie, Cara L. Frankenfeld, and Matthew A. Makara, "The Spatial Food Environment

of the DC Metropolitan Area: Clustering, Co-Location, and Categorical Differentiation," *Applied Geography* 35 (2012): 300–307.

21. Mingyang Li and Baabak Ashuri, "Neighborhood Racial Composition, Neighborhood Wealth, and the Surrounding Food Environment in Fulton County, GA," *Applied Geography* 97 (2018): 119–27.

22. L. V. Moore, A. V. Diez Roux, J. A. Nettleton, D. R. Jacobs, and M. Franco, "Fast-Food Consumption, Diet Quality, and Neighborhood Exposure to Fast Food: The Multi-Ethnic Study of Atherosclerosis," *American Journal of Epidemiology* 170 (2009): 29–39; Jeannette Eckert and Igor Vojnovic, "Fast Food Landscapes: Exploring Restaurant Choice and Travel Behavior for Residents Living in Lower Eastside Detroit Neighborhoods," *Applied Geography* 89 (2017): 41–51.

23. Pasquale E. Rummo, Katie A. Meyer, Annie Green Howard, James M. Shikany, David K. Guilkey, and Penny Gordon-Larsen, "Fast Food Price, Diet Behavior, and Cardiometabolic Health: Differential Associations by Neighborhood SES and Neighborhood Fast Food Restaurant Availability in the CARDIA Study," *Health & Place* 35 (2015): 128–35.

24. D. A. Alter and K. Eny, "The Relationship between the Supply of Fast-Food Chains and Cardiovascular Outcomes," *Canadian Journal of Public Health* 96, no. 3 (2005): 173–77; Lewis B. Morgenstern, James D. Escobar, Brisa N. Sánchez, Rebecca Hughes, Belinda G. Zuniga, Nelda Garcia, and Lynda D. Lisabeth, "Fast Food and Neighborhood Stroke Risk," *Annals of Neurology* 66, no. 2 (2009): 165–70; T. Dubowitz, M. Ghosh-Dastidar, C. Eibner, M. E. Slaughter, M. Fernandes, E. A. Whitsel, C. E. Bird, A. Jewell, K. L. Margolis, W. Li, Y. L. Michael, R. A. Shih, J. E. Manson, and J. J. Escarce, "The Women's Health Initiative: The Food Environment, Neighborhood Socioeconomic Status, CMI, and Blood Pressure," *Obesity* 20, no. 4 (2012): 862–71.

25. Helen Lee, "The Role of Local Food Availability in Explaining Obesity Risk among Young School-Aged Children," *Social Science & Medicine* 74 (2012): 1193–1203; Shannon N. Zenk, Elizabeth Tarlov, Coady Wing, Stephan A. Matthews, Kelly Jones, Hao Tong, and Lisa M. Powell, "Geographic Accessibility of Food Outlets Not Associated with Body Mass Index Change among Veterans, 2009–14," *Health Affairs* 36, no. 8 (2017): 1433–42.

26. Dubowitz et al., "Women's Health Initiative"; Kristen Cooksey-Stowers, Marlene B. Schwartz, and Kelly D. Brownell, "Food Swamps Predict Obesity Rates Better Than Food Deserts in the United States," *International Journal of Environmental Research and Public Health* 14 (2017), http://www.doi.org/10.3390/ijerph14111366; J. Currie, S. DellaVigna, E. Moretti, and V. Pathania, "The Effect of Fast Food Restaurants on Obesity" (working paper 14721, National Bureau of Economic Research, 2009); B. Davis and C. Carpenter, "Proximity of Fast-Food Restaurants to Schools and Adolescent Obesity," *American Journal of Public Health* 99, no. 3 (2009): 505–10; J. N. Bodor, J. C. Rice, T. A. Farley, C. M. Swalm, and D. Rose, "The Association between Obesity and Urban Food Environments," *Journal of Urban Health* 87, no. 5 (2010): 771–81; R. W. Jeffrey, J. Baxter, M. McGuire, and J. Linde, "Are Fast Food Restaurants an Environmental Risk Factor for Obesity?," *International Journal of Behavioral Nutrition and Physical Activity* 3, no. 2 (2006), http://www.doi.org/10.1186/1479-5868-3-2; F. Li, P. Harmer, B.J. Cardinal, M. Bosworth, and D. Johnson-Shelton, "Obesity and the Built Environment: Does the Density of Neighborhood Fast-Food Outlets Matter?," *American Journal of Health Promotion* 23, no. 3 (2009): 203–9.

27. Mika Matsuzaki, Brisa N. Sánchez, Maria Elena Acosta, Jillian Botkin, and Emma V. Sanchez-Vaznaugh, "Food Environment near Schools and Body Weight: A Systematic Review of

Associations by Race/Ethnicity, Gender, Grade, and Socio-economic Factors," *Obesity Reviews* 21 (2009), http://www.doi.org/10.1111/obr.12997; Adenantera Dwicaksono, Ian Brissette, Guthrie S. Birkhead, Christine T. Bozlak, and Erika G. Martin, "Evaluating the Contribution of the Built Environment on Obesity among New York State Students," *Health Education & Behavior* 45, no. 4 (2018): 480–91.

28. "Designated Regional and Ethnic Exploration of Factors Affecting Present and Potential Consumer Attitudes and Appeal toward Burger King Restaurants" (prepared by J. Greene Associates–Qualitative Research Services for Kabon Consulting Inc., November 1973), 2, box 26, folder 9, CRJP.

29. S. B. Austin, S. J. Melly, B. N. Sanchez, A. Patel, S. L. Buka, and S. L. Gortmaker, "Clustering of Fast-Food Restaurants around Schools: A Novel Application of Spatial Statistics to the Study of Food Environments," *American Journal of Public Health* 95 (2005): 1575–81; Naa Oyo A. Kwate and Ji Meng Loh, "Separate and Unequal: The Influence of Neighborhood and School Characteristics on Spatial Proximity between Fast Food and Schools," *Preventive Medicine* 51, no. 2 (2010): 153–56; Brian Elbel, Kosuke Tamura, Zachary T. McDermott, Dustin T. Duncan, Jessica K. Athens, Erilia Wu, Tod Mijanovich, and Amy Ellen Schwartz, "Disparities in Food Access around Homes and Schools for New York City Children," *PLOS ONE* 14, no. 6 (2019), https://www.doi.org/10.1371/journal.pone.0217341.

30. Ann Forsyth, Melanie Wall, Nicole Larson, Mary Story, and Dianne Neumark-Sztainer, "Do Adolescents Who Live or Go to School near Fast-Food Restaurants Eat More Frequently from Fast-Food Restaurants?," *Health & Place* 18 (2012): 1261–69.

31. Elaine Wong, 2009. "Popeye's 'Chicken Queen' Tells It Straight," *Adweek*, May 31, 2009.

32. Micki McElya, *Clinging to Mammy: The Faithful Slave in Twentieth-Century America* (Cambridge, Mass.: Harvard University Press, 2007).

33. Rudd Center for Food Policy and Obesity, AACORN, and Salud America!, "Food Advertising Targeted to Hispanic and Black Youth: Contributing to Health Disparities" (University of Connecticut, 2017); Rudd Center for Food Policy and Obesity, Council on Black Health, and Salud America!, "Increasing Disparities in Unhealthy Food Advertising Targeted to Hispanic and Black Youth" (University of Connecticut, 2019).

34. KFC Corp., "Pride 360," n.d., accessed January 6, 2011, http://www.kfc.com/pride360/default.htm; KFC Corp., "Rules & Regulations," n.d., accessed January 6, 2011, http://www.kfchitmaker.com/rules.

35. McDonald's Corp., "What Is 365 Black?," n.d., accessed January 6, 2011, http://www.365black.com/365black/whatis.jsp.

36. McDonald's Corp., "Feedback," n.d., accessed January 6, 2011, http://www.365black.com/365black.

37. Sonya A. Grier and Vikki C. Lassiter, "Understanding Community Perspectives: A Step towards Achieving Food Marketing Equity," in *Advances in Communication Research to Reduce Childhood Obesity*, ed. Jerome D. Williams, Keryn E Pasch, and Chiquita A. Collins (New York: Springer, 2013), 343–66.

38. *Crawford v. McDonald's USA LLC and McDonald's Corporation*, United States District Court for the Northern District of Illinois Eastern Division, 2020.

39. Amy L. Best, *Fast-Food Kids: French Fries, Lunch Lines, and Social Ties* (New York: New York University Press, 2017), 124–25.

40. Best.

41. Frederick C. Harris, *The Price of the Ticket: Barack Obama and the Rise and Decline of Black Politics* (New York: Oxford University Press, 2012), 120.

42. Tom Burrell, *Brainwashed: Challenging the Myth of Black Inferiority* (New York: Smiley Books, 2010), x.

43. Burrell, 137.

44. Burrell, 113.

45. Burrell, x.

46. Harris, *Price of the Ticket*, 100.

47. Maggie Dickinson, *Feeding the Crisis: Care and Abandonment in America's Food Safety Net* (Berkeley: University of California Press, 2019), 35.

48. Bruce G. Link and Jo Phelan, "Social Conditions as Fundamental Causes of Disease," *Journal of Health and Social Behavior* 36 (1995): 80–94.

49. "Final Report on Exploratory Attitude and Usage Study to Assess the Marketplace Dynamics Facing Kentucky Fried Chicken in Select Black Communities" (prepared for Mingo–Jones Advertising Inc. by Tri-Ad Research Services, August 1985), box 32, folder 16, CRJP.

50. Surabhi Bhutani, Dale A. Schoeller, Matthew C. Walsh, and Christine McWilliams, "Frequency of Eating Out at Both Fast-Food and Sit-Down Restaurants Was Associated with High Body Mass Index in Non-Large Metropolitan Communities in Midwest," *American Journal of Health Promotion* 32, no. 1 (2018): 75–83; Sean C. Lucan, Frances K. Barg, Alison Karasz, Christina S. Palmer, and Judith A. Long, "Concepts of Healthy Diet among Urban, Low-Income, African Americans," *Journal of Community Health* 37 (2012): 754–62.

51. I would have included the photograph I have of this poster, but the resolution was not high enough to reproduce in print.

52. Punam Ohri-Vachaspati, Zeynep Isgor, Leah Rimkus, Lisa M. Powell, Dianne C. Barker, and Frank J. Chaloupka, "Child-Directed Marketing Inside and on the Exterior of Fast Food Restaurants," *American Journal of Preventive Medicine* 48, no. 1 (2015): 22–30.

53. Student research staff conducted street observations in 2007.

54. From in-person observation conducted by the author, July 2019.

55. "A Mission to Serve Lunch in the Capitol," *NYT*, January 20, 2009.

56. Sabrina Strings, "Obese Black Women as 'Social Dead Weight': Reinventing the 'Diseased Black Woman,'" *Signs: Journal of Women in Culture and Society* 41, no. 1. (2015): 123.

57. Strings, 123.

58. For a book-length analysis of food shaming and policing of Black Americans, see Psyche Williams-Forson, *Eating While Black: Food Shaming and Race in America* (Chapel Hill: University of North Carolina Press, 2022).

59. Dickinson, *Feeding the Crisis*, 132.

60. *Personal Responsibility in Food Consumption Act: Hearing before the Subcommittee on Commercial and Administrative Law of the Committee on the Judiciary, House of Representatives*, 108th Cong. 5 (2003).

61. *Personal Responsibility in Food Consumption Act*, 1–2.

62. Todd G. Buchholz, "Burgers, Fries, and Lawyers," *Policy Review*, February/March 2004, 56.

63. *Personal Responsibility in Food Consumption Act: Hearing before the Subcommittee on Commercial and Administrative Law of the Committee on the Judiciary, House of Representatives*, 108th Cong. (2003).

64. *Common Sense Consumption: Super-Sizing versus Personal Responsibility: Hearing Before the Subcommittee on Administrative Oversight and the Courts of the Committee on the Judiciary*, 108th Cong. 2 (2003).

65. *Common Sense Consumption*, 9.

66. *Common Sense Consumption*, 3.

67. LaVonna Blair Lewis, David C. Sloane, Lori Miller Nascimento, Allison L. Diamant, Joyce Jones Guinyard, Antronette K. Yancey, Gwendolyn Flynn, and Reach Coalition of the African Americans Building a Legacy of Health Project, "African Americans' Access to Healthy Food Options in South Los Angeles Restaurants," *American Journal of Public Health* 95, no. 4 (2005): 668–73.

68. Joshua Sbicca, *Food Justice Now! Deepening the Roots of Social Struggle* (Minneapolis: University of Minnesota Press, 2018).

69. Ordinance 180103, effective September 14, 2008, Los Angeles City Council.

70. Gilda Haas, executive director, Strategic Actions for a Just Economy, to Planning and Land Use Management Committee, Los Angeles City Council, July 21, 2008.

71. Roland Sturm and Aiko Hattori, "Diet and Obesity in Los Angeles County, 2007–2012: Is There a Measurable Effect of the 2008 'Fast-Food Ban'?," *Social Science & Medicine* 133 (2015): 205–11.

72. Sturm and Hattori. Health data came from the California Health Interview Survey, a random sample of state residents totaling almost 142,000 respondents across the three years. It asked how many times in the past week they had consumed fast food, non-diet soda, fruit, and vegetables excepting fried potatoes. BMI was also measured by self-report. The study compared respondents in South Los Angeles (N = 495 on average across the three waves) to those elsewhere in city (N = 9,406 on average).

73. Sturm and Hattori, 210.

74. Adam Chandler, "Why the Fast-Food Ban Failed in South LA," *The Atlantic*, March 24, 2015.

75. Robert Creighton, "Cheeseburgers, Race, and Paternalism: Los Angeles' Ban on Fast Food Restaurants," *Journal of Legal Medicine* 30 (2009): 249–67.

76. Manny Fernandez, "Pros and Cons of a Zoning Diet: Fighting Obesity by Limiting Fast-Food Restaurants," *NYT*, September 24, 2006; Los Angeles City Planning Commission report on case CPC-2007-3827-ICO, 2007.

77. Hannah Garth, "Blackness and 'Justice' in the Los Angeles Food Justice Movement," in *Black Food Matters: Racial Justice in the Wake of Food Justice*, ed. Ashanté M. Reese and Hannah Garth (Minneapolis: University of Minnesota Press, 2020), 107–30.

78. Angel Jennings and Doug Smith, "South LA Ban on New Fast-Food Restaurants Has Little Effect," *Los Angeles Times*, May 9, 2015.

79. Lyle Harris, "Seventh St. Corridor Gets a Fast-Food Restaurant," *Washington Post*, September 29, 1983.

80. Naa Oyo A. Kwate, "No. 11 Racial Patterning of Fast Food," in *The Street: A Photographic Field Guide to American Inequality,* edited by Naa Oyo A. Kwate (New Brunswick, N.J.: Rutgers University Press, 2021), 115–23.

81. Zachary W. Brewster and Sarah N. Rusche, "Quantitative Evidence of the Continuing Significance of Race: Tableside Racism in Full-Service Restaurants," *Journal of Black Studies* 43 (2012): 893–911.

82. Suzie Amer, "Minority Report: Are Ethnicity and Tipping Related?," *Restaurant Business,* November 15, 2002.

83. Rachel Meltzer and Sean Capperis, "Neighbourhood Differences in Retail Turnover: Evidence from New York City," *Urban Studies* 54, no. 13 (2017): 3022–57.

84. Ann Maxwell and Daniel Immergluck, *Liquorlining: Liquor Store Concentration and Community Development in Lower-Income Cook County Neighborhoods* (Chicago: Woodstock Institute, 1997).

85. Google Maps Street View, accessed November 2019, https://www.google.com/maps.

86. "From Fish Market to Rentals, First Look at KP Developers Forthcoming Harlem Rentals," *CityRealty,* April 24, 2017, https://www.cityrealty.com/nyc/market-insight/features/future -nyc/from-fish-market-rentals-first-look-kp-developers-forthcoming-harlem-rentals/10543. "Affordable Lottery Launches for Harlem Apartments from $1,850," *CityRealty,* June 12, 2019, https://www.cityrealty.com/nyc/market-insight/features/affordable-housing/affordable-lottery -launches-harlem-apartments-1850-month/32821.

87. Irvine (Jimmy) Hines, "Horn and Hardart Colored Employees to Entertain Big Crowd at Renny, This Saturday," *New York Age,* April 15, 1939.

88. Will Ellis, "The Harlem Renaissance Ballroom," *AbandonedNYC,* May 24, 2012, https:// abandonednyc.com/2012/05/24/the-harlem-renaissance-ballroom/.

89. Naa Oyo A. Kwate and Ji Meng Loh, "Fast Food and Liquor Store Density, Co-Tenancy, and Turnover: Vice Store Operations in Chicago 1995–2008," *Applied Geography* 67 (2016): 1–13.

90. Jackelyn Hwang and Robert J. Sampson, "Divergent Pathways of Gentrification: Racial Inequality and the Social Order of Renewal in Chicago Neighborhoods," *American Sociological Review* 79, no. 4 (2014): 726–51.

91. R. J. Sampson, *Great American City: Chicago and the Enduring Neighborhood Effect* (Chicago: University of Chicago Press, 2012).

92. Thomas A. Hirschl and Mark R. Rank, "Homeownership across the American Life Course: Estimating the Racial Divide," *Race and Social Problems* 2 (2010): 125–36.

Conclusion

1. The project appeared in the fall of 2015 on Everyday Incarceration (@everydayincarceration), an Instagram account.

2. Michael Owen Jones, "Dining on Death Row: Last Meals and the Crutch of Ritual," *Journal of American Folklore* 127, no. 503 (2014): 3–26.

3. Victor Ray, "A Theory of Racialized Organizations," *American Sociological Review* 84, no. 1 (2019): 29.

4. Mark Bittman, "The True Cost of a Burger," *NYT,* July 15, 2015; Eric Schlosser, *Fast Food Nation: The Dark Side of the All-American Meal* (Boston: Houghton-Mifflin, 2001).

5. James Baldwin, "An Interview with James Baldwin by Studs Terkel, December 29, 1961," in *James Baldwin: The Last Interview and Other Conversations,* ed. Quincy Troupe (New York: Melville House, 2014), 26.

6. James Baldwin, *Notes of a Native Son* (New York: Dial Press, 1963), 96.

Index

Page numbers in italic refer to illustrations.

382n8; of drive-in customers, 91, 99–101,
382n10, 382n12, 395n42; in response to
activism, 162, 170, 173
police violence, 7, 97–98, 115, 117, 163–64,
235, 381n61
Ponzie, Johnnie, 289
Popeyes Chicken and Biscuits, 234–35, 291,
293, 297, 318; commercials, 336; name
change, 332; referenced by Barack Obama,
339–40
Powell, Tracy, 291
predatory inclusion, 250–59
President's Advisory Council on Minority
Business Enterprise, 193–94, 200, 393n15
Prince & Joy's Drive-In, 211
Prince Castles, 68
Proctor, Frank B., 25
Procter & Gamble, 79
Prohibition, 13, 67
protests, 98, 106, 125, 279, 316, 344, 386n58;
of Burger King, 142, 162, 245; of drive-
ins, 100; of KFC, 107; of McDonald's, 106,
108–9, 166–73, 178–79, 200, 202, 243–44,
395n50; of White Castle, 22. See also
boycotts
psychographics, 233, 267, 272, 278
ptomaine poisoning, 43–44, 372n37
public housing, 35, 38, 47, 111, 134, 136, 137,
161, 211, 222, 234, 244–45, 385n54, 405n62
public transit, 26, 53, 58, 110, 134, 241, 301–2,
319
Puerto Rican communities, 199, 204, 213, 245,
409n57
PUSH International Trade Bureau (PITB),
269, 272

Qahaar, Eugene, 290
Queens, New York City, 47, 60, 204, 213, 239,
286

racial covenants, 38, 44, 46, 76, 240, 257–58,
261–82, 290–92, 312; and Breadbasket,
160–61. See also Operation PUSH

racial purity, 18, 26, 32, 52, 54, 286
racial stereotypes, xvii, 41–42, 65, 79–80, 106,
233, 246, 307, 317, 339, 342, 406n12
racial turnover of neighborhoods, 107, 109,
127, 133, 139, 141, 160; in Cleveland, 163,
176–77; White flight, 68, 70–71, 115, 148,
150–53, 241, 409n57
racism, xvi, 20, 35, 41, 137, 144, 159, 239, 289,
332, 364n3; in advertising, 18, 79, 302; and
business leaders, 144, 146, 154, 169–70,
183, 189, 196, 214, 253, 316, 325–28, 397n3;
in policy, 48, 93, 131, 198, 200, 251, 304,
309, 373n52, 381n58; reverse racism, 169;
violent, 7–8, 16, 98, 110, 113–15, 117, 120,
235, 368n88, 386n61. See also Ku Klux Klan;
lynching; mob violence; redlining; White
flight; White supremacy
radio, 79, 379n4, 406n12; Burger King commercials, 263, 276, 278; KFC commercials,
267, 277; McDonald's commercials, 267,
320; Popeyes commercials, 336
railroad service jobs, 19, 21–22, 64, 408n42
Rangel, Charles, 410n69, 423n84
Ray, Victor, 354
Reagan, Ronald, 183, 282, 300–301, 310
real estate, 7, 25, 47, 126, 130, 301, 324,
369n101; and Burger King, 237, 272; developers, 37, 48, 346, 348–49; and KFC, 107,
277, 317; and McDonald's, 84, 106, 244,
250–51, 348, 405n62; racism in, 16, 28, 272;
and White Castle, 285
Red Barn, 130, 186
redlining, xvii, 35, 126, 250, 325, 344–47;
by Burger King, 292; by KFC, 270; by
McDonald's, 326–27; in Miami, 73
Red Summer (1919), 7
Reese, Ashanté, 309
Regal Theater, 37, 137, 397n3
Reich, Thomas M., 212–13
Renaissance Ballroom and Casino, 349
Rensi, Ed, 423n84
reparations, 178–79
respectability, 68, 100, 105, 128, 180; food

Naa Oyo A. Kwate is associate professor at Rutgers, The State University of New Jersey. She is author of *Burgers in Blackface: Anti-Black Restaurants Then and Now* (Minnesota, 2019) and editor of *The Street: A Photographic Field Guide to American Inequality*.